GENDER AND HIGHER EDUCATION

Gender and Higher Education

EDITED BY BARBARA J. BANK

The Johns Hopkins University Press   Baltimore

© 2007, 2011 by Barbara J. Bank
All rights reserved. Published 2011
Printed in the United States of America on acid-free paper
9 8 7 6 5 4 3 2 1

The Johns Hopkins University Press
2715 North Charles Street
Baltimore, Maryland 21218-4363
www.press.jhu.edu

Library of Congress Cataloging-in-Publication Data

Gender and higher education / edited by Barbara J. Bank.
    p.   cm.
  Includes bibliographical references and index.
  ISBN-13: 978-0-8018-9782-5 (pbk.: alk. paper)
  ISBN-10: 0-8018-9782-3 (pbk.: alk. paper)
  1. Educational equalization—United States.   2. Women—Education
(Higher)—United States.   3. Education—Study and teaching (Higher)—
United States.   4. Education, Higher—Social aspects—United States.
I. Bank, Barbara J.
  LC213.2.G44   2011
  378.1'9822—dc22   2010017550

A catalog record for this book is available from the British Library.

This one-volume work is a selected edition of *Gender and Education: An Encyclopedia* (*Two Volumes*), edited by Barbara J. Bank, originally published in two volumes in hard cover by Praeger Publishers http://www.praeger.com, an imprint of Greenwood Publishing Group, Inc., Westport, CT. Copyright © 2007 by Barbara J. Bank. Paperback edition by arrangement with Greenwood Publishing Group, Inc. All rights reserved.

Special discounts are available for bulk purchases of this book. For more information, please contact Special Sales at 410-516-6936 or specialsales@press.jhu.edu.

CONTENTS

III: Gender Constructions and Controversies in the Academic Curriculum

PREFACE

The aim of this book is to reflect the current state of scholarship, research, and practice concerned with gender and higher education. Although there have been long-standing interests in and debates about the suitability of various amounts and types of higher education for men and women, the development of multifaceted research and scholarship on gender and higher education had its beginnings in the 1960s and 1970s. Stimulated by the social movements of that period, particularly by what we now call second-wave feminism, much of this research focused on girls and women whose education many viewed as inferior to that of boys and men. Indeed, had this book appeared in the 1970s or 1980s, its title probably would have been *Women and Higher Education*. Already in those decades, however, theoretical developments within feminism and education were turning scholarly attention from women's disadvantages to the broader, more complex issues surrounding the many social meanings of gender and the many ways gender is embedded in educational practices and the institutional structures of colleges and universities. It is these broader, more complex issues that are discussed in the introduction to this book and are illuminated by its chapters and their overviews.

The chapters are a combination of essays that originally appeared elsewhere, essays that have been extensively revised from their original publication, and new chapters prepared expressly for this book at my invitation. With one exception, the previously published chapters appeared in *Gender and Education*, a two-volume encyclopedia that I organized and edited for the Greenwood Publishing Group, Inc., published under their Praeger colophon in 2007 and also available as an e-book from ABC-CLIO. The exception is chapter 26 in part III, titled "Literary Studies" and authored by Annette Kolodny. It originally appeared under the title "Afterward: How the Florence Howe Award Helped Change Literary Studies" in *Diversifying the Discourse: The Florence Howe Award for Outstanding Feminist Scholarship, 1990–2004*, edited by Mihoko Suzuki and Roseanna Dufault, and published by the Modern Language Association of America in 2006. I am grateful to the Modern Language Association of America for permission to reprint this chapter. Thanks also to the Greenwood Publishing Group for granting permission to the Johns Hopkins University Press to reprint 40 of the essays that originally appeared in *Gender and Education: An Encyclopedia* (Praeger, 2007).

Of these 40 essays, 33 retain the basic organization and content that they had in the encyclopedia, although most of them have been updated and revised. At the editor's request, 7 of the 40 essays have undergone extensive revisions. In most cases, these revisions were requested because the encyclopedia version of the chapter had a substantial focus on elementary or secondary schooling that was deemed irrelevant to a book focused on higher education. I am grateful to Ronald Anderson, Stephanie Woodham Burge, Mary Frederickson, Rachel Hile, Michelle Paludi, Cynthia Pelak, and

Virginia Vincenti for their willingness to refocus and rewrite their chapters. Thanks are also due to those who responded with enthusiasm and expertise to my requests for new chapters on important topics that had been neglected in the encyclopedia: Elizabeth Allan, Brent Bilodeau, Judith Glazer-Raymo, Jeni Hart, Jill Hermsen, Lisa Plume Hallen, Abbe Herzig, Jackie Litt, Christian Matheis, Susan Staffin Metz, Kristen Renn, Tiffani Riggers, Linda Sax, Jennifer Silva, and Sheryl Ann Tucker. Drawing on their educational activities, research, and scholarly writings, they authored or coauthored nine new chapters, each of which is a valuable addition to the book.

Seven features of the encyclopedia have been retained in this book. First, all authors were asked to focus on gender, but no single definition of that term was imposed on them. As a result, the chapters vary considerably in the ways in which gender is conceptualized and analyzed. Although some authors seem to use gender in an unexamined manner to refer, simply, to men and women, or even males and females, a careful reading reveals that these authors, along with their more gender-analytic colleagues, conceive of gender as an unequal social construction that is amenable to change. Thus it seems fair to say that *inequality* and *malleability of gender* are central themes throughout the book, and readers should be alert to the different ways in which authors develop these themes or take them for granted.

Second, all authors were asked to provide a brief summary and status report for their topic that could be comprehended by academics, students, and members of the general public who are not experts on that topic or on gender and higher education as a field of study. In other words, the chapters are not meant to be like those in a handbook that are aimed at scholars, researchers, and educational practitioners who want a long, detailed review of the literature on a particular topic replete with citations and references for each assertion made by the author.

Given the educated but general audience for which authors were asked to write, the third encyclopedia feature they were asked to incorporate into their chapters was clear, nontechnical language. In those few places where technical terms are required, authors were asked to provide definitions or examples to make the terms clear to students and general readers. A fourth encyclopedia-style feature is the practice of beginning a chapter with an introductory overview (in many cases, much like a summary) but avoiding a repetitive summary at the end of the chapter. This practice also helps to keep the chapters shorter, thereby allowing more chapters on more topics.

A fifth encyclopedia-style feature is the limited number of citations and references found in most of the chapters. Limiting citations proved a difficult task for many authors who are used to giving generous credit to almost all who have written on the topic of their chapters. Following instructions from the publisher of the encyclopedia, the editor was particularly firm with those authors whose chapters originally appeared in that work, and I am willing to take criticism from those readers who do not find the expected citation to themselves or others in those chapters. More citations appear in some of the chapters prepared especially for this book, although even these chapters contain fewer references than some authors originally proposed or than would appear in a handbook chapter on the same topic. Regardless of the number of citations, however, every chapter is followed by a helpful list of references and further reading that direct readers to works from which they can obtain more detailed information about the topic of the chapter and more extensive citations and references.

Where appropriate, these lists also contain references to previous work by the authors on which they based their chapters for this book. Although the readers of this book do not have to be expert researchers and scholars, the authors were selected because of their demonstrated accomplishments in the topical areas with which their chapters are concerned. For some of the authors, their previous work on the topic of their chapters is extensive and intensive enough that the chapter in this book is primarily a reprise of this earlier work. For others, more attention is given to the research, writings, and practices of scholars and educators other than the author. In all cases, the recommended readings contain many citations and references to the broader literature on which the chapter is based.

The sixth and seventh encyclopedia-style features adopted in this book are the arrangement of chapters into topical parts and the alphabetical arrangement of chapters by title within each part. The division into topical sections is not found in all encyclopedias but has become more common over time. The use of alphabetical order by title is very common, and both features have the advantage of helping readers locate specific chapters on particular topics quickly and easily. Alphabetically arranged chapters also offer flexibility to the reader, but they do not provide clues about the relationships among the chapters. To find these clues, readers should consult the overview to each part of the book for information about the ways in which the topics of the chapters in that part might be compared and contrasted to other chapters. Because this book is likely to be used as a supplementary text reader in a broad array of college courses, not all instructors or students will want to follow the suggestions in the editor's overviews about the ways in which chapters are related to one another and about the order in which they might be read. Leaving the chapters in alphabetical order is a signal that they can be read in whatever order meets the goals of the readers of this book.

It is the editor's hope, however, that all readers will give careful attention to this preface and to the introduction that follows. Both are designed to orient the reader to the entire book. The introduction discusses how the meanings of gender have evolved historically and what it means to put gender in the center of the analysis of higher education. Although sometimes used as a synonym for sex, gender is a more complex construct. To inquire about gender is to ask more than how the two discrete groups known as men and women compare to each other. In contrast to sex, gender is less binary, less biologically based, more interactive and socially constructed, and more sensitive to the multiple ways in which maleness and femaleness (or masculinity and femininity) can be enacted, altered, performed, and undermined.

Following the introduction, the book is divided into six parts. As the overviews indicate, the editor considers all the chapters appearing in the same section to be relevant to one another, along with a few chapters from other parts of the book that are mentioned in those overviews. An index is located at the end of the book, providing more options to access information quickly.

The chapters in part I are focused on theoretical perspectives and educational research. The theories and research approaches covered were selected because they have something important to say about gender that is relevant to a full and sophisticated understanding of the contemporary nature of higher education, especially in the United States. More than the other chapters in this section, chapters 1, 3, 4, and 6 are primarily and directly concerned with education and educational change: chapters 3 and 6 focus on college student development, with chapter 3 giving major attention to male and female development, and chapter 6 focuses on lesbian, gay, bisexual, and transgender identity development; chapter 4 describes feminist critiques of educational research and practices, and chapter 1 explains the theory of higher-educational institutions known as academic capitalism and then applies it to the analysis of gender inequities.

The other chapters in part I focus more directly on women and gender and less centrally on higher education. For historical reasons elaborated in the overview to part I, these chapters can be divided into three groups. One group consists of the early feminist criticisms of gender inequality and male domination, known as liberal and radical feminism (chapter 7) and Marxist feminism or feminist reproduction theory (chapter 5). Because academic capitalism draws on radical and Marxist feminism, Chapter 1 could also be included in this group as well as in the education-centered set of chapters described above. The second group consists of chapters 2 and 8, focused on Black, multicultural, and global feminisms that criticized earlier feminist theories for being White-oriented, European-centered analyses and sought to broaden these analyses by emphasizing race, culture, and ethnicity. The third group, chapters 9 and 10, as well as the overview to part I, discusses two postmodern theories—poststructuralism and queer theory—that criticize feminist theories for using analytic language that re-creates the gender dualism and male domination feminists seek to destroy. These last two chapters in part I end by showing the effects that poststructuralism and queer theory have had on educational research and practices.

The overview and chapters in part II focus on the different kinds of institutionalized higher education in the United States that men and women experience at the present time or have experienced in the past. With the exception of distance education, discussed in chapter 13, all of these institutions tend to be campus based. Of the campus-based institutions, the ones that did not originate either to support or to exclude certain kinds of people and their cultures are the community colleges, discussed in chapter 12. In contrast, chapters 14 and 17 focus on colleges specifically designed to educate African Americans and members of American Indian tribes, respectively, and the overview to part II discusses what the U.S. government now calls "minority-serving" institutions of higher education. Although all chapters give attention to ways in which institutions of higher education are gendered, chapters 11, 15, 16, and 18 explicitly review the extensive literatures concerned with the origins, history, benefits, and shortcomings of coeducational public, private, denominational, and Catholic institutions in comparison and contrast to single-sex institutions, including military academies.

Part III is concerned with the official academic curriculum of higher educational institutions, a term that refers primarily to their accredited courses and the degree programs associated with those courses. Authors who wrote the chapters that appear in this section were asked to focus on the ways in which the curricular areas discussed in their essays have been gendered. In particular, they were asked to discuss ways in which their curricular areas are gender exclusive, as well as the ways in which they are gender inclusive, and the reasons for whatever gender constructions and controversies characterize the curricular fields with which they are concerned. Most authors also discuss the comparative participation rates and achievements of men versus women in particular academic majors and fields of study.

It would be impossible for one small book to contain a chapter on each of the many curricular areas that can be found in institutions of higher education. Although the chapters are presented in alphabetical order, the overview to part III reveals that the section's first chapter presents information about most of the different academic fields men and women have chosen as their majors across the past 35 years, and the remaining chapters were selected to represent four different patterns of gendering in the curriculum of higher education: numerically feminized fields of study (chapters 24 and 30, concerned with home economics and teacher education, respectively); numerically masculinized fields of study (chapters 20, 31, 22, 27, covering, respectively, science, technology and computer science, engineering, and mathematics, or the STEM fields as they are currently called); canonically masculinized fields of study (chapters 25 and 26, discussing history and literary studies, respectively); and emancipatory fields of study (the remaining chapters—21, 23, 28, 29, and 32—analyzing Black studies, feminist pedagogy, men's studies, multicultural education, and women's and gender studies, respectively).

Part IV is devoted to gender constructions and achievements in what has historically been known as the extracurriculum, but is now called the cocurriculum by some educators, especially those working in the fields of student affairs and services. As the overview and chapters in part IV demonstrate, some components of the extracurriculum, such as college athletics and cheerleading, fraternities, the Reserve Officers' Training Corps (ROTC), and sororities, have had major influences on the ways in which dominant forms of masculinity and femininity have been constructed among students in higher education. Contrasting alternatives to these dominant forms of gender construction have been offered by other components of the extracurriculum discussed in part IV, such as service-learning programs, women's centers and, more recently, campus centers and programs designed to support lesbian, gay, bisexual, transgender/transvestite, queer, questioning, and intersex students, faculty, and staff. There are, of course, many components of the extracurriculum that are not discussed in this book. In part, this is due to space limitations, but it is also true, as indicated in the overview to part IV, that many extracurricular clubs, activities, and programs have not yet been studied from a gender perspective.

One of the interesting anomalies of higher educational institutions is that they are places where students are often officially exhorted to become "all that they can be." Yet when they look about them, students observe a work place that is highly sex segregated, with women concentrated in secretarial work, part-time employment, teaching, and low-level administrative positions and men overrepresented among technical staff, full professors, well-funded researchers, and high-level administrators. Although discussed in other sections of the book, this division of labor is examined most closely in part V, which contains an overview and chapters that focus on the men and women who are the faculty, advisors and mentors, and administrators in higher education.

The overview of part VI begins with a discussion of the meaning and nature of policies concerned with gender and higher education. The overview also describes some of the complexities of the policy process and some of the ways in which theoretical controversies about the nature of gender differences have influenced debates about the kinds of policies that have been or should be implemented to promote gender equity, foster the highest levels of educational achievement among men and among women, and deal with specific gender-related problems. The chapters in part VI examine a broad range of such policies in the United States and provide a large number of insights into the conditions under which governmental and organizational policies concerning gender and higher education are more or less likely to be successful.

Although first because of the alphabetical ordering of chapters, the chapter on affirmative action that appears in part VI is also appropriately first because it provides a review of the broad range of affirmative action policies that shape the rights, opportunities, and behaviors of administrators, faculty, and students on college and university campuses. Subsequent chapters focus on more specific policies and constituents. Chapters 45, 49, and 50, for example, focus on evaluation policies, policies proposed by university women's commissions, and work-family policies, respectively, all of which affect primarily faculty and other employees in higher education. In contrast, chapters 46, 47, and 48 focus on students in their respective examinations of sexual harassment policies, students' rights, and the effects of Title IX on college athletics.

Information about the authors is given in the list of contributors that appears at the end of the book. I greatly appreciate the cooperative spirit, excellent chapters, and good cheer provided by all the authors. Together we have produced a work that provides a brief but intelligent and interesting review of research, scholarship, current practices, issues, and debates about gender and higher education in the United States.

GENDER AND HIGHER EDUCATION

Introduction

For those who believe that the social structures and processes known as higher education cannot be fully understood unless attention is paid to gender, it always comes as a surprise to discover how many books concerned generally with institutions of higher education or, more specifically, with college degree programs, declining academic standards, faculty development, student services, academic management, institutional financing, governing policies, and other education-related matters either pay no attention to gender or devote a single chapter to "women-and-the-topic-with-which-this-book-is-concerned." Entire issues of well-regarded educational journals still appear without a single article that takes account of gender. Professional meetings are held during which all the papers concerned with women and gender are relegated to a few sessions, while most of the others sessions discuss education-related theories, research, and practices as if gender didn't matter. In contrast to these tendencies to ignore or marginalize women and gender, this book places gender in the center of its analysis of higher education. All the topics with which its chapters are concerned—from theoretical perspectives and educational research, through the history and contemporary organization of institutions of higher education, their curricula, extracurricula, faculty, and administration, to higher education policies—are viewed through a gender lens.

But what does *gender* mean? This question can best be answered by taking a long look back at the scholarship and research concerned with the education of males and females, boys and girls, men and women and the ways in which the conceptual framing of that scholarship has changed over time from an emphasis on biologically based sex to sex-role theory to a concern with women and sex equity to a focus on gender identities that are malleable, unequal, intersectional, and institutionalized. What accounts for these changes in terminology and conception?

In the decades leading up to the 1970s, there was a considerable amount of writing and research concerned with what was then called sex differences in education. Should males and females attend the same schools? Should they be classmates? Do they need the same amount of education? Should they take the same courses, or should they take courses tailored to their special interests? Do they have the same amount of intelligence? Do they perform equally well in different subject-matter areas of the academic curriculum? How close are their test scores and grades? Do they want the same kinds of extracurricular activities? Should they have the same rights and privileges, or do females need more protection, such as curfew hours at college? Some of these questions could be answered with findings from well-conducted research, but many were based on, and answered with, untested or poorly tested assumptions about the essential differences between males and females.

Even in this early period, there were educators and social scientists who were uncomfortable with these assumptions about essential differences and the language in which they were expressed. *Male* and *female* carried too much of a biological connotation, they argued, and writing about *sex differences* ran the likely danger of being read as talk about biologically based and determined differences or the less likely danger of being confused with differences in sexuality. To these educators and social scientists, however, many of the differences in interests and performance and even test scores of boys and girls or men and women were due wholly or primarily to social circumstances. To call attention to the social origins of sex-linked preferences and behaviors, many adopted the language of role theory.

To role theorists (see, e.g., Biddle, 1979), much of human behavior could be understood as the result of the social positions or identity labels that people assumed in society. Attached to these social positions or identity labels were certain prescriptive or proscriptive expectations for behaviors, usually called social norms. When a person assumed or aspired to a particular social identity, that person had to learn the appropriate norms, preferably to internalize them as self-expectations, and to use those norms as a guide for his or her behaviors. This process of role learning, known as socialization, sometimes took a long period of time, and some people learned their roles better than others. Those who took up a particular position but failed to conform to the social norms attached to that position were likely to receive negative sanctions, and if their nonconformity persisted at a high level, they were likely to find their right to a particular position or identity claim challenged or even abrogated. Although role theory worked particularly well when applied to occupational positions, such as teacher, it also had some advantages in research and scholarship concerned with what came to be known as *sex roles*.

Talk about sex differences easily implied biological causality, but talk about differences in sex roles forced hearers to consider the social nature of what was being discussed. The term *role* came from the theater, and just as it would be difficult to assign biological cause to the different roles that people played on the stage, so too the language of sex roles made it harder to assign biological causality to the different role behaviors of males and females. Standing alone and apart from the language of roles, the terms *male* and *female* still seemed to carry too many biological assumptions. As a result, sex-role theorists tended to use terms like *male sex role* or *female sex role* or to drop the male/female nomenclature entirely in favor of writing about boys and girls or men and women, terms that designate social positions better than *male* and *female*. Much attention was given to research and scholarship concerned with role development across the life cycle (e.g., Gordon, 1972), including the ways in which boys and girls learned their sex roles at home and in schools; the role conflicts (i.e., contradictory expectations) experienced by students caught between the sex-role norms of their teachers and their peers; and the ways in which sex roles changed as students moved up through the school years. The roles of teachers and educational administrators also attracted researchers (such as Gross, Mason, and McEachern, 1958), though most of these investigations focused more on occupational roles than on sex roles.

When second-wave feminism emerged and flowered in the United States and around the world in the 1960s and 1970s, the focus quickly shifted from sex roles to sex equity (see Stockard et al., 1980). What had previously been viewed by role theorists as predictable—and fairly benign or even beneficial—sex differences in classroom behaviors, course choices, academic achievements, and educational outcomes were now reconceptualized as unjust, unfair, and unacceptable sex inequities, most of which favored boys over girls and men over women. A policy agenda for eliminating these inequities was developed for education (Klein, 1985), as for other social institutions: Tracking of boys into certain kinds of courses and girls into others should be eliminated, and the entire curriculum should be equally available to both sexes. Women should be admitted to male-only colleges and universities, including those in the Ivy League, on the same bases as men. Curricular materials that ignored or denigrated women should be replaced with materials that were free of misogynist biases. Teachers at all levels of education should be made aware of their different behaviors toward males and females and should be required to treat students in an equitable manner. Schools that put resources into extracurricular activities for boys, such as athletic teams, should put equivalent resources into extracurricular activities for girls. Secondary school teachers, school counselors, and faculty in higher education should make certain that their advice to students about academic matters, personal life, educational plans, and occupational goals were completely free of traditional, stereotypic assumptions about appropriate roles for men and women.

In the early years of second-wave feminism, much of the research documenting unequal educational opportunities and outcomes between boys and girls and many of the arguments favoring equity continued to use the language of role theory and of sex inequalities (see, e.g., Stacey, Béreaud, & Daniels, 1974; Weitzman, 1979). As time went on, however, that language was gradually superseded by the language of gender. Sex differences became gender differences or gender inequalities. Sex equity became gender equity (Klein, 1985, 2006). Male and female sex roles became masculinities and femininities. Socialization, role-learning, and role-playing became processes of "doing gender" (West & Zimmerman, 1987) and of gender construction (Ferree, Lorber, & Hess, 1999).

There were many reasons for these changes. One was the fact that sex-role theory put such a heavy emphasis on early childhood socialization as the time when people learned their sex roles. This emphasis led to a form of social essentialism that was objectionable to second-wave feminists, including activists seeking sex equity and participants in the emerging discipline of women's studies. Social essentialism was the notion that because boys and girls were socialized into different sex roles at very early ages, they internalized essentially different identities, beliefs, preferences, and behaviors. Because these differences were so deep seated, they were the source of much social stability and continuity. This argument was not much different from the arguments about essential biological differences between the sexes that sex-role theory had rejected. Although *social* essentialism did leave open the possibility that what was socially induced could be socially changed, the internalization of sex roles deep inside of (properly socialized) boys and girls meant that change was likely to be a long and psychologically difficult process of resocialization. This was not an image of men and women compatible with a feminist movement seeking rapid social change. A focus on the socially constructed nature of gender was much more in tune with the times.

Another reason for moving away from the language of sex-role theory was its tendency to focus on one type of appropriate male sex role, usually styled as instrumental and task oriented, and one type of appropriate female sex role, usually styled as expressive, sociable, and nurturant. Within the theory, it was assumed that these sex roles were normative in the sense that they were consensually agreed-upon standards for behavior. All boys were taught to conform to the expectations of the male sex role, though some did so better than others, and all girls were expected to internalize the female sex role. At the societal level, the two roles were thought to be complementary and to provide stability to institutional life, especially in the family, where the complementary roles of nurturant mother and work-oriented father modeled the explicit sex-role socialization of their daughters and sons. While some feminists did not want to give up their claim to expressiveness and nurturance, and a few exalted these kinds of "female" behaviors, most advocated a more historically and culturally informed understanding of the many lines of behavior that had been, were currently, and could become characteristic of men and women. From this perspective, there was not just one appropriate and consensually supported male sex role and one complementary female sex role, but rather many masculinities and femininities, some of which were more oppositional than complementary.

Even though some of these masculinities and femininities were more socially acceptable than others, these evaluations varied across time and place. The most admired, honored, and dominant form of masculinity, conceived as hegemonic masculinity by Connell (2005), is not enacted by or expected to be enacted by all men, even at a single time and place, and it is subject to resistance and change as well as complicity and support. Similarly, societies advance a model of what Connell calls "emphasized femininity" as an admired and honored ideal, but most women are not expected to conform to this type of femininity, and some resist it strongly. It was this recognition of variation, change, and resistance that made the concept of gender, a term that encompassed multiple masculinities and femininities, so much more acceptable to historians, international comparative scholars, and many feminists than the concept of consensual and complementary sex roles.

This emphasis on multiplicity and the effort to avoid universalizing claims about the categories of men and women has also been particularly important in the emergence of Black, multicultural, and global feminisms; in the formulations of postmodern and queer theories with their insistent rejections of either/or dualisms; in the development of theories and campus resources focused on lesbians, gays, bisexuals, and transgendered persons; and in the founding and evolution of the academic fields of Black studies, women's and gender studies, multicultural studies, and men's studies (see essays in parts I, III, and IV). Among the many kinds of masculinities and femininities one might consider are those that intersect with different social classes, race-ethnicities, and sexualities. And, certainly, when one's eyes are on inequalities, this list would have to be extended to include religion, age, and physical disabilities.

One important thing that gender theories share with sex-role theory is the firm assertion that gender (sex roles) and the masculinities and femininities that comprise it are not simply characteristics of individuals but are also embedded in social interactions, social structures, and cultural forms. Although the two theories do not conceptualize interaction, structure, and culture in the same way, they both insist on the externality of gender (or sex roles), sometimes called gender institutionalization, as well as its internality in the form of self-identities. Some gender theorists (e.g., Risman, 2004) insist not only that gender is embedded in the division of labor, tasks, goals, and social relationships that define institutional structures, such as education, but also that gender is a social structure in its own right because it is a socially constructed hierarchy of power and status. In this view, hegemonic masculinity entails dominance not only over women but also over other forms of masculinity. And although hegemonic masculinity may be embodied in specific individuals, such as the star quarterback on a university football team, its power derives not from the athlete himself but from the authority accorded to that form of masculinity in the structure and culture of the university in which that masculinity is socially constructed. It is this gender hierarchy of authority and power built into structures and cultures by interaction processes and, in turn, shaping how people think about and present themselves that readers should have in mind when they encounter the language of "gendered education" throughout this book.

The language of gender and gendering has not totally eclipsed earlier ways of talking and writing about differences between boys and girls or men and women in education and other social institutions. Every year I receive requests to renew my memberships in a variety of different professional organizations. The forms supplied for this purpose by most organizations ask that I indicate my "sex" as either male or female, and the form supplied by a few others ask that I use those same choices to indicate my "gender." Not only do these renewal forms assume that people can be easily divided into two contrasting categories, seemingly rooted in biology, but some use the term gender as a label for this dualism. Clearly this was not what scholars had in mind when they developed theories of gender encompassing multiple, intersectional masculinities and femininities in opposition to theories concerned with male/female dualism and sex differences. Yet one can hardly object when an organization asks simplistic questions about sex or gender because it wants to pursue greater gender equity, perhaps by determining whether it no longer has proportionately more females among its members than among its officers.

Similar questions and goals characterize much of the research summarized in this book. Students are assigned to one of only two gender categories (male or female, men or women) on the basis of faculty observation, self-reports, or administrative records, and that assignment is used to calculate gender differences in course selection, academic fields, classroom behaviors, academic performance, educational attainments, or graduation rates. Or, if the researcher's interest is in school personnel, faculty and administrators may be separated into males and females and this dichotomy used to contrast their behaviors, career patterns, salaries, and other work outcomes. Research of this type is one of the major foundations on which claims about gender (in)equities in education are based, and readers will find a good deal of it summarized and analyzed in parts III and V.

The insights of gender theories are not ignored in these sections, however, nor in the other parts of this book. Many authors give attention to the variability among men and among women, with several essays focusing on the intersectionality of gender with race-ethnicity, social class, and/or sexuality, and some essays examining changes in gender-related behaviors or outcomes over time or across types of schools. Many of these chapters look at the ways in which gender is constructed and built into the social structures and cultural forms of education, including institutional contexts (part II), the academic curriculum (part III), the extracurriculum (part IV), and higher education policies (part VI). The extent to which specific chapters examine the ways in which gender is malleable and embedded in intersectional identities, social interactions, and institutional structures varies considerably. This variation depends on the topic of the chapter, the kinds of research that are available concerning that topic, and the judgment of authors about how best to characterize the current state of scholarship on gender and education for the topic with which their own chapter is concerned.

This is an exciting time to be involved in the study of gender and education. It is a time in which this broad topic is the focus of multiple theories and research alternatives along with interesting theoretical and methodological debates (see part I); is producing interesting research findings, many of which are presented throughout this book; and is witness to the enormous changes in the status of women and men in higher educational institutions that are mentioned and analyzed by many contributors.

To characterize these times as exciting is not the same as calling them happy. For those with a commitment to deepening their knowledge about and understanding of gender and the ways in which it shapes and is shaped by higher education, this book answers many questions but also raises many. For those with a commitment to gender equity in education, the good news about the elimination of many forms of gender bias contained in this book is tempered with disheartening information about the many kinds of gender inequities that continue to exist in the institutional and organizational structures and cultures of higher education in the United States. But rather than using our time to argue about whether the glass of knowledge about gender and higher education and the glass of gender equity in education are half full or half empty, this is a good time to think about how to fill both glasses to the brim. This book contains many suggestions about the kinds of theories, research, scholarship, policy initiatives and implementation, and educational practices that can help accomplish these two tasks.

REFERENCES AND FURTHER READING

Biddle, B. J. (1979). *Role theory: Expectations, identities, and behaviors*. New York: Academic Press.

Connell, R. W., & Messerschmidt, J. W. (2005). Hegemonic masculinity: Rethinking the concept. *Gender & Society, 19*, 829–859.

Ferree, M. M., Lorber, J., & Hess, B. B. (1999). *Revisioning gender*. Thousand Oaks, CA: Sage Publications.

Glasser, H. M., & Smith, J. P., III. (2008). On the vague meaning of "gender" in education research: The problem, its sources, and recommendations for practice. *Educational Researcher, 36*(6), 343–350.

Gordon, C. (1972). Role and value development across the life cycle. In J. A. Jackson (Ed.), *Role* (pp. 56–105). London: Cambridge University Press.

Gross, N., Mason, W. S., & McEachern, A. W. (1958). *Explorations in role analysis: Studies of the school superintendency role*. New York: John Wiley & Sons.

Klein, S. S.(Ed.). (1985). *Handbook for achieving sex equity through education*. Baltimore: Johns Hopkins University Press.

Klein, S. S. (Ed.). (2007). *Handbook for achieving gender equity through education*. Second edition. Mahwah, N.J.: Lawrence Erlbaum Associates.

Risman, B. (2004). Gender as a social structure: Theory wrestling with activism. *Gender & Society, 18*, 429–450.

Stacey, J., Béreaud, S., & Daniels, J. (Eds.). (1974). *And Jill came tumbling after: Sexism in American education*. New York: Dell.

Stockard, J., Schmuck, P., Kempner, K., Williams, P., Edson, S. K., & Smith, M. A. (1980). *Sex equity in education*. New York: Academic Press.

Weitzman, L. J. (1979). *Sex role socialization: A focus on women*. Palo Alto, CA: Mayfield.

West, C., & Zimmerman, D. (1987). Doing gender. *Gender & Society, 1*, 125–151.

I
Theoretical Perspectives and Educational Research

Their failure to take gender—and especially women—seriously was one of the criticisms of educational theories, research, and practices made by participants in the second-wave feminist movement of the 1960s and 1970s. According to these critics, psychological and social scientific theories—and the educational theories based on them—often assumed that suppositions and observations about "human beings" or "mankind" or "students" applied equally well to men and women. Examples of such theories were those concerned with college student development which at that time assumed that cognitive and identity development proceeded in the same way for all students, with no attention paid to differences in gender. Despite this shortcoming, these theories were very popular and generated a huge volume of research, the findings from which were usually applied to women even if all the research subjects were men.

As chapter 3 ("College Student Development") reveals, it was not until the 1980s that challenges to these theories began to appear in the form of studies designed to assess whether the theories could be generalized to women as well as men. Findings suggesting that developmental processes and outcomes differ across gender types led to the formulation of the *female* student development theories and, subsequently, the *male* student development theories, described in chapter 3, and also to the theories of developing sexual orientations and gender identities described in chapter 6 ("Lesbian, Gay, Bisexual, and Transgender Identity Development Theories").

Criticisms by second-wave feminists of educational research and practices were similar to those leveled against education-related theories. According to these criticisms, much of the attention of educational researchers and practitioners was directed toward the educational achievements and problems of boys and men. Underlying these male-centered practices and research projects were assumptions about the greater importance of higher education for men than for women, who were often assumed likely to "waste" advanced educations either by becoming full-time homemakers or by putting family ahead of careers. Thus it was considered neither surprising nor important during this historic period that women were less likely than men to complete undergraduate degrees or to enroll in graduate and professional degree programs. Instead, it was deemed far more important that men, rather than women, receive the kinds of education that would allow them to be productive, successful members of the work force, and it was generally accepted that research should be focused on the ways to increase the likelihood of this outcome.

Feminists of this period considered the assumptions about women that underlay so much of educational research and practice to be nothing more than prejudice. Their commitment to social change led these feminists to advocate the kinds of education for women that would allow them to qualify for all of the jobs available to men, not just those traditionally considered appropriate for women. Women should have equal educational and occupational opportunities with men. To these ends, second-wave feminists turned the research lens away from a focus on men's greater educational achievements than women's and toward the barriers preventing women from the greater achievements of which feminists assumed they were capable. This led to a large body of research evidence concerning the ways in which gender and other social identities, such as race-ethnicities, social classes, and sexualities, affected the ways in which students were treated in schools and the ways in which they experienced schooling. And since schools are also major employers, researchers also increasingly concerned themselves with the ways in which gender affected the occupational lives and prospects of teachers, academics, and administrators at all levels of education.

It was not just the content of research that underwent changes, however. Research methods and procedures were also challenged and altered. The terms *feminist research, feminist scholarship*, and *feminist methodology* appeared with increasing frequency from the mid-1970s to the present time, although the meanings of those terms were constantly being interrogated. Central to the feminist critique and reformulation of research methodology and procedures were the beliefs that much of so-called objective research was really male centered, that male-centered research either omitted women from study or presented a distorted view of them, and that women's experiences could better be understood by researchers who are reflexive about the research process, adopt the standpoint of those they study, and are sensitive to the ethical and political implications of their research. Additional information about feminist research methodology can be found in chapter 2 ("Black Feminism, Womanism, and Standpoint Theories") and chapter 4 ("Feminist Critiques of Educational Research and Practices") in this section of the book and in most of the chapters concerned with the academic curriculum that appear in part III.

The feminist scholars and activists who had so much influence on developmental theories and on educational research did not represent a single unified form of feminism. Indeed, they did not—and still do not—fully agree with one another about how best to conceptualize gender or education or equity. Yet it would be inconceivable that anyone would try to think or write about gender and higher education without paying attention to the major arguments of feminist theories and of the postmodern theories that critiqued and extended them. The feminist theories that gained most popularity and influence in the 1960s and 1970s were liberal and radical feminisms, discussed in chapter 7 ("Liberal and Radical Feminisms"), and Marxist feminisms, more recent versions of which are discussed in chapter 5 ("Feminist Reproduction Theory") and chapter 1 ("Academic Capitalism").

An emphasis on *individualism*, including individual learning, is often said to be a characteristic of liberal feminism, and there is some truth in this characterization because liberal feminism, like all forms of liberal theory, does place an emphasis on individual effort and competitive achievement. However, liberal feminism draws attention to group differences, particularly gender differences, and to the ways in which some groups, particularly women, have systematically been discriminated against and denied equal opportunities. Thus the analyses of gender and education conducted by liberal feminists lead from individual to social structure and back again. To make individual competition fair, there must be a structure of equal opportunities, especially in the schools where individuals obtain the knowledge, skills, and credentials that allow them to compete effectively in the job market. To its many critics, liberal feminism is regarded as politically naive in its failure to recognize the complex ways in which gender oppressions are intertwined with other forms of oppression, such as those of race and class; in its tendency to draw a line between public and private life; and in its simplistic notion that individual learning and achievement depend on educational and job opportunities, along with reproductive choices, rather than on institutionalized arrangements of economic, social, and political power.

In contrast to liberalism's emphasis on individualism and equal opportunities, the central focus of radical feminism is on *patriarchy*, the system of male power that is embedded in higher education and in all of the other institutional arrangements of contemporary societies. In contrast to Marxist forms of feminism which put a heavy emphasis on social class hierarchies and class exploitation, radical feminism's emphasis on patriarchy places male dominance and women's oppression at the center of its analysis. Education is not so much a liberal feminist project whereby women can gain credentials and gender equity as it is a revolutionary process of unmasking the denials by teachers and scholars of the many ways in which men have sought and gained control of women's minds and bodies. Marginalized women, such as witches and goddesses and lesbians, who resist male power and male constructions of womanhood, are valorized by radical feminists, and traditional female traits, such as nurturance and intuition, are given positive status. The best education for women is one based on their own experiences, history, and cultural production that will help them overcome compulsory heterosexuality and patriarchal control.

The call for a revolutionary change in education is also characteristic of Marxist-based theories that see existing educational institutions as major sites for the *reproduction of social-class inequality* and, in the case of Marxists feminisms, for the *reproduction of gender inequality* as well. In other words, schools, colleges, and universities are sites for the preparation and reproduction of a hierarchically stratified, gendered workforce and polity in which women are trained for lower-status jobs and second-class citizenship. This is a sharp contrast to the view of liberal feminism that sees higher education as a set of venues in which women can gain liberatory knowledge and skills. More information about the differences between these theoretical approaches and about the development of neo-Marxian feminism can be found in chapter 5.

Drawing on both radical and Marxist feminisms is academic capitalism, a structural approach to education described in chapter 1 that focuses on recent changes in contemporary colleges and universities in the United States, Canada, Australia, and the United Kingdom. The central argument of academic capitalism is that colleges and universities have undergone a shift from a public good knowledge/learning regime to an academic capitalist knowledge/learning regime with the result that patriarchy is becoming further entrenched in higher education institutions by the rational economic agenda characteristic of this newer regime. The resource imbalances across departments and units that are now becoming commonplace in institutions of higher education disadvantage women faculty and students, who tend to be concentrated in academic fields with fewer economic resources and market opportunities than those available in predominantly men's fields. Thus, academic capitalism both highlights the reproduction of inequalities stressed in Marxist feminism and endorses the view of radical feminism that a complete restructuring of colleges and universities may be necessary to abolish the patriarchy that is embedded in Western systems of higher education and to achieve gender equity.

Early versions of liberal and radical feminisms were criticized for their acceptance of sexual dualism, or the notion that almost everyone can be divided into two sexes (male and female), and their emphasis on the sexual divide as the most crucial division among humankind. Early Marxist-based feminisms, in turn, were criticized for not taking gender seriously enough and for making social class inequalities paramount. As chapters 1, 5, and 7 reveal, these criticisms led to modifications in the theories over time. Most notably, radical feminism opened the door to lesbian feminism and to the broad range of sexualities and affectionalities described in chapter 6, Marxist feminisms struggled to become a dual-systems theory with equivalent emphasis on class and gender, and all forms of feminism—especially feminist reproduction theory —became less focused on the national scene and more global in scope. Some of these changes came in response to the development of feminisms that were not Eurocentric, such as those focused on in chapter 2 ("Black Feminism, Womanism, and Standpoint Theories") and chapter 8 ("Multicultural and Global Feminisms").

To Black, multicultural, and global feminists, a major problem with the male-female dichotomy is that it tends to lump together all males and all females. Instead of talking about differences between men and women, they ask, "What men and what women are you talking about?" This question immediately calls attention to the enormous variation among women and among men. Black feminism draws particular attention to the intersectionality of gender, race-ethnicity, and class, and reminds other feminists, as well as educational researchers more generally, that the world looks quite different to White middle-class women than it looks from the standpoint of poor Black women. Like Black feminists, multicultural and global feminists also reject female chauvinism, by which they mean the tendency for relatively privileged women—most often White, Western/Northern, middle-class, heterosexual, and well-educated women —to assume, incorrectly, that their way of seeing the world is the way all women see it.

Although Black, multicultural, and global feminists reject the notion that all women are basically alike, a position sometimes called female essentialism, they do not want to turn women of different social classes, race-ethnicities, nationalities, and sexual orientations against one another. Instead, they want women of different backgrounds to come together in mutually respectful alliances to fight against social inequalities not only across gender lines but also across all the lines that separate "us" from "them." It is the desire to expose these lines of division and inequality, along with a preference for social justice over traditional social hierarchies, that unite the very different versions of feminism described in part I.

In recent years, all versions of feminism have found themselves the targets of the postmodern criticisms discussed in chapter 9 ("Postmodern and Poststructural Theories") and chapter 10 ("Queer Theory"). Advocates of poststructural and queer theories argue strongly against other theories that view maleness or heterosexuality or femaleness or homosexuality as fixed identities attached to individuals because of their biology or socialization. Instead, they want people to recognize the ways in which language is used to *construct* identities and to make them appear to be stable and coherent. In the case of gender, a central poststructural concern is with the ways in which power arrangements in contemporary society create systems of *discourse*, such as literature or art or law or research reports, that create particular versions of human subjects. Most of these versions, such as male and female, are dichotomies, and queer theorists and other postmodernists argue that these dualistic categories are never natural or neutral. Instead, they create and maintain power relations. Whether the dichotomy is male and female per se or some other dualism related to gender, such as masculinity/femininity, rationality/emotionality, or heterosexual/homosexual, the underlying assumption is that one side of the dualism is superior to the other. Women will never attain equality with men as long as language and ideology continue to constitute them as inferiors. And because they are creators and purveyors of dominant forms of language and ideology, institutions of higher education bear major responsibility for the perpetuation of gender inequities, although they also provide a venue in which to deconstruct gendered and other forms of power relations.

Many educators and feminists reject postmodernist approaches to gender. There is more to gender than language and other texts, they argue, and they call attention to the structurally embedded material conditions that benefit men and heterosexuals in comparison to women and homosexuals. By denying this materiality and the divisions of gender, postmodernists undermine the ability of people to organize around identities, such as women or lesbians or feminists, into social movements that can effectively fight for gender equity and against the concentration of power and privilege in the hands of heterosexual men.

Other feminists are more willing to accept some of the insights of postmodern theories, particularly the deconstruction of power relationships based on the rejection of dualisms that lump together all women or all homosexuals or all people of some other particular identity. They accept the notion that it is only by rejecting such dualisms that students and faculty can stop being complicit in the normalization of some people versus the marginalization and oppression of others. As not only chapters 9 and 10 but also the chapter on university women's commissions in part VI of this book reveal, even well-intentioned efforts to achieve gender equity can perpetuate negative, demeaning, and self-defeating stereotypes of the women these efforts are designed to help. To avoid such pitfalls, some feminists are willing to join with postmodernists in fostering educational practices and policies that may have less of an identity focus than developmental or feminist theories but that may ultimately be more empowering.

CHAPTER 1

Academic Capitalism

AMY SCOTT METCALFE AND SHEILA SLAUGHTER

Academic capitalism refers to the market or marketlike behaviors of institutions of higher education and those working within them to secure external resources. At the heart of academic capitalism is the notion that, in times of financial stress or uncertainty, individuals and organizations often adopt market-based strategies to strengthen or bolster their relative position in the economy. At times, these actions contradict nonprofit status and allow market values to enter the public sector. Articulated first in the work of Slaughter and Leslie and later by Slaughter and Rhoades, academic capitalism is not a gender theory per se, but it does highlight aspects of resource imbalance that have plagued women in academe for as long as they have been permitted by men to participate in coeducational higher education.

The Entrepreneurial University

Academic capitalism was first explored at length in Slaughter and Leslie's *Academic Capitalism: Politics, Policies, and the Entrepreneurial University* (1997). In this book, the authors drew upon the work of sociologists of science and economists to foreground their examination of the forces that drove the restructuring of higher education in the 1980s and 1990s in four English-speaking countries (Australia, Canada, the United States, and the United Kingdom). The study included three levels of inquiry: international, national, and institutional. At each level they employed a different theoretical framework and data collection method, with concepts ranging from globalization to professionalization.

At the international level, they looked to theories of global political economy to help explain shifts in resource allocation for higher education. They found that the move from an industrial to a postindustrial economy had and continues to have repercussions for the process of worker education (from basic education to just-in-time and lifelong learning), the process of production (from physical to mental), the location of managerial power (shifting from oligopolistic corporations tied to the nation-state to multinational corporations that are still largely oligopolies), and the role of innovation in pursuit of profit. They also found that globalization has four primary implications for higher education: (1) the constriction of monies available for discretionary activities such as postsecondary education; (2) the growing centrality of technoscience and fields closely involved with markets, particularly international markets; (3) the tightening relationships between multinational corporations and state agencies concerned with product development and innovation; and (4) the increased focus of multinationals and established industrial countries on global intellectual property strategies. As time spent in the latter phase of research and development decreased, the differences between basic and applied research became less salient, and all research had entrepreneurial potential. In short, growing global markets, also known as the process of globalization, led to the development of national funding policies that targeted university-based entrepreneurial research (research that has market relevance and commercialization potential) while simultaneously reducing block grants (undesignated funds that accrue to universities, often according to formulas) to higher education institutions, thus leading academics to increase their direct engagement with the market.

At the national level, Slaughter and Leslie examined the higher education finance data of the four countries, using Pfeffer and Salancik's (2003) resource dependency theory as an interpretive lens. Resource dependency theory contends that organizations are influenced by external agents that provide support in the form of money or other assets. The degree to which this occurs depends upon the relative magnitude of the resource exchanged and the criticality of the resource to the functions of the focal organization. Using this framework, they found that changes in national policies had measurable effects on spending patterns for higher education in the four countries. The relative decline in block grants from national governments to institutions (compared to other sources of support) resulted in a shift of expenditures from areas not likely to be able to generate their own revenues (e.g., libraries, building maintenance, on-campus instruction) to areas of potential income growth (such as sponsored research, continuing education, and student services). Although Slaughter and Rhoades (2004) have reconsidered resource dependency as a central tenet of academic capitalism because of the realization that higher education is much more involved in the external environment and not nearly as dependent as previously portrayed, the notion that organizational behavior and values can be understood through patterns of revenue generation and expenditure still holds.

Finally, at the institutional level, Slaughter and Leslie examined the ways that faculty and administrators engaged in marketlike behaviors and how this affected their concept of their profession and their labor. Qualitative interviews with academics were analyzed using a conceptualization of professionalization as a process in which organizational, political, and economic skills are equally as important as, if not more important than, knowledge, theory, expertise, and altruism. They drew from Weber's (1958) notion of "state capitalism" to understand publicly paid university employees as "state-subsidized entrepreneurs," who implement their academic capital by engaging in production. Although they focused primarily on technology transfer activities in the sciences and engineering, Slaughter and Leslie concluded that the faculty role is changing as a result of national policy shifts regarding the ways in which the state distributes funds to higher education. In the 1980s and 1990s, resource allocation patterns changed so that higher education institutions could no longer rely on unrestricted block grants from government and, therefore, had to encourage academics to pursue competitive research grants and other sources of revenue. In many instances, tuition restrictions were also lifted, and students bore more of the cost of their education than before. This final section of Slaughter and Leslie's book served as a foundation for the development of a fully conceptualized theory of academic capitalism that appeared in Slaughter's collaboration with Rhoades.

Higher Education in the New Economy

In *Academic Capitalism and the New Economy: Markets, States, and Higher Education* (2004), Slaughter and Rhoades explored the internal organizational dynamics of revenue-seeking behavior in higher education. Building on their previous work, the book continues to develop the thesis of academic capitalism by situating state-sponsored academic entrepreneurialism in a networked, global political economy. Like descriptions of the increasingly global and interconnected New Economy, the theory of academic capitalism includes the ideas of flexibility, risk, and entrepreneurial behavior seen by economists as particularly salient to success in global markets.

Slaughter and Rhoades theorize that colleges and universities are shifting from a public good knowledge/learning regime to an academic capitalist knowledge/learning regime. The notion of a "regime" as a dominant discourse or paradigm comes from Foucault's (1977, 1980) use of the word to describe the intersections between power and knowledge.

In the public good knowledge/learning regime described by Slaughter and Rhoades, academic research is considered to be collective labor toward a common good. This way of thinking about academic production is in keeping with Robert Merton's norms of disinterested science (communalism, universality, free flow of knowledge, and organized skepticism) and Vanevar Bush's social contract model, in which government funds universities to pursue "basic" science in a discovery-oriented environment that, once released into the knowledge commons, provides the foundation for product development in the consumer market. In the public good knowledge/learning regime, the academic production process is removed from the market, buffered by government laboratories and corporations that developed basic science into applied science. Implicit in this concept of academic research is the notion that the social sciences, and particularly the arts, although contributing to the public good, are not in the foreground of knowledge production. That position is taken by the sciences. This hierarchical conception of disciplines is reinforced by the state through research funding patterns that favor science and engineering and the lack of government articulation with the social sciences and arts. However, as long as state-government funding to institutions of higher education continues to support the social sciences and the arts through faculty positions in order to maintain the largely undergraduate educational functions of the university, these areas survive, but they are somewhat isolated from entrepreneurial departments and colleges that are close to the market.

In contrast to the public good knowledge/learning regime is the academic capitalist knowledge/learning regime that Slaughter and Rhoades describe as valuing knowledge privatization and profit taking in which institutions, inventor faculty, and corporations have claims that come before those of the public. Higher education becomes more connected to the marketplace in this regime, often in the form of partnerships with industry, start-up companies, equity interests, distance learning activities, strategic alliances, and idea laboratories. The values that drive the academic capitalist knowledge/learning regime do not replace Mertonian norms and the notion of basic science, but the public good is redefined as what is good for economic development as the public sector (institutions and governments) takes an even stronger role in shaping local, national, and global economies. However, academic freedom and the knowledge commons (peer review), which were critical values for the public good knowledge/ learning regime, are interrupted by knowledge claims that occur through intellectual property agreements and the commercialization of research products in the new regime. In other words, the academic profession is weakened as individual or corporate (private) ownership of knowledge capital is asserted.

Yet the privatization of knowledge, meaning the shift from serving the public good to the private good, is not reserved for the sciences and applied fields in the academic capitalist knowledge/learning regime. The social sciences and the arts are afforded more contact with the market as education itself becomes commoditized in the form of distance education, prepackaged curricula, and continuing/contract education programs. In the academic capitalist knowledge/learning regime, all disciplines become open markets, including the traditional teaching, research, and service functions of the university itself.

The process by which the academic capitalist knowledge/learning regime becomes ascendant is further theorized by Slaughter and Rhoades as having four components: the development of new circuits of knowledge, interstitial organizational emergence, intermediating networks, and extended managerial capacity.

Universities create new inter- and intraorganizational linkages when knowledge no longer moves primarily within scientific, professional, or scholarly networks. The rise of information and communications technologies has aided in the formation of alternative circuits of knowledge, where academics are connected to others outside higher education on a scale never seen before. In addition, the increase in the number of technology administrators on campuses to aid in the installation and support of these electronic networks has itself created a new knowledge domain in academe, where technical expertise is often a pathway to organizational power and influence (as seen in the executive cabinet role of the chief information officer).

As aids to the formation and sustainability of these new circuits of knowledge, interstitial organizations emerge to manage new activities related to generation of external revenues. Examples of these new organizations, found within higher education institutions, are economic development offices, trademarks and licensing offices, and technology transfer offices. These interstitial organizations at the boundary of higher education are often tied to networks that intermediate between public, nonprofit, and private sectors.

Intermediating organizations that exist between the public and private arenas are independent entities such as foundations, professional associations, consortia, and think tanks. These organizations are in the position to bring together boundary-spanning individuals from the state, market, and higher education (often from the interstitial units) to work collectively toward expanding the academic capitalist knowledge/learning regime.

The new circuits of knowledge, interstitial organizations, and intermediate organizations are populated by academic managers, whose numbers and influence increase in the academic capitalist knowledge/learning regime. These managers have increased their capacity to engage the market, redrawing the boundaries between universities and the corporate sector. As these academic managers become more professionalized, their positions in the academy are strengthened, and their influence on the direction of higher education is increased.

Academic Capitalism and Feminism

Slaughter and Rhoades drew upon the work of several social theorists concerned with social class hegemony because the academic capitalist knowledge/learning regime is central to the production of the middle and upper middle classes. Women were not foregrounded as a group in constructing the theory of academic capitalism in large part because men were seen to be the most active in constructing the academic capitalist knowledge/learning regime. Indeed, this regime is in part constructed to continue to give men some of the privileges they have historically held as a result of higher education. Academic capitalism can therefore be seen as a gender theory because it explains how patriarchy is becoming further entrenched in higher education institutions by a rational, economic agenda, despite the modest or significant gains of individual women.

The theory of academic capitalism draws heavily upon theorists who have been influenced by the economic inequality theories of Karl Marx and are also concerned with how power plays out in organizations and society. They do not focus on what to Marx was the central dynamic of social change, the struggle between capital and labor, with labor understood as the working class. Rather, these theorists see actors and organizations as players in the power dynamics that constitute societies. Gramsci (1971), for example, saw the state as more than the executive committee of the bourgeoisie; indeed, he saw the state as a (relatively) independent sector, in which class dynamics played out in a variety of unexpected ways. Gramsci also theorized ideological hegemony, which went beyond Marx's concerns with consciousness/false consciousness. Although these theorists understand the power of capital arrayed in global corporations and would at least acknowledge a business class and the power of elites, they look beyond the raw power of capital, concentrating on ideology, hegemony, and the normative and technical power held by the upper middle class. They see the upper middle class, whether deployed in academe, the bureaucratic state, or a small, innovative corporate sector, as fluid, strategic, and self-interested, able to wield power in ways that further the organizations and groups with which they are involved.

Traditionally, higher education served middle and especially upper-middle-class men as a form of credentialization that allowed them to occupy professional, scholarly, and managerial positions in society. Until the 1970s, women were either excluded from many professional schools or were subjected to admissions quotas that severely limited their numbers. Other than at women's colleges, only small numbers of women were professors in the 1950s and 1960s; and almost none were to be found at research universities. As women's social movements gained them space in the academy, men were forced to share their privileges. This was not a win-win situation unless the professional, scholarly, and managerial positions expanded by the number of women seeking these positions, which did not occur.

As women made gains in higher education—and indeed they did, now constituting over half of all graduates—men became active in constructing the academic capitalist knowledge/learning regime as a strategic effort to continue their historic privileges. They were the leaders and the beneficiaries of the market and marketlike activities that are the hallmark of academic capitalism. For example, men lead women in the number of patents derived from academic labor, are more often than women the CEOs of spin-off companies created from academic pursuits, and are more likely to benefit from the licensing of university research products. This is not to say that women were or are not actors in the new circuits of knowledge, interstitial and intermediating organizations, and expanded managerial sector through which academic capitalism has become incorporated in colleges and universities. They study and work in these sectors, but they are more often handmaidens to entrepreneurial men than entrepreneurs themselves. Of course, given the complexities of third-wave feminism, there are some women who are highly successful in the academic capitalist knowledge/learning regime. But even among the highly successful women, almost none are as successful as men, and most women do not do as well in the new roles made possible by the academic capitalist knowledge/learning regime as do men. In other words, the academic capitalist knowledge/learning regime has allowed men to recapture the historic benefits they received from an exclusively male higher education system.

Therefore, by including academic capitalism in a feminist theoretical framework, one is able to examine the historically imbedded and actively reinforced patriarchy of academe. Academic patriarchy has resulted in areas of the college or university that are closer to the market being predominantly male while the areas with stronger ties to the social welfare function (social work, education, nursing) involve more women. Salaries in the feminized fields are lower (for both men and women), and the social sciences and humanities receive far less governmental funding and support than male-dominated areas like science and engineering. In many cases, this has led enterprising educators in various nonpreferred fields (e.g., education professors who copyright tests and measurements, learning enhancement devices and techniques, distance education modules; fine arts faculty who copyright Web design, electronic art, graphic design) to increase revenues through market activity. However, this has generally benefited relatively few individuals in nonpreferred fields because of (1) the lack of external infrastructure such as federal mission agencies that fund research in these areas, (2) the feminization of these fields, and (3) the ensuing low stature of these fields in status and prestige hierarchies. In other words, despite market activity, there has not been widespread salary improvement in these areas. While these disparities have been explained as functions of the external labor market, academic capitalism can be used to highlight the active marginalization of fields that are not central to international competitiveness and global capitalism, which has subjugated women's work and women's epistemology throughout the world. Because of the social reproductive function of higher education, the relative position of women and their value in the academic arena is critical and, to a large extent, foreshadows the future place of women in society, politics, and economics. Academic capitalism theory is therefore particularly well coupled with radical feminism because both theoretical approaches agree that "revolutionary" restructuring of the academy may be necessary to redress the historical patriarchy that is imbedded within the systems of higher education.

REFERENCES AND FURTHER READING

Bush, V. (1990). *Science—the endless frontier: A report to the president on a program for postwar scientific research*. Washington, DC: National Science Foundation. (Original work published 1945)

Foucault, M. (1977). *Discipline and punish: The birth of the prison* (A. Sheridan, Trans.). New York: Vintage Books.

Foucault, M. (1980). *Power/knowledge: Selected interviews and other writings, 1972–1977* (C. Gordon, Trans. & Ed.). New York: Pantheon Books.

Gramsci, A. (1971). *Selections from the prison notebooks* (Q. Hoare & G. Nowell-Smith, Trans. & Eds.). New York: International Publishers.

Merton, R. K. (1973). The normative structure of science. In N. W. Storer (Ed.), *The sociology of science: Theoretical and empirical investigations* (pp. 267 278). Chicago: University of Chicago Press. (Original work published 1942)

Pfeffer, J., & Salancik, G. R. (2003). *The external control of organizations: A resource dependence perspective.* Stanford, CA: Stanford University Press. (Original work published 1978)

Slaughter, S., & Leslie, L. (1997). *Academic capitalism: Politics, policies, and the entrepreneurial university.* Baltimore: Johns Hopkins University Press.

Slaughter, S., & Rhoades, G. (2004). *Academic capitalism in the new economy: Markets, state, and higher education.* Baltimore: Johns Hopkins University Press.

Slaughter, S., & Rhoades, G. (2005). Academic capitalism and the new economy: Privatization as shifting the target of public subsidy in higher education. In R. A. Rhoads & C. A. Torres (Eds.), *The university, state, and market: The political economy of globalization in the Americas* (pp. 103–140). Stanford, CA: Stanford University Press.

Weber, M. (1958). *From Max Weber: Essays in sociology* (H. H. Gerth & C. W. Mills, Trans. & Eds.). New York: Oxford University Press.

CHAPTER 2

Black Feminism, Womanism, and Standpoint Theories

EVANGELINE A. WHEELER

Black feminism is the nexus between the Black liberation and the women's liberation movements, but it has its own distinct ideologies. Black feminist thought consists of specialized knowledge created by African American women that clarifies a standpoint of and for Black women. In other words, Black feminist thought encompasses theoretical interpretations of Black women's reality by those who actually live it. Black feminist perspectives stress how various forms of gender, race, and class oppression work together to form a matrix of social domination. These oppressions are deeply interwoven into social structures and work together to define the history of the lives of Black women in America and other women of color worldwide. The history of these cultural oppressions can be traced back to the era of U.S. slavery, during which time a social hierarchy developed locating White men at the top, White women next, followed by Black men, and finally at the bottom, Black women. Because of the wide scope of these oppressors and the 400-year history associated with them, Black feminist writers and theorists reason that Black women have developed a distinct perspective and cognizance that provides them with keen social and economic survival skills, including utilizing everyday strategies of political resistance.

The particular interactions of oppressions faced by Black women daily have forced particular perspectives on social reality. Black feminists are highly critical of oversimplified models of oppression that suggest that Black women must identify as either Black or women, women first and Black second, or Black first and women second. Black feminists believe that when the lives of African American women are improved, there will be progressive development also for African American men, their families, and their communities. Black feminism can be identified with the celebrated historical tradition of Black female activists' commitment to empowering themselves to create a humanistic community for all.

Because middle-class White women within the traditional feminist movement have been accused of focusing on oppression primarily in terms of gender while paying scant attention to issues of race or class, theories of Black feminism were forged in resistance to this felt marginalization. It has been argued, too, that oftentimes Black women had avoided the women's movement based on fear of interrogation by their own community members who linked racism with the women's movement. Articles in the anthology *Words of Fire: An Anthology of African-American Feminist Thought* (Guy-

Sheftall, 1995) contain some examples of this. Michelle Wallace, in her article "Anger in Isolation: A Black Feminist's Search for Sisterhood," suggests that the women's movement simply exploits Black women to help it build integrity. bell hooks, in "Black Women Shaping Feminist Theory," complains of the assumption in the women's movement that all women share a common oppressor. The Black feminist critique of racism has demanded that White women claim responsibility for their own racism and not require Black women to either educate White women on issues of race or to applaud their efforts at becoming less racist.

Black Feminist Activism and Scholarship

The Black feminist movement developed in the United States during the late 1960s and early 1970s as groups like the Combahee River Collective (which emphasized capitalism as the primary source of oppression for Black women) and the National Black Feminist Organization (NBFO) reacted to the sexism and homophobia of the male-dominated Black civil rights movement and the racism of the White feminist movement. In 1977, the Combahee River Collective, a grassroots Black feminist organization in Boston that had begun as a chapter of the NBFO, issued a position paper that analyzed the intersection of oppression in Black women's lives and asserted the legitimacy of feminist organizing by Black women. The Collective's work broke significant new ground because it was explicitly socialist, addressed homophobia, and called for sisterhood among Black women of various sexual orientations. In fact, the early commitment of Black lesbian feminists was crucial to building the movement in the 1970s, at a time when many heterosexual Black women were reluctant to identify themselves as feminists.

The NBFO emerged from meetings held among African American women at the New York offices of the National Organization for Women in May and August 1973. The NBFO pledged itself to address problems of discrimination faced by African American women because of their race and gender. The NBFO sought to change the portrayal of African American women in the mass media, raised consciousness about sexual abuse in the African American community, and fought for higher wages and greater political influence for African American women. Chapters were organized in several major U.S. cities including Chicago and Detroit, but the national organization dissolved in 1977. *Sage: A Scholarly Journal on Black Women*, the first explicitly Black feminist periodical devoted exclusively to the experiences of women of African descent, was founded in 1984 at Spelman College, a traditionally Black women's college in Atlanta, Georgia. Barbara Smith and Audre Lorde were cofounders of Kitchen Table: Women of Color Press, the first independent press to focus on the work of feminists of color. Among its publications were the now-classic *Home Girls: A Black Feminist Anthology* and *This Bridge Called My Back: Writings by Radical Women of Color*.

Patricia Hill Collins, a major thinker in Black feminist theorizing, in her landmark 1990 book *Black Feminist Thought: Knowledge, Consciousness, and the Politics of Empowerment*, describes major themes in the construction of Black feminist thought, all generated from a Black woman's point of view. Most importantly, Black women empower themselves by creating self-definitions and self-valuations that enable them to establish positive self-images and to repel negative, controlling representations of Black womanhood created by other people. Some of these negative, pathological, controlling images are known as "mammies," "matriarchs," "welfare queens," and "Jezebels." Such racist stereotypes are operative myths in the minds of many, allowing an easy disregard for the extent to which Black women are victimized in society. Black feminists stress the importance of positive self-definition as part of the journey toward social and political empowerment.

In order to help alleviate the psychological and economic suffering of Black women and to help them gain political power, Black feminists advocate a separate area of academic study that focuses exclusively on articulating and understanding the lived experiences of Black women. A typical contemporary Black feminist can be broadly described as an African American woman academic who believes that female descendants of American slavery share a unique set of life experiences importantly distinct from those of Black men and White women. The emergence of Black women's studies in colleges and universities during the 1980s and the creation of a community of African American women writers such as Toni Morrison, Alice Walker, and Gloria Naylor, among a great many others, have created institutional locations where Black women intellectuals can produce specialized thought. One style of scholarship, for example, first describes activist traditions dating from abolitionist times and then investigates instances of contemporary activism in formal organizations and in everyday life and work. Black women's history, documenting social structural influences on Black women's consciousness, and Black feminist literary criticism, exploring Black women's self-definitions, constitute two focal points in Black women's intellectual work. However, the suppression of Black feminist thought in mainstream scholarship and within its Afrocentric and feminist critiques has meant that Black women intellectuals have traditionally relied on alternative institutional locations to produce specialized knowledge about the Black women's standpoint. While Black women can produce knowledge claims that contest those of mainstream academia, academia often does not grant that Black women scholars have competing knowledge claims based in another knowledge validation process. Thus any credentials controlled by mainstream academia can be denied Black feminist scholars on the grounds that their research is not credible. Many Black women scholars, writers, and artists have worked either alone, as did Maria W. Stewart, or within African American community organizations, like Black women in the historic club movements and in contemporary churches. In terms of professional advancement in an academic career, a focus on helping the socially and politically disadvantaged become self-determining usually lies outside the definitional boundaries of traditional disciplines like psychology, for example, so a Black feminist orientation is not very likely to enhance one's career.

Black feminists combine academic intellectual thought and political activism. Black women intellectuals use examples of lived experiences like working in factories, working as domestics, obtaining good health care, organizing communities, and mothering in their theorizing and written scholarship. They have the job of reinterpreting experiences so that African American women are aware of their collective knowledge, enabling them to feel empowered instead of oppressed. The Black feminist movement does not mobilize through an institutionalized formal organization. Black feminist collectives operate through local communities in decentralized, often segmented, ways referred to in the literature as "submerged networks." Such gatherings of women with Black feminist views have existed throughout the history of Blacks in America, but the label of feminist was rarely attached to the activity. Some informal networks include self-help groups, book clubs, "sistah" parties and gatherings, and explicit political education groups.

Womanism

Novelist and essayist Alice Walker in 1983 introduced the term "womanist" as a more culturally acceptable label for people uncomfortable with the label of Black feminist. Walker first used the term in the context of her collection of poems *In Search of Our Mothers' Gardens: Womanist Prose*. The need for this term arose from the early feminist work that advocated social change such as the right for women to move from the domestic sphere to the working and professional spheres away from home. This feminist agenda ignored the fact that many Black women were not housewives and had in fact been working outside the home most of their adult years to help support their families. Black women were already working women outside the home, but not out of personal choice, and certainly not usually as a matter of personal fulfillment. Similarly, the Black liberation movement focused largely on equality first for African American men, while the community's women were inadvertently (and temporarily) left in the background. With the increasing use of the term, both African American studies and women's studies programs began to incorporate womanism into university courses, and historians, for example, are regarded as womanist historians if they have incorporated the views and experiences of African American women in their accounts of history. Another term, "Africana womanism," places Africa at the center of analysis as it relates to women of African descent, wherever in the world they may live. Thus, the terminology Africana womanism, not Black feminism, womanism, or any other term perhaps more appropriately fits the woman of the African diaspora.

Black Feminism and Standpoint Theory

A standpoint is a particular intellectual place from which people see and understand social reality. A related metaphor is that of a "lens" through which we view the world differently depending on which lens we happen to be looking through. A standpoint helps in articulating a social group's perspective about its lived experiences and in mapping the practices of power structures that oppress them. Standpoint theories, like that of Black women, claim to represent the world from a particular socially situated perspective that can lay a claim to special kinds of knowledge, an epistemic privilege or authority.

Black feminist standpoint theories reject the notion of an unmediated truth, arguing that knowledge is always mediated by myriad factors related to an individual's or group's particular position in the sociohistorical landscape. The basic insight of standpoint theories is that members of oppressed groups, like Black women, have special kinds of knowledge by virtue of their marginalized status in society. From knowledge gained via their particular standpoint, Black women can best embark upon political empowerment achieved through a raised group consciousness. Even if Black women cannot make good on the claim that their standpoint has *privileged* access to reality, it may offer alternative representations of reality that are more *useful* to the group than are other truthful representations. As feminist standpoint theory developed, it focused more on the political nature of the standpoint, and it has attempted to attend to the diversity of women by incorporating the standpoints of other marginalized groups like those of Black women. Black feminist standpoint theory is a type of *critical theory*, whose aim it is to empower the oppressed to improve their situation. It is a position from which emancipatory action can be taken.

Feminist standpoint theory derives from the Marxist position that the socially oppressed classes can access knowledge unavailable to the socially privileged, that different social groups have different points of view for gaining knowledge, particularly knowledge of social relations. It appropriates the Marxist belief in the epistemological superiority—or at the very least, equality—of the perspective of the oppressed classes. In the Marxist view, workers do not have this standpoint to begin with. They attain it by gaining collective consciousness of their role in the capitalist system and in history, since several aspects of the workers' social situation enable them to attain an epistemically privileged perspective on society. Workers are oppressed, central to the capitalist mode of production, and endowed with a cognitive style based on their practical productive material interaction with nature. Oppression gives them an objective interest in the truth about whose interests are really served by the capitalist system. They have a special view of capitalism. Because under capitalism the standing of all other classes is defined in relation to them, in coming to know themselves, and their class position, workers come to know their society as a totality.

Marxism offers the classic model of a standpoint theory, claiming an epistemic privilege over fundamental questions of economics, sociology, and history on behalf of the standpoint of the proletariat. And so feminist standpoint theory considers knowledge of marginalized groups as equally important as that produced by dominant groups. A marginalized standpoint like that of Black women is important because it not only can view the dominant group from unflattering angles but also can view many other different standpoints and critique them. When these situated facts from different standpoints form a pattern, the patterns themselves could be seen as knowledge. The epistemic privilege of the oppressed is sometimes cast, following W. E. B. Du Bois, in terms of "bifurcated consciousness," the ability to see things both from the perspective of the dominant and from the perspective of the oppressed and, therefore, to comparatively evaluate both perspectives.

Black women are oppressed and, therefore, have an interest in representing social phenomena in ways that reveal rather than mask certain truths. As in Hegel's description of the master-slave relation, the subordinate slave is dependent upon the dominant master; it is in his or her interests to understand the master. Likewise, a subordinate group's standpoint is more complete as its members have a greater reason to understand the dominant group's standpoint and little reason to maintain the status quo. Black women also have direct experience of their oppression, unlike Black men or White women, whose privilege enables them to ignore how their actions affect Black women as a class. Every standpoint theory must offer an account of how one gains access to its situated knowledge. This depends on whether membership in the group whose perspective is privileged is defined objectively, in terms of one's position in a social structure, or subjectively, in terms of one's subjective identification as a member of the group.

In the early 1980s, Nancy Hartsock developed what she called "the feminist standpoint," a concept that attempted to adjust the Marxist idea that one's perspective is dependent only on one of the two major class positions in a capitalist society. Hartsock suggested instead that the position of women is structurally different from that of men, that the lived realities of women's lives are profoundly different from those of men. She argued that the sexual division of labor forms the basis for a feminist standpoint. Just as Marx's understanding of the world from the standpoint of the proletariat enabled him to go beneath bourgeois ideology, so a feminist standpoint can allow us to understand patriarchal institutions and ideologies as perverse inversions of more humane social relations. Hartsock thus attempted to translate the concept of the standpoint of the proletariat, by analogy, into feminist terms.

There is no homogeneous women's experience and hence no singular women's standpoint, since women see things differently from different social locations; different marginalized groups have different social, economic, and symbolic viewpoints. For Black women, the logic of an epistemology that grounds epistemic privilege in oppression is to identify the multiply oppressed as multiply epistemically privileged. Within feminist theory, this logic has led to the development of Black feminist epistemology. Thus Patricia Hill Collins grounds Black feminist epistemology in Black women's personal experiences of racism and sexism and in cognitive styles associated with Black women. She uses this epistemology to supply Black women with self-representations that enable them to resist the demeaning racist and sexist images of Black women in the wider world and to take pride in their identities. Black women are "outsiders within" having enough personal experience as insiders to understand their social place but also enough critical distance to empower critique.

Standpoint theorists argue about its history, its status as theory, and its relevance to current thinking, some arguing that standpoint theory provides a circular basis for deciding which standpoints have epistemic privilege. Considering many standpoints in the production of knowledge has been criticized on the grounds that it opens the way for relativistic knowledge. But in fact the collection of many standpoints works toward a more robust empirical representation of epistemology. The many different representations of a single phenomenon, such as a historical event, can be critically evaluated to determine what patterns arise out of the accounts of the phenomenon as it happened. Many different standpoints are accessed in an attempt to create a more robust account of a phenomenon. The consideration of many different standpoints, including that of Black women, gives an opportunity for the entirely polemical or plainly false standpoints to be seen as nonobjective.

Implications for Higher Education and Research

In the history of White women's education in the United States, higher education for women was shaped by notions of something called true womanhood, which was not applied to Black women. Higher education also was based on perceived cognitive and intellectual differences between men and women, so women were educated primarily in the domestic arts. Black women, however, had no practices of separation from their men, so education for Black women came to emphasize education for men and women alike, with the ultimate goal of racial uplift. Feminist perspectives of nineteenth- and twentieth-century Black women originated in teachings that stressed how necessary it was for all of the community's members to be educated. White women who entered teaching jobs after graduating from high schools typically left their careers behind when they got married. Black women typically continued to work, not always because of economic necessity, but sometimes because of the need to participate in the empowerment of their community and to inculcate generations of students with Black feminist thought.

Black feminist pedagogy is dedicated to raising the political consciousness of all students by introducing an Afrocentric orientation to understanding the world, emphasizing the roles of race and gender as critical to understanding all social and historical phenomena, and instilling in students the motivation toward political activism.

The presence of the Black feminist standpoint in education as an alternative episte-mology is important because its existence challenges not only the content of what currently passes for truth but simultaneously challenges the process by which that truth was derived. Black feminist pedagogy as a philosophy of liberation enables stu-dents to take revolutionary action to change their communities, both local and global. To respectfully teach about theorizing from a Black woman's standpoint requires a re-jection of the concept of education as value-free and instead demands an embrace of a pedagogy based on ethics and civic engagement. Presenting situatedness as the foun-dation of reality and knowledge rejects the elitism of academic thinking.

Since much of Black feminist thought is contained in the works of Black women writers, literary criticism by Black feminist critics provides an especially fertile source of Black women's ideas. Black feminist standpoint theories offer a critique of conven-tional epistemologies in the social and natural sciences. Ways of knowing informed by the motive of caring for the community's needs will produce more valuable represen-tations than ways of knowing informed by the singular interests of the dominant. They will produce representations of the world in relation to universal human inter-ests rather than in terms of the interests of dominant classes, heretofore ideologically misrepresented as universal interests.

Black feminist research is conducted primarily to solve real-world problems. The researcher and the research participants become engaged in a dialogue whereby the researcher uses her knowledge and skill to stimulate a new awareness within the com-munity. An important aspect in this applied research is the respect given to the par-ticipants. Acknowledgment of their capability and potential to produce knowledge themselves is made. The standpoint theorist or activist should at any time *situate* her-self within the plane of her research topic to validate or justify her knowledge claims. One's epistemological standpoint lends her authority when doing research in any field of the social sciences. Such a participatory approach to research requires a com-mitment to the empowerment of the people being studied.

Historical accounts of events are recorded and put forth as objective truths, but official accounts of events are rarely presented from a Black woman's standpoint. An African proverb describes this position well: Only when lions have historians will hunters cease being heroes. The dominant class writes history from its standpoint, and the marginalized standpoint is oftentimes considered alternative, or indeed subver-sive, history. The dominant class considers its own standpoint history to be objective and correct, whereas the marginalized historical perspective is often deemed a subjec-tive interpretation of the same events. According to standpoint theory, the closest a historical account can get to objectivity is to consider the many different standpoint perspectives of a single event and to deconstruct each account to derive the patterns that emerge. But as critics would readily point out, the ethereal nature of objectivity arises upon realization that deconstruction is done from a particular standpoint and then reconstructed from another particular standpoint. Just as traditional European American standpoint history depicting the appropriation of Native American land shows White immigrants as diplomatic and considerate toward Native Americans, the Native American historical accounts tell quite a different story, instead depicting the systematic and cruel destruction of native civilization. Black feminist historians will give different accounts of Black women's history.

Black feminist standpoint theory is especially relevant in the scientific method. Validity in scientific method is created by the reproduction of results over many testings of a single hypothesis. To consider a single epistemological standpoint as universally valid is to test a hypothesis over and over again from the same standpoint in the same conditions. For science to proceed, and for scientific arrogance to be overcome, many standpoints must be introduced into the scientific community as valid modes to verification of a single scientific hypothesis. Many case studies in the sciences ranging from the field of pharmacology to sociology have fallen subject to being viewed by one singular epistemological standpoint, namely that of the dominant class. Scientific studies conducted solely on the dominant class and then generalized to Black women are often misapplied.

Gender theorists began by studying the concept of gender itself, ignoring issues of race, asking about the meaning of the differences between men and women with respect to several social and psychological variables. Many feminist proponents of gender theory rested their analyses on universal presumptions about the significance of gender and the specific characteristics of masculinity and femininity that were based on White women's experience of gender, which Black feminism argued against. Sojourner Truth, in her famous 1851 speech, *Ain't I a Woman?* made at a women's rights convention, is used on this point. Truth argued that femininity conceptualized as passive and weak, like the description of White women in the constructed notion of true womanhood, did not apply to her and most other Black women, yet she and they could equally be called woman.

REFERENCES AND FURTHER READING

Collins, P. H. (1990). *Black feminist thought: Knowledge, consciousness, and the politics of empowerment*. New York: Routledge.

Guy-Sheftall, B. (Ed.). (1995). *Words of fire: An anthology of African-American feminist thought*. New York: New Press.

Harding, S. G. (1991). *Whose science? Whose knowledge? Thinking from women's lives*. Ithaca, NY: Cornell University Press.

Harding, S. G. (2004). *The feminist standpoint theory reader: Intellectual and political controversies*. New York: Routledge.

Perkins, L. (1993). The role of education in the development of Black feminist thought. *History of Education, 22*(3), 265–275.

Smith, B. (1977). *Toward a Black feminist criticism*. Trumansburg, NY: Crossing Press.

CHAPTER 3

College Student Development

TIFFANI A. RIGGERS AND LINDA J. SAX

There is a vast empirical literature on college student development that examines how students create identity and how they develop cognitively during the college years. Such work is informed by a variety of theories that help us to explain the nature and process of change during college. For the most part, this research is informed by theories of cognitive and identity development that consider students in the aggregate (i.e., do not consider how the process of development may differ in terms of students' gender, race, or other characteristics). However, critiques of these theories have given rise to the notion that perhaps the process of development differs for different types of students. In the case of gender, the question is whether traditional theories of student development apply equally to women and men, or whether the two genders develop in unique ways during the college years.

In response to these critiques and related questions, theoretical perspectives on college student development have been continually evolving. Women's development is now better understood as distinct from men's, and there is a growing interest in understanding the unique nature of development specifically for male college students. As theories continue to advance, they will serve to better inform empirical research on men's and women's development in college. In fact, a recent large-scale study of gender differences in the impact of college (Sax, 2008) supports the notion that college student development differs for women and men both in the nature of change that occurs and in the forces that affect change. However, the study emphasizes that gender differences in student development are not always clearly aligned with gender-based theoretical perspectives. Additional research is needed to assess the validity of existing theoretical perspectives on women's and men's development and to address the applicability of theories to each gender as a whole, given the vast diversity *within* the male and female college student populations.

General Student Development Theories

Initially, theories relevant to college student development did not focus on differences of gender but presumed that the developmental process applied equally to men and women. While some of these theories are now applied primarily to men and some have been answered with concomitant theories applying to women (Kohlberg's and Gilligan's moral development theories are notable examples), it is valuable to briefly review the foundational theories that have informed the field of college student development.

Identity Development

Erik Erikson is generally considered the father of identity development. His theory of development is lifespan oriented with the traditional-age college student appearing in his fifth stage (Identity versus Role Confusion) (Erikson, 1968). In this stage, Erikson posited that both men and women begin to construct their identity based on surrounding influences and experiences. The goal of this stage is to develop commitment both to the self and to relationships with others. Upon completion of this stage, Erikson believed that individuals would be prepared to develop lasting relationships and authentic intimacy. Transition between stages is proposed to occur as individuals experiences a "crisis" (or moment when they are forced to confront a changing paradigm or internal development). After the individual resolves the crisis, he or she can move to the next stage of development.

CHICKERING'S THEORY OF IDENTITY DEVELOPMENT

Chickering proposed seven stages, or "vectors," that college students pass through in developing their identity (Chickering & Reisser, 1993). The term *vector* is used to indicate that the stages are directional and that each seems to have increasing magnitude or influence on the student as she or he accomplishes it. In the first two vectors (Developing Competence and Managing Emotions), students gain intellectual, practical, and interpersonal skills. These skills establish a foundation from which individuals can create healthy relationships in the next two vectors (Moving through Autonomy toward Interdependence and Developing Mature Interpersonal Relationships). While traversing these two vectors, students begin to act more confidently in their relationships, develop a broader understanding of differences, and internalize an active tolerance and acceptance of these differences.

The interpersonal relationships (which can be romantic or platonic) developed in the fourth vector are believed to be vital in Establishing Identity, Chickering's fifth vector. Chickering acknowledges that an individual may have multiple identities (e.g., female, African American, and lesbian) and notes that the student may not establish identity in each dimension at the same time. A student who has accomplished this vector will demonstrate an increased comfort with him or herself—physically and emotionally. Chickering also suggests that a student who has completed this vector will be more self-assured and have a more secure sense of self. In the final two vectors, Developing Purpose and Developing Integrity, students utilize the skills and confidence gained in establishing their identities to direct them as they pursue their goals and relationships. In these stages, students become more confident in the ability to integrate outside influences (such as family) with their own goals and purposes. Students also demonstrate a stronger sense of belief in personal values and morals and are more able to integrate their beliefs and actions.

In the past 20 years, research has been conducted to test Chickering's original theory and determine if it is equally generalizable for both men and women. Chickering and Reisser, for example, suggested that women place a greater importance on the element of interdependence (a reliance on mutual support of others) over independence (a sense of self-sufficiency; autonomous behavior) and that women develop interdependence prior to independence (while men may do the converse). Foubert,

Nixon, Sisson, and Barnes (2005) found that women develop mature interpersonal relationships earlier than men but that later stages, such as developing purpose, occurred around the same time for both.

MARCIA'S THEORY OF EGO-IDENTITY DEVELOPMENT

James Marcia (1966) also utilized an Eriksonian perspective on identity development in constructing his theory of identity development and status. Marcia focuses on two specific psychosocial tasks that may occur simultaneously or separately: Exploration and Commitment. In Exploration, the theory suggests that men and women will differentiate themselves from their peers and view themselves as individuals as they search for an identity that defines who they are. The completion of the Commitment task brings about a sense of stability and comfort with the explored and chosen identity.

In each of these two tasks of identity formation, Marcia suggests that men and women may encounter four responses. The first is a precrisis response in which the individual's identity is "diffused," or unclear. In this stage, the young man or woman has not explored his or her identity with any real effort and is uninterested in doing so. Likewise, this individual is not necessarily committed to any concrete aspect of his or her identity; an ambivalent attitude toward ideological issues is likely present as well. Some students may exhibit a "foreclosed" response to crisis, or an unreflected and unquestioning adherence to a set of beliefs or values about one's self and the world. These values and beliefs are often taken from the parent(s) or other influential adults (e.g., teachers, coaches) and may also be influenced by peers. Students encountering a "moratorium" response are in the midst of identity crisis and are actively searching for who they are. The search is conscious and intentional, and though they may not have reached a stage of commitment, men and women in this stage are fully involved in exploring their beliefs and values and determining who they will be. Finally, students whose response is "identity achievement" have reached a stage of commitment to their various identities. Like Chickering, Marcia leaves room for identity to develop across multiple dimensions, including gender-role, political, religious, and occupational.

Cognitive Development

Cognitive development theories are primarily concerned with how individuals make sense of the world around them. The theories generally typify how individuals interpret events in light of their own experiences and biases. Theories in this category also demonstrate the development that occurs as an individual's ability to make meaning becomes more sophisticated. In the same way that identity theories are rooted in Erikson's model, cognitive development theories are rooted in the work of Piaget (Evans, Forney, & Guido-DiBrito, 1998).

Cognitive theorists suggest that mental structures serve as filters or lenses as each person views the world (Abes, Jones, & McEwen, 2007). These structures are thought to occur for all people regardless of cultural situation, though the timing of the development may vary (Evans et al., 1998). Thus, much like identity theories, cognitive theories often operate as stage theories; individuals must pass through a series of stages as they become more developed. Movement between stages is believed to be caused by a sense of disequilibrium when the individual experiences a mental conflict (i.e., an event that does not unfold as the individual expects). At this point, individuals will try to assimilate the experience into existing understandings, and if this is not possible, they will create a new filter or lens. In this way, experiences of the world are put into places wherein the individual can use them to make meaning of events and relationships.

KOHLBERG'S MORAL DEVELOPMENT THEORY

Kohlberg's (1971) theory was widely used, initially, to apply to development of both men and women, though now it is generally applied only to men (because his sample consisted primarily of men). In this theory, Kohlberg suggests an orientation for upholding justice as the highest stage of development. The theory is a lifespan stage theory, which states that development of morality and ethics begins at infancy. In the earliest stages, children's morals are formed by conceptions of good and bad. Children obey (a parallel to behaving morally in this stage) because there are physical consequences to obedience and disobedience; punishment and reward figure heavily. As individuals mature, the foundation of morality becomes more other-centered, meaning that behavior is governed by approval and respect for order or authority (concepts of loyalty to others over self become important), regardless of personal consequences. The final stages of Kohlberg's theory emphasize universal logic and behavior. In these stages, individuals have a greater understanding of and exhibit active compliance with the social contract (generally held beliefs about good people and behaviors). While individuals acknowledge that others may have different beliefs and values, they also believe that there is a universal way of behaving that causes no harm to others and punishes those who do cause harm (an enactment of justice). Kohlberg relates these behaviors with adherence to a "Universal Ethical Principle," an abstract social agreement about just and unjust behavior by which individuals seek justice because it is right (not necessarily to help *people* per se but because justice is the highest ethical behavior).

Kohlberg's research assistant Carol Gilligan (1982) later challenged the theory as being too androcentric and devaluing characteristics inherent in female moral development. She also critiqued his belief that women are unable to achieve the same level of moral and ethical development as men (because he did not observe women behaving in the same ways regarding justice as men). Her companion theory is presented below, in the section on women's cognitive development theories.

PERRY'S SCHEME OF INTELLECTUAL AND ETHICAL DEVELOPMENT

Perry (1970) based his work heavily on the work of Piaget and Kohlberg in developing a theory of intellectual and ethical development. The theory was developed after studying the intellectual developmental patterns of both men and women, but he has been criticized for his exclusive use of men in illustrating his theoretical concepts.

Perry's goal of creating a conceptual map of ethical development resulted in a model in which individuals occupy nine positions through their collegiate experience. Perry eschewed the word *stage* when constructing his model, deeming its implication of temporal development too strong. He preferred instead the word *position*, which emphasizes a location through which a student must pass, but does not emphasize duration. Perry's theory suggests that students begin college believing in strict categories of right and wrong (dualism). In these early positions, authorities are thought to have possession of all knowledge, and the student serves as a receptacle for learning (though if a professor challenges previously determined knowledge, the student may exhibit disequilibrium). In later positions, the student acknowledges the possibility of multiple truths but may now consider that he or she is wrong when faced with opposing views. As students continue to develop, they gain a sense of relativism and begin to critique their own and others' conceptions of truth, eventually determining a personal sense of ethics. This personal sense of ethics coincides with a determination of identity and sense of self in context of the larger community, culture, and world.

For Perry, the most important part of students' intellectual and ethical development is not the actual position itself but the period spent transitioning between positions, as that is when the development of intellect and ethics occurs. Perry emphasizes that while the positions are somewhat directional (that each position must be completed before reaching the next), they are not exclusively positive (an individual may regress when faced with new information or experiences). Perry's theory suggests that different aspects of ethical development may occur at different times in a person's life, indicating the process is more like an ever-expanding loop than a straight line.

BAXTER MAGOLDA'S EPISTEMOLOGICAL REFLECTION MODEL

In a qualitative, longitudinal study of college women and men, Marcia Baxter Magolda (1992) identifies patterns of knowing that are gender related but makes special effort not to distinguish between specifically male and female developmental patterns. She suggests that students show a decline in Absolute Knowing (a dualistic perspective of truth) during their college years, and a gain in Transitional and Independent Knowing (which takes into account the contextual nature of truth). Baxter Magolda emphasizes that knowledge is constructed by the individual in a context of societal, relational (i.e., formed through friends, romantic partners, etc.), and familial beliefs and values and proposes that development is transactional and relative, for both women and men. She proposes that women and men may approach these cognitive changes differently but that both will demonstrate transformation. Her theory has many similarities to Perry's, but because her data were analyzed in terms of gender, she is able to offer more information about differences and similarities between women and men.

Absolute Knowers see a clear distinction between true and false, believing that authorities hold answers. In this phase, knowers focus on receiving knowledge from an authority figure (like a professor) and mastering it. Receiving Knowledge was demonstrated more often in women, while men were more likely to strive for Master Knowledge. Mastery behavior is often more vocal and interactive in challenging authority, while receptive behavior is more silent and collaborative.

Transitional Knowers demonstrate a growing belief in the uncertainty of truth. These knowers expect to engage in dialogues about knowledge (rather than just receiving it or memorizing it) and begin to take an active part in the construction of knowledge. Students at this stage exhibit Interpersonal Knowing (learning through interactions with others) and Impersonal Knowing (learning through debate or challenge with others). Baxter Magolda relates Interpersonal Knowing to women's behavior and Impersonal Knowing to men's but notes that both genders demonstrated a more active approach to gaining knowledge in these stages. In the Independent Knowing stage, the instructor who was formerly an authority now serves as a guide or facilitator. Students in this stage are interested in understanding each other's interpretation of truth and knowledge. These knowers demonstrate two distinct patterns: Interdependent Knowing (interactive creation of knowledge, through which one develops one's own thoughts but also receives and incorporates others' ideas) and Individual

Knowing (less interactive than Interdependent Knowing, but the individual is still interested in learning about others' ideas).

Male and female behaviors converge in the final stage, Contextual Knowing (in which knowledge depends on context and may be truer in some settings than others). Baxter Magolda offers, however, that this stage is unlikely to be evident in undergraduate college students but rather in an individual's lifetime. When observed, the behaviors are typified by a student who believes in the contextual and relative nature of truth. This student may adhere to a certain set of truths, but these beliefs are supported by evidence. Ultimately, Baxter Magolda found more similarities than differences among men and women; thus her theory focuses more on students as learners in general. This theory can be used to reemphasize the value of all students as learners and the importance of students' discovering their own voices.

Female Student Development Theories

In the early 1970s, researchers began to raise questions regarding the generalizability of popular student development theories. They noticed gender and racial inequities in the samples used to develop the theories, in which the participants often were primarily white males. Additionally, some of the theories presumed women to have less capacity for development because their observed behavior and development were different than the theory prescribed (e.g., Kohlberg). Researchers criticized these theories for a lack of attention to gender and a lack of specificity regarding the differential development of both women and men. While critiquing the popular theories, researchers used a distinctly feminist theoretical approach. This approach addresses the development of both men and women from independent perspectives, acknowledging that men and women may not develop in the same ways, but not assigning deficit to either gender. In response, a number of theories were developed that identified the developmental trajectory of women separate from the trajectory of men. In addressing the development trajectories of women, researchers noted that women often encountered similar stages as men, but the result of completing the stage was different.

Josselson's Theory of Identity Development in Women

Ruthellen Josselson (1987) took a qualitative and longitudinal approach to testing and critiquing Marcia's identity development theory, ultimately creating a theory of women's identity development. Josselson used Marcia's four levels and reframed the activities that occur within each level based on her 20-year study of 60 women. She suggests that Marcia's theory was based on decision making rather than content or context. Josselson notes that women appear more likely to develop their identity in light of their community and world context, a more other-centered model than men utilize.

In particular, Josselson establishes that women's identity development takes place while women negotiate relationships. Women are more focused on the nature of the person they want to become than on exterior identifications such as occupation, relationship status, and religion that are the predominant identities for men (according to Marcia's theory). Josselson's theory illuminates the different ways women and men use relationships in identity formation. Whereas men might utilize relationships to create distinct, individual identities for themselves, women are thought to depend on relationships to inform their personal identity and to help them maintain their connection to others.

Gilligan's Theory of Women's Moral Development

Gilligan (1982) observed that women were often omitted or overlooked in many of the developmental theories being developed and used in higher education. Her main concern was that men were often considered the basis for normative behavior and development, leaving women to appear underdeveloped, immature, or in some cases abnormal. As Kohlberg's former research assistant, she particularly noted that Kohlberg did not include women in his sample and yet generalized his findings to both men and women. Beginning to study moral development herself, she discovered that there was another line of moral reasoning that was not accounted for in Kohlberg's model. She believed Kohlberg's findings identified a "justice voice" and that she had identified a "care" (or mercy) voice.

Gilligan presents a moral development perspective for women, suggesting that women and men have the same capacity for development but that each gender develops differently. While Kohlberg's theory focused on understanding rules and rights (a more male way of development) in moral development and behavior, Gilligan's focuses on the power of relationship and community. She argues that the justice voice stresses autonomy and independence, whereas the care voice emphasizes interdependence and connection. Gilligan's theory is a stage theory, like Kohlberg's, and the stages themselves parallel Kohlberg's with the exception of the achievement needed to move to the next stage. In Gilligan's early stages (childhood), the individual makes decisions based on her self-preservation and self-interest. In the middle stages, individuals begin to gain a sense of responsibility for others and an orientation toward sacrifice of the self in order to achieve consensus and remain connected to others. Gilligan's final stage, like Kohlberg's, centers on the idea of doing no harm to others. In particular, Gilligan states that women's ethical and moral behavior at this stage takes into account the effect of the outcomes on others' psychological and physical well-being rather than abstract principles of justice (such as those posited in Kohlberg's theory).

Belenky, Clinchy, Goldberger, and Tarule's Theory of Women's Ways of Knowing

Gilligan and Perry are foundations of the theory of Women's Ways of Knowing (Belenky, Clinchy, Goldberger, & Tarule, 1986). Belenky et al. utilized the meaning-making aspects of the earlier moral and ethical development theories to study how women identify knowledge and truth. Theirs is a critique and response to Perry's work and, as such, focuses on women to determine what aspects of development might be missing from his theory. They propose five separate perspectives (rather than stages) that a woman may have as she assesses the world around her. Though they did not propose that the perspectives build on each other in a stagelike way, some authors (e.g., Kuk, 1990) suggest that the perspectives seem to exhibit increasing complexity of cognitive thought and thus are similar to Perry's stages.

The first perspective is Silence, when a woman demonstrates an automatic, unthinking obedience, which is indicative of her sense of powerlessness and of being subject to an external and dominant authority. Women experiencing this perspective are often younger or deprived of status in some way, either educationally, socially, or economically. Women may still be silent in the next perspective, Received Knowledge; however, they are actually learning about truth by listening to others. There is a strong belief that truth is held by an external authority and that the woman herself does not have the power to create knowledge.

Women who have the perspective of Subjective Knowledge understand that they have some power to create truth. The development of this perspective often occurs as a woman encounters the failure of an authority figure. She begins to believe that truth may be different for different people and in different situations and that it is created by society. In the next perspective, Procedural Knowledge, two different types of knowing —Separate and Connected—act in tension. Separate Knowers strive for an objective search for truth (excelling in critical thinking skills and objective reasoning), while Connected Knowers place a more subjective filter on the information they are hearing and sharing. Connected Knowers make no effort to objectify their own perspectives and expect that what they are hearing from others is conveyed through a subjective lens of the speaker. The final perspective of this theory is Constructed Knowledge. This is the most complex stage and is typified by the ability to integrate both the objective and subjective into personal truth. Belenky et al. suggest that women who attain this perspective are able to fully listen to others without losing their own sense of self.

Male Student Development Theory

As is evident in the foregoing sections, in the late twentieth century many of the general student development theories were reconceptualized and applied solely to men, and as a result, scholars sought to discover developmental theories that specifically addressed women. While many of the earlier theories were largely based on research with predominantly male samples, researchers are now seeking to determine if the general theories indeed characterize men's development authentically. This new direction of research has focused thus far on the identity development of men in light of the different behaviors of men and women on college campuses (Harper, Harris, & Mmeje, 2005) and on challenges to the stereotypical views of masculinity (O'Neil, 1981; Davis, 2002). The absence of specific models regarding men's identity and cognitive development (such as those that exist for women) is notable, and research has initially focused on the gendered nature of manhood rather than specific stagewise development models.

Men's identity development research utilizes social psychological perspectives combined with other relevant disciplines to challenge the ways that education has previously looked at men and masculinity. Researchers (e.g., Davis, 2002) suggest that masculinity, like femininity, is an artifact of our culture and socially constructed, but they note that men and women have differential ways of communicating, experiencing challenge, and constructing identity. In particular, Davis (2002) notes two specific conflicts of self-expression. The first occurs when men desire to express their thoughts and feelings but are constrained by social pressures to conform to noncommunicative stereotypes of male behavior. The second occurs in determining when face-to-face communication with other men is appropriate, as opposed to nonverbal or indirect communication methods.

One particularly salient finding across the research is men's fear of femininity in identity expression and the identity conflict created for men by experiencing external definitions of identity or having identity ascribed to them by others (O'Neil, 1981; Davis, 2002; Harper et al., 2005). These received identities often begin at home (passed from parent to child) and may be influenced by peers and then are emphasized upon arrival in the college environment, because of the gender norms that exist on any given college campus, or a peer-group effect. The fear of being feminine (or having femininity ascribed to them) can lead men to increased depression and psychological stress (Good & Wood, 1995). However, because of the gender norms on campuses, male students are significantly less likely to seek help regarding their emotional problems. Men also report feeling as though supportive campus structures are not as available for them as they are for women (Davis, 2002).

Harper, Harris, and Mmeje (2005) offer a theoretical model of male development and behavior that rests heavily on the basis of social construction of gender. They suggest that men come to college socialized to their gender roles and behaviors and that in college they may experience disequilibrium about the role of masculinity and femininity in their personality. The conflicts that they experience regarding their gender identity often lead to increased misbehavior, including acts that may lead to campus judicial intervention (such as vandalism, assault, and rape). These behaviors, as well as drug and alcohol abuse, serve as exercises in "proving" their maleness. These role conflicts can also have effects on the academic life of college men. For instance, men may conceal academic ability to avoid negative consequences from male peers for performing above the level that is socially accepted (Czopp, Lasane, Sweigard, Bradshaw, & Hammer, 1998) or may struggle to stand up to other men who want to "hang out" rather than study (Vianden, 2009). Role conflicts may also make it difficult for men to connect with faculty members in meaningful ways, as some may consider it a weakness to disclose that they did not comprehend course content or did poorly on a test. As a result, men may refrain from seeking out faculty members beyond the classroom (Vianden, 2009).

The Harper et al. (2005) model begins with the man's socialization into a type of masculinity prior to college (both at home and at school) that rewards tough behavior and results in more frequent referrals to authority figures for discipline. The social construction of maleness also figures heavily in their model, and the authors suggest that the behaviors learned prior to college are reinforced by the gender norms on campus. When men arrive in college, however, their masculine identities may be challenged, creating a gender role conflict (O'Neil, 1981) if they are unable to succeed in ways that they have in the past. The failures they encounter (in the classroom or other areas) further reinforce the fear of femininity and may influence an active response to reclaiming male identity, which then may result in misbehavior and judicial response. The authors suggest that these conflicts may cause men to have difficulty in developing the competencies that Chickering and Reisser (1993) describe unless the men perform behaviors that are socially accepted by their male peers. Harper et al. suggest that these factors all influence men as they learn how to behave on a college campus and as they construct their male identities.

REFERENCES AND FURTHER READING

Abes, E. S., Jones, S. R., & McEwen, M. K. (2007). Reconceptualizing the model of multiple dimensions of identity: The role of meaning-making capacity in the construction of multiple identities. *Journal of College Student Development, 48*(1), 1–22.

Baxter Magolda, M. B. (1992). *Knowing and reasoning in college: Gender-related patterns in students' intellectual development.* San Francisco: Jossey-Bass.

Belenky, M., Clinchy, B., Goldberger, N., & Tarule, J. (1986). *Women's ways of knowing.* New York: Basic Books.

Chickering, A. W., & Reisser, L. (1993). *Education and identity* (2nd ed.). San Francisco: Jossey-Bass.

Czopp, A. M., Lasane, T. P., Sweigard, P. N., Bradshaw, S. D., & Hammer, E. D. (1998). Masculine styles of self-presentation in the classroom: Perceptions of Joe Cool. *Journal of Social Behavior and Personality, 13*(2), 281–294.

Davis, T L. (2002). Voices of gender role conflict: The social construction of college men. *Journal of College Student Development, 43*(4), 508–521.

Erikson, E. (1968). *Childhood and Society* (2nd ed.). New York: Norton.

Evans, N. J., Forney, D. S., & Guido-DiBrito, F. (1998). *Student development in college: Theory, research, and practice.* San Francisco: Jossey-Bass.

Foubert, J. D., Nixon, M. L., Sisson, V. S., & Barnes, A. C. (2005). A longitudinal study of Chickering's vectors: Exploring gender differences and implications for refining the theory. *Journal of College Student Development, 46*(5), 461–471.

Gilligan, C. (1982). *In a different voice: Psychological theory and women's development.* Cambridge, MA: Harvard University Press.

Good, E. G., & Wood, P. K. (1995). Male gender role conflict, depression, and help seeking: Do college men face double jeopardy? *Journal of Counseling & Development, 74,* 70–75.

Harper, S. R., Harris, F., Mmeje, K. C. (2005). A theoretical model to explain the overrepresentation of college men among campus judicial offenders: Implications for campus administrators. *NASPA Journal, 42*(4), 565–588.

Josselson, R. (1987) *Finding herself: Pathways to identity development in women.* San Francisco: Jossey Bass.

Kohlberg, L. (1971), Stages of moral development. In C. M. Beck., B. S. Rittenden, and E. V. Sullivan (Eds.), *Moral Education.* Toronto: University of Toronto Press.

Kuk, L. (1990). Perspectives on gender differences. *New Directions for Student Services, 51,* 25–36.

Marcia, J. E. (1966). Development and validation of ego-identity status. *Journal of Personality and Social Psychology, 3*(5), 551–558.

O'Neil, J. M. (1981). Patterns of gender role conflict and strain: Sexism and fear of femininity in men's lives. *Personnel and Guidance Journal, 60,* 203–210.

Perry, W. G. (1970). *Forms of intellectual and ethical development in the college years: A scheme.* New York: Holt, Rinehart & Winston.

Sax, L. J. (2008). *The gender gap in college: Maximizing the developmental potential of women and men.* San Francisco: Jossey-Bass.

Vianden, J. (2009). Improving first-year students' out-of-classroom faculty interactions. *E-source for College Transitions, 6*(5), 1–17.

CHAPTER 4

Feminist Critiques of Educational Research and Practices

LUCY E. BAILEY

Feminist critiques of traditional approaches to educational research and practices surfaced in the eighteenth century, emerged with greater vigor and variety in the 1960s and 1970s, and have expanded today into a substantive body of scholarship that questions and revisions what it means to produce knowledge about education and the social world. Broad in scope and diverse in expression, feminist research draws from an array of methods, philosophies, models, and disciplines to pursue questions about educational knowledge and schooling processes. Central to such pursuits is the conception of education as a social and economic system with profound power and possibility to shape human lives. As such, it is a crucial arena for feminist work. Researchers with varied goals have worked within and against conventional approaches to analyze male power and demonstrate the centrality of gender to education, social life, and the creation of knowledge. Early feminist critiques of educational research and practices explored the varied effects of historically male-dominated social systems and male bias in scientific thought on women's opportunities. More recent critiques encompass a wider array of topics, ranging from policy inequities to women's under-representation in administrative positions to the varied ways gender, race, and class shape educational theories.

Despite the growth and diversity of feminist inquiry since the civil rights and women's movements in the United States, the visibility of feminist methodologies in some fields and their near invisibility in others speak to still untapped potential in researchers' use of these resources. This variable use also reflects a certain degree of unfamiliarity with, confusion about, or reluctance to engage with feminist methodologies that merits redress. Indeed, the complexity of contemporary educational concerns necessitates that researchers utilize an array of tools and techniques to approach their work effectively. Although feminist scholars have diverse interests, training, and theoretical allegiances, feminist approaches to research share some common characteristics: a spirit of critique, recognition of the centrality of gender and other key identities in social life, the promotion of equal educational opportunities and practices, and principles of feminist methodology that guide the vision and practice of research. These "guiding principles" (Fonow & Cook, 1991) offer researchers concrete tools for traversing steadily shifting educational terrain as new educational imperatives and issues emerge.

Contemporary feminist critiques of educational research and thought have antecedents in the eighteenth century. Upper-class Anglo-European women protested the practice of denying women educational opportunities based on their perceived physical and intellectual inferiority to men. Arguing that education, law, government, and other social institutions were androcentric—centered on men's needs, aspirations, and social roles—women advocated formal education to aid them in raising future citizens, carrying out their domestic and social responsibilities, and serving as moral guides for others. Some with more radical visions for the time refuted male philosophers' claims that women were inherently too emotional and passive to bear the responsibilities of autonomous citizenship. Others protested scientists' diligent efforts to pinpoint the exact source of women's presumed inferiority in the fibers and processes of the body. Scientists variously examined skull size, brain weight, genitals, and menstrual cycles for evidence of women's arrested and inferior development.

Indeed, women's assumed emotionality was the basis for excluding them from research endeavors as well. Considered "unreliable" witnesses for verifying scientific experiments believed to require an objective and neutral stance, women were barred from the Royal Society of London until the twentieth century (Haraway, 1997, p. 32). Yet as early as the mid-1700s, some men and women questioned the presumption that research approaches based on such beliefs and exclusions could be considered neutral, objective or value-free. This important critique of claims to "objectivity" in traditional research remains central to contemporary feminist thought.

In the early twentieth century, feminist researchers in education, anthropology, and psychology examined the powerful notion of "sex difference" long presumed as fact. Researchers questioned the attribution of intellectual, personality, and behavioral differences between men and women solely to "natural" (biological) causes rather than family and educational (social) experiences. Feminists thought examining the belief in "natural" differences systematically was important given its continued use as justification for denying women various social roles and opportunities, including equal education. Investigating "sex difference" from a variety of angles, researchers discovered social causes of differences that appeared to exist across sex and race. This pioneering body of scholarship collectively contributed to undermining the notion of absolute biological difference and highlighted the role research can play in questioning commonly held beliefs used to limit human potential. If difference has a social basis, this research suggested, education can contribute to altering the direction of human lives.

More recent feminist critiques emerged as part of a larger surge of academic revision in the wake of the civil rights and women's movements. During the 1960s and 1970s, scholars in varied disciplines began questioning with greater intensity the traditional content, processes, and techniques that constituted knowledge in their fields. The development of women's studies in higher education, the passage of Title IX, and the establishment of a special interest group called "Research on Women in Education" in the American Educational Research Association, the country's largest educational association, testify to the growing salience of gender in education. In this spirit of revision and change, feminist researchers scrutinized the methods for conducting research and establishing knowledge in education. A key critique focused on claims that educational research proceeds from a "disinterested," "objective," or "value-free" stance. Feminists made clear that excluding women historically from research samples, generalizing to women the results of research conducted with men, and seeking explanations for women's presumed inferiority are neither objective nor value-free processes. Indeed, such research not only perpetuates male domination and inequality but does so in the powerful guise of scientific and "disinterested" knowledge.

Feminists also argued that White men's numerical dominance in research positions, doctoral programs, and the university professoriate inevitably influenced the direction and analysis of educational research. This argument captured a growing belief at that time: that all research is laden with researchers' subjective beliefs, social ideas prominent in a given time period, and prevailing assumptions about the best approach for conducting research. These sometimes invisible factors influence what we study, how we study it, and what we conclude. For example, analysis of research during this period found male researchers more likely than females to judge women as susceptible to influence. Female researchers were more likely than men to ask questions about sex differences in psychological research. Similar patterns were visible on the basis of race and class. White women's pioneering research included primarily White participants and overlooked race and class differences influential in research findings.

Feminist scholars also questioned assumptions of "universality" in educational research that overlook gender as a central force shaping social organization and research processes. For example, psychologist Carol Gilligan's work *In a Different Voice* (1982) challenged Lawrence Kohlberg's foundational research that proposed a "universal" model of moral development (a model applicable to all) yet found girls' behavior to be less moral than boys when judged by that model. Approaching her research with consciousness of gender, Gilligan found that females were not less moral than boys but held different conceptions of morality based on an ethics of care and connection. Her findings indicated that theories such as Kohlberg's based on male norms may not only have limited applicability to female experience but can distort understanding of the social world when accepted as universal. Subsequent work on caring, nurturing, and reproduction emphasized sex/gender difference. Similarly, feminist research on social security and higher education has shown that policies and practices that may appear "gender neutral" often reflect male career patterns. For example, tenure-track time lines do not take into account gendered elements of lived experience such as kinship work and reproductive labor. Although universities generally provide professors between five to six years to achieve tenure, this time line is at odds with the biological parameters of childbearing and research findings on female professors' scholarly productivity, which can increase later in their professional careers once childbearing and family responsibilities lessen.

Feminists continue to challenge research claims to universality because they also render differences *among* women invisible and limit understanding of the complexity of the social world. Though earlier feminists primarily focused on sex/gender difference with insufficient attention to other aspects of identity and subjectivity, contemporary feminists consider differences among women as fundamental considerations in conceptualizing, conducting, and analyzing research. Class, race, ethnicity, sexuality, nationality, and ability are social constructs as well as aspects of lived experience that intersect with and enrich the construct of gender. Making universal claims based on partial norms erases such diversity. For example, research that revisited Gilligan's premise with the added analytic attention to race and class found African American women and men to share commonalities in moral decision making. Similarly, research with Latina mothers has shown that they sometimes engage differently with their children's education than what White middle-class norms dictate. Also, the growing body of research into American girlhood has identified clear differences in the ways race and class shape girls' experience with and expressions of classroom engagement, desire, peer culture, cheerleading, teen pregnancy, and prom.

Despite the salience of difference to educational theory and practice, conventional educational research continues to mobilize universal claims and initiate studies with insufficient attention to the complexity of diverse social positioning. Even as feminist methodologies grow increasingly diverse and complex, these historical patterns of exclusion continue to necessitate researchers' attention. Psychological research examining concepts such as achievement, motivation, and development have sometimes overlooked gendered inflections of such concepts or their varied expressions across social groups. Major textbooks intended to overview educational research do not include critical forms of inquiry or feminist research. Methodologists have noted research patterns in which female victimization rather than agency is emphasized, findings on dominant groups are generalized to others, identity intersections are ignored, heterosexuality and Whiteness are presumed, or Western bias leads to culturally insensitive research practices or conclusions limited to a Western perspective.

Contemporary feminist research practices, both within and outside of higher education, are interdisciplinary, drawing from an array of methods, beliefs, models, philosophies, data sources, and disciplinary practices to create knowledge. Feminists use different theories (frameworks that explain and organize) and epistemologies (frameworks for coming to understand and know what we know) to approach their investigations. Such frameworks are often highly contested, fueling productive discussion and revision of existing approaches. For instance, scholars have struggled to explore how culture shapes women's and men's lives without simplifying and reinscribing such differences as absolute. Others have debated the significant implications of poststructuralism and postmodernism for feminist research, fields of thought in which scholars critique and deconstruct concepts and systems long assumed as fixed and foundational to human understanding of the world: science, reason, knowledge, truth, progress, gender. Tensions have surfaced among those who utilize materialist approaches to research women as embodied subjects positioned unequally in social structures and those who draw from poststructuralist thought to analyze how language creates the categories people inhabit, including the very category of "woman," how categories of knowledge develop and function, and what constitutes "legitimate" research. Scholarly debates in the wake of poststructuralism are complex, nuanced, and productive. They have fueled increasingly innovative and reflexive approaches that push the boundaries of what it means to produce knowledge about the social world.

Feminist Methods and Methodologies

Researchers generally distinguish between methods and methodology. Methods are commonly grouped in the broad categories of *qualitative* methods (tools or techniques that generally use words, artifacts, and images as data) and *quantitative* methods (tools or techniques that generally use numbers as data). The specific purpose of any research project determines which methods researchers use to collect and analyze information. For instance, even though some perceive quantitative methods as a male-centered approach to research, feminist scholars have found quantitative methods particularly useful for exploring the breadth of phenomena, for obtaining grants, and for influencing public policy. Researchers may employ either quantitative or qualitative methods, or a combination of these, such as oral history, surveys, statistics, focus groups, ethnography, document analysis, participant observation, and autobiography —among many other choices.

The term *methodology*, in contrast, refers to the theory of how research should proceed and the guiding rationale for the design, methods, and analyses utilized. Although feminist scholars revise methodologies as they debate central concepts and face new social complexities, researchers proceeding from a feminist methodological stance are guided by certain principles. First, feminist research proceeds from the assumption that gender, race, class, and sexuality, among other elements of identity, are central to the organization of social life, to lived experience, and to the inquiry process. Researchers investigate issues and produce knowledge with gender, gender relations, gender and power, and the fluctuating nexus between gender and other social locations in mind.

Second, feminist research assumes that inquiry is not a value-free or objective process. Researchers are shaped by their social location, lived and embodied realities, and ideas available in any given historical moment. These interpretive, critical, or deconstructive research approaches contrast with conventional educational research dominated by the scientific paradigm termed "positivism." Although positivism is only one way to conceptualize the social world and approach the knowledge-gathering process, its preeminence in education has shaped beliefs regarding what science can—and should—look like. This dominance is reinforced by current research funding patterns in the wake of No Child Left Behind (NCLB) legislation (2001). Despite scholars' advocacy of an expansive definition of science, governmental funding since 2001 has been directed almost exclusively to positivist, evidence-based research. The positivist paradigm posits a physical and social world that researchers armed with appropriate tools, methodological objectivity, and systematic data procedures can understand, predict, and control. Positivism emphasizes empiricism (sense experience) as the foundation of knowledge and advocates researcher distance from and neutrality toward his/her object of inquiry. To feminist researchers, however, disinterestedness, neutrality, prediction, and control are neither attainable nor necessarily desirable stances for inquiry into the complexity of the social world. They argue, as do others, that research requires varied belief systems and methodologies.

A third element of feminist methodology is *reflexivity*. This concept, also present in other research traditions, refers to researchers' responsibility to analyze their own research practices. The specific research project shapes what components of reflexivity researchers utilize. In its earlier formulation, feminist methodology guided researchers to reflect on their research methods, to explore research participants' own reflections on the subject of research, and significantly, to use these reflections to analyze how larger social forces such as power and hierarchy shape the research process. More recently, scholars have expanded the concept of reflexivity. Researchers consider how their allegiances and identities relate to their topic, how these features shape their methodological choices, research practices, and the knowledge created, how findings may influence social thought, and how audience, topic, and methods may influence presentation and reception of findings.

Patti Lather and Chris Smithies's study *Troubling the Angels: Women Living with HIV/AIDS* (1997) offers a clear example of the multilayered use of reflexivity in feminist work. The authors use qualitative inquiry to explore women's diverse experiences living with HIV/AIDS. Throughout the text, Lather and Smithies recount their own research struggles, trace women's experiences with HIV/AIDS, incorporate participants' reflections on the researchers' work, and ponder the possible implications of their findings for social thought concerning HIV/AIDS. They emphasize their reflexive practices through a split text format, separating group interviews from their own reflections. This format highlights the centrality of researcher reflexivity to creating knowledge about women's lives—essential reflections in a project attempting to trouble the boundaries between researcher and participant and to represent women's struggles living with a devastating virus. In contrast to research approaches in which the scientist appears as a "disembodied knower" devoid of personal investments in the research process who merely reports results, the methodological choice described above is explicitly feminist in that it approaches research inquiry and the creation of knowledge as processes imbued with gendered power and renders the researchers' process of meaning-making visible. In this view, researchers' training and social location can shape the inquiry process in rich and meaningful ways. Those committed to understanding knowledge as *constructed* rather than *found* must reflect consciously on the ways their research practices shape knowledge.

A fourth principle of feminist methodology is its orientation to action and social change. Feminist researchers are committed to identifying and changing fundamental inequities that social institutions, including education, reflect and perpetuate. Despite their diverse theoretical commitments, feminists share a common insistence that their work contributes to intellectual, social, and political transformation. Education is a central site for such transformation. This orientation differs from research designed to explain, predict, or simply explore phenomena. While explanation or understanding may be goals of feminist inquiry, they are accompanied by an explicit call to analyze power relations, alter inequities, and promote human agency. Feminist research practice, as a type of social relationship, must also reflect this commitment to transformation. Specifically, feminist educational research may provide calls to action; reinterpretations of established theory; models for transformative research processes; analyses of existing research, policy, or law; recommendations for developing new research, policy, or law; greater understanding of racial, gender, and class stratification in education and recommendations for change; visions of equitable teaching practices; consciousness-raising; advocacy for underrepresented groups in curriculum, teaching, and leadership; and guidelines for program development or revision.

Feminist educational researchers express this orientation to action and social justice in varied ways. Pioneering research that identified widespread discrimination against people of color and other women in academic tracking, teaching practices, curriculum, and popular culture offered specific corrections for such inequities. Other scholars have highlighted Chicana and postcolonial feminism, women's activism in teacher unions, and working-class girls' anger as examples of women's resistance to racist, Western, and patriarchal power historically. In light of the historical dominance of men and masculine thought in education, some researchers advocate radical structural changes such as returning to single-sex schools or home schooling. Some theorists propose new approaches to learning. For example, in an incisive use of terms still potent today, Adrienne Rich (1977) urged women to "claim" rather than simply "receive" their education. Rich argued that women's historically passive and yielding approach to their learning demonstrates how profoundly conventional sex-role socialization and male-centered knowledge has muted women's voices, usurped their agency, and diverted them from pursuing affirming and transformative knowledge. Actively claiming one's education, Rich asserted, might be the very "difference between life and death" for women (1977, p. 231). Contemporary research echoes Rich's call for voice as scholars document the gendered constraints teachers and parents continue to place on girls' bodies, voices, and agency in classrooms and playgrounds.

This orientation to action may also produce concrete resources to better women's lives. Lather and Smithies (1997) designed their text in part as an educational resource to correct misconceptions about HIV/AIDS and to provide information for women and their families living with the virus. Researchers investigating sexual harassment and bullying in K–12 schools and on college campuses have reviewed legal cases, clarified terminology, and offered resources for administrators to address these issues. Feminists studying sex education have recommended comprehensive programs that better serve adolescents than abstinence-only education programs that portray adolescent females as potential victims, suppress healthy female desire, and promote married heterosexuality as the only acceptable form of human sexuality. Autobiographical and biographical scholarship has probed the fluid boundaries between women's experiences and their social context. Policy researchers have studied NCLB, Affirmative Action and Title IX of the Higher Educational Amendment Acts of 1972 to clarify gaps between the vision and application of these mandates. They have highlighted how Title IX is applicable to sports, cheerleading, women's presence in science, technology, engineering and math, and the schooling of pregnant teens to emphasize the necessary changes school workers must make to ensure equal educational opportunity.

A fifth element of feminist methodology is concern with ethical and political implications of the research process. Central to this concern is the relationship between participant and researcher: Who has the right to speak for whom? Who is included and excluded? What kind of relationship should researchers have with participants? What role should participants play in conducting and analyzing research? Historically, some researchers have exploited and manipulated subjects or assumed a hierarchical stance privileging the researcher's authority and expertise. Conventional practice continues to advocate that researchers hold a neutral, distanced stance in the conduct of research to prevent bias from influencing study results. In contrast, in feminist practice, researchers often seek ways to disrupt constructions of researchers as "experts" and participants as "objects of research." Caring, emotionality, and other affective elements are welcomed as potentially enriching for the research endeavor as well as characteristics to analyze for knowledge about the social world. Like the conceptual difference between doing research "on" people and doing research "with" people (Lather & Smithies, 1997), feminist researchers might approach their participants as potential collaborators, rich sources of information, and partial experts on their own lives. This conceptual difference is not meant to cast research subjects in a net of romanticism that erases researchers' contributions to the research process or to coax subjects to participate beyond their abilities or desires. Rather, it reflects efforts to reduce inequities in the research process and foreground the humanity and subjectivity of participants. Collaboration among scholars, collaboration with participants, democratic research designs, and participant feedback on research findings are common ways feminist researchers have attempted to create more equitable research relationships.

Concern with the ethical and political dimensions of research has also necessitated grappling with its representation. Contemporary research has been shaped by the "crisis of representation," a phrase that refers to a period of intense academic questioning that began in the 1970s and centered on the degree to which research can actually capture and present aspects of social life. Researchers often approach their endeavors with the conviction that careful choices in design, methods, and analysis will ensure that findings and their presentation in statistics, graphs, texts, or films reflect social reality as closely as possible. In contrast, researchers engaged in the productive ferment wrought by the crisis of representation often conceptualize research findings as partial, situated, contextual, and co-constructed in complex relationships between researchers, participants, and audiences.

Feminist methodologists have also considered how to represent the marginalized groups and often sensitive issues they study and how their research findings might be circulated and consumed. For example, researchers studying gay students, sex workers, people living with HIV/AIDS, and school-aged mothers and pregnant teens have recognized the groups they study are highly stigmatized in society—stigma to which research may unintentionally contribute. Thus, included in researchers' methodological considerations is how to represent participants sensitively. Changes in methodological practices have spurred the development of experimental forms of data representation such as performance, poetry, drama, blended narratives, and photography. Whether representational forms are conventional or experimental, feminist researchers conceptualize inquiry as an inherently political process and strive to anticipate the possible consequences of their representational choices.

Although feminist thought continues to shape educational practice, educational fields have not incorporated feminist theories and methodologies equally. Indeed, objections to feminist research as politically driven and not "real" research limit its use. Governmental initiatives that fund randomized experimental trials and other positivist scientific research to the exclusion of other forms of science may increase this pattern. Psychology has produced significant scholarship on sex roles, sex differences, and adolescent development and identity, while feminist research in career, technical, and vocational education is scarce. Male critical theorists continue to overlook gender as a substantive category of analysis in the workings of capitalist power. Educational research sometimes focuses on counting males and females in a given discipline rather than applying a feminist analysis to the forces leading to numerical inequities or curricular initiatives that interrupt them. Educational leadership has used feminist methods since the 1980s to examine diverse issues: institutional factors limiting women's advancement, the experiences of women of color in administration, and "leadership" as a masculine, White, and heterosexist concept. Feminist pedagogy (studies on the science of teaching) offers rich scholarship on institutional hierarchies and classroom power relations, and feminist research in mathematics, science, and reading is growing. Curriculum theorists and literary scholars have analyzed the Western and Eurocentric thought shaping language use, classroom practices, and curricular materials. Across fields and disciplines, feminist methods remain a rich resource for educators to utilize in their shared quest for greater understanding of the social world. As pressing educational concerns continue to emerge, feminist approaches can contribute to the power of education to transform human lives.

REFERENCES AND FURTHER READING

Fonow, M. M., & Cook, J. (1991). *Beyond methodology: Feminist scholarship as lived research*. Bloomington: Indiana University Press.

Fonow, M. M., & Cook, J. (2005). Feminist methodology: New applications in the academy and public policy. *Signs: Journal of Women in Culture and Society*, *30*(4), 2211–2236.

Haraway, D. J. (1997). *Feminism and technoscience*. New York: Routledge.

Lather, P. (1991). *Getting smart: Feminist research and pedagogy with/in the postmodern.* New York: Routledge.

Lather, P., & Smithies, C. (1997). *Troubling the angels: Women living with HIV/AIDS.* Boulder, CO: Westview Press.

Reinharz, S. (with Davidman, L.). (1992). *Feminist methods in social research.* New York: Oxford University Press.

Rich, A. (1979). *On lies, secrets, and silence: Selected prose.* New York: Norton.

Skelton, C., Francis, B., & Smulyan, L. (2008). *Gender and education.* London: Sage.

St. Pierre, E., & Pillow, W. S. (2000). *Working the ruins: Feminist poststructural methods in education.* New York: Routledge.

Young, M. D., & Skarla, L. (2003). *Reconsidering feminist research in educational leadership.* New York: State University of New York Press.

CHAPTER 5

Feminist Reproduction Theory

JO-ANNE DILLABOUGH

Pierre Bourdieu, some might say, was not a feminist. Indeed, the now late French social theorist was often regarded by feminist theorists in France and beyond the borders of continental Europe as largely uninterested in questions of gender and social inequality. This broad claim notwithstanding, from the early 1990s onward Bourdieu did in fact argue that concerns over the nature and significance of *masculine domination*—a term closely aligned with symbolic domination and far more complex in nature and constitution than its wording suggests—can be identified to greater or lesser degrees in all aspects of social life. Bourdieu went on to argue that masculine domination, as it pertains primarily to culture and social class, has its greatest effect in social institutions where the maintenance of an apparently stable and rational social order is a key national project par excellence. Consequently, he pointed particularly to education as a powerful site for the reproduction of gender inequality, as well as conceptualizing it as a spatially organized site for the accumulation of specific forms of gendered capital, ideological assertions, and the subsequent class formation of social stratification.

The efforts of gender theorists in education, especially *feminist reproduction theorists*, dating back to the 1970s, have reflected many of Bourdieu's concerns about masculine domination and the forms of educational control operating in relation to wider capitalist interests in globalizing contexts. Feminist reproduction theory, arguably the form of educational feminism aligned most closely with Marxist and neo-Marxist feminist thought, has therefore been most centrally concerned with what Bourdieu (1998) eloquently referred to as the "constancy of structure" in gender relations: a study of how "categories of understanding" about "sex" and "gender" and their material effects reproduce a *constant* and "deeply sedimented" gendered division of labor that is embodied in public consciousness and asserted through class relations in education (see also McNay, 2000).

Arguably, it has been the reproduction theorists, or those who might be deemed class theorists, concerned with gender inequality, particularly those aligned with concerns about women's relationship to the political economy (such as Madeleine Arnot and Lois Weis) and, more recently, feminists interested in cultural theory (such as Beverley Skeggs, Diane Reay, Lisa Adkins, and Angela McRobbie) who have committed in part to Bourdieu's belief that education and other social forces in the cultural field (e.g., media) play a very substantial part in reproducing (not merely regulating) gender, race, and class divisions in the state. Feminist reproduction theorists have also struggled to unpack contemporary misconceptions, including those made by some gender theorists, such as liberal and maternal feminists, about the potential eradication of social inequality through liberal and relational models of educational access and opportunity. Following a Marxist interest in history, feminist reproduction theorists incorporated into their theory a social history of women's oppression in the nation-state (e.g., feminist historical materialism). In this way, they were able to draw upon the heuristic principles of historical materialism to expose the relationship between masculine hegemony, class stratification, and material interests. Feminist scholars in this theoretical camp were therefore able to engage in class critiques of the state in order to reveal its binary conceptions of the abstract male citizen and domestic sphere as ultimately underwriting women's political participation in the state. They also conceptualized the state as emphatically asserted from the viewpoint of a male history in face of many other competing social interests.

It is for these reasons that reproduction theorists are often viewed as the critical consciousness of the field—providing a *"critical political semantics"* (see Fraser & Gordon, 1995) of a system that still largely privileges men over women, White students over minority ethnic students, and elite classes over the "working classes" and economically disadvantaged youth. As such, feminist reproduction theory, and the Marxist ideas it draws upon, have made major contributions to the study of gender inequality in schools. The theory has not been without criticism, however, and in the current political and policy contexts, limitations of the theory and related gender research have also emerged.

Reproduction Theory and the Study of Gender Equality

In the second half of the twentieth century, largely following the work of European social theorists, sociologists in the United Kingdom and the United States, and the political force of the international second-wave feminist movement, researchers began to concern themselves with education's role in the reproduction of gender and class relations in the state (e.g., Arnot, formerly MacDonald, 1980; Bowles & Gintis, 1976). In particular, the rise in feminist social movements in the 1960s and 1970s played a critical role in allowing reproduction theorists to rethink the nature of egalitarian postwar aims of education and their significance in eradicating gender inequality. The historically derived argument raised by reproduction and neo-Marxist feminists was that national education systems were characteristically modeled on a classed notion of citizenship and civic participation reflecting a residual public/private split. The public/private distinction noted by reproduction theorists referred to the manner in which the liberal democratic nation-state and its associated national education systems had been built upon a division between the rational male citizen (i.e., legitimate public participant) and the ascription of women to the realm of the private (as caregiver, teacher). The basic premise of Marxist feminist critiques of the nation-state was, therefore, that liberal socialization theories and their implicit commitment to traditional gender roles implied an assumption of conformity to state ideals (traditional male and female roles) and a focus upon a male-centered economy rather than the recognition of gender equality and the dismantling of substantial class distinctions across and among women through education.

An emphasis upon the reproduction of the social and economic order by the educational Marxists of the 1970s thus led to a feminist version of *social reproduction* theory

(MacDonald, 1980). Informed primarily by Bowles and Gintis (1976) and British and European Marxist movements, feminist sociologists conceptualized education as an institutional tool of capitalism that reproduced the position of women in the domestic sphere and, in particular, the subordination of working-class girls into a social status residing outside the domain of legitimate citizenship. In these conceptualizations, social class served as the social category that not only prefigured but determined girls' educational experiences, identities, and forms of consciousness.

In this early version of gender reproduction theory, the study of school structures (e.g., curriculum subjects, educational policies, streaming) and their links to the economy was privileged over issues of cultural identity, difference, resistance to dominant power formations, and modalities of social agency (see Arnot & Dillabough, 1999, for an elaboration on these points). While such theories offered few practical suggestions in relation to girls' emancipation through education or to the corresponding need for a more egalitarian notion of education extending outward from an expanded democracy, the critique of the liberal state and the concepts of "freedom" and "equality" through education were crucial to the critical power of reproduction theory to question the apparently egalitarian gender principles put forward by Western liberal states.

At the level of sociological theory, then, many reproduction feminists were forced to reject Emile Durkheim's late nineteenth-century imagined concept of education for national stability or nationhood because it raised substantial problems of gender inequality and led to economic instability for women, particularly if socialization into the realm of the domestic field often equated with economic disadvantage, family violence, or single parenthood for women. Scholars concerned with gender equity would, therefore, need to recognize the significance of the relationship between the economic sphere and the state's construction of the domestic sphere and their effect on the institutional culture of schooling as it pertained both to women's history in the liberal state and to girls' and women's employment futures. As Arnot and Dillabough (1999) argued following the insights of well-established Marxist feminists, this recognition of the political barriers to women's rights in the state led to an understanding of education as the site for the preparation (and reproduction) of a hierarchically stratified gendered workforce, with women being prepared for lower status, marginalized or domestic/service positions in the labor market (see, for example, Spender, 1987).

Reproduction feminists were therefore the most obvious and sustained critics of both Durkheim's state socialization theory and liberal accounts of sex roles (including sex-role theory), the socializing aims of which undermined women's claims for equity and emancipation. Not only did the public/private split pose problems for women in terms of access to a more diverse set of educational opportunities, but it also undermined the very premises of liberal equality in postwar democratic nation-states. From the perspective of reproduction and Marxist feminists, education could thus be seen to support a "patriarchal conception of civil society" (see Deitz, 2003), both founded upon, and realized through, the structural practices of education. Education feminism was heavily influenced by such currents and began to address what Dale Spender (1987) identified as the "patriarchal paradigm" of state education, focusing largely upon the constraining effect of social structures on girls' and women's lives (see also Arnot & Dillabough, 1999). As Arnot (2002) suggested, a key challenge facing reproduction theorists was to assess the degree to which education functions as a cultural force in making girls and women "classed and sexed subjects."

Feminist reproduction theory, now well established, therefore stands in marked contrast to the liberal feminist account of sex differences, with its goal of challenging the liberal view that gender differences are somehow linked to individual traits and abilities or liberal equality practices rather than attributable to objective divisions in the social world and structural constraints in society (Dillabough, 2002). In its earlier versions, it also stood against poststructural accounts of power as located primarily in the functional manifestation of language because it remained concerned with objective social class relations and materiality as playing a constraining role in women's lives. In its more recent forms, such divisions between approaches are much harder to detect, and it would seem that much intellectual bridging between neo-Marxist approaches and postmodern approaches has taken place.

Contrary, then, to liberal perspectives suggesting that gender equality has now been achieved or to poststructural accounts that focus upon linguistic forms of cultural power, feminist reproduction accounts have provided gender theorists with the theoretical tools for continuing to view education as a form of both institutional power and social constraint and, therefore, as central to the maintenance of an unequal gender/social order. For example, in recent years, critical feminist policy researchers have demonstrated that, despite the assertion of liberal claims of access and "equality of opportunity" policies, *White middle-class* girls and boys continue to dominate the higher echelons of academic achievement and the labor market. It is therefore ongoing class stratification and the reassertion of middle-class ideals through education policy that largely explain social differentiation, not perceived individual differences, the apparent abilities of children, or equity policies per se. *Achievement, performance, and school choice* in education therefore serve as "markers of economic privilege" (Reay & Lucey, 2003) and are fundamentally tied to issues of power, social mobility, and the historical division between the public and private spheres. What might then sometimes be seen as advancements in girls' educational performance (and it is clear that gender performance patterns have changed in some national contexts over the past 30 years), feminist reproduction theorists argue, must therefore be understood and read within the larger context of social class relations. And, as long as a concern with gender differences and performance remains at the center of equality debates, gender will continue to emerge as a determining force for the achievement of equality irrespective of other social relations. This singular emphasis in much of the equality literature and in popular culture on gender differences in achievement ultimately prioritizes gender above all other categories, thus obscuring the significance of other factors such as economic changes, the rise in standardized testing, female employment, retrenchment, migration patterns, and the elimination of ESL training, in shaping students' educational experiences.

In more recent years, while many liberal feminists have continued to claim that gender equity policies explain girls' exemplary post-1980 K–12 achievement results cross-nationally, feminist reproduction theorists have assessed the changing nature of economic capital and its broad and largely negative effect on male and female youth in schools (globally and in the global "south") as well as its influence over the current configuration of teacher's work and educational policy. To my mind, it is this *critical consciousness* or *critical political semantics* that puts into question the success stories that are often told by liberal feminists and the media about girls' and boys' achievement in schools and higher education, as so many of these success stories are contingent upon performing in a highly competitive, colonial system of education that is largely neo-liberal in form. According to a reproduction approach, it is still evident that social differentiation, and not the democratization of social relations, remains at the heart of the liberal democratic project. Here, then, is one of the central contributions of feminist reproduction theory to sociology of education—an ability to question the line dividing the colonial public and the private in schools and to expose the class mechanisms by which such gendered and racialized divisions are reproduced. By contrast, liberal feminism has proved to be fundamentally ahistorical and in so doing has failed to acknowledge the state-related barriers to girls' successes in schools and the labor market. By contrast, and somewhat paradoxically, the postmodernists and poststructuralists have also failed to acknowledge the part played by materiality in the formation of gender inequality.

Limitations of Feminist Reproduction Theory and Its Account of Education

What might be some of the shortcomings in, and objections raised to, the fundamental presuppositions of the type of project feminist reproduction theorists have undertaken in education? The first, originating paradoxically in the work of postmodern, poststructural, and postcolonial/cultural studies approaches, is that reproduction theorists have been seen to devalue the part played by diverse women's movements and broader elements of, for example, culture, race, and sexuality in the recontextualization of gender relations and social inequality. The primary explanation for this shortcoming is that reproduction theorists are seen to be too constrained by metatheoretical explanations of social inequality, such as class conflict. The key problem, then, was that feminist reproduction accounts had raised a seemingly narrow perspective on gender and class to preeminent status and reduced the multiplicity of potential social processes and forms of identification shaping gender inequality in schools (such as compulsory heterosexuality) to single-factor explanations tied to the political economy.

Yet, while the pressure to conceptualize "gender" more broadly was crucial to more ethically conceived gender theories, some aspects of this pressure also discouraged some reproduction theorists from continuing to study macro-level concepts of education and their complementary effect on differently positioned girls' and boys' educational experiences. By the end of the 1980s, government initiatives seemed to be the prime motivation behind many gender equity research projects. Some reproduction theorists, while still concerned with the state, suddenly seemed trapped in the liberal rhetoric (e.g., voice research as individual liberal narrative, performance studies) and therefore left behind many of the macro issues that had once so concerned them. This reality was further compounded by the fact that postmodern and poststructural feminists were far less focused on issues of class and social structure or had removed social class from the equation altogether. The most obvious and somewhat paradoxical outcome of this dual framing of equality outside of a structural paradigm was that novel structural mechanisms (associated with globalization, or local-global relations) shaping inequality in the late twentieth century went largely unassessed and still remain, to greater or lesser degrees, hidden from public view.

A second and related objection finds its most forceful formulation in neoliberal political policies rather than in theory or research per se. For example, the ongoing pressure for researchers extending from larger neoliberal research agendas in the 1990s has meant that *sometimes* the work of gender researchers aligns with government policy rhetoric by endorsing, even if tacitly and unintentionally, some of its alarmist and essentialist claims about gender inequality (e.g., "boys' underachievement," "disruptive masculinities," "girls' global academic successes"). Precisely because class stratification had not managed to retain its dominance in social theory, many gender researchers, including some reproduction theorists, ultimately conflated their equity concerns with the school effectiveness and performance agenda and an overwhelming concern with gender differences.

The preoccupation with universal gender differences in achievement, much of which seems driven by larger concerns about student success in a global economy, has diminished the status of feminist sociological theories of the state in the study of gender inequality. Although concerns about gender and achievement need not be unrelated to equity or the social concerns of a state, *the sociological explanations for reported differences* in achievement and other equity concerns are diminishing not only in status but also in currency. Particularly in the United States, there is a peculiar tendency within some reproduction approaches to turn toward liberalism and neoliberal practice as a response to changing political economies and global demands rather than toward ethical and sociological questions about girls' and boys' engagement with education as class and racialized expressions of their social location in the state.

A third objection, a constraint that might be seen as theoretical or epistemological, can be derived from an analysis of the presuppositions of some reproduction accounts in explaining how social change has influenced men and women's experiences of, successes within, and barriers to, education. This objection questions whether reproduction theory (in its efforts to secure a theory of the "constancy of structure," pace Bourdieu) may, despite its own sustained critiques of liberalism, have inadvertently obscured an analysis of the relationship between gender equality and social change. In earlier moments, the project of feminist reproduction theory was to secure an account of how education, as a contradictory and complex social structure, subordinates girls and women. Yet those who object might ask if reproduction theorists have failed to acknowledge the late modernizing influences and geographical changes that continue to transform the micro and macro patterns of educational experience and exclusion for diverse girls, women, boys, and men over time. Nor have reproduction theorists adequately assessed the role that girls' and women's agency has played in mitigating structural barriers to gender equality. The most obvious late twentieth-century example might be the ways in which more fluid gender identifications (e.g., sexuality) have reconstituted the very meanings of gender relations in schools and their influence on equity on a larger cultural scale (see Rasmussen & Harwood, 2003). The consequence of this potential failure has been that some of the most important questions about young peoples' differential relationship to novel social and structural arrangements remain substantially unanswered, as do questions about youth agency and subjectivity.

Finally, and perhaps most importantly, during and after the rise of the civil rights movement, reproduction theorists were faced with the reality that educational expansion for girls and women (a key argument of the Marxist feminists)—as the primary mechanism for responding to broader social problems rooted in gender and class inequalities—was a necessary but insufficient strategy for addressing those inequalities reflected within the operation of the education system itself. Against a background of the rise of migration racism throughout Europe, North America, and the Antipodes and clearer feminist recognition of other forms of social inequality, class egalitarianism came under greater academic scrutiny. Clearly, the study of gender and class conflict was not enough. Feminist sociologists began to turn to the development of analytical

frameworks sufficiently sophisticated for addressing the complex and interrelated issues of culture and gender and identity together with their role in shaping educational/
social exclusion. Together with the challenges presented by a range of influential social
theorists (including, for example, Judith Butler, Michel Foucault, and Jacques Derrida),
educational scholars began to build a systematic agenda through which to critique the
Marxist/reproductive projects of education, particularly in their failure to sufficiently
contribute to social justice and to larger identity debates about the "self" in social theory. At the center of this critique lay the charge that the reproduction theorists had
devoted themselves to charting the outcomes of educational inequality rather than
exploring gender identity and the subtle microcultural processes of exclusion operating through schooling. The exposure of such cultural processes have brought to the
fore the problems raised by egalitarianism as the defining premise for the success of
gender equity. It also became clear that gendered conceptions of education articulated
by reproduction theorists sometimes remained too narrowly conceived in addressing
the demands of the labor market rather than confronting larger and burgeoning questions of culture difference.

Many of these limitations have emerged as a result of a return to an emphasis upon
gender differences and achievement rather than determining, as an interdisciplinary
and cross-national project, how diverse education systems function in a changing
global, market-oriented, and highly unequal social order. Such limitations have also
emerged in part as a failure to respond to compelling and widespread theoretical
changes in the social sciences.

To remain committed to an understanding of how education produces gender differentiation (as an expression of other social relations), we would, as many feminist
sociologists have argued, need a "generative theory" (see Arnot, 2002; McNay, 2000)
that could account for the contemporary relationships among, for example, gender,
culture, history, social formations, education, debates about the subject, and the economy. Such a theory would need to address micro-level concerns raised about gendered
discourse (e.g., racialized constructions of masculinity and femininity in schools), discursive identities, risk, biography, and culture while at the same time ensuring a commitment to a critical assessment of the role of education as a movable and changeable
apparatus of globalizing state. This work would also need to consider more seriously what
contemporary feminist debates in social theory have to offer to education principally
in relation to a study of human agency, culture, and identity, such as a much more
sophisticated account of how contemporary male and female youth read, internalize,
and respond to the changing economic and cultural order. If theorists and researchers
were to focus their sights on the development of such a generative framework, gender
differences in education would not be constructed as *essential*, as purely *successful*, or as
the only equity issue on the podium but rather as markers of economic, cultural, and
social privilege that are far more complex than liberal accounts or the media suggest.

In moving forward to create a complex theoretical framework for understanding
how schools and societies in late modernity continue to shape gender relations, theorists and researchers must be certain to avoid the mistakes of the past, particularly
the failure to be more comprehensive in their ethical reach. If "class stratification"
and "gender" stood at the center of the project of feminist reproduction theorists in
earlier years, these now need to be seen as conceptual tools that remain necessary but
could never be seen as sufficient or representative enough for the present theoretical
landscape.

REFERENCES AND FURTHER READING

Arnot, M. (1982). Male hegemony, social class and women's education. *Journal of Education, 164*(1), 64–89.

Arnot, M. (2002). *Reproducing gender*. London: RoutledgeFalmer.

Arnot, M., & Dillabough, J. (1999). Feminist politics and democratic values in education. *Curriculum Inquiry, 29*(2), 159–190.

Bourdieu, P. (1974). The school as a conservative force: Scholastic and cultural inequalities. In J. Eggleston (Ed.), *Contemporary research in the sociology of education* (pp. 32–46). London: Methuen.

Bourdieu, P. (1998). *Masculine domination*. Stanford, CA: Stanford University Press.

Bowles, S., & Gintis, S. (1976). *Schooling in capitalist America*. London: Routledge & Kegan Paul.

Deitz, M. (2003). Current controversies in feminist theory. In N. W. Polsby (Ed.), *Annual review of political science* (Vol. 6, pp. 399–431). Palo Alto, CA: Annual Reviews.

Dillabough, J. (2002). Gender equity in education: Modernist traditions and emerging contemporary themes. In B. Francis & C. Skeleton (Eds.), *Investigating gender: Contemporary perspectives in education* (pp. 11–25). Milton Keynes, UK: Open University Press.

Dillabough, J. (2003). Gender, education, and society: The limits and possibilities of feminist reproduction theory. *Sociology of Education, 76*(4), 376–379.

Fraser, N., & Gordon, L. (1995). A genealogy of dependency: Tracing a keyword of the U.S. welfare state. In J. Brenner, B. Laslett, & Y. Arat (Eds.), *Rethinking the political* (pp. 33–60). Chicago: University of Chicago Press.

MacDonald, M. (1980). Socio-cultural reproduction and women's education. In R. Deem (Ed.), *Schooling for women's work* (pp. 13–25). Boston: Routledge & Kegan Paul.

McNay, L. (2000). *Gender and the subject*. Cambridge, MA: Polity Press.

Rasmussen, M. L., & Harwood, V. (2003). Performativity, youth and injurious speech. *Teaching Education, 14*(1), 25–36.

Reay, D., & Lucey, H. (2003). The limits of "choice": Children and inner city schooling. *Sociology, 37*(1), 121–142.

Spender, D. (1987). Education: The patriarchal paradigm and the response to feminism. In M. Arnot & G. Weiner (Eds.), *Gender and the politics of schooling* (pp. 143–154). London: Hutchinson.

CHAPTER 6

Lesbian, Gay, Bisexual, and Transgender Identity Development Theories

KRISTEN A. RENN AND BRENT L. BILODEAU

For students who are lesbian, gay, bisexual, or transgender (LGBT), colleges and universities can be important settings for developing sexual orientation and gender identities. Identity development along many dimensions (e.g., gender, race, ability, social class, and sexual orientation) occurs during college for students of all ages, from those who attend college immediately after high school to those adult learners who return to postsecondary education later in life. Understanding the context and processes of LGBT identity development can help faculty and administrators who work with students in classrooms and out-of-class settings such as residence halls, athletics, and academic and career advising. Theories of LGBT identity development are typically drawn from the fields of psychology and sociology, although there is a growing body of research specifically on the experiences and identities of college students.

Lesbian, gay, and *bisexual* describe sexual orientations, whereas *transgender* describes gender identity. Sexual orientation describes an individual's pattern of emotional, romantic, or sexual attraction to people of the same or different genders; attraction to the same gender is *gay* (for men) or *lesbian* (for women), to a different gender is *heterosexual*, and to either or all genders is *bisexual*. Gender identity describes a person's internal sense of self as male, female, or between or outside these two categories. *Transgender* is used as an umbrella word for a broad range of individuals whose gender identity differs from biological sex assignment and societal norms for gender expression; a person whose gender identity matches sex assignment and societal norms is *cisgender*.

On many campuses social, support, and political alliances of lesbian, gay, and bisexual (LGB) people also include transgender (trans or T) people, to form the common abbreviation LGBT (sometimes GLBT or some other arrangement). It is important to remember, however, that sexual orientation and gender identity are separate, but related, domains of identity. Policies and programs in place to assure nondiscrimination toward LGB people often do not provide protection for transgender people.

LGB Identity Development

The development of LGB identities has been a research subject since the 1970s. Before 1973 when the American Psychiatric Association removed homosexuality from the list of mental disorders, scholars focused on psychological treatment of lesbians and gay men, and little was known about the development of healthy LGB identities. Student affairs administrators in the United States treated gay and lesbian students as either disciplinary problems or candidates for counseling. Since the 1970s, researchers in psychology, sociology, and higher education have produced a substantive body of literature on LGB identities and experiences in higher education. This literature focuses almost entirely on students, with only a little theorizing on the identities of nonheterosexual faculty and staff.

LGB identity theories can be grouped into those that are more stage based and linear and those that take a lifespan or ecological approach. Both are useful to understanding identity development, though the trend is away from linear models toward nonstage theories that account for multiple, intersecting domains of identity (e.g., race, ethnicity, religion). As a group, LGB identity theories assume that the nonheterosexual individual is growing up in a society where heterosexuality and discrimination against people in same-sex relationships are the norm, conditions that currently hold true in the United States and throughout the world. An important developmental task in any of the theories is resisting the heterosexual norm and concomitant expectations placed on individuals.

Stage Models of LGB Identity

Stage models typically describe sexual orientation identity as moving from an initial stage of first awareness of self as nonheterosexual through discovery of self as LGB, through immersion in LGB communities and relationships, to an integrated identity in which sexual orientation is one aspect of the self. In the first stage, individuals may struggle with internalized fears about being lesbian, gay, or bisexual and resist feelings of same-gender attraction. As they begin to recognize and accept that they may not be heterosexual, they may explore the history and culture of LGB people through media (traditional and online), literature, and film, creating an understanding of the possibilities for healthy, positive LGB identity. Stage models describe a period of experimentation with same-gender sexual activity, often accompanied by a growing sense of personal normalcy. An immersion in LGB community may precede, follow, or accompany this experimentation, and some stage models indicate that rejection of the heterosexual norm, sometimes in anger and activism, is typical. LGB people "come out of the closet" (frequently abbreviated as "come out") as LGB to friends, family, and important others. Finally, individuals reach a point of healthy integration of LGB identity with other aspects of identity and life roles (e.g., worker, partner, family member). Proponents of stage models argue that although there are distinct stages or phases through which individuals pass, they are not necessarily linear, and often the process is fluid, with stops, starts, and backtracking.

Critics of stage models point out that many of them were created out of clinical samples of cisgender, adult men and women, most often lesbian or gay, not bisexual. The research samples were also overwhelmingly White and sometimes from narrow geographic regions. One criticism of these models is that they focus on the process of coming out to self and others as nonheterosexual and that the degree of "outness" defines the individual's stage. Also, the notion that a healthy endpoint is an integrated identity, not one that is predominantly focused on LGB identity, has been questioned for the ways that it appears to privilege an assimilated, nonactivist identity that is not desirable or possible for all LGB people, especially not for those who do not conform neatly to gender expectations. Masculine lesbians or effeminate men, for example, might not have societal approval to integrate their sexual orientation identities as easily as might lesbians and gay men who conform more closely to expected expressions of gender. The integration of LGB identity may also be more complicated for individuals who are in racial and ethnic minority groups, participate in conservative religious traditions, are from working-class families, or are people with disabilities. In spite of these criticisms, the stage models are widely taught and used, in part because many LGB people report that these models do represent their experiences with identity development.

Ecological and Lifespan Theories of LGB Identity

Lifespan and ecology theories assume sexual orientation identity is a social construction and attempt to account for the complexity of contexts and individual characteristics that affect its development. Bilodeau and Renn (2005) summarized a growing body of research on LGBT identities in adolescents, bisexuals, people of color, and women. These studies provide a broader base from which to understand the specificity of identity development among people of color in the U.S. and internationally. Research shows that LGB identities have different names and meanings across cultures, including some cultures in which sexual orientation and gender are blurred and some in which gender and heterosexuality are considered so fixed that the idea of same-sex relationships does not even exist. Ecological approaches, such as those that account for the specificity of time, place, and culture in LGB identity, are a valuable addition to the stage models.

Anthony D'Augelli (1994) presented a lifespan approach to sexual orientation identity development that also accounts for cultural and individual differences. He posited three sets of interrelated variables involved in identity formation: (1) personal actions and subjectivities, which are perceptions and feelings about sexual orientation, as well as sexual behaviors and the meanings individuals attach to them; (2) interactive intimacies, which are relationships with family, peers, and intimate partners, as well as the meanings attached to them; and (3) sociohistorical connections, which are norms, policies, laws, and values specific to geography, culture, and historic time period. This triad interacts within an individual's developmental context to create incentives and obstacles for LGB identification and acting on same-gender attraction.

D'Augelli further delineated six "identity processes" in which development occurs. They are not stages, either linear or hierarchical, and they operate more or less independently:

exiting heterosexuality
developing a personal LGB identity
developing an LGB social identity
becoming an LGB offspring
developing an LGB intimacy status
entering an LGB community

Some individuals might have very well-developed LGB personal and social identities, for example, but not have come out to their families. Others might have strong intimate relationships but not be identified strongly with an LGB community. This model does not rely on degree of "outness" as a measuring stick for LGB identification, nor does it prescribe a likely order of events in individual development. It also accounts for the ways LGB people may make meaning of their identities differently in different contexts and in different points in their lives. Colleges and universities often provide opportunities for several of these processes (developing personal and social LGB identities, entering an LGB community, developing an LGB intimacy status).

Weaknesses of ecological and lifespan approaches to LGB identity development include their lack of specificity of developmental trajectory, which can make it difficult to design educational programs and interventions that support individual growth. If the stage models present a more or less linear way of understanding how individuals develop, the ecological and lifespan approaches leave the order undetermined. The fluidity and person-specific nature that is their strength in explaining the *processes* of identity development leave open some weaknesses in explaining the *content* of developmental experiences. Yet, like the stage models, these theories are popular among student affairs professionals and other educators because they resonate with individual experiences.

Studies of LGB College Students

The stage, ecological, and lifespan models were developed primarily on noncollege samples and have been brought into the field to study LGB college students. There is a growing body of literature on the experiences and identities of LGB college students, focusing on traditional-age students (those ages 18–24 who come directly from high school) and mainly psychological in nature, with a few ethnographic studies as well. This literature can be divided into three categories: studies of student experiences, of campus climate, and of LGB identity development.

Studies of student experiences include those that aim to make LGB students more visible and to describe their campus experiences in student organizations, in the classroom, on athletic teams, and so forth. Often these are qualitative, single-campus studies, though a few researchers have done multisite studies. Student experiences related to LGB issues include the experiences of heterosexual students and the effects of college on their attitudes toward LGB people; overall, evidence indicates that college has the effect of decreasing anti-LGB attitudes and increasing support for LGB people and gay rights.

Campus climate studies are often single-campus studies conducted by a student affairs division or an office responsible for multicultural/diversity issues more broadly. Climate studies sometimes include faculty and staff as well as students, and sometimes LGB campus climate is included as part of a larger study of gender or racial climate. Multicampus climate studies have been important historically in demonstrating the need for improving policies, programs, and practices aimed at combating anti-LGBT violence and ending discrimination. Susan Rankin (2005) is a leader in the field of LGBT campus climate research.

LGB identity development among college students is now well studied. It seems clear that in addition to the utility of the stage, ecological, and lifespan models, studies specific to higher education are useful in understanding how best to create academic and out-of-class environments that promote LGB student development and learning. The interplay between LGB identity and academic work—for example, when a student writes a class paper on lesbian history or conducts research on gay parents—shows that LGB identity motivates students to work harder academically by giving them a stake in the outcome of their work; at the same time, the paper or research provides information and experiences that strengthen identity pride. Other studies show that peers play an important role in LGB identity development, and LGB student organizations may provide both challenge and support to LGB identity.

Transgender Identity

Transgender identity in higher education is less well understood than are lesbian, gay, or bisexual sexual orientations. As stated at the outset, *gender identity* describes a person's internal sense of self as male, female, or between or outside these two categories, and *transgender* describes a broad range of individuals whose gender identity differs from biological sex assignment and societal norms for gender expression. A sample of terms related to *transgender* includes *transsexual, male to female (MTF), female to male (FTM), cross-dresser, genderqueer*, and *gender nonconforming*. It is important to note that not all individuals whose identity is gender atypical use the term *transgender*. *Gender variant* is emerging as a phrase that is used interchangeably with *transgender*. Though these definitions are common in the United States, many non-Western cultures define transgender identities by a unique language related to cultural norms. Across cultures, gender identity and sexual orientation are often seen as more integrated identities, in contrast to the Western medical and psychiatric tradition differentiating gender identity from sexual orientation.

Transgender Identities: Medical and Psychiatric Perspectives

In the United States, models for responding to the needs of transgender persons have been heavily influenced by the American Psychiatric Association's (2000) *Diagnostic and Statistical Manual of Mental Disorders, Fourth Edition, Text Revision (DSM-IV-TR)*, which bases "treatment" for transgender individuals on a diagnostic category referred to as gender identity disorder (GID). Treatment options range from psychotherapy to sex reassignment surgery. While a number of practitioners and scholars regard *DSM IV-TR* as invaluable for addressing the needs of gender-variant individuals, others disagree. A growing number of practitioners and scholars have been highly critical of the current classification of transgender identity as GID, citing its highly pathologizing nature. Yet, in order to access sex reassignment surgery, an individual must first undergo psychological treatment, essentially being documented as having a mental illness. Some scholars and transgender activists assert that medical and psychiatric treatment perspectives overly emphasize transition from one gender to another, to become either male or female. These approaches marginalize genderqueers, androgynous persons, gender-benders, transsexuals who do not desire surgery, and the expanding gender-variant identities embraced by today's youth.

Transgender activists and allies have focused their attention on the American Psychiatric Association's pending new manual, *DSM-V*, with an intended publication year of 2012. Pressure to remove GID from *DSM-IV-TR* has been compared to the 1973 removal of homosexuality as a mental illness classification. A number of practitioners and scholars call for the creation of healthy, transgender-positive human development models.

Human Development Perspectives on Gender Identity

While still marginal, emerging scholarship provides an alternative to western medical and psychiatric perspectives. Studies that included transgender students, for example, suggest that their gender identity development experiences followed the developmental pattern posited by D'Augelli (1994) for LGB individuals. As applied to transgender students, identity development occurs in the context of the simultaneous development of the gender-variant person's self-concept, relationships with family, connections to peer groups, and community. This perspective has been termed *life-span*, as it views gender identity development and unique social contexts as variable over a lifetime.

In addition, a notable contribution is Arlene Ishtar Lev's (2004) *Transgender Emergence: Therapeutic Guidelines for Working with Gender-Variant People and Their Families*. The text utilizes a nonpathologizing lens that honors diversity and recognizes the role of oppression in the developmental process of gender identity formation. Of particular value is Lev's identity model, which examines social structures related to biological sex assignment, gender identity, social gender role, and sexual orientation. Lev demonstrates the societal expectation that biological sex assignment predicts male or female identity, which then predicts gender role as "masculine man" or "feminine woman" and heterosexual orientation to the presumed "opposite" sex. Instead, Lev posits that these four categories are fluid, with loose couplings between dimensions allowing for a continuum across categories. In this new formulation, biological sex assignment does not necessarily predict the male-female binary, nor does masculinity attach only to male-men (or femininity only to female-women). In this approach, sexual orientation, too, is fluid once sex and gender binaries are rendered mutable.

Specific to higher education, Bilodeau (2009) found that transgender students reported that institutional policies, norms, and structures restricted their ability to express their gender identities as the students experienced them. The requirement to self-identify as either "male" or "female" on institutional forms, for example, meant that a student who was biologically and legally female, but living as a man, had to choose between a legally correct answer and one that represented the student's lived identity. For the many students who identified not as male or female, but as gender-queer or gender variant, the requirement to indicate one sex or the other was itself burdensome. Sex-segregated facilities and student activities (e.g., residence hall room assignments, fraternities, sororities, intercollegiate athletics) posed another barrier for transgender students. Terming this phenomenon "genderism," Bilodeau pointed to the many ways that forcing adherence to a strict gender binary caused not only transgender but also cisgender people to make compromises at best and suffer harassment and violence at worst.

Critiques of studies of transgender students focus on the dearth of research in the area and the design of the few studies that exist. Small convenience samples are the norm, and researchers rely on nonlongitudinal approaches, missing opportunities to see how identities might change and develop over time. The near invisibility of the transgender population on campus, however, and the difficulty of identifying them among students, faculty, staff, and graduates have made studying transgender identity in higher education exceptionally challenging. Ecological and lifespan models, in combination with Lev's (2004) proposal and Bilodeau's (2009) notion of genderism, offer promising directions for future research in the area. Queer, feminist, and postmodern approaches to the study of gender identity, summarized by Bilodeau and Renn (2005), also offer promising directions for future research.

Intersections of LGBT and Other Identities

The recent emergence of research on the intersections of sexual orientation and gender identities with race, religion, social class, and ability marks a new direction for theories about college student identities. Sometimes called *intersectionality*, this way of describing identities takes into account the simultaneous experience of self as belonging to multiple social groups and the ways that one's identity and experiences are influenced by the cultures and expectations of these multiple groups. For example, the identity and experience of an African American Christian lesbian will differ in meaningful ways from that of a Filipino genderqueer student or a White gay man who is also deaf. Studies of LGBT students rarely isolate entire samples drawn on lines as specific as these examples, but researchers are increasingly attentive to groups such as LGBT students of color and LGBT students at faith-based institutions. Intersections with LGBT identity are sometimes considered in studies of African American students, for example, or students with disabilities, or other groups defined by an identity other than sexual orientation or gender identity.

Studies focused on intersectionality show that LGBT students sometimes experience discrimination in social groups in which they are a minority, just as students of color sometimes experience discrimination in predominantly White LGBT communities. Transgender students often report feeling isolated among groups of LGB students who do not understand how genderism operates to constrain gender identity and expression on campus. On the more positive side, LGBT students sometimes report that other aspects of their identities provide a source of resilience and support. Elisa Abes (Abes & Kasch, 2007) is the leading scholar in this area and has argued for using multiple theoretical perspectives, including queer theory and constructivism, to understand intersectionality and the ways that students make meaning of their identities.

Globalization and LGBT Identities

Globalization and internationalization affect all aspects of higher education, including the ways that LGBT student identities are understood. The concepts of sexual orientation and gender identities are not universal, and the ways that LGBT students experience identity in the United States may be radically different from the ways that LGBT students in other regions construct identity and community. For example, homosexual activity, if not gay identity, is illegal and carries substantial penalties up to and including death in many countries. Not surprisingly, LGBT students in these nations do not form visible communities. Even in places where same-sex marriage is permitted (e.g., South Africa), social values may be so strongly antigay that the threat of violence keeps most students from organizing openly. Non-gender-conforming female students, called tomboys or *boyah* (plural *boyat*) in some Islamic cultures, have organized through online social networking sites (e.g., Facebook.com), though they are targeted by government and media as being socially undesirable, confused lesbians. Yet there are signs that higher education faculty and staff in countries that officially discourage homosexuality (e.g., China) are taking steps to support LGBT students and to create friendlier campus climates for these students. The approximately 100 male-to-female transgender students—called lady-boys or third-gender people—at Thailand's Suan Dusit Rajabhat University are permitted to dress in female clothing, which would otherwise be considered a violation of the university's dress code that requires men to wear trousers and ties.

It is not clear what the effects of globalization will ultimately be on the construction of LGBT identities in college students, but the increasingly international and transient nature of the global student and faculty population is likely to bring into contact individuals with varying understandings of their own and others' expressions of sexual orientation and gender identity. International students coming to the United States from more conservative cultures, for example, express dismay with attempts on the part of LGBT students and student affairs staff to make them more accepting of homosexuality. Openly LGBT scholars from more tolerant cultures must, when they study or research abroad in more conservative regions, come to terms with religious, cultural, and political proscriptions on the expression of LGBT identities. Ecology and lifespan theories of identity development suggest that in each case—students unaccustomed to casual acceptance of LGBT peers and LGBT students studying in less tolerant cultures—there is the possibility for the kind of individual sense-making that promotes identity development.

REFERENCES AND FURTHER READING

Abes, E. S., & Kasch, D. (2007). Using queer theory to explore lesbian college students' multiple dimensions of identity. *Journal of College Student Development, 48*(6), 619–636.

American Psychiatric Association. (2000). *Diagnostic and statistical manual of mental disorders* (4th ed.). Washington, DC: Author.

Bilodeau, B. L. (2009). *Genderism: Transgender students, binary systems and higher education.* Saarbrücken, Germany: VDM Verlag.

Bilodeau, B. L., & Renn, K. A. (2005). Analysis of LGBT identity development models and implications for practice. In R. L. Sanlo (Ed.), *Gender identity and sexual orientation: Research, policy, and personal perspectives: New directions for student services, No. 111* (pp. 25–40). San Francisco: Jossey-Bass.

D'Augelli, A. R. (1994). Identity development and sexual orientation: Toward a model of lesbian, gay, and bisexual development. In E. J. Trickett, R. J. Watts, & D. Firman (Eds.), *Human diversity: Perspectives on people in context* (pp. 321–333). San Francisco: Jossey-Bass.

Lev, A. I. (2004). *Transgender emergence: Therapeutic guidelines for working with gender-variant people and their families.* New York: Haworth Clinical Practice Press.

Rankin, S. R. (2005). Campus climates for sexual minorities. In R. L. Sanlo (Ed.), *Gender identity and sexual orientation: Research, policy, and personal perspectives: New directions for student services, No. 111* (pp. 17–24). San Francisco: Jossey-Bass.

CHAPTER 7

Liberal and Radical Feminisms

CHRIS WEEDON

For more than 200 years liberal feminists have been important advocates of women's education, campaigning for equality of access and provision. Liberal feminism has argued that women are as rational as men and that gender should not affect the forms that education takes. In the late 1960s and 1970s, radical feminism criticized existing educational provision as part of a patriarchal order that served men's interests and imbued women with knowledge and ideas that perpetuated their subjection to patriarchy. It argued for education for women that would enable them to understand the working of patriarchal power and heterosexism in order to resist and transform the patriarchal order.

Liberal Feminism

Since the 1700s, liberal feminism has fought to extend the rights and duties of liberal political discourse to women, focusing on civil rights, education, political and religious freedom, individual choice, and self-determination. It has addressed gender inequalities through campaigns for inclusion within civil rights legislation, access to education, and equality of opportunity. The defining feature of individuals for liberal theory is rational consciousness. Liberalism has thus tended to legislate for abstract individuals, taking little account of the unequal power relations of class, gender, and race that structure societies and work against equality. As many feminists have pointed out, liberal ideas have also perpetuated a dualism based on a mind/body split. Indeed, it was the meanings ascribed to the bodies of women and people of color that were, and in some societies still are, used to justify their exclusion from education and other human rights. Such practices often appeal to the idea of women as equal in worth but naturally different in their biological and social roles.

The liberal feminist struggle for inclusion goes back to the early 1700s when British feminist Mary Astell voiced women's demands for equality with men. Writing in the 1790s, at the time of the French Revolution, Olympe de Gouges in France and Mary Wollstonecraft in Britain argued powerfully for rights for women. In *A Vindication of the Rights of Woman*, Wollstonecraft (1792/1975) suggested that, given comparable education and socialization, women would be as rational and capable as men. This exemplifies the discursive framework within which subsequent liberal feminist activism can be located. Over the last few centuries, liberal feminism like liberalism more broadly has been a force for positive social change. Today, it is still the intellectual basis for a wide range of social and cultural practices that constitute individuals as apparently free, autonomous, and rational subjects. Moreover, as a political and moral philosophy, liberalism continues to offer the promise of self-determination and freedom to people who are denied education and civil and political rights.

Over the centuries, liberal feminists have campaigned for equal access to education and the professions, property rights, the vote, and all other rights enjoyed by men. They have argued for women's equality on the basis of sameness, insisting that, given equal education, women are as rational and capable of holding public office and administering property as men. To make these arguments, liberal feminists have inevitably played down women's differences from men—whether these differences are understood as biologically determined or as socially produced—arguing that gender difference should neither determine how one is regarded as a human being nor how one is educated. In the fight for equal access to education and jobs, the liberal feminist strategy of disregarding differences that result from women's roles as childbearers and carers made it difficult to attend to the structures producing women's dual role. Only in moments of crisis, such as war, have liberal democracies given meaningful attention to this problem.

The failure of liberal feminism to tackle structural problems impeding women's equality, combined with the liberal tendency to view interpersonal and domestic issues as private, helped give rise in the late 1960s to new and more radical forms of feminism. Critiques of liberal feminism took issue with its failure to challenge a normative dualism that defines human beings as rational entities. This view of human beings tends to be at the expense of their bodies and emotions, masking the structural power relations that continue to govern women's lives, in particular those governing the control and exploitation of women's reproductive capacity and sexuality. The forms of feminism that challenged liberal feminism from the late 1960s onward included radical feminism, lesbian feminism, new forms of socialist feminism, Black, Third World, postcolonial, postmodern, and queer feminisms.

Critiques of liberal feminism argue that it is weakest when addressing issues of women's sexuality and reproductive power within a discourse of individual rights. Contemporary liberal feminism, like its historical antecedents, tends to retain the public/private divide in which issues to do with sexuality and reproduction are viewed as private questions of individual choice. The main strategy adopted by liberal feminism is to create the conditions for such choices, and here education is seen as crucial. The failure to give due attention to other forms of power—in particular, class, race, and heterosexism as they affect choices—limits liberal feminism's potential effectiveness in bringing about change. For example, having children and a career are seen as basic liberal feminist rights. Yet such a lifestyle can usually only be achieved at the expense of other women—usually working-class women—who are forced to work in domestic and childcare jobs at low rates of pay. Fundamental changes in the structures of working life, the sexual division of labor, and provisions for domestic and child-care responsibilities would be necessary to enable all women to have children and acceptable paid work.

While the case of child rearing may be relatively straightforward, the issue of sexuality raises much more difficult questions. For example, most liberal feminists oppose censorship, arguing that adults should be allowed to choose whether or not to participate in pornography and prostitution. It is the implicit theory of subjectivity underpinning liberal feminism, which sees women as rational, knowing, sovereign subjects formed by good education, that is at issue here. This raises the question of how to account for the internalization of oppressive gendered forms of subjectivity and women's apparent complicity in the exercise and reproduction of oppressive patriarchal practices. How does one deal with the rights and choices of prostitutes and other sex workers in industries that, other feminist argue, are profoundly detrimental to all women? It is necessary to move outside liberal feminist discourse into radical feminism or poststructuralist feminism with their different ideas of education for alternative ways of approaching these issues. Challenges to the liberal feminist discourse of educated free choice have come from a range of alternative feminist perspectives. Thus, for radical feminists, both prostitution and pornography are best understood as part of a broader strategy of male control of women's bodies, which a radical education should be able to unmask. Sexuality and reproduction are, however, precisely those areas which liberalism had tended to place in the realm of the private and the personal (i.e., beyond politics and power).

Feminists of all types have challenged this assumption, insisting that the personal —the sphere of private life—is a site of political struggle. Radical feminists have put much of their energy into fighting for women's autonomy in the areas of sexuality and procreation. This has included campaigns against pornography and prostitution. Contemporary socialist feminists also see control of sexuality and procreation as fundamental to women's oppression but tend to focus on the economic aspects of the problems. It is perhaps poststructuralist feminist critiques that have raised the most fundamental questions about these practices and the liberal feminist assumption of educated, free individual choice. They challenge the very notion of the individual that lies at the heart of liberalism, decentering the primacy of rational consciousness and offering radically different models of subjectivity, contesting views of meaning that see it as a mirror of reality.

The example of biology can throw light on what this means. Biology has long been used to define and justify women's inequality as natural. It has been used to prove the inevitability of the sexual division of labor and of gender roles, from nineteenth- and twentieth-century attempts to deny women education and the vote to recent sociobiology, which sees women as naturally subordinate to men by virtue of their genes. Whereas liberalism disregards biological difference and radical feminism gives it new meanings, postmodern approaches seek to deconstruct the various meanings of biological difference and their role in constituting gendered subjectivity. Here biological theories are seen as a field of competing discourses seeking to define, in this instance, the meaning of womanhood. These discourses structure institutional practices and shape the subjectivities of women and men. In doing so, they produce and reproduce power relations that, from a feminist perspective, are patriarchal. Poststructuralists would thus argue that pornography is a powerful cultural form that helps shape sexual identities and sexual practices in profound ways that liberal feminism does not address. The liberal individual whose education has provided her with the ability to makes choices about pornography is already shaped by discourses of gender and sexuality that preclude objective free choice.

Radical Feminism

The emergence of radical feminism in the late 1960s was, in part, a reaction to the liberal feminist failure to challenge many aspects of women's oppression and to Marxist attitudes toward women. The sexist structures of both traditional left politics and of the key mobilizing struggles of the 1960s (the anti-Vietnam and civil rights movements) were also the springboard for the new women's movement that was partially formed in answer to the prejudice and sexism experienced by women in these campaigns.

Radical feminism rejects both the theoretical frameworks and political practice of liberalism and orthodox Marxism. Radical feminists argue, on the one hand, against liberalism—that women's liberation cannot be achieved by a theory and practice that make provisions for the rights of abstract individuals, irrespective of social class and gender relations. On the other hand, radical feminism argues that women's oppression cannot be reduced to class oppression and the economic and social structures of the capitalist mode of production. In opposition to Marxism, radical feminism regards women's oppression as the primary and fundamental form of oppression. Gender is seen as an elaborate system of male domination, which is at the basis of all social organization. The term used to signify this universal system of male domination is *patriarchy*. While both radical and socialist feminisms use this term, in radical feminism it refers to a system of domination that pervades all aspects of culture, education, and social life and can be found in all cultures and at all moments of history. Patriarchy in radical feminist discourse stresses the common oppression of women irrespective of historical, cultural, class, or racial differences.

Early radical feminist writing developed explicitly in relation to Marxism. For example, Shulamith Firestone's influential text *The Dialectic of Sex* (1972) used a Marxist framework but replaced the key Marxist terms with those concerned with sexual oppression. As radical and revolutionary groups developed, however, they became divorced from left-wing politics, drawing in women who were not already socialists, and became increasingly separatist, placing greater emphasis on critiques of heterosexism.

Education in radical feminism is a process of unmasking the ways in which patriarchal institutions—including schools, universities, and mainstream scholarship—have colonized women's minds in the interests of patriarchy. Radical feminists have looked to history and anthropology to gain evidence of the universality of women's oppression. A powerful example of such work is Mary Daly's *Gyn/Ecology* (1979). Part of the project of this book is to show the connections between women's oppression across a range of cultures and history and to unmask how male dominated scholarship has sought to deny the universal oppression of women. Daly rejects arguments that hide women's shared oppression by insisting on cultural relativism and argues that all these practices are examples of the universal repression of women. Like most radical feminist writers, Daly does not speculate on the cause of women's oppression beyond its necessity for the maintenance of male supremacy and power. Like other radical feminists, she locates the primary mechanisms of male control of women not in male ownership of the means of production but in male control of women's minds and bodies, in particular their sexuality and their reproductive powers. Where women elude such control, they are destroyed as, for example, widows and spinsters who are burned as witches or Indian brides who outlive their husbands and then are subjected to sati. Much male energy, however, goes into preventing women from ever becoming a threat, and patriarchal education plays a key role here.

Radical feminism theorizes patriarchy as an all-encompassing set of power relations aimed at securing male control of women's minds and bodies. In early radical feminist thought, women's bodies were given a foundational status as both the focus of women's oppression and the basis of women's positive difference from men. Little account was taken either of different types of female bodies or the effects of race and class on women's oppression. From the early radical and revolutionary texts of the late 1960s and 1970s to the present, radical feminists have privileged issues of women's sexuality, control of fertility, violence against women, and sexual exploitation. The liberation of women from patriarchal power requires learning to see these areas of women's experience differently. Radical and revolutionary feminist politics breached the public/private divide, focusing on the personal as a key site for political action. The personal for women under patriarchy is bound up with the meaning, status, and control of their bodies, which soon became the unifying focuses in radical feminist analyses.

Radical feminism aims to enable women to decolonize their minds of patriarchal meanings. Taking as role models marginalized figures such as witches, mystics, goddesses, and wise women, radical feminists created a discourse of strong and resistant women who elude patriarchal control and embody strength, wildness, and self-determination together with traits more usually ascribed to women such as intuition, emotion, and fertility. Their failure to include non-White figures limited the appeal of such discourse to Black women. Traditional female traits and values are given a new and positive status, challenging the supremacy of traditionally male traits such as reason and objectivity. The devalued qualities, central to traditional ideas of femininity, are seen as necessary to the wholeness of both women and men. To reinstate their importance is a first step toward radically transforming patriarchal understandings of reason and emotion.

With its emphasis on the body, radical feminism placed the question of difference in sharper focus than previously but failed to take account of the racialized female body. Endorsing the binary oppositions between woman and man, radical feminists seek to transform and revalue the meaning of the terms "female" and "woman," celebrating the female body as a site of strength, endurance, creativity, and power. Knowledge and education are central to this project. In her powerful and poetic text *Woman and Nature: The Roaring Inside Her* (1984), Susan Griffin, for example, exposed how man has used science and religion over the centuries to colonize both woman and nature and to shape them in his own interests. Man, she argues, has sought to gain ascendancy over woman and nature by separating himself from them and cultivating forms of rationality denied to women. The themes of Griffin's work have subsequently become central to a broad-based ecofeminist movement, which takes issue with many of the assumptions and practices of modern science. From an ecofeminist perspective, political and social issues ranging from AIDS and reproductive technology to nuclear weapons and Third World poverty are seen as related, and this holistic approach encourages new forms of spirituality.

In the 1970s, radical feminist writing attempted to develop a universally valid and transhistorical account of women's oppression under global patriarchy, which could be the basis for a universal sisterhood. In doing so, it privileged a particular interpretation of gender relations over all other forms of power. Differences of class, race, and ethnicity became less significant or sometimes invisible. Founded on theories of female difference that were often grounded in women's biology, radical feminism, particularly in the 1970s, proved both inspirational and empowering for many women but excluded others. It celebrated what had previously been denigrated: women's bodies, sexuality, traditionally feminine qualities, and women's capacity for motherhood. Subsequent critiques of the failure of much radical feminism to pay attention to differences of class, race, and culture have led to greater attention to these issues on the part of more recent radical feminist writers (see Bell & Klein, 1996).

Heterosexuality as an Institution

A primary focus of radical feminist critique is heterosexuality. In her influential essay "Compulsory Heterosexuality and Lesbian Existence" (1980), American lesbian feminist and poet Adrienne Rich argued that heterosexuality is an institution and cornerstone of patriarchy, not a natural preference. She asked how and why lesbians have been forced into hiding and why even feminist scholarship has neglected their existence. This, she suggested, weakens its accuracy and transformative power.

Rich developed an analysis that starts from the proposition that, far from being innate, heterosexuality is systematically imposed on women through wide-ranging forms of mental and physical violence. Patriarchal education and the control of knowledge play significant roles in securing the reproduction of the institution of heterosexuality. Included among the ways in which male power has denied women their own sexuality over the centuries are both repressive practices, such as genital mutilation, and male-defined forms of knowledge and science, such as psychoanalysis and sexology. Culture and education also play a key role, for example through images of lesbianism in the media and literature and the exclusion of the history of lesbianism. All this works to ensure that female sexuality is expressed only in the interests of male pleasure and reproduction.

Rich's argument shares much with other radical feminists. It offers a global account of the institution of patriarchy, which is both cross-cultural and transhistorical, drawing on examples from a range of cultures and historical moments. As in Daly's work, this strategy results in male power appearing monolithic and all encompassing. Yet, unlike much radical feminist writing, Rich does not limit the female and the feminine to those areas traditionally so defined. She argues that it is patriarchy itself that limits women to traditionally feminine areas—restricting women's access to education, the professions, and public life. Male power seeks to withhold knowledge by means of the noneducation of women. For example, education reproduces sex-role stereotyping that discourages women from working in science and technology, while the informal structures of educational institutions also work to exclude women.

As in much radical feminist analysis of heterosexuality's role in securing global patriarchy, questions of how class, race, and cultural difference affect the meaning and materiality of patriarchal practices are not addressed. Social practices are interpreted only in terms of their role in the reproduction of heterosexuality. In the process, the cultural specificity of particular practices is rendered invisible. For example, few postcolonial feminists now would accept interpretations of arranged marriages, purdah, and the veil as simple expressions of global patriarchal power. Their functions are much more complex and context-specific, and this needs to be understood in order to realize possibilities for resistance and transformation, which might be undertaken from within the patriarchal order. What Rich's analysis does make clear, however, is the role of these practices in upholding norms of heterosexual marriage, which reinforce patriarchal power.

The radical feminist critique of compulsory heterosexuality is taken up and theorized differently in the work of Judith Butler (1990, 1993), who focuses on embodied subjectivity and theorizes the ways in which the materiality of the body is gendered according to a heterosexist matrix. Starting from the premise that bodies are part of certain highly gendered regulatory schemas, Butler suggests a way of theorizing these schemas via the concept of performativity. In other words, gendered subjectivity is acquired through the repeated performance by the individual of discourses of gender. Moreover, Butler argues that there is no gender identity behind these performances of gender. Performativity is, for Butler, a reiterative and citational practice. Drawing on Foucault (1981), Butler insists that the body is an effect of power, that embodied subjectivity is discursively produced, and that there is no sex outside of culture. This involves a decentered notion of the subject and of agency very different from those of radical feminism. Butler locates resistance and the possibilities of transforming the status quo within the discursive field, which produces both existing power relations and forms of subjectivity. Education thus has a key role to play in the transformation of patriarchal, heterosexist power, and it is a precondition for new forms of agency that can transform aspects of material discursive practices and the power relations inherent in them.

A central tenet of radical feminist thought is that existing theory, education, and scholarship—like the academy more generally—are both male defined and patriarchal. They are male defined in their norms, values, and objects of study, which exclude women's history, experience, and interests. They are patriarchal in the meanings and values that they produce and reproduce. As such, they cannot serve as a source of useful knowledge for women. To develop useful and self-affirming knowledge, women need to start from their own experience of their personal lives, of politics, and of their own history and cultural production.

Problems of Eurocentrism

In their different ways, both liberal and radical feminisms appeal to what they see as universal norms and values. Liberalism maintains that all people share essential human qualities and deserve respect, full access to human rights—including education—and the opportunity to realize their full potential. Radical feminism promotes the idea of shared oppression and a resistant global sisterhood. Both stand accused of blindness to racism and of Eurocentrism based on an uncritical assumption that Western norms, values, and ideas of progress are the realm of feminism. While blindness to questions of race has led to the tendency to read White women's experience as common to all women, Eurocentrism implies that Western feminist aspirations should be the measure for all societies. Black, Third World, and postcolonial feminists have challenged the race blindness and Eurocentrism of both liberal and radical feminist theory and politics. They have questioned the terms on which non-White and non-Western women are included and the class and racialized interests represented in particular forms of education, scholarship, political strategies, and campaigns. In critiques of feminist scholarship and colonial discourses, postcolonial feminists argue that both liberal and radical feminisms demonstrate how much Western feminist writing about Third World women depicts them as a singular category defined by their victim status. This effect is achieved by the implicit assumption that (White) Western feminism is the best judge of the cultural practices of other groups and societies. The universal aspirations of liberal feminism, like those of radical feminism and Marxism, are called in to question because they render invisible historical specificity, agency, and the localized operations of power, both negative and positive, wherein lies the potential for resistance.

REFERENCES AND FURTHER READING

Bell, D., & Klein, R. (Eds.). (1996). *Radically speaking: Feminism reclaimed*. London: Zed Books.

Butler, J. (1990). *Gender trouble*. New York: Routledge.

Butler, J. (1993). *Bodies that matter*. New York: Routledge.

Daly, M. (1979). *Gyn/ecology*. London: Women's Press.

Firestone, S. (1972). *The dialectic of sex: The case for feminist revolution*. London: Paladin.

Foucault, M. (1981). *The history of sexuality: Vol. 1. An introduction*. Harmondsworth, UK: Penguin.

Griffin, S. (1984). *Woman and nature: The roaring inside her*. London: Women's Press.

Rich, A. (1980). Compulsory heterosexuality and lesbian existence. *Signs, 5*(4), 631–660.

Wollstonecraft, M. (1975). *A vindication of the rights of woman*. Harmondsworth, UK: Penguin. (Original work published 1792)

CHAPTER 8

Multicultural and Global Feminisms

ROSEMARIE TONG

Multicultural and global feminisms are two related modes of feminist thinking that emphasize women's differences, disagreements, and situated identities, even as they strive to identify both commonalities in women's experiences and opportunities for women to work together to achieve shared goals. Although the terms *multicultural feminism* and *global feminism* are often used interchangeably, strictly speaking, multicultural feminism focuses on the different kinds of women living within a nation-state, whereas global feminism highlights the complex relationships between women in one nation-state and women in other nation-states. Common to both multicultural feminism and global feminism, however, is resistance to two key ideologies that feminists have rejected: so-called female essentialism and so-called female chauvinism. Female essentialism is the view that there exists some sort of Platonic form, "Woman," which each woman in the world either embodies or should strive to embody in precisely the same way. Female chauvinism is the tendency of relatively privileged women—for example, White, Western/Northern, middle-class, heterosexual, and well-educated women—to assume, incorrectly, that their way of seeing the world is the way all women see it.

Multicultural Feminism

Although some of the world's nation-states have fairly homogeneous populations, very few of them have populations that are as homogeneous as the population of Iceland, say. Most nation-states are very multicultural. Within their historically constructed boundaries are a wide variety of peoples who, as a result of migration, immigration, forced resettlement, territory seizure, or enslavement are now located in one or another of the world's geographical areas. Among these multicultural nation-states is the United States, where, in large measure, the concept of multicultural feminism first arose in self-conscious form. It is therefore as good a context as any in which to analyze the assumptions and development of multicultural feminism.

In order to appreciate the significance of U.S. multicultural feminism, it is important to understand the reasons for its emergence and rapid ascendancy. Throughout the 1960s, 1970s, and 1980s, U.S. feminists focused mainly on the gender differences between men and women. They stressed the degree to which, in the West, qualities such as self-assertion, rationality, a sense of justice, physical strength, and emotional restraint were associated with masculinity, whereas qualities such as connectedness to others, emotionality, physical weakness, and caring were associated with "femininity." They also debated the extent to which these traits were biological givens or social constructions and whether masculine traits were better than feminine traits or vice versa.

Some feminists sought to establish that women had the same intellectual, physical, and moral capacities as men and that, if women were given the same educational and occupational opportunities men had, women could be men's full equals. Like men, women could be chief executive officers of large corporations, army generals, neurosurgeons, and football players. Other feminists countered that it was a mistake for women to try to be like men because women's ways of knowing, doing, and being were just as good as, if not better, than men's. They argued that equal treatment of men and women requires equal recognition of men's and women's different needs, interests, and values. Women should not strive to become like men. On the contrary, they should celebrate their difference from men.

Both sameness feminists and difference feminists had crucial points to make about the relationship between men, maleness, and masculinity on the one hand and women, femaleness, and femininity on the other hand. For sameness feminists, the primary enemy of women was sexism—the view that women are not able to do what men do and are appropriately relegated to the domestic sphere. In contrast, for difference feminists, the primary enemy of women was androcentrism—the view that men are the norm for all human beings and that women should become like men (Fraser, 1997, pp. 48–49).

Significantly, the debate between sameness and difference feminists was never resolved because by the mid-1980s, feminists' nearly exclusive focus on the category of gender came into question. Lesbians, women of color, and other marginalized women pointed out that official feminism—the kind of feminism that held sway in the academy and determined which issues counted as feminist—was not a feminism for all women but a feminism for privileged women. They also stressed that gender is neither the only nor necessarily the main cause of many women's oppression. Depending on her race, ethnicity, class, religion, sexual orientation, age, health status, or level of education, one woman's oppression may be another woman's liberation. Just because some college-educated housewives in suburbia would rather be sitting in a corporate office than driving to a soccer game does not mean that female assembly-line workers would rather work in a sweatshop than stay at home with their children. More generally, the fact that some women find that matters related to their sexuality and reproductive capacities and responsibilities play the greatest role in their oppression does not mean that all women find this to be the case. For some women, not sexism, but racism, ethnocentrism, classism, heterosexism, ableism, and/or ageism are the major contributors to their low status.

Repentant about its relative neglect of women's differences and its failure to push marginalized women's concerns to the forefront of its agenda, U.S. academic feminism determined to reorder its priorities. Discussions of sexism and androcentrism were replaced by discussions of interlocking systems of oppression (gender, race, and class) and women of color's and other marginalized women's multiple jeopardies. Although a privileged White woman may hit her head against a glass ceiling or two in her lifetime, she will not have to face the kind of obstacles a Native American woman with few or no job skills, severe diabetes, clinical depression, and an alcoholic husband has to face. Nor will she have to contend with the kind of hardships that an undocumented Mexican woman in the United States accepts as her lot—as the price of admission to a better life for her children. As multicultural feminists see it, sexism, racism, classism, ableism, elitism—indeed all the "isms" that divide people—interlock and choke whomever they catch in their grip. Oppression is a many-headed beast capable of rearing any one of its heads depending on the situation. The whole body of the beast is the appropriate target for multicultural feminists who wish to end its reign of terror and, depending on her situation, each woman must pick and choose her battles.

In an attempt to give voice to women whose voices have been previously silenced, multicultural feminists have urged disadvantaged women to educate advantaged women about their concerns. But women of color and otherwise marginalized women have not always welcomed these overtures. They claim that it should not be their responsibility to explain themselves to privileged women in terms that privileged women can understand, thereby ironically contributing to the reigning state of affairs in which privileged women are "us" and underprivileged women are "them." On a related issue, many disadvantaged women point out that they do not want to join feminist groups that are populated mainly by advantaged women. They prefer starting their own organizations and working on behalf of women whose condition and experiences are most like their own. Finally, many women of color and other previously marginalized women eschew the label "feminist" either because of popular misconceptions about it or because they prefer to identify themselves as womanists rather than feminists. Conceived by Alice Walker, the term *womanist* refers to a certain kind of feminist, one who is committed to helping an entire people, men as well as women (Walker, 1983, p. xi).

For all its virtues, there are some problems with multicultural feminism. First, it is not clear precisely what is meant by the term *culture*. Sometimes the term denotes a group of women who, on account of their race or ethnicity, share a tradition or history that distinguishes them from other groups of women. But at other times, the term *culture* is used more expansively to include groups of women who feel that something about them—for example, their sexual orientation to women or their disabled physical condition—is the glue that holds them together and makes them a "we."

Second, the differences among women within a culture may be just as great or even greater than the differences between some of them and the women in another culture. For example, a well-educated Asian American woman whose millionaire great-grandparents immigrated to San Francisco from Hong Kong may have far more in common with an Anglo-American woman whose millionaire great-grandparents made a fortune in banking than with an Asian American woman, newly immigrated to the United States, who spent her childhood in a Laotian village working on her family's small rice field.

Third, and related to the second point, it is not clear which characteristics make a woman a true or authentic representative of her culture. Must she be an average or typical woman in her culture? Or must she instead be a disadvantaged as opposed to an advantaged woman in her culture? These questions are perceptively addressed by Uma Narayan, an Indian woman, who immigrated to the United States and now teaches at a prestigious U.S. university. She claims that her opposition to women-harming Indian cultural practices are often dismissed as the views of a Westernized woman who has betrayed her culture when in fact they are the views of many women (and men) who live in India and want to reform their native culture (Narayan, 1997, p. 128).

Fourth, to the extent that culture is linked with race or ethnicity, an increasing number of people in the United States (and, of course, elsewhere) are members of more than one culture. In the 2000 U.S. census, about seven million people identified themselves as belonging to more than one race or some other race than the racial categories used in the census. Increasingly, people wear their multiracial and multiethnic backgrounds proudly. Specifically, parents of children whose race or ethnicity is blended report that their children find White/non-White oppositions of little if any interest, meaning, or concern to them. Race and ethnicity take a backseat to the kind of music, clothes, foods, and lifestyles a person prefers. My own two sons are a blend of Chinese and Czech genes. One looks Hispanic, the other looks Native American. Significantly, both of my sons refuse to label themselves as anything in particular. They like being "other."

Fifth, and by way of a summary of some of the points raised above, if it is to be fully successful, multicultural feminism needs to examine more carefully the concept of *whiteness*. If by "White" is meant an organic tradition with its own customs, self-understandings, music, art and literature, and more, then there is no unitary White culture. People with white skins do not belong to one White culture. Rather, they participate in, or at least have their roots in, for example, Italian American, Irish American, Polish American, or Hispanic American communities. Much the same can be said about people with black skin or yellow skin. Depending on whether a Black person's family has recently immigrated to the United States from Haiti or has been here since the first of the slave days, that person will identify his/her culture as Caribbean rather than African American or vice versa.

In contrast, if by *White* is meant not a nonexistent White culture but a hegemonic power structure bent on maintaining its privileges and prerogatives, then multicultural feminists still need to rethink this use of the term white. In the United States, *White*, as a hegemonic power structure, is the result of the intersection of two facts: namely, which kind of people were most populous in the United States for nearly two centuries (they happened to have white skins) and which kind of people were first to seize the reigns of U.S. society's economic, political, and cultural institutions (they also happened to have white skins). But today (as in the past, though to a far lesser degree) having a white skin does not guarantee membership in the U.S. power elite. For example, poor White women with minimum-wage jobs too meager to pay both their food and rent bills are not members of the power elite, though affluent African American lawyers and Asian American Wall Street tycoons probably are. There still is an "us" and a "them," but the composition of this hegemonic dichotomy is starting to change in response to U.S. demographics and attitudinal shifts.

Whatever conceptual problems multicultural feminism may have, it has enriched U.S. feminism. Women's studies courses and texts no longer present gender issues in abstraction from race and class issues. Thematic courses on women as workers may include articles on White teenaged girls from Minnesota who have run away from their homes and now must eke out a living in Atlanta's seamy sex industry; upper-middle-class African American women working in Fortune 500 companies; and undocumented Mexican American women working as nannies or maids for Texas legislators. Gender issues will be discussed in each of these articles but in ways that show how a woman's age, race, and class shape them. Similarly, discussions about reproduction-controlling technologies (contraception, sterilization, and abortion) and reproduction-aiding technologies (donor insemination, in vitro fertilization, and cloning) stress that whether one or more of these technologies is or is not oppressing depends largely on a particular woman's race, class, age, sexual preference, religion, marital status, and so forth. For some women, the right not to reproduce is most important to them. They either do not want children or they want to control the number and spacing of their children. For other women, however, the right to reproduce is their major concern. Pressured to be sterilized or to use long-term contraceptives by policy makers or health care professionals who view them as unfit to be mothers, poor women who want large families may feel aggrieved. Moreover, poor women with infertility problems may wish that they, as well as rich women with infertility problems, could afford steep out-of-pocket in vitro fertilization costs. As they see it, their desire to have children is no less intense than rich women's.

Convinced that women (and men) must understand the ways in which their own and others' race, class, and gender empower or, alternatively, disempower them, multicultural feminists have sought to transform the curricula of women's studies, feminist studies, and gender studies programs to achieve this educational goal. Increasingly, the materials and texts used in these curricula reflect the fact that, after 2030, people with white skins will no longer constitute the majority of the U.S. population. At least with respect to sheer numbers, the "them"—the people of color—will have become the "us." Multicultural feminists live in happy anticipation of this major social shift, seeing in it opportunities for women to break out of all the bipolar patterns of human domination and subordination that have restricted their thought and action.

Global Feminism

Global feminism differs from multicultural feminism because it focuses not on women in any one nation-state but on how the condition of women anywhere in the world affects the condition of women everywhere else in the world. Agreeing with multicultural feminists that feminism cannot ignore women's cultural differences, global feminists nonetheless strive to create alliances among women worldwide. They share two goals in common. The first is to convince all nations to honor women's rights to make free choices about matters related to their reproductive and sexual capacities and responsibilities. Without the ability to control their own bodies and the course of their destiny, women cannot feel like full human persons. The second, co-equal goal of global feminists is to bring women (and men) together to create a more just social and economic order at the global as well as national order. Global feminists are activists as well as theorists; they are bent on creating a new world order in which all people, no matter where they live, have enough food, shelter, clothing, health care, and education to live full human lives (Bunch, 1984, p. 250).

Global feminists realize that women must forge strong global networks in order to eliminate the disparities that exist between the world's wealthy people and the world's poor people. For them, universal sisterhood is not a natural state of affairs but an ideal to achieve. Before women can embrace each other and work together as a team, they must do the hard work of confronting each other. Among the biggest walls to tear down is the wall between women in the so-called First World and women in the so-called Third World.

The First World / Third World opposition, which has increasingly been replaced by either the developed nations/developing nations contrast or the North/South contrast, bears the stamp of the world's colonial past. Because of their power, people in developed nations view themselves as the Self—progressive, literate, and enlightened—

and people in the developing nations as the Other—backward, illiterate, ignorant. Having given up their aspirations to control the world's developing nations militarily and politically, the world's developed nations seem bent on controlling them economically and culturally.

Among the ways the developed nations control developing nations economically is related to what is now referred to as the Southern debt. About 30 years ago, when interest rates were relatively low, many developing nations borrowed large amounts of money from developed nations. Unfortunately, interest rates rose steeply, and the developing nations were unable to pay the interest on their loans. In order to prevent the world economic system from crashing, the International Monetary Fund and the World Bank rescheduled the debts of many developing nations. As part of this bailout scheme, they required the affected developing nations to adjust the structure of their economies to facilitate their integration into the global economic system. In order to earn enough foreign currency to finance their rescheduled external debts, however, developing nations have had to export as many inexpensive goods as possible or allow their people to work for large transnational companies located in their boundaries. As a result of this state of affairs, most developing nations have not been able to produce their own consumer goods and are forced to import them from developed nations (Jaggar, 2002, pp. 119–121). Not only are these goods costly, they bear the cultural imprint of the world's developed nations: Nike sneakers, Camel cigarettes, Coca-Cola, Ford cars, Levi's blue jeans, and Dell computers. The so-called McDonaldization of the world seems harmless enough on the surface, yet it may signal the recolonization of the South by the North (Bunch, 1984, p. 249).

Global feminists think that women, even more than men, are used to service the Southern debt, thereby participating in their nations' continuing plight. Nevertheless, many women in developing nations decide to work for relatively low wages in the multinational companies located in their homelands. They do so to help support their struggling families or to avoid having to work in the sex tourism industry that caters to men from developed nations. These men pay for the sexual services of women in the developing countries they visit.

Because of their nations' condition, women in developing nations are often much more focused on economic, social, and political issues than on the sexual and reproductive issues that have tended to preoccupy the interest of women in developed nations. As a result of women's different priorities, women's conversations at international conferences have sometimes dead-ended. In fact, at each of the three international women's conferences the United Nations sponsored during the International Decade for Women (1975–1985)—in Mexico City (1975), Copenhagen (1980), and Nairobi (1985)—as well as at Forum 85, a loosely confederated group of 157 nongovernmental organizations, problems emerged among women who represented so-called First World, Western, Northern, and developed nations on the one hand and women who represented so-called Third World, Eastern, Southern, and developing nations on the other. Fortunately, by the 1995 women's conference in Beijing, global feminists had helped women resolve some of their cross-cultural differences and to appreciate some of their commonalities. Typical of the kinds of educational tools global feminists use to draw women together are studies such as one done on low-income urban women in Brazil, Egypt, Malaysia, Mexico, Nigeria, Philippines, and the United States. Despite their differences, all the women who were studied used their status as mothers to justify their sense of reproductive entitlement. They reasoned that because they, and not the men in their lives, bear the greatest burdens and responsibilities of pregnancy, childbearing, and child rearing, they have earned the right to make the crucial decisions in these areas (Petchesky & Judd, 1998, p. 362).

Although global feminists think it is vital to acknowledge that political, religious, and cultural contexts make the situations of women different around the world, they also think it is vital to acknowledge that the biological characteristics of females make *some* situations of women similar around the world. Global feminists urge women to read books about and by each other, to see films and documentaries that reveal each other's everyday lives, and, if possible, to travel to each other's nations to meet each other face to face. In recognizing each other's shared frailty and mortality, global feminists think women will be inspired to care enough about each other to produce globally just policies aimed at eliminating the patterns of domination and subordination, of arrogance and cruelty, that have characterized human relationships for too long.

REFERENCES AND FURTHER READING

Bunch, C. (1984). Prospects for global feminism. In A. M. Jaggar & P. S. Rothenberg (Eds.), *Feminist frameworks: Alternative theoretical accounts of the relations between women and men* (3rd ed., pp. 249–252). New York: McGraw-Hill.

Fraser, N. (1997). *Justice interruptus: Critical reflections on the "postsocialist" condition.* New York: Routledge.

Jaggar, A. M. (2002). A feminist critique of the alleged southern debt. *Hypatia, 17*(4), 119–145.

Narayan, U. (1997). *Dislocating cultures: Identities, traditions, and third-world feminisms.* New York: Routledge.

Petchesky, R., & Judd, K. (Eds.). (1998). *Negotiating reproductive rights: Women's perspectives across countries and cultures.* London: Zed.

Tong, R. (1998). *Feminist thought: A more comprehensive introduction* (2nd ed.). Boulder, CO: Westview Press.

Tong, R. (with Anderson, G., & Santos, A.). (2001). *Globalizing feminist bioethics: Cross-cultural perspectives.* Boulder, CO: Westview Press.

Tong, R., Donchin, A., & Dodds, S. (Eds.). (2004). *Linking visions: Feminist bioethics, human rights, and the developing world.* Lanham, MD: Rowman & Littlefield.

Walker, A. (1983). *In search of our mothers' gardens.* New York: Harcourt Brace Jovanovich.

CHAPTER 9

Postmodern and Poststructural Theories

BECKY FRANCIS

Postmodern and poststructural theories have presented a strong challenge to the humanist perspectives in which second-wave feminist thinking tended to be couched and have inspired the powerful and insightful research of many contemporary feminist scholars in the field of education. To understand this challenge and the contributions of these theories, it is useful, first, to understand that poststructuralism is a branch of postmodernism that places particular emphasis on the ways in which socially and culturally produced patterns of language, known as discourses, construct people and the power relationships among them in particular ways.

Poststructuralism has had particular appeal and implications for feminist research on gender and education because it explicates the ways in which the gendered nature of society is caused by discourses that position all people as male or female and present these gender categories as relational. Despite its appeal and contributions to the exploration of some of the theoretical complexities of feminism, poststructuralism has also challenged feminism, particularly its tendency to categorize people by gender and its claims to being a movement that will emancipate women. Poststructuralism aims to deconstruct such feminist claims that are seen as oppressive productions of a singular, powerful truth. In response, feminists have criticized poststructuralism for being apolitical and morally vacuous while at the same time recognizing that it has provided innovative and valuable understandings of gender performances and power relations.

Distinctions between Postmodernism and Poststructuralism

Although the terms *postmodernism* and *poststructuralism* are often conflated in the literature, and key poststructuralist and postmodernist thinkers have been influenced by each other's work, there are distinctions between the two theoretical movements. *Postmodernism* is an umbrella term incorporating those theorists who critique modernism and the enlightenment philosophical positions and assumptions that underpin it, such as the progressive nature of history; the prevalence of reason; the discoverability of scientific and philosophical "truths"; and the humanist view of the self as a rational, agentic, coherent subject. Key thinkers influencing this broad movement have been Jean Baurillard and Jean-François Lyotard, whose work has had particular influence in art, film studies, and cultural studies. Postmodernism and its critique of accepted "rational" narratives and positions has also provided foundational inspiration for theoretical movements such as queer theory.

While far from being a unitary or unified theoretical position, *poststructuralism* has a more specific referent than postmodernism in that it emerged in response to the structuralist movement in literary criticism and its semiotic analysis of "signs." The best-known pioneers of poststructuralist theory—Roland Barthes, Jacques Derrida, Julia Kristeva, and Michel Foucault—were all strongly influenced by structuralism and in many cases adopted aspects of structuralism in their early work. But, disillusioned with the "science of signs," as with the inadequacies and effects of ideologies, these theorists began to work against the apparent certainties of structuralism by, for example, revealing how the text can "play" free of the intentions of the author. In this sense poststructuralism is a specific branch of the postmodern movement. It has developed a particularly challenging (both intellectually and politically) corpus of theoretical work, and the works of Derrida and Foucault, especially, have been highly influential in the political and social sciences. Foucault's work was particularly applicable in the social sciences because, in developing his "genealogical" approach to the study of institutions and values as changing because of socioeconomic transformations in particular historic periods, he elaborated the poststructural view of text and language as *discourse.* "Discourses" are socially and culturally produced patterns of language that constitute power by producing objects (or subjects) in particular ways (a housewife, for example, could be positioned as fulfilling her natural role through traditionalist discourses of gender essentialism, or she could be positioned as a victim of oppression in some types of liberal feminist discourse).

Whereas much poststructuralist scholarship develops the deconstructive element so central to Derrida's position, Foucault's work has been particularly influential among Western feminists because of its contribution of theoretical tools applicable in social science research and its ability to address specific conundrums that have confronted feminist theory. Judith Butler has drawn on his work in her development of the concepts of subjectivity and performativity, and in education his ideas have inspired exciting new explorations and theorizations.

The Appeal of Poststructuralism for Researchers in Gender and Education

Second-wave feminist researchers were quick to identify the powerful role that educational institutions played in the reproduction of gendered inequalities. During the 1970s and 1980s, feminist researchers created a body of challenging and influential work that drew on social learning theories to explain women's lack of power in society as resulting from a process of socialization beginning in the family and reinforced in schools. It was argued that education taught girls to "know their place" in the gender order through a hidden curriculum of taught sex roles and assumptions concerning the comparative inferiority of girls. However, there was growing criticism of social learning theories and the notion of a "reproduction of roles." Research began to illustrate how young people do not simply take up roles in any passive or uniform way but are active in constructing their own positions. Concepts of resistance and analysis of change in social relationships over time were used to challenge notions of social reproduction and debate the perceptions of a fixed subjectivity that underpinned such understandings.

Poststructuralist theory offered an alterative position that provided a radical critique and rereading of enlightenment, humanist views of subjecthood. In some areas there were already overlapping ideas between feminist and poststructural positions, and in others poststructuralism offered exciting readings that addressed problems facing feminist theory in the late twentieth century. There were five key elements contributing to poststructuralism's appeal to feminists: scepticism toward enlightenment concepts of reason and objectivity; a new view of the self; discourse and power; deconstruction of sex/gender; and the emancipatory potential of discourse analysis.

Like feminists, poststructuralists are skeptical of the discourses of scientific enlightenment that maintain a rational approach and the possibility of analytical objectivity. They share with feminists a strong objection to the separating of the reasoning mind (constructed as male) from the emotions and body (constructed as female).

With regard to the self, poststructuralism offered a view of selfhood that was radically different from that produced in socialization and sex-role theories and that addressed some of the limitations identified in notions of "reproduction of roles." Poststructuralism saw the self (and behavior) as produced by text, as fragmented and fluid rather than fixed and rational. Foucault saw the self as positioned and positioning others in discourses, shifting in construction depending on the discursive context. This theory appears to offer an explanation of selves and behaviors that can incorporate the notions of resistance and contradiction that proved so problematic for sex-role theory. The self is passively positioned in certain discourses but is at the same time active in *positioning* in other discourses. According to Foucault (1980), wherever there is discourse there is resistance: For instance, if a self is positioned as powerless by one discourse, it is possible that s/he may position her/himself as powerful via an alternative discourse. Moreover, discourses themselves are not static but alter over time as the social institutions that produce them change.

This poststructuralist discourse analytic position offered a new perspective on power and power relations that was highly attractive to feminists. Particularly, it provided an explanation for some of the theoretical complexities that have challenged feminism, such as the ways in which power is constituted between women (and between men), as well as between men and women. In the late twentieth century women of color, working-class, gay, and disabled feminists drew attention to the dominance of feminist agendas by White, middle-class, heterosexual, and able-bodied women and the ways in which these women's practices were often marginalizing or silencing the issues faced by women from less-advantaged sections of society. Hence, feminists were made aware that oppressive power relationships are not only dependent on gender but can occur as a result of a host of other factors and can exist between women. Foucault's view of power as operated via discourse rather than existing as the possession of particular groups or individuals was able to address this theoretical problem. Foucault (1980) saw individuals as constantly both undergoing and exercising power, via discourse.

If selves are constructed through ever-shifting and competing discourses, gender/sex positions are also deconstructed by this poststructuralist approach. Poststructuralism can explain the gendered nature of society as caused by discourses that position all people as male or female and present these categories as relational. This not only answers some of the previously discussed questions concerning resistance to gender roles inexplicable by sex-role theory but challenges gender essentialism. Radical and *difference* feminists have sometimes maintained that an "essential feminine" exists linking all women as a group. In contrast, other feminists have critiqued essentialist positions as self-subverting because they effectively explain and therefore, in a sense, *legitimize* the difference between women's and men's social power. Poststructuralist theory can challenge and deconstruct essentialist binary dichotomies of masculine/feminine.

The emancipatory potential of discourse analysis is embedded in the notion that people are not only positioned in discourse but also active in positioning others, and this emancipatory potential of discourse analysis has been interpreted as positive and embraced by some feminists. For instance, Davies (1989, 1997) argues that the analysis of gender discourse will provide us with a new understanding of the way in which power is constituted and the ways in which we are positioned within that discourse. She and others maintain that this raises the possibility of our creating *new* gender discourses and, thus, reconstituting ourselves through discourse. (Such interpretations have been contested, however, by those who stress the deterministic aspects of poststructuralism.)

The Deconstructive Challenge to Feminism

Despite the apparently beneficial contributions of poststructuralist discourse analysis and theories of power and subjectivity for feminist research, there are important epistemological tensions between notions of feminism as a "movement" and poststructuralist positions. These emanate from feminism's origin as an emancipatory movement in contrast to poststructuralism's deconstructing tendencies. For example, although feminism is a notably "broad church" in terms of the theoretical positions and aims of its proponents, feminists share a focus on gender, usually framed by an understanding of gender inequalities, and an intention to challenge and change such inequality. As such, feminism constitutes an emancipatory movement, and its origins are lodged in liberal conceptions of "rights," which are arguably imbued by "enlightenment" humanist views of selfhood and agency. The feminist narrative can then be understood in postmodernist terms as a truth narrative or "metanarrative," which bears a "will to truth" and the evocation of a progressive history in the belief that the world can be improved via human project. Postmodernism aims to deconstruct such metanarratives, which are seen as oppressive in their apparent tantalization and production of singular "truth," and hence their exercise of power.

Some feminists have argued that because feminism is so multifaceted and has not sought to claim coherence in the same way as many other ideologies, it should not be read as a metanarrative. Others have argued fiercely that the retention of the underpinning feminist narrative as an emancipatory movement rooted in liberal humanism is essential to the coherence, positivity, and power of feminist discourse. Some theorists have argued that feminism's focus on gender difference is founded on the notion of a universal female (and a universal male) subject—a position that would also be challenged by poststructuralist theory that deconstructs totalities and illuminates difference. However, while liberal and radical feminist positions have often alluded to the experience and oppression of all women based on their gender (even if recognizing inequalities between different groups of women), feminists drawing on poststructuralist theory are arguably developing a position that goes beyond "founding subjecthood." For example, in the work of key poststructuralist feminists such as Judith Butler and Bronwyn Davies, there is no founding male or female subject—rather, subjects are constituted as male or female, masculine or feminine via gender discourses, which subjects take up as their own and reproduce in performances of gender.

There is continuing dispute as to whether feminism's broadly emancipatory position renders poststructuralism a fruitless, even dangerous, theoretical pursuit for feminists. These issues have been debated vigorously in the field of gender and education. Some feminists have identified the potentially conservative and reactionary threads of poststructuralist theory and the articulation of such aspects by some of postmodernism's key proponents. These feminist critics maintain that poststructuralism undermines the feminist movement and robs feminists of their most effective conceptual tools. They assert that the label "poststructuralist feminist" is an oxymoron, the combination of such oppositional positions being theoretically untenable.

Conversely, a further line of critique of much "poststructuralist feminist" work has stemmed from "strong" poststructuralists within this field, who observe humanist (modernist) notions of agency and "choice" resurfacing within this work. An example is provided by the optimistic position noted above—that subjects can be encouraged to reflect on discourses and understand the ways in which they are positioned and, in turn, learn to take up alternative discourses with which to challenge oppressive ones. This perspective has been criticized as evoking a humanist understanding of subjectivity in assuming the potential for "rational" choice, agency, and coherence of action and, hence, to be at odds with dominant poststructuralist theory (see, for example, the debate between Bronwyn Davies and Alison Jones in *Gender and Education*, 1997).

In addition, there are further specific criticisms with which feminists have charged poststructuralism. For example, they assert that it has not provided an adequate explanation of the nature and source of power and the way in which it is exercised against women. But it is undoubtedly the poststructuralist deconstruction of metanarratives and "truth discourses" that has aroused most anxiety among feminists and deliberation as to the value of poststructuralist work for feminist positions. The two key criticisms are, first, that poststructuralism is profoundly apolitical. Poststructuralism's rejection of truth discourses and its dispersal of identity render it a negative/nihilistic theory unable to engage in theoretical or practical work for social change. This focus on deconstruction rather than construction results in political nihilism and fatalism, thus causing political and ethical paralysis.

The second criticism concerns poststructuralism's inability to judge the value of discourses. Specifically, it has been observed that without "grand narratives" it becomes impossible to generalize about power relations. As noted above, the identification of discourses and interrogation of their powerful effects on subjects and society at large (exemplified in the work of Foucault) is one of poststructuralism's most influential contributions in the social sciences. However, while poststructuralist discourse analysis is useful for "opening up" or deconstructing discourse, it is theoretically unable to privilege one reading over another. Likewise, the poststructuralist refusal of truth claims or "totalizing" statements leaves political researchers bereft of the ability to evaluate the *relative* importance and influence of different discourses. In order to circumvent this problem, some political researchers have adopted terms such as "prevailing discourse" or "dominant discourse" in order to construct political interpretations, yet often it is noticeable that the methods by which such categorizations have been formulated go unarticulated.

Deconstruction does not necessarily constitute *opposition*, only critique (see, for example, Foucault, 1990). Yet some have queried whether a theory that deconstructs other theories but appears to provide nothing with which to replace them can be relevant to emancipatory positions. Other writers argue that, more than simply failing to help feminism, poststructuralism is an androcentric, even reactionary, theory because it undermines the arguments and "truth claims" of oppressed groups and incapacitates movements by infecting them with theoretical paralysis, hence protecting the status quo.

Feminist theorists have been at the forefront of those attempting to articulate satisfactory accommodations of these theoretical tensions and to develop new theoretical pathways that address such tensions. Particularly, such writers have attended to issues of agency and to reclaiming notions of solidarity as well as difference.

Productivity of Poststructuralist Research in Gender and Education

Poststructuralist theory, and indeed postmodernism more generally, have had a profound effect on gender research in education. Feminist researchers in the 1970s and early 1980s spoke confidently of "the girls" and "the boys" as two distinct groups in schools, but researchers drawing on poststructuralist theory have critiqued such homogenizing labels. They have pointed to the immense difference and diversity among different subjects labeled "boys" or "girls" and documented the shifting power positions among these pupils depending on the discursive context. Such analyses have also reinvigorated more structuralist approaches in gender and education, with researchers drawn to identify the ways in which factors such as social class and ethnicity inflect power relations and resources within and across gender groups.

Researchers have applied discourse analysis to education policy documents, illuminating the gendered assumptions and powerful gender discourses at work in these texts. Poststructuralist researchers have inverted the traditional view of gender as "given" and naturalized in the classroom, identifying instead the ways in which schooling creates and heightens gender difference by obsessively delineating pupils (and teachers) according to "random" categories of gender and instilling gendered practices and behaviors through institutional and curricula practices and constructions. Such research has documented the ways in which pupils and teachers take up gender discourses and make gender their own and the myriad ways in which these subjects are "gendered" in educational discourse and via classroom dynamics. Such research has developed a particularly rich vein of poststructuralist or poststructuralist-influenced work in education. The work of Bronwyn Davies provides an excellent example of this approach. From her examination of gendered interaction and gender discourse in the preschool and primary school (1989), Davies concluded that gender discourse presents the social world as split into a clear, relational dichotomy of male/female duality. Children construct the taking up of these relational gendered positions as vital for social competence and identity and, thus, engage in "gender category maintenance work" in order to visibly demonstrate their gender allegiance. Hence, poststructuralist research has provided explanations for processes (such as the development of gender identity and the incentive for girls to adopt gender identities if they are not inherent), which had previously puzzled researchers of gender and education.

Following from this deconstruction of gender categories, some feminists argue that the terms "woman" and "girl" may be misleading and redundant, implying a fixity and homogeneity that do not exist. It has been argued, therefore, that such terms should be jettisoned, or at least used with far more care, in gender and education research. However, it may be said that gender categorization remains a conundrum for researchers in the field. This is partly because gender difference/inequality is generally felt to be the central theme of feminist work and, hence, relinquishing those categories might mean abandoning a central point of analysis, and partly, perhaps, because the use of gender categorizations is so ubiquitous in schooling. It is common practice in schools to evoke gender categories in speech and in practice and to delineate between "the girls" and "the boys." Feminist research has shown how such gender distinctions permeate diverse aspects of school life including aspects as disparate as classroom management, seating arrangements, expectations and interests, friendship groups, use of playground space, and so on.

An obvious criticism of such analytical work is that it pleasures in critique and in the identification and deconstruction of current discursive practices but suggests or builds nothing in their place. This argument applied widely to poststructuralism might be seen as particularly pertinent in education, which is, at least ostensibly, a constructive program to which change (i.e., increased education) is integral. There are exceptions, however. To refer again to Bronwyn Davies's important work as an exemplar, Davies has been a pioneer in attempting to apply poststructuralist theory to classroom practice for emancipatory (feminist) purposes. Following her study with preschool children (1989), she concluded that it is only through the deconstruction of the "gender dualism" that assigns traits and modes of behavior to one gender or the other (and which children take up as fundamental to their gender identities) that children will be able to break from the rigid, gendered positions to experiment with different ways of being. In her further work, she embarked on an ambitious program to actually teach children about poststructuralism in order to enable children to understand the nature of gender discourse and its restrictions on their lives and provide them with the tools to deconstruct the gender dichotomy themselves. Her book *Shards of Glass* (1993) describes her endeavors in this area.

Of course, without a feminist "regime of truth" stating that gendered behavior is an (erroneous) social construction leading to inequity, children would be provided with no reason or incentive to deconstruct current discourses or to challenge the gender dualism. Hence, the *feminist* aspect remains imperative in such action research and pedagogical practice. Without the addition of such emancipatory position, apolitical poststructuralism, which joys in deconstruction and textual play, cannot, by its very nature, be used for *reconstruction* in the sense that many feminists would wish to attempt. However, the combination of these two theoretical positions—though not without its theoretical permutations and challenges—has opened up fertile paths in gender and education research and provided innovative new readings of gender performance and power relations in educational contexts.

REFERENCES AND FURTHER READING
Butler, J. (1990). *Gender trouble*. New York: Routledge.
Davies, B. (1989). *Frogs and snails and feminist tales*. Sydney, Australia: Allen & Unwin.
Davies, B. (1993). *Shards of glass: Children reading and writing beyond gendered identities*. Cresskill, NJ: Hampton.
Davies, B. (1997). The subject of post-structuralism: A reply to Alison Jones. *Gender & Education, 9*(3), 271–283.
Foucault, M. (1980). *Power/knowledge: Selected interviews and other writings, 1972–1977*. New York: Pantheon.
Foucault, M. (1990). *Politics, philosophy, culture: Interviews and other writings, 1977–1984*. New York: Routledge.

Jones, A. (1997). Teaching post-structuralist feminist theory in education: Student resistances. *Gender & Education, 9*(3), 261–269.

Nicholson, L. (Ed.). (1990). *Feminism/postmodernism.* New York: Routledge.

Simons, J. (Ed.). (2004). *Contemporary critical theorists: From Lacan to Said.* Edinburgh, Scotland: Edinburgh University Press.

CHAPTER 10

Queer Theory

SUSAN TALBURT

Queer theory is a field or approach of study that was named in the early 1990s and entered the field of education over the following years. Informed by lesbian and gay studies, as well as feminist and poststructural theorizing, queer theory is less a systematic method or framework than a collection of approaches to questioning normative assumptions about sex, gender, and sexuality. Queer theory challenges assumptions that homosexual and heterosexual are fixed, discrete categories; that sex is biological and gender is its cultural manifestation; and that sexuality constitutes identity. It frequently draws on feminist analyses of gender; however, queer theory centers sexuality as its object of study, recognizing that gender and sexuality are inextricably linked but not synonymous. As a term of affiliation, *queer* understands both identities and affiliations among subjects as partial, temporary, and contextual. Queer theory seeks to take into account the intersections of race, class, gender, and ethnicity, as they constitute the sexuality of the subject and the power relations within which he or she is constituted. In the field of education, queer pedagogy does not teach for or about identities but studies processes that differentiate subjects as "normal" or "deviant," seeking to disrupt categorization and foster new forms of relation and affiliation.

Queer politics developed in the late 1980s partly as a rejection of the assimilationist politics of the mainstream gay and lesbian movement. Activist groups such as Queer Nation brought attention to the proliferation of a variety of queer sexual practices, identities, and identifications that subvert and challenge traditional beliefs about gender and sexuality. This activism, which included not only lesbians and gay men but also bisexual, intersexed, transgendered, and transvestite subjects, dramatized both gender and sexual fluidity. While often discomforting for many, the term *queer* is intended to invoke a past of bigotry and hatred and to rewrite a present that affirms a variety of nonnormative expressions of sexualities and genders. Even as identity could be said to be sedimented in the term *queer*, queer theory and activism use the term to work against stasis and normalization associated with the naming of identities.

Drawing from political movements, feminist and poststructural theories, and lesbian and gay studies, queer theory initially developed primarily in the humanities, including history, cultural, and literary studies, although numerous fields, such as legal studies, the social sciences, and education increasingly engage with its critique of the normalization of heterosexuality and corresponding sex and gender roles. For example, as (homo)sexuality entered public, legal, and policy discourse in the 1990s, educational research turned attention to inquiry into (homo)sexuality and the use of queer theory. After three decades of educational research into gender and schooling, scholars have begun to draw on queer theory to understand the workings and implications of sexuality and gender in school practices, pedagogy, and curriculum.

A central aim of queer theory is the denaturalization of what appear to be stable categories by studying the construction of sex and gender and how these categories have produced and affected differently positioned subjects. Unlike lesbian and gay studies, which sought to create a distinctive history, tradition, and body of knowledge about gay and lesbian individuals and cultures, queer theory seeks to disrupt ideas of discrete, fixed identities by underscoring the ways in which sexuality and its meanings are constructed, contingent, and relational. Queer takes up poststructuralism's conceptualization of identity as unstable, relational, and changing to refuse the normalization that a fixed definition would confer on sexual subjects. For queer theory, categories such as man, woman, homosexual, or heterosexual are never natural or neutral. In this sense, it questions heteronormativity, or the idea that heterosexuality is natural.

While recognizing a need for the interrogation of normalcy, critics of queer theory contend that its emphasis on sexuality over gender runs the risk of ignoring gender differences and returning the universal male subject to the center of theorizing. Others question whether its refusal of a foundation for identity or community limits its political potential.

Essentialism and Constructionism

Queer theory intervenes in debates regarding whether gender and sexuality are essential or constructed. Essentialists consider identity to be natural, innate, and fixed over the course of one's life, as suggested by ideas that people are "born that way." Essentialists understand homosexuality as a universal phenomenon that has existed across time and cultures. Essentialism can lead to views that sexual identity is attached to certain behaviors, such as "coming out" as gay or lesbian, which serves as a marker of authenticity as one takes up a gay or lesbian identity. Although some argue that it constitutes a conservative stance, essentialism has been used as a strategy to secure civil rights for gay men and lesbians. Activists have drawn on essentialist discourses to argue that if homosexuality is a historical constant that is biological or innate and cannot be changed, gay men and lesbians should be conferred rights.

Constructionists, on the other hand, understand gender and sexuality to be "made" rather than "born," a creation of cultural and social contexts. While they may not argue against a biological basis of sex, they often separate gender as a cultural phenomenon that is not essential to one's identity. Thus, constructionists posit that homosexuality is not universal but has different cultural meanings in different sociohistorical contexts. Constructionists contend that their analyses of social and cultural variation offer a means of political intervention in that the social and cultural can be changed. At the same time, its critics argue that constructionism sends a message that homosexuality can be changed because it is cast as a "choice."

Both views, but particularly essentialist stances, can be attached to an "ethnic model" of gay and lesbian politics, which positions lesbians and gays as an identifiable minority population, different but equal, that can demand recognition, equal rights, and legal protections. Identity politics, the idea that a personal identity converges with a group identity to constitute identifiable needs and concerns, has enabled collective representation for women, gay men and lesbians, and African Americans. However, the representation of a coherent, unified community has also revealed profound divides along lines of race, ethnicity, nationality, class, and gender with, for example, women and African Americans arguing that their needs are excluded and that the community that is represented is largely White and male. Thus, queer theorists have suggested that the use of identity as the grounds to constitute a community or a politics is of limited value in that it excludes other elements that contribute to subjects' sense of identity. For queer theorists, community is provisional and politics coalitional. Each depends on interests and connections in a context.

Questioning Categories of Identity

While queer theory shares affinities with constructionism, it takes its critique of essential identities further by questioning the very attachment of sexuality to identity. Queer theory criticizes an "ethnic model" of sexual identity because of its underlying acceptance of the logic that sexual orientation is determined by the gender of one's sexual object choice and that this orientation constitutes an identity.

In a move that breaks with essentialist and constructionist understandings of identity, Eve Kosofsky Sedgwick pointed to two contradictory views, minoritizing and universalizing, of homosexuality. A minoritizing view understands homosexuality as the identity of a small, consistent, and discrete population. A universalizing view understands same-sex desire as relevant to people across a spectrum of sexualities. The second, less common view suggests that homosexuality is not the property of an individual or a group but is implicated in the definition and production of all subjects, regardless of identity. While a minoritizing view defines identity categories as discrete, a universalizing view argues that homo/heterosexual definition is intertwined and constitutive of all subjects. This relational view of the meanings of sexuality and identity leads queer politics and theory to shift their focus to difference rather than identity. Difference precedes identity and is constitutive of subjects' positions.

Following from the insights of deconstruction, queer theory understands binary oppositions as sets of categories that are inherently unequal. Heterosexual, for example, is valorized and homosexual subordinate. Just as an opposition such as man/woman sustains its hierarchical structure through such oppositions as rational/emotional, active/passive, and strong/weak, heterosexual/homosexual is implicated in a number of oppositions, such as, to borrow from Sedgwick, natural/artificial, health/illness, majority/minority, public/private, and innocence/initiation. Because the valorized term in a binary opposition depends on the subordinated term for its meaning, the meanings of the dominant term shift in relation to changes in the subordinated term's meanings. In this way, homosexual is always both internal and external to heterosexual. Thus, following a universalizing view, homosexual definition affects individuals across a range of genders and sexualities.

Queer theory denaturalizes categories of homosexuality and heterosexuality by revealing their contextual, historicized nature as they are constituted through relations of power. For example, a number of historians have pointed out that in the late nineteenth century, the field of sexuality experienced a significant paradigm shift when medicine, the law, and the state ceased to focus on identifying homosexual acts and began to name homosexual identities. Some have called this shift from naming "behaviors" to codifying the homosexual as a "type" of person to be the founding of modern homosexual—and, by corollary, heterosexual—identities. It is the basis of minoritizing views of homosexuality. Yet queer theory goes beyond constructionist stances that point to historical variation by deconstructing the operations of power that create knowledge of constructed categories rather than discovered identities.

Much of queer theory's emphasis on power and knowledge in constructing the "truth" of the homosexual is based in the work of Michel Foucault. In his first volume of *The History of Sexuality*, Foucault questioned what he called the "repressive hypothesis," or the belief that in the nineteenth century there was a prohibition against speaking about sexuality. He argued instead that the "prohibition" functioned as an "incitement to discourse," or a proliferation of discourses about sexuality. Part of this incitement to speak of sexuality was a belief that in revealing the secrets of their sexualities, subjects could produce a knowledge that would reveal the "truth" of who they were. For example, psychoanalysis as a practice asks subjects to speak of their sexuality in the search for an underlying truth of the self. Drawing a link from Christian confessional practices to modern psychoanalysis, Foucault argued that as subjects are called on to confess their emotions, thoughts, and desires, they are placed in a power relation to an authority figure who interprets speakers' narratives seemingly to reveal, but actually to produce, a "truth" of the self. And this "truth" is an effect of power.

In tracing the workings of power and knowledge, Foucault conceptualized three processes of objectification that are integral to the ways in which one becomes a (sexual) subject: dividing practices, scientific classification, and processes of subjectification. Dividing practices categorize subjects, such as the homosexual and the heterosexual; scientific classification creates modes of inquiry that claim scientific status and create expert knowledge about these subjects; and subjectification refers to the meaning-making processes through which subjects form the self. Queer theorists argue that as educators and educational researchers seek to understand subjects, their capacities, and their cultures, they create scientific "knowledge" to classify individuals and corresponding practices that divide and regulate subjects who come to know and understand themselves through these discourses.

Following from Foucault, queer theorists argue that the contemporary imperative for lesbians and gay men to "come out" is a relic of this confessional impulse and maintains systems of power that would divide the heterosexual from the homosexual to produce "truths" about each. Even as coming out serves an important function of disclosing what Sedgwick (1990) has called the "open secret"—unacknowledged knowledges of the existence of nonheterosexual subjects—it also reinforces the homo/heterosexual binary.

Queer theory, then, breaks with feminist and lesbian and gay identity politics based on voicing and making visible identities to question the very formation and basis of identities. By positioning *queer* not as a noun or identity but as a verb—an ongoing process of identification with or against others—queer theory seeks to open up alternatives to processes of normalization. To understand *queer* as a "doing" rather than a "being," queer theorists argue, creates possibilities for new forms of relation.

Gender and Sexuality as Constitutive Performance

Compulsory heterosexuality assumes a linear congruence, or causality, among a subject's sex (male or female), gender identity (masculine or feminine), and (opposite sex) sexual object choice. Homosexuality deviates from this normative sex-gender-desire system through same-sex sexual object choice. At the same time, inappropriate gender expressions for a certain sex—what some call gender inversion—can be conflated with homosexuality. For example, a "sissy boy's" feminine behaviors, even if his desires are heterosexual, often result in homophobic taunts or diagnoses of gender identity disorder, which is thought to lead to adult homosexuality.

Judith Butler's analyses of compulsory heterosexuality—or the heterosexual matrix's normative regulation of gender, sexuality, and identity—has had an influence across fields, including education. Butler extends Foucault's work to include gender, demonstrating how the regulation of gender enforces heteronormativity. She cautions that the claiming of marginalized identities, such as woman or lesbian, is complicit with the very heteronormative regimes identity politics seeks to resist. Fundamental to her argument is that feminism should not take "woman" as a foundational category, not only because its meaning is not universal or transparent, but also because the use of the category reinforces binary views of gender relations and of the categories male and female. By arguing that gender is a cultural expression of biological sex, she says, feminists reiterate patriarchy's determinism and leave little room to account for change or resistance.

Butler (1990) demonstrates that the continuity of sex-gender-desire is regulated by a system of compulsory heterosexuality that demands that subjects express appropriate, intelligible behaviors. For Butler, gender is an effect of repeated gendered performances. In other words, gender is not authentic but must be repeatedly performed or expressed in order to seem real. Behaviors are not an expression of a gender identity; rather, subjects attain a gendered identity through their gendered behaviors. Expressions or performances of gender, which are said to be its natural results, are instead its constitution. They do not express an inner core or essence; rather, a gender identity is the effect of a subject's performances. To understand gender as a fiction focuses on the potential for agency as individuals create their own practices and identities. Yet performativity is not a voluntary performance, as subjects' performances and their intelligibility to others depend on the terms of the heterosexual matrix. Thus the proliferation of subversive performances of gender and sexuality reveals that they are not natural or foundational but contingent.

Present Educational Practice

Queer theory has slowly entered educational research and practice. Increasing attention to the needs of lesbian, gay, bisexual, and transgender (LGBT) youth in the media and among educators during the 1990s precipitated interest in issues of sexuality and schooling. For several decades, researchers, activists, and youth development workers have documented ways in which LGBT youth are at risk for suicide, verbal and physical assault, drug and alcohol abuse, sexually transmitted diseases, homelessness, dropping out of school, and depression. Advocates have used these depictions of victimized LGBT youth to justify inclusive practices, such as curricular change, the formation of Gay-Straight Alliances, and the creation of "safe space" programs in schools. Thus, educational practice related to sexuality focuses on supporting and offering resources to LGBT teachers and students, enabling LGBT individuals to "come out" of the closet, and teaching positive images of LGBT individuals and cultures.

Queer theorists have challenged prevailing images of queer youth as victimized by society, family, and educational institutions. Lost in these depictions, they argue, are understandings of queer youth that include pleasure, agency, and creativity. In response, activists argue that with such a controversial topic as schools and (homo)sexuality, the suffering of LGBT youth offers an important fulcrum to focus attention on the need to combat homophobia and its effects in schools.

These corrective approaches are informed by ethnic models of identity and multicultural inclusion. Educators argue that offering positive representations through the curriculum and role models through teachers will build self-esteem for LGBT youth and tolerance among non-LGBT youth. Queer theorists critique such projects as perpetuating divisions of "queer" and "straight" people and cultures. These divisions participate in normalization by codifying LGBT and non-LGBT identities as stable, separate, and predictable by constructing particular types of knowledge about and for each group. Because curricular approaches must decide what kinds of representation, how much, where, and for whom, the naming of difference runs the risk not only of being prescriptive rather than descriptive but also of failing to challenge norms. While recognizing these dangers, some educators express reticence to pursue a queer critical analysis or deconstruction of LGBT images, identities, and representations in schooling as efficacious when there has previously been little positive mention of such identities.

Queer theorists also express concern that positive representations and programs make a further division between those who are and are not "out" of the closet. They argue that being "in" or "out" in educational contexts is more complex than these dichotomies reveal. The valorization of "coming out" and speaking the truth of the self can function as a White middle-class norm that ignores ethnic and racial community and family ties that mediate the desires of youth to "come out." It further reinforces ideas that sexuality reveals a "truth" of the self.

Queer theorists argue that inclusive educational practices predicated on identities are limited in their transformative potential. For example, efforts to create gender equity do not challenge inequitable gender structures or the ways categories of identity themselves can be oppressive. Similarly, efforts to offer LGBT students resources, support, safety, or inclusion focus on mediating the effects of the interpersonal marginalization of the "other" rather than the privileging of the "normal," thereby leaving intact structures of privilege and oppression. Conversely, efforts that would teach accurate images and tolerance presume that education should offer knowledge to counter stereotypes or myths resulting from exclusion or distortion in the curriculum. While such approaches have the potential to expand knowledge, they presume that accurate portrayals of the LGBT individuals are possible and can be received rationally, regardless of students' implications and investments in the knowledges being studied. In other words, while these approaches may help students understand others, they may not challenge the ways in which they understand the dynamics of their own positioning, particularly in relation to systems that privilege some and marginalize others. Fundamentally, education predicated on models of ethnic identity fails to examine how processes of differentiation and subordination work as norms are constituted.

Queer Pedagogy

At this early stage of its development, queer theory offers a trenchant critique of traditional, identity-based models of inclusion as well as some ways for educators to approach subject matter and processes of teaching and learning differently. Consonant with queer theory's refusal to fix itself or its subjects of study, queer pedagogy offers no codified method or content.

Queer theory argues that mainstream approaches that seek to function as an antidote for homophobia or a cure for low LGBT self-esteem are tantamount to assimilationist demands for equal cultural representation that will expand ideas of normal to include gay and lesbian people. Traditional pedagogies target heterosexual ignorance—assuming that knowledge will stop homophobia and homosexual isolation—presuming that curricular images and faculty role models will enhance self-esteem. They reinforce binary oppositions of tolerated and tolerant, or oppressed and oppressor.

Rather than replacing absences or distortions with accurate representations that would normalize queer subjects, queer pedagogy works against the constitution of knowable or known subjects and instead prizes unintelligibility, or the impossibility of knowing homosexual or heterosexual. Queer pedagogy rejects the notion that curriculum can appeal to rational subjects who will cognitively process information that leads to tolerance. Knowledge and the "transmission" of knowledge are not something to be mastered. Instead, queer pedagogy focuses on how individuals come to know—how knowledge is produced through interaction. Pedagogy becomes a problem of knowledge, of how students learn or read, and what relations they form to knowledges. Queer pedagogy draws from the psychoanalytic insight that learning involves an "unlearning" in which ignorance is not necessarily a lack of knowledge but an attachment to certain forms of knowledge and a resistance to new knowledges. Thus, queer pedagogy takes into account how students learn from or refuse to understand their implications in new knowledges. It asks students and teachers to study their own learning and relations to texts and to inquire into their resistances, identifications, and disidentifications. The problem, then, is not filling in accurate information but engaging students in conversations about their own subject formation and the identifications they take up or refuse.

Queer pedagogical approaches ask students and teachers to consider their own complicity with and relationships to oppression. Through a curriculum that includes multiple voices, students do not search for a "truer" story but for multiple, often contradictory, stories that might destabilize and change dominant narratives. Integral to such education is participants' rethinking the self in relation to binaries of normalcy/deviance. As they deconstruct privilege and marginalization, students must engage affect and cognition in reading their own locations and the implications of their actions. For example, autobiographical work as a queer curriculum practice involves studying one's own narratives to examine differences within oneself and in one's relations with others. Rather than repeating comfortable narratives and categories of identity or resisting new narratives, students must work through an "unlearning" in order to create new knowledges.

As part of a project of studying processes of differentiation and normalization, queer theorists ask for curricular and pedagogical approaches that highlight the relational and unstable nature of identity. Thus, rather than teaching about sexuality as attached to specific acts or discrete identities, teaching and learning focus on sexuality as implicated in social relations and in pleasure. In decentering the homosexual/heterosexual binary, queer curriculum focuses on understanding differences within and among persons rather than differences in categories of persons. For example, a "queering" of the traditional curriculum, such as the literary canon, investigates usually invisible and potentially queer pleasures and desires in seemingly "straight" texts. Heterosexuality itself can then be revealed as unstable and as sometimes queer.

Refusing to objectify difference, queer pedagogy is not interested in who or what lesbian and gay people are but in examining the social relations that create and result from divisions of heterosexual normalcy / homosexual deviancy. Following queer theory's questioning of binary oppositions, queer pedagogy asks for rethinking the stable identities upheld by gender and sexual dichotomies and encourages the formation of identifications beyond given binaries. With a goal of disrupting processes by which some subjects are normalized and other subjects marginalized, queer pedagogy seeks not to produce identities and knowledges about identities but to foster recognition of teaching, learning, and social relations themselves as fluid and variable. A goal is not the formation or recognition of identities but the proliferation of new relations and affiliations.

REFERENCES AND FURTHER READING

Butler, J. (1990). *Gender trouble: Feminism and the subversion of identity*. New York: Routledge.

Foucault, M. (1978). *The history of sexuality: Vol. 1. An introduction* (R. Hurley, Trans.). New York: Vintage.

Jagose, A. (1996). *Queer theory: An introduction*. New York: New York University Press.

Kumashiro, K. (2002). *Troubling education: Queer activism and antioppressive pedagogy*. New York: RoutledgeFalmer.

Rasmussen, M. L., Rofes, E., & Talburt, S. (Eds.). (2004). *Youth and sexualities: Pleasure, subversion, and insubordination in and out of schools*. New York: Palgrave Macmillan.

Pinar, W. F. (Ed.). (1998). *Queer theory in education*. Mahwah, NJ: Lawrence Erlbaum.

Sedgwick, E. K. (1990). *Epistemology of the closet*. Berkeley: University of California Press.

Talburt, S., & Steinberg, S. R. (Eds.). (2000). *Thinking queer: Sexuality, culture, and education*. New York: Peter Lang.

II
Institutional Structures and Contexts

OVERVIEW

The chapters in this section focus on the institutional contexts in which men and women obtain higher education in the United States both at the present time and in previous historical periods. When people think of higher educational institutions, they usually think of physical locations characterized by certain kinds of people, buildings, furnishings, equipment, supplies, and activities. We ask people, "*Where* did you get your degree?" and most people will give the expected answer by naming a college or university located in a particular place. Or we might ask, "*Where* did you go to college?" and be told the names of one or more institutions of higher education, each with a specific locale. Despite the ubiquity of these questions and answers, not everyone transits from home to a building or campus of buildings for his or her higher education. Students enrolled in distance education can successfully pursue courses and degree programs without ever leaving home. And, although most of us think of institutions of higher education as places where students and faculty come together to engage in processes of teaching and learning, students enrolled in distance education can complete their courses, and even their entire degree, without ever being in the same physical location as their teachers. The furnishings, equipment, and supplies of distance education also tend to be somewhat different from what is found in most college buildings, with contemporary distance education using media and technology to transmit curricular content that satisfies governmental requirements from certified teaching personnel to officially enrolled students.

It is the conformity to legal requirements governing curriculum, certification of teaching personnel, enrollment, and progress of students that turns educational practices into institutional contexts, or formal education, as it is sometimes called. Many people in the United States come to college campuses to attend lectures, concerts, plays, and informal discussions, and increasing numbers of people worldwide learn a great deal via the Internet and electronic mail. Although they may qualify as forms of education, these teaching and learning activities do not qualify as the kinds of formal education described in chapter 13 ("Distance Education") or in any of the other chapters in part II. To be an educational institution, the teaching-learning relationships and processes must be legally recognized and regulated. In most countries, this legal framework for education is established at the national level, sometimes in response to international conventions, and in some nations, states or provinces have most of the constitutional authority over education, usually exercised in the United States through a statewide coordinating or governing board that delegates some of its powers to the governing boards and administrators of community colleges, private and public colleges, and state universities.

Within this legal framework, educational institutions develop their own values, regulations, and social structure. *Social structure* refers to the different kinds of people who constitute an institution, such as students, faculty, and administrators; the activities of those people, sometimes called the division of labor; and the ways in which those people and their activities are linked or related to one another. To understand the social structure of higher education and its relationship to gender, it is necessary to answer two questions: What institutions of higher education are available, and who has access to them? *Availability* refers to the number and kinds of higher education that have been legally established and to the historical mandates and regulatory framework that determine who may participate in them and how. As chapter 15 ("Men's Colleges and Universities") and other chapters in part II make clear, the United States has moved from a situation in which fully accredited institutions of higher education were totally unavailable to women and members of most minority groups who wanted to attend them as students or work in them as regular faculty or administrators, to a situation in which it is illegal for colleges and universities to bar women and minorities from these positions.

Whereas availability is largely a matter of established legal rights, *accessibility* refers to the extent to which people of varying identities are encouraged or discouraged from taking positions in various kinds of institutions of higher education or in the various programs offered by those institutions. Are women welcome to enroll or to pursue an academic career in a particular college? Are Blacks discouraged from attending a particular university or aspiring to become its chief academic officer? While it is certainly true that a college or university that is unavailable to a particular group is also inaccessible to them, the reverse is not necessarily the case. As the chapters in this book make abundantly clear, even after they have been allowed into formerly all-White male colleges and universities, White women, Blacks, and other minority group members have often been made to feel like "outsiders" who do not belong.

Thus it is hardly surprising that "outsider" groups have established their own institutions of higher education. As chapter 18 ("Women's Colleges and Universities") makes clear, White women began establishing these institutions in the antebellum period when men-only colleges and universities were unavailable to them. Even after both private and public coeducational colleges and universities appeared on the national scene, enrollments at women's colleges continued to grow, and new women's colleges continued to be established. In part, this was due to an acceptance of the arguments against coeducation summarized in chapter 11 ("Coeducational Colleges and Universities"), but it also represented a desire to obtain one's higher education in an accessible institutional context in which women were prized and felt comfortable, a college *for* women, not just a college available to women.

Higher education institutions for African Americans, now known as historically Black colleges and universities (HBCUs), were established prior to the Civil War in the North and, mostly, after the war in both the North and South at a time when almost none of the existing men's, women's, or coeducational colleges and universities in the

United States would admit Blacks. As chapter 14 ("Historically Black Colleges and Universities") makes clear, all but three of the HBCUs existing today are coeducational and have been so since their founding. This adoption of coeducation was also true of the Black common schools and probably resulted from two traditions: the mixed-sex form of informal education practiced in Black churches and families, including slave families, prior to the Civil War and the commitment to the tradition of coeducation carried by northern missionary teachers who flocked south to teach former slaves during the Reconstruction period. The proportions of girls and women enrolled in the Black common schools were higher than the proportions of males, a pattern that continued into the twentieth century and may have resulted from a different relationship between schooling and jobs for the two sexes. It is possible, for example, that there was more demand for boys than girls in agricultural labor. In addition, schoolteaching, one of the few nonmanual jobs open to large numbers of African Americans, tipped from being a predominantly male occupation to a predominantly female one well before the end of the nineteenth century, just as it had tipped earlier in White schools. And this feminization of teaching was one of the primary forces driving up demand for secondary and higher education for women of all races.

The establishment of HBCUs was also fostered by state and federal laws. In the closing decades of the nineteenth century, racial segregation across public schools was legally established throughout the southern states, a process upheld by the Supreme Court in its infamous *Plessy v. Ferguson* decision of 1896. Support for a racially segregated system of higher education also came from the federal government in the form of the second Morrill Act of 1890, which specifically required states practicing racial segregation in public higher education to establish land-grant institutions (largely agricultural and vocational) for the Black population. These institutions also took on the tasks of teacher training and educating Blacks for public service jobs. It was not until 1954 that the Supreme Court—in its famous *Brown v. Board of Education of Topeka, Kansas*, decision—finally overthrew the *Plessey v. Ferguson* decision by declaring that "separate is not equal" and mandating racially integrated public schools.

Although it sometimes took federal troops to enforce it, this decision plus the civil rights legislation that followed it eventually had the effect of making education at what had been all-White public institutions available to African Americans and to other racial-ethnic minorities. As was true of predominantly White women's colleges after coeducation became available, most HBCUs did not disappear just because racial segregation in higher education became illegal. Many Americans continued to view HBCUs as special places with a proud and courageous history of racial uplift, colleges *for* Blacks and not simply colleges available to Blacks when other colleges were not. Thus support for these institutions continues—and is now built into the American legal structure— even though they enroll increasing numbers of Whites and only a small proportion of Blacks who currently attend colleges and universities in the United States.

The importance of having access to institutions of higher education in which one can feel a sense of belonging is also clearly seen in the establishment and development of tribally controlled colleges and universities (TCUs), described in chapter 17 ("Tribal Colleges and Universities"). These institutions of higher education have existed in the United States for about 40 years and have been recognized and supported by the federal government since 1978. It is noteworthy that the reasons for their founding was to protect and enhance American Indian tribal cultures while at the same time preparing tribal students to live biculturally in both their own cultures and non-Indian cultures.

Like women's colleges and HBCUs before them, TCUs are clearly meant to be accessible to the students they seek to serve. They aim to be places that instill in their students pride in their identity and in people like themselves, not just to be available places to earn college credits and degrees. All TCUs are coeducational and have been since their founding and, as noted in chapter 17, women and men have functioned as equal partners in the tribal efforts to establish TCUs.

Unlike tribal colleges, military institutions of higher education do not construct themselves as places that are equally accessible to men and women. Indeed, for many years they were not even available to women. Chapter 16 ("Military Colleges and Academies") describes and analyzes the difficulties women faced in making these institutions available. Making them fully accessible is proving even more difficult. Historically, these institutions have supported a military culture that is hierarchical and highly masculinized. A soldier was conceived as someone who was manly, disciplined, brave, strong, and loyal to country and to military comrades. Although this image has undergone some modification now that military colleges and academies have become coeducational, one cannot read chapter 16 or the chapter about the Reserve Officers' Training Corps that appears in part IV without concluding that the cultural climate of military institutions is not yet fully welcoming or comfortable for women. The challenge these institutions continue to face is to become more accessible to women by developing a military-supportive culture in which women are not harassed or objectified and in which "soldier" is not posited as the opposite of everything that is feminine or womanly.

Of all the institutions examined in part II, community colleges seem to be the only type that was not intended either to support certain kinds of people and their culture or to exclude them. As chapter 12 ("Community Colleges") indicates, community colleges are public institutions, and many of them had their origins as junior colleges that grew out of secondary schools. As such, they were coeducational and usually open to students of all races and ethnicities. Because of their low cost, their open admissions policies, and their vocationally linked programs, community colleges also attract high proportions of students from lower- and working-class backgrounds, but the United States is not a country that values or seeks to preserve, support, and enhance working-class culture. Thus it is not surprising that most community colleges—despite their name—have not embraced the cultural strengths of working-class or minority racial-ethnic communities and have, instead, been defensive about enrolling students from low socioeconomic and weak academic backgrounds and have worked hard to help those students achieve upward social mobility. Whether this orientation makes the cultural climate of community colleges seem alien to many of their students or whether the low costs and large enrollments of economically disadvantaged students helps them identify with these institutions is a question that has attracted little research or commentary. As a result, it is difficult to know the extent to which students at community colleges see them as welcoming and accessible compared with students attending and evaluating other institutions of higher education.

The eight institutional structures of higher education examined in part II do not exhaust all of the types of colleges and universities that have existed in the United States. Among those founded to serve the needs of students with specific cultural identities are the denominational (mostly Protestant), Roman Catholic, and elite private colleges and universities. A small number of these institutions continue to be particularly accessible to specific religious and social-class groups around whose values, beliefs, and cultural forms campus programs and activities are organized. The vast majority of these institutions, however, no longer cater to specific religious groups, and most elite institutions now try to attract students from lower socioeconomic and minority racial-ethnic backgrounds by means of scholarship programs. In addition, accreditation requirements, transfer policies, and the desire to be eligible for public funds, especially those that support students, have brought most of these institutions under state and federal regulations. As a result, these religious and private institutions have become more like their public counterparts, and discussions of them appear in chapters 11, 15, and 18, focused on coeducational, men's, and women's colleges and universities, respectively.

In recent years, federal laws have recognized *minority-serving institutions* as a distinct category of colleges and universities eligible for targeted federal appropriations. Except for HBCUs and TCUs, which are usually included in this category, most minority-serving institutions are given this label because they enroll a specified proportion of minority students and not because of the amount or type of services they provide for those students. Thus, in 1992, Congress created a category called Hispanic-serving institutions to encompass all accredited and degree-granting public or private nonprofit institutions of higher education with 25% or more full-time undergraduate Hispanic students, one-half of whom are low income. Similarly, in an education budget bill passed by Congress and signed by President Bush in 2007, the definition of minority-serving colleges included "predominantly Black colleges," in which 40% or more of the undergraduates are Black and at least half of all undergraduates are low-income or first-generation college students. Other minority-serving colleges recognized by Congress and the Department of Education (DOE) are those enrolling relatively high proportions of Asian and Pacific Islanders, Alaska Natives, American Indians, and Native Hawaiians. Unlike women's colleges, HBCUs, and TCUs, most of these colleges were not specifically established *for* the minority groups that now attend them.

No systematic efforts have been made by Congress or the DOE to determine whether and how minority-serving institutions truly serve their minority students. Research into this matter is clearly needed especially because, as chapters 11 and 12 ("Coeducational Colleges and Universities" and "Community Colleges") reveal, merely increasing the proportion of a particular group, such as women, in an institution of higher education is no guarantee that members of that group are given full access to all programs and positions, treated as well as members of the dominant group, or made to feel welcome and valuable. Undoubtedly, many campuses in the United States are trying to provide their minority students with opportunities, resources, and services that are identity affirming. What is far less clear is whether such minority-serving provisions increase along with the size of the minority group on campus. One suspects that the opposite might even be true, with more minority services provided on those campuses that have few minority students and are trying to recruit more. In any case, it is not certain whether minority-serving institutions are different structures than other coeducational institutions of similar size, resources, and political jurisdiction that enroll smaller proportions of the same minority group.

Certainly, it does not require a government designation as "minority-serving" for such services to be established. Congress and the DOE do not take account of sexualities or affectional orientations in their definitions of minority-serving institutions, and no special funds are made available to campuses that happen to enroll high proportions of gay men, lesbians, or transexuals. Yet the first chapter in part IV describes a broad range of campus resources and supports designed to make institutions of higher education more open and accessible to lesbians, gays, bisexuals, transexuals, transvestites, queer, questioning, and intersex students, faculty, and staff.

The existence of such programs serves as a reminder of the multiplicities of gendered identities that exist on campuses and of the intersectionalities of these identities with the many others—race, ethnicity, social class, marital status, age, parental status, religion, etc.—with which these gendered identities intersect. And the recognition of gender multiplicities and intersectionalities, in turn, serves as a reminder of the fact that even institutions that truly serve women, racial-ethnic minorities, or the economically disadvantaged may be *for* only some of the people who claim each of these identities.

CHAPTER 11

Coeducational Colleges and Universities

BARBARA J. BANK

Coeducation refers to the education of males and females at the same institution. The founding of Oberlin College in 1833 is generally recognized as the beginning of coeducational higher education in the United States, although it was not until 1841 that Oberlin granted to women the first college degrees equal to those granted to men. Prior to this time, men and women received their higher education at single-sex institutions, with male-only institutions greatly outnumbering those available to women. Some new small colleges, especially in the Midwest, quickly followed Oberlin's lead, as did the University of Iowa, which has continuously admitted women, as well as men, since its opening in 1855. However, coeducation was not adopted by already-existing institutions until the Civil War, when their shortage of students prompted some all-male institutions to admit women for the first time in their histories. Some of these institutions reverted back to male-only policies after the war was over, but there were economic, ideological, and political developments in the following 150 years that fostered both the trend toward coeducation in newly founded colleges and universities and the trend toward making available to women what had formerly been male-only institutions. Chief among these were the larger enrollments and reduced costs that resulted from educating women in the same institutions as men, the struggles of feminist movements for gender equity, and the legal framework governing higher education in the United States.

Coeducation was not unopposed, however. From the early 1800s onward, controversy raged about what form of higher education, if any, was necessary or suitable for women. The exact content of these debates varied across place and time, but it is possible to identify three major themes that characterized most of the opposition to coeducation. These themes concerned women's enrollment in higher education, women's place within coeducational institutions (once they were allowed to enroll), and women's treatment within coeducational institutions—especially in contrast to the treatment of men. Opposition to making higher education available to women ranged from nineteenth-century arguments against allowing women to receive any form of higher education to subsequent attempts to bar them from specific institutions. Efforts to confine women to "appropriate" places within coeducational institutions began at the turn of the twentieth century and continued until the 1970s, when concerns shifted to the ways in which women were being treated in those institutions. Although those who expressed these critical concerns have not stopped the trend toward co-education, they have made it clear that having equal rights to enroll in institutions of higher education and in all of their programs does not ensure that women and men are receiving equally good educations.

Conditions Fostering Coeducation in the United States

Prior to the Civil War, most institutions of higher education were small, poor, and short lived. Only two state universities—South Carolina and Virginia—received regular state appropriations. Their student bodies consisted of the sons of the planter aristocracy rather than a cross section of young men from various social classes. In those two states, as in others, students from more humble backgrounds were more likely to attend denominational colleges established by a large variety of religious groups. These colleges proliferated from the 1850s into the 1890s, with many of them being established by missionaries along the ever-moving American frontier and, after the Civil War, in the South among former slave populations.

Because their goal was to provide higher education for all of their church members and converts, religious denominations often tried to provide education for both men and women. In older, more populated, and wealthier parts of the United States, this effort sometimes took the form of establishing separate institutions for men and, usually later, for women, but in the Midwest and West, and among ex-slaves in the South, denominational colleges were more likely to be coeducational and to have multipurpose curricula, including teacher training, that appealed to women as well as men. Coeducation was no guarantee, however, that denominational or even state institutions would be successful. Nevertheless, the growing demand for schoolteachers during and after the Civil War and the growing willingness of school officials to hire women for these jobs created a need for women's higher education that could not be met only by women's colleges, which, by 1870 were already greatly outnumbered by coeducational institutions of higher education.

It would be a mistake to assume that the missionaries, religious groups, philanthropic donors, and state legislatures responsible for the proliferation of coeducational institutions were guided by ideologies that favored gender integration and equity. It is more likely that most of them held the traditional views of gender typical of their times and regarded coeducation as more of an economic necessity than a matter of justice. Even the strongest advocates for women's education often failed to embrace the political goals of the first-wave feminists who were active on behalf of women's rights, including suffrage, from the 1830s to the 1920s. While it is certainly true that these educational leaders championed women's rights to higher education, it is also true that they often accepted gender segregation and advocated more protective single-sex rather than coeducational colleges for women. To obtain support for their efforts to provide women with high-quality educations, these advocates for women's colleges often used traditional assumptions about gender differences such as the notion that women were naturally more pious, gentle, and virtuous than men. When coupled with a solid education, they argued, women's essential goodness could have beneficial influence on sons, husbands, and other men and, through them, on social and political life.

Even those who advocated or wanted access to coeducation made use of arguments based on assumptions about the essential nature of women. The presence of women on campus, it was claimed, would have beneficial effects, including a softening influence, on male students. Because of their daily interactions with women in an educational environment, college men would exhibit better manners than those of the rowdy fraternity boys at some of the established male-only institutions. And under the tutelage of their women peers, college men would also increase their appreciation of the arts, music, and other refinements.

This tendency to defend higher education for women on the grounds that it would improve the lives of men continued into the second half of the twentieth century. When Mabel Newcomer published her history of women's higher education in 1959, she expressed the belief of her contemporaries—as well as that of earlier historical periods—when she wrote that neither the advocates nor the opponents of college education for women seriously questioned that homemaking is woman's most important role and went on to claim that attending college actually made women better wives, mothers, housekeepers, and community workers than noncollege women.

Newcomer's congratulatory stance regarding higher education for women came under attack in the 1960s and 1970s when second-wave feminism emerged as a popular and powerful social movement. Feminists argued that women should not be required to put mothering and other family duties ahead of all other roles, and they should not live their lives through their husbands and children. Echoing a demand made by first-wave feminists more than 100 years earlier, the second-wave feminists said that the time had come to admit women to the elite male universities (and to all other male-only institutions). Once that happened, women's colleges would have no further justification because they were nothing more than a consequence of gender segregation and traditionalism, and they had failed in both the nineteenth and twentieth centuries to embrace, let alone lead, the fight for political and economic equality for women. Single-sex colleges also were charged with creating an artificial world that prevented women from working closely with men on serious endeavors and from competing with men academically. Although they were viewed as far from perfect alternatives, coeducational colleges and universities were considered to be more reflective of the "real world." They also became, in the decades leading into the twenty-first century, the sites of much feminist activity and many successes in the battle for equal rights and opportunities.

These successes and the earlier successes of those who promoted coeducation in the 1800s and early 1900s were greatly facilitated by the legal framework for higher education that evolved after the passage of the Morrill Land-Grant Act in 1862. That act affirmed the importance of public higher education by making public lands available to states to endow colleges. Even though the legislation did not specifically list the education of women as one of the goals that public colleges should meet, most parents assumed that land-grant institutions should educate their daughters as well as their sons, and women gradually established their right to attend. After the funding for public higher education was improved under the second Morrill Act of 1890 and was extended to African Americans, these public institutions underwent considerable expansion and went on to become the largest coeducational institutions in the country.

Legal changes concerned specifically with gender and schooling did not appear at the U.S. federal level until the 1970s. Most important to the struggle for gender equity within public institutions has been Title IX of the Education Amendments of 1972, which provided that no person in the United States could, on the basis of sex, be subjected to discrimination in any education program or activity receiving financial assistance from the federal government. Despite many efforts by educational institutions to interpret "program or activity" as narrowly as possible, and despite some support for these narrow interpretations by the courts, the Civil Rights Restoration Act of 1987, passed over the veto of President Ronald Reagan, specified that Title IX applied to all the operations of a college or university, not only those programs or activities that directly received federal funds.

Another important legal milestone on the road to gender equity in higher education was the law passed in 1975 directing that women be admitted to America's military service academies in 1976 and thereafter. Also put into the service of coeducation was the Fourteenth Amendment to the U.S. Constitution, which the Supreme Court used as the basis for its decision in 1996 that the Virginia Military Institute (VMI) had to admit women. That decision, in effect, made all U.S. public colleges and universities coeducational and brought to an end the right of any public college or university to bar all women (or all men) from enrolling.

By the time of the VMI decision, almost all private colleges and universities that had begun as male-only institutions had already become coeducational, with Columbia University, in 1983, being the last of the Ivy League colleges to admit women to its undergraduate programs. As was true of most other major men's universities in the United States, Columbia had begun admitting women to graduate work in the 1890's, a move that was justified largely on the grounds of the prohibitive cost of trying to establish separate graduate programs for women and was legitimated by the even earlier admission of American women to successful graduate work in Swiss and German universities that served as models for graduate education in the United States.

Opposition to and Criticism of Coeducation

The traditional assumption about their destiny as homemakers that was used to justify women's higher education was also used to oppose that education. Of course, opponents did not stress the essential goodness of women and their gentle, civilizing influence on men and children. Instead, they argued that women had physical and mental limitations that would be stretched to the breaking point if they attempted to undertake a program of higher education similar to that pursued by men. One of the more influential expressions of this prejudice was contained in *Sex in Education*, published in 1873 by Dr. Edward H. Clarke, an eminent professor in the Harvard Medical School who warned about horrible outcomes—such as hysteria, uterine disease, and derangements of the nervous system—that higher education posed to women's health and well-being. In his history of women's education, Thomas Woody (1929) said that such arguments should have been laid to rest in the 1840s, by which time many women had shown that they could master difficult subjects without ill effects, but the assertions of women's essential inability to do rigorous college work, and the inappropriateness of their attempts to do so, lasted well into the twentieth century.

Particularly concerned with gender improprieties, sexual temptations, and moral development was the Roman Catholic Church, which strongly resisted, first, all higher education for women and, later, coeducation. No Catholic college in the United States admitted women until 1895, when the first Catholic women's college was established. Catholic colleges for men did not begin to admit women until the second decade of the twentieth century, and then only on a limited basis, mostly for teacher training. Even by 1940, women had been admitted to only 10 of the 74 Catholic colleges and universities that had begun as male-only institutions, although by that time an equivalent number of Catholic colleges for women had been established. Most analysts attribute the resistance to coeducation by the Catholic Church to its tradition of training priests and the religious in sex-segregated monasteries and convents as well as to strong ideological concerns about sexual morality. It seems likely, also, that the cost of maintaining sex-segregated educational institutions was greatly reduced as long as they could be staffed primarily by nuns and priests.

Assumptions about women's essential weaknesses were also used as reasons for barring them from military academies and colleges, which, as noted above, did not become coeducational until fairly recently and then, usually, as a result of legislative or judicial coercion. Prior to becoming coeducational, these institutions viewed themselves as male preserves and as proving grounds for a particular kind of aggressive, competitive, and militaristic masculinity. Admitting women, it was believed, would threaten masculine claims to superiority and destroy the culture of the institutions.

Similar fears were expressed as part of the "reaction against coeducation" that occurred during the Progressive Era, from 1890 to 1920. The years leading into that era had seen large increases in the numbers of women students, as well as major changes in the nature of higher education. Enrollment figures for 13 state universities in the Midwest and West in 1907, presented by Charles Van Hise, president of the University of Wisconsin, showed that women outnumbered men at seven of these universities, sometimes by a sizable margin. Although men outnumbered women at the other six institutions, the average size of the differences was considerably smaller. Clearly, women had become a numerical force on coeducational campuses, and many educators felt that something had to be done about this "problem."

The "reaction against coeducation," despite its name, was not an attempt to bar women from higher educational institutions on grounds of their intellectual or physical inferiority. Instead, it was an attempt to limit women's power and presence by finding a place for them in coeducational institutions where they would not be a competitive threat to men. The rhetoric of "essential inferiority" of women was rejected in favor of a rhetoric of "essential difference" between the sexes. This rhetoric was central to several speeches given by the president of Harvard University, Charles W. Eliot, including one at the inauguration of Wellesley's new president in 1899, in which he suggested that higher education for women should be different from that of men because it was likely that women's intellects were as dissimilar from men's as were their bodies.

Although Eliot spoke at a time when no women were admitted to undergraduate degree programs at Harvard, President William Rainey Harper of the University of Chicago, which had been a coeducational institution since its opening in 1892, used similar rhetoric to justify the decision to segregate men and women students for the first two years of their undergraduate education. Segregation, Harper argued, would improve coeducation by helping each sex develop "manly" or "womanly" ideals. He thought it was a pedagogical and social mistake to assume that men and women should be trained to be just as nearly alike as possible. Several other coeducational universities followed the lead of Chicago, segregating some undergraduate courses, especially those in the liberal arts and sciences that were offered in multiple sections. Still other universities dealt with the "women problem" by establishing various kinds of quota systems. Stanford University, for example, set a quota in 1904 of one female for every three males admitted to undergraduate degree programs, a practice it continued until 1933.

A more insidious solution to the problem was advocated by Wisconsin's President Van Hise (1908), who suggested that the best form of segregation was the "natural segregation" that occurred because of choices "freely made" by the students. Colleges of engineering, law, business, agriculture, and medicine at Wisconsin and other universities were open to women, he noted, but few women had taken advantage of their offerings. As a result, they were essentially men's colleges. In contrast, the newly established colleges of home economics had a strong appeal for women (but not men) and could serve as a model of professional education for women. Natural segregation, said Van Hise, would occur on all college and university campuses if they would develop more professional courses that appealed to one sex but not the other.

In the following decades, President Van Hise's proposal was to achieve considerably more success than President Harper's. Not only were students increasingly tracked by gender, but superbly trained women scientists were also kept out of departmental faculties in chemistry and biology and psychology in colleges of liberal arts and sciences and encouraged, instead, to teach in or to head departments of nutrition or household science or child development in colleges of home economics. Other career programs "for women" that were established on university campuses during this era included social work, library science, and nursing. The establishment of colleges of education, independent of colleges of liberal arts, also contributed to gender segregation and changed the nature of teacher training.

The tracking of men and women into separate "places" in higher education continued throughout the twentieth century, especially in such predominately "female" fields as education, health sciences, home economics, and library science, where the proportion of bachelor's degrees awarded by U.S. institutions to men has never risen above 25% and has remained fairly stable over recent decades. The proportion of engineering degrees awarded to undergraduate women was far below that level throughout the century, but that proportion increased dramatically from less than 1% in 1970–71 to more than 20% by 2001–2. In other fields that were historically male dominated, American women have narrowed the gender gap even more, substantially increasing their annual proportions of business baccalaureate degrees, graduate degrees at both the master's and doctoral levels, and professional degrees in law to the point that they have either equaled or surpassed American men.

Despite substantial gains for women in higher-educational achievements, it is not uncommon to hear claims that American women are still far from catching up with their male counterparts. Undoubtedly, some of these claims are due to the speed with which changes in enrollments and degree completions have been occurring; there seems to be a time lag between what women are achieving in institutions of higher education and reports of their accomplishments. Another reason for these claims about women lagging behind seems to be a misunderstanding of what it means when government documents, such as those made available by the U.S. Department of Education's National Center for Education Statistics, announce gender differences in degrees earned. Take, for example, the document showing that women and men earned 47.7% and 52.3%, respectively, of the doctoral degrees awarded by U.S. institutions of higher education in the 2003 to 2004 academic year. Reports of these figures in the media and elsewhere often interpreted them to mean that American women still had some catching up to do. That interpretation ignored the fact that more than a quarter of the doctoral degrees included in these calculations were given to international students, or what the U.S. government calls nonresident aliens, who are much more likely to be men than women. If one wants to know whether more *American* men than women are earning doctoral degrees, these nonresident aliens would have to be removed from the calculations. When this is done, it turns out that in 2003–4, women had already surpassed men, with 53% of all doctoral degrees awarded to Americans by U.S. institutions going to women and 47% of those degrees going to men.

Although some of the examples used to support claims about American women's higher-educational disadvantages compared to American men do not hold up under careful scrutiny, there is some good evidence that gender inequalities in the distribution of students across courses and major fields can still be found, and most of these inequalities favor men over women. The women's fields that men continue to avoid are generally lower-paying, lower-prestige fields than engineering, where women still lag far behind, despite steady increases, and computer and informational sciences, where increases in women's baccalaureate and master's degree attainments up to the beginning of the twenty-first century have since been reversed. Even when women do enter very high-paying "men's fields," such as medicine, they tend to pick specialties that pay less than those chosen by their male counterparts.

Such differences have been disappointing to those who thought that once women could enroll in the best educational institutions and degree programs available to men, their educational choices and attainments would also equal those of men. Some of the explanations offered for why this has not happened focus on the unequal treatment of men and women in coeducational institutions. One kind of unequal treatment has been called "the chilly climate for women" (Hall & Sandler, 1982), a phrase that refers to the many ways in which male students demand and receive more attention than female students. Classroom observers have reported that professors take the comments of their males students more seriously, allow them to monopolize class discussions, make more eye contact with them than with women students, and are even more likely to remember their names. As a result, women are more likely to sit silently. When they do answer questions or make comments, they are far more likely than their male peers to do so in a soft voice or a hesitant manner, making it more likely that their ideas will be ignored or trivialized. While the "chilly classroom climate" has been accused by some researchers of silently robbing women of knowledge and self-esteem, it seems likely that it may be those women who already lack high levels of self-confidence and assertiveness who are deterred by the "chilly climate" from pursuing male-dominated fields of study in favor of retreats to traditional women's fields where they feel less "chilled."

Another drawback of coeducational institutions that has been found to interfere with the performance of women students is sexual harassment. Because the definition of sexual harassment includes a hostile environment, there is some overlap between harassment and the "chilly climate" for women. In addition to an intimidating environment, however, sexual harassment includes outright assaults, both verbal and physical. Many of these attacks come from male students, sometimes in the form of date rape or gang rape, but faculty have also been found guilty of soliciting sexual favors from their students in return for good grades or other academic rewards. Like the assaults and rapes, most of these solicitations come from men and are directed at women. Although most colleges and universities enacted policies against sexual harassment in recent decades, most campus surveys support the conclusion that harassment of women students by male faculty is still occurring, albeit somewhat less blatantly than in the past, and harassment of women students by male peers continues to be widespread. Many women are too embarrassed, humiliated, intimidated, and afraid to report harassment, preferring instead to simply remove themselves from contact with the harasser, even if this means dropping certain classes or avoiding certain campus activities that might have facilitated their academic success and future careers.

Although research has not appeared indicating the extent to which efforts to escape sexual harassment drive women out of "masculine" fields of study into traditionally women's fields, a mountain of evidence supports the conclusion that these women's fields have proportionately more women faculty, as well as students, than the traditional men's fields. The lack of women faculty has often been cited as one of the reasons women do not feel as if they belong or are welcome at certain institutions or in certain fields of study. Although the assertion seems to be based more on faith than on evidence, women's aspirations and achievements are predicted to be higher if they attend colleges or universities that provide them with successful female faculty who can serve as role models and mentors. This argument has been particularly common among advocates of women's colleges who point out, correctly, that those colleges have proportionately more women faculty and administrators than similar coeducational colleges and universities.

The gender of faculty may be less important than the kinds of expectations they have for their students and whether those expectations depend on the gender of their students. The same could be said about campus administrators and their expectations for their faculty members and students. Echoing President Eliot's speech in 1899, Lawrence Summers, the 27th president of Harvard University, opined in a speech given in January of 2005 that essential, innate differences between women and men might be one reason fewer women than men have successful careers in science and mathematics. Undermining subsequent claims by Summers's defenders that this opinion was just his way of stimulating discussion were the facts that the percentage of women offered tenured faculty positions at Harvard had declined every year since 2001, when Summers assumed the presidency, and that in the 2003–4 academic year preceding his talk, only 4 of 34 tenured job offers for Harvard positions went to women. Not only did Summers endorse some of the same beliefs about gender differences that had kept women out of Harvard for more than 300 years following its founding in 1636, but his remarks and the hiring practices of the institution he headed also served as reminders that it would be wrong to assume that the admission of women to Harvard's student body and to its faculty should be interpreted to mean that women were truly the equals of men. At Harvard and throughout U.S. higher education, the fight for coeducation has been won, but the goal of gender equity has not yet been reached.

REFERENCES AND FURTHER READING

Gordon, L. D. (1990). *Gender and higher education in the progressive era*. New Haven, CT: Yale University Press.

Hall, R. M., & Sandler, B. R. (1982). *The classroom climate: A chilly one for women?* Washington, DC: Association of American Colleges.

Miller-Bernal, L., & Poulson, S. L. (Eds.). (2004). *Going coed: Women's experiences in formerly men's colleges and universities, 1950–2000*. Nashville, TN: Vanderbilt University Press.

Newcomer, M. (1959). *A century of higher education for American women*. New York: Harper & Brothers.

Solomon, B. M. (1985). *In the company of educated women*. New Haven, CT: Yale University Press.

Van Hise, C. R. (1908). Educational tendencies in state universities. *Publications of the Association of Collegiate Alumnae Magazine, Series III* (17), 31–44.

Woody, T. (1929). *A history of women's education in the United States* (Vol. 2). New York: Science Press.

CHAPTER 12

Community Colleges

BARBARA K. TOWNSEND

Community colleges have long served as the initial step in baccalaureate attainment for many women and minorities. They have also been considered diverting institutions that channel lower-income students, especially minorities and often women, into occupational programs rather than into transfer programs that lead to the baccalaureate or into four-year colleges and universities. At the faculty and administrative levels, there are higher percentages of women faculty and women presidents than in any other institutional type. While their presence could be regarded as signaling institutional receptiveness to women faculty and leaders, some have interpreted their presence as a marginalization of women faculty and presidents. That is, they are consigned to teach and lead in the lowest-tier institutions in higher education.

Is the community college a ghetto for students, including women, from the lowest socioeconomic status (SES) quintiles and for women faculty and even women presidents, or is it a paragon of opportunity? Because they offer education "higher" than secondary schools but "lower" than baccalaureate-granting institutions, community colleges are sometimes considered to be on the margins of higher education. These institutions are also considered marginal because they enroll a high percentage of students from low socioeconomic and weak academic backgrounds. Many of these students are women and minorities. Community college faculty are also considered marginal within the professoriate because they work with many academically marginal students, do not teach upper-division courses, are not required to do research, and rarely have doctorates (about 20% hold a doctorate, often obtained after starting to teach at the community college). The presidency of a community college could also be viewed as a less impressive accomplishment for women (and men) because of some people's negative perceptions of the institution.

Such an interpretation ignores how community colleges have provided millions of women and minority students with the opportunity for higher education and consequent economic advancement. While it is true that community colleges, like all institutions, are gendered institutions whose practices have not always served and do not currently serve women as well as they could and should be served, it is also true that community colleges have, in their own way, enabled many women students and faculty and staff to achieve their goals. Largely because of the influence of women faculty and staff and as part of their orientation to the needs of their immediate community,

community colleges have developed programs for particular groups of women students, such as adult women students and those needing child-care services. These institutional efforts have facilitated educational attainment for many individuals. Additionally, community colleges in general are known for their supportive, student-oriented environment designed to help students unsure of their abilities and often needing academic remediation. This kind of environment helps all students, including women and minorities.

Short of the country's economic structure being upended and its educational structure being radically changed, community colleges will continue to provide access to higher education, including baccalaureate attainment for millions of women students, a positive employment venue for many women faculty, and frequent leadership opportunities for women aspiring to be institutional presidents.

What Are Community Colleges?

Positioned between high schools and four-year colleges and universities, community colleges are generally public two-year institutions whose highest degree offering has been the associate degree. As of fall 2001, more than 1,100 community colleges in the United States enrolled almost six million credit-bearing students and over five million noncredit students.

Community colleges have a comprehensive offering of programs, meaning they offer certificate and degree programs in occupational fields as well as the associate of arts, or AA, degree. As the first two years of a baccalaureate degree, the AA is termed the academic or "transfer" degree. It is this degree program that links community colleges to higher education since participation in it has historically been a step toward enrollment in a four-year college or university. Community colleges' other associate degrees are typically designed to lead to immediate employment upon degree receipt.

Female students have received the majority of associate degrees for the past few decades. Women students are more apt to be in the transfer degree program than are men students, and minority students are less apt to be in these programs than in occupational programs.

The curriculum of these institutions, like that of four-year colleges, is still dominated by gender-identified fields of study. For example, women are the majority of students in nursing and education programs, while men dominate enrollments in automotive mechanics and electronics. Also, women are more likely to be in the lower-status vocational programs such as child development and clerical and office support, whereas men are more likely to enroll in higher-status fields such as criminal justice, information systems technology, and industrial technology.

According to recent research from the Community College Research Center at Teacher's College, Columbia University, women who do not earn an occupational credential such as a certificate or degree receive less benefit economically from their course work than do men students. In other words, earning an occupational community college credential advantages women economically over men, although it is not clear why. This situation is particularly true for female students from low socioeconomic backgrounds. There is some evidence that male community college students in occupational programs come from lower socioeconomic and weaker academic backgrounds than do female students.

Gender Composition of Community Colleges

If judged by numbers alone, community colleges would seem to be receptive to, even embracing of, women. Like all of higher education, women students have dominated enrollments for almost three decades. In 2001, more than 57% of community college students were female, according to U.S. Department of Education data. Many of the women (and men) who attend community colleges are "nontraditional" students, meaning they do not enroll immediately after high school graduation and attend full time. Rather, community college students are often older (currently the average age of first-time college-goers at community colleges is 24), have family responsibilities, attend part time, and work full time. Additionally, a large percentage of community college students are minorities. In fact, community colleges have a greater percentage of minority students than do four-year colleges.

Sensitive to the needs of their students, many of whom are working adults with children, community colleges have been higher education leaders in offering extended hours of operation, courses at locations other than the main campus, and courses throughout the day and evening, as well as on weekends. The availability of classes and services, combined with the low tuition, has meant that many women could afford to attend college, both financially and timewise. Additionally, community colleges have offered noncredit programs, often funded by federal programs, whose audience is primarily women, such as welfare-to-work and job-training programs.

Women students who attend community colleges have many role models among community college faculty and administrators. Women faculty constituted 50% of the faculty at public two-year schools in 2004, according to American Association of University Professors (AAUP) data; around 40% of department chairs, according to a 1998 study by Miller and Creswell; and 27% of community college presidents in 2000, according to American Council on Education data. These percentages far exceed those in four-year institutions, where there are fewer women faculty, department chairs, and presidents, particularly at the university level. However, minority females still lack many minority role models, female or male. Only around 15% of community college faculty and approximately 20% of community college presidents are from racial and ethnic minority groups. Given the numerous retirements of faculty and administrators that are currently occurring and will occur over the next few years, there is even more opportunity for women, including minority women, to be hired as faculty and senior-level administrators.

The presence of women staff is also strong numerically in community colleges. Numerically, there is almost parity between female and male executive, administrative, and managerial staff. Among nonprofessional staff, women were 63% in fall 2001, according to the National Center for Education Statistics. However, these staff positions reflected the gendered nature of work: Women held 93% of the clerical and secretarial positions, while men held 91% of the skills/crafts and 74% of the service/maintenance positions.

A major reason for the large number of women among community college students and faculty is that the institutions' historical development has been conducive to admitting female students and hiring female workers. The two-year college was initially promoted at the beginning of the twentieth century partly to divert students from universities that preferred to focus on upper-division course work and faculty research. Various university presidents such as William Rainey Harper at the University of Chicago believed that the junior college, as it was initially called, could provide the general education generally offered in the first two years of college. It was thought that many students completing this junior college course of study would be satisfied and no longer pursue higher education, while the more academically talented and dedicated would transfer to four-year colleges and universities. Both public and private two-year colleges were created, with the public ones frequently developing as the 13th and 14th years of high school. With its roots in coeducational high schools, the public two-year college initially offered a free or low-cost education to both female and male students desirous of inexpensive postsecondary education but perhaps unwilling to leave home to seek it. Many women students fit this profile, partly because families were more likely to invest in the education of sons than daughters and to be concerned about their daughters leaving home to go away to study. Thus, from the very beginning of public two-year colleges, women students were accepted, if not welcome.

Women students, like men students, chose to use these institutions for their own ends. While institutional leaders developed gender-based terminal curricula such as home economics and secretarial programs for women students, many women chose to enroll in the transfer program so that they could pursue the baccalaureate if they desired. Also, according to a 1995 study by John Frye, the initially gendered curricula frequently were transformed by infusion of more academic content sought by women students.

After World War II, the public junior college became known as the community college, and the mission of providing education to all who sought it, known as the "open access" mission, was emphasized. Consequently, many women (and minorities) began their higher education at the community college because of its low cost, geographic availability, and general lack of admission standards (e.g., no national standardized test scores were required).

Students were not the only women who increasingly joined the community college during this period. With the tremendous expansion in the number of community colleges, built at the rate of one a week in the mid-1960s, institutional leaders, desperate to fill faculty staffing needs, were willing to hire women as faculty. Since community college faculty during this time period frequently came from high school faculty, there was a relative abundance of available women to be faculty. The four-year sector was also expanding during this time period, so many men seeking faculty positions were wooed to four-year colleges and universities rather than to community colleges.

Influenced by the civil rights movement and the women's movement in the 1960s, community college women, just like women at four-year colleges and universities, began to press for gender equity in salaries and promotions as well as a positive environment free from sexual harassment and sexual stereotyping and discrimination. Some sought the creation of institutional day care and women's centers and women's studies courses and programs for their students. Consequently, under the rubric of meeting community needs, during the 1970s a number of community colleges began to offer reentry programs for older women students as well as women's and ethnic studies programs. Institutional leaders, motivated by concerns for enrollment and institutional growth, accepted the necessity for these programs as well as the growing enrollment of women and minority students.

While there is less institutional focus currently on reentry programs for women, given the younger age of the average community college student, courses focusing on gender issues, as well as studies focusing on racial/ethnic minority groups, are available at many community colleges nowadays. Day care is often available, particularly in institutions with an early childhood education program. Thus women's needs were addressed by community colleges when women mobilized to get them met.

Examples of national mobilization that have led to the increased presence of female faculty and administrators, especially presidents, include the development of the National Institute for Leadership Development (NILD) and the American Association for Women in Community Colleges (AAWCC). For over 20 years, NILD has emphasized the preparation of women community college administrators for the attainment of college presidencies. The AAWCC, created in 1973, has a broader focus. It seeks equity for all women in two-year colleges, including students. Its members focus on such activities and issues as support services for adult women students as well as equal pay for equal work.

Organizations like the AAWCC and NILD operate from a liberal feminist perspective that believes in improving women's situations so that they are on equal footing with men. Thus these organizations focus on issues of equal pay for equal work, an environment free of sexual harassment and stereotyping, and so forth. They want to level the playing field rather than disrupt it or upend it, as socialist or radical feminists would wish to do. Undergirding these organizations' efforts to improve community colleges as educational and work sites for women students, faculty, and staff is the implicit assumption of capitalism as the appropriate economic system.

Although radical and socialist feminists may view community colleges as instruments serving to maintain the capitalistic structure with its inherent stratification by social class (a particularly popular interpretation in the 1970s and 1980s), doing so ignores the reality that individuals can derive great educational, social, and economic benefit from attending them. Attending them is often the *only* choice for some students, given their financial situation and family commitments and, sometimes, their academic background. At the curricular level, it is true that community colleges, like other higher education institutions, have curricula that are often stereotypical in their gender-based enrollment patterns, but they do provide curricular choice for individual students.

Institutional Environment for Women Faculty

The environment of community colleges for women has primarily been studied in terms of women faculty. From a liberal feminist perspective, community colleges currently seem to be more positive workplaces than are four-year institutions, at least as measured by faculty salaries, faculty perceptions of work environment, and prominence of women faculty and senior-level administrative leadership. With regard to salary, a 2004 study by the AAUP found that the discrepancy between full-time female and male faculty's salaries at community colleges was only between 4% and 7%, compared with four-year colleges, where women faculty earn from 11% to 22% less than male faculty, depending upon the type of four-year institution.

Recent national surveys of faculty members' perceptions about their work also indicate that female community college faculty, in the aggregate, are generally positive about their work environment. A 1998 national study by Huber indicated that 85% of women faculty (and 82% of minority faculty) believed they were treated fairly, compared to 75% of faculty at other institutional types. Huber also found that only 17% of community college faculty perceived problematic gender issues among their students.

In their 2002 national study, Hagedorn and Laden found that female and male faculty had similar, generally positive perceptions about the community college climate. However, women and minority faculty were more likely than male or White faculty to disagree that claims of discrimination were overstated.

Although community college women faculty may be generally pleased with the climate at the macro level, there may be more negative perceptions of climate at the micro or single-institution level. For example, John Wolfe and Carney Strange's 2003 qualitative study of a small rural two-year campus found that the few female faculty at the institution experienced a negative climate. The women attributed this climate largely to the lack of sufficient female faculty to present a counterperspective to the male-dominated culture. Similarly, Townsend and LaPaglia found in a 2000 study of faculty in Chicago City Colleges that women and minority faculty were more apt to perceive discrimination on the basis of gender and race/ethnicity than were White male faculty.

There are various reasons community college faculty, both female and male, might be better satisfied than faculty at other institutions. Two major reasons are belief in the community college mission of open access to those who might not otherwise participate in higher education and the lack of pressure to publish. In particular, many women faculty work at community colleges because of their need to balance family and community commitments with their professional work. Additionally, if it is true that women prefer teaching to research, as some studies indicate, then the community college is a good institutional fit because of its emphasis on teaching.

Another positive influence on climate is the less competitive nature of the institution with regard to promotion and tenure. Not all community colleges have tenure; instead they offer faculty a series of long-term contracts. Additionally, not all have academic rank; at some institutions all faculty are labeled instructors. Even in those institutions with rank and tenure, the path to tenure is shorter (typically three years), and the granting of tenure and rank is dependent upon educational credentials, teaching, and institutional service. Thus promotion and tenure are more easily earned in community colleges than in universities and in many four-year colleges. In spite of this, however, a greater percentage of men are tenured in those public two-year colleges with tenure: 68.3% of the men compared with 62.2% of the women, according to data in the 2005 *Chronicle of Higher Education Almanac*.

Although there is much that is positive, relatively speaking, about community colleges as work sites for women faculty, there is little evidence that institutional leaders (who were almost exclusively male until the 1970s) took the initiative to make these institutions female friendly. Rather, it was women faculty and staff, especially in the 1970s and early 1980s and continuing into the present, who pushed for gender equity in hiring, salaries, and promotion and tenure. It was women faculty, staff, and students who pushed for women's studies and women's centers. As a 2005 study by Wolf-Wendel, Ward, Twombly, and Bradley indicates, even today, with women faculty in equal proportion to men faculty and with over one-fourth of presidents being female, there seems to be little if any institutional leadership in developing family-friendly policies and practices such as rooms in which women faculty (or students) could use a breast pump or breastfeed their child. There is little institutional leadership in developing family leave policies so that faculty and staff would not have to use their accumulated sick leave when they need to give birth and recover from the birth.

Despite these shortcomings, community colleges generally provide a more positive work environment for faculty than do most four-year institutions. That is not to say that the environment is ideal. Its structural arrangements are often still marked by traditional views of faculty (e.g., it is assumed that their child-care needs will be met by stay-at-home wives). But the mere presence of so many women faculty and so many women presidents ensures that women's voices can and will be heard, even if at times they have to moderate their messages for colleagues (including women) still bound by gender stereotypes.

Given women's higher representation, greater salary equity, and higher levels of satisfaction in community colleges compared with universities, it seems fair to suggest that university voices that claim women faculty are marginalized by working in the community college reflect an elitist assumption that the only acceptable institutional workplace is the research university. These voices devalue faculty who choose to value teaching and a set of professional responsibilities that enable them to balance work and family life in a more manageable way. These voices also implicitly devalue the students served by these faculty.

What Does the Future Hold for Women in Community Colleges?

For women students, certain trends in the development of community colleges may affect their access to the institution and to the baccalaureate degree. Many community colleges in the twenty-first century seem to be changing the extent to which they focus on open access for those students who would not normally enroll in higher education. There is a growing trend for honors programs, including the provision of free tuition for students in these programs. Also, postbaccalaureate students, those who already have a bachelor's degree or higher, are attending community colleges to improve their current job skills or develop new ones. Additionally, because of escalating tuition costs in all of higher education, community college attendance is a fiscal bargain. Thus many traditional-age students who would normally have started at four-year institutions are choosing (or being coerced by their parents) to attend community colleges. What these enrollment trends mean is that lower SES students, many of whom are first-generation college students, unaware of the need to register early for popular classes, may find there is little or no space for them. Many low SES minority and women students may thus find that access to higher education is more difficult.

Counterbalances to these enrollment trends are two important curricular developments. The first is the development of the baccalaureate degree offered by community colleges. Over 20% of states have authorized selected community colleges to create baccalaureate programs in vocationally oriented, high-demand fields such as education and nursing. These two fields will increase the number of women in baccalaureate programs, while other fields such as applied and manufacturing technology and criminal justice will primarily increase the number of male students. A second curricular development is the growing willingness of some four-year institutions to accept the associate of applied science (A.A.S.) or "terminal" degree as equivalent to two years of the baccalaureate, whereas in the past many of the courses taken for this degree would not be accepted. Thus, women who have the A.A.S. in such fields as nursing or food services would be able to obtain the baccalaureate at a four-year institution more easily.

For women faculty and senior-level administrators, it is likely that even more jobs will become available because of retirements of the faculty and institutional leaders who were hired during the great growth period of community colleges in the 1960s and early 1970s. Community colleges may well be the first (and perhaps only) institutions where female and male faculty reach parity in salary and rank.

REFERENCES AND FURTHER READING

Frye, J. (1995). Women in the two-year college, 1900 to 1970. In B. Townsend (Ed.), *Gender and power in the community college: New directions for community colleges, No. 89* (pp. 5–14). San Francisco: Jossey-Bass.

Hagedorn, L. S., & Laden, B. V. (2002). Exploring the climate for women community college faculty. In J. Palmer (Ed.), *Community college faculty: Characteristics, practices, and challenges: New directions for community colleges, No. 118* (pp. 69–78). San Francisco: Jossey-Bass.

Huber, M. T. (1998). *Community college faculty attitudes and trends, 1997*. Menlo Park, CA: Carnegie Foundation for the Advancement of Teaching.

Miller, M. T., & Creswell, J. W. (1998). Beliefs and values of women in community college leadership. *Community College Journal of Research and Practice, 22*(3), 229–238.

Townsend, B. K. (Ed.). (1995). *Gender and power in the community college: New directions for community colleges, No. 89*. San Francisco: Jossey-Bass.

Townsend, B. K., & LaPaglia, N. (2000). Are we marginalized within academe? Perceptions of two-year college faculty. *Community College Review, 28*(1), 41–48.

Townsend, B. K., & Twombly, S. B. (1998). A feminist critique of organizational change in the community college. In J. Levin (Ed.), *Organizational change in the community college: New directions for community colleges, No. 102* (pp. 77–86). San Francisco: Jossey-Bass.

Wolf-Wendel, L., Ward, K., Twombly, S. B., & Bradley, S. (2005, April). *Faculty life at community colleges: The perspective of women with children*. Paper presented at the annual meeting of the American Educational Research Association, Montreal, Canada.

Wolfe, J. R., & Strange, C. C. (2003). Academic life at the franchise: Faculty culture in a rural two-year branch campus. *Review of Higher Education, 26*(3), 343–362.

CHAPTER 13

Distance Education

CHRISTINE VON PRÜMMER

As distance education—often in the guise of e-learning—is on the rise, it becomes increasingly important to look at gender issues in this educational field. Even where a majority of distance students and teachers are women, they tend to have little or no representation in the definition of content and in shaping the teaching and learning process. In 1982, women distance educators initiated "WIN," the Women's International Network, within the International Council for Distance Education (ICDE) in order to address gender issues and redress the underrepresentation of women in leadership positions. The first tangible WIN product was the book *Toward New Horizons for Women in Distance Education* (Faith, 1988), with contributions from women from all corners of the world. Twenty years later, ICDE is once again a male-dominated organization, and WIN no longer exists as a recognized network within the established distance education world. Nevertheless, the issues and comparative research initiatives as well as the networking of women in the field continue. In 2004, for instance, the United States Distance Learning Association launched the International Forum for Women in E-Learning. And, at the present time, gender continues to be an important category of analysis and action in distance education.

The Field of Distance Education

Essentially, *distance education* denotes a system of teaching and learning that does not require classroom attendance. The term literally refers to the geographical distance between teachers and students. Instead of meeting face to face on campus, they are in separate locations, the teaching and learning process usually occurring at separate times. The prominent characteristic of distance education, therefore, is the use of media and technology to transmit content and to enable interaction and communication between teachers and students and between students.

The use of media and technologies has contributed to the changes that "distance education" has undergone since its beginnings in the mid-1800s. Originally, letters were exchanged, as teachers wrote down the subject matter and sent course "letters" to students in remote areas. Students worked through the written and printed materials, did the assignments, and mailed their solutions and possibly queries to the teaching staff, who in turn mailed back their comments and evaluations. Consequently, in the early days, distance education was called "correspondence education."

As new media and technologies were developed, the printed course materials were increasingly supplemented and sometimes supplanted by these new teaching and learning tools. "Correspondence education" evolved into "distance education," which made use of telephone, radio, audio- and videocassettes, and television in order to enhance its teaching. Increasingly, elements of personal contact were introduced into the teaching and learning process. Audio- and to some extent videoconferencing simulated person-to-person interaction.

From the 1980s onward, with the advent of personal computers and information and communication technologies (ICTs), distance education experienced dramatic changes in its delivery and communication methods as well as in its image. By the mid-1990s, distance education had entered the Worldwide Web in a big way. The Internet seemed to offer unlimited possibilities not only for course delivery and for studying but also for interaction and collaboration and for administrative purposes. The terms *online education, electronic campus*, and *virtual university* became nearly synonymous with the term *distance education*. There is even a persistent tendency to argue that *distance education* is now obsolete and has been superseded by the more up-to-date terms *online education* or *e-learning*. On the other hand, it is argued that providing education online is just one of the ways of organizing a teaching and learning system at a distance and that the use of the Internet and other ICTs does not fundamentally change the character of distance education. In fact, there is now a trend toward "blended learning," which utilizes a mixture of media and technologies as well as some face-to-face events.

Issues of Equity

From the beginning, the world of distance education has been closely associated with issues of equal access to education. Originally meant to provide education for people in remote areas, distance education also became a means of extending educational opportunities to anyone who could not attend classes in person. Apart from geographical distance, reasons that prevent children or adults from attending traditional educational institutions may lie in social, cultural, or personal factors. Social class, for instance, may be a distancing factor, as people from a lower- or working-class background cannot afford better schooling for their children or traditionally do not value advanced education. Cultural factors may prevent people of certain religious or ethnic backgrounds from providing their children, especially their daughters, with higher education. Or the mainstream culture may deny minority groups access to educational opportunities. Personal factors may be at work when a potential student is disabled, has to take care of children or other family members, works full time at a job, or is imprisoned or institutionalized.

This shift in focus was accompanied by a corresponding shift away from the original concept of "teaching at a distance" manifested, for instance, in the term *distance teaching university* (DTU) for providers of tertiary distance education. The new terms *open learning* and later *open and distance learning* (ODL) and finally *open, distance, and flexible learning* show a twofold commitment: an emphasis on open access and an emphasis on the learning process and the needs of learners.

International comparisons show that this redefinition process occurs at different speeds and in different ways as distance education providers start from different institutional premises and philosophies. Many DTUs, especially in Anglo-Saxon countries, explicitly started as "open universities," with few or no admission requirements, enabling students without formal educational prerequisites to study for a degree. The British Open University is a prominent and early example. Other DTUs, such as the German FernUniversität, require formal entrance qualifications of students entering a degree program. For these universities, the meaning of "open" may lie in the increased provision of continuing education and opportunities for professional development and lifelong learning.

Women and Distance Education

The goal of providing equal access to education through the provision of ODL inevitably leads to a concern with gender. In countries and cultures the world over, including Western, industrialized societies, girls and women—especially those from a minority background—are educationally disadvantaged compared with their male counterparts. This may be attributed to material factors as well as to cultural or religious factors regarding the role of women and men in society, and often these reasons overlap. On the material level, for instance, it may be argued that a family lacks the money to cover the cost of sending all children to school or that the family income needs to be supplemented through putting children to work. Yet where limited financial resources make it necessary to set priorities as to which child should get an education or attend secondary school and university, boys tend to be systematically preferred over girls regardless of intellectual ability and individual wishes. On the level of cultural and religious factors, it may be argued that a woman's place is in the home and that she does not need higher education or vocational training in order to fulfill her "natural" duties as housewife and mother. There may also be a concern that "too much" education could corrupt a woman's moral standing and make her unfit for her "proper place" in the private sphere of her future family. On the other hand, as future "head of household" and breadwinner, a boy is expected to get an education, possibly complete a degree, in order to obtain employment and start a career and take his "proper place" in the public sphere.

Looking at distance education as a second chance for people previously excluded from (higher) education, it is easy to see that women on the whole are more in need of such additional educational opportunities. This is especially true where gender discrimination meets discrimination based on class, race, or other factors affecting equal access. Women are also more likely to live in situations that make it difficult or impossible to attend face-to-face classes or to afford the direct costs (e.g., tuition fees, books) and indirect costs (e.g., child care) associated with attending classroom-based educational programs. It is therefore reasonable to expect that women are the larger target group of distance education. This is reflected in the fact that many distance teaching institutions such as the British Open University or the Canadian Athabasca University have a majority of women students. Yet there are others such as the German Fern-Universität or distance education programs in parts of Africa and Asia where women students are the minority.

The New Learning Environment of the Virtual University

At the beginning of the twenty-first century, both traditional and ODL institutions are increasingly concerned with ways in which the seemingly unlimited possibilities of ICTs and the new media can be employed to create new learning environments. The last few years have seen rapid developments in ICTs, resulting in the widespread availability of multimedia computers and Internet access among the population of Western, industrialized societies. Also, ICTs are constantly improved and increasingly powerful. New features are developed allowing more data to be transmitted and handled at greater speed and creating new dimensions of interactivity and communication.

This has had profound effects on distance education institutions, with regard both to potential student populations and to the organization and delivery of ODL. ICTs can provide the means to reach larger and more distant and divergent target groups more quickly and at lower cost. As "distributed learning" replaces the more traditional forms of distance education, ODL becomes less dependent on the availability and reliability of postal services and is less subject to time constraints inherent in "snail mail" communication.

Easily the most obvious difference between distance education and campus-based education is the physical learning environment in which students and staff are situated. Traditional face-to-face teaching and learning takes place within the walls of an institution, with both teachers and students present in the same room, giving and attending a lecture or seminar or participating in exercises and lab experiments. In this setting, the educational environment is structured to a large extent by the school or university, which provides the classrooms and equipment, library and lab facilities, as well as opportunities on the campus for informal exchanges and communication between the students and between students and staff. To the extent that a university provides student housing, it also influences the students' personal learning environment.

A distance teaching university, by contrast, traditionally does not provide a teaching and learning environment for its students. Since there are very few or none of the usual attendance requirements, the DTU has no need for a campus in the classic sense or for university buildings as physical structures with classrooms, laboratories, lecture theaters, libraries, meeting places, or cafeterias where students habitually meet each other and their teachers face to face. Distance education materials are delivered to the students wherever they direct them to be sent. The students, relieved from the necessity of being present at a specific place at a specified time, are in turn responsible for setting up their own learning environments.

Both the campus-based and the home-study learning environments are defined, and distinguished, by the physical whereabouts of the students and the teachers. This is different for the new learning environment of the virtual university, which, in principle, can supplement or replace traditional teaching systems and, in fact, originates as often from "conventional" face-to-face institutions as it does from DTUs. Students can enter the "virtual" university regardless of their "real" learning environment, provided they have access to the necessary technology.

Gender Issues in the Virtual University

Concerns about new learning environments have also spurred debate about whether the new world of online teaching and virtual studying might be as closed to women as traditional universities were until the turn of the twentieth century. The opposite viewpoint holds that gender differences have all but disappeared as a result of ICTs. In order to find answers to these questions, it is necessary to look at some recent research data on gender equality in e-learning and on issues concerning women students.

Looking at DTUs as forerunners to the electronic campus, we continually find empirical evidence of the ways in which different distance education systems affect the participation of women and gender differentiation in areas such as access, course choice, learning styles, and communication patterns (see especially the comparative research done by Gill Kirkup and Christine von Prümmer on the situation of women students at the British Open University and the German FernUniversität since 1985: Kirkup & von Prümmer, 1990, 1997; von Prümmer, 2000). There is no evidence to suggest that gender is less of an issue in the virtual university, although it is all too easy to forget that the new technologies are as gendered as their predecessors from which they developed and to assume that women automatically have equal opportunities to enter and succeed in the virtual university. Yet gender-specific and feminist research shows that women often have less access to the technologies, less control over the ICTs in their homes and places of work, and less confidence and competency in using the technology (Kirkup, 1996; von Prümmer & Rossié, 2001). Combined with everyday institutional androcentrism and with the fact that students' private lives on the whole are still characterized by the gendered division of housework and child care, these factors could lead to systematic discrimination against women in the virtual campus unless special measures are taken to ensure gender equity.

ICTs have the potential to facilitate communication and interaction between the students and between students and staff in distance education settings. They are therefore especially attractive for women distance students who tend to prefer connected learning styles and opportunities for exchange and cooperation otherwise missing in their distance learning environment. At the same time, there is empirical evidence that communication processes in newsgroups and electronic discussions are frequently dominated by men and their styles of discourse—often highly competitive and declamatory—which may be uninteresting or off-putting to women (Balka & Smith, 2000). In order to ensure equity of access for both men and women, care must be taken to construct the virtual university as a women-friendly learning environment and to counteract dysfunctional developments.

In looking at gender and the use of ICTs, it is also helpful to distinguish more clearly between the technology and its application: On the one hand, there is the basic technology and the know-how to operate the hardware and software—the engineering and informatics side of ICTs. On the other hand, there is the use of the Web as a means for communication and information gathering through electronic channels. It seems that the technology as such is still very much a man's thing (and men do their best to mystify it and keep women out), while communication and interaction is something women enjoy and excel at.

This distinction helps to explain why surveys continually show that it is mostly husbands or male partners who decide which computer is purchased, why men have more sophisticated and better-equipped machines, why women are less experienced and less enthusiastic about mastering the complex processes of setting up their own equipment, connecting to the university server through an Internet services provider, and joining a discussion forum only after installing the appropriate conferencing software package. Once their systems are hooked up and functional, women are free to participate in online activities and—much like driving their car or using software packages for data analyses—can safely forget about the underlying hardware, the electronic fuel injection, and the computer programming that make it all possible. If the concept of *open* distance learning is taken seriously, it cannot afford to neglect issues of equity and overt or latent discrimination. While it is true that many women have discovered the Internet and its potentials, research findings also confirm that gender differences still exist with respect to access and control over resources, social division of labor and time management, learning styles, and learning environments.

Surveys on computer access and use of ICTs for distance studies show that in Western, industrialized countries such as Germany, over 90% of distance education students have access to a computer for study purposes, but there are still a significant number of distance students without high-speed Internet access. While there are still differences between the students in different subject areas—people studying mathematical and technical subjects are more likely to have a computer, but people studying education, social sciences, and the humanities are less well equipped—the *overall* results show hardly any gender differences. This result might be interpreted as showing, first, that gender has become irrelevant with regard to the new technologies and, second, that mandatory computer and Internet access would not be a problem for (prospective) students.

Looked at more closely, though, the survey data show the usual gender-differentiated patterns where women

- mostly have access to only one computer, usually at home, while many men can access more than one computer and often have a suitable PC at their place of work;
- have less sophisticated equipment and software, especially as far as multimedia and ICT features are concerned;
- are more likely to leave the purchasing decision to their husband/partner;
- face more restrictions in using the technology and have less control over the computer, which is likely to be used by other family members;
- have less Internet access than men, especially at work, and must rely slightly more on the provision of the technology in study centers and other external sources; and
- often have less experience, less interest, and less confidence in using the multimedia and ICT features of a computer.

In order to ensure equal opportunities for women in e-learning, specific consideration must be given to these patterns of computer usage. On the basis of research and experience, it is clear that the virtual university must not be left alone to develop "naturally," following technological advances and software revolutions without regard to their social effects. In order to enable women to participate fully in the virtual university, factors that hinder this equal participation must be identified and measures taken to redress gender imbalances.

On the whole, ODL institutions seem to have embarked on a process toward becoming virtual universities. Most DTUs, and many universities set up in the traditional teaching mode, have introduced Internet-based courses and degree programs. Some existing DTUs are in the process of transformation; some new DTUs have been established outright as "virtual universities." In this situation, it is necessary to look at the students whom these universities serve and to assess their needs and wishes with regard to learning and communicating through electronic media as well as their access to the electronic campus as demonstrated by the availability of the necessary equipment and know-how. There is a tendency to assume that more and better equipment, more sophisticated computer programs, more powerful data transmission, and increased communication facilities equate to higher-quality education. But is this true? There is evidence to the effect that better servers in the university do not automatically mean better service for the students, especially with regard to gender-specific patterns in access and study conditions.

In addition to issues of access and exclusion, the question of how to serve women students in a virtual learning environment, as in any other ODL context, touches on two spheres: First, the virtual university must be designed as a women-friendly, non-discriminatory place, and second, students' personal environments and life situations must be taken into account. In this context, it is interesting to note that the virtual learning environment tends to be seen as a closed system and that, consequently, there is little concern with the "outside" circumstances such as the conditions under which students study and their access to the computer and the Internet. Yet these circumstances have profound effects on the ways in which women and men are able to organize their lives around their studies and to pursue their academic interests successfully.

To the extent that ICTs replace the traditional media and access to advanced technologies becomes an essential prerequisite for studying in the virtual university, there is an increasing danger that women will be disproportionately disbarred from entering and enjoying the virtual learning environment if gender issues are ignored and the definition and construction of the virtual university is left to the existing male-dominated, androcentric academic and political decision-making processes or to "market forces." To offset this, one area of support and services for (potential) women students might be measures promoting the necessary computer literacy and user confidence as well as supplying easy-to-use software with instructions that can be followed by people who are not familiar with computer jargon and do not aspire to become computer experts.

Another area in which gender sensitivity is essential is the field of content, presentation, and curriculum. Women's studies and gender studies have been shown to be effective in redressing some of the existing imbalances of an androcentric educational system by focusing on previously neglected issues and by looking at these from a different standpoint. The success of these programs suggests that one of the ways to promote women's participation in the virtual campus is the inclusion of women's and gender studies in the curriculum, dealing specifically with gender-related issues and developing women-friendly ways of using the new technologies for teaching and learning processes. Examples of this are courses offered for credit within various master's of distance education degree programs such as the Gender Issues in Distance Education course at the Canadian Athabasca University.

In order to ensure that the virtual campus will not be a place without women or a place in which women are passive participants who "consume" the education they cannot get any other way, women themselves must be prepared to embrace the new world of ICTs, to take a critical look at the dangers and also at the advantages inherent in virtual teaching and learning processes, and to be involved in shaping their own new learning environments.

This will not be an easy task, as many projects in this area ignore the social and political implications, thereby adversely affecting the chances of women. For instance, the proponents of virtual universities tend to focus on the technologies at the expense of the human element. There are many cases where seemingly endless amounts of money are being spent on buying the hardware and little or no money is spent on hiring and training the staff who will have to work with this technology or on making sure all students and staff are computer literate. There is also a tendency for funding bodies and decision makers to focus on subject areas that have an obvious affinity to technology, such as the male-dominated fields of computer science and electrical engineering, and to be less open to developments in "unlikely" subject areas such as philosophy and literature that are more popular with women students.

Considering the limited resources and the high costs of developing high-quality teaching materials and maintaining effective and conducive structures for interaction, it is very important that women from different universities, and from different countries, are given the opportunity to set up networks for cooperating and for sharing not only their course materials but also their teaching and learning experiences and the results from their evaluation research. In this way, it is possible to avoid duplication, both of materials and of mistakes, and to build up a larger store of courses by and from women.

REFERENCES AND FURTHER READING

Balka, E., & Smith, R. (Eds.). (2000). *Women, work and computerization: Charting a course to the future*. Dordrecht, Netherlands: Kluwer.

Faith, K. (Ed.). (1988). *Toward new horizons for women in distance education: International perspectives*. London: Routledge.

Kirkup, G. E. (1996). The importance of gender. In R. Mills & A. Tait (Eds.), *Supporting the learner in open and distance learning* (pp. 146–165). London: Pitman.

Kirkup, G. E., & von Prümmer, C. (1990). Support and connectedness: The needs of women distance education students. *Journal of Distance Education, 5*(2), 9–31.

Kirkup, G. E., & von Prümmer, C. (1997). Distance education for European women: The threats and opportunities of new educational forms and media. *European Journal of Women's Studies, 4*(1), 39–62.

Kramerae, C. (2001). *The third shift: Women learning online*. Washington, DC: American Association of University Women. Information on the report retrieved June 30, 2006, from http://www.aauw.org/research/3rdshift.cfm

Spronk, B. (2002). *Globalisation, ODL and gender: Not everyone's world is getting smaller*. Retrieved June 30, 2006, from http://www.iec.ac.uk/resources/globalisation_paper_bs_2002.pdf

von Prümmer, C. (2000). *Women and distance education: Challenges and opportunities*. London: RoutledgeFalmer.

von Prümmer, C., & Rossié, U. (2001). Gender-sensitive evaluation research. In E. J. Burge & M. Haughey (Eds.), *Using learning technologies: International perspectives on practice* (pp. 135–144). London: RoutledgeFalmer.

CHAPTER 14

Historically Black Colleges and Universities

MARYBETH GASMAN

Issues of racial equality have long received special attention at historically Black colleges and universities (HBCUs). One consequence of this focus, however, is that issues of gender equality are sometimes swept under the rug—rarely discussed, except among a small group of feminists. This "sweeping" is quite evident in the research on HBCUs, where the focus is almost entirely on males. Discussion of women or the relationships between men and women within the Black college context is limited. In the words of Black feminist scholar Patricia Hill Collins, many Black college women have found themselves in the position of "outsider-within"—meaning that their gender puts them in a disadvantaged position within the racialized Black college community.

Most HBCUs were founded in the aftermath of the Civil War, with the exception of three in the North: Lincoln University and Cheyney University in Pennsylvania and Wilberforce in Ohio. With the end of the Civil War, the daunting task of providing education to over four million formerly enslaved Blacks was shouldered by both the federal government, through the Freedmen's Bureau, and many northern church missionaries. As early as 1865, the Freedmen's Bureau began establishing Black colleges, resulting in staff and teachers with primarily military backgrounds. During this period, most Black colleges were colleges in name only; like many White colleges in their infancy, these institutions generally provided primary and secondary education. From their beginnings, most Black colleges, unlike their historically White counterparts, provided coeducational training. Black women, like Black men, were seen by the White missionaries and Whites in general as potential workers in need of training. Only Barber Scotia College and Spelman College, founded in 1867 and 1881, respectively, were solely dedicated to the education of women. Morehouse College, founded in 1867, was the only Black college for men.

The benevolence of the White missionaries was tinged with self-interest and sometimes racism. The missionaries' goal in establishing these colleges was to Christianize the freedmen (i.e., convert formerly enslaved people to their brand of Christianity). And while some scholars see the missionaries' actions as largely well meaning, many others do not. According to a more radical group of scholars, the idea of a Black menace was at the forefront of the minds of these missionaries, who believed that education would curb the "savage" tendencies of the former slaves but should not lead to full-blown social equality. The education provided to Black college students was a mixture of liberal arts and industrial training: Classical texts were taught side by side with manual labor skills for men and household duties for women (both for their own homes and for those White homes in which they might work). Many Black colleges also provided teacher training.

With the passage of the second Morrill Act in 1890, the federal government again took an interest in Black education, establishing public land-grant Black colleges and universities. This act stipulated that those states practicing segregation in their public colleges and universities would forfeit federal funding unless they established agricultural and mechanical institutions for the Black population. Despite the wording of the Morrill Act, which called for the equitable division of federal funds, these newly founded institutions received fewer monies than their White counterparts and thus had inferior facilities. Just as before the act, women who attended these schools learned household duties, such as how to cook, clean, make brooms, and sew. On the other hand, men were trained in brick making and laying, farming, blacksmithing, and other forms of manual labor.

It was not until the turn of the twentieth century that most Black colleges seriously began to provide college-level liberal arts education. Institutions such as Fisk in Tennessee, Dillard in Louisiana, and Howard in Washington, DC, exemplified this approach, schooling their male and female students in the classics. For the most part, these colleges prepared students for teaching positions in schools and colleges and for public service.

Today, according to the federal government, there are 103 HBCUs, both public and private. Three of these institutions are single sex: Spelman College (female) and Morehouse College (male) in Georgia and Bennett College (female) in North Carolina. At these institutions as well as the other 100, there have historically been gender disparities that continue today. These disparities and the discrimination that causes them are manifest within the ranks of students, faculty, and administration. Each of these groups provides a unique lens through which to view the problem.

Students and Gender Roles

During the early years of Black colleges, female students were sheltered by the administration; their lives were shaped by institutional policies designed to control their behavior. In the eyes of the White missionaries, Black women had been stripped of their feminine virtue by the experiences of slavery and therefore had to be purified before they could assume the responsibilities of the home. Typically during the late 1880s, female Black college students were not allowed to leave the campus without a member of the administration escorting them. By contrast, men were free to come and go as they pleased. At most institutions, the dean of women lived on campus in order to watch over the "fragile" and "impressionable" young college girls. The dean of men, on the other hand, lived off campus, as did the other upper-level administrators. During the mid-1920s, many female students at Black colleges and universities urged campus administrators to grant them greater autonomy, noting that it would help them learn self-reliance—a skill that they saw as essential to assuming leadership roles. These same women fought vehemently against the repressive religious customs used to rear their race and gender. These practices were generally imposed by White and Black male administrators, many of whom were also ordained Baptist ministers. In particular, the administrators often used the biblical writings of Saint Paul as a rationale for relegating women to second-class status. Women were told that, according to the Bible, patient waiting was to be held above the development of one's talents.

In spite of the heavy hand of religion and the resulting sexism, Black colleges during the late 1800s and early 1900s offered a surprising number of opportunities for Black female students to participate in traditionally male activities. For example, at Talladega College, women were able to join the rifle club. On the other hand, women participated in social service sororities such as Alpha Kappa Alpha and Delta Sigma Theta. While sometimes focused on the superficial aspects of appearance and socialization, these organizations were also active in suffrage and civil rights activities as well as other national causes.

During the 1950s and early 1960s, Black women on Black college and university campuses were instrumental in the civil rights movement. Women at both Bennett College and Spelman College participated in sit-ins and lunch counter demonstrations. The administrators of these women's colleges, now Black rather than White, were supportive of the student actions. However, this was not the case at all Black colleges and universities. At some public Black institutions, which were under the close supervision of state government authorities, administrators declined to help both male and female student protesters who had landed in jail.

Many of these young HBCU women were fearless, working diligently to make change within their communities and within the country as a whole. For example, Barbara Harris and Diane Nash, both Fisk University students, were jailed along with 63 other male and female students who protested Nashville's segregated lunch counters. Although they were offered an opportunity to make bond ($100), they chose to go to jail because, in their minds, paying the bond would be a capitulation to the South's Jim Crow legal structure. Ironically, as these female students were fighting on behalf of civil rights, they were still being treated as fragile accessories to men by their college administrations. For example, at the same time that students at Bennett College were marching in the streets and attempting to desegregate lunch counters, they were required to take a course called "The Art of Living," which focused on becoming a successful homemaker.

In the early 1970s, Patricia Gurin and Edgar Epps completed a research study that sought to understand the advantages and disadvantages gained by Black male and female students at HBCUs. Surveying 5,000 African American students, this study was comprehensive and its results compelling. The researchers found that undergraduate women at HBCUs were considerably disadvantaged. In particular, the educational and career goals of female students were significantly lower than those of their male peers. Not only were these Black women less likely to aspire to the Ph.D., but they were more likely to opt for low-prestige careers in the female sector of the nation's job market (e.g., teaching and the health professions). This seminal research also showed that the patriarchal environments at many HBCUs compounded the problem. Other researchers have found that social passivity and disengagement on the part of Black women, most likely caused by institutional environments, helped explain why these individuals did not have higher career aspirations. Scholars in the mid-1980s found that although women were actively engaged in the classroom and in extracurricular activities, they spent less time interacting with individual faculty members. This practice could result in fewer discussions about graduate school and less support for nonfemale career fields. More recently, researchers have shown more equal gains for men and women from the HBCU experience. It appears that women have overcome some of the barriers placed before them, breaking away from passivity. However, at many campuses, an at-mosphere persists that encourages women to cede to male counterparts in class dis-cussions and in student leadership positions.

Studies have shown that African American female students at HBCUs feel a higher level of anxiety than their male counterparts. In addition, when surveyed, they felt less competent and were often less assertive than males. Sadly, other studies have re-vealed that female students were more willing to take on positions and roles that made them seem less competent in order to avoid threatening their male peers. Despite these feelings of insecurity, women's academic performance at HBCUs outpaces that of Black males. A recent study showed that at most HBCUs, the percentage of Black women on the honor roll was larger than the percentage of women enrolled at the institu-tions. For example, at Clark Atlanta University in 2005, women accounted for 69% of the student body but made up 84% of the dean's list. Likewise, at Howard University, women made up 60% of the student body but accounted for 70% of the honor roll. On average, the percentage of women on deans' lists at HBCUs exceeded their enrollment by 10%.

Currently, the nation's HBCUs enroll approximately 250,000 African American stu-dents, with a large proportion attending private four-year institutions. HBCUs grant roughly 28% of bachelor's degrees, 15% of master's degrees, 9% of doctoral degrees, and 15% of professional degrees awarded to African Americans. Black women outpace Black men at all educational levels. Despite generally favorable statistics for degree attain-ment for women, the majority of these degrees are in traditionally female-dominated programs. Over 70% of Black women's degrees earned at HBCUs are in the health pro-fessions or education. Black women, much like White women, hold positions in ser-vice areas and are less likely to hold jobs in the sciences. Here certain Black colleges are trying to make gains. For example, of the Black women who enter graduate programs in the sciences, 50% are from Spelman College and Bennett College—schools that have special programs preparing their students for scientific fields. Moreover, HBCUs represent the top 20 institutions overall in the placement of Black women in graduate programs in the sciences at all U.S. institutions of higher education. Xavier University in New Orleans, in particular, sends more Black women into U.S. medical schools than any other institution in the country. Some recent research has shown that Black col-lege and university women are now selecting majors that were once exclusively male—including math, technology, engineering, and science. However, they are still aspiring to the lower level positions within these fields.

Although HBCUs were established to educate African Americans, and this popula-tion continues to make up the majority of these institutions' student bodies, they also educate a substantial number of White, Latino, and Asian students. In the student bodies of some HBCUs, such as Lincoln University in Missouri, White commuters, many of whom are part-time students, constitute the majority. African American stu-dents, however, continue to outnumber Whites among full-time, residential students at Lincoln. Other institutions, such as Bluefield State, Delaware State, and Kentucky State have between 18% and 26% non-Black students. Most of these students are women, adding to the large percentages of women at HBCUs overall.

Gender in the Faculty Ranks

During the early years at Black colleges, the faculty consisted mainly of White missionary men and women. Most, in fact, were White, unmarried women from the

Northeast. As more African Americans gained college degrees that prepared them for teaching, they slowly trickled into the faculties of Black colleges. In addition, free Blacks from the North, who had been trained as teachers prior to the end of the Civil War, came south to assist with teaching.

By the turn of the century, both the White and Black female faculty members (and for that matter, the Black male faculty) were kept under the tight control of White college presidents who, for the most part, were puppets of newly wealthy White industrialist philanthropists. These philanthropists included men such as John D. Rockefeller, Andrew Carnegie, and Julius Rosenwald, who funded and sat on the boards of these institutions. Faculty members typically implemented the types of curricula supported by these philanthropists, who funded only those institutions that agreed with their educational philosophies.

still run by white men

Many HBCUs developed rigid puritanical and patriarchal codes of behavior for their female faculty. For example, in 1913, the board of Howard University decided to institute a policy stating that any female teachers who married would be required to resign their positions—married women were deemed incapable of handling both teaching and wifely duties. Unmarried female faculty members were seen as a separate class, and their actions were always subject to great scrutiny.

Although Blacks gradually supplanted Whites in the presidential offices, they sometimes continued the domineering leadership styles of their predecessors. This remained a problem through the 1960s and 1970s. Although there have not been any empirical studies in this area, individual testimonies abound of the difficult situation women were placed in under autocratic and male-dominated leadership. Unfortunately, the oppressive styles of some Black college presidents and their unfair treatment of faculty have been used by White outsiders to demonstrate the inferiority of Black colleges in general. This has made it difficult for faculty and staff at those colleges to raise questions about leadership at Black colleges without engendering charges of racist complicity with these institutions' outside detractors. However, as Black women who have actual experiences with these problems have come forward with more nuanced accounts, it has become easier to offer a balanced critique of Black male leadership. For example, in a painful report of the years she spent at Black colleges entitled "Black Women in Academia," Margaret Walker Alexander points in particular to her days at Livingstone College in North Carolina and Jackson State University in Mississippi (Alexander, 1995). According to Alexander, every time she succeeded in making a creative contribution within these institutions, she was replaced by a man. The institutions' presidents constantly questioned her intelligence and dedication.

Black women account for just over 6% of full-time faculty members in academia overall. Just over half of these women are employed at HBCUs. In the area of promotion and tenure, women continue to lag. According to data compiled by the National Center for Education Statistics in 2000, approximately 30% of men at HBCUs hold the rank of full professor, and 26% hold the rank of associate professor. In contrast, only a little over 20% of female faculty members are full professors, and 19% are associate professors.

Studies have shown that female faculty members at HBCUs are hesitant about discussing issues related to fairness in employment, workplace climate, and professional development. In a 2001 survey of 1,000 female faculty members at HBCUs, over 45% said that they had been discriminated against because of their gender. When asked to give specific examples of the discrimination, these same women refused, noting that they were uncomfortable providing details because of fear of retribution. Research shows that women at HBCUs are promoted at a slower rate, receive lower salaries, and are more likely to teach part time. Some scholars attribute this situation to the fact that women have to juggle family, work, and community responsibilities. Moreover, Black female professors typically have more academic responsibilities than their male counterparts. They are looked to for advice by young women, are asked to serve on numerous committees, and are often required to be the voice of the college in the local community. It is interesting to note that male and female faculty members at HBCUs start out with approximately the same salary, but they do not progress at the same rate. By the time Black male and female faculty members reach the rank of full professor, Black women receive only 89% of the salaries earned by men.

When asked their opinion in research studies, Black female faculty claimed that fewer opportunities exist for them to work collaboratively; they are rarely asked to do so by their male peers. As collaboration is a time for mentoring of junior faculty by senior faculty, this situation works to the disadvantage of females. In addition to less collaboration and mentoring, Black females sense a lack of support from the administration that manifests itself in less funding for research and teaching innovations.

Administrators: Where Are the Women?

Traditionally at HBCUs, women have not played prominent roles in administration; in most instances, they were not given the opportunity. Early on, the leadership of these institutions was handpicked by the wealthy White philanthropists who supported the institutions, and these individuals put their trust in the hands of mainly White men. By and large, it was not until the mid-twentieth century that even Black men would assume leadership roles at Black colleges and universities. There were a few exceptions, however. Mary McLeod Bethune started her own school for girls in 1904, which became coeducational Bethune-Cookman College in 1923. She served as a strong leader of the institution for 40 years, bringing the cause of African American higher education to the attention of the nation's political and business leaders. Although most people in Daytona Beach, where the college was located, including some of her close friends, thought she would not succeed and the school would fold, Bethune worked diligently, and her efforts and charisma attracted the attention of James Gamble, cofounder of Procter and Gamble. Gamble supported Bethune's college for years and also served as the chair of the institution's board of trustees. While Bethune was the first Black female president of a coed institution, Willa Player was the first Black female president of a Black women's college. In 1955, she took over the leadership of Bennett College in Greensboro, North Carolina, after having served as a faculty member and vice president at the institution. During her tenure at Bennett, President Player was continually asked to justify the existence of a Black women's college, as very few people saw the value in separate education for Black women.

Beginning in the 1920s, the dean of women position became a permanent fixture at coeducational institutions of higher education, and this provided a leadership opportunity for Black women. HBCUs chose women who were refined and cultured to act as role models and disciplinarians for their college women. As in the case of female faculty members, their behavior was scrutinized by the male administration. At most institutions, they were required to live on campus. In fact, it was not until 1929 that Juliette Derricotte, the dean of women at Fisk University, was allowed to live off campus. Other HBCU were slow to follow Fisk's example.

Lucy Diggs Slowe, the first dean of women at Howard University (1922–1937), was a powerful and groundbreaking leader within both the HBCU community and higher education in general. She challenged the exclusion and underrepresentation of women at Howard, especially within the institution's policy-making bodies. Moreover, she took public stands at the university, speaking out on gender-based salary discrimination and demanding equal living conditions for women. Her bold nature angered many of her male peers, who were used to being openly condescending to Black women. In one instance, when Slowe acted as a representative of several female students who had been sexually harassed by a Black male professor, she received a letter attacking both her credibility and that of the students. The accuser asserted, "You forget that you are merely the Dean of Women and not the custodian of morals of the male teachers of Howard University. It is my opinion if you had something to do and two classes to teach as the other Deans, you wouldn't hear so much" (Mills in Bell-Scott, 1979, p. 22).

Lucy Diggs Slowe's views on empowering women did not gain favor with then Howard University president Mordecai Johnson. A graduate of all-male Morehouse College, Johnson hired Black women for the faculty but still held paternalistic views. Slowe was in no way conventional and did not match Johnson's ideas of what a Black woman should be. From the time that Johnson arrived at Howard in 1926 until Slowe's death in 1937, they quarreled over issues of equality for Black women.

With these exceptions, there were very few female administrators at Black colleges or universities until the 1950s and even then women mainly filled the role of dean of women. In fact, Spelman College, which many would consider the premiere Black women's institution in the United States, did not have a Black female president until Johnnetta B. Cole in 1987. Although women's colleges have historically been less resistant than coed institutions to employing women in the upper echelons of administration, only in the mid-1970s did Spelman and Bennett begin to fill these positions with women with any regularity.

The lack of Black female representation in the administration still plagues Black colleges and universities today. Only 15 out of the 103 presidents of HBCUs are women. With few exceptions, these women are the heads of the smallest, least well-known Black colleges—those with fewer than 1,000 students. Men typically lead the larger and more prestigious HBCUs and are paid much higher salaries than their female counterparts. In a pattern that mirrors higher education overall, women in administration are typically found in the student and external affairs divisions (development, alumni relations, and public relations). They are particularly underrepresented in the chief academic officer position. On average, at HBCUs, this position is held by Black males in their early fifties who are married with children. Most are promoted from within the institution and hold doctoral degrees awarded in the academic disciplines. This is significant, as more women receive degrees in more applied fields of study, especially in education and social work.

The women who are in chief academic officer positions tend to be older than their male counterparts, have been tenured longer, and are much more likely to be single. And, by and large, few of these women (who have been discouraged by male-dominated institutional policies) have any aspiration for the presidency. Of note is the fact that male chief academic officers are more frequently asked to serve as acting president when the president is on leave. An explanation for this may be that male administrators within Black colleges and universities take the professional background and socialization of their male colleagues more seriously than that of their female colleagues. Males tend to be integrated into the cultural milieu of the institution more quickly than females.

Much like their White female counterparts at predominantly White institutions, Black female administrators and faculty often face a chilly climate—sometimes experiencing incidents of sexual harassment. According to several Black feminist scholars, HBCUs lag behind their predominantly White institutional peers with regard to anti-sexual-harassment education and policies. Some speculate that Black women have not fought as vehemently as Whites because they fear that feminism will demand that they give up their fight against racism. For example, with the exception of Spelman and Bennett, very few Black colleges and universities have women's studies programs. In more recent years, there have been gains in the area of gender relations at HBCUs. At Hampton University, for instance, President William Harvey has hosted forums on male and female relationships within the Black college community and beyond. More importantly, he has made a priority of the understanding of sexism and the incorporation of nonsexist values into the curriculum. And Xavier University in New Orleans has targeted these types of programs specifically at Black men to ease on-campus gender relations.

In 2003, Johnnetta B. Cole and Beverley Guy-Sheftall authored *Gender Talk: The Struggle for Women's Equality in African American Communities*. Although this book covers areas beyond Black colleges, it is significant in that both Cole and Guy-Sheftall work at Black colleges. Johnnetta Cole was the president of Spelman (1987–1997) and is currently the president of Bennett College. Likewise, Beverley Guy-Sheftall is a full professor of women's studies at Spelman College and the founding director of the Women's Research and Resource Center. Both of these women struggled in a male-dominated Black college environment, pushing a feminist agenda, and often feeling the push back. More importantly, together they have spoken out publicly about the rift between Black men and women within the context of Black colleges but also within the larger Black community. This conversation, being facilitated from within Black colleges, is essential to making change in the area of gender relations and equity at these institutions.

REFERENCES AND FURTHER READING

Alexander, M. W. (1995). Black women in academia. In B. Guy-Sheftall (Ed.), *Words of fire: An anthology of African American feminist thought* (pp. 454–460). New York: New Press.

Bell-Scott, P. (1979). Schoolin' "respectable" ladies of color: Issues in the history of Black women's higher education. *Journal of the National Association of Women's Deans and Advisors of Colored Schools*, 22–28.

Bonner, F. (2001). Addressing gender issues in the historically Black college and university community: A challenge and call to action. *Journal of Negro Education, 70*(3), 176–191.

Cole, J. B., & Guy-Sheftall, B. (2003). *Gender talk: The struggle for women's equality in African American communities*. New York: Random House.

Gurin, P., & Epps, E. G. (1975). *Black consciousness, identity, and achievement: A study of students in historically Black colleges*. New York: Wiley.

Guy-Sheftall, B. (1982). Black women and higher education: Spelman and Bennett colleges revisited. *Journal of Negro Education, 51*(3), 278–287.

Washington, E. (1993). *Uncivil war: The struggle between Black men and women*. New York: Noble Press.

CHAPTER 15

Men's Colleges and Universities

LESLIE MILLER-BERNAL

College education was originally just for men, in particular, wealthy, White, Protestant men. But in the nineteenth century, especially after the end of the Civil War, women gained access to some men's colleges, many women's colleges were founded, and more colleges opened as coeducational institutions. Nonetheless, men's colleges remained prestigious. They did not just exclude women; they celebrated a hegemonic or dominant form of masculinity, particularly at times when women's ascendancy threatened male privilege. At the end of the 1960s, when demographic, economic, and cultural factors combined to favor coeducation, all but a handful of men's colleges admitted women.

Today, men's colleges are virtually an extinct form of higher education. Although women can now attend virtually all institutions of higher education in the United States, their experiences in formerly men's colleges and universities, particularly at first, were not entirely positive. To transform formerly men's institutions into coeducational colleges in the true sense of the word—where women are coequal with men—is not easy. Traditions, campus iconography, staffing, and "old-boy" connections all mean that women begin as marginalized outsiders. With the support of key leaders and a strong commitment to fight subtle as well as blatant inequities, colleges and universities have the potential to become as good places for women to study as they have been for men. Such transformations do not happen automatically, however; they take persistent efforts.

Early History

College education was for men only for about 200 years—between 1636 when Harvard opened and 1837 when Oberlin admitted its first women students to the same degree program as men. Nine colleges were founded during the colonial era. In addition to Harvard, they were William and Mary (1693), Yale (1701), Princeton (1746), University of Pennsylvania (1751), Columbia (1754), Brown (1764), Rutgers (1766), and Dartmouth (1769). All of these colleges were small, associated with a particular Protestant denomination, had a curriculum focused on the study of classics, and stressed oratory rather than written work. Since professions of the time, such as law and medicine, did not require a college degree, many students attended for only a few years. At college, White, Anglo-Saxon gentlemen gained prestige and connections with others who might further their careers. The most common future occupation of male students was clergyman.

Student life in early all-male colleges was bleak. Students were subject to many petty rules administered by faculty, and their only extracurricular activities were literary or debating societies and sometimes dramatics or music. Student-faculty relations were so bad that until the end of the Civil War, violent rebellions occurred quite frequently; in a few instances, professors or others involved in the fray were killed.

Colleges were founded at an increasingly rapid rate over the course of the nineteenth century. While in 1800 only 25 degree-granting institutions existed, this number more than doubled in 20 years, reaching 52 by 1820. Forty years later, this number had increased almost fivefold to 241. As they proliferated, colleges gradually became more like the institutions we know today. The curriculum became somewhat varied with the addition of a few practical courses and modern languages. Some colleges, notably Harvard, allowed students to choose courses among electives. Many more extracurricular activities, especially sports, developed after the Civil War and played a key role in eliminating students' violent rebellions. One aspect of college education remained about the same as it had before, however: Most colleges were for wealthy, White, Protestant men, and large segments of the public believed that this was appropriate, since only men were expected to enter the public sphere.

Excluded groups used various methods to try to enter these male bastions. Women and their allies petitioned authorities at men's colleges, sometimes asking only for permission for women to take the colleges' exams so as to be able to verify that they were college graduates, but in other cases, to take classes, too. When enrollments at men's colleges fell in response to war or to economic depression, they were more receptive to such petitions. A few, like Middlebury College in 1883, then accepted women on an experimental basis but stayed all-male in terms of college personnel and facilities much longer. Many people, including some women, believed that it was better for women to attend institutions designed specifically for them—academies and seminaries and then the new women's colleges, most of which opened after the Civil War ended.

Beginning in the late eighteenth century, Catholics formed their own institutions, as did African Americans, or Whites acting on their behalf, about 60 years later. Various orders of priests, particularly the Jesuits, established Catholic men's colleges, beginning with Georgetown, which opened in 1789. About 100 years later, women religious (often called nuns) opened colleges for women. Black colleges, on the other hand, were almost all coeducational from the start; some even had women on their faculty. Notable exceptions to this coeducational pattern, however, were two Black colleges that exist today: Morehouse for men, which opened in 1867, and Spelman for women, which opened in 1881.

One way that men's colleges accommodated women's pressure to be allowed entry was to establish annexes or coordinate colleges for them. Harvard was the first institution in the United States to try this compromise. Radcliffe opened as Harvard's unobtrusive annex in 1879. Others soon followed, with probably the best known being Sophie Newcomb (1887), the coordinate of Tulane in New Orleans; Barnard (1889), the coordinate of Columbia in New York City; and Pembroke (1891), the coordinate of Brown in Providence. Coordinate colleges varied in terms of their independence from the men's institutions, which were always larger and richer. Barnard was one of the most independent, with its own faculty, president, and board of trustees. Today it is unusual among coordinates in being an autonomous degree-granting institution.

While single-sex institutions were common in the Northeast and South, they were less common in the Midwest and West. Still, women's positions in coeducational colleges and universities were not always secure. Frequently, a separate curriculum was established for women students and, in certain periods, women were subject to quotas, as they were at Stanford, or even banned from an institution that had been coeducational. Such reactions to women were particularly common in the late nineteenth and early twentieth centuries during a period characterized by fears that U.S. culture was being "feminized" or weakened by women and immigrants. Wesleyan, which had gone from being a men's college to being coeducational, excluded women in 1913; women were not readmitted until the coeducational wave of the 1970s. The University of Rochester had an even more complicated history. After opening as a men's institution in 1850, it finally succumbed to pressure (and money) from Susan B. Anthony and her allies and admitted women in 1900. But under another president, women's presence at the university was believed to stand in the way of its desired research reputation, so the university became all-male again by establishing a coordinate college for women, which opened in 1914 and lasted until 1955, when, once again, Rochester became a coeducational university.

Men's colleges not only excluded women, they celebrated manliness. The stress on men students' physical activities and strength, stoicism, and endurance received particular attention at the end of the nineteenth and beginning of the twentieth century. Theodore Roosevelt, later president of the United States, exemplified the type of student admired at Harvard in the 1880s: a good student but not a "grind," physically strong and very active, and involved in many clubs that fit the life of a gentleman. All team sports were believed to be character building and the best preparation for men's careers because of the discipline and rough give-and-take they required. But football, which became a dominant college sport beginning in the 1880s, played a particularly key role in the development of "manly men." More than any other sport, it enabled men to engage in controlled aggression and risk taking in front of audiences that often included admiring women.

Another part of the gradually developing collegiate culture that reinforced qualities judged to be masculine were the social or Greek fraternities. Begun in the 1820s at Union College but dominant after the end of the Civil War, fraternities used secret hazing rituals to promote solidarity and reward such stereotypical manly characteristics as stoicism and fearlessness. Fraternities also permitted men to restrict their social circles further to people who shared social status or interests. Different fraternities got reputations for particular types of men—upper-class men or men good in a sport such as football, for example. At times fraternities at the top of the prestige hierarchy became influential in their institution and able to affect such college policies as admissions. Excluded groups, Jews and African Americans, formed their own fraternities in the early twentieth century.

Men's Colleges in the Early to Middle Twentieth Century

Although coeducation became the dominant form of higher education in the late nineteenth century and educated an increasing percentage of college students in the twentieth, being all male enhanced an institution's status. Of eight prestigious eastern colleges (later known as the Ivy League), six were all male: Brown, Columbia, Dartmouth, Harvard, Princeton, and Yale. The other two, Cornell and University of Pennsylvania, were coeducational, although women within them were separate to some degree. The "Ivies," particularly the "Big Three" (Harvard, Yale, and Princeton), were viewed as the American counterpart to the all-male colleges of Cambridge and Oxford in Great Britain.

Prestige was maintained not only by longevity and being all male but also by a college or university's class and ethnic homogeneity, particularly after World War I. By then, some rich Irish Catholics, but very few Catholics whose families originated in southern or Eastern Europe, were students at the Ivy League colleges. Because few African Americans applied to predominantly White institutions, elite colleges did not see them as a threat. Concern focused on the percentages of Jewish students that had risen during the first two decades of the twentieth century. Princeton, Yale, Harvard, Columbia, and other institutions instituted quotas to reduce the numbers of Jews as a way of increasing their status.

The two world wars inevitably had a negative impact on enrollments of men's colleges as young men joined the military. Colleges survived with the help of the federal government, which paid them to help train members of the armed forces. During World War I, more than 500 colleges and universities participated in the Students' Army Training Corps, with a later benefit being large donations for building facilities, particularly football stadiums, named in honor of students who had died serving their country. Similar training programs existed during the Second World War. The navy, for example, chose 131 campuses to provide 120,000 navy men with the kinds of courses they needed.

Between the wars, a greater percentage of the population attended college as higher education came to be viewed as essential to social mobility. Elite men's and women's colleges increased their tuition substantially for the first time, making them much more expensive to attend than state universities. Even during the Great Depression they found they could enroll a sufficient number of students, virtually all of whom had to be wealthy, since very few scholarships existed. The vast majority of students attended coeducational institutions, including such newer college forms as the two-year junior college and teachers' colleges, developed as part of a greater commitment to mass higher education. The Catholic colleges founded during this era remained exceptions to the coeducation trend, however, as did a few women's colleges that opened on the East and West Coasts.

At the end of World War II, college and university enrollments boomed, particularly among men, as many veterans took advantage of the G.I. Bill to further their education. Not only did this result in the proportion of women at colleges declining (although their absolute numbers rose), but it also resulted in colleges' having more mature students who rebelled against the traditional restrictions of college life. Student bodies became more diverse as colleges, sensitized by the war against the Nazis, became more open to Jews and Blacks. Partly as a result of cold war politics and the perceived need to keep up with the Soviet Union after its Sputnik success, the federal government of the United States poured money into higher education, enabling colleges and universities to expand and modernize their facilities. Thus several factors converged to make the 1950s and 1960s a "golden age" for higher education.

The Move to Coeducation Beginning in the Late 1960s

The situation changed dramatically by the end of the 1960s. Campuses were rocked by students protesting racism, the Vietnam War, campus policies that treated them as less than responsible adults, and curricula that seemed irrelevant to many social issues. Enrollments were no longer increasing at such a rapid rate, although women's enrollments were rising faster than men's. Commentators warned about the new depression of higher education, just as many administrators were worrying about how they would pay back loans or fill up dormitories and classroom spaces. For men's colleges, coeducation seemed like a good solution to these problems.

Students and the faculty who taught them increasingly took coeducation for granted, as very few had experienced any other type of education. Men's (and women's) colleges seemed more and more out of step with a social order that claimed to value integration of races, ethnic groups, and the sexes. While people associated with women's colleges saw the value of women's-only spaces, especially as research spawned by the women's movement buttressed these claims, no corresponding justifications of men's colleges existed. Moreover, administrators at men's colleges knew that by opening their doors to women they would get excellent students who would raise their colleges' academic standards. Other benefits that college personnel believed would come from coeducation were civilizing men students, reducing their disruptive and anti-social behavior, and providing them with a normal, healthy social environment. Administrators and trustees were also responding to pressure from their students, since a majority of them wanted their institutions to become coeducational. Among reasons advanced for making men's colleges coeducational, concerns about women's education and gender equity were almost entirely absent.

Opposition to admitting women existed as well. Many alumni, in particular, did not want their college to change in this fundamental way. The compromise popular in the late nineteenth century—not becoming fully coeducational but establishing coordinate colleges for women—once again surfaced and in a few cases was implemented. Hamilton, a small, conservative men's college in central New York State, developed a coordinate women's college in 1968 that was very different from itself—progressive, with a high percentage of Jewish students—but took over the coordinate college 10 years later. At the end of the 1960s, Yale began to negotiate with Vassar about establishing coordinate relations at virtually the same time that Princeton engaged in similar discussions with Sarah Lawrence. In the latter two cases, however, coordination was rejected, and all four institutions became coeducational before 1970. Princeton's rationale for preferring coeducation over coordination and its detailed plans to implement the change to coeducational status were written up as a committee report. This "Patterson Report" of 1968 became widely known and emulated.

Within a relatively short period of time, virtually all men's colleges, even Catholic ones, admitted women. In some cases, it took federal or court action to bring about this change. In the case of the University of Virginia, for example, courts mandated in 1969 that this public institution admit women and do so at a faster pace than the university had wanted. Congress required the five federal military academies to admit women in 1976. Considering the intimate association of the military with masculinity, the idea of women passing strenuous physical tests and enduring the ritual humiliations at a place like West Point helped to dismantle gender stereotypes.

One of the most sensitive issues involved men's colleges that were associated with women's colleges. A common solution was for the two institutions to merge, although in fact that usually meant that the older, richer, larger, and more powerful men's institution subsumed the smaller women's college, as happened with Brown and Pembroke in 1971. In some cases, the women's coordinate was weakened so that it ultimately became little more than a residential unit. Such was the case with Sophie Newcomb at Tulane and Douglass at Rutgers, although protests in 2005 over the plan to merge all colleges at Rutgers demonstrate that even this degree of separation has been important to women. Barnard College was more successful in its negotiations with Columbia. Not only did Columbia admit women later (1983) than all the other Ivies, but Barnard remained an independent women's college.

Experiences of Women in the Formerly Men's Colleges

Most men's colleges did little to prepare for the entry of women beyond making some adjustments to the physical plant. They seldom considered how the preponderance of men among faculty and staff, the all-male iconography around campus, the traditions and college songs that celebrated manliness, the dominance of fraternities, and the attention paid to male sports would affect women students. Moreover, the first cohorts of women were often a small minority of all students and subject to the experiences of other minorities: being treated as tokens who could speak for their group, being marginalized, and having their behavior carefully scrutinized. They received media attention as the first "coeds," particularly at the more famous men's colleges like Yale. Some of the new women students did not mind such attention, but others became bitter.

Unlike the "coeds" of the past, these women were entering male strongholds at a cultural moment when traditional gender roles were being questioned. The women's movement had made such concepts as sexism part of the lexicon and raised people's awareness of the myriad ways women were disadvantaged. Issues like date rape, sexual harassment, sexist language, and the "chilly climate" in coeducational classrooms were acknowledged and debated. Empowered by this movement, the new women students, sometimes assisted by key allies among administrators and faculty, protested the subordinate status they had been expected to assume. Typically, as at Johns Hopkins in the early 1970s, women formed campus liberation groups and organized conferences to which they invited famous women to speak. Not all women students were equally involved, however. Minority women, who experienced racism as well as sexism, often formed their own campus organizations.

Moreover, many institutions lacked basic support for the women students. Although Title IX was passed in 1972 at the beginning of the coeducation movement, it faced court challenges and was poorly enforced for years. As a result, sport facilities for women were vastly inferior to those for men. Generally, it took women themselves to organize and pressure their colleges for resources such as athletic coaches, decent locker rooms, and more women's teams. A famous incident occurred at Yale in 1976 when crew members went to a physical education director's office and bared their breasts, which had been inscribed with "Title IX," to protest inequality in athletic facilities. Outside of the sports arena, women had to fight for health services, including female contraceptives and abortion counseling. Women's resources centers became popular as places where women could maintain feminist libraries, run programs on issues important to them such as eating disorders, sponsor lesbian-bisexual support groups, and, in general, feel safe and acknowledged.

Men's colleges typically had a low percentage of women faculty, administrators, and trustees. Local as well as outside pressures, including law suits charging colleges with discrimination in hiring and pay, led colleges to try to improve their gender ratios. The emergence of academic fields in which women typically dominate, particularly women's studies, also encouraged colleges and universities to hire more women. By 2005, about 38% of full-time faculty members were women, but their representation was 10% less at research institutions, which are more prestigious.

In many men's colleges, pockets of sexism or even misogyny remained even after women students were admitted. Fraternities, secret societies at Yale, and eating clubs at Princeton continued to bar women and were places where women were sometimes harassed or raped. In many small colleges, and some larger ones, fraternities have been weakened or disbanded; Princeton's and Yale's exclusive clubs now admit women. Yet incidents in which women are abused or used as sexual objects for football recruiting continue to occur. Today they are more likely to create protest and lead to sanctions than they were in the past, however.

Some formerly men's colleges responded more quickly and completely than others to the challenges of moving toward becoming gender-equal institutions. Factors affecting responses include the wealth of the institution, how firmly entrenched a male-dominant ethos was, and leadership, particularly by powerful women. A wealthy institution like Princeton, for example, was able to appoint more women faculty and top women administrators (including in 2001 a woman president) and to provide financial support for women students and needed facilities for them. Massachusetts Institute of Technology and Duke University are two well-known institutions that have embarked on major studies of gender relations on their campuses and instituted many reforms to try to assist women better.

Men's College since the 1990s

In the 1990s, a decade after virtually all private men's colleges admitted women, controversy erupted over the admission of women to two southern state military institutions: Virginia Military Institute (VMI) and The Citadel in South Carolina. The case became well known as the media focused on a young woman, Shannon Faulkner, who had applied to The Citadel but eventually found the scrutiny and harassment too much and left. Nonetheless, the case went all the way to the Supreme Court, which ruled that even a parallel program for women at a women's college (which VMI was establishing) would not provide women with equal protection or the same access to privileges that graduates of these two institutions received. Women were admitted, but as of 2009, they remained a small minority of all cadets, less than 10%.

Today only a handful of private men's colleges remain: Wabash College in Indiana; Hampden-Sydney in Virginia; Morehouse in Atlanta, Georgia; and Catholic Saint John's in St. Cloud, Minnesota. Additionally, there is a tiny exclusive, nontraditional, private two-year men's college, Deep Springs in California. Of the four-year men's colleges, two are closely associated with women's colleges: Morehouse with Spelman and St. John's with College of St. Benedict. They thus can offer their men students a partly coeducational experience. Even the more complete men's colleges, Wabash and Hampden-Sydney, have been somewhat affected by the women's movement. Unlike men's colleges of the past, their faculties contain women—almost 30% at Hampden-Sydney and slightly over 20% at Wabash. In addition, Wabash offers an area of concentration (not a major, though) in gender studies. On the other hand, each of them has national fraternities—10 at Wabash and 11 at Hampden-Sydney (60% of Wabash men belong to one of them; 22% of Hampden-Sydney men do). Ties to values of the past are evident. Wabash is governed by a "Gentleman's Rule," and a plaque on one of Hampden-Sydney's front gates notes the meaning of a Latin motto, "When you graduate, you will be a changed person, an educated person. And you will be a man."

REFERENCES AND FURTHER READING

Brubacher, J. S., & Rudy, W. (1997). *Higher education in transition: A history of American colleges and universities* (4th ed.). Somerset, NJ: Transaction.

Horowitz, H. L. (1988). *Campus life: Undergraduate cultures from the end of the eighteenth century to the present.* Chicago: University of Chicago Press.

Miller-Bernal, L., & Poulson, S. L. (Eds.). (2004). *Going coed: Women's experiences in formerly men's colleges and universities, 1950–2000.* Nashville, TN: Vanderbilt University Press.

Thelin, J. R. (2004). *A history of American higher education.* Baltimore: Johns Hopkins University Press.

Townsend, K. (1996). *Manhood at Harvard: William James and others.* New York: Norton.

CHAPTER 16

Military Colleges and Academies

DIANE DIAMOND

Military colleges and academies are historically archetypal masculine institutions. The first women who entered these institutions as cadets generally encountered strong opposition to their presence. Hostility ran the gamut from malicious comments to outright sexual harassment. The women's motives for attending were questioned; their achievements were not acknowledged. Unsurprisingly, the single greatest obstacle to women's successful integration was the attitudes of male cadets.

The first female cadets fought an uphill battle to gain the acceptance of their male peers. It was often difficult for male cadets to accept that women had chosen to attend "their" school, not to make a point as feminists, to find husbands, or because they were lesbians, but simply because they wanted the challenges and benefits that came from a military college/academy education. As the percentage of female cadets increased, women became established at the institution, and male cadets who chose to attend an all-male military college/academy were replaced by those who chose to attend a coeducational military college/academy, prejudicial attitudes generally began to abate, and female cadets gained acceptance.

At most U.S. military colleges and academies today, women are found throughout the ranks, from first-year cadets to upper-class leaders, from military trainers to professors, and female cadets feel welcomed and accepted. Today, women are viewed as valued members of the military college/academy community.

What Are Military Colleges and Academies?

Military colleges and academies are postsecondary institutions that provide a general education as well as training in military tactics and military strategy. These institutions educate and train future military officers by developing cadets in four critical ways: academically, physically, militarily, and morally-ethically.

Military colleges and academies maintain spartan military environments and regimens where incoming students receive indoctrination aimed at transforming them into cadets. As part of this process, entering cadets are typically given closely cropped haircuts, issued uniforms, and taught the proper way to march, salute, and address those with seniority. They rise early and their days are highly regimented, filled with military, athletic, and cadet activities, in addition to academic classes. A typical day might include marching, military drill, discipline, class, and extracurricular activities.

In the United States, there are two kinds of military colleges and academies: federal (government-run) and state-run or private-run. Graduates of the federal service academies are awarded bachelor of science degrees and are commissioned in their service-specific branch of the United States armed services for a minimum of five years. About 18% of the U.S. military officer corps are academy graduates. Unlike the federal academies, graduates of state and private military colleges and academies are not required to join the military after graduation. Nonetheless, some military colleges have high commissioning rates among their graduates.

Integral to military training and a prominent characteristic differentiating military from other institutions of higher education is the heavy emphasis placed on physical training and testing. In order to maintain this emphasis once women were admitted, almost all U.S. military colleges and academies developed a system of "equivalent training," or "gender norming" with separate physical fitness standards for male and female cadets based on established physiological differences between men and women. During the early years of coeducation, many male cadets found it difficult to accept gender norming and railed against what they perceived as lower standards for women. These men pointed to gender norming as confirmation that women had lesser abilities and an unfair advantage. Even today, gender norming remains a point of contention for male cadets who do not accept or understand that the standards set for women require the same expenditure of effort as those set for men. Unlike all other U.S. military colleges and academies, Virginia Military Institute (VMI) maintains a single physical fitness standard for its male and female cadets. While a single physical fitness standard may appear to be gender neutral, it is, in fact, based on a standard developed by and for men. For the sake of strict equality, VMI disregards actual physiological differences. However, since VMI's physical fitness standard is based on the male body, fewer women than men pass VMI's physical fitness test. Thus, VMI's "gender neutral" standard actually places VMI female cadets at a disadvantage because it is, in actuality, a male standard applied to both male and female cadets.

The Legal Framework for Coeducation

Military colleges and academies have traditions as archetypal masculine domains from which women have historically been excluded. Several conditions propelled these institutions toward coeducation, including the dramatic influx of women into the workforce, the attempt to pass the Equal Rights Amendment, and the changes in the military during and after the Vietnam War. Following that war, the United States shifted to an all-volunteer force. To maintain sufficient manpower, the military dramatically increased the number of women in the armed services and expanded the assignments available to women. Between 1972 and 1976, the number of women in the armed services rose from 45,000 (1.9%) to 110,000 (just over 5%) of military personnel. Prior to 1975, the U.S. Army had a separate corps for women, the Women's Army Corps (WAC). In June 1975, the Secretary of the Army told Congress that the Women's Army Corps was no longer needed and that its removal would ensure full integration of women into the army. Congress resolved that women could not be fully integrated unless it dissolved the separate corps status of the WAC, which it finally did in 1978.

Meanwhile, in 1972, the U.S. Naval Academy denied admission to two women nominated by Senator Jacob Javits of New York and Congressman Jack McDonald of Michigan. The legislators responded by introducing bills in both houses making it illegal for the services to deny admission to the academies on the basis of sex. In 1974, while these bills were still before Congress, the U.S. Merchant Marine Academy amended its admission requirements, making it the first federal service academy in the United States to enroll women students. That same year, Norwich University (a private military college) began admitting women into its corps of cadets. Whereas both the Merchant Marine Academy and Norwich University voluntarily undertook coeducation, the Army, Navy, Air Force, and Coast Guard academies fought to remain all male. The fight over coeducation included divisive argument in Congress and resistance from the Department of Defense. Despite opposition, on October 8, 1975, the president of the United States signed into law a bill directing that women be admitted into America's service academies in 1976. Although the Army, Navy, Air Force, and Coast Guard academies had no choice but to comply, they did so grudgingly.

In time, most state and private military colleges and academies voluntarily joined the federal service academies as coeducational institutions. Two notable exceptions were The Citadel and VMI, state-funded military colleges that undertook lengthy court battles to remain all-male institutions. Their court battles ended when the U.S. Supreme Court ruled that "Virginia Military Institute's all-male admissions policy violated women's constitutional right to equal protection." Although they could have relinquished state funding and become private institutions, both instead decided to admit women into their corps of cadets.

In the fall of 2006, the last U.S. all-male military college (Valley Forge Military College) became coeducational. Speaking on the advent of coeducation, the dean of Valley Forge Military College remarked, "This shift brings new diversity into the classroom and will strengthen our academic programs, while bringing us inline with the service academies and our military structure."

The History of Coeducation

The first female cadets at the military colleges and academies were tokens. They were highly visible, viewed as representatives of their social group, experienced performance pressure, were stereotyped, and found that the differences between them and the men were exaggerated. They stood out because of their identity as women, but their individuality was subsumed by their membership in the out-group. Those women who were unsuccessful were viewed as representative of all women; those who succeeded were considered exceptions to the rule.

Not only were the first female cadets tokens, they were under extraordinary pressure to blend in and conform to masculine standards of behavior. To gain the acceptance of their male peers, they downplayed their femininity, tried to keep up with the men, did not make too much of women's solidarity, and avoided anything that would draw additional attention to themselves as women.

Keeping up with male cadets in the physical arena determined, in large measure, the women's acceptance by their male peers. They found that it was not enough to be outstanding women; they had to be as good as, or better than, the men. Women who could keep up with the men were judged "not like other women," and therefore acceptable. At the same time, female cadets could not be too feminine or too masculine, or for that matter, too successful, so that the men would not feel threatened by their achievements. Female cadets who attained leadership positions were seen as threats to male authority, their successes frequently dismissed as acts of favoritism. Male cadets would complain that women who received leadership positions were selected as a result of political correctness, to fill a quota, or because the women were only judged relative to other women instead of relative to all cadets. Some male cadets also maintained that the women were usurping leadership positions that rightfully belonged to men. Female cadet leaders not only had to contend with male cadet opposition but also with the inherent difficulties of a leadership role and male cadets who found it difficult being led by a woman.

In addition to all the physical and emotional difficulties of cadet training, the first female cadets routinely encountered both subtle and overt harassment. Frequently it took the form of sexist remarks and condemnations. An alumna from one of West Point's first coed classes recalled one insidious form of gender harassment she experienced as a cadet: "Sexist cadences [i.e., poems in marching rhythm such as, "I don't know but I've been told, Eskimo p—— is mighty cold"] were allowed all of the time. My innocence did not allow me to see the inappropriateness of these cadences back then. At the time, I just thought they were traditions that were passed down from class to class. I guess that I also assumed that we were talking about those 'other girls' and not me" (Interview with author, 1997).

Harassment, however, went beyond sexist cadences. Female cadets endured verbal affronts, rude jokes, sexual innuendo, and taunting from classmates as well as still more odious harassment including male cadets urinating or ejaculating on the women's belongings. Blatant forms of discrimination were in fact the norm in the early years of coeducation at the federal service academies, with female cadets reluctant to report possible date rape, sexual assault, or sexual harassment to their cadet chain of command. Female cadets at nonfederal military colleges also experienced harassment. For example, in the third year of coeducation at VMI, the cadet chosen to be the next regimental commander (the highest-ranking cadet) was expelled after he was accused of seeking sexual favors from three freshmen women.

In their efforts to be seen as soldiers rather than women or sex objects, the first female cadets were afraid to wear makeup or skirts. Their male peers found it difficult to accept them as women and as cadets at the same time. Several years into coeducation, female cadets were still hesitant to be seen as feminine because, in the highly masculine environment of the military college/academy, femininity was equated with weakness. Today, female cadets are more confident about their femininity, no longer afraid to be women and cadets at the same time. Nevertheless, female cadets are still under some pressure to conform to the male ethos of the military college/academy. And female cadets still must negotiate public perceptions of femininity and successful performance of their role as cadets. Gender was, and remains, the most significant issue structuring the women's experience as cadets.

The greatest obstacle to the acceptance of women at military colleges and academies was, and remains, the attitudes of men. Some male cadets held highly traditional views about women, believing that women had no place in a man's world such as the military. Others were more concerned that standards would be made more lax to accommodate the women. Some men feared a loss of esprit de corps, others that their institution, and they by affiliation, would suffer a loss of prestige following the admission of women. Some questioned why women wanted to be there; others thought women were only attending to prove a point. And some male cadets would neither speak to nor voluntarily work with female cadets. A minority of men, however, saw coeducation as a change that would be beneficial to the institution, to cadets, and to the armed services overall.

A major step toward accepting coeducation occurred when male cadets realized that women were attending for the same reasons men do—the challenges, opportunities for rigorous military training, quality education, patriotism, institutional prestige, and institutional alumni network, to name a few. Some women come from military families; some come to prepare for a military career. Moreover, the federal service academies provide a free high-quality education, albeit with a five-year commitment.

By training alongside women, some male cadets began to develop cross-sex friendships and to see female cadets not as out-group members but as individuals with similar goals and aspirations. The presence of women sometimes even became a source of motivation. In time, the majority of male cadets came to accept the women, and some even came to acknowledge the benefits of coeducation.

The Benefits of Coeducation

Women, men, and the military colleges and academies all benefit from coeducation. Coeducation offers women access to specialized military training at schools to which they were previously denied admittance. Coeducation also pushes women to do their best and achieve more than they thought they could. Male cadets also benefit from coeducation. By training alongside women, male cadets learn that female cadets are capable of doing what they (men) do. Coeducational military colleges and academies provide male (and female) cadets with models of women achievers and prepare them to be part of a diverse team. Women also serve as a unique form of motivation for men: If even one woman accomplishes a difficult task, men often feel compelled to do likewise so as not to be bettered by a woman.

Coeducation not only teaches male cadets how to work with women, it supplies "real world" training. Whereas an all-male education is good preparation for an all-male world in which women are relegated to peripheral roles, coeducation is good preparation for the real world in which women figure prominently, not only as mothers, teachers, and girlfriends, but also as subordinates, peers, and superiors.

Like their students, military colleges and academies also benefit from coeducation. Coeducation enables state and private military colleges and academies to mirror not only the federal service academies but also the armed services in general. Coeducation has helped military colleges and academies increase both the number and quality of their applicants. And coeducation has helped schools with declining admissions raise their cadet numbers. On an organizational level, the admission of women has helped make military colleges and academies more professional. Whereas profanity and mistreatment were commonplace in many all-male military colleges and academies, once women became established, such behavior became less acceptable. Thus coeducation helps transform military colleges and academies from boys' schools to schools of leadership.

The possibility also exists that coeducation in military colleges and academies may eventually benefit the armed services. While training at most military colleges and academies today, women are established members of the corps of cadets and can aspire to anything that men can. However, the same cannot be said of women in the armed services. Ironically, most military colleges and academies today are actually more progressive than the armed services for which they train their cadets. So after four years of being equals, the rules change in the military and women are second-class citizens.

While this seems like ominous news, the progressive stance taken by many military colleges and academies may actually presage changes in the armed service themselves. Coeducational training may serve as the impetus for change, since graduates of these military colleges and academies will be the future military leaders, and military leaders who received their training in a coeducational environment will be more comfortable with the idea of men and women working together than military leaders trained in an all-male environment. Consequently, the future holds promise for a more fully integrated armed services, one that offers women greater opportunities for advancement.

The Importance of Institutional Support for Women

Although it takes only four years for a military college or academy to transition from all-male classes to all-coed classes, it takes far longer for coeducation to become naturalized. Coeducation begins with the admission of the first women but to succeed requires time and a long-term commitment on the part of the institution before those within its walls fully accept coeducation. Since women first entered military colleges and academies, several factors have helped to improve the experience of female cadets at most of these institutions. First, women are now found at all levels of the institutions, from upper-class leaders to professors and military officers. Second, there has been an increase in the number of women who serve as cadets, faculty, and military trainers. Third, the chain of command is clearly supportive of women, sending the message that women are valued members of the community. These visible, consistent, and strong organizational supports for women demonstrate to both male and female cadets that the administration is serious about supporting women and is concerned about the safety and well-being of female cadets.

Because of these improvements, at most military colleges and academies today, female cadets no longer feel isolated from one another, are more comfortable associating with other women and expressing their femininity, and are better able to garner the support they need to succeed. These changes have helped make military colleges and academies more welcoming to female cadets.

Most military colleges and academies have also made concerted efforts to reduce sexism and prejudice based on gender. Some institutions have instituted "sensitivity training" related not only to gender issues but also to racial tolerance and sexual harassment, emphasizing that everyone is a soldier first, sexless, classless, colorless. By supporting their female cadets, enjoining male cadets to treat women appropriately, prosecuting improper behavior, and working to educate cadets about equity, harassment, and fair treatment, military colleges and academies have helped to reduce prejudice and gender bias.

At institutions that steadfastly support coeducation, resistance to coeducation diminishes over time, women become established, and both the military college/ academy and those within it become acclimated to coeducation. However, if the institution does not fully embrace coeducation, women will remain peripheral members. In 2003, the reports by women at the U.S. Air Force Academy of pervasive problems with sexual harassment demonstrated that time alone will not produce attitudinal change if the environment is not conducive to such change. Thus, whereas short-term transitional programs are necessary to initiate change, they are not in themselves sufficient to establish long-term institutional transformation. Such change requires a concerted long-term commitment of institutional leaders who actively support and enforce policies of change. By downplaying the seriousness of the sexual harassment and disparaging female cadets who came forward to report abuse, U.S. Air Force Academy administrators and officers created an atmosphere that condoned and perpetuated discriminatory behavior. The Air Force Academy has since undertaken a rigorous training program aimed at preventing sexual misconduct, and the academy has shown improvement; the rigorous training has been credited for decreasing the number of reported cases of sexual misconduct.

The Current State of Gender Integration

Female cadets today are far better off than were the first female cadets. Today, the experience of female cadets is generally positive, and gender relations quite good. Nevertheless, current female cadets generally have no difficulty offering up examples of gender bias ranging from sexist e-mails to a common misperception among male cadets that all female cadets are overweight. Gender bias even endures at military colleges and academies that have been coeducational for decades. For example, in a survey of graduating seniors at West Point conducted by the U.S. Military Academy Office of Policy, Planning and Analysis in 2001, 99.2% of female cadets reported that they had heard members of the corps of cadets make disparaging remarks about women at West Point, with slightly more than half of them responding "frequently." Even if such remarks are spoken in jest, they create a subtly hostile environment that serves to remind women of their marginal status.

In a report issued in August of 2005, a Pentagon task force faulted the military academies for harassment, hostile attitudes, and inappropriate treatment of women, including jokes and offensive stories of sexual exploits, derogatory terms for women, offensive gestures, repeated and unwanted propositions for dates or sex, and offers to trade grades for academic favors. While this report credited West Point and the Naval Academy with progress in addressing sexual harassment and assault issues, it nonetheless called for placing more women in leadership roles at the academies and admitting more women as cadets and midshipmen. The task force study demonstrates that, although the federal service academies have made progress in incorporating women into their corps of cadets, gender integration is not yet a fait accompli.

In all the military colleges and academies, the transition to coeducation has not been easy. These institutions are tough under the best of circumstances, with rigorous athletic, military, and academic requirements. With all of the added obstacles the first women encountered, it is impressive that some managed to graduate. The first female cadets showed that women were capable of handling the rigorous physical and military courses and could succeed in the traditionally masculine domain of the military college/academy. Contemporary female cadets continue to prove their competence as hardworking members of their corps of cadets, successfully mastering the rigors of military college/academy life. Although some military colleges, such as VMI and The Citadel, are still in the nascent stages of coeducation and all must continue their efforts to improve gender relations, at most military colleges and academies today, female cadets are welcomed, accepted, and valued members of their military college/academy community.

REFERENCES AND FURTHER READING

Barkalow, C. (1990). *In the men's house: An inside account of life in the army by one of West Point's first female graduates*. New York: Poseidon.

Campbell, D., & D'Amico, F. (1999). Lessons on gender integration from the military academies. In F. D'Amico & L. Weinstein (Eds.), *Gender camouflage: Women and the U.S. military* (pp. 67–79). New York: New York University Press.

Diamond, D., & Kimmel, M. S. (2004). "Toxic virus" or lady virtue: Gender integration and assimilation at West Point and VMI. In L. Miller-Bernal & S. L. Poulson (Eds.), *Going coed: Women's experiences in formerly men's colleges and universities, 1950–2000* (pp. 263–286). Nashville, TN: Vanderbilt University Press.

Diamond, D., Kimmel, M. S., & Schroeder, K. (2000). What's this about a few good men? Negotiating gender in military education. In N. Lesko (Ed.), *Masculinities at school* (pp. 231–249). Thousand Oaks, CA: Sage.

Janda, L. (2001). *Stronger than custom: West Point and the admission of women*. Westport, CT: Greenwood.

Yoder, J. D. (1989). Women at West Point: Lessons for token women in male-dominated occupations. In J. Freeman (Ed.), *Women: A feminist perspective* (3rd ed., pp. 523–537). Palo Alto, CA: Mayfield.

CHAPTER 17

Tribal Colleges and Universities

WAYNE J. STEIN

In the late 1960s and early 1970s, the founders of the tribally controlled colleges and universities (TCUs) movement undertook the challenge of entering and working to change a system of education for American Indian people in which they had been denied input and had seen a concentrated effort to eradicate all things American Indian. Today, the movement continues the efforts of educational exploration, initiative, and development that began in the summer of 1968 with the founding of Navajo Community College in Tsaile, Arizona. TCUs can best be described as small, tenacious institutions of higher education that serve the smallest and poorest minority group in the United States (American Indians) in difficult and challenging circumstances. TCUs are generally underfunded, with overworked administrators, faculties, and staffs, and are viewed by the rest of American higher education with some wonderment at their ability not only to survive but also to survive with panache.

It was among the founders of the TCUs that an important trend began in the TCUs movement that is still prevalent today within the TCUs, namely, the leadership roles of women in all aspects of the TCU movement. Women make up nearly 50% of the founders of TCUs over their 42-year history to date. Traditionally, American Indian women had been equal partners in all decisions made among the tribes of American Indians. This tradition nearly disappeared once American Indian people became a subjugated people. Indian societies began reflecting the norms of the majority society that had conquered them and, thus, relegating Indian women to near second-class status.

The founders advocated a philosophy that supports a dual mission, which is still adhered to by leaders of the TCUs, to protect and enhance their own cultures including values, traditional stories, and languages while at the same time embracing many of the tools of standard postsecondary education. TCU leaders recognize that they cannot just prepare tribal students to be proficient in their own cultures but must also prepare them to be proficient in the non-Indian world that surrounds the tribal communities. They have to prepare their students to live biculturally in two very different worlds.

Many in the American Indian world believe that TCUs are the best thing to have happened for American Indians in the 120 years since the last free American Indian people were relegated to a reservation. Today TCUs constitute .01% of postsecondary education in the United States, yet the American Indian College Fund (AICF) states that TCUs educate nearly 18% of the entire American Indian student population enrolled in higher education within the United States.

TCU History

Nowhere in Indian country during the 1960s were events moving more quickly concerning American Indian control of Indian education than in the Navajo Nation. Political and educational leaders formed Dine, Inc., a community-based and nongovernmental education organization, with the intention of taking control of the education of Navajo students. One area of Indian education that the founders of Dine, Inc., desired to address immediately was higher education. The attrition rate of 90% or more experienced by Navajo students attending colleges off the reservation demanded innovative solutions. The participants in Dine, Inc., began exploring the possibility of a community college for the Navajo people. This was not a totally new topic of discussion, but never before had it been approached with such seriousness.

After much preparation by Dine, Inc., the Navajo Nation founded and chartered Navajo Community College in July of 1968 in Tsaile, Arizona. Though underfunded and forging a completely new path in higher education, Navajo Community College (now called Dine College) survived and succeeded, encouraging a number of other tribes to found and charter their own tribal college during the seventies, eighties, nineties, and into the twenty-first century.

As early as 1972, however, leaders of the fledgling TCU movement recognized that unity among the small number of TCUs was essential to promoting the TCUs as a viable option for Indian people in higher education. Thus the American Indian Higher Education Consortium (AIHEC) was born of political necessity. Since its inception, AIHEC has provided a significant and vital support role to the TCUs as their national representative.

One of its most important activities has been that of advocate in Washington, DC, for the TCUs, charged with securing and maintaining the principal funding source of the colleges. The TCUs interact with the federal government much as state-supported institutions do with their state governments. AIHEC was able to convince Congress and President Carter in 1978 that funding the TCUs was part of the trust responsibility that the federal government had with American Indian peoples through its treaty agreements and obligations.

The Tribally Controlled Community College Act of 1978 has had a stabilizing influence on the tribal college movement, even though the TCUs have never been fully funded through the congressional appropriation process at the level ratified by the act. Title I of the Tribal College Act, in fiscal year 2000, authorized $6,000 per American Indian student FTE (full-time equivalent). Based on the Consumer Price Index since 1978, however, the authorization per student FTE should have been $8,450 by 2005 to have kept pace with inflation. Either figure is considerably higher than the actual amount of $4,447 per student FTE actually appropriated in the 2005 federal budget for funding Title I of the Tribal College Act. TCUs are still $3,000–$4,000 per student and a decade behind in funding compared to their non-Indian state-supported mainstream counterpart institutions.

The tribal colleges do seek funding vigorously from a number of sources other than the Bureau of Indian Affairs and the Tribally Controlled College Act. These include other federal agencies, philanthropic organizations such as the W. K. Kellogg

Foundation and the Bush Foundation, and corporations. These additional funds are targeted to specific high-priority tasks by the individual TCUs as they are identified and funds are secured. Upon occasion, AIHEC, the national organization of the TCUs, will also seek grants from these sources to carry out membership-wide projects needed by all the TCUs or by the central office of AIHEC itself to improve its infrastructure. These additional funds can be instrumental in carrying forward much-needed educational programs within TCUs.

The important effort by the TCUs to build a diversified funding base was enhanced in 1989 with the founding of the American Indian College Fund. AICF has an independent board of directors yet is answerable to AIHEC as its chartering agent. It has raised significant amounts of funding, and AICF reports that between 1989 and 2005 it distributed more than $27 million in scholarships and an additional $18 million in grants to the TCUs. Several years ago, AICF was able to start a major capital fundraising effort, Sii Ha Sin / Campus Construction, and has used that initial investment to raise another $87.5 million from state, local, tribal, and federal sources. Currently there are 80 projects under way, totaling 730,000 square feet of classrooms, dormitories, libraries, administration buildings, and cultural centers. Fitting these additional funding sources into the tribal colleges' fiscal designs allows the colleges to begin examining new programs, new curricula, new forums, new buildings, and advanced degrees for their students and communities.

An important initiative of the TCUs and AIHEC has been the development and publication of the *Tribal College Journal*. The journal has led the way in informing the world about the TCU movement, has played a vital role in spreading the news among the TCUs of innovative programs they can share, and has begun an important research agenda on behalf of the TCUs. It has also become a major source of information to indigenous people around the world on "how to start their own community controlled institution of postsecondary education and keep it viable over time," and to non-Indians interested in the TCU movement.

The initiatives developed by the TCU presidents and AIHEC have led to many innovative and productive outcomes. Three of the most important are the Capture the Dream Project; the passage of Public Law 103-32 by the U.S. Congress; and executive orders signed by presidents Clinton and George W. Bush. The recently completed Capture the Dream Project was the W. K. Kellogg Foundation's $25 million American Indian Higher Education Initiative. It focused on strengthening the faculties and internal programs of TCUs; addressing cultural, language, and sovereignty issues of tribal communities; and improving the relationships between TCUs and mainstream institutions of higher education.

PL 103-32 is the legislation that identifies the Equity in Education Land-Grant Status Act of 1994, by means of which the U.S. Congress gave land-grant status to the TCUs. This important piece of legislation now helps to preserve and expand a solid agriculture, programmatic, and financial base for all TCUs. In addition, the executive orders signed by presidents Clinton and Bush serve as important reminders that the TCUs are constituents of the entire federal government and are part of a larger federal mandate to provide American Indian education. Executive Order No. 13021, signed by President Clinton on October 19, 1996, promoted TCUs' access to all federal programs and instructed relevant government agencies to explore ways in which they might assist TCUs to carry forward their mandate to serve American Indian communities. On July 3, 2002, President Bush signed Executive Order No. 13270, creating two potentially powerful new advocacy tools for TCUs: the President's Board of Advisers on Tribal Colleges and Universities and the White House Initiative on Tribal Colleges and Universities.

Missions and Curricula of TCUs

Though their functions are much more similar than different, there is a sharp distinction between non-Indian institutions of higher education and TCUs. Both strive to serve their communities as comprehensive institutions providing programs that respond to community and student needs. Their differences lie in funding sources, jurisdiction, and cultural factors, not educational goals. Today, the TCUs and non-Indian institutions generally remain separate in the political and fiscal arenas, but not in spirit. Generally, an atmosphere of educational exchange, mutual trust, and mutual appreciation exists between the two systems.

Today there are 37 TCUs, 36 in the United States and 1 in Canada, ranging in location from Alaska to Michigan and Arizona. TCUs serve numerous American Indian tribes, but all adhere to several basic principles in their mission statements. Each has stated that the needs to preserve, enhance, and promote the language and culture of its tribe is central to its existence. The colleges serve their communities as resources to do research on economic development, human resource development, and community organization. Each provides quality academic programs for students seeking two-year degrees for transfer to senior institutions. Several TCUs have developed four-year and master's programs in areas where they felt the greatest need existed within their communities. Wherever possible, each college provides vocational and technical programs that help ensure that students can find decent jobs in their communities upon completion of their studies.

The top four areas in which associate's degrees were awarded by TCUs in 2002 were liberal arts and sciences, education, business, and health. Typical academic and teaching curricula offered today at a TCU are two-year associate of applied science degree programs, associate of arts degree programs, and associate of science degree programs and one-year certification programs. Associate of applied science degree programs combine practical coursework and general education designed to prepare students for immediate entry into the world of work the day after graduation. Typical disciplines for associate of applied science degrees are human services, computer science and information systems, tribal language arts, office technology, and tribal administrative practices.

Associate of arts degrees and associate of science degrees are awarded for successful completion of academic programs designed to prepare students intending to transfer to four-year colleges or universities upon completion of their education at a tribal college. Typical areas of study leading to associate of arts degrees include general studies, business administration, tribal or Native American studies, and the social sciences. Typical courses of study leading to associate of science degrees are business administration, health sciences, and pre-engineering.

TCUs have also embraced the technical and trade curricula that are needed by their students to secure employment in the students' home community. One-year certificate programs are designed by the tribal colleges to respond to local community employment opportunities. Students are prepared within a sharply focused vocational program with much hands-on practical experience. Such programs are as wide-ranging and diverse as the communities and tribal colleges that create them.

Four tribal colleges—Sinte Gleska University, Oglala Lakota College, Haskell Indian Nations University, and Salish Kootenai College—have instituted four-year baccalaureate programs in human resources, social sciences, and education. A major stride by a TCU in curriculum development, considering the financial hardships and isolation it has endured, is Sinte Gleska University's success in developing and receiving accreditation for the first-ever master's degree program in education at a TCU. This growth is illustrated by the fact that, in 1972, Sinte Gleska University, then Sinte Gleska College, offered only 22 courses in a scattering of disciplines from psychology to math with 13 administrators and faculty making up the entire college staff.

Each college has had to travel the accreditation path alone, but morale and expertise have been liberally shared among members to the benefit of all TCUs. This accreditation effort has so far resulted in 34 of the 37 TCUs gaining full accreditation as institutions of higher education, with the other 3 TCUs in candidacy status. TCUs have spent the last 40 years doing their best to meet the requirements of outside agencies of higher education to serve their students and communities. That does not mean that they neglected their mission statements, which require they make a special effort to enhance, protect, and teach about their own cultures and languages. However, many in leadership roles at the TCUs believe that the time has come to reexamine the total curriculum of their institutions and focus on the development of a curriculum that is "indigenous" and less reflecting of mainstream higher education curricula yet still meets the needs of their students and communities in the twenty-first century.

The Personnel of TCUs

The boards of trustees of TCUs are a reflection of their communities, with a nearly 100% level of local American Indian community members serving on the boards. It is not uncommon, however, to find boards of trustees of the TCUs to be made up of nearly all women. Boards of trustees for TCUs play the important role of buffers between tribal politics and the colleges. They also often act as mediators among policy makers, as personnel selection committees, and as the local watchdogs of and for the TCUs. These important responsibilities make TCU boards of trustees unique in Indian country because of the autonomous nature of their authority as granted by the tribal charters founding the TCUs. However, board members do keep in mind how their decisions will affect their communities and their long-term relations with their chartering tribal governments.

Administrators and faculty of tribal colleges are a mixture of American Indians and non-Indians. About 80% of TCU administrators are American Indian, and about 63% of TCU faculty members are non-Indian. Women make up 50% of administrators and faculty of the TCUs. At present 17 of the 37 current presidents of TCUs are women, and most TCUs have had a woman president at some time during their institutional histories. Whatever the race or gender of a TCU administrator or faculty member, however, her or his strongest characteristic is dedication to the students and to the missions of the colleges as has been emphasized by numerous accreditation site-visit teams. In almost every report, the accreditation associations evaluating the TCUs have written about the importance of the dedication of TCU administrators and faculty.

Faculty problems experienced by TCUs generally fall into three main areas. First is the difficulty of finding and keeping science and mathematics instructors. Second is the high turnover among faculty who find life on Indian reservations too isolated and culturally different. Third, and toughest to solve, is the fact that, as the colleges mature and their student populations grow, salaries generally remain low among TCU faculty. The issue of underfunding facing the TCUs is a serious one, but nowhere is it more serious than in recruiting, hiring, and keeping good faculty, administrators, and support staff.

TCUs continue to focus on their students and the special abilities and needs these students bring to their colleges. Dine College and all subsequent TCUs recognized that mainstream institutions of higher education were not adequately serving American Indian students, especially those from geographically isolated reservations. The reasons were many. The social isolation of Indian students on off-reservation campuses, culture shock, and poverty were some of the main contributors to the 90% attrition rate experienced by Indian students in mainstream colleges and universities.

Students at TCUs are older, on average, than undergraduate students at other institutions of higher education. Sixty-six percent of them are female, with females outnumbering males in every age category from under 18 to over 65. Women students are often single heads of households, and many students of both sexes speak English as their second language, are poor, and, prior to their tribal college experience, have found formal educational settings to be a hostile environment for them. One American Indian student told her teacher after attending class at a TCU that, for the first time in her life, she felt welcome when she entered the classroom. At no time before, including all of her elementary and secondary school years, had she ever felt welcome in her classes. She had always felt as if she were an unwanted visitor. Her experience at the TCU changed that for her, and she now looked forward to going to class with great anticipation each day.

In 1968, Dine College served 300 mostly Navajo students. In 2003, according to the AICF, TCUs served more than 30,000 students representing 250 tribes from across the United States, Mexico, and Canada. TCU personnel work closely with each student to help design a program that will fit his or her individual needs and abilities. This concern for the individual student has played an important role in the high retention rates of first-generation American Indian students within the TCUs. Retention rates for the TCUs can be measured in two ways: (1) the conventional fashion, which counts as a dropout any student who leaves college before completion of a degree program, in which case TCUs have a retention rate of approximately 45%; or (2) a more accurate method begun by the TCUs, which labels as "stop-outs" those who leave and then return within a quarter to continue their studies. By measuring in this fashion, the colleges' retention rate is approximately 75% to 80%. Students who stop-out generally do so because of financial difficulties or because they have been put on academic probation. A recent study by AICF found that after one year of completing their studies, 91% of TCU graduates were either working or pursuing advanced degrees. The significance of this 91% figure for students working or in advanced education becomes more apparent when it is compared to the finding that more than 50% of the adult population residing on an Indian reservation is usually out of school and unemployed.

Prospects and Challenges Facing TCUs

Sinte Gleska University, Oglala Lakota College, and Salish Kootenai College have demonstrated that it is possible for TCUs to offer advanced degrees. Many of the TCUs are now researching advanced curriculum options for their students and are seriously studying the move to become four-year institutions. This latest focus of TCUs, expanding to become four-year colleges, is a strong indication of how optimistic these institutions are about their futures.

TCUs have become one of the strongest allies of the United States federal government in carrying out its unique trust responsibilities in education on behalf of American Indian people. The federal government's support of TCUs has led to the best direct education being provided to American Indians today who live on reservations. AIHEC has also become a major source of administrative and educational technical assistance for the TCUs, especially the more recently founded TCUs.

Even with all the positives that have transpired over the past 42 years in the TCU movement, there are still major obstacles facing American Indian tribes that desire to develop and found new TCUs. The two major obstacles to such developments are funding for such efforts and maintaining the community's will to persevere in the face of all the difficulties of trying to start and maintain such institutions. Scattered across the western half of the United States, there are only 36 TCUs serving their tribes on geographically isolated reservations, but there are approximately 300 tribal nations of American Indians in the United States. This means that only about 10% of all reservations are being served by their own TCUs. Leaders of the TCU movement believe that there is much room for growth in the movement when adequate resources are secured for that growth in partnership with the federal government.

At the 2002 World Indigenous Peoples Conference on Education held on the Nakoda Reserve west of Calgary, Alberta, Canada, the World Indigenous Higher Education Consortium was founded among the indigenous peoples of the world to regain control of the postsecondary education of their peoples. Recently TCUs and AIHEC have embarked on a new outreach program and are now communicating regularly with their sister indigenous-controlled institutions from around the world. AIHEC is at the forefront of the development of this worldwide organization that will bring the international indigenous higher education institutions together as important and self-controlled research and program development entities.

REFERENCES AND FURTHER READINGS

American Indian College Fund. (2003). *Facts: Educating the mind and spirit*. Denver, CO: Author.

American Indian Higher Education Consortium. (2002). *Tribal college map*. Alexandria, VA: Author. Available at http://www.aihec.org/colleges/TCUmap.cfm

Benham, M., & Stein, W. J. (Eds.). (2002). *Renaissance of American Indian higher education*. Mahwah, NJ: Erlbaum.

Boyer, P. (1997). *Native American colleges: Progress and prospects*. Princeton, NJ: Carnegie Foundation for the Advancement of Teaching.

Stein, W. J. (1992). *Tribally controlled colleges: Making good medicine* (American Indian Studies, Vol. 3). New York: Peter Lang.

CHAPTER 18

Women's Colleges and Universities

LISA WOLF-WENDEL AND BECKY EASON

Women's colleges and universities are institutions with a mission to serve the educational needs of women. Most of these institutions enroll some men, either at the graduate level or in certain programs. Women's colleges and universities in the United States, which numbered approximately 214 institutions at their peak in 1960, today number fewer than 80 institutions. Although few in number, women's colleges and universities today, as in the past, are extremely diverse in size, location, selectivity, sponsorship, and other institutional characteristics. Despite their diversity, women's institutions of higher education, particularly women's undergraduate colleges, have been found to provide their students and graduates with more positive outcomes than coeducational colleges. When the characteristics of women's colleges that account for these positive results are identified, it is possible for women's colleges to serve as models for other institutional types and for those other types of institutions to learn the lessons that women's colleges can teach about how best to educate undergraduate students.

Characteristics of Today's Women's Colleges and Universities

Women's colleges and universities in the United States educate less than 1% of all women attending postsecondary institutions and award 1% of all degrees conferred —15,000 bachelor's degrees in 2000, with a total enrollment of 95,873 (93% of whom are women). Estimates are that fewer than 5% of college-going high school seniors will even apply to attend a women's college or university. These women's institutions tend to be small, ranging in size from 94 to 5,000 full-time students, and most of them are private institutions, with more than half affiliated with a religious denomination, most often with the Roman Catholic Church (33%). According to *U.S. News and World Report*, women's undergraduate colleges are disproportionately more likely than co-educational liberal arts colleges to have class sizes under 20 students. In terms of geographic location, almost half of U.S. women's colleges and universities are located in the Northeast; 33% are located in the South; there are three women's institutions of higher education in California; and the rest are scattered around the country. Many women's colleges and universities have cooperative relationships with nearby coeducational institutions. For example, Scripps College in California is part of the Claremont Colleges Consortium; Smith College and Mount Holyoke College are aligned with Amherst, the University of Massachusetts, and Hampshire College; and Bryn Mawr has a cooperative relationship with Haverford College and Swarthmore College. These types of cooperative relationships allow individuals to take classes from any of the campuses, to participate in extracurricular activities, and even to share in cooperative living arrangements.

While the most selective women's colleges, those known as the Seven Sisters, receive the lion's share of attention in the media and in the research literature, women's colleges and universities represent a diverse array of institutions. The Seven Sisters are the oldest, most selective, and most well endowed of the women's colleges. The Seven Sisters include Barnard, Bryn Mawr, Mount Holyoke, Radcliffe, Smith, Vassar, and Wellesley, although Vassar and Radcliffe are no longer women's colleges. There are also two historically Black four-year women's colleges (Spelman and Bennett) and approximately six two-year women's colleges. There are currently three public institutions of higher education for women—Douglass College of Rutgers University, Mississippi University for Women, and Texas Women's University. Seventeen women's institutions of higher education grant master's degrees, while 47 grant bachelor's degrees. Women's colleges range in selectivity from very selective to nonselective. Some of the institutions that grant master's degrees admit men to these programs, although their undergraduate population continues to be open only to women. From a resource perspective, the women's colleges and universities also vary greatly—from those with healthy endowments (including the Seven Sisters) to those institutions that are entirely dependent on tuition revenue to cover operating expenses. Interestingly, in a review of the top colleges by the *Princeton Review*, 4 of the 10 listed with the nicest residence halls were women's colleges, as were 3 of the 10 with the most beautiful campuses, and 3 of the 20 with the best college food.

Though women's colleges and universities do not represent a single mold, they do share some common traits. For example, they serve women of color and nontraditional-aged women in higher proportions than comparable coeducational institutions. The explanation for this is twofold. First, serving women, in all their diversity, is a major component of the mission of many of these institutions. Second, in order for the existing women's colleges and universities to survive with their original missions still intact, many had to be creative in attracting and retaining women students. As fewer than 5% of high school women will even consider applying to a women's college, many women's colleges have had to focus their attention on attracting older women, part-time students, and transfer students. Women's colleges and universities are also more likely than their coeducational counterparts to grant undergraduate degrees to women in the more male-dominated fields.

Women's Colleges Outcomes

Research, both quantitative and qualitative, demonstrates that women's undergraduate colleges are among the most empowering environments wherein women are taken seriously and ultimately experience success. Graduates of women's colleges tend to hold higher positions and earn higher salaries than their coeducational counterparts. Despite the fact that women's college graduates account for fewer than 4% of all college-educated women, 20% of women in Congress and 30% of *Business Week's* list of "Rising Women Stars in Corporate America" are graduates of women's colleges. Further, 33% of the women board members for the 1992 Fortune 1000 companies were women's college graduates, and they were overrepresented among the women who were the highest-paid officers in Fortune 1000 companies. Approximately 14% of cabinet members in state government are women's college graduates, and 90% of women's college alumnae have participated in at least one civic or professional organization since graduation. Further, research shows that women's college graduates tend to be more involved in philanthropic activities after graduation than their coeducational counterparts. Famous women's college graduates include but are not limited to Jane Addams, Madeleine Albright, Pearl S. Buck, Barbara Bush, Rachel Carson, Hillary Rodham Clinton, Marian Wright Edelman, Nora Ephron, Geraldine Ferraro, Betty Friedan, Lillian Hellman, Katharine Hepburn, Jeane Kirkpatrick, Nancy Pelosi, Nancy Reagan, Cokie Roberts, Diane Sawyer, and Gloria Steinem.

Graduates of women's colleges are more than twice as likely as graduates of coeducational colleges to receive doctoral degrees, to enter medical school, and to receive doctorates in the natural sciences. Women's college graduates disproportionately pursue doctorates in math, science, economics, and engineering. Indeed, graduates of women's colleges are more likely to hold traditionally male-dominated jobs upon graduation, such as lawyer, physician, or manager. Nearly half the graduates of women's colleges have earned advanced degrees.

Compared to women at coeducational institutions, students at women's colleges are more satisfied with their overall college experience and express higher levels of self-esteem and leadership skills. Women at women's colleges are said to participate more fully in and out of class than women at coeducational institutions. Some suggest that this is because they observe women functioning in the top jobs of the college: 90% of women's college presidents are women, and 55% of the faculty are women. Others suggest it is because there are more leadership opportunities available only to women at these colleges. Whatever the reason, students at women's colleges report greater satisfaction with their college experiences—academically, developmentally, and personally.

Some critics have questioned the results of individual studies on the efficacy of women's colleges, especially those that focus on the effect of attending a women's college on career and postgraduation outcomes. These critics focus on those studies that use institutions rather than individuals as the unit of analysis and the fact that the studies cannot adequately control for individual student background characteristics. In addition, some critics suggest that the relative success of graduates of women's colleges may be a dated phenomenon. In other words, when women students began to have access to prestigious men's colleges, did claims about women's colleges remain true? This question assumes that the success of women's colleges is due to the fact that the "best" women students could not attend the "best" schools in the country. It also assumes that studies of women's colleges focus on the most elite of these institutions. A third critique about the research on women's colleges is that it fails to account for the self-selection of students. In other words, some suggest that women who choose to attend women's colleges are somehow predestined to be successful and that one cannot credit the institution at all for the outcomes produced.

The best way to address such critiques is to examine the literature on women's colleges in its totality rather than to look at one study at a time. Indeed, studies taken one at a time represent only pieces of a larger puzzle. Research is most powerful when conclusions are drawn from a wide variety of studies using different methods, sources of data, and time periods. Reviewing the literature makes clear that the majority of studies on women's colleges, including those that control for both institutional and individual characteristics of students, come to the same conclusion. Therefore, although it is impossible to randomly assign students to attend either a women's college or coeducational college, the self-selection argument appears specious. Further, it is not only dated studies that make claims about the positive outcomes associated with women's colleges, as current studies using contemporary college attendees also come to the same conclusions. Given the totality of the research on women's colleges, one can safely conclude that, despite differences among methodologies and approaches, the extent of overlap, the consistency, and the corroboration in the research findings are so great as to warrant the conclusion that a woman attending an all-women's college, compared with her coeducational counterpart, is more likely to achieve positive outcomes such as having higher educational aspirations, attaining a graduate degree, entering a sex-atypical career, and achieving prominence in her field.

Historical Legacy

A brief history of women's education in general and of women's undergraduate colleges in particular helps to put today's women's colleges into the proper historical context. In the colonial period, it was widely believed that women were intellectually inferior to men and that educating women might lead to health problems and eventually to a decreased ability to bear children. And, since education in the colonial period was aimed at preparing men for the clergy, there was no real impetus to provide higher education for women. Formal higher education was not an option for women during this era.

In the early 1800s, several seminaries for women only were founded to provide girls with a liberal education, equivalent to a high school education. Graduates of these seminaries were prepared to be mothers, wives, and teachers. These seminaries were not immediately classified as colleges, although schools such as that founded in 1821 by Emma Willard modeled their curriculum, in large part, after that offered at the most prestigious men's colleges of the day. Other women-only institutions, such as those founded by Catherine Beecher in 1824 and 1832 and Mount Holyoke Seminary, founded by Mary Lyon in 1837, became prototypes for today's women's colleges and were seen by many as the best way to educate women.

There are several women-only institutions that claim to be the first "college." Georgia Female College was chartered by the state legislature in 1836; its curriculum, however, was more similar to a high school's than that of a college. In 1853, Mary Sharp College in Tennessee was founded; its curriculum looked very similar to the four-year degree program offered at the men's colleges. Similarly, Elmira Female College in New York, chartered in 1855, offered a true collegiate course. In the early days of women's access to higher education, single-sex institutions were the norm. By 1860, there were approximately 100 women's colleges in existence, about half of which offered a collegiate-level curriculum.

Also by 1860, several institutions, including Oberlin, began experimenting with coeducation. The passage of the Morrill Land-Grant Act during the Civil War led to the creation of land-grant institutions, all of which were coeducational. During this period, normal schools and public high schools also began to emerge as educational alternatives for women. These factors offered women a broader array of educational options, which affected the growth and popularity of women's colleges. By 1880, more than 20,000 women were enrolled in college, a figure that represented 33% of the college-going population. Approximately half of these students were enrolled in women-only institutions.

By 1880, there were 155 women's colleges that awarded college degrees. As is true today, these early women's colleges represented a diverse array of institutions. Among them were institutions that were religiously affiliated and independently controlled, including a large number of Catholic institutions. Some of these women's colleges were highly selective, while others had open admission; some were urban, others were rural, and some offered a liberal arts curriculum, while others offered vocational training programs. Many of these women's colleges were founded in the South and Northeast. In the Midwest and West, coeducation was the norm during this era. The women's colleges in the South were widely perceived as "finishing schools" and were not taken seriously by many in higher education.

After the Civil War, the women's colleges of the Northeast, especially the Seven Sisters, wished to demonstrate that women were as capable of achieving advanced education as were men. These institutions replicated the classical curriculum of the most elite men's colleges. Indeed, compared to other educational options for women through normal schools and coeducational institutions, the curriculum at these women's colleges focused on liberal education rather than on preprofessional programs. These women's colleges not only replicated the curriculum of the men's colleges, they also required students to meet the admission standards of the men's schools. This created enrollment problems, as few women had the necessary background in Greek and Latin. Finding qualified faculty willing to teach at these women's colleges was also a significant problem in the early days. One solution to these dilemmas was the founding of coordinate colleges, institutions that shared the faculty and curriculum of men's colleges but that operated as separate institutions. These institutions, including Radcliffe, Pembroke, and Barnard, were considered women's colleges because the male and female students did not take classes together and because the institutions had different administrators. The Seven Sisters served as an enduring model of high-quality education for women.

Between 1890 and 1910, undergraduate enrollment at women's colleges increased by 348%, while the gain of female students at coeducational colleges was 438%. Over a similar period, male student attendance in college increased by only 214%. By the turn of the century, coeducation had become the norm for women. Among the arguments in favor of coeducation were that separate education was economically wasteful, that women were equal to men and should therefore be educated with them, that single-sex institutions were unnatural, and that coeducation would be helpful in taming the spirits of young men. By 1920, women students represented 47% of the student body in colleges and universities. Indeed, the 1920s were a high point in women's education, and in many cases women outnumbered men in undergraduate colleges. During this era, 74% of the colleges and universities were coeducational, and the vast majority of women in higher education attended these institutions. Women's colleges, however, continued to attract sufficient numbers of students to remain viable.

The 1930s through 1950s were marked by a return to more traditional views about the role of women in society, a view that emphasized women in the home and family. By 1950, the percentage of women in higher education dropped to a low of 30%, and enrollment at many women's colleges began to decline precariously. The 1960s and 1970s saw a more pronounced shift away from single-sex institutions toward coeducation. During this period, the most prestigious exclusively male colleges and universities began to admit women to their undergraduate programs, and many women's colleges also became coeducational. Many of the women's colleges that decided not to admit men closed because of financial exigency during this period. Indeed, many small private liberal arts colleges, both coeducational and single sex, closed during this era. To many, the replacement of single-sex education with coeducation was seen as part of women's attainment of parity with men. In fact, many believe that the shift away from single-sex institutions to coeducational ones served both sexes better. Some argued that if one believed that women should attend women's colleges, it somehow implied that women are different or inferior to men. Others argued that women who attend single-sex institutions do not learn to deal with men and, therefore, are less ready to compete and function in the "real world." As a result, the number of women's colleges today has declined to fewer than 80 institutions.

Most of the women's colleges that survived the decline in the 1970s transformed themselves from women's colleges to "colleges for women." These institutions purposefully rededicated themselves and their institutional missions to serve women students. The Women's College Coalition, founded in 1972, was created to support these institutions and to increase the visibility and acceptability of women's colleges. Title IX of the Educational Amendments of 1972 barred institutions from discriminating in admissions by gender. While private women's colleges have been relatively free to continue admitting predominantly women, this act had a significant effect on public women's colleges. The Supreme Court ruled in 1982 that Mississippi University for Women, one of the three remaining public women's colleges, must admit men seeking admission to all of their programs. The university did so, but it continues to maintain an explicit mission to serve women. In 2005, the Rutgers board of governors proposed ending Douglass's tenure as a stand-alone, single-sex institution, thereby placing its status as a public women's college in jeopardy. Despite their many successes, women's colleges are struggling to remain a viable option on the higher education landscape. Their future tenuous, they nonetheless can serve as models for ways to successfully educate women.

Lessons Learned from Women's Colleges

The positive outcomes associated with attending a women's college has led some researchers to explore the characteristics of these institutions to see how they can serve as models for coeducational institutions. Seven institutional traits stand out as being descriptive of how women's colleges facilitate the success of their women students. These traits can serve as lessons that other institutions might wish to follow to create environments that facilitate the success of women students. These lessons include (1) clarify and communicate a mission that puts women at the center; (2) believe women can achieve and hold them to high expectations; (3) make students feel as if they matter; (4) provide strong, positive role models; (5) provide ample opportunities for women to engage in leadership activities; (6) include women in the curriculum; and (7) create safe spaces where women can form a critical mass.

With regard to the first lesson, women's colleges typically have focused missions that permeate their culture, values, decisions, physical environment, rituals, and history. The education of women is central to this mission and is intentionally reflected in curriculum decisions, publications, and at numerous decision-making points day to day and over the long term. While coeducational institutions do not have the luxury of being able to focus exclusively on women, by purposefully considering the needs of women, such institutions may be better able to serve this group of students.

Just as women's colleges were initially established to refute the notion that women could not succeed in serious academic pursuits, today's women's colleges continue to demonstrate the importance of holding women students to high academic standards and believing in the capacity of women students for success. Having high expectations and encouraging students to achieve are among the main characteristics of women's colleges that are worthy of emulation. At women's colleges, the most common approach to getting students to "aim high" involves faculty telling students that they have potential, telling them that they are capable, and telling them what is expected of them. Faculty members at women's colleges suggest the importance of not giving up too early on students who are having academic difficulties, especially in male-dominated fields. This is a trait that should be emulated across all institutional types.

Women's colleges are known for the level of support and caring that students receive from faculty and administrators. Support from constituents at women's colleges includes not only guidance related to academic issues but also support and advice on personal matters. Research demonstrates that some degree of personal support on a campus is pivotal for student success in that students need to feel that they are noticed, that what they say or do is important, and that they are appreciated. Institutions that are able to create an environment where students feel cared for are more likely to have students who are motivated to learn and who have a strong sense of institutional loyalty.

By the composition of their employees, women's colleges clearly communicate that the options for women are varied and the doors of possibility are open wide. Without the presence of women at all levels on a college campus, a significant statement is made about whether women should be in those positions, whether they can succeed in such positions, and whether women students should aspire to such positions. That is, the presence of women in leadership roles and within the faculty communicates a great deal about women's options and choices.

Women's colleges provide a large variety of opportunities for women to be involved in the life of the campus, both in and outside of class. These opportunities help students develop strong leadership skills, keep them active in their institutions, and facilitate their overall success. At women's colleges, women are not only expected, but also obligated, to hold all of the available leadership positions. Institutions that expect women students to be involved and active members of the community are more likely to graduate successful students.

Women's colleges often infuse women into the general curriculum via classroom examples, lectures, and assigned readings. Topics pertaining to women can be found as a major part of extracurriculum—presented through planned, often required lectures, speaker series, and discussion groups. Providing opportunities for students to learn about themselves and about others who have been historically marginalized is important. Including the voices of women is not something one does merely to enhance the self-esteem of underrepresented students. Instead, the infusion of diversity into the curriculum helps all students understand how to succeed and how to fight societal discrimination and injustice.

Women at women's colleges believe that one of the factors that make these institutions successful is that not only are women in the majority but the institution also offers a supportive peer culture that creates a feeling of safety among students. Research suggests that the proportion of different types of individuals within an institution affects both how they are viewed by the organization and how they fit in. Having a critical mass means more than just adding more students from a particular group; it also means consciously paying attention to the needs of that group and providing a supportive climate. It means fostering an effective community, which entails, among other things, incorporating diversity, creating a shared culture, and promoting caring, trust, and teamwork. The strength of a women's college is that being around peers who share certain characteristics makes one feel comfortable, safe, supported, and included. Moreover, having this critical mass expands how one perceives limitations, assets, and possibilities. In contrast, the absence of this supportive peer culture makes one feel isolated and limited.

Many of the characteristics inherent at women's colleges parallel traits associated with successful academic institutions for men and women students. What sets women's colleges apart from most coeducational institutions, however, is the purposefulness with which the former respond to the needs of their women students. The success of women is central to the values held by campus constituents. This belief undergirds most of the actions of both the institutions and the individual campus constituents. These are environments in which the situation for women is not only favorable but also empowering—colleges where there is a critical mass of women faculty, colleges where women are nurtured and challenged, and colleges where woman-related issues dominate campus discussions. These colleges act intentionally to take women seriously.

Women's colleges exhibit these traits in different ways, exemplifying the idea that "successful" colleges are not all alike. While separate examinations of the characteristics of each institution are illuminating, it is important to understand that the whole of these institutions is greater than the sum of their parts—one cannot look at a single element in isolation. Instead, it is the combination of characteristics, the ethos of these institutions, that makes them unique and able to facilitate the success of their students. What sets women's colleges apart from other campuses is that they are purposeful in their adoption of structures, policies, practices, and curriculum that are sensitive to the needs of women.

REFERENCES AND FURTHER READING
Harwarth, I., Maline, M., & DeBra, E. (1997). *Women's colleges in the United States: History, issues, and challenges*. Washington, DC: U.S. Government Printing Office.
Lasser, C. (Ed.). (1987). *Educating men and women together: Coeducation in a changing world*. Urbana: University of Illinois Press.
Purcell, F. B., Helms, R. M., & Rumbley, L. (2005). *Women's universities and colleges: An international handbook*. Rotterdam, Holland: Sense Publishers.
Riordan, C. (1994). The value of attending a women's college: Education, occupation and income benefits. *Journal of Higher Education, 65*(4), 486–510.
Solomon, B. M. (1985). *In the company of educated women: A history of women and higher education in America*. New Haven, CT: Yale University Press.
Tidball, E., Smith, D., Tidball, C., & Wolf-Wendel, L. (1999). *Taking women seriously: Lessons and legacies for higher education from women's colleges*. Phoenix: ACE/Oryx Press.
Wolf-Wendel, L. (1998). Models of excellence: The baccalaureate origins of successful African American, European American and Hispanic women. *Journal of Higher Education, 69*(2), 144–172.
Women's College Coalition Web site. www.womenscolleges.org

III

Gender Constructions and Controversies in the Academic Curriculum

OVERVIEW

The chapters in part III examine gendering processes within the official, academic curriculum of institutions of higher education. The term *official, academic curriculum* refers to the accredited courses offered by educational institutions. Usually the curriculum is listed in the printed or electronic materials educational institutions use to describe themselves, such as their institutional Web sites, course schedules and catalogs, or faculty and student handbooks. These listings are often accompanied by short descriptions of the goals and content of each course, but a full understanding of the curriculum requires additional information about each course, such as all the topics that will be covered, the content of the course readings, the various assignments and tests students will have to complete, and what the teacher will say about the course materials. This information can be gleaned by examining course outlines, handouts, and tests; reading the textbooks and other course-related materials, including students' test answers and papers; attending class meetings and listening to the course-related comments of teachers and students; and watching or listening to audiovisual materials and student reports presented in class. As indicated, the curriculum is not just a list of accredited courses, or even a statement of goals and intentions relevant to those courses, but also a set of practices.

These practices affect the extent to which certain courses and the fields of study (e.g., departments, programs, majors, minors) that they constitute are accessible to people of various identities. As in part II, *accessibility* refers to the extent to which a field of study is open and welcoming to academically qualified students and workers (teachers, staff, administrators) of particular identities, not just legally available to them. Consistent with the goals of this book, the primary emphasis of the chapters in part III is on *gender* identities, and the authors whose chapters appear in this section were asked to discuss the ways in which their particular component of the academic curriculum has been gender/culturally stereotyped or exclusionary as well as the efforts that have been made to make their curricular field of study more gender/culturally inclusive and equitable. Gender accessibility results both from the practices of departmental and program faculty, administrators, staff, and students with regard to men and women (or various kinds of men and women) and from the responses of those men and women to the practices they encounter.

One indication of the gender accessibility that students have to various programs in the academic curriculum is the proportion of men and women students who complete degrees in those programs. Chapter 19 ("Academic Programs: Undergraduate, Graduate, and Professional") provides readers with an overview of the proportions of men and women graduates from U.S. colleges and universities who completed their degrees in various academic programs in 1975–76, 1990–91, and 2005–6. By comparing men's and women's degree completions over time, it is possible to learn which degree programs have become more or less gender segregated or desegregated and which ones have become more masculinized or feminized numerically. Gender accessibility is only one of the possible reasons for changes in the gender composition of degree programs. Other reasons are discussed below, at the end of chapter 19, and in the other chapters in this section.

The topics of those other chapters were selected to represent four different patterns of gendering in the curriculum of higher education. The first pattern could be called *numerically feminized fields of study* and includes education, discussed in chapter 30 ("Teacher Education") and home economics, discussed in chapter 24 ("From Home Economics to Family and Consumer Sciences"). In addition to education and home economics, now called family and consumer sciences (FCS), other academic fields described in chapter 19 that have the characteristics of numerically feminized fields of study include health professions and related sciences (including nursing) and public administration and social services professions (including social work). All of these fields have more than a century-long history of enrolling and graduating proportionately more women than men, and none has witnessed a substantial increase in recent years in the number and proportion of men who select these fields of study.

At the present time in the United States, the majority of teachers at the elementary and secondary school levels are women. That this was not always the case has been widely documented by historians and other social scientists who use the term *feminization of teaching* to describe the process of change that occurred in the nineteenth century as the majority of men teachers became a minority and women assumed the overwhelming majority of teaching positions. By the start of the twentieth century, women constituted the majority of teachers in all regions of the United States, and by 1910, they were the majority in every state. Although U.S. census figures reveal some fluctuations in the size of this majority over time, the proportion of all teachers in the United States who were women in 1900 (74.9%) was about the same as the proportion who were women in 2000 (75.5%). Not all of these teachers received bachelor's degrees in education, nor did all who received those degrees enter the teaching profession. Nevertheless, women were also the majority of degree recipients in education throughout the twentieth century, and according to the most recent *Digest of Education Statistics*, issued by the Department of Education, women received 84,790, or 79.1%, of the 107,238 bachelor's degrees in education awarded in 2005–6.

Like education, FCS has been a numerically feminized field since its inception as home economics in the nineteenth century. Although the 20,775 bachelor's degrees in FCS awarded by U.S. institutions of higher education in 2005–6 was less than a fourth of the number awarded in education that year, the proportion of those FCS degrees that were awarded to women was substantially higher than for education: 18,339, or 88.3%. Despite the fact that women constitute such large majorities of graduates in

FCS and education, chapter 19 reveals that neither field attracts as large a proportion of all women graduates as it once did. Nevertheless, the label *numerically feminized fields of study* remains appropriate, as both fields continue to attract substantially more women than men, and neither field has seen more than a tiny increase since the 1970s in its proportion of all male graduates. (Education has actually witnessed a substantial decline.) These gendered patterns of degree completion suggest that men may find education and FCS less accessible than women do, although both fields have been characterized by efforts to attract more men, especially during the past 40 years. Nevertheless, chapters 24 and 30 detail many ways in which these academic fields—and the occupations to which they are linked—have been shaped by historic processes that have structured them in a feminized manner.

The academic programs that present the sharpest contrast to the numerically feminized fields of study are the *numerically masculinized fields of study* characterized historically and at the present time by the higher graduation rates of men and the substantially lower graduation rates of women. At the present time, these fields are often called the STEM fields (an acronym for science, technology, engineering, and mathematics), and chapters 20 ("Biological and Physical Sciences"), 31 ("Technology and Computer Science"), 22 ("Engineering"), and 27 ("Mathematics"), along with chapter 19, present information about the ways in which STEM fields have been gendered and about the reasons many women find them to be inaccessible. Of the academic fields covered in these chapters, the only one that now grants bachelor's degrees to a higher proportion of women than it did in the 1970s and earlier is the biological sciences, and a higher proportion of women than of men now receive their bachelor's degrees in that field. In contrast, table 1 in chapter 19 also reveals that the proportion of women receiving their bachelor's degrees in the physical sciences was about the same in 2005–6 as it had been in the mid-1970s and early 1990s, but the proportions of women taking degrees in computer sciences, engineering, and mathematics increased slightly from 1975–76 to 1990–91 but then dropped and was lower in 2005–6 than it was fifteen years earlier.

Even though it is not large, this drop comes as a shock to those who expect to see more evidence of a positive effect on academic programs of the criticisms of higher education advanced by second-wave feminism and by the Black Freedom Movement of the 1960s. Not only did these social movements criticize gender and racial segregation in many institutions of higher education and their degree programs, but the social movements also mounted formidable challenges to the traditional undergraduate and graduate curriculum: Traditional curricula ignored or distorted the experiences and contributions of men of color and all women, and they also failed to engage critical issues of justice, equality, power, and community service, all of which were regarded by the political activists as crucial components of a quality education. Criticisms of this type gave rise to new academic programs that can be called *emancipatory fields of study*, including those discussed in chapters 21 ("Black Studies and Black Women's Studies"), 29 ("Multicultural Education"), 32 ("Women's and Gender Studies") and 28 ("Men's Studies"). Cutting across these and other academic fields has been a major effort to develop feminist pedagogy, which, as chapter 23 ("Feminist Pedagogy") explains, is a grassroots and unofficial policy initiative that takes different forms, but all of its advocates are united in a passionate—and sometimes dangerous—effort to transform teaching and learning processes to the greater advantage of girls and women.

When the emancipatory fields of study first emerged on college campuses, their courses were usually taught by members of traditional disciplines under a cross-listing arrangement. Thus, for example, a member appointed in romance languages might teach a course on French feminism that was listed for credit in both the language department and the women's studies program. Or a sociologist might teach a course on race relations for credit in both the sociology department and Black studies. Arrangements such as these meant that criticisms of the traditional disciplines, as well as the new subject matter offered by faculty committed to the emancipatory fields of study, were embedded in traditional disciplines in ways that gave them access to and influence over departmental students and the curricula offered to them. However, not all established departments welcomed such incursions. Some refused to cross-list courses with the emancipatory programs even when some of those programs eventually achieved departmental status, and others allowed faculty to teach cross-listed courses only as part of a voluntary overload. Even in those traditional departments that seemed to welcome involvement with the newer emancipatory fields of study, there was resistance to curricular changes. Many of the older, well-established disciplines had a canon—an accepted, recognized list of "sacred" texts or of important persons, ideas, and events— around which their curriculum had come to be organized, and they were loath to change it. Although usually defended on the grounds of importance or excellence, disciplinary canons were also centered on the ideas, writings, and activities of White, middle- and upper-class men. For these reasons, I refer to these disciplines as the *canonically masculinized fields of study*.

On most college and university campuses, two of the larger and more influential canonically masculinized fields of study are history and English. Chapters 25 ("History") and 26 ("Literary Studies") provide information about some of the ways in which those fields have been challenged by feminists over the past 40 years and about the responses to those challenges within the disciplines. Whereas chapter 26 sounds an optimistic note about the growing acceptance of feminist literary studies over time, chapter 25 takes a more cautious stance, one that recognizes that the ways in which educators and historians teach and write about U.S. history have "changed dramatically over the last three decades" but also documents the ways in which foundational courses in U.S. history continue to be male centered. Unfortunately, space limitations did not permit inclusion of chapters discussing the impact of feminism on the many other canonically masculinized fields of study (e.g., art history, foreign languages and literature, music, philosophy, sociology), but it seems likely that the same mixture of change and resistance documented in chapter 25 would characterize all of these fields, albeit with some showing more change than others.

In addition to the criticisms by second-wave feminism of the existing academic disciplines for their male-centered subject matter and pedagogy and for excluding or discriminating against women, feminists also complained about assumptions throughout the curriculum concerning the appropriateness and normality of particular forms of masculinity (rational, instrumental, assertive, technologically oriented) and femininity (expressive, intuitive, nurturant) that make some men or women (but not others) suitable for certain kinds of academic pursuits. These assumptions, argued the feminists, produce differences in the extent to which men and women participate in the various disciplines. Support for these arguments can be found in the chapters on the STEM disciplines found in this part of the book. These chapters suggest that STEM disciplines—with the exception of biology—do present themselves as stereotypically masculine and, therefore, less accessible to women students. The same tendency, in reverse, was suggested above about the numerically feminized fields of study, such as teacher education and home economics, whose long history of association with women's work may serve as a bar against male participation. Similar arguments might be made with regard to other degree patterns identified in chapter 19. The rising proportion of men taking degrees in the arts, for example, might be due to the rising use of "masculine" electronic technologies in design-related fields. And, conversely, the rising proportion of women taking degrees in communications may be due to the decline in emphasis on communications technologies and the rising concern with interpersonal and organizational communications, journalism, and public relations.

More research is necessary to test these and other possibilities. What seems clear, however, is that the criticisms feminists made of academic fields of study 40 years ago are still valid. Despite many efforts to increase the accessibility of all fields to women and men of all types, most academic fields continue to be either numerically feminized, numerically masculinized, or canonically masculinized. In addition, some academics fear that the emancipatory fields of study are becoming more conventional and less critical or innovative and may themselves be adding to the gender gaps in higher education. For those who are troubled by such gaps and would like to see them closed, the chapters in this section provide several examples of successful curricular transformations and offer many suggestions about additional ways in which the official curriculum can root out its heavy and continuing emphasis on the accomplishments and traditions of affluent White males by putting gender and cultural pluralism at its core.

CHAPTER 19

Academic Programs: Undergraduate, Graduate, and Professional

STEPHANIE WOODHAM BURGE

Young women's striking advances within higher education represent a significant example of social change in the United States. Historically, young men were more likely to enroll in and graduate from college, as well as achieve postgraduate and professional degrees. Since the late 1980s, however, young women's educational attainment has kept pace with men's. Among contemporary cohorts, young women's educational achievements surpass those of men in terms of earned bachelor's and master's degrees. Furthermore, in 2006, young women's attainments of doctoral degrees and first-professional degrees were at parity with men's.

Despite women's remarkable strides in higher education, gender inequality in the workplace, measured by both occupational sex segregation and the pay gap between men and women, remains persistent. Women's stalled progress in the workplace, despite substantially higher educational attainment, is a puzzle for scholars. What explains patterns of persistent gender inequality at work, despite women's increasing educational achievements? Part of the answer lies in the fact that young women and men pursue different fields of study in higher education, whether at the undergraduate or graduate level. Studies of occupational sex segregation and gender inequality in earnings often treat educational achievements similarly, regardless of the degree's academic program or the credentials earned. Yet many elite and lucrative occupations require specific educational credentials as prerequisites for entry into these careers. For this reason, researchers and educators need to attend to patterns of sex segregation in academic programs, in addition to gender-related trends in the overall number of earned degrees.

Historical overviews of gendered pathways in American higher education show considerable changes in patterns of sex segregation of academic programs since the 1970s and in particular that much of this change has been due to young women's entry into some traditionally male-dominated fields. While this change has been most notable in the distribution of women and men across fields of study for undergraduate degrees, some of these changes have also occurred at the graduate level. Potential explanations for women's inroads into some male-dominated academic programs such as business include a gender convergence in young adults' career expectations and evaluation of extrinsic work rewards, such as compensation and prestige. Scholarly research on men's low and declining representation in traditional women's fields, such as education, and women's continued underrepresentation in physical science, technology, engineering, and math (STEM) programs suggests the importance of resilient gender differences in adolescents' valuation of family, self-efficacy, and work preferences.

Gender-Related Trends in Educational Attainment

According to the National Center for Education Statistics (1978, 1993, 2007) women earned approximately 46% of the bachelor's degrees, 46% of the master's degrees, and 23% of the doctoral degrees awarded in the United States in 1975–76. Of the first-professional degrees (including law, theology, and various fields of medical study) awarded that year, fewer than one out of five were conferred on women. By the beginning of the 1990s, the gender gap in bachelor's and master's degrees had reversed; women earned approximately 54% of these degrees. Similar gender-related trends occurred in the distribution of doctoral and first-professional degrees. In 1990–91, women earned 37% of doctoral degrees and 40% of first-professional degrees, a striking increase since the mid-1970s. More recently, women's educational achievements have surpassed those of men at nearly every level of educational attainment. For example, in 2005–6, women earned nearly 58% of bachelor's degrees, 58.5% of master's degrees, and almost half of doctorates and first-professional degrees conferred by degree-granting institutions in the United States.

At the same time that young women's educational achievements have skyrocketed, women also have carved new inroads into academic programs traditionally dominated by men. Since the mid 1970s, considerable shifts have occurred in the distribution of women and of men across academic fields of study in undergraduate, graduate, and professional degrees. Yet there remains evidence that men and women who enroll in American higher education continue to pursue gender-differentiated educational pathways, and the trend toward gender integration of academic programs seems to have stalled among contemporary cohorts.

Trends in Gender Segregation of Bachelor's Degrees

Have patterns of sex segregation of bachelor's degrees changed as much as gender-related trends in overall educational attainment? Table 1 presents the percentages of women and men achieving bachelor's degrees from U.S. degree-granting institutions in major fields of study in the academic years of 1975–76, 1990–91, and 2005–6 (National Center, 1978, 1993, 2007). In the mid-1970s, 23% of male college graduates earned business degrees, 16% earned social science or history degrees, and almost 9% earned engineering degrees. In total, these three majors accounted for almost half of the college degrees earned by men in 1975–76. By contrast, just 6.7% of women earned a business degree and far fewer than 1% earned an engineering degree. Among female college graduates of the mid-1970s, education, social sciences and history, and health professions and sciences (including nursing) were the top three majors. Majors in education accounted for more than one-fourth of the bachelor's degrees earned by women in 1975–76.

Other fields of study, though not as prevalent in the 1970s, were also highly segregated by gender. For example, men were 3.8 times more likely to major in architecture, 3.9 times more likely to earn agricultural degrees, and 3.4 times more likely to major in physical science than women. On the other hand, women were four times more likely to major in foreign languages and family and consumer sciences and approximately twice as likely to major in English, public administration and social service professions

Table 1. Bachelor's Degrees Conferred in the United States by Sex of Student and Field of Study (%)

Major	1975–76		1990–91		2005–6	
	Men	Women	Men	Women	Men	Women
Agriculture and natural resources	3.1	0.8	1.8	0.7	1.9	1.3
Architecture	1.5	0.4	1.1	0.7	0.9	0.5
Area studies (ethnic, cultural, and gender)	0.3	0.4	0.4	0.5	0.4	0.6
Arts (fine, visual, and performing arts)	3.3	6.1	3.1	4.4	5.1	6.0
Biological and biomedical sciences	7.0	4.5	3.9	3.4	4.2	5.0
Business, management, and marketing	22.8	6.7	26.2	20.0	25.3	18.5
Communications	2.5	2.1	4.1	5.4	4.5	5.7
Computer and information sciences	0.9	0.3	3.5	1.2	6.0	1.1
Education	8.3	26.8	4.7	14.8	3.6	9.9
Engineering	8.9	0.3	13.5	1.9	10.6	1.7
English language and literature/letters	3.3	6.3	3.5	6.0	2.7	4.4
Family and consumer sciences / human sciences	0.1	4.0	0.3	2.3	0.4	2.1
Foreign language, literature, and linguistics	0.7	2.8	0.7	1.5	0.9	1.6
Health professions and related sciences	2.3	10.1	1.9	8.4	2.0	9.3
Interdisciplinary studies	3.5	3.5	4.1	4.8	3.8	6.2
Mathematics and statistics	1.9	1.5	1.5	1.2	1.3	0.8
Philosophy and religious studies	1.2	0.6	0.9	0.5	1.2	0.5
Physical science	3.4	1.0	2.2	0.9	1.9	1.0
Psychology	4.5	6.4	3.2	7.2	3.2	8.0
Public administration and social service professions	1.1	2.3	1.1	2.0	0.7	2.1
Social sciences and history	15.6	11.4	13.6	9.5	12.8	9.4
Theology	0.8	0.4	0.7	0.2	0.9	0.3
Other fields of study	2.9	1.3	4.1	2.7	5.8	3.9
Index of dissimilarity	0.40		0.29		0.28	

(including social work), and the fine and applied arts as men. Few academic majors were gender integrated in the mid-1970s, with only interdisciplinary studies claiming the exact same proportion of men's and women's college majors. The index of dissimilarity score of .40, shown in table 1 for the 1975–76 academic year, means that 40% of women and men would have had to change majors in order for male and female college graduates to be proportionately distributed across major fields in that year. An index score of .00 would indicate that women and men are proportionately distributed across all academic majors (no sex segregation), and a score of 1.00 would indicate that women and men do not earn degrees in the same academic fields (complete sex segregation).

By 1990–91, young women had made considerable progress into previously male-dominated academic majors. For example, women and men were almost equally likely to earn biology degrees, and the gender gap in proportion of business degrees declined from 16.1% in 1975–76 to 6.2% in 1990–91. Moreover, some fields of study, such as communications, that were relatively gender integrated in the mid-1970s had feminized by 1991, meaning that women were then more likely to earn degrees in these majors compared to men. Two important changes in women's educational attainment facilitated their growing representation in previously male-dominated majors. First, as noted above, women's proportion of college enrollments increased significantly between 1975–76 and 1990–91, as evidenced by the reversal of the gender gap in bachelor's degrees. Second, during this period, a considerable proportion of women shifted away from education majors; only about 15% of women bachelor's-degree recipients earned education degrees in 1990–91, compared to 27% in 1975–76.

While considerably more women earned degrees in STEM fields in the early 1990s than in the mid-1970s, women's proportional achievements in these majors continued to be far outpaced by men. For example, although women's proportional representation within engineering increased more than sixfold from 1975–76 to 1990–91, the gender gap in engineering grew larger during this same period. Similar patterns occurred in computer and information sciences. By contrast, women continued to earn proportionately more education and health science degrees than men. Nevertheless, table 1 shows that between 1975–76 and 1990–91, the index of dissimilarity declined to .29, meaning that roughly three out of ten male and female college graduates would have had to change majors to have an equivalent dispersion of women and men across college majors.

The twenty-first century is dually characterized by historically unparalleled educational achievements for women and by resilient patterns of gender inequality in the sex segregation of college majors. Table 1 shows that the most prevalent undergraduate majors for women graduates in 2005–6 were business, education, social sciences and history, and health professions and sciences, in that order. Business and social sciences/history were also the two most popular majors for men in 2006, but they were followed by engineering and computer science, majors that lead to more highly compensated jobs than those associated with a bachelor's degree in education or the health sciences. In majors such as engineering and physical sciences, the gender gap in earned degrees narrowed slightly between 1990–91 and 2005–6; however, increased gender integration in these fields stemmed more from men's lower likelihood of achieving degrees in these majors than from women's enhanced degree attainment. The gender gap in proportions of some majors, such as business, computer science, and mathematics, actually increased between 1990–91 and 2005–6. Feminized fields such as psychology, health sciences, and public administration grew increasingly gender segregated between 1990–91 and 2005–6. Women's attainment of biology degrees outpaced men's by the twenty-first century, a noticeable change from 1991, when similar proportions of men and women earned degrees in biological science. Finally, the gender composition of architecture and social sciences/history remained fairly stable between the early 1990s and 2006. Because declines in the sex segregation of some academic majors were offset by increases in the segregation of other majors, the overall level of sex segregation remained fairly stable between 1990–91 and 2005–6, resulting in an index of dissimilarity for the latter year of .28.

Trends In Gender Segregation of Graduate Degrees

How do patterns in sex segregation of graduate degrees compare to those we have seen in bachelor's degrees? Tables 2 and 3 present results of my calculations based on data from the National Center for Education Statistics (1978, 1993, 2007) showing historical trends in women's and men's representation across fields of study in master's and doctoral degrees. Aside from showing gender-related trends for specific majors, the tables reveal two important differences across levels of degrees. First, levels of sex segregation in graduate fields of study have been more stable and have remained some-

Table 2. Master's Degrees Conferred in the United States by Sex of Student and Field of Study (%)

Major	1975–76		1990–91		2005–6	
	Men	Women	Men	Women	Men	Women
Agriculture and natural resources	1.7	0.3	1.4	0.6	1.0	0.7
Architecture	1.5	0.5	1.4	0.7	1.3	0.7
Area studies (ethnic, cultural, and gender)	0.3	0.3	0.4	0.3	0.3	0.4
Arts (fine, visual, and performing arts)	2.7	3.0	2.4	2.7	2.4	2.2
Biological and biomedical sciences	2.7	1.4	1.5	1.4	1.5	1.4
Business, marketing, and management	22.5	3.4	32.7	15.2	35.1	17.6
Communications	1.1	0.9	1.1	1.5	1.1	1.4
Computer and information sciences	1.3	0.3	4.2	1.5	5.2	1.3
Education	27.3	56.9	13.3	37.7	17.1	37.6
Engineering	9.4	0.4	13.7	2.0	10.8	2.2
English language and literature/letters	2.3	4.2	1.7	2.9	1.2	1.7
Family and consumer sciences / human sciences	0.1	1.4	0.2	1.0	0.1	0.5
Foreign language, literature, and linguistics	0.7	1.6	0.4	0.8	0.4	0.7
Health professions and related sciences	2.5	5.8	2.9	9.3	4.5	11.4
Interdisciplinary studies	1.2	1.2	1.2	1.4	1.2	1.5
Mathematics and statistics	1.5	0.9	1.3	0.8	1.1	0.6
Philosophy and religious studies	0.5	0.3	0.5	0.3	0.4	0.2
Physical science	2.8	0.6	2.4	0.8	1.5	0.7
Psychology	2.5	2.5	2.1	4.4	1.7	4.4
Public administration and social science professions	4.8	5.0	3.6	6.8	3.2	6.4
Social sciences and history	6.5	3.5	4.5	2.9	3.5	2.5
Theology	1.3	0.7	1.9	0.9	1.5	0.7
Other fields of study	2.6	4.8	5.2	4.3	3.5	3.2
Index of dissimilarity	0.38		0.39		0.35	

what higher overall than in undergraduate fields of study. Second, among doctoral degrees, levels of sex segregation have actually increased very slightly since the mid-1970s because women's strides in educational achievement at the doctoral level have been primarily concentrated within feminized fields of study.

This concentration of women in feminized fields of study can also be seen at the master's degree level. Table 2 shows that well over half (56.9%) of women who earned master's degrees in 1975–76 majored in education, and the remaining 43% were primarily distributed across fields that were either women dominated (e.g. health sciences and English) or fairly gender integrated (e.g., public administration and psychology). Several of women's inroads during these years into other fields of study at the master's level were in gender-integrated or women-dominated fields such as health sciences, public administration, and psychology rather than traditionally male-dominated fields of study such as STEM.

Similar trends can be observed in men's participation in sex-segregated majors. For example, although 27% of master's degrees earned by men in 1975–76 were awarded in education, by 2006, men's representation in education had declined to 17%, signaling a relative shift out of the field of education. By comparison, between the mid-1970s and 2005–6, men's tendency to earn master's degrees in business grew substantially

Table 3. Doctoral Degrees Awarded in the United States by Sex of Student and Field of Study (%)

Major	1975–76		1990–91		2005–6	
	Men	Women	Men	Women	Men	Women
Agriculture and natural resources	3.3	0.8	3.8	1.6	2.5	1.8
Architecture	0.3	0.2	0.4	0.2	0.4	0.3
Area studies (ethnic, cultural, and gender)	0.5	0.7	0.4	0.5	0.3	0.5
Arts (fine, visual, and performing arts)	1.7	2.2	1.9	2.5	2.2	2.7
Biological and biomedical sciences	10.1	9.3	10.4	10.4	10.2	10.4
Business, marketing, and management	3.4	0.7	3.7	2.2	3.7	2.4
Communications	0.6	0.6	0.6	0.8	0.7	0.9
Computer and information sciences	0.8	0.3	2.4	0.6	3.9	1.1
Education	19.7	33.3	11.3	26.8	9.3	17.9
Engineering	10.5	0.8	19.3	3.3	20.8	5.5
English language and literature/letters	3.8	10.4	2.6	5.4	1.8	2.7
Family and consumer sciences / human sciences	0.2	1.6	0.3	1.3	0.2	1.0
Foreign language, literature, and linguistics	1.7	5.3	0.9	2.0	1.5	2.3
Health professions and related sciences	1.6	2.1	2.8	6.3	6.8	18.8
Interdisciplinary studies	0.7	1.1	0.7	0.9	1.7	2.1
Mathematics and statistics	2.9	1.2	3.2	1.3	3.2	1.4
Philosophy and religious studies	1.8	1.1	1.4	0.8	1.5	0.6
Physical science	11.9	3.8	13.9	5.8	11.0	4.9
Psychology	6.7	10.5	5.4	14.4	4.7	13.0
Public administration and social service professions	0.7	1.3	0.8	1.7	1.0	1.5
Social sciences and history	12.4	11.5	7.9	7.3	7.7	6.2
Theology	3.8	0.5	3.8	0.9	3.9	1.1
Other fields of study	0.8	0.5	2.2	2.8	0.8	0.8
Index of dissimilarity	0.30		0.34		0.32	

(from 22.5% to 35.1%) and men's representation within STEM master's degrees either remained fairly constant (as in the case of engineering) or increased substantially (as in the case of computer science).

Women's substantially increased representation within business master's degrees (most typically MBA degrees) represents a notable exception to this trend toward sex-typed degree programs at the master's level. Between 1975–76 and 2005–6, women's tendency to earn master's degrees in business, as opposed to other fields of study, jumped from 3.4% to almost 18%. Despite women's significant inroads into the traditionally male-dominated field of business, men did not carve similar pathways into traditionally female-dominated graduate master's programs. Consequently, while sex segregation of master's degree programs, as indicated by the index of dissimilarity, declined between 1975–76 and 2005–6, this decline was small (from .38 to .35), and most of the decline stemmed from women's shift away from education programs to business programs.

As shown by table 3, sex segregation of doctoral degrees actually increased slightly between 1975–76 and 2005–6 (from .30 to .32), primarily because women's increased likelihood of earning doctoral degrees was accompanied by a tendency to pursue sex-segregated fields such as education, health sciences, and psychology. Similarly, as echoed in undergraduate and master's programs, men's doctoral degree attainment during this same period of time tended to be concentrated largely in STEM fields. In fact, STEM fields comprised more than one-third (36.2%) of men's doctoral degrees in 1975–76 and nearly half of doctoral degrees awarded to men in 1990–91 and 2005–6 (49.2% and 49.1%, respectively). With the exception of biology doctoral degrees, women's proportional representation within STEM fields lagged men's considerably.

Trends in Gender Segregation of First-Professional Degrees

As noted above, first-professional fields encompass law, theology, and various fields of medical education. The latter include chiropractic, dentistry, medicine, optometry, osteopathic medicine, pharmacy, podiatry, and veterinary medicine. For two reasons, sex segregation of first-professional degrees looks somewhat different than sex segregation of traditional academic fields of study. First, when compared to majors at the undergraduate and graduate levels, first-professional degrees are awarded in fewer areas of study, which can result in an underestimation of the amount of sex segregation across fields that confer first-professional degrees. Second, much of the sex segregation that occurs within medical and legal professions develops after the point that first-professional degrees are awarded. For example, after doctors have received their medical degrees, they typically pursue postgraduate residency programs and medical fellowships that allow them to develop additional fields of specialty, such as dermatology, neurology, pediatrics, oncology, neurology, orthopedic surgery, etc. Similarly, in the legal profession subspecialties exist that differ substantially in remuneration levels and within which women and men are not evenly distributed. Yet, even with those caveats in mind, examining trends in sex segregation of first-professional degrees over time is still instructive regarding the extent to which women and men have completed degrees in similar fields at this elite level of education.

In 1975–76, women earned only 16.4% of first-professional degrees awarded. Among those women, nearly two-thirds (63.6%) earned a law degree and nearly one-quarter (22.3%) earned a degree in medicine, with 5% or fewer earning degrees in the other first-professional fields. By contrast, young men were somewhat more evenly distributed across professional degrees: just under half earned law degrees, over one-fifth (21.3%) earned medical degrees, 10% earned a degree in theology, 9.8% earned dental degrees, and just over 5% earned degrees in either chiropractic medicine (2.7%) or veterinary medicine (2.4%). Nevertheless, because *both* women and men were overwhelmingly concentrated in two fields (law and medicine), the sex segregation index for professional degrees in 1975–76 was comparatively lower (.17) than for other academic degree programs (see tables 1–3), and most of this segregation in first-professional degrees was due to the proportionately greater representation of men than women in dentistry and theology and women's proportionately greater representation in law.

Between 1975–76 and 1990–91, few of the overall trends in women's and men's distribution across professional degrees changed. One exception was the erosion of the gender gap in dentistry degrees, which narrowed considerably from 7.4% in 1975–76 to 1.2% in 1990–91. The biggest change, however, was not in the gender distributions across professional fields of study but rather in the substantial increase in women's share of all first-professional degrees. Whereas the dissimilarity index dropped only slightly from .17 to .13, the proportion of all professional degrees awarded by U.S. institutions to women rather than men shot up from 16.4% to 40.4%.

By 2005–6, women earned just under half (49.8%) of all first-professional degrees awarded in the United States, and women's and men's distributions across academic programs were fairly similar. Still, among these more contemporary cohorts, there are some patterns of sex segregation, such as women's greater likelihood of pursuing veterinary medicine and pharmacy and men's proportionately greater degree attainment in law, dentistry, theology, and chiropractic medicine. Consequently, the dissimilarity index in 2005–6, while very low compared to other graduate degrees, still hovered around .11.

Explanations for Trends in Gender Segregation of Academic Majors

Young women's rising educational attainment, coupled with resilient gender inequality in the workplace, represents an anomaly to scholars. A primary cause of women's stalled advancement in the workplace despite their significant educational gains is that sex segregation within higher education continues to be a dominant feature of the American educational system. Research shows that career advancement and earnings depend not only on amount of education but also upon the academic major pursued during one's years of higher education. Furthermore, entrance into many scientific careers requires advanced credentials of a particular type that can only be obtained from appropriate degree-granting institutions. Thus, understanding the reasons underlying women's uneven progress into academic majors that can lead to elite occupations represents a critical step in understanding persistent gender inequality in careers.

Explaining Declines in Gender Segregation in Previously Male-Dominated Majors

As shown by trends of women's degree patterns since the mid-1970s, young women have made considerable progress in several previously male-dominated majors such as business, communications, and biology. What may account for the decline of sex segregation in these fields? Cohort change in young women's and men's occupational expectations and work values provides some clues. Research on early career goals of youth during the 1960s and 1970s revealed pronounced gender differences in occupational expectations that reflected sex-stereotypic roles within paid work. Among high school seniors in the 1970s, girls expected to work in service-oriented occupations such as teaching, nursing, and other social service occupations, whereas boys expected to work in more competitively oriented environments that involved entrepreneurial activity, small partnership, and corporate activity. However, recent work on the transition to adulthood suggests that gender differences in adolescent career goals have all but disappeared among contemporary cohorts. These shifts in young women's career goals away from traditionally female-dominated occupations such as teaching may have facilitated women's increased interest in academic majors such as business.

Historically, young men have valued paid employment more than young women. Yet since the 1980s, there has been significant convergence between young women and men in their prioritization of paid work. Recent studies indicate that young women and men are now equally likely to view careers as centrally important in their lives, and in some studies, girls are found to be even more likely than boys to value work as a central goal. In addition, past research found that young men tended to value the extrinsic rewards of work (e.g., income, power, and opportunities for advancement) more than young women. Among contemporary young adults however, women and men tend to evaluate the importance of extrinsic work rewards similarly. Furthermore, young women's valuation of extrinsic work rewards has increased more rapidly than young men's, which has contributed to the erosion of the gender gap in extrinsic work values. Young women's growing commitment to paid employment and interest in the pecuniary rewards associated with work may also explain their increasing propensity to pursue previously male-dominated academic majors, especially business.

While women have made considerable strides into business majors, men have not similarly moved into traditionally female areas of study such as education, health, and humanities. To date, scholarship on the gender segregation of academic majors has focused almost exclusively on women's progress (or lack thereof) into various college majors. Therefore, missing from this literature is an explanation for men's (relative) lack of involvement in traditionally female academic majors that tend to lead to service-oriented careers such as teaching, nursing, and social work. Though there is only a paucity of research on this topic, resilient differences in women's and men's work values may lend some clues. For example, though gender differences in valuation of extrinsic work rewards are subsiding among contemporary youth, men continue to place less emphasis on nonpecuniary aspects of work (such as social service) that have often attracted women to teaching and nursing careers.

Explaining Continuing Gender Segregation in STEM Programs

While sex segregation of academic majors has declined considerably since the 1970s, women's continued underrepresentation in STEM programs remains an example of persistent gender inequality in higher education in the twenty-first century. Women's lower access to these majors has garnered substantial scholarly, media, and political attention recently for two primary reasons. First, women's underrepresentation in STEM represents a significant loss of talent for science endeavors that fuel economic prosperity. Second, women's lower selections of math and physical science majors have sizeable implications for gender inequality in the workplace, since many lucrative occupations require advanced math and science credentials. Scholars offer a variety of explanations for women's lower interest in and attainment of math and science majors, including women's *lack of academic preparation, lower math self-efficacy, greater valuation of intrinsic work rewards*, and continued *valuation of family*.

Past research on women's underrepresentation in math and science college majors focused on gender differences in *academic preparation*, since advanced coursework in math and science during secondary school fosters success in science at the college level. Gender differences in math and science participation and achievement are few while students are in primary or junior high school. Among high school students, earlier cohorts of young women tended to be less likely to take advanced course work in math and science, but studies of contemporary high school students suggest that gender differences in the number and level of math and science courses taken during secondary school have eroded. However, the course-taking gender gap has shrunk more in math than in science. Therefore, young women's lower achievements in math, science, and engineering majors may stem in part from a lack of earlier educational preparation, especially in STEM fields, during secondary school.

Self-efficacy in math and science means that a person has feelings of capability and competence in those subjects. Students' self-efficacy in math and science promotes interest in future mathematical and scientific endeavors as well as persistence within those fields. Some evidence indicates that broad cultural beliefs about gender negatively affect young women's self-efficacy in math and science (Correll, 2001). Specifically, those cultural beliefs about gender that privilege men's competency in math and science over women's infuse young women's self-perceptions of their (in)ability to perform math and science tasks. Consequently, in order for young women to feel equally competent in math and science, their actual performance in these subjects may have to *exceed* men's performance. To the extent that contemporary young women continue to receive gendered messages about men's greater competency in math and science, women's lower self-efficacy in math and science may explain their lower achievements in math and science majors in college.

While gender differences in the valuation of extrinsic work rewards such as salaries and prestige may be subsiding, young women's and men's *valuation of the intrinsic rewards from work* remain notably different. Although young women's valuation of extrinsic rewards has increased, women continue to value intrinsic work rewards such as helping others and self-fulfillment. Young women's and men's different valuation of intrinsic work rewards may explain women's lower achievements in physical and computer science, math, and engineering majors. In contemporary studies of early-life orientations, girls tend to value compassion and purpose in life more than boys, whereas boys tend to value materialistic goals more. Young women may also have less interest in science majors because they have greater interest in helping others, working with people rather than things, and seeking intrinsic rather than extrinsic rewards from work, which are aspects of gendered behavior shaped by cultural norms. In fact, the gender gap within subfields of science tends to be smaller in science majors that are directly linked to helping others, such as premedicine and biology, which are common majors in the United States for those intending to pursue medicine or veterinary science at the postbaccalaureate level.

Women's advancement in certain academic majors may also be limited by their continued *valuation of family*, despite their rising educational achievements and career ambitions (Jacobs, 1995). Women's responsibility for family may continue to channel them into academic majors that lead to careers perceived to be better fits for balancing work and family. While young women's career goals have risen, women continue to value family more than men. Furthermore, contemporary young women expect more work and family conflict than do young men, and both young women and men anticipate resolving work/family conflict through women's career sacrifices. Therefore, young women may avoid academic majors leading toward careers that they perceive to be incompatible with balancing work and family demands.

Several ethnographic studies suggest that one reason women do not pursue or persist within math and science majors during college is due to their perception that scientific careers do not lend themselves to work and family balance (Seymour & Hewitt, 1997). However, other studies indicate that valuing family negatively affects women's science achievements, but gender differences in adolescents' valuation of family are not large enough to fully explain the gender gap in undergraduate and graduate science achievements (Xie & Shauman, 2003). Perhaps other causes, such as those mentioned above, combine with family valuation, as well as some gender-biased conditions of scientific training and work, to explain this persistent gender gap.

REFERENCES AND FURTHER READING
Correll, S. (2001). Gender and the career choice process: The role of biased self-assessments. *American Journal of Sociology, 106*(6), 1691–1730.

Jacobs, J. A. (1995). Gender and academic specialties: Trends among recipients of college degrees in the 1980s. *Sociology of Education, 68*(2), 81–98.

Johnson, M. K., Oesterle, S., & Mortimer, J. T. (2001). Adolescents' anticipations of work-family conflict in a changing societal context. In S. Hofferth & T. J. Owens (Eds.), *Children at the millennium: Where have we come from, where are we going?* (pp. 233–261). London: Elsevier Science.

Marini, M. M., Fan, P. L., Finley, E., & Beutel, A. M. (1996). Gender and job values. *Sociology of Education, 69*(1), 49–65.

National Center for Education Statistics. (1978). *Digest of Educational Statistics, 1977–78*. Washington, DC: U.S. Government Printing Office.

National Center for Education Statistics. (1993). *Digest of Education Statistics, 1993*. Washington, DC: U.S. Government Printing Office.

National Center for Education Statistics. (2007). *Digest of Education Statistics, 2007*. Washington, DC: U.S. Government Printing Office.

Seymour, E., & Hewitt, N. (1997). *Talking about leaving: Why undergraduates leave the sciences*. Boulder, CO: Westview Press.

Xie, Y., & Shauman, K. (2003). *Women in science: Career processes and outcomes*. Cambridge, MA: Harvard University Press.

CHAPTER 20

Biological and Physical Sciences

SUE V. ROSSER

The impact of women's studies and scholarship focused on gender has emerged more slowly and made fewer inroads in the natural and physical sciences than it has in the humanities and social sciences. Although women's health concerns became one of the forces motivating the women's movement in the 1960s, women scientists and engineers tended not to be heavily represented in the leadership of women's studies on most campuses. Nationally, directors of women's studies and much of the scholarship on women emerged initially from the humanities, followed by the social sciences, and only more recently from the biological and physical sciences.

Gender construction in the official curriculum of the biological and physical sciences has not been mainstreamed as widely or penetrated as deeply as it has in the humanities and social sciences. This may result from the relatively small number of women in science and engineering and even smaller number of women scientists involved with women's studies. Not until a substantial number of women populated the ranks of the faculty in humanities and social sciences did gender construction transform the mainstream curriculum.

Now, the research and its reflection in curricular content demonstrate an increase in the critiques of androcentric bias, topics studied, diversity of approaches used, and disciplinary and interdisciplinary background of the scholars and teachers. The pedagogical techniques exemplify increased attention to how gender construction in society as a whole can be reinforced or resisted in reaching students in the classroom.

Women in Science

The dearth of scientists in women's studies resulted partially from the very small number of tenure-track women faculty in senior positions in science, technology, engineering, and mathematics. Although 57.5% of BS degrees, 58% of MS degrees, and 43.8% of all Ph.D. degrees went to women in 2000, women comprise a smaller percentage of the degrees in the physical sciences, computer science, and engineering. For example, women received 40.3% of the BS degrees, 35.5% of the MS degrees, and 23.2% of the Ph.D. degrees in the physical sciences and only 20.4% of the BS degrees, 20.7% of the MS degrees, and 15.7% of the Ph.D. degrees in engineering in 2000 (Commission of Professionals in Science and Technology, 2002). Although women received

28% of the BS degrees, 33.3% of the MS degrees, and 16.5% of the Ph.D. degrees in computer science in 2000, a recent report reveals that only 0.3% of women first-year college students express an interest in majoring in computer science. This represents an 80% decline in interest between 1998 and 2004 (Foster, 2005).

The small number of women receiving degrees in the sciences and engineering results in an even smaller percentage of women faculty in these fields. Only 26.5% of science (including social and life sciences) and engineering faculty at four-year colleges and universities are women. The percentage of women in a particular discipline varies from relatively high percentages in psychology to much lower percentages in the physical sciences and engineering. Elite or research institutions (the Carnegie category Doctoral/Research—Extensive) have the smallest percentage of women faculty in the physical sciences and engineering.

Objectivity, Androcentric Bias, and Gendered Research in Science

In addition to the small number of women scientists and engineers, strong cultural traditions of masculinity and objectivity in science threatened to keep science studies separate from the theories of cultural and social construction of knowledge production acceptable in humanities and social sciences. Most researchers in the behavioral, biomedical, and physical sciences are trained in the scientific method and believe in its power. Few, however, are aware of its historical and philosophical roots in logical positivism and objectivity. Positivism is premised on the assumption that human beings are highly individualistic and obtain knowledge in a rational manner from immediate sensory experiences that may be separated from their social conditions. This leads to the belief in the possibilities of obtaining knowledge that is both objective and value free, the cornerstone of the scientific method.

Longino (1990) has explored the extent to which methods employed by scientists can be objective and lead to repeatable, verifiable results while contributing to hypotheses or theories that are congruent with nonobjective institutions and ideologies of the society. According to Longino, background assumptions are the means by which contextual values and ideology are incorporated into scientific inquiry. The institutions and beliefs of our society reflect the fact that the society is patriarchal. Even female scientists have only recently become aware of the influence of patriarchal bias in the paradigms of science.

A first step for feminist scientists was recognizing the possibility that androcentric bias would result from virtually all theoretical and decision-making positions in science being held by men. Not until a substantial number of women had entered the profession could this androcentrism be exposed. As long as only a few women were scientists, they had to demonstrate or conform to the male view of the world in order to be successful and have their research meet the criteria for "objectivity."

In the past two decades, feminist historians and philosophers of science, anthropologists, and feminist scientists have pointed out the bias and absence of value neutrality in science, particularly biology. By excluding females as experimental subjects, focusing on problems of primary interest to males, utilizing faulty experimental designs, and interpreting data based in language or ideas constricted by patriarchal parameters, scientists have introduced bias or flaws into their experimental results in several areas. These flaws and biases were permitted to become part of the mainstream of scientific thought and were perpetuated in the scientific literature for decades. Because most scientists were men, values held by them as males were not distinguished as biasing; rather they were congruent with the values of all scientists and thus became synonymous with the "objective" view of the world and the aspects of it studied.

The demonstration that contextual values, including gender, bias not only the scientific research of individuals but also what is accepted as valid science by the entire scientific community represents one of the major contributions that feminism has made to science. In her 1999 book *Has Feminism Changed Science?* Londa Schiebinger examined how the presence of women in traditionally male disciplines has altered scientific thinking and awareness, concluding that feminist perspectives have had little effect on mathematics and the physical sciences but more impact on biology, including medicine, archaeology, reproductive and evolutionary biology, and primatology.

A small number of women have worked in both women's studies and science to include gender in the science curriculum and science in the women's and gender studies curriculum. Now, most campuses boast women in science and engineering (WISE) programs for students; each year numerous conferences, journals, and anthologies focus on women and science, and the National Science Foundation and other federal agencies award multimillion-dollar grants to facilitate institutional transformation to advance and retain women in science and engineering.

Within the sciences, substantial differences exist between the biological sciences and the physical sciences in the extent to which gender construction has permeated the official curriculum. Some of these differences reflect differences between the number of women in biology and the number of women in the physical sciences.

An overarching theme emerging from studies underlines that the social usefulness of science and technology, especially to help human beings, attracts and retains women in science. One can see this appeal in the number of women in the biological sciences who undertake research centered on animals and, in many cases, human health. On a more abstract level, the connection between gender and biology and the impact of gender on biological research becomes evident. Given the high costs of sophisticated equipment, maintenance of laboratory animals and facilities, and salaries for qualified technicians and researchers, virtually no experimental research is undertaken today without governmental or foundational support. The choice of problems for study in research is substantially determined by a national agenda that defines what is worthy of study—that is, worth funding. The lack of diversity among congressional and scientific leaders may allow unintentional, undetected flaws to bias the research in terms of what we study and how we study it. Feminist critiques revealed the impact of distinct gender bias in choice and definition of health research problems.

Cardiovascular research became the poster child demonstrating the extent to which the data for the studies done only with male subjects could not be extrapolated to women. Cardiovascular diseases and AIDS stand as classic examples of diseases studied using a male-as-norm approach. Aspects of this approach included research designs that failed to assess gender differences in cardiovascular disease, case definitions that failed to include gynecologic conditions and other symptoms of AIDS in women until 1993, and exclusive use of males as research subjects in clinical trials.

Exclusion of women from clinical drug trials was so pervasive that a survey of clinical trials of medications used to treat acute myocardial infarction found that women were included in less than 20% and the elderly in less than 40% of those studies (Gurwitz, Nananda, & Avorn, 1992). Thus, individuals most likely to benefit from the medications were excluded in most trials. The Women's Health Initiative, established in

1990, seeks to fill these gender gaps in research and practice by collecting baseline data and determining interventions to prevent cardiovascular disease, breast and colorectal cancer, and osteoporosis.

Similarly, it was clear in the early primatology work that particular primate species, such as the baboon and chimpanzee, were chosen for study primarily because their social organization was seen by the observers as closely resembling that of human primates, where the male was dominant. Subsequent researchers forgot the obvious limitations imposed by such selection of species and proceeded to generalize the data to universal behavior patterns for all primates. It was not until a significant number of women entered primatology that the concepts of the universality and male leadership of dominance hierarchies among primates were questioned and shown to be inaccurate for many primate species, such as the bonobos.

The influence of gender in research in the physical sciences becomes less evident where the materials and bodies studied lack the sex and gender evident in animals. In *Gender and Boyle's Law of Gases*, published in 2001, Elizabeth Potter demonstrates that gender and other social conditions, such as his conservative political and religious beliefs, influenced Boyle's choice of the mechanistic, rather than animistic, model to explain his law of gases.

The choice of particular technologies to develop from basic research may also reflect male priorities. Male dominance in engineering and the creative decision-making sectors of the workforce may result in similar bias, particularly design and user bias. Shirley Malcom, director of education and human resources for the American Association for the Advancement of Science, suggested that the air bag fiasco suffered by the U.S. auto industry serves as an excellent example of gender bias reflected in design; this fiasco would have been much less likely had a woman engineer been on the design team. Since, on the average, women tend to be smaller than men, women on the design team might have recognized that a bag that implicitly used the larger male body as a norm would be flawed when applied to smaller individuals, killing rather than protecting children and small women.

Influences of Women's Studies Research and Theories on the Sciences Curriculum

In many ways, the gender construction in the official curriculum of biological and physical sciences mirrors the categories of scholarship in women's studies as a whole and the emerging development of the field. Recovery of lost texts and missing women characterize some of the earliest scholarship in the late 1960s and early 1970s as women's studies emerged as the academic arm of the women's movement with the establishment of the first programs in 1969–70. The search for where and why women were missing from all fields was a necessary first step in beginning to understand how their absence led to flaws, distortions, and biases in each discipline. History of women in science and their impact upon the different disciplines and subfields continues to be an active research area today. Work in the history of science has blossomed to include roles of institutions in general, particular types of institutions such as women's colleges, the national laboratories, outstanding women such as Nobel laureates, the lives of ordinary women scientists, as well as the reflection of gender in men's scientific theories.

Recognition that basic data on the number of women relative to men receiving degrees in science, mathematics, and engineering and on their employment status, rank, salary, and professional progress and attainments were crucial to women and science came early. After successful lobbying of Congress, the Science and Engineering Equal Opportunities Act of 1980 was passed. The National Science Foundation was required to collect data each year on the status of women and other underrepresented groups; in the 1990s the data collection included the rates of participation in science of persons with disabilities. Building on these foundational data, current scholars provide statistical documentation and analyses of more subtle factors and obstacles that now deter women.

The revelations from the data on number of women coupled with documentation of differential socialization and educational environments for women and men scientists led to questions about the impacts of these differences. Would women's differing interests, life experiences, and perspectives lead them to ask new questions, take different approaches, and find alternative interpretations leading to new theories and conclusions?

Just as women's studies scholars revealed that the assumption that male experience coincided with human experience constituted a form of androcentric bias that rendered women invisible and distorted many research results, these same scholars mistakenly assumed that the experience of all women was the same. Women of color, working-class women, and lesbians pointed out that their experiences as women and as scientists did not fit the depictions that emanated from a White, middle-class, heterosexual perspective. This revelation led to the recognition that gender did not represent a homogeneous category of analysis and that gender needed to be studied in relationship to other oppressions of race, class, nationalism, and sexual orientation.

Age or developmental stage becomes another aspect of diversity that can modify the experience of even the same woman throughout her life course. The comments of senior women scientists and engineers reveal the new, subtle forms of gender discrimination and discounting they encounter, after successfully overcoming barriers to establishing their career and balancing it with family responsibilities.

The past 20 years underline the influence of globalization and the significance of understanding international perspectives and movements. Much in the same way that, early on, in its eagerness to discover the influence of gender, women's studies suffered from the failure to recognize diversity among women, scholars now acknowledge the constraints of not understanding the experiences of women in different countries and cultural contexts.

Although enrollment of foreign graduate students in science and engineering increased by 35% from 1994 to 2001, it peaked in 2001 when 41% of doctorates awarded in the United States went to non-U.S. citizens. Although nearly 30% of the actively employed science and engineering doctorate holders in the United States are foreign born, as are many postdocs (National Science Board, 2004), very little research has focused on immigrant women scientists. One study (Xie & Shauman, 2003) found that immigrant women are only 32% as likely as immigrant men scientists and engineers to be promoted, partly because the women tend to immigrate for their husband's career.

Some of the junior women scientists and engineers interviewed as part of another study (Rosser, 2004) comment explicitly on their experience of becoming established in the United States after immigration and compare the status of scientists in their country of origin with that of U.S. scientists. Only a few of these women provide insights that shed light on how the experiences of immigrant women scientists differ from those of their U.S.-born colleagues.

As women's studies entered a stage that focused on the analysis of gender as a so-cial category, critics began to question the ways in which gender determines the struc-ture of social organizations, systems of cultural production, and the roles and defini-tions of masculinity and femininity. One of the greatest contributions of women's studies in all fields has been to broaden the definitions, language, and categories of knowledge. Scholars explored how the scientific hierarchy, including the language and metaphors of scientific theories and descriptions used, both reflected and reinforced gender roles. They uncovered the historical roots of modern science in a mechanistic model in which objectivity became synonymous with masculinity and that encour-aged the domination of male scientists over women, nature, and organic models of the world.

Similarly, for many years, women's health was synonymous with obstetrics and gynecology. Not only did this define women in terms of reproduction, leaving out huge chunks of the life span, it also reinforced the male-as-norm approach to the rest of disease. Looking at all of health and disease and all of the body as part of women's health stands as a critical contribution to the women's health movement. When viewed from women's perspectives, new issues enter the definition of "health" issues. For ex-ample, domestic violence is now considered a major health issue.

Women's studies, science, and medicine all suffer when theories and research be-come too disconnected from the daily lives of people, particularly women. Women's studies is currently in a phase of recognizing the significance of rejoining theory and practice; it places emphasis upon refocusing on the personal experiences and daily lives of women.

Many women scientists and engineers, while appreciating the issues raised about objectivity, questioned the translation of "high theory" into the practice of science and the relevance of such theories in their own lives as scientists, where they still en-counter substantial discrimination. The science wars that developed from postmodern theories and increasing globalization drew attention to the necessity for the refusion of theory and practice. For many women teaching and practicing science, this dichotomy between theory and practice appeared to be a false separation. Grounded in laboratory practice, the fusion of theory and practice in science classrooms and laboratories has a long tradition.

Further evidence of the fusion of theory with practice comes from a current focus of feminist science studies on the personal experiences and daily lives of women scientists. These studies also reflect interdisciplinary approaches in their use of post-colonial theories, oral histories, and ethnographies as theoretical and methodological approaches to science studies.

Rosser (1997) suggests 20 pedagogical techniques developed by feminists and women's studies faculty that could be more widely employed in science classrooms:

1. Expand the kinds of observations beyond those traditionally carried out in scien-tific research. Women students may see new data that could make a valuable con-tribution to scientific experiments.
2. Increase the number of observations and remain longer in the observational stage of the scientific method. This would provide more hands-on experience with vari-ous types of equipment in the laboratory.
3. Incorporate and validate personal experiences women are likely to have had as part of the class discussion or the laboratory exercise.

4. Undertake fewer experiments likely to have applications of direct benefit to the military.
5. Propose more experiments to explore problems of social concern.
6. Consider problems that have not been considered worthy of scientific investigation because of the field with which the problems traditionally have been associated.
7. Formulate hypotheses focusing on gender as a crucial part of the question asked.
8. Undertake the investigation of problems of a more holistic, global scope rather than the more reduced and limited-scale problems traditionally considered.
9. Use a combination of qualitative and quantitative methods in data gathering.
10. Use methods from a variety of fields or interdisciplinary approaches to problem solving.
11. Include females as experimental subject in experimental designs.
12. Use more interactive methods, thereby shortening the distance between the observer and the object studied.
13. Decrease laboratory exercises in introductory courses in which students kill animals or render treatment that may be perceived as particularly harsh.
14. Use precise, gender-neutral language in describing data and presenting theories.
15. Be open to critiques of conclusions and theories drawn from observations differing from those drawn by the traditional male scientist from the same observations.
16. Encourage uncovering of other biases such as those of race, class, sexual orientation, and religious affiliation that may permeate theories and conclusions drawn from experimental observation.
17. Use less competitive models to practice science.
18. Discuss the role of scientist as only one facet that must be smoothly integrated with other aspects of students' lives.
19. Put increased effort into strategies such as teaching and communicating with nonscientists to break down barriers between science and the layperson.
20. Discuss the practical uses to which scientific discoveries are put to help students see science in its social context.

Like specific pedagogical techniques, the broader models for phases of curricular transformation developed by women's studies scholars for other disciplines have been modified for the sciences (Rosser, 1997):

Stage 1. The absence of women is not noted. This is the traditional approach of the curriculum, in which the perspective of the White, Eurocentric, middle- to upper-class male is considered the norm and the absence of others is not noted.
Stage 2. Women are added onto existing science curriculum, structures, and design, without changing or attempting to accommodate them to fit women's interests and needs.
Stage 3. Women's concerns and approaches are seen as a problem, anomaly, or deviant from the norms of science, as barriers that prevent women from entering science are identified.
Stage 4. The focus is on women as workers, users, and scientists and on developing curricula that will attract them to the field.
Stage 5. Science is redefined and reconstructed to include all.

Although few would argue that stage 5 has been fully achieved, there is little doubt that the curriculum in the biological and physical sciences is less androcentric, more female friendly, and generally more inclusive than ever before.

REFERENCES AND FURTHER READING

Commission of Professionals in Science and Technology. (2002). *Professional women and minorities* (14th ed.). Washington, DC: Author.

Foster, A. (2005). Student interest in computer science plummets. *Chronicle of Higher Education, 51*(38), p. A-31.

Gurwitz, J. H., Nananda, F. C., & Avorn, J. (1992). The exclusion of the elderly and women from clinical trials in acute myocardial infarction. *Journal of the American Medical Association, 268*(2), 1417–1422.

Longino, H. (1990). *Science as social knowledge: Values and objectivity in scientific inquiry*. Princeton, NJ: Princeton University Press.

National Science Board. (2004). *Science and engineering indicators—2004*. Arlington, VA: Author.

Potter, E. (2001). *Gender and Boyle's law of gases*. Bloomington: Indiana University Press.

Rosser, S. V. (1997). *Re-engineering female friendly science*. New York: Teacher's College Press.

Rosser, S. V. (2004). *The science glass ceiling: Academic women scientists and the struggle to succeed*. New York: Routledge.

Schiebinger, L. (1999). *Has feminism changed science?* Cambridge, MA: Harvard University Press.

Xie, Y., & Shauman, K. (2003). *Women in science: Career processes and outcomes*. Boston: Harvard University Press.

CHAPTER 21

Black Studies and Black Women's Studies

MAULANA KARENGA

The intellectual roots and data sources of Black studies, in a general sense, reach back in history to societies like ancient Egypt, Mali, and Songhay, which had institutions of higher learning, established an intellectual tradition of study of themselves and the surrounding world, and left a rich and varied body of documents for critical examination. However, Black studies, as a self-defined and organized discipline in the modern university, has its origin in the social and academic struggles of the 1960s. Indeed, the defining process for the emergence of Black studies is the Black Freedom Movement in both its civil rights and Black power phases. The critical issues of freedom, justice, equality, power, political and cultural self-determination, educational relevance, community service, and social engagement are all found in the fundamental and formative concerns that shape the early and continuing self-conception of Black studies.

These focal concerns are, of necessity, framed by overarching and pervasive concepts of race, class, and gender and the disciplinary imperative to engage these constraints on human freedom and human flourishing both intellectually and socially. Thus, Black studies develops a self-understanding as both a site of critical intellectual study, production, and transmission and an agency and instrument of social change in the interest of African and human good. It self-consciously builds on an activist-intellectual tradition evident in African culture as early as ancient Egypt and continuing through the nineteenth and twentieth centuries as expressed in the work and activities of activist-intellectuals such as Anna Julia Cooper, W. E. B. Du Bois, Carter G. Woodson, Ida B. Wells, Mary McLeod Bethune, Ella Baker, Malcolm X, and Martin Luther King Jr. The paradigm that evolves here is one of acquisition and use of knowledge and skills to address critical social issues in the interest and service of community, society, and the world. That Black studies was conceived and constructed in the midst and interest of the Black Freedom Movement clearly influenced its reaffirmation of this activist-intellectual tradition and drew it inevitably not only toward confronting the race, class, and gender issues in society and the academy but also eventually toward a critical self-questioning and confrontation with these issues within the Black community and within the discipline itself, especially issues of gender.

Pan-African in scope, the discipline began with the fundamental assumption that the Black initiative and experience in the world represented a special cultural truth worth studying and knowing and that it offered a rich source of paradigms of human excellence and achievement and thus for understanding humanity in its varied and various ways. Moreover, Black studies understood itself, along with other ethnic studies, as a necessary corrective for the existing monocultural curriculum and focus in the academy and argued that quality education, by definition, was a culturally pluralistic or multicultural education.

Finally, Black studies also understood itself as an emancipatory project in an intellectual and social sense. It thus linked intellectual emancipation with social liberation and knowledge acquisition with the obligation of service and social action. And it embraced the concept and imperative of mutually beneficial relations between campus and community as put forth by Nathan Hare, architect of the first Black studies program.

In the course of its development, Black studies has demonstrated its capacity to broaden its core of original concerns and includes in its core curriculum areas vital to its self-understanding and continued development in the face of new demands and challenges in the academy and society. In the midst of its critical and persistent search for truth and meaning in history and society from an African vantage point, it poses the African initiative and experience as a rich resource for critical intellectual study. Moreover, it offers a rigorous intellectual challenge and alternative to established-order ways of understanding and engaging social human reality. And as an emancipatory educational and social project, it self-consciously offers an African contribution to understanding and approaching the world and to multicultural efforts to initiate polices and practices that constantly expand the realm of human freedom and human flourishing. Within this overarching framework, Black studies conceived and structured its mission around three disciplinary pillars: cultural grounding, academic excellence, and social responsibility.

Cultural Grounding

From its inception, Black studies saw African culture—continental and diasporan, ancient and modern—as the foundation and framework for its intellectual, pedagogical, and social practice. Discussion of the centrality of culture evolved in the discipline first around the early call for a Black frame of reference advanced in Kawaida philosophy, a theory of social and cultural change developed in the 1960s by Maulana Karenga. Afterward, it appears in discourse around the theory of Afrocentricity developed by its founding theorist Molefi Asante in the late 1970s and early 1980s. For Kawaida and Asante, Afrocentricity, or African-centeredness, is a methodology and orientation that places Africans at the center of their own culture, treats them as active subjects rather than passive objects of history, and engages African ideals and ways of being human in the world as the fundamental point of departure for intellectual production in the discipline. Contrasted to this is the Eurocentric approach, in which European culture is the fundamental source for ideas and research agendas. The African-centered vision critically defined requires that Black studies root itself in African culture as a dynamic and varied and living practice and constantly dialog with it, asking it questions and seeking from it answers to the fundamental concerns of humankind, and from this ongoing process continuously bringing forth the best of what it means to be African and human in the world.

Academic Excellence

The emphasis on academic excellence develops in the context of establishing both the value and durability of the discipline and Black studies scholars' own commitments to the highest level of teaching and intellectual production. Concern was also directed toward a similar deep intellectual grounding for Black studies students who had initiated the struggle for Black studies and had put forth as one of their priorities the demand for a relevant education. A relevant education for Black studies scholars and advocates meant one that was meaningful, useful, and reflective of the social realities of society and the world. Thus an early stress of the discipline was on social service, service learning, and political involvement as component parts of the Black studies project.

Social Responsibility

The emphasis on social responsibility evolves out of both the ancient and ongoing African activist-intellectual tradition and the origin of Black studies in the midst of the Black Freedom Movement and the social and academic struggles that defined this process. The emancipatory role assigned to education, as key to intellectual and social liberation within this tradition of activist scholarship, calls into being a process of critique and corrective of domination in its various forms. This critique and corrective are parallel and complementary processes in Black studies and rooted in the ancient African understanding that poses knowledge not simply as a personal possession or pursuit but also as a social good to be shared and used to improve the human present and enhance the human prospect.

The Emergence of Black Women's Studies

As Black studies continued to develop, it underwent the ongoing critical self-questioning associated with growth and expansion. It thus began to expand its curriculum to continuously include additional areas of studies deemed essential to its mission. The additions included Black women's studies, classical African studies (especially of ancient Egypt), Afrocentric theoretical and philosophical studies, popular cultural studies, expanded offerings of ethics, and various forms and kinds of diaspora studies. Among these additional fields of focus, Black women's studies stands out as one of the most invigorating and expansive. This was so not only because of the generative discourse and debates that occurred around its essentiality even indispensability to the discipline but also because of the valuable scholarship that evolved within this vital area and from its exchange with other fields of focus.

The history of the emergence of Black women's studies as a vital component part of Black studies is informed and shaped by several factors. The first factor, as mentioned above, is the ongoing self-questioning of the discipline itself as it develops and seeks to constantly expand and meet the internal and external challenges related to its mission. Within this general developmental self-questioning was the specific concern about the core conception of the discipline itself as an emancipatory project and how its structure and functioning expressed this commitment. Black studies had come into being denouncing all inequalities, injustices, and constraints on human freedom and flourishing. It now discovered it had to confront the contradiction of having a male-privileging curriculum and often a similar faculty hiring practice, although it understood itself as an emancipatory educational and social project.

The contradiction, however, is brought to the forefront in a strong and sustained way by the intellectual and practical struggles waged by Black women within the discipline itself, and these struggles form the second factor shaping the emergence of Black women's studies. These Black studies scholars and advocates struggled to create and sustain space for teaching and research in Black women's studies and to establish it as an indispensable component part of Black studies. Not only did they challenge male-centered interpretations of African and human reality and the relationships that such interpretations created, they also produced and posed alternative visions. Among some of the early works in the 1970s that raised important Black women's studies issues are Toni Cade's *The Black Woman*, Joyce Ladner's *Tomorrow's Tomorrow*, Inez Smith-Reid's *"Together" Black Women*, Mary Helen Washington's *Black-Eyed Susans*, Sharon Hurley and Rosalyn Terborg-Penn's *The Afro-American Woman: Struggles and Images*, and Roseann P. Bell, Bettye J. Parker, and Beverly Guy-Sheftall's study *Black Bridges: Visions of Black Women in Literature*. These works raised critical issues of race, gender, and class and called for correctives.

In the 1980s and 1990s, early Black women's studies literature was built on and expanded in various fields, especially in literature. Among the most notable are LaFrancis Rodgers-Rose's *The Black Woman*; Gloria Hull, Patricia Bell-Scott and Barbara Smith's *All the Women Are White, All the Blacks Are Men, but Some of Us Are Brave*; Paula Giddings's *When and Where I Enter: The Impact of Black Women on Race and Sex in America*; Vivian Gordon's *Black Women, Feminism, and Black Liberation*; Delores Aldridge's *Black Male-Female Relationships*; bell hooks's many books, including *Talking Back: Thinking Feminist, Thinking Black*; Darlene Clark Hine's multivolume *Black Women in American History*; Patricia Hill Collins's *Black Feminist Thought*; Clenora Hudson-Weems's *Africana Womanism: Reclaiming Ourselves*; Niara Sudarkasa's *The Strength of Our Mothers: African and African American Women and Families*; and Rosalyn Terborg-Penn and Andrea Benton Rushing's *Women in Africa and the African Diaspora*. These early writings laid the basis for a continuously expansive literature and discourse.

A third factor shaping the emergence of Black women's studies was the key role Black women played in building and developing the two major professional organizations of the discipline, the African Heritage Studies Association (AHSA) and the National Council for Black Studies (NCBS). Black women scholars were in the vanguard of the move for self-determination and self-definition in the discipline and collaborated in both the intellectual and practical founding of AHSA in 1968. Since then, they have played a fundamental role in its maintenance, development, and leadership. Some of the important pioneers in this process are Shelby Lewis, Barbara Wheeler, Barbara Sizemore, Charshee McIntyre, Nancy Cortez, and Inez Smith-Reid.

Likewise, the founding of NCBS was due in great part to the conceptual and organizational initiative of Bertha Maxwell Roddy, who issued the call for the founding of NCBS. Black scholars around the country joined her at the University of North Carolina, Charlotte, in 1975 to engage in dialog on critical issues in Black studies. From this initiative, she created interest in building NCBS and, along with other women, played a central role in its conception, formation, and development and served as its first chair. These women played leadership roles not only in the founding and development of NCBS and AHSA but also in the definition and development of the discipline itself. Among the most noted, in addition to Maxwell Roddy, are Delores Aldridge and Carlene Young who, along with women leaders in AHSA, have continuously advanced women's intellectual and social issues in both Black studies discourse and organizational practice. Through this process, they have not only enriched Black studies discourse but also expanded the discipline itself.

Another factor operative in the shaping of the emergence of Black women's studies is the development of creative tension between Black womanists and feminists and

White feminists and between Black studies and women's studies. Black studies had always understood the discipline as composed of studies of Black men and women, male and female, family and community. Thus it resisted efforts to place Black women's studies in women's studies programs for several reasons. First, it was seen as compromising the integrity of the discipline, dividing and separating its component parts and locating them in different areas of study and administration. Second, it was argued that this violated departmental and discipline autonomy and self-determination and represented White racial disregard for these academic and political principles. It was also seen as a contradiction to White women's claiming the importance of women's self-determination and then denying self-determination to Black women and other women of color. Third, it was contended that Black women are a central subject in Black studies and only a topic in White women's studies, for there the central theories, concepts, figures, and focus are rooted in White culture. Finally, it was argued that, although there were commonalities among various kinds of women, there were also basic differences that required, as a matter of self-determination, that each group of women speak with their own voice in the context of their own community.

Tensions also revolved around issues of differing emphases on race and gender and calls by Black womanists and feminists for White feminists to recognize the race and class nature of their own feminism and the privileged position of White women in the White patriarchy, which worked to Black women's and Black people's disadvantage.

A fifth factor that aided in shaping the development of Black women's studies is the critical revisiting of the unequal male/female relations in the Black Freedom Movement and the resultant critique of sexism in its philosophy and practice. This criticism became a central and expanded discourse with a persistent demand for inclusion and the end of inequality in participation, power, and representation in the discipline and social relations. In this continuing process, there are also genuine efforts by many male scholars to be self-critical and self-corrective and a developing literature on ethical and mutually beneficial bases for improving the quality of male/female relations and representation in the discipline and society.

Womanism

Within the ongoing growth and expansion of the discipline of Black studies, Black women's studies has continued to develop and define itself through its intellectual and professional initiatives and the discourse created around these. Especially significant is the development of an expanding literature and discourse of womanism. Womanism, like feminism, has many forms, reflecting both the sociohistorical and cultural contexts in which it evolves and the various thinkers and groups who constructed and advanced it as an intellectual and political project. Moreover, the major forms evidence within them variations by different thinkers. This reflects the fact that there is an open-textured and unfinished character to the project, involving not only constant internal self-interrogation but also ongoing critique of and correctives for the established order of things.

The history of womanism is also a much-discussed issue. It is placed in its ancient origins in the sociohistorical and cultural context of ancient Africa and in its modern origins in the early struggles of African women and people against external domination (i.e., imperialism, colonialism, and the holocaust of enslavement). Thus, although the term "womanism" was coined in the early 1980s, some of its fundamental concepts, especially in Africana, African feminist, Afrocentric, and Kawaida womanism, are rooted in ancient African values such as the shared dignity of human beings, male and female; complementarity of the sexes with the Cooperian stress on equality and mutual respect; male/female partnership in healing, repairing, and reconstructing the world; cultural grounding; community commitment; and moral and social agency.

Womanism as a modern intellectual and political initiative evolved in the midst of social struggle and attendant discourse and discussion within the Black Freedom Movement and the Black Studies Movement and between Black and White women over common and differing issues and concerns and the need to have a voice and vision authentically African. In this regard, it reflects both conflict and confluence with Black and White feminist thought and practice. Thus African American feminism or continental African feminism, while staking out space for an authentic and independent Black voice, nevertheless uses feminism and feminists to define their project. Africana womanists like Clenora Hudson-Weems and Kawaida womanists like Tiamoyo Karenga and Chimbuko Tembo argue, however, that authenticity of voice and vision requires cultural grounding, that feminism and feminists are culturally and historically specific to White women's experience, and that Africana womanism is the correct and most useful term for Black women's emancipatory project. African feminist womanists, like Oyeronke Oyewumi, also reject the use of feminism as a historically and culturally specific global political project growing out of White women's experience and as possibly imperialist. However, Oyewumi sees the category feminist as transhistorical and indicative of female agency and self-determination, both deeply rooted in traditional African culture. Beverly Guy-Sheftall embraces both womanism and feminism as categories to define her stance, using them interchangeably.

Given these considerations, forms of womanist and feminist discourse, while distinct, often overlap and interrelate. Thus, even in articles or books designated Black or African feminist, the issues addressed and the methodology used to engage them will often reflect a womanist approach and understanding, a self-consciously and distinct Africana women's voice and vision.

REFERENCES AND FURTHER READING

Aldridge, D., & Young, C. (Eds.). (2000). *Out of the revolution: The development of Africana studies*. New York: Lexington Books.

Asante, M. (1998). *The Afrocentric idea* (Rev. ed.). Philadelphia: Temple University Press.

Asante, M., & Karenga, M. (Eds.). (2006). *Handbook of Black studies*. Thousand Oaks, CA: Sage.

Du Bois, W. E. B. (1973). The field and function of the Negro college. In H. Aptheker (Ed.), *W. E. B. Du Bois: The education of Black people: Ten critiques, 1906–1960* (pp. 83–102). New York: Monthly Review Press. (Original work published 1933)

Hare, N. (1969). What should be the role of Afro-American education in the undergraduate curriculum? *Liberal Education, 55*(March), 42–50.

Hudson-Weems, C. (1993). *Africana womanism: Reclaiming ourselves*. Troy, MI: Bedford.

Karenga, M. (2002). *Introduction to Black studies* (3rd ed.). Los Angeles: University of Sankore Press.

Marable, M. (2000). *Dispatches from the ebony tower: Intellectuals confront the African American experience*. New York: Columbia University Press.

Mazama, A. (2002). *The Afrocentric paradigm*. Trenton, NJ, and Asmara, Eritrea: Africa World Press.

Stewart, J. (2004). *Flight in search of vision*. Trenton, NJ, and Asmara, Eritrea: Africa World Press.

CHAPTER 22

Engineering

SUSAN STAFFIN METZ

> One's creativity is bounded by one's life experiences. By failing to attract a
> diverse engineering work force, we diminish what engineering can contribute
> to society and society pays an opportunity cost . . . in designs not thought of . . .
> in solutions not produced.
>
> William A. Wulf, former president, National Academy of Engineering

Women continue to be underrepresented in engineering education and professional
practice despite over 30 years of research, programming, government reports, and discussion across all sectors. Why do women opt out of engineering? Extensive research
indicates that many factors dissuade women from engineering. These factors include
a lack of awareness and understanding of what engineers do; the isolating social and
academic climate that is prevalent in many engineering schools; the lockstep, rigid
curriculum that requires early commitment often to the exclusion of other interests;
and the perception of the difficulty of balancing a career and family. However, the persistent stereotypes and pervasive lack of knowledge about engineering deter women
from even considering the field as a career choice.

It is critical that the United States cultivate the scientific and technical talents of
all its citizens, not just of those who have traditionally worked in science, technology,
engineering, and mathematics (STEM) fields. Women and minorities are entering the
U.S. workforce at an unprecedented rate, and demographics indicate that this trend
will escalate. It is incumbent on the engineering profession and those who care about
solving the challenges of our world to attract capable students from all demographic
groups to the study and practice of engineering and increase the engineering literacy
of all Americans. This cannot happen if parents, educators, and students do not possess a full understanding of the field and its contributions. Research indicates that this
is not yet the case and that there is considerable work to be done if women and other
underrepresented groups are to become more engaged in the engineering enterprise.

Understanding Engineering

In 2003, the American Association of Engineering Societies (AAES) commissioned
a Harris poll to determine the public understanding of and attitudes toward engineering and engineers. According to the poll, 66% of Americans feel they are "not very or

not at all well informed about engineering and engineers." Women were less interested in engineering than men, with only 28% indicating they were "very or somewhat" interested, compared with 53% of men (AAES/Harris Poll Interactive, 2004).

Recently, Harris Interactive fielded an online youth survey for the American Society for Quality (2009). The survey found that boys are more likely than girls to say they are interested in an engineering career and boys are more encouraged by their parents to think about an engineering career. In addition, the survey results indicated three major reasons all students ages 8–17 may not be interested in engineering: (1) a lack of knowledge about engineering; (2) a preference for a more exciting career than engineering; and (3) a lack of confidence that they will succeed in engineering because of their math or science skills.

What Attracts Women to Engineering?

Changing the Conversation, a study conducted by the National Academy of Engineering (2008), selected and tested messages that were likely to improve the public understanding and appeal of engineering with male and female teens and adults. The first and second choices of messages chosen by boys were "Engineers make a world of difference" and "Engineers are creative problem solvers." Girls also rated "Engineers make a world of difference" first, but their second choice was "Engineering is essential to our health, happiness and safety." Interestingly, African American girls who were 16 and 17 and Hispanic girls in all age groups tested found this second message significantly more appealing than teenage boys.

Changing the Conversation also contends that current messages tend to ignore the more inspiring aspects of engineering such as creativity, teamwork, and communication and instead emphasizes the need for superior mathematics and science skills. For girls, it is critical to highlight specific examples of how engineering affects the world rather than dwelling on the need to develop technical skills. Students who choose to be doctors do so to save lives, not to master anatomy and organic chemistry. Engineers must stop emphasizing the need to excel in math and science and instead talk about their ability to improve the quality of life for people around the globe.

Another study conducted by the WGBH Educational Foundation (2005) to understand what attracts high school women to engineering generated the following results:

- High school girls believe that engineering is for people who love math and science. They don't have an understanding of engineering, show an interest in it, or think it is for them. They perceive engineering as a profession for men.
- Engineering study is portrayed as very challenging, requiring superior math and science skills. Messages do not include benefits and rewards of being an engineer.
- Professional interests for girls hinge on relevance—the job is rewarding and the profession is for someone "like me."
- Career motivators for high school girls include enjoying their job, having a favorable work environment, making a difference, earning a good salary, and having flexibility in their schedule.
- High school girls react positively to personal and informational stories.

In the Women's Experiences in College Engineering (WECE) project, involving over 20,000 undergraduate women at 53 institutions, the vast majority of students knew they were going to be engineering majors before they entered college, primarily because of parental encouragement (Goodman, Cunningham, & Lachapelle, 2002).

Without the benefit of parental encouragement, students need to depend on other sources of information that are often unreliable and laced with traditional stereotypes and misperceptions. This research also found that attraction to the kind of work female students think engineers do such as helping society solve problems, building and designing, improving the environment, and exploring outer space draws women to engineering.

Significant similarities and differences between male and female perceptions of engineering are illustrated in Anderson and Gilbride's (2005) study of 2,500 Canadian high school students. They found that males and females acknowledge that engineering heavily involves mathematics and the use of machinery. In fact females ranked "uses lots of machinery" as their second overall statement to describe engineering, compared with males, who ranked that statement fourth. This perception may discourage women from pursuing engineering, since they have been traditionally discouraged from jobs that involve heavy machinery or manual labor.

Margolis's and Fisher's book *Unlocking the Clubhouse* (2002) further illuminates the differences between a young man's and a young woman's decision to pursue a career in technology. "Computing with a purpose," the concept of using the computer as a tool to enable processes and solutions that have an impact on human and social contexts, makes the study of computer science compelling and meaningful to women. However, when male and female students were asked to provide descriptions of the typical computer science student, about 50% of all respondents said that the image of the computer science student "is not me." Gender differences are telling, with 69% of female and 32% of male computer science majors viewing themselves as different from most of their peers whose lives do not revolve around the computer. In fact, nearly two-thirds of the women question whether they belong in computer science because they do not identify with the typical male computer science student.

This raises an interesting issue. Who are the students who do belong in the technical professions? If we buy into the stereotypes—which include White or Asian male, excels in and loves math and science, and prefers machines to people—we severely limit the type of students who can see themselves succeeding in engineering. Expanding the perception of engineers and engineering is imperative if we want to attract a diverse and talented pool of individuals, thereby enriching the engineering field.

Girls Are Prepared to Study Engineering

Although many female high school students are prepared to pursue an engineering degree, most simply choose not to. They have taken the upper-level math and science classes necessary to major in engineering in college. In terms of standardized tests, very little difference exists between genders in performance. The average score for 17-year-old girls on the National Assessment of Educational Progress in 2004 was 305, compared with 308 for boys. Standardized Achievement Test scores in mathematics continue to show only a slight gap in scores between genders. Overall, females and males are equally prepared upon graduating high school to enter a college engineering program (Commission on Professionals in Science and Technology, 2009).

Interest in engineering and other fields can be assessed by reviewing data from Preliminary Standardized Achievement Tests (PSAT), which ask students to indicate their intended college major. As students progress through high school and beyond, the number of engineering-interested students falls significantly below the number of engineering-ready students. Among 1.5 million high school juniors taking the PSAT in

2008, only 8% indicated that they planned to major in engineering. The strongest intended major among males was engineering (15.2%), while females most frequently indicated an interest in the health professions and sciences (25.1%) (Commission on Professionals, 2009).

Furthermore, while the number of males enrolling in engineering has declined since 2003, women have experienced a steady decline in engineering since 2001, and the percentage drop has been even greater. During this period, total enrollment for women in four-year engineering schools in the United States fell from 78,468 in 2001 to 69,869 in 2006. Consequently, in 2006 women were a mere 17.2% of the students enrolled in undergraduate engineering programs. The decline of women in college engineering programs is especially alarming in light of the fact that in 2005 women earned 58% of all bachelor's degrees, nearly half of all degrees in law (48%) and medicine (46%), 41% of the masters in business administration, and 36% of Ph.D.'s in natural science but only 18.2% of the doctorates in engineering. Breaking down the engineering degrees by field, it is interesting to note how unevenly distributed women are in different engineering disciplines. For instance, in 2006, women received nearly 42% of the bachelor's degrees in biomedical engineering, 36.2% of the bachelor's degrees in chemical engineering, and 32.1% of the bachelor's degrees in industrial engineering. Disciplines in which women are in short supply are mechanical and computer engineering, each at a level of 13.3%, and electrical engineering, at 14.2% women. Interestingly, the two largest disciplines, mechanical and electrical engineering, are fields that attract extremely low percentages of women.

Women of different racial and ethnic backgrounds are also unevenly distributed among 2006 undergraduate engineering degree recipients. Review of male and female students within specific racial and ethnic groups shows that African American women received the highest percentage of bachelor's degrees (32%) in engineering within the African American community, followed by Asian American women (24.7%), Hispanic women (23.3%) and White women (16.8%) (Commission on Professionals, 2009).

Engagement Is Critical

How do we engage students, particularly women and minorities in the United States, in the engineering enterprise? A recent study by Jolly, Campbell & Perlman (2004) proposes the following trilogy of closely entwined characteristics that are necessary for students to advance in the sciences and quantitative fields. The trilogy includes

- *Engagement*: an orientation to the sciences or quantitative disciplines demonstrated by awareness, interest, and motivation
- *Capacity*: the knowledge and skills needed to advance to increasingly complex content in the sciences and quantitative disciplines
- *Continuity*: access to institutional and programmatic opportunities, material resources, and guidance that support advancement to increasingly complex content in the sciences and quantitative disciplines

While the level of each characteristic may vary, the presence of all three characteristics is necessary to successfully pursue an engineering career. If engagement is missing, there is no desire to develop understanding. If capacity is lacking, there are no basic skills on which to build knowledge and interest. If there is no continuity, students are unable to apply the knowledge learned (Jolly, Campbell, & Perlman, 2004).

The engagement, capacity, and continuity model offers sound insight regarding the underrepresentation of women in engineering. While it remains important to improve continuity and capacity for all students, engagement is the key to getting more females involved in engineering. Continuity has increased as a result of Title IX, which provides for equal opportunities in school for young men and young women, at least for predominately White upper- and middle-class students. As mentioned previously, capacity in mathematics is very similar and is improving for both male and female students in this demographic group. Girls graduate from high school with skills and knowledge equivalent to those of their male peers, but substantially fewer girls continue in engineering and science, which suggests distinct differences in engagement between boys and girls.

If Women Enroll in Engineering, Will They Stay?

Imagine that a publicity campaign for the field of engineering has been so successful that Americans are fully informed and well versed in the practices of engineers. Equal numbers of women and men are driven to major in engineering to contribute to a world with significant challenges relating to health care, security, environment, energy, infrastructure, knowledge management, and more. They are eagerly anticipating the start of their freshmen year in one of many outstanding engineering schools in the United States.

If this scenario ever becomes a reality, the engineering community will need to focus on how to retain these academically talented students who are motivated by factors that may be considerably different than those that historically drew students to engineering. Are engineering schools willing and able to deliver a curriculum that incorporates contemporary motivational factors and relinquishes some of the traditional but arguably less necessary fundamentals? Are engineering schools willing to assess their academic and social climate and implement policies and practices that facilitate success for all students?

Many female students who switch out of engineering cite school climate factors that contribute to feelings of isolation, low self-confidence, and a lack of connection to the department as a reason for leaving (Goodman, Cunningham, & Lachapelle, 2002). Losing interest and attraction to another field are also key factors for women who leave engineering. Some engineering schools have conducted climate assessments through surveys, interviews, and focus groups to understand the experience of their engineering students in order to identify policies and programs that could improve the experience. This exercise is an important step to create a more productive academic and social environment for all engineering students (Project to Assess Climate in Engineering, 2009).

In 2000, the Accreditation Board for Engineering and Technology laid the framework for a potentially more innovative curriculum with more latitude by focusing on student outcomes instead of required courses. Many engineering schools are making their curriculum more appealing by

- integrating engineering design courses in freshmen and sophomore years
- including teamwork experiences in courses
- offering opportunities for undergraduates to do research with faculty
- providing support centers for faculty seeking to improve teaching methods
- employing various forms of technology in the classroom to improve pedagogy

Nourishing students' interest in engineering by using examples in class that highlight relevant applications of engineering principles will engage students. Is it also possible to maintain the quality of an engineering education and integrate substantial components of economic, political, and cultural fundamentals to attract a more diverse population to the profession? This approach could result in educating students to have a core engineering education whose primary areas of interest lie in other fields such as law, politics, medicine, and journalism, among others. Consider the benefits to someone in Congress who needs to make decisions about energy policy being engineering literate.

While changes in curriculum and pedagogy are being developed, tested, and implemented at varying degrees in many engineering schools, other programs and opportunities can be offered to students. Service learning is an emerging area that has the potential to attract students who are motivated to make a difference in the world by working in teams to define, design, build, and test engineering solutions to assist local agencies in providing much-needed care to people within their jurisdiction. Service learning attracts women and underrepresented minorities in disproportionate numbers (Coyle, Jamieson, & Oakes, 2005). An exciting option for students who seek an experience outside the United States is Engineers Without Borders (EWB), a nonprofit humanitarian organization established to partner with developing communities to improve their quality of life. EWB engages and trains responsible engineers and engineering students to implement sustainable projects in developing communities worldwide. Additionally, more schools are making study-abroad options more accessible to engineering students by increasing flexibility in the curriculum. Notably, this strategy has the potential to attract more women to engineering and to retain them in engineering because women students participate in study abroad programs at disproportionately higher rates overall.

ACKNOWLEDGMENT
Thanks to Simmee Silton, science instructor for the Discovery Museum in Acton, Massachusetts, for her editorial contribution to this chapter.

REFERENCES AND FURTHER READING
AAES/Harris Poll. (2004). American perspectives on engineers and engineering: Final report. Retrieved April 14, 2009, from http://www.aaes.org/harris_2004_files/frame.htm

American Society for Quality. (2009). Engineering image problem could fuel shortage. Retrieved April 14, 2009, from http://www.asq.org/media-room/press-releases/2009/20090122-engineering-image.html

Anderson, L. S. & Gilbride, K. A. (2005). Image of engineering among Canadian high school students. Proceedings of the *8th UICEE Annual Conference on Engineering Education, 1–4.* Kingston, Jamaica: UNESCO, International Centre for Engineering Education.

Commission on Professionals in Science and Technology. (2009). All statistical information presented is available from sources on www.cpst.org.

Coyle, E. J., Jamieson, L. H., & Oakes, W. C. (2005). EPICS: Engineering projects in community service. *International Journal of Engineering Education, 21*(1), 139–150.

Goodman, I. R., Cunningham, C. M., & Lachapelle, C. (2002). *The Women's Experiences in College Engineering (WECE) Project final report.* Cambridge, MA: Goodman Research Group.

Jolly, E. J., Campbell, P. B., & Perlman, L. (2004). *Engagement, capacity and continuity: A trilogy for student success.* GE Foundation. Retrieved July 18, 2006, from www.campbell-kibler.com

Margolis, J., & Fisher, A. (2002). *Unlocking the clubhouse*. Cambridge, MA: MIT Press.

Project to Assess Climate in Engineering (2009). Study supported by the Alfred P. Sloan Foundation. Suzanne G. Brainard, principal investigator; Susan Staffin Metz, coprincipal Investigator. http://depts.washington.edu/paceteam/

National Academy of Engineering. (2008). *Changing the conversation: Messages for improving public understanding of engineering*. Washington, DC: National Academies Press.

WGBH Educational Foundation. (2005). *Extraordinary women engineers final report*. Reston, VA: American Society of Civil Engineers.

CHAPTER 23

Feminist Pedagogy

BERENICE MALKA FISHER

Why do some teachers describe what they do as "feminist pedagogy"? What issues arise when instructors use this approach? Feminist pedagogy is the name applied by many late twentieth- and early twenty-first-century teachers to their ways of teaching women's or gender studies and other courses with a feminist orientation. Writings and discussions about this topic tend to focus on college and university settings, where most of these courses are offered. Those who see themselves practicing feminist pedagogy share a commitment to social justice for women. But such teachers diverge in how they view social justice and how they hope to promote it in the classroom.

Although feminist pedagogy is often described as employing certain techniques (e.g., sitting in a circle, keeping journals that include personal reactions, engaging in action projects), these methods may be used by teachers who lack commitment to women's liberation. Feminist teachers may or may not adopt particular strategies in their version of feminist pedagogy. Thus the differences and similarities in feminist teaching are best understood not by describing techniques but by looking at what feminist teachers hope to achieve in their classrooms. Four major goals are equality, caring, collective resistance, and deconstruction. A given teacher may work toward several goals. She (or he) might combine one or more of them with other perspectives and practices (such as spirituality, psychoanalysis, or theater) that inform her teaching.

The Liberal View of Education: Feminist Teaching for Equality

Many teachers of women's studies and related classes are attracted to the liberal view of education for equality and freedom that dominates Western industrial societies. Drawing on these liberal values, feminists have opposed the exclusion of females from access to equal education: Like boys and men, women and girls must be provided the knowledge and intellectual tools that all individuals need to make independent decisions. Feminist teaching for equality means making sure that student development is unfettered by discrimination (e.g., barring females from certain schools or courses of study) or attitudes that discourage female talent and ambition. The curriculum, too, must be free of gender bias: Everyone should learn to identify and reject the gender stereotypes and misinformation that permeate virtually every field of study. A truly liberal education prepares female students to develop as full human beings, to participate as equals in a democratic society, and to compete successfully in a capitalist world.

This approach to feminist teaching has both strengths and weaknesses. Its strengths lie in the insistence on equal treatment and on cultivating the ability and yearning that girls and women bring to their schooling. No one calling himself or herself "feminist" is likely to dispute these principles. The weaknesses of this approach lie in the temptation to view learning as a narrowly rational process and in a tendency to minimize the impact of race, class, sexuality, physical ability, nationality, and other areas of inequality. A woman may be disadvantaged by her gender but privileged in terms of social class. Or she may be disadvantaged not only by gender but also by race and class. For an individual woman, equal educational opportunity may help her to escape the limits of her situation—to become what is sometimes called an "exceptional" woman. But the liberation of some women as individuals, however rewarding, leaves unjust social structures in place.

Feminist Pedagogies Based on Caring

In response to these weaknesses, feminist teachers have called into question the individualism on which the liberal view is based. The liberal ideal of individual achievement, critics note, applies unequally to men and women. The model for the fully developed, independent individual is male. This model ignores the fact that women's caring activities support the striving of such "independent" men and that women are expected to compensate for the damage done to males by a competitive society. While women are praised for their roles as nurturers, liberal societies often denigrate caring. In higher education institutions, especially research universities, women faculty are often encouraged to take on caring-related work (e.g., advising students) and demeaned for pedagogical practices that seem too caring by labeling them "touchy-feely," "mothering," or "therapy."

In contrast to the liberal perspective, feminist pedagogies based on caring pay special attention to relationships among individuals. Feminist scholars point out that caring can be cultivated in men as well as women and suggest that schooling should develop the caring capacities of both boys and girls. In college and university teaching, feminists have contrasted the distanced teaching style of many academics with a more "connected" approach in which teachers guide students into jointly constructing new ways of knowing. Rather than remaining remote, instructors share their own intellectual struggles. Teachers need to nurture women students in particular so that they can become fully connected to the public world.

There are many impediments to creating a culture of caring in the classroom. Students in women's studies and other feminist-oriented courses can find texts and discussion about women's oppression quite painful. Female students may realize that they themselves have been physically, emotionally, or intellectually harmed. Female as well as male students may be urged to consider how they have profited from gender oppression. Such classroom dynamics easily evoke fear, anxiety, denial, guilt, anger, and feelings of helplessness and isolation in the face of so much systemic injustice. Course requirements may raise students' fears that they cannot live up to the teacher's feminist caring ideals and consequently could be punished through humiliation or low grades.

When the exploration of injustice includes race, class, and other socially defined differences, such fears are often expressed as a concern about "safety." Depending in part on the identity of the teacher and the mix of students, a White student may feel unsafe in expressing confusion or guilt about her or his lack of awareness of racism. An

African American student may feel that it is not safe to describe his or her own experiences of racism. A White teacher's attempts to express caring toward a student of color may easily (and too often correctly) be seen as patronizing. A lesbian teacher who acknowledges her sexual orientation may find that disclosure about this identity leads some heterosexual students to feel "unsafe" or to interpret her caring gestures (usually incorrectly) as sexual harassment.

As these examples suggest, no matter how sincerely feminist teachers try to foster caring in the classroom, socially structured inequalities deeply influence what students and teachers are willing to say and do. A general commitment to care does not dissolve the tensions that arise over differences of power and privilege. Indeed, as feminist critics have noted, a caring attitude that fails to recognize conflict resulting from inequality of power and privilege easily turns into pity for the less fortunate or a kind of controlling maternalism that perpetuates injustice.

Feminist Pedagogies of Collective Resistance

Unlike teaching theories that put caring at their center, feminist pedagogies of collective resistance pay special attention to how power differences affect the relation of students and their teachers to questions of gender injustice. These pedagogies were directly or indirectly inspired by social justice movements and theories that proliferated in the 1960s—including the civil rights and Black power movements, community organizing, radical student and national liberation struggles, Mao Tse-tung's revolutionary thought, and Paulo Freire's Brazilian blend of socialism and Catholicism. In part because of the influence of Marxist and socialist ideas, activists often emphasized "consciousness raising"—the process of people talking to others in similar circumstances about their common experiences of oppression. Such discussions were seen as a catalyst for resisting injustice and transforming society into a just one.

In this spirit, radical feminists developed a specifically feminist version of consciousness raising in which women would share their experiences and feelings of gender oppression, analyze these accounts, and develop actions to promote women's liberation. Socialist feminists included attention to class exploitation in their discussions. Black feminists drew on community traditions of Black women talking together about their oppression by White and Black men as well as by White women. Women of color from numerous ethnic and national traditions, lesbians, women with disabilities, older women, and other feminist activists adapted the collective approach to their particular experiences of oppression.

Moved by such social justice initiatives, many feminist teachers in higher education have sought to integrate some form of consciousness raising into their classrooms. Such teachers place great value on building community through sharing experiences and relating them to theories and acts of resistance to injustice. But, as with teachers trying to practice a pedagogy of caring, there are serious obstacles to this approach. The first concerns the tension between intellectual expertise and the process of learning from everyday experience. Experience, as teachers know, is not an infallible guide to knowledge. At times teachers cite personal experiences that are permeated by classist, sexist, or racist assumptions. A White student studying nursing implies that Black women are "lazy" because she thinks that the aides in the hospital where she is interning are not doing their jobs. Although a feminist teacher might respond by citing research to show that such thinking is prejudiced, feminist teaching for collective resistance suggests another path: that the teacher employ her expertise to help the class as a whole explore the structural conditions (e.g., hierarchy, occupational segregation, profitability) that lead to such conflicts at work. This approach puts everyone in the picture and suggests a shared responsibility for remedying injustice.

Yet accounts of experience also can produce powerful teaching moments and important opportunities for learning by teachers as well as students. The very disciplines in which feminist academics have been educated are permeated with false and questionable assumptions. Feminist scholarship, too, contains misperceptions and gaps, many resulting from an insufficient understanding of differences in power and privilege among women.

For instance, a student with a physical disability might draw on her own experiences to point out that the course and its texts assume that all women are able bodied. Her words might spark a general sharing of experiences and discussion about how the range of disabilities relate to gender oppression. If the teacher has not integrated disability consciousness into her understanding of oppression, this sharing might serve as a stimulus to her own disability education: to learning about experiences of disability as well as theories and projects for change.

The problems associated with integrating experience into the classroom are exacerbated by the tendency in higher education to denigrate emotions (often considered "feminine"). Sharing experiences can bring out strong feelings. Teachers employing a pedagogy of collective resistance are faced with the challenge of helping students explore the assumptions embedded in their feelings. If a student becomes angry in response to a feminist text on the subject of battering, a feminist teacher can help both the student and class to explore the meaning of that anger or any other responses the students might have. One student may be angry because she or someone close to her has experienced battering, or because she blames battered women for their situation, or because she thinks she should not have to read about such painful things in a college course. Another student may be angry because he is afraid he will be identified with such abuse, or because he actually condones it but cannot admit this, or because he is horrified by male violence. A feminist teacher can help students bring their perspectives into discussion of larger questions raised by the course: about what constitutes harm, about responsibility, about the relation of political life to education.

The third area of tension for feminist teachers concerns their attempts to use bureaucratic authority in a positive way. Although consciousness raising emphasizes the equal authority of participants, feminist teachers have various degrees of bureaucratic authority over students including, in particular, the power to enforce rules, to evaluate through grading and other means, and to give or withhold institutional support. The tension between this power and student awareness of its potential for harming or helping them can create an almost insuperable barrier to working together to understand and seek alternatives to gender injustice.

At the base of this tension is the question of trust: whether it is possible for students to trust teachers who have the power to do them harm. There is no simple formula for cultivating trust, but pedagogies of collective resistance stress how consciousness raising enables students to get to know each other and the teacher. When teachers as well as students are able to tell their stories, students are more likely to have a realistic picture of the risks involved in sharing experiences, feelings, and ideas. During a discussion about the impact of sexism on schooling, a female student may want to bring up her own fears of intellectual inadequacy. She may be understandably worried that this information could be used to harm her academic standing in the class or the school.

Her ability to trust the teacher and her classmates is strongly affected by what she knows about their own experiences and values. If the teacher—taking into account the risks to herself and the students—is willing to share her own story of intellectual insecurity and growth, she may be able to draw the whole class into this discussion.

Teachers who seek to practice a feminist pedagogy of resistance pay special attention to the kinds of harm that result from unequal power relations. Even where the student population is relatively homogeneous, differences in privilege become apparent. Yet many feminist teachers and activists have argued that, rather than being a liability, differences among women can be a source of great collective strength. Some have sought to explore this potential by working with the concept of "bridging"—an intellectual and political role that women of color, often lesbians, have been able to play in showing the points of connection between the many and seemingly incompatible social locations they occupy. Another related concept is "positionality"—the notion that social positions like gender and class are not simple or fixed but consist of complex and potentially changing relationships that involve both privileges and disadvantages (a person might be advantaged by heterosexual preference but disadvantaged by class, and both positions might change). Concepts like these help teachers and students to describe the complicated and shifting networks of commonalities and differences entailed in any problem of gender injustice they seek to understand and solve. A more subtle understanding of difference enables teachers and their students to evaluate feminist or nonfeminist texts or policies in terms of what has been omitted—such as consideration of how age or nationality impacts opportunity—as well as what is named.

Feminist Pedagogies of Deconstruction

Feminist teachers of all varieties pay attention to how women have been excluded from mainstream definitions of knowledge. But for teachers identified with a feminist pedagogy of deconstruction, the dynamics of exclusion have more far-reaching implications. Inspired by the work of French theorists such as Michel Foucault and Jacques Derrida and, sometimes, by the "queer" activism of the 1980s and 1990s, these feminists focus on how language (or "discourse") continually constructs the world into mutually exclusive and hierarchically arranged opposites (or "binaries"). Gender or racial or sexual distinctions such as man/woman, White/Black, and gay/straight assume that all individuals can be categorized in one or the other group and that one in each pair must be dominant. By uncritically employing these categories, the critics argue, feminists themselves reproduce the patterns of oppressive thought they should be disrupting. Feminist teachers who value caring and connection, the critics continue, too often assume that people called women are more naturally caring than those called men. Similarly, feminist teachers trying to practice a pedagogy of collective resistance often falsely assume that sharing a common identity (such as "woman" or "lesbian") will lead to a common understanding of injustice and collective resistance to it.

The alternative offered most frequently by deconstructionists is teaching for criticism: the continuous process of taking apart any kind of text—whether an academic article or a film or an everyday conversation—to reveal how it erases and demeans certain people or events or activities. A teacher might show the students how a manifesto demanding "lesbian" rights actually excludes from consideration bisexual, transgender, or pansexual people whose sexual preferences and behaviors resist such categorization.

The same instructor might help the students deconstruct a text that takes for granted categories like "working class" or "women of color." This teacher might point out instead that "selves" are complex and fluid social constructions, dependent upon often changeable sexual histories or class positions or racial identities. From this viewpoint, nothing can be taken as "natural"—neither anatomy nor any social distinctions based upon it.

In some respects, pedagogies of deconstruction present a profound critique of pedagogies based on caring and collective resistance. Deconstruction refuses to accept any linguistically determined fate—whether it involves feminist teachers believing that they should be especially nurturing or students being characterized in certain ways because they are a "woman," or a "woman of color," or a "lesbian of color," or a "working-class lesbian of color." Yet this refusal comes at a high price. In the context of such critical teaching, little room is made for the kind of compassionate connection that pedagogies of caring value and try to cultivate. Indeed, the emphasis on criticism tends to reproduce the reason/emotion split pervading higher education.

The deconstructionist criticism of identity politics (that is, the view that political analysis and resistance grows out of sharing a common identity) also can reinforce relations of dominance and subordination in the classroom that feminist teachers are committed to challenging. In this approach, experience becomes highly suspect—not a beginning point out of which discussion can be generated but material for deconstruction. The emphasis on criticism makes it more difficult for students to use their experiences and feelings to voice their own reservations about the texts or their teachers. Teachers, not students, are experts in criticism, and expertise in deconstruction becomes the standard of success in both teaching and learning.

Imagine a lone student who identifies as a working-class lesbian of color sitting in a class in which the teacher models criticism by deconstructing the categories through which the student describes herself. The criticism may be perfectly sound—or not. But there are the real-life consequences for this student's relationships in the classroom and for connections to others outside the classroom. Perhaps the student feels liberated by being freed from the constraints of these categories. Or perhaps she becomes even more isolated, more hesitant to participate in class or skeptical of political groups that promote collective action by women like herself. The contexts in which the student lives her life, the subtle or not-so-subtle power dynamics of the classroom as well as the structures of inequality that she encounters outside that classroom, profoundly shape the implications of the critical viewpoints she is being taught.

Contexts for Feminist Pedagogies

All feminist teachers continuously make intellectual, ethical, and political choices about what and how they teach. Feminist teachers drawn to the liberal vision of society question inherited limits and biases and base their teaching choices on belief in the autonomous and rational individual. Teachers who put caring at the center of their work reject rampant individualism and give priority to teaching assignments and techniques that support caring and connection. Partisans of collective resistance to injustice condemn oppression and exploitation and try to create the kind of classroom community that cultivates the search for common understandings and solutions amid difference and conflict. Deconstructionists challenge fixed meanings and assign texts and set requirements according to which binary distinctions they decide are most in need of criticism.

Yet the meaning of any pedagogical choice depends on its context. In choices related to feminist teaching, two factors are especially influential. The first is the actual institutional and social context in which feminist teachers do their work. Whatever their preferred pedagogy, such teachers are affected by the size and mission of the school, the kind of department in which they work, the nature of the student body, and their position within the institution—or whether they do not have a regular position and must move from school to school. Given the particular combination of conditions, teachers may find themselves adopting, combining, or rejecting different goals for feminist teaching: stressing individual development at one point, responding in a caring mode at another, encouraging the collective spirit for a certain classroom task and emphasizing criticism for a different one, and integrating other perspectives that seem appropriate.

The second important factor influencing the practice of feminist pedagogy is the political and intellectual climate of the institutional, local, national, and global context in which a feminist teacher works. The costs and benefits of putting any theory of feminist pedagogy into practice influences how teaching is actually done. For instance, a teacher who gravitates toward a feminist pedagogy of resistance might find considerable support in a small liberal arts college with a history of defending political activists. But if that college is located in a city or state or province that has a conservative leadership or in a country where the government actively suppresses social justice values by limiting civil liberties and withdrawing financial support, the teacher's ability to fulfill the potentials of feminist teaching may become highly problematic.

If teachers attempting to practice feminist pedagogy share a commitment to social justice for women, such teachers also share the challenge of trying to realize their commitment in the face of backlash. Feminist teachers often must cope with intense opposition to their efforts. They may be fired, penalized, or undermined by rules and reorganizations aimed at hampering their work. Yet feminist teachers have rich resources to draw on: their transformative values, their passionate scholarship, and their continued dedication to forging connections between their classrooms and feminist activism. Through innovative writing, ongoing debates, and conferences and workshops devoted to trying to answer the question, "What is feminist pedagogy?" they show that the challenge is being met and that the work of feminist teaching continues to nurture both their students and themselves.

REFERENCES AND FURTHER READING

Armstrong, A. E. & Juhl, K. (Eds.). (2008). *Radical acts: Theatre and feminist pedagogies of change*. San Francisco: Aunt Lute Books.

Bannerji, H., Carty, L., Dehli, K., Heald, S., & McKenna, K. (Eds.). (1991). *Unsettling relations: The university as a site of feminist struggles*. Toronto, Canada: Women's Press.

Belenky, M. F., Clinchy, B. M., Goldberger, N. R., & Tarule, J. M. (1986). *Women's ways of knowing: The development of self, voice, and mind*. New York: Basic Books.

Cohee, G. E., Daumer, E., Kemp, T. D., Krebs, P. M., & Lafky, S. A. (Eds.). (1998). *The feminist teacher anthology: Pedagogies and classroom strategies*. New York: Teachers College Press.

Diller, A., Houston, B., Morgan, K. P., & Ayim, M. (Eds.). (1996). *The gender question in education: Theory, pedagogy, and politics*. Boulder, CO: Westview.

Felman, S. & Laub, D. (1992). *Testimony: Crises of witnessing in literature, psychoanalysis, and history*. New York: Routledge.

Feminist pedagogy: An update [Special issue]. (1993). *Women's Studies Quarterly, 21*(3 & 4).

Fisher, B. M. (2001). *No angel in the classroom: Teaching through feminist discourse*. Lanham, MD: Rowman & Littlefield.

Gallop, J. (Ed.). (1995). *Pedagogy: The question of impersonation*. Bloomington: Indiana University Press.

Garber, L. (Ed.). (1994). *Tilting the tower: Lesbians, teaching, and queer subjects*. New York: Routledge.

hooks, b. (1994). *Teaching to transgress: Education as the practice of freedom*. New York: Routledge.

Keating, A. (2007). *Teaching Transformation: Transcultural classroom dialogues*. New York: Palgrave Macmillan.

Luke, C., & Gore, J. (Eds.). (1992). *Feminisms and critical pedagogy*. New York: Routledge.

Macdonald, A. A., & Sánchez-Casal, S. (2002). *Twenty-first century feminist classrooms: Pedagogies of identity and difference*. New York: Palgrave Macmillan.

Maher, F. A., & Tetreault, M. K. T. (1994). *The feminist classroom*. New York: Basic Books.

Naples, N. A., & Bojar, K. (Eds.). (2002). *Teaching feminist activism: Strategies from the field*. New York: Routledge.

Weiler, K. (1991). Freire and a feminist pedagogy of difference. *Harvard Educational Review, 61*(4), 449–474.

CHAPTER 24

From Home Economics to Family and Consumer Sciences

VIRGINIA B. VINCENTI

Family and consumer sciences (FCS), the name adopted in 1994, represents a new and broader vision of the field dealing with individual and family well-being, previously called home economics (HE). From its founding in the early twentieth century to the present, the field in higher education has prepared professionals for positions in government including the cooperative extension service and federal agencies such as USDA, state consumer protection units, and county offices and programs; in social service and nonprofit organizations; business; and industry.

Today's college and university programs offer associate, bachelor's, master's, and doctoral degrees in FCS and its specializations (family science and child development; gerontology; marriage and family therapy; hospitality management; dietetics, nutrition, and food science; consumer economics and family resource management; housing and interior design; and merchandizing, apparel design, and textile science) that graduate tens of thousands of students annually. These programs began as a movement to improve the daily lives of individuals in families, save society from family breakdown, and create professional career opportunities for women in the late 1800s when expansion of science, capitalism, industrialization, immigration, and urbanization were dramatically changing American society.

Nineteenth-century U.S. historical documents reference the need to educate women for their culturally defined roles. Catharine Beecher's 1841 publication, *A Treatise on Domestic Economy*, became the first comprehensive text for girls and a popular manual for women, detailing fulfillment of their role in Victorian ideology. Blocked by culturally defined gender roles from entering the clergy like her father and several brothers, Beecher shifted her attention to educating girls in her seminaries and women through her publications. She prepared females to be society's moral leaders through their roles as mothers, homemakers, and teachers, the latter a job previously limited to males. Her seminaries for young girls and teachers offered more intellectually challenging education than generally available during her lifetime (1800–1878).

However, it was the negative impacts of the industrial revolution on sanitation and home life during the second half of the nineteenth century that motivated a group of educated women to make a difference. Professional employment was scarce, almost nonexistent for married women. Because educated women were barred from many fields, they created new professional opportunities that used science to free home-makers from the drudgery of housework to save time and energy for loftier pursuits.

After the 1862 Morrill Land-Grant Act established colleges to promote the liberal and practical education of the industrial classes, campus and informal community-based programs developed to provide practical education for women like the agricultural and mechanical arts that prepared men for their agrarian roles in working-class American society. Women were not entirely welcome in higher education or in male-dominated professional societies, which either denied women's entry or marginalized them. Except for the eastern private women's colleges, established for the middle and upper classes, women's entrance into higher education was primarily through HE.

Near the end of Beecher's life, Ellen (Swallow) Richards—a two-time Vassar College graduate, the first woman to attend Massachusetts Institute of Technology (MIT), and later an MIT chemistry instructor—emerged as a leader of the HE movement in its transition to a profession. Richards finished her second bachelor's degree in 1873, did extensive graduate work, but, according to Jerome B. Wiesner, 1979 MIT president, she was not awarded a master's degree although she probably qualified for a Ph.D. Richards taught and did research at MIT until her death in 1911. She never rose above the rank of lecturer, even though some who were awarded full faculty status, her husband included, had only bachelors' degree. She became a leader in the movement to create opportunities for women in science (Rossiter, 1982, p. 12).

During the 1890s and later at Cornell University opposition to having women faculty was so intense that their status was lowered to the nonfaculty rank of lecturer, thus setting a precedent for future appointments. Faculty argued that the university would lose status by appointing women to professorships, higher salaries were unnecessary because unmarried women did not have families to support (a common fallacy), they were not as well educated as most men (though agricultural faculties generally lacked doctorates), and most telling, they did not want women to compete with men (Rossiter, 1982).

This marginalization and concern for human well-being led Richards, other educated women, and several men to create the new profession. When Melvil Dewey invited Richards to the Lake Placid Club in upstate New York to develop an HE regents' exam, Richards encouraged him to host a conference for those interested in improving daily life and unifying their independent efforts in schools, communities, and higher education. The resulting Lake Placid Conferences on Home Economics (1899–1908) led to the 1909 establishment of the American Home Economics Association (AHEA) and its *Journal of Home Economics*. The conferees discussed the impact of immigration, industrialization, and lack of public understanding of scientific applications to improve daily life in homes and families. They wanted their new profession to address poor housing, overcrowding, food adulteration, unhealthful and unsafe living and working conditions, factory pollution, growing poverty, and communicable diseases—then the leading cause of death. They developed practically oriented interdisciplinary curricula for different educational levels including natural sciences, arts, humanities, and the emerging social sciences. They rejected capitalism's laissez-faire approach to the plight of the poor and the social Darwinian notion of eugenics. Instead, they embraced euthenics, a science of developing human well-being by improving living conditions.

The debate about women's appointment to professorships at Cornell continued until 1911, when the faculty voted in favor of professorial appointments for women but only because they were in the Department of Home Economics, established in

1907. After a long, contentious argument, the faculty, while remaining generally opposed in principle, did not object to professorial appointments for women in the Department of Home Economics. To the Cornell faculty, home economics was of such low status because of its female composition and content that full professorships for women were tolerable there (Rossiter, 1982).

From 1917 through 1945, the country and the profession were preoccupied with World War I, the Great Depression, and World War II. During and after World War II dramatic societal change challenged the cultural concept of women's work. This societal upheaval profoundly affected homes and families. Although home economists were working to help families deal with change, to those trying to rid women of stereotypic roles to gain entrance into traditionally male careers, home economics became the enemy.

During the 1960s, the profession grew dramatically as it developed specializations, made its rhetoric more gender neutral, focused more on paid careers, increased research productivity, and recruited males into the field. The U.S. Office of Education, the Federal Extension Service, and HE land-grant university units sponsored a 1961 French Lick, Indiana, conference to redesign HE curricula at the secondary, college, and adult levels. Subsequent workshops developed outlines of fundamental concepts and generalized principles. Simultaneously, other professional options opened for women, reducing the proportion of women enrolled in HE in higher education.

Research funding had been hard for the HE field to obtain. However, Iowa State's dean of the College of Home Economics, Helen LeBaron, who served on the White House vocational education panel, made sure the 1963 Vocational Education Act included HE research funds (Rossiter, 1997). President Johnson's effort to create the Great Society provided opportunities for home economists, but prejudicial attitudes trumped them. Rather than helping home economists fund research and earn prestige, it signaled to powerful academic men that, however trivial HE had once seemed, it was becoming lucrative enough to take over (Rossiter, 1997). As men moved in and gained administrative positions, their units were also given more institutional resources than they had received when unmarried female professionals led them.

The largely male National Association of State Universities and Land-Grant Colleges (NASULGC) reduced the field's visibility and organizational status. Its executive committee sought and received $200,000 in 1964 from the Carnegie Corporation to study HE, which was consistent with Carnegie's interest in the status of American women. This grant went to Earl J. McGrath and Jack T. Johnson. McGrath was the director of Columbia University's Teachers College Institute of Higher Education, where he had done similar studies of other areas of professional education, including one on liberal arts and home economics (Rossiter, 1997). Jack T. Johnson was McGrath's associate at Teachers College (McGrath & Johnson, 1968).

Their charge from NASULGC presidents was biased toward the elimination of home economics land-grant programs, unlike their charges in reviews of other professions. Recognizing the hostility of the land-grant university presidents, soon after McGrath and Johnson were selected and even before they got under way, home economics administrators offered to cooperate fully (M. East, personal communication, summer 2003), providing data that might otherwise have been suppressed if control had remained in the hands of the NASULGC presidents. Had the home economists been less proactive and more confrontational, the report might have reinforced McGrath's and Johnson's initial negative perceptions of the field.

By 1965 the 1963 Vocational Education Act had appropriated up to $12 million for home economics research and by 1967, $22.5 million. What looked like a huge improvement, however, suddenly backfired on home economics units. In 1966 NASULGC eliminated the Division of Home Economics and reduced its status to a Commission of Home Economics within the Division of Agriculture, eliminating the field's place in the executive committee. In response, the division members established their own organization, the Association of Administrators of Home Economics (AAHE). Before the study was complete, land-grant presidents moved ahead with their plans, renaming, reorganizing, and replacing HE departments with new curricula.

As McGrath and Johnson reviewed the data home economists supplied and the data they had collected themselves, their orientation toward the profession changed. The resulting report recommendations were positive about the future of the field. The report criticized federal and state legislation and agreements foundational to HE education, extension, and research in land-grant institutions for not providing enough freedom or stimulation to enable HE, particularly extension, to meet current challenges (McGrath, 1968). It recommended a thorough review at the highest governmental levels, including investigation of the confining relationships between county government and agrarian interests, to assure that home economics could and would redesign its programs and services to meet the needs of American society. McGrath reported that he had no doubt about HE's future but was firmly convinced that the schools training HE professionals would grow in size, strength, and position in American higher education. He further concluded from the study that the profession would gain nothing by changing the name "home economics" (McGrath & Johnson, 1968).

Rossiter (1997) concluded that the heart of home economists' problems in the 1950s and 1960s was not really declining enrollments or lack of faculty doctorates, as was so often claimed then, but the hostility and related communication gaps between "a new breed of ambitious university presidents who wanted to get rid of home economics, whatever it was, and the many women deans who tried repeatedly and futilely to define the field and to improve and expand their programs with little outside support." The women deans tried to outlast the presidents, graduate more Ph.D.s, and garner more research funds. However, when such support was suddenly forthcoming, many of the strongest women deans were nearing retirement. Male administrators on several major campuses seized the opportunity to reshape the formally female HE units into the somewhat more gender-neutral "nutritional sciences," "human development," or "human ecology." Such reforms "grew out of the ageism and misogyny of the time" (pp. 97, 115–116).

Although the university presidents quietly filed the report they had planned to use against HE, the NASULGC Commission on Home Economics administrators used the positive aspects of the McGrath and Johnson report to increase support for their programs. They quickly approached the NASULGC senate and received funding to "study, analyze and implement the report recommendations," using it to hold a 1968 conference, and mail the report to AAHE and *all* NASULGC members (Higgins, 1968). The report helped maintain HE higher education units and even helped obtain increased support for some of the institutional units originally funded under the second Morrill Act of 1890 (F. Byrd, telephone interview, May 5, 1995).

In 1979 Brown and Paolucci published an AHEA-commissioned reconceptualization of the profession. It called for more emphasis on curricula focused on reason, ethics, cultural and self-reflection, and identifying and framing underlying perennial

problems distinct from current symptomatic ramifications. It emphasized finding solutions that increase societal and familial justice. Just as previously male-dominated
professions are becoming gender neutral, HE as a female-dominated profession has
sought gender neutrality as well. However, outside forces such as federal vocational education and USDA legislation and appropriations, reduction in FCS university teacher
education programs, and inertia toward specialization in the field has limited the impact of this reconceptualization.

By the mid-1980s, increasing specialization within the field was weakening the
interdisciplinary approach. Extension administrators, teacher educators, and some specialized faculty worried about this fragmentation, but many others were indifferent or
unsupportive. Consequently, higher education units adopted more than 30 names for
themselves, either to emphasize their programs' integrative nature (e.g., family and
consumer sciences) or to accommodate the particular combination of specializations
included in their individual units (e.g., design, family, and consumer sciences). New
professional organizations drew members from specific work settings and specializations. Nationally, this proliferation of names and organizations further exacerbated
identity confusion.

To stimulate critical thinking and improve articulation of the profession and its
contributions to society, AHEA initiated an annual competitive commemorative lec-
tureship in 1984, its 75th anniversary. Marjorie Brown, professor of home economics
education at the University of Minnesota, honored for her professional and intellectual contributions, was the first selected. She shocked her audience by chiding the profession for conforming to society and being dominated by individualism and strongly
influenced by business and industry. She claimed the profession still subscribed in-
appropriately to economic materialism, a nineteenth-century view that physical and
economic conditions in society and the home naturally precede political-moral, social-
psychological, and cultural improvement. This emphasis on the physical aspects of
daily life in homes and acceptance of positivistic empirical science and technology led
to internal inconsistencies between the profession's philosophy and professional practice. Brown urged the profession to be more self-critical and to stop compromising its
commitment to families simply to gain or keep business and industry positions. Subsequently Brown published two volumes in 1985 on the profession's history leading to
its current state in the 1980s and a third in 1993 reconceptualizing the profession.

By 1992 the profession's identity problem had become so severe that five major
professional HE organizations sponsored the 1993 Positioning the Profession for the
21st Century meeting in Scottsdale, Arizona. After much deliberation, the attendees
selected "family and consumer sciences" as the profession's new name and developed
a new conceptual framework reaffirming its integrative approach to improving individuals, families, communities, and the environments in which they function. This
new name and framework were intended to escape the stereotypic connotations of
"home economics" that had plagued the profession and to broaden its focus to include
improvement of individual, family, and community well-being; influence the development, delivery, and evaluation of consumer goods and services; and bring about
public policy and societal change. Some who attended the conference felt it had created a new profession that transcended HE.

At their respective 1994 annual meetings, all five national associations adopted
the conceptual framework, and four changed their organizations' names to incorporate "Family and Consumer Services." The fifth, AAHE, became the Association of

Administrators of Human Sciences because "human sciences" implies equality with "agricultural sciences," with which HE programs in land-grant institutions are often closely tied by tradition and funding. Although many higher education units changed their names to FCS after 1994, multiple names still exit. For some higher education programs, the new name has dramatically increased enrollments and attracted more male students.

The profession remains committed to enhancing the quality of personal life for individuals and families well beyond housework, not because it is women's responsibility as some still accuse the field of perpetuating, but because this aspect of life is important to all people and to the well-being of society. However, societal bias continues to view this mission as gendered. Since two-thirds of the U.S. economy consists of consumer spending, much advertising is for consumer goods. Advertisers exaggerate the difficulty, time consumption, and unpleasantness of even simple domestic tasks for women, busier than ever with moneymaking, personal improvement, and children's activities. They promote women's status as depending on clean, sweet-smelling homes; quick, no-prep meals; and premeasured ingredients (Elias, 2008).

REFERENCES AND FURTHER READING

Brown, M. M., & Paolucci, B. (1979) *Home economics: A definition.* Alexandria, VA: American Home Economics Association.

Elias, M. J. (2008). *Stir it up: Home economics in American culture.* Philadelphia: University of Pennsylvania Press.

Higgins, N. R. (19, 20 January 1968). Minutes, Executive Board meeting, AAHE, p. 3.

McGrath, E. J. (1968). The changing mission of home economics. *Journal of Home Economics, 60*(2), 85–92.

McGrath, E. J., & Johnson, J. (1968). *The changing mission of home economics: A report on home economics in the land-grant colleges and state universities.* New York: Teachers College Press.

Ralston, P., & Vincenti, V. (1997). *Teaching in land-grant and state universities: New perspectives in human science.* Washington, DC: Board on Human Sciences, National Association of State Universities and Land-Grant Colleges.

Rossiter, M. W. (1982). *Women scientists in America: Struggles and strategies to 1940.* Baltimore: Johns Hopkins University Press.

Rossiter, M. W. (1997). The men move in: Home economics in higher education, 1950–1970. In S. Stage & V. B. Vincenti (Eds.), *Rethinking home economics: Women and the history of a profession.* (pp. 96–117). Ithaca, NY: Cornell University Press.

Stage, S., & Vincenti, V. B. (Eds.). (1997). *Rethinking home economics: Women and the history of a profession.* Ithaca, NY: Cornell University Press.

Vincenti, V. B. (1983). Antecedents of reformism. *Journal of Home Economics, 75*(3), 26–31.

Vincenti, V. B. (1987). Science and sexism: The historical influence on home economics today. *Journal of Home Economics, 79*(4), 45–49.

Vincenti, V., & Smith, F. (2004). Critical science: What it could offer all family and consumer sciences professionals. *Journal of Family and Consumer Sciences, 96*(1), 3–70.

Vincenti, V. B. (1990). Home Economics in higher education: Communities of convenience or purpose? *Home Economics Research Journal, 19*(2), 184–193.

CHAPTER 25

History

MARY E. FREDERICKSON

At the beginning of each new academic year, one can almost hear the wheels turning as thousands of college professors and high school teachers assemble a broad array of lecture notes, textbooks, primary documents, photographs, and films and gear up for another term of teaching the history of the United States survey course. Still the mainstay of U.S. culture requirements at most American colleges and universities, and certainly the backbone of the advanced placement curriculum completed by college-bound students across the nation, foundation courses in U.S. history come as close to a disciplinary canon as anything else.

In this post-9/11 world, many teachers and professors scramble to make these courses as relevant as possible by adding new material—on U.S. foreign policy in the Middle East, Latin American immigration, and U.S. relations with post-Soviet Russia and China. Historians strive to prepare students for the twenty-first century by encouraging them to scrutinize the past more carefully and systematically than ever before in order to understand the challenges facing the United States in the twenty-first century as the nation wages two wars, confronts a struggling global economy, meets global health crises, and deals with relentless poverty within and beyond our national boundaries. The economic, social, and political issues facing the United States have rarely been greater. In a climate permeated by despair and pessimism, solutions to these problems appear elusive at best.

Given the preponderance of national and international challenges we face, why is it germane at this juncture to reexamine the construction of gender in the American past? The fact is that it has never been more important to analyze gender, to understand how national cultures reinforce gender-linked behavior, and the ways in which gendered symbols permeate the cultural formation of nation states. The various ways people in the United States have used gender to tell their national story reveal a great deal about us as a people. For academics, the challenge is to teach students to untangle the tangled skeins of the American past, including the unresolved paradoxes of gender, and then reevaluate U.S. history on their own terms.

As students undertake these tasks, they must ask some fundamental questions about gender and history in America: What roles have men and women played in the development of the United States? What economic positions have men and women occupied over time and why? How has power been distributed in American society from the founding of the republic up to the present? In what ways have women and men contributed to the development of American culture? How does one move beyond a male/female binary when discussing the role of gender in American society, past and present? A gendered study of American history, like analyses that carefully consider race, ethnicity, and class, provides a richer and more nuanced understanding of the past, one that reflects more accurately the multiple experiences of a majority of the American people. Moreover, the contemporary world cries out for analyses that take into consideration changing constructions of masculinity and femininity, both in the United States and in other nations and cultures. At this historical moment we need more sophisticated ways of understanding how gender has worked in the past in order to make sense of contemporary global politics and the myriad of cultural performances being enacted on the world stage.

One can make a plausible argument that the way educators and historians teach and write about U.S. history has changed dramatically over the last three decades. The work of feminist historians and the "new" social history, from the 1970s through the 1990s, resulted in the production of college-level textbooks that no longer focus solely on political and military history, moving from one presidential administration to the next, analyzing U.S. history war by war, and offering detailed biographies of a short list of White male captains of industry. Students in the early twenty-first century are introduced to a more diverse set of historical characters than earlier generations of Americans came to know, and most become familiar with a range of political and social movements set in motion by Americans representing both majority and minority viewpoints. Women and men from a complex array of ethnic and racial backgrounds have shaped American culture and worked from the beginning to be included as part of the body politic, to be recognized as citizens. Many of these efforts have been gendered, as evidenced for example by the fact that American women worked for over 150 years to obtain suffrage and property rights within the nation recognized as the world's greatest democracy. Men struggled with different gender expectations: compulsory military service and the role of breadwinner, for example.

The long fight for women's suffrage clearly exemplifies the connections, and disconnections, between the "enterprise of women's history" and the "story of the American past." In this regard, changes in U.S. survey courses have been remarkable in many respects. Classes once narrowly defined have given way to courses that openly address the American past in terms of politics, foreign affairs, economic change, and cultural and social transformation over 500 years. On the other hand, while major revisions in the U.S. foundation courses are real, one must ask whether or not the ways in which gender figures into most survey courses has actually gone beyond the "add women and stir" recipe for curricular reform.

Women make more appearances in most survey courses taught in the twenty-first century, but most of the time representations of women in these courses remain marginal. Despite the progress that has been made, the difficult challenges of transforming the U.S. curriculum regarding gender lie not behind us but ahead. Historians are at a point where they must work hard to protect the gains that have been made, even as they move ahead to promote more significant change. After 30 years of good work, they still have a long way to go before they can proclaim victory in terms of successfully gendering public understanding of the American past. This statement is applicable across the gender spectrum, for at this point more is known about women's history, in terms of the construction of female roles, than about male roles and the development of masculinity. Historians still know precious little about what happens when they forgo heterosexuality as normative and open themselves to understanding the realities of homosocial and homosexual relationships, networks, and life experiences. Americans with transgendered identities have barely begun, in Kathi Kern's (1996) words, to "feel as part of history."

So where do things stand and what needs to be done? A close examination of the way U.S. history is taught reveals that historians from across the country have put enormous energy into revising the curriculum. This has been crucial work because these courses are the seed corn of the profession: At any one time in the United States, in four-year colleges, community colleges, and high schools (public and private), approximately three million students are enrolled in introductory U.S. history courses. Educators have devised ingenious new ways of teaching the survey, but the American history narrative that forms the basis of most U.S. survey courses is still, despite all of the changes and the enormous amount of work that has been done, courses inherited from the past in which, as historian Linda Kerber (1997) suggests, the lessons seem to march in a well-laid-out sequence from Columbus to as close to the present as the instructor can get before the semester or school year ends. She argues that, because of the need for efficiency and coverage (although she would agree that this is probably not the only reason), historians adopt a structure in which matters related to women are less important than those related to men.

A close analysis of U.S. history survey syllabi confirms this argument and suggests that, while significant changes have been made, the version of American history most frequently available to students remains dominated by male-centered stories and gender-differentiated versions of the past. A close reading shows that, without question, the broad range of U.S. history books available for college and high school students, like the survey courses they support, have changed dramatically. A simple measure of index entries referring to women can track the evolution of women's inclusion in survey texts. In 1963, the first edition of John Blum's *The National Experience* included six topical entries under the heading "women" in its index. The eighth edition of that work, published in 1993, included 14 topical references to women. Tracing women's inclusion across the four editions of Nash et al.'s *The American People* reveals a similar pattern: the first edition (1986) included 54 topical references to women; the fifth edition (2001) 120 references. The seventh edition (2006) has 152 index entries, including headings for "feminism," "gender," and "women's movement." And so it goes with every U.S. history textbook. So far, not one textbook, even among those written by authors averse to women's history, has reduced the number of references to women in later editions.

What is striking about U.S. history survey texts is that, once one moves beyond the indexes, with their ever-increasing numbers of references to women, women become significantly less visible. Tables of contents are particularly bad. If women appear at all, and usually they do not, they surface in 1830–1860 in subchapter headings such as "Women, Families, and the Domestic Ideal" and make rare appearances in subheadings such as "Rebirth of Feminism" and "Feminism, Antifeminism, and Women's Lives." That's it. Let me emphasize this: As a rule, women do not appear in any form in chapter titles in U.S. history textbooks. If they appear in tables of contents at all, they emerge in chapter subheadings, and then only rarely. The exceptional textbook in this regard has one to three references to women in subheadings (out of an average of 500 subheadings per text).

If one looks at charts in these texts, women disappear almost completely. An occasional chart illustrates, for example, the "Occupational Distribution of Working Women, 1900–1998" or "Marriages and Divorces, 1890–1997," but many texts do not have a single chart that incorporates data about women's lives. You may well be asking, "Are men mentioned in chapter titles or subheadings in these texts?" That is a good question, for the word *man* or *men* is not used as often as are references to specific men. For example, in many recently published textbooks, male political leaders are regularly referred to by name in chapter headings and subheadings (e.g., "Progressivism and the Republican Roosevelt" or "Senator Douglas and the Kansas-Nebraska Act, 1854"). What about broader references to gender as a category of historical analysis? Almost none.

Textbook maps tell the same story. Although maps appear at first glance to be gender neutral, when one looks at list after list of the maps included in survey texts, it is striking how gendered they actually are: War campaigns are mapped by the movement of soldiers, not the involvement of civilian populations. Farm tenancy is mapped according to the number of male tenants. Elections results are mapped with a presumption of universal suffrage, even in the many decades when the suffrage was anything but universal. The standard map including women shows pro- and antisuffrage states. A powerful message is given to students in terms of what is important enough to appear on a map: Land acquisitions (most in the years when in most states women could not, by law, hold property in their own name) are very important (many maps). Conversely, the average number of maternal deaths in childbirth does not appear on maps or charts in any contemporary U.S. survey textbook. Paintings and photographs, on the other hand, often seem to be the vehicles by which women are most frequently brought into the survey text.

Over the last three decades, there is no question that scholars and teachers have worked diligently to transform the U.S. history survey course in order to make the past more relevant and accessible to a broader range of American students. In many ways, they have been extremely successful in reshaping foundation courses in U.S. history, especially as far as gender is concerned. But when considered as a whole, has the story of the past told to U.S. students actually become more complex and inclusive over the last quarter century? What do students take with them when the course ends? What kind of foundation are history surveys providing? What will the long-term effects of 9/11 be on the narratives historians and their students write about the American past? Most important, what should the future be?

Clearly, the time has come to change the paradigms used to teach American history. In many ways, past efforts to introduce gender as a category of analysis should embolden educators to try some additional new strategies. Let me suggest two avenues that I see as promising in terms of further transforming the ways American history is taught, particularly regarding gender and the construction of masculinity and femininity, as well as forms of sexuality that transcend the male/female binary. First, digital technology and the Worldwide Web offer a way to supersede the linear chronological track traditionally followed in teaching U.S. history. Second, historians and educators need to begin to seriously analyze gender and women's history in the United States from a global perspective.

Digital technology and the Web have transformed multiple aspects of people's experience and consciously and unconsciously changed their worldview. The future is now because students already live in this new world. A revolution many believe to be as profound as the Gutenberg invention of moveable type is well under way, and this new technology is in the process of changing the ways people teach, write, and think. A Web-based approach to the history survey has the potential to hasten the paradigm shift many have been seeking and make it easier to integrate women and gender into the American historical narrative. If used to disrupt the rigid linearity and unswerving chronological schema of the history survey, the Web and the Internet will alter existing paradigms and teach in ways that expand discussions of gender and multiculturalism beyond male/female, beyond Black/White/Brown. The converse is true as well, for there is no guarantee that the digital humanities will not replicate paper-based scholarship and teaching in perpetuating traditional gendered parameters in the study of U.S. history.

Thousands of U.S. survey courses in colleges and high schools across the country now regularly use Web-based materials. Each year brings an exponential increase in the number and quality of archives available online. The array of photographs, maps, primary documents, rare books, and manuscript collections that faculty and students can access from library, classroom, or home is truly astounding: the rich archives stored by the History Cooperative; virtual tours at sites ranging from Ellis Island to the Holocaust Museum to the National Underground Railroad Freedom Center; specific Web sites accessible to students and faculty including Ed Ayers's Valley of the Shadow (http://valley.vcdh.virgina.edu), the Documenting the American South project at the University of North Carolina, Chapel Hill (http://docsouth.unc.edu), and the Triangle Factory Fire Web exhibit created by the ILR School at Cornell University (http://www.ilr.cornell.edu/tranglefire/) to name a few. Hundreds of Web sites now contain elaborate documentary projects for teachers and students of U.S. history. Katharine Sklar and Tom Dublin's Women in Social Movements Web site (http://womhist.alexanderstreet.com/) includes 79 projects and over 2,400 documents and attracts 10,000 visitors a month from 90 countries. The AP Central Web site has been enormously successful in making online sources on women's history available to thousands of high school teachers across the country and also as a model for cooperative projects with both the Smithsonian Institution and Columbia University. The Library of Congress American Memory Project (http://memory.loc.gov/ammem/index.html) provides free and open access to written documents, sound recordings, still and moving images, prints, maps, and sheet music that document the American experience. The American Social History Project Center for Media and Learning (http://www.ashp.cuny.edu/) has revitalized interest in all aspects of U.S. history for teachers and students.

Access to the Web is also making a more transnational approach to U.S. history a reality. The tens of thousands of overseas visitors to the Women in Social Movements Web site make visible the global community of researchers and students committed to researching aspects of the American past. Scholars from China to Norway to the United States are responding to increasing global interdependence and interaction by rethinking the geographical and chronological boundaries that delineate the history, geography, and culture of America. Those committed to expanding our knowledge of gender and women's history are particularly well equipped to participate in the project of internationalizing American history. Existing academic programs in comparative women's history provide important models for new efforts to internationalize American history. Students engaged in courses of study that emphasize a comparative approach will be better equipped to connect America to other parts of the world and to address the multitude of global challenges and opportunities that face the United States.

History teaches people about themselves, and nothing is as integral to the construction of a self as gender. Individually, as a people with unique personal histories, and collectively, as citizens sharing in the experiences of civil society and national identity, those who live and work in the United States need ways to understand how gender shapes, and has shaped, their lives. Americans who honestly open themselves to studying the history of colonial America and the United States in all its complexity in terms of gender—and class, race, and ethnicity—may be able to understand where they came from and how their nation reached this place we call the present. History lessons about gender are integral to this process, for they provide clear ways to enrich the past and the means to achieving a future that is sustainable in a rapidly changing world.

REFERENCES AND FURTHER READING

Berkin, C., Crocco, M., & Winslow, B. (Eds.). (2009). *Clio in the classroom: A guide for teaching U.S. women's history*. New York: Oxford University Press.

Blom, I. (1991). Global women's history: Organizing principles and cross-cultural understanding. In K. Offen, R. R. Pierson, & J. Rendall (Eds.), *Writing women's history: International perspectives* (pp. 135–150). Bloomington: Indiana University Press.

Frederickson, M. (2004). Surveying gender: Another look at the way we teach United States history. *History Teacher, 37*(4), 476–483.

Interchange: The promise of digital history. (2008). *Journal of American History, 95*(2), 452–491.

Kerber, L. (1997). The challenge of opinionative assurance. *National Forum: The Phi Kappa Phi Journal, 77*, 9–13.

Kern, K. L. (1996). To feel as part of history: Rethinking the U.S. history survey. *AHA (American Historical Association) Perspectives, 34*(5), 7–8.

Lindenmeyer, K. (2003). Using online resources to re-center the U.S. history survey: Women's history as a case study. *Journal of American History, 89*(4), 1483–1494.

Yang, M. M. (Ed.). (1999). *Spaces of their own: Women's public sphere in transnational China*. Minneapolis: University of Minnesota Press.

Zinsser, J. P. (1996). And now for something completely different: Gendering the world history survey. *AHA (American Historical Association) Perspectives, 34*(May-June), 11–12.

CHAPTER 26

Literary Studies

ANNETTE KOLODNY

It is impossible to overstate the impact and continuing importance of the Florence Howe Award for Feminist Scholarship since its inception in 1974. For recent generations of scholars who grew up with feminist inquiry as part of their college curriculum, a brief look backward may be in order. Graduating from high school in 1958 and from college in 1962, as I did, I don't think I even realized how invisible women were in the education I had just received. To be sure, we knew that George Eliot was a woman. Jane Austen and Emily Dickinson were usually introduced to us in high school. We were told that Harriet Beecher Stowe had written an antislavery best-seller that helped foment support in the North for civil war, but no teacher actually assigned *Uncle Tom's Cabin*. In high school civics courses or college history surveys, names like Margaret Fuller, Elizabeth Cady Stanton, and Susan B. Anthony were mentioned as women ahead of their time who had agitated for female suffrage. But while we read *about* them, we never read anything written *by* them. Although Lorraine Hansberry's *A Raisin in the Sun* was *the* Broadway hit of 1959, the year I was a sophomore English major at Brooklyn College in New York, no women of color were on any reading list. And only because one of my sisters began to explore her sexuality, tapped into a closeted lesbian grapevine, and brought home a much-worn copy of Radclyffe Hall's 1928 novel *The Well of Loneliness* did I divine there might be anything like a tradition of lesbian literature. With precious few exceptions, then, for my generation, women were either absent from the arts and public life, or they were the invisible helpmates of significant males.

Then, as the 1960s progressed, personal and political discontents exploded—and came together: the civil rights movement, the anti–Vietnam War movement, the United Farm Workers' movement, the early gay and lesbian rights movement, the beginnings of the environmental movement, and the general questioning of unjust authority and inequitable treatment between and among groups in the United States. What we then called the women's liberation movement was a part of it all, and many of us came to it through our prior involvement in one or more of the other great catalysts of the decade.

To be honest, literature was a small part of the mix. Nonetheless, the heady days of consciousness-raising groups and the women's liberation movement of the late 1960s and early 1970s revealed the slight presence of women in almost every textbook or reading assignment from grade school through college. Whether we studied literary texts in graduate school or in small independent reading groups, anything we could find written by women fed our desires to recover a sense of our past, our prior accomplishments, and our shared sisterhood across lines of race, religion, ethnicity, class, region, and sexual preference. Those of us who studied literature in graduate programs in the late 1960s and early 1970s were determined to rediscover our literary foremothers, even when our male professors told us there weren't any. And we were determined to examine all the ways in which literatures—by men and by women both—had constructed and deconstructed femininity and gender roles. Our first triumphs were archival: We discovered a wealth of women writers dating back to Sappho. Our second triumph was to teach ourselves and our students how to read the codes and nuances, the subterranean resistances, and the acts of outright courage inscribed in women's texts. Our third triumph was the renewal of theory: We grappled with the inadequacies of available modes of literary analysis and, when necessary, invented our own.

By 1974, there was a wealth of new feminist scholarship on the general subject of gender and literature. But the women who produced that scholarship were dismissed as faddish, or they were said to be working on second-rate writers. Too many of those women (myself among them) were denied promotion and tenure. At least part of the reason women were failing to make it through the promotion and tenure process was that, in addition to a general hostility toward our feminist work, we had too few venues in which to place our essays, and most university presses were still hesitant about developing lists in the new feminist scholarship. Since we couldn't publish, we were perishing.

In my area of American literature, for example, the major and oldest established journal in the field—the journal of the American Literature Section of the MLA—is *American Literature*. But in the years before 1974, the vast majority of the articles and book reviews in that journal were written by male scholars and the few women authors who received attention (mainly from male scholars, of course) included Anne Bradstreet and Emily Dickinson or, less frequently, Flannery O'Connor, Eudora Welty, Ellen Glasgow, Edith Wharton, and Willa Cather. The first article to appear in *American Literature* with even a modestly feminist point of view was Blanche H. Gelfant's fine study of Willa Cather, "The Forgotten Reaping-Hook: Sex in *My Ántonia*," which appeared in the March 1971 issue. Even so, feminist critics continued to submit their work to that journal, as to many others, albeit with little success. Several feminist friends of mine papered their bathroom walls with their rejection slips.

Then, in 1974, the Women's Caucus of the Modern Language Association named a prize for Florence Howe, one of the caucus's founders, a previous MLA president, a visionary pioneer in the field of women's studies, and a cofounder of the Feminist Press. The caucus thereby effectively announced that the new feminist scholarship was important and here to stay. That scholarship could be weighed, it could be judged, and it could be held to the highest standards of excellence. Feminist scholarship also now carried the imprimatur of approval from a group within the prestigious Modern Language Association. With the initiation of the award, nonfeminist and mainstream journals that had previously been closed to feminist scholarship gradually became more receptive.

Even a journal like *American Literature* began to change under the rising pressure of the profession's grudging acceptance of feminist approaches. Beginning with the March 1974 issue, *American Literature* carried two decidedly feminist articles, both written by feminist critics about women writers: Cynthia Griffin Wolff's "Lily Bart and the Beautiful Death" and Claire Katz's "Flannery O'Connor's Rage of Vision." From then on, feminist critics and feminist approaches were no longer invisible in the pages of this esteemed journal. Additionally, an entirely new pantheon of women writers soon began to appear in the articles and the book reviews alike—everyone from Djuna Barnes and Adrienne Rich to Zora Neale Hurston and Phillis Wheatley. Aiding that process of acceptance was the fact that mainstream journals like *American Literature* sought out at least one token feminist to add to their editorial boards. Thus feminist submissions could be assured of at least one potentially sympathetic reader. With more and more articles by and about women appearing in journals, moreover, the same university presses that published the journals increasingly recognized the growing demand for scholarly and critical books by feminists. By 1980, several prestigious university presses could point to impressive lists in the general areas of feminist theory and gender and literary history. Winners of the Florence Howe Award (along with the honorable mention recipients), especially, had little trouble getting their book manuscripts vetted by university presses. A great deal had changed.

While the advent of the Florence Howe Award cannot, by itself, account for all this, that award was certainly a major player in the pressure for acceptance because it gave our enterprise a new legitimacy. Indeed, had they had the opportunity, many of the long-established journals would have carried even more feminist materials. But another factor had now entered the equation: the new journals that women themselves were establishing.

The early and mid-1970s saw the introduction of several feminist journals that provided even more welcoming venues for the publication of the new feminist scholarship. *Off Our Backs* had been publishing since 1970; *Quest: A Feminist Quarterly* began publishing in 1974; and from 1972 on, several distinguished and slightly more mainstream feminist journals began appearing. In 1972, Wendy Martin founded *Women Studies: An Interdisciplinary Journal*; that same year *Women's Studies Quarterly* began publication (enlarged from what had formerly been the *Women's Studies Newsletter*); and *Feminist Studies*, under the editorship of Claire Moses, made its first appearance. In 1973, Janet Todd was the founding editor of *Women and Literature*. Two years later, *Signs: A Journal of Women in Culture and Society* appeared under the editorship of Catharine R. Stimpson, and *Frontiers: A Journal of Women's Studies* published its first issue. In 1976, *Camera Obscura: A Journal of Feminism and Film Theory* began publication, and in 1978, *Women's Studies International Quarterly* made its first appearance. Simultaneously, nonfeminist mainstream journals began to devote special issues to the subject of women and feminism. In the winter of 1975, for example, the journal *Diacritics* published the special issue *Textual Politics and French Feminism*.

I retell this well-known history only to emphasize the fact that as the 1970s progressed, mainstream journals found themselves competing with the new feminist journals for articles that used feminist critical approaches. And everyone wanted to publish a Florence Howe Award winner. Yet all this publishing activity did not immediately translate into significantly increased success for feminist critics in the promotion and tenure process. Annette Niemtzow, who in 1975 published one of the best feminist studies of Henry James in *American Literature*, was later denied promotion and tenure at Bryn Mawr. Despite the recent appearance of my first book, *The Lay of the Land: Metaphor as Experience and History in American Life and Letters*, in 1975, I was denied promotion and tenure in the English department at the University of New Hampshire.

Subsequently, I initiated one of the earliest Title VII discrimination suits and sued the university for sex discrimination and anti-Semitism. That lawsuit resulted in many important case law precedents and was finally settled out of court in October 1980. But during those long five years, even though I continued to do research and publish, I was never sure I would really have a career. In fact, my essay "Dancing through the Minefield: Some Observations on the Theory, Practice, and Politics of a Feminist Literary Criticism" was written during a bleak period when I was contemplating the end of what was then my brief career in academe. But in 1979 the as yet unpublished essay won the Florence Howe Award, which by itself gave me the courage to fight on. For that, I am forever grateful for what this award meant to me personally.

Now, as a seasoned veteran of the culture wars, I have come to understand what the Florence Howe Award meant to the academy in general. It validates the worth of every critic and scholar who engages in feminist practice. Beyond that, the award has continued to signify the fact that feminist scholarship forever transformed the shape and the subject matter of literary inquiry in the United States and around the world. After all, we continue to discover new women writers, both past and present, and we continue to experiment with both theory and critical methodology. As this collection of Florence Howe Award winners (in Suzuki & Dufault, 2006) makes clear, we are no longer constrained by language or by geography. Our reach is increasingly global— and will continue to be so. As a result, feminist scholarship continues to widen the discourse of and about literary matters. At its inception, the Florence Howe Award helped to give our enterprise, in all its diversity, both legitimacy and visibility. It does that still, even today. That is the award's gift to us all.

REFERENCES AND FURTHER READING

Gelfant, B. H. (1971). The forgotten reaping-hook: Sex in *My Ántonia*. *American Literature, 43*, 60–82.

Hall, R. (1990). *The well of loneliness*. New York: Anchor. (Original work published 1928)

Hansberry, L. (1994). *A raisin in the sun*. New York: Vintage. (Original work published 1959)

Katz, C. (1974). Flannery O'Connor's rage of vision. *American Literature, 46*, 52–67.

Kolodny, A. (1980). Dancing through the minefield: Some observations on the theory, practice, and politics of a feminist literary criticism. *Feminist Studies, 6*, 1–25. Reprinted in Warhol & Herndl (1997).

Niemtzow, A. (1975). Marriage and the new woman in *The portrait of a lady*. *American Literature, 47*, 377–395.

Stowe, H. B. (1994). *Uncle Tom's cabin; or, Life among the lowly*. New York: Norton. (Original work published 1852)

Suzuki, M., & Dufault, R. (Eds.). (2006). *Diversifying the discourse: The Florence Howe award for outstanding scholarship, 1990–2004*. New York: Modern Language Association of America.

Warhol. R. R., & Herndl, D. P. (1997). *Feminisms: An anthology of literary theory and criticism* (2nd ed.). New Brunswick, NJ: Rutgers University Press.

Wolff, C. G. (1974). Lily Bart and the beautiful death. *American Literature, 46*, 16–40.

CHAPTER 27

Mathematics

ABBE HERZIG

The presumed objectivity of mathematics has led to a cultural blindness in the discipline to personal issues and to an academic mathematics that is organized to neither acknowledge nor accommodate social identities or issues. Consequently, mathematicians have largely ignored issues of gender and race, and students who do not correspond to the disciplinary cultural norm (male, White, childless, self-assured) are often at a disadvantage.

Consistent with this blindness in mathematics, the exodus of students from mathematics has often been described as a "leaky pipeline," a metaphor that poses students as passive participants in their education whose progress is affected only by the forces of fluid dynamics. A "leaky pipeline" does not address why students of some groups stay in mathematics while others leave in greater proportions, and it fails to recognize the roles of competitiveness and individualism in attrition. By combining all students into one undifferentiated volume of "fluid," this metaphor allows educators and policymakers to overlook the very human implications of the postsecondary educational environment in mathematics. A more promising metaphor might be that of a journey, suggesting that there is a destination, and that there are or should be different paths through advanced work in mathematics. This metaphor puts the onus of achievement not only on the student but also on the educational system, and it can easily incorporate the likelihood that some travelers have the privilege to be better equipped for their journeys than others or that they may encounter fewer obstacles along the way.

The participation of females in advanced mathematics decreases at every educational stage. Although more than half of all college students are female, women have earned only about 40% of bachelors degrees awarded in the mathematical sciences in the United States in recent years. One study on undergraduate attrition reports that mathematics has the highest attrition rate among all disciplines except for the health professions. Mathematics has also been reported to have one of the highest differences in the undergraduate attrition rates of women and men, with women more likely to leave mathematics than men. Over the past decade, approximately 30% of graduate students in the mathematical sciences have been women. In 2007–8, women earned 31% of doctorates, and African Americans, Native Americans, and Latinos combined earned only 9%. Despite earning three-tenths of doctorates awarded that year, women of all race-ethnicities comprised only 26% of the new doctorates who were hired by doctoral-granting departments. In the fall of 2007, only 19% of full-time faculty in mathematics were women (and thus female graduate students had proportionally few female role models among the faculty).

The largest drop in women's participation in mathematics occurs at the graduate level, the focus of this chapter. The training of graduate students—like the training of students at all levels—requires the acquisition of mathematical knowledge, participation in mathematical practices, and the development of a sense of belonging in mathematics. The last of these factors is most often overlooked, but perhaps most critical, in addressing gender inequities in postsecondary mathematics. Obstacles to women's belonging include characteristics of mathematics departments that make them inhospitable to women and discourses about graduate mathematics education that construct women as incompetent.

Belonging in Mathematics

According to sociocultural theories, learning entails students' appropriation of knowledge, participation in practices, and developing a sense of identity or belonging within the discipline (Boaler, 2002). Each of these dimensions is critical for students' development as mathematicians. Mathematics graduate programs in the United States are primarily structured to provide training in mathematical scholarship, and recently there has been a growing emphasis on training graduate students in practices of the profession, but little attention has been paid to students' development of a sense that they have a place within mathematics.

Building students' sense of belongingness in mathematics has been proposed as a critical feature of an equitable K-12 education. A similar construct has been proposed at the graduate level, with research implying that students' involvement or integration into the communities of their departments is important for their persistence. Students in several programs have described the importance of having a "critical mass" of women or students of color. Graduate women in mathematics and science have reported feeling isolated or alienated in their male-dominated departments and have described ways that they feel that they do not fit in.

Mathematicians and mathematics students have commonly been stereotyped as lacking in social skills and without interests outside of mathematics. Suzanne Damarin (2000) analyzes discourses surrounding mathematical ability and concludes that there is "a discourse of mathematics ability as marking a form of deviance and the mathematically able as a category marked by the signs of this deviance" (p. 78). In addition to being marked as women, mathematical women are further marked by the stereotypes of the mathematically talented, and women are constructed as deviant separately within each marked category. First, their mathematical ability defines them as deviant. Second, given common stereotypes of mathematics as a male domain, mathematical women are marked among mathematicians as not really one of them. For women of color and women who are mothers, the marking is even more complex, leaving them distanced from each of those communities to which they might otherwise belong. Women who choose to pursue mathematics must be willing to endure these multiple constructions of themselves as deviants and may be marginalized from the mainstream community of the mathematically able.

Obstacles Women Face in Postgraduate Mathematics

While all students face some challenges to belonging, for women and people of some racial and ethnic groups, coming to belong in mathematics is even more difficult. Challenges faced by women in graduate mathematics fall into two categories. In the first are aspects of graduate education that make graduate school an inhospitable environment for women: negative or absent relationships with faculty, ineffective styles of communication and competition, unfamiliar epistemology, and conflicts with family responsibilities. The second category entails ways that the discourses surrounding graduate mathematics education construct women as incompetent or incapable of mathematics: notions of autonomy and independence, beliefs about talent and who is capable of doing mathematics, and confidence.

Negative or Absent Relationships with Faculty

Students who have limited or negative relationships with faculty have fewer avenues to develop the knowledge, practices, and sense of belonging that are critical to success in graduate school. Encouragement from people influential in students' lives plays an important role in students' decisions to enroll and persist in graduate studies. Both women and men have acknowledged the importance of encouragement and moral support from family members. Students who are treated as junior colleagues are more likely to stay enrolled in graduate school and complete degrees, and conversely, students who feel they are treated as "adolescents" are less likely to complete degrees. Few mathematics graduate students report having received moral support or encouragement from faculty or mentors within their departments or programs, although when such encouragement was offered, it made a big difference to them.

Negative interactions with faculty are pervasive for women in science. Various forms of discrimination women face in their relationships with faculty have been documented, including professors who would not take on women students and advisors who did not seem to tap into their professional networks as vigorously for their women students as they did for men. Women have been excluded from the informal social networks of their laboratories or departments, treated as "invisible," and had their contributions marginalized, as well as having been the objects of openly sexist behavior, including unwanted sexual advances from faculty, tolerance by colleagues of public sexist comments, and professors who openly state that women are not as smart, dedicated, or talented as men.

Ineffective Styles of Communication and Competition

Despite the collaborative nature of much of their work, some mathematicians have described the intense competition of their work worlds, including the confrontational atmosphere at conferences and relationships with their Ph.D. supervisors in which "arrogance, bullying, favoritism, and the need for tenacity all featured" (Burton, 2000, p. 4). Communication styles commonly used in mathematics can be meant to impress and mystify rather than to explain and illuminate, and confrontational language is a normal part of mathematics discourse. Common terms used in mathematics like "we claim," "the proof is trivial," "it is obvious," and "it is commonly known that," can be intimidating. This assertive communication style may be a mode of communication that is uncomfortable for some students, particularly women.

Sandra Keith (1988) argues that the mode in which mathematics is usually written and spoken is one of advocacy, of claims and assertions, one which generally ignores its audience. Given research reports that women use fewer declarative sentences in conversation than men, it seems likely that the language of mathematics may be more easily adopted by men than women. And, according to Keith, "it is a language which, particularly when spoken, is frequently confused with impatience, frustration, and defensiveness. Mathematical 'arguments' in the rhetorical sense of the word, move easily into 'argumentative' encounters" (p. 8). The forms of communication used by women may make it particularly difficult for their attempts at mathematical communication to be accepted. Consequently, these students may not fit faculty expectations for graduate students and may be judged to be incompetent.

Positive interactions with peers are important to students' experiences and persistence in graduate school. The perceived competition of graduate study has been cited as a factor in students' decisions to leave graduate school and in enrolled students' dissatisfaction with their experiences in graduate school.

Unfamiliar Epistemology of Graduate Mathematics

Some students are attracted to mathematics because of its abstract nature. Other students have reported disillusionment with how far removed their studies or research in mathematics or science was from meaningful or relevant questions. In several studies, frequent causes students cited for leaving mathematics and science were the seeming meaninglessness of their work and its irrelevance to social issues or to the people or issues in their lives.

Graduate study in mathematics is largely focused on traditional, theoretical mathematics. As a result, "many researchers lack the broad knowledge needed to address real-world problems . . . and the system of education is more or less self-contained, with graduates teaching what they have been taught in the same manner they have been taught" (National Research Council, 1992, p. 15).

Mathematics is often taught in highly abstracted ways, with little or no explicit connection to other mathematical ideas, ideas outside of mathematics, or the mathematical "big picture." Some authors have argued that women tend to be more interested in relationships and interaction among ideas than men, and in science women are more eager to learn how scientific ideas and facts fit together than are men, who may be more content to examine information out of context. Some feminist writers challenge the predominance of abstraction in mathematics; for example, Betty Johnston (1995) claims that abstraction in mathematics is a consequence of modern industrial society, based on the idea of separating things into manageable pieces, apart from their context. She further argues that this abstraction of mathematics is a masculine artifact, a way of denying the social nature of mathematics.

Conflicts with Family Responsibilities

Numerous studies have failed to find evidence that having dependents has an impact on persistence or attrition in graduate school or on research productivity in science overall. However, these studies have been plagued by sample selectivity and other biases. For example, scientists who faced the most serious obstacles to combining an academic career with family life might no longer participate in science, skewing the sample of those who remain; further, most studies on scientific productivity focus on elite scientists. While much of this research studies the impacts of family responsibilities on scientific productivity, they do not study the ways in which a career in science affects the decisions scientists make about marriage and family. To avoid conflicts with the demands of their careers, some scientists (particularly women) have decided not to marry or have children, to postpone having children until their careers were more established, or to have fewer children than they had originally planned; these decisions were made more commonly in the natural and physical sciences than in the social sciences.

Doctoral students with dependents generally take longer to complete their degrees, and the impact of having dependents is substantially greater on women than on men, particularly in the physical sciences and mathematics. Women graduate students in science who marry or have children have been described by faculty as not serious about their studies or as unreliable and not worth the investment; men who marry or have families do not face the same biases.

In order to accommodate family life, women in science often choose to pursue careers in industry, and those who remain in academe tend to aspire to jobs in small teaching colleges rather than research universities. Both women and men graduate students in science and mathematics have left graduate school because of a perceived imbalance between family and work responsibilities. Women have reported the double bind of combining motherhood with graduate school, as they felt that they were not able to devote enough time or energy to either. These perceived conflicts for women, between life in and out of mathematics and science, may explain why women graduate students have been reported to be less likely to be married and have families than male graduate students.

Women are more likely to make career compromises to follow a spouse than are men and are more affected by the concurrent timing of the graduate school, tenure, and childbearing clocks than men. What makes women faculty attractive as role models for women graduate students might not be their professional success as much as their ability to combine a successful career with a family life.

An additional obstacle facing students with family responsibilities is family-unfriendly scheduling, which limits the ability of some students to participate in the practices and activities of the department. Certainly some of the effect of family life on graduate student progress could be ameliorated by appropriate institutional responses, such as affordable child care, support for part-time study, flexible deadlines and a slower pace for students who are also parents, financial support, and flexibility in scheduling.

Independence and Autonomy

Women graduate students in science and mathematics have been stereotyped as less capable and competitive than men, and as a result, they may not be taken seriously by faculty. Starting from a young age, women's socialization can lead them to look for interaction, attention, and reinforcement rather than to be autonomous and independent learners. This pattern of socialization can work against them in the eyes of their advisors, especially in a disciplinary culture like that found in mathematics, where work is expected to be individualistic and independent. Consequently, female graduate students' styles of interaction may be different than those expected by male faculty and may be misinterpreted as inferior.

In effect, autonomy and independence are double-edged swords for women in science, as it takes a certain amount of support or belonging to enable a student to take risks. As noted above, male students may have enhanced relationships with faculty, which provide them with increased opportunities to develop a sense of belonging. This feeling of acceptance is a prerequisite for independent and autonomous work. Denied the same degree of relationships with faculty, female students may find it more difficult to act independently.

Beliefs about Talent and Who Can Do Mathematics

Mathematicians' beliefs in the importance of "talent" or "ability" can lead them to virtually ignore doctoral students in their first several years of the program, describing instruction as providing an opportunity for students to discover or prove whether they possess that talent. Some faculty have described feeling that they were doing students a favor by helping them avoid wasting time if they were unlikely to "have what it takes" to make it in graduate mathematics. These beliefs provide an explicit obstacle to students' participation in the program, in that only after they have proven themselves would they have opportunities to participate in meaningful ways in mathematics practice. This forms a double bind, since it ignores the ways that meaningful participation might enhance students' abilities and skills at mathematics.

This faculty belief in talent moves the focus of doctoral education from fostering students' development as mathematicians to filtering out students without the prerequisite talent or ability. In contrast, treating ability (as opposed to achievement or knowledge, for example) as the major reason for children's educational success has been found to interfere with their motivation to learn, their use of effective learning strategies, and their engagement with the content of the curriculum. Although the effects of different attributions for success have not been studied at the graduate level, one might imagine similar processes at play.

Confidence

Confidence has been described as an important feature in a graduate student's persistence toward a degree and as an influence on students' career plans and their persistence in pursuing them. Mathematics students need confidence in their abilities in order to persevere in solving mathematics problems, both in course work and in research.

In some research, men in science and mathematics have appeared more confident than women, despite the lack of significant differences in GPAs between men and women. While women have reported entering graduate school with lower self-confidence than men, their confidence is often further eroded by experiences within graduate school.

Confidence and ability are often intermingled in the research literature, as researchers describe students' confidence in their abilities and frequently its relationship to gender. However, most authors discuss confidence and ability without defining these constructs and without problematizing their often gendered connotations and implications. Some authors have constructed students as talented not because of any measurable, definable attribute but rather because they possess fluency with particular practices and behaviors that are consistent with expectations in schools. Similarly, graduate students may be described as confident when they exhibit the practices and behaviors that are valued within the mathematical community. Students who behave differently than the ways commonly accepted—as may be the case for women—are therefore constructed as lacking in confidence, and in some cases, in ability.

Enhancing women's opportunities and success in mathematics requires explicit attention to minimizing each of these obstacles, which are more severe for women than for men, and to building more avenues for women to come to feel that they belong in mathematics.

REFERENCES AND FURTHER READING

Bass, H. (2003). The Carnegie Initiative on the Doctorate: The case of mathematics. *Notices of the American Mathematical Society, 50,* 767–776.

Boaler, J. (2002). The development of disciplinary relationships: Knowledge, practice, and identity in mathematics classrooms. *For the Learning of Mathematics, 22,* 42–47.

Burton, L. (2000, November). *Strangers in paradise? The construction of mathematics as a male community of practice.* Paper presented at the 5th Symposium on Gender Research, Kiel, Germany.

Damarin, S. K. (2000). The mathematically able as a marked category. *Gender and Education, 12*(1), 69–85.

Grant, L., Kennelly, I., & Ward, K. B. (2000). Revisiting the gender, marriage, and parenthood puzzle in scientific careers. *Women's Studies Quarterly, 28,* 62–85.

Herzig, A. H. (2004). Becoming mathematicians: Women and students of color choosing and leaving doctoral mathematics. *Review of Educational Research, 74*(2), 171–214.

Herzig, A. H. (2004). "Slaughtering this beautiful math": Graduate women choosing and leaving mathematics. *Gender and Education, 16*(3), 379–395.

Johnston, B. (1995). Mathematics: An abstracted discourse. In P. Rogers & G. Kaiser (Eds.), *Equity in mathematics education: Influences of feminism and culture* (pp. 226–234). London: Falmer Press.

Keith, S. (1988, June). *Women and communication in mathematics: One woman's viewpoint.* Paper presented at the 10th Annual Meeting of the National Women's Studies Association, Minneapolis, MN.

Lacampagne, C. B., Campbell, P. B., Herzig, A. H., Damarin, S., & Vogt, C. M. (2007). Gender equity in mathematics. In S. Klein (Ed.), *Handbook for achieving gender equity through education* (2nd ed.) (pp. 235–254). Mahwah, NJ: Lawrence Erlbaum Associates.

National Research Council. (1992). *Educating mathematical scientists: Doctoral study and the postdoctoral experience in the United States.* Washington, DC: National Academy Press.

Sonnert, G., & Holton, G. (1995). *Who succeeds in science? The gender dimension.* New Brunswick, NJ: Rutgers University Press.

CHAPTER 28

Men's Studies

ROBERT HEASLEY

Men's studies is the study of gender as it applies to the experience of boys and men. Scholars of men's studies develop theory and carry out research that explores what it means to have a biological designation of being male in the context of culture, society, and human interaction. They critically examine how maleness is interpreted and how it is experienced within societal institutions such as family, religion, workplace, politics, and education. In the field of education, men's studies research may relate to such perplexing questions as whether boys really do learn differently than girls, why males are pursuing college education at lower levels than females, as well as ways to reduce male bullying and create campus environments that support many ways of being masculine.

Men's studies, which is sometimes located within or associated with women's studies or gender studies, can best be understood as a broad interdisciplinary field of study that provides, in whatever discipline it surfaces, a critical examination of how our concepts of masculinity are influenced by and influence society. Beginning in the mid-1970s and into the 1980s, a variety of academic departments at colleges and universities began to offer courses focused on men and masculinities. The term *masculinity* itself came to be pluralized, acknowledging the broad range of ways males are and can be "masculine."

Like women's studies, men's studies has its roots in a broader social movement that began as a series of small men's groups in the 1960s and 1970s that were concerned with increasing their understanding of their relationships with women and with one another. Although many of the early participants in the men's movement considered themselves feminists and supporters of women's rights, other branches of the men's movement also emerged that were indifferent to feminism or were antifeminist. Some of the academics active in men's studies as either faculty or students are also active in the men's movement, usually in the more progressive and profeminist branch of that movement. Men's studies scholars have also conducted research into the men's movement and have presented the results of their investigations to students in classes and to colleagues at professional conferences.

The major contribution of men's studies, however, has been to help students, educators, and other practitioners to think more analytically about gender and, specifically, about the needs of boys. The traditional view of males is that they are different from females and share a common predisposition to separate themselves from any-thing considered feminine. This assumption has led, in the past, to the expectation that all males will want to be or should be athletic or competitive. Schools thus empha-sized programs and activities that accentuated those "masculine" qualities instead of providing equal levels of support for boys pursuing noncompetitive and nonathletic activities. Boys who do not fit into the desired ways of being male are marginalized.

Such practices, say men's studies scholars, not only fail to acknowledge the many differences within male experiences of gender but also contribute to maintenance of a gender hierarchy, wherein certain types of masculine expression are valued over others. That negative effects—including bullying, higher dropout rates, poorer educational outcomes, and school violence—may result from such socialization of males goes un-examined. Recent scholarship indicates that boys in the United States and elsewhere are increasingly rejecting education (especially in the humanities) in part because of its association with femininity. Thus men's studies scholars find that when social insti-tutions such as schools excessively reinforce traditional male gender expectations, so-ciety struggles to keep boys actively engaged in intellectual pursuits.

Beginnings and Development of the Men's Movement

The men's movement, including men's studies, is rooted in Western culture by three historical developments: the psychoanalytical movement started by Sigmund Freud in the late nineteenth century, the suffrage movement, and the second wave of the feminist movement beginning in the 1960s.

Freud and later psychoanalysts, such as Karen Horney, questioned the assumption of biological "givens" related to males and females. They raised questions about the influence of parents on children's gender-related behavior, arguing that factors such as a boy's rivalry with his father and fear of castration (becoming too close to his mother) were the basis of psychological trauma. While psychoanalytic theories have been chal-lenged and criticized, these theorists importantly asserted that neither masculinity nor femininity was fixed. Rather, they saw that how boys and girls expressed them-selves as male and female occurred within a social context. In the case of boys, atten-tion was paid to the relationship between mother and son and the importance of the son separating from the mother, leading to the belief that boys would become like girls if they did not detach from the feminine.

Such perceptions of gender had implication for education. Boys were encouraged to participate in "male" educational and social opportunities that devalued the asso-ciation of boys with anything perceived to be feminine. As a result, organizations such as the Boy Scouts of America were founded in the early 1900s. The mission of the Boy Scouts was to instill in each boy the "manly qualities" that he would not find in areas where women were influential, including family and elementary education. In this context, the relationship of a boy to education came to be valued less than his relation-ship to adventure and activities that took place outside of the home and school.

On social and political levels, the suffrage movement in the late nineteenth and early twentieth centuries raised serious questions about gender, far beyond women's right to vote. The suffrage movement called into question women's overall relation-ship to and dependence on men, raising uncomfortable questions about men and the meaning of masculinity. After all, if women could have access to the voting booth and could advocate for social and political causes, then what would come next—access to men's colleges and high-status careers, even economic independence? This meant that institutions created for males—for the socialization and education of boys—could be called into question. What, after all, did it mean (and did it take) to be a man?

Answers to these questions during the early part of the twentieth century were often premised on the assumption that males had qualities that were special if not superior to qualities of women, with significant educational implications. Intellectuals and political leaders maintained that boys should be seen as *essentially* different from girls. School curricula reflected this; children of each sex were encouraged to study topics appropriate for their sex—woodshop for boys, home economics for girls. Until the rise of feminism in the 1960s, most colleges and universities gave preference to male applicants and guided males into careers traditionally assumed appropriate for men (and females into traditionally women's careers). Emphasis within the curriculum represented particular ways of being gendered. Literature and history focused on male heroes whose behaviors accentuated male desire and need for adventure, war, and independence, while females were portrayed as dependent and homemakers. Females were represented as one-dimensional, based on the assumption that the ideal woman (and thus all women—or at least all White women) would desire to be limited to these roles.

What men's studies scholars would later point out is that the focus on these particular ways of being male also severely limited how males are perceived and how boys are socialized. The emphasis on separate curricula, on separate spheres in terms of exposure to ideas and ways of thinking, while limiting girls and women's access to opportunity, also limited males' perception of the desirability of anything identified as feminine. Effects continue; recent studies of educational choices of males and females show male students devaluing the study of literature and the "soft" sciences like psychology or sociology, since these are seen as less worthy of male attention, while engineering and chemistry are pursued in part for their value as "hard" sciences. Not surprisingly, careers in these latter areas are more highly rewarded.

Prior to the development of women's studies and, more recently, men's studies, such institutional assumptions and curricular decisions regarding men went without question. But after second-wave feminists began advocating for inclusion of women in educational institutions and programs where only males had been allowed and for including the study of women's lives in all academic arenas, education experienced significant changes throughout the latter half of the twentieth century.

What was also occurring, though less visibly, was a new emphasis on examining the implications of gender on males. By the early 1970s, both mass-market publications and scholarly writing emerged that challenged assumptions society held regarding males. These writers joined feminists in questioning the perception that males had innate and superior qualities compared to females or that males were even distinctively different from females at the levels previously assumed. The second wave of feminism's message to males was that they should question what effect gender had on their lives and they should question the gendered arrangements in institutions such as family and schools that contributed to problems experienced by both females and males.

Those who began to focus on the study of men raised questions about whether masculinity, along with expectations and assumptions made in its name, was really just a set of social assumptions that was now being threatened by social change. As they started to document, in men's lives, like women's, gender can be expressed in a range of ways. The differences between males and females were found to be less dramatic than previously thought, and they found more variation than previously assumed in the way males "are"—both across and within cultures.

Three quite different and sometimes oppositional approaches to understandings of men's lives evolved in the 1970s and 1980s that continue to frame debates about men and masculinity in the men's movement and, to a lesser extent, within men's studies. These have come to be called the men's rights/father's rights, mythopoetic, and profeminist approaches.

Men's rights advocates see males as experiencing societal oppression from being used as "machines," as workers and providers in an increasingly materialistic culture, while not receiving support equal to that of women for being engaged as parents (e.g., being less likely than mothers to gain custody of children in divorce cases). They have responded sometimes angrily to feminists, arguing that women's issues are not more important than men's are, nor should women's rights receive priority over the rights of men. In the 1990s, a related movement, the Christian-based Promise Keepers drew very large audiences, calling on men to return to traditional roles of husbands and providers.

The *mythopoetic* men's movement got its name from the reliance of movement leaders on analyses of men's lives that are based on ancient myths and archetypes (deep unconscious themes). Mythopoetic writers and self-help workshop leaders, including Robert Bly and Sam Keen, suggest that maleness is, in its essence, different from femaleness and femininity. While not taking political stances like the men's rights movement, they often see men as being victims of feminism and father loss/single motherhood. They emphasize ritual, mutual support, the importance of "unleashing the wild man within," as well as the importance of mentoring boys as they become men.

A third branch of the men's movement that evolved during the same period takes a *profeminist* approach and thus provides a critique of the men's rights perspectives. Men and women taking this perspective assert that, while gender relationships in a patriarchal culture are based on an imbalance of power between men and women, men are also negatively affected because social institutions privilege and benefit certain types of masculinity over others, and in the process, devalue not only women but all that is perceived as feminine. Beginning as a set of informal, antisexist men's groups in the 1970s, the organization that is now known as the National Organization for Men Against Sexism began holding annual conferences on men and masculinity in 1975 that were and still are attended by men and women exploring these perspectives on a personal and intellectual level.

While these three approaches to understanding men's lives offer differing perspectives, each has contributed to the growing discussion about men and gender. They have led to the formation of a range of national organizations of activists, academics, and practitioners focused on programs as divergent as interventions to stop men's violence, advocacy for fathers' access to children following divorce, support for men who are trying to overcome addictions to pornography, informational campaigns about men's health problems, and various efforts designed to end the devaluation of the feminine and of homosexuality among males.

Men's Studies as a Scholarly and Professional Field

Like the men's movement, men's studies is a response to the feminist movement and to the women's studies programs of academic research and theory that grew from that movement. Beginning in the 1960s, feminists began to advocate strongly for the academic study of gender in addition to calling for a range of social and political changes needed to reduce inequality between men and women. Feminists called attention to "gender" as a core human identity around which much of the social world is organized and which deserves multidisciplinary study.

Similarly, men's studies has made conceptualizations of the male gender role visible as a focus of study in a range of disciplines. Men, and particular expressions of masculinity that are predominant at a given point in time, have historically gone unexamined. For instance, school and campus shootings are often associated with "kids" or "students" acting out rather than being reported and investigated as a gender—specifically male—problem comprising a set of patterned behaviors associated with masculinity, such as boys' access to and likelihood of using guns, greater exposure to bullying and violence, lower emotional self-awareness, and lower likelihood than females of seeking help.

Men's studies advanced as courses began to be offered in universities and colleges, served by a growing body of literature in scholarly books and journal articles. Important early scholarly works that stressed the ways in which patriarchy and sexism disadvantage men, as well as women, included *The Forty-Nine Percent Majority: The Male Sex Role* by Deborah S. David and Robert Brannon (1976) and *The Myth of Masculinity* by Joseph Pleck (1981). The American Psychological Association formed a men's studies division in the 1980s. As indicated above, regional and national conferences on men and masculinities were organized during this period, drawing together those working in the emerging fields of domestic violence / battering intervention, profeminist activism and scholarship, and those pursuing personal changes in their lives that called for a new vision of what it meant to be a man.

Philosopher Harry Brod (1987) in *The Making of Masculinities* laid a foundation for theorizing masculinity as a product of social norms and values that change and adapt to societal dictates over time. Gender, for males, came increasingly to be viewed as a social construction that is a product of social forces, with specific forms of masculinity being idealized to the extent that they serve to support social order. In a culture that devalues homosexuality, males are socialized to devalue homosexuals in exchange for being perceived as appropriately "masculine." At the same time, males are given encouragement and rewards for overtly sexualizing women as a means of demonstrating a particular type of heterosexuality (one that is dominant over females). Similarly, in alignment with a culture that values competition, schools place an emphasis on competitive sports, and males are rewarded if they compete for athletic, economic, or personal gain. Boys who are not competitive—or not athletic—are devalued.

By the 1990s a more developed literature began to surface among scholars, presenting theory and research on men overall and in specific arenas of men's lives such as education, sports, sexual orientation, religion, literature, and media. The American Men's Studies Association, founded in 1991, sponsors annual conferences featuring papers by professors, students, researchers, and practitioners. Some indication of the rapid growth of the literature in men's studies can be seen in the fact that *Men's Lives* (Kimmel & Messner, 1997), an anthology often assigned as required reading in college courses concerned with sex and gender, appeared in seven editions between 1997 and 2006, each of which contained a substantial amount of new material. Additionally, a number of books and journal articles addressing masculinities in the context of race and ethnicity, social class, and age have contributed to an understanding that the field of men's studies has become an important area of study providing rich insight into the diversity of men's lives and critical analysis of the notion of masculinity and its effects. Men's studies courses also often interrogate feminist and queer theories concerned with the effects of gender on sexuality and sexual identities.

In *Masculinities*, R. W. Connell (1995) made a major contribution to the field, identifying as hegemonic the form of masculinity against which all other ways of being male are measured, one which requires women to perform "emphasized femininity." He argues that hegemonic masculinity (the dominant perceptions and enactments of what it means to be male) prevents alternative forms of masculinity from gaining legitimacy and keeps problems associated with traditional masculinity from being acknowledged. This reconceptualization challenges the linear conception of masculinity, in which some males are seen as being more or less "masculine" than others, based on some normative definition. By challenging this conception and the dichotomous conception in which males are seen as either masculine or not, scholars have begun to understand the wide-ranging variations of male behavior. For instance, in the school context, males who prefer to participate in activities and interactions predominantly involving female students might be considered "less masculine" than those participating in male-only sports and might be labeled as "sissy," "queer," or "fag" by other males. Different sports are seen as more or less masculine, for example football as compared with gymnastics, resulting in boys shying away from pursuing "nonmasculine" activities as well as devaluing those males who do participate. Often school administrators, teachers, and parents attribute greater value to sports considered the most masculine, even if without intention. By examining the meaning of such behaviors, men's studies scholars introduce ways of understanding their influence.

Recent research on boys and men, accompanied by further theorizing, continues to accentuate the importance of viewing masculinity as a socially negotiated experience while acknowledging physiological differences between males and females, as well as among males. Men's studies scholars in the social and behavioral sciences explore topics such as male violence, sexuality, boys and men's emotional self-awareness, and boy's school failure and dropout rates. At the same time, scholars in religious studies, history, literature, and the arts and popular culture seek to critically examine the representation of masculinities and the voices of men in their respective fields of study.

The field of men's studies continues as a broad range of ongoing courses taught in a variety of disciplines—many located within the social sciences, but increasingly incorporating the humanities. These courses are supplemented by projects such as dissertations examining the representation of masculinity in literature or film and college-based conferences or programs addressing men's studies or men's issues on campus. Several colleges and universities have developed overarching programs related to men's studies, notably Saint John's University in Minnesota, which has created a men's center for leadership and service that has organized three major conferences addressing issues related to the college male. Hobart and William Smith College in New York State offers an interdisciplinary minor in men's studies, while other colleges are considering similar programs. The American Men's Studies Association has initiated a project to collect syllabi and related course material and make them available on its Web site to encourage the development of more courses about men and masculinities on more campuses.

The scholarship of men's studies, although still relatively new, serves to advance a greater depth of understanding of the influence of both biological and social factors on men's lives and our concepts of masculinity, thus creating new understandings of boys' and men's realities and the influence of gender on males. The results of their studies produce knowledge that will continue to be of value to educators in reaching their goal of effectively teaching all students, of all genders.

REFERENCES AND FURTHER READING

Brod, H. (Ed.). (1987). *The making of masculinities: The new men's studies*. St. Leonards, NSW, Australia: Allen & Unwin.

Connell, R. W. (1995). *Masculinities*. Berkeley: University of California Press.

David, D. S., & Brannon, R. (Eds.). (1976). *The forty-nine percent majority: The male sex role*. Boston: Allen & Unwin.

Kimmel, M. S., & Messner, M. A. (Eds.). (1997). *Men's lives*. New York: Allyn & Bacon.

Pleck, J. (1981). *The myth of masculinity*. Cambridge, MA: MIT Press.

CHAPTER 29

Multicultural Education

RENÉE J. MARTIN

Over the past 40 years a variety of definitions of multicultural education have emerged. There is evidence to suggest that much of the literature and (by extension) the resulting pedagogy concerned with multicultural education ignores gender and has a tendency to focus upon issues of race and ethnicity. An analysis of social class is also usually ignored, as are the complex ways in which social class, race, and gender intersect. Of the five prevailing approaches to multicultural education, the one known as multicultural social reconstructionist education makes this intersectionality central. It attempts to create an understanding of how race, social class, and gender coalesce to create systemic patterns of institutionalized oppression.

Five Approaches to Multicultural Education

In the 1980s, Christine Sleeter and Carl Grant developed a taxonomy identifying five prevailing approaches to multicultural education. While the first four approaches espouse theories advocating transmission of the dominant culture, the fifth approach, multicultural social reconstructionism, is grounded in critical and liberatory theory and advocates transforming schools and social institutions. Social justice advocates and liberatory pedagogues believe, therefore, that this can be an effective pedagogical approach to redress issues of gender inequity as well as other forms of social injustice.

The first approach chronicled by Sleeter and Grant (1994), known as *teaching to the exceptional or culturally different*, asserts that teachers should assist students in acquiring knowledge, skills, and attitudes that will enable them to participate successfully in the culture of the dominant group. This approach is used to teach children a sense of their own distinct cultural ethnicity or heritage or to teach about a particular historically marginalized group. It is primarily used when members of a historically marginalized group are represented in a school or class. Students are encouraged to acknowledge their racial and ethnic identities but are asked to assimilate those identities into the cultural mainstream. Critics contend that the approach centers on a deficiency orientation wherein all groups are measured against and expected to conform to a dominant White, Western cultural norm. A further criticism of the approach is that it ignores social class and gender.

Of the approaches discussed by Sleeter and Grant, one that remains popular is the *human relations* approach. This approach attempts to foster positive, individual relationships among students of diverse racial and ethnic backgrounds but ignores gendered issues. The overarching goal is to replace tension and hostility with tolerance and to do so with personal interaction. It can be argued that although women and men have had thousands of years of personal interaction, interaction has not ameliorated gender-based inequality. In fact, it has been asserted that personal, especially sexual, relationships between women and men sometimes exacerbate gender inequities. Sexual relationships often bind women and men together in traditional and sometimes inequitable social relationships that make it difficult to remediate or even call attention to inequities.

Criticism of this approach centers on a failure to educate students to think critically about how categories of difference originate or why various groups have been marginalized and oppressed. Issues of race and ethnicity are of primary importance, and issues of gender and social class are subsumed. Tension between girls and boys is sublimated and depicted as a natural part of the maturation process. Consequently, the harassment of girls that has been widely reported by researchers during the past two decades is overlooked. Girls receive the message that harassment is natural, and boys develop a sense of entitlement to girls and to the school environment.

Additionally, students who are taught from a human relations approach are not asked to wrestle with the moral or ethical implications of gender inequities or to investigate the ways in which women are victimized when men are advantaged. This approach also suggests that people should tolerate rather than accept and value individual and group differences.

The *single-group studies* or *ethnic additive* approach educates students about a historically marginalized group. This is done primarily by teaching about members of the group at certain points in the curriculum or at particular junctures during the year as in the designation of February as Black History Month or March as Women's History Month. The approach is aimed at dispelling the myth that schooling is a neutral process by attempting to be more inclusive and helping students understand how schools have supported the status quo through the perpetuation of stereotypes. Further, it addresses some of the systemic issues of inequality such as in the exclusion of women's accomplishments from the curriculum. One version of this approach peripherally infuses women into the curriculum. For example, women may appear in certain parts of the curriculum as in a chapter titled "Women in Science" in a science textbook. The peripheral infusion (either in a text or at certain times of the year) suggests that women have not been an integral part of a discipline, that indeed their accomplishments are limited to a chapter often located at the end of the text, which is further complicated by the fact that many teachers never reach the end of a textbook. The ethnic additive approach relegates women, their lives, and accomplishments to the margins of the canon and sends a message that women are not as highly valued for their contributions as their male counterparts.

The approach known as *multicultural education* is an effort to strengthen the knowledge base by transforming the curriculum so that, on the surface, it presents diverse perspectives. The approach attempts to free curricular materials of gender stereotypes but is limited in that it fails to acknowledge multiple forms of diversity as complex and inextricably linked. With this approach, there is scant attention to social class and its effects on women's lives. This approach may acknowledge the accomplishments of women in some superficial ways; for example, schools have become more adept at supporting women's athletics and displaying their trophies. However, girls are often relegated to the use of lesser facilities, less popular schedules, and lesser celebrations of their victories. When women's lives and accomplishments are included, they are often co-opted by a perceived need for fairness, usually under the guise of sameness for boys and men.

An illustration of this occurred when the National Organization for Women advocated a Take Your Daughters to Work Day. Schools could have been at the forefront of a discussion acknowledging that many occupations remain closed or difficult for women to enter. They might have countered the bogus claim that boys are also discriminated against by educating children and using data about occupational segregation and wage disparities. Instead, there was virtually no outcry as conservative groups balked and insisted that boys be allowed to accompany parents to work. While many schools would assert that they have initiated a multicultural education approach as described by Sleeter and Grant, it is clear that the approach does little to probe the depths of gender equity issues.

Further, the multicultural approach presents a dominant cultural perspective but avoids delving into causal factors that undergird issues of oppression. Topics such as homophobia are considered taboo in most schools and are therefore virtually absent from the curriculum. Homophobic epithets are commonplace in school hallways and on playgrounds, where many students report that playing games such as "Smear the Queer" are still part of playground culture. Homophobia does not exist in isolation. It is inextricably linked to the privileging of that which is masculine over that which is feminine, and it plays an important role in fostering school violence.

While critical educators recognize that some approaches to multicultural education actually impede students from adequately addressing gender equity, the approach advocating education that is multicultural and social reconstructionist or *multicultural social reconstructionism* (MCSR) is widely considered to be the most efficacious. A derivative of liberatory, critical, and feminist theories, MCSR is characterized by eight objectives. MCSR (1) views culture as a product of power relationships; (2) helps students investigate issues of inequality in their own environments and encourages them to take action regarding those conditions; (3) conceptualizes culture and identity as complex and dynamic; (4) organizes a curriculum that incorporates students' backgrounds, learning styles, and experiences; (5) uses schools as laboratories to prepare students to participate actively in a democratic society; (6) builds a curriculum that enables students to become agents of change; (7) creates an environment that celebrates diversity; and (8) teaches students to build coalitions and develop cooperative learning strategies.

The MCSR approach advocates that students question the status quo and challenge existing inequalities, implying a shared responsibility to work actively toward redressing systemic inequities. It recognizes that knowledge is political and not neutral and that schools are arenas of struggle, resistance, and transformation. It is predicated on the belief that intellectual tension opens up new possibilities of interaction between teachers and students and affords them an opportunity to challenge dominant social forces. Most importantly, this approach views culture as a product of power relations and encourages students to recognize and confront power structures. It also calls for a restructuring of the social institutions that transmit the dominant culture to entities that challenge and therefore destabilize the current societal paradigm.

Multicultural social reconstructionists insist upon a recognition of the complex ways that racial, gender, and class oppressions intersect. An MCSR approach has the potential to unite students across oppressions so that various forms of oppression are not viewed as competing with each other. For example, students of color may perceive that the history of racism, including the enslavement of African Americans, is so horrific that no other form of oppression can compare to it. Rather than pursuing the idea that racism and sexism are competing oppressions, critical pedagogues seek unification to achieve a common goal: in essence, the eradication of all forms of oppression. When students unite for the common good across oppressive conditions, strength and commonality of purpose can be realized.

An MCSR educational approach prompts students to interrogate oppressive social relationships in order to help shape a society that is more equitable, democratic, and just. It calls upon students to rethink cultural norms and value structures that reify the status quo. Further, it establishes classrooms as democratic sites of empowerment and underscores the need for critical dialogue and the enactment of counterhegemonic principles, thereby enhancing the potential to transform traditional relationships of power and domination while simultaneously calling attention to the representative voices of historically marginalized groups.

Critical multicultural pedagogy does not merely seek to transform the society but also functions as a means of investigation. It promotes rigorous thinking and the development of students' intellects, thereby asking them to interrogate complex, synergistic social relationships. It encourages students to search for new perspectives as well as alternative lenses and to transgress social boundaries.

Positionality as a Liberatory Tool

Positionality refers to the race, class, and gendered identities that people occupy in society and the ways in which the culture situates those identities, as well as the power that they are able to accrue as a result of those positionalities. The construct of positionality acknowledges that people are all raced, classed, and gendered and that those identities are relational, complex, and fluid positions rather than essential qualities. Because all positions are partial, they represent stances and points of view that are problematic and that must be problematized. Students who understand the construct of positionality are able to question the legitimacy of their worlds, the construction of their personal identities, systems of rewards, relationships of power, moral positions and ethical tenets that function to uphold or deny power, and access to institutions and resources to which they have become accustomed.

Understanding the construct of positionality is essential to the effective implementation of an MCSR approach, which requires that educators and their students interrogate their positionalities as raced, class, and gendered individuals. Positionality does not define people in terms of fixed identities but by their location within shifting relational networks. It questions what happens when positionalities are depicted as mutually exclusive and what occurs when multiple positions exist. Further, it questions what tensions arise as a result of the interplay among various positions.

For example, many young women are discouraged from pursuing so-called masculine activities, occupations, or sports. What occurs for girls who are talented athletes who also find themselves on the brink of adult femininity as it has been constructed by the dominant culture? Even if they have the strength, stamina, and talent, few possess the psychological acumen that is needed to endure the stigma associated with girls who play football, wrestle, box, or play ice hockey. A salient factor in the battle to overcome gender oppression is a cultural preoccupation with normative masculinity and femininity. Walkerdine (1990) noted that American society is overflowing with social fictions of what it means to be feminine or masculine. She contends that these fictions are so deeply embedded in society that they can take on the status of fact, especially when they are incorporated into and regulated by powerful social institutions such as schools or media.

Gender oppression in the form of homophobia is used as a powerful deterrent to advocating for equity. The quest for equity is viewed as a direct threat to the status quo and the perpetuation of a world in which men are accorded disproportionate power, access to resources, and the ability to govern those resources. In order to deter women from interrogating issues of gender inequality, some men have devised heinous epithets such as labeling feminists "femi-Nazis," thereby equating women's quest for liberation with one of the most horrific genocidal events in the history of the world. Antifeminist propaganda routinely depicts women who attempt to engage in non-traditional activities or occupations as masculine, man haters, and lesbians. Similarly, men in American society are apprehensive about violating the culture's prevailing masculine code of behavior. Goals to overcome sexism have been historically ascribed to women. Some men, fearing that they will be labeled homosexuals, have expressed disdain for any affiliation with "women's issues." There is pressure for men to adopt what Jackson Katz has called a "tough guise," a hypermasculine persona that projects an image of men as physically powerful, muscled, and the polar opposite of anything in the culture that might be viewed as female or feminine. The guise of masculinity exists as an unwritten code of behavior that restricts men and encourages them to use physical prowess and power over others to project manhood.

Positionality also encourages us to ask what occurs when multiple positions exist. It asks us to consider what tensions arise as a result of the complex interplay among various positions. Racism, sexism, and elitism have interdependent effects on patterns of discrimination based on the positionalities of race, gender, and class. The discrimination is rationalized through a network of prejudices founded largely on cultural biases in the form of myths and stereotypes that Vega noted are unconsciously passed from one generation to the next. The ways in which positionalities are situated determine our access to power, our ability to control our lives, and our ability to effectuate our goals. Gender is always situated within racial and social class positionalities. Being a woman does not mean definitively that one will be treated a particular way. It is one thing to be a wealthy, heterosexual, African American woman in the United States, and it is quite another to be an African American lesbian who lives in poverty.

Positional knowing prompts us to interrogate the links between race and gender. What positionalities collide for a person of color who is female in American society? Women of color, for example African American women, have written extensively about the tensions that arise between the obligation they feel to defend and support African American men as well as to defend themselves against racism while simultaneously grappling with the sexism and issues of gender that are also present in their lives. MCSR affords people an opportunity to investigate the tensions and resonances that hold possibilities for understanding the complexities of their positionalities.

Among the questions for those who embrace an MCSR approach is how to best invoke its principles in order to effectively teach students about issues of gender equity and social justice. Doing so can be a fairly daunting task. Various authors have discussed the fact that the dominant culture and its institutions have colonized students' minds. Students arrive in classrooms with a wealth of knowledge about what it means to be feminine or masculine and predicate their identities on the importance attached to traditional depictions of those roles in society. The task for critical educators is to find ways to tap into the tacit knowledge that students bring to schools and to excavate the landscape of their intellectual terrain in ways that do not alienate them from that knowledge but that cause them to unearth its nuances.

Critical multicultural pedagogy has the potential to enable students to identify contradictions and initiate alternatives to the status quo. It encourages them to pose questions such as, What characterizes the cultural contexts in which women live, work, and learn? What are the cultural paradigms for female success? What multiple and often contradictory positionalities intervene when we attempt to create alternatives to inequitable practice? And, what kinds of pedagogical and institutional practices are possible when we admit that we are doubtful, that the world contains ambiguities, and that we are vulnerable?

There are risks and problems associated with advocating an MCSR approach. Issues arise because schools are not designed to interrogate the status quo; rather they tend to perpetuate it. Standardized testing and the invocation of national initiatives such as No Child Left Behind have exacerbated the attempts of those whose goal it has been to reform education. Most colleges of teacher education have failed to substantively integrate issues of social justice across their teacher education curricula. Isolated courses, which often completely ignore issues of gender and social class in favor of superficial attention to race, tend to prevail. Consequently, many teachers enter classrooms ill equipped to adequately address issues of social justice and, specifically, of gender justice. For many of the reasons cited earlier, gender has not been regarded as a substantive issue. A cursory glance at teacher education programs aimed at addressing school violence underscores the fact that few if any consider the gendered nature of school bullying, harassment, and shooting. Additionally, the scholastic underachievement of girls is rarely highlighted, while numerous recent texts have focused on whether or not boys are being left behind. Finally, the culture at large permits and encourages stereotypes and gender injustices in virtually all of its institutions. There is little incentive for teachers to invoke curricular approaches that oppose those injustices, and this is evidenced in the research that indicates that employing an MCSR approach is not yet a reality in most schools. While using an MCSR approach to educating about issues of gender equity constitutes high-risk pedagogy, it must be noted that its use affords educators opportunities to display how women and men might live authentic lives to their fullest potential. Consequently, there can be no doubt that the risk is outweighed by the potential benefits of this approach to multicultural education.

REFERENCES AND FURTHER READING

Alcoff, L. (1988). Cultural feminism versus poststructuralism: The identity crisis in feminist theory. *Signs: Journal of Women in Culture and Society, 13*(3), 405–436.

Bartlett, K. (1990). Feminist legal methods. *Harvard Law Review, 103*(4), 829–888.

Haraway, D. (1988). Situated knowledges: The science question in feminism and the privilege of partial perspective. *Feminist Studies, 14*(3), 575–599.

hooks, b. (1989). *Talking back: Thinking feminist, thinking Black*. Boston: South End Press.

Kincheloe, J. (2004). *Critical pedagogy*. New York: Peter Lang.

Maher, F. A., & Tetreault, M. K. T. (1993). *The feminist classroom*. New York: Basic Books.

Sleeter, C. E., & Grant, C. A. (1994). *Making choices for multicultural education: Five approaches to race, class, and gender* (2nd ed.). Columbus, OH: Merrill/Macmillan.

Vega, F. (1978). *The effect of human inter-group relations education on the race/sex attitudes of education majors* (Unpublished doctoral dissertation). University of Minnesota, Minneapolis.

Walkerdine, V. (1990). *Schoolgirl fictions*. London: Verso.

CHAPTER 30

Teacher Education

PEGGY PLACIER

Gender has been a central construct in teacher education since the inception of formal programs in the United States and other countries. In many nations, a majority of students in teacher education—a vast majority in primary or elementary education—are women. However, the most recent *Handbook of Research on Teacher Education*, edited by Cochran-Smith, Feiman-Nemser, McIntyre, and Demers (2008), does not include a chapter devoted to gender but only brief discussions of gender as one aspect of the teaching population or teacher identity.

Within teacher education, gender has been and can be viewed as a structural principle, a social problem, or an identity. As a structural principle, gender has differentiated and stratified teacher education curricula and programs. As a social problem, gender in teacher education has periodically captured policy attention, albeit for different, and sometimes contradictory, reasons. As a facet of identity, gender is regarded as a social construction that can best be understood and analyzed within recent critical, feminist, or postmodern treatments of teacher education. How gender is understood has important implications for educational policies. It also seems likely that current policy debates about educational achievement will have implications for teacher education programs, including how gender is treated in teaching and research.

Gender as Structural Principle

From a functionalist perspective, places called schools need people called teachers. Before the establishment of public school systems in the United States, men far outnumbered women as schoolteachers. Women taught children, of course, but in the home context. Women in early New England established "dame schools" in their homes that provided beginning reading instruction and a form of day care. An educated young woman might become a tutor or governess for children of an affluent family. But teaching in a school as usually depicted was either a temporary occupation for men studying to enter more respected professions such as the clergy, law, medicine, or an esteemed position in a private college preparatory institution for boys. Teachers were schoolmasters.

Through the nineteenth century, several trends converged to change this pattern in teaching and, thus, in teacher education. Early in the century, advocates of Republican Motherhood (the idea that mothers, as the first teachers of future male citizens, were important to the welfare of the new republic) supported the creation of secondary and postsecondary institutions for women. Even some who believed in the intrinsic value of women's education adopted the discourse of Republican Motherhood to gain sponsorship for women's schools. Therefore, a growing number of middle-class women pursued advanced formal education.

In the period before the Civil War, northern states passed laws establishing state-supported elementary schools for the masses, creating a surge in demand for teachers. New states admitted during westward expansion established public schools as a matter of course. Advocates and providers of women's education, as well as state education leaders, presented a variety of arguments for recruiting educated, unmarried women into teaching. Women teachers, like ideal mothers, would be morally pure and gentle guardians for young children. They would be more likely to stay on the job than men because their economic opportunities were severely limited. Finally, and some think most importantly, self-sacrificing women would make few complaints about low salaries and exploitative working conditions; therefore, they would provide a cheap and compliant workforce for the burgeoning public schools (Clifford, 1989; Spring, 2005).

At women's schools, such as the Troy Female Seminary and Mount Holyoke College, as well as state normal schools, young women enrolled in classes specifically designed for teacher preparation. Schoolmarms increasingly replaced schoolmasters; by 1860, women outnumbered men in teaching. A teacher might travel west to find a teaching position in a new frontier community or in a federal or church-affiliated school designed to "civilize" Native American children. After the Civil War, southern state constitutions were rewritten to create segregated public school systems, and federal funds supported new freedmen's schools. Northern teachers, both White and Black, went south. At the turn of the century, women taught thousands of immigrant children in urban schools to speak English and become loyal American citizens. Women who embarked on these challenging ventures often saw themselves not only as independent risk takers but as missionaries—religious, political, or social (Hoffman, 1981).

However, the supply of formally prepared women teachers did not meet the demand. Local control of hiring meant that local school boards might prefer men or applicants with little formal preparation. The pay and working conditions in many schools, as well as the common restriction that women could not continue to teach after marriage, did not resolve the problem of teacher turnover. These conditions still made teaching a short-term occupation that hardly seemed to warrant extensive preparation. Nevertheless, formal teacher education grew, provided by a variety of private and public institutions. Historically Black colleges and universities (HBCUs) had a mission of meeting the demand for Black teachers in segregated schools after the Civil War. HBCUs were somewhat more likely to encourage both men and women to pursue teaching because employment opportunities for educated African American men were meager. In some states, teachers could work in elementary schools if they had graduated from a high school teacher preparation program; these programs enrolled almost exclusively women. Finally, many teachers were hired to teach without formal preparation and later attended summer teacher institutes, often held at regional teachers colleges, to learn about pedagogy. Eventually, all states adopted regulations requiring formal teacher education at the college level for certification to teach in public schools (Clifford & Guthrie, 1988).

Another structural pattern that affected teacher education was gender stratification between elementary and secondary teachers, as well as between teachers and administrators. Early public schools were often ungraded one-room elementary schools with lone female teachers. Public secondary schools did not really multiply until the late nineteenth century. Men with bachelor's degrees in the disciplines predominated in high schools and earned higher salaries than elementary teachers. The "principal teacher" in a graded elementary school up until the 1920s was often a female teacher with part-time administrative duties. Colleges of education began offering new graduate degree programs in school administration. As the principal's role professionalized and became separated from teaching, men displaced women at this level. Men in teacher education programs often planned to teach for only the minimum number of years required by state or local policies before leaving to pursue the principalship.

These gender patterns continue to influence teacher education today. The vast majority of students in U.S. teacher education programs are White females. After desegregation, most positions for African American teachers, who had been restricted to Black schools, were eliminated. HBCUs today produce far more African American teachers than predominantly White institutions, but the numbers are still small. Most preservice teachers in early childhood and elementary education are White women, while White men compose about half of the students in secondary programs. Women have made inroads in traditionally male-dominated secondary disciplines such as math, science, and social studies and to a more limited extent in vocational fields, such as agricultural education. In addition, White women are now a majority of teacher education faculty in the United States, although in many countries men still predominate in the faculty ranks.

Critics of teacher education today continue to question whether teachers need special preparation in how to teach if they have adequate knowledge of curriculum content. For decades, these critics have assailed the quality of teacher education, including the academic abilities of education students and their instructors. In these critiques, authors do not explicitly mention gender, but it is interesting that equal derision is rarely leveled at historically male-dominated professional schools such as engineering and law. Some critics recommend cutting back or even disbanding formal teacher education to provide more open entry into teaching through an unregulated labor market. They propose that open entry might diversify the teacher population in terms of gender and ethnicity.

Although the specific historical causes differed, in European and South American countries, there was a similar shift from male to female teachers in the past century, especially at the primary levels. A common factor is the spread of universal primary education, with a resulting demand for large numbers of low-salaried teachers. There is evidence of the importance of gender in the politics of teacher education in countries as dissimilar as Germany, Mexico, Australia, Sri Lanka, and Argentina (Ginsburg & Lindsay, 1995).

Gender as Social Problem

Current studies and commentaries on education in the United States often begin by noting, or even bemoaning, that the majority of teachers are White, middle-class females, while the student population is becoming more ethnically diverse. Moreover, low-income students of color are more likely to have low scores on standardized achievement tests that, in today's political context, are considered to be a key indicator of school and teacher ineffectiveness. While gender equity advocates argue that schools disadvantage girls, others worry about how boys, especially African American boys, fare in schools where most teachers are White women. According to this demographic argument, the proportion of White, middle-class women in teacher education programs is a problem because they may not be capable of effectively teaching their low-income students of color, thus contributing to the "achievement gap." Their misunderstandings of African American male students in particular may be a factor in the incidence of school disciplinary infractions, which have increasingly severe consequences under zero-tolerance laws.

From a conflict theory perspective, an important question has been, Do schools systematically advantage or disadvantage certain groups of students? Tyack and Hansot (1992) point out that for the past two centuries, U.S. education critics have alternated between identifying schools as having a "boy problem" or a "girl problem." According to the boy problem, female teachers do not understand boys and try to feminize them by limiting their physical activities and pursuits of "masculine" interests. According to an outmoded version of the girl problem, schools might push girls too hard academically, making them physically and intellectually unfit for wife- and motherhood. The more recent version of the girl problem, presented most notably in a report from the American Association of University Women (AAUW) published in 1992, is that schools disadvantage girls through low academic expectations, less teacher attention, and gender stereotyping in the curriculum.

These gender conflicts have had several effects on teacher education. The approach to the girl problem since the 1970s, and especially since the AAUW report, has been for teacher educators to integrate gender equity content into the curriculum to a limited extent, often as one topic under the broad headings of "multicultural education" or "diversity." Preservice teachers today are more aware of potential gender biases in textbooks and language, for example. However, for future teachers to examine their sexist assumptions and unconsciously biased interactions with male and female students—as gender equity advocates propose—would require much more extensive curriculum revision.

The boy problem in the early twentieth century brought about implementation of curriculum reforms such as manual training, physical education, and extracurricular sports intended to retain more boys in school. Recently, boy problem discourse has been revived in support of a call for more men in teaching. Some teacher education programs are actively recruiting men, especially minority men, and especially in elementary education. Alternative teacher education programs for people who are changing careers (e.g., retiring from the military or from a math/science-related occupation) may attract men who want a faster route into teaching than attending a two- to four-year program with a cohort of young women. Once an occupation is identified as "female," it is stigmatized, and men entering it may feel that their masculinity, career ambition, or even sexual orientation is suspect.

Teacher educators in other countries, if the available literature is any indication, pay some attention to gender equity in the curriculum but do not seem to claim that women teachers disadvantage their male students. The United States has experienced a backlash against the feminist movement and gender equity policies, which may contribute to the revival of the boy problem in education policy arguments in this country. Other countries also do not have the same racialized histories as the United States, where the teacher education literature repeatedly identifies the predominance of *White* female teachers as the problem.

Gender as Identity

From critical, feminist, and postmodern perspectives, gender is one aspect of a teacher education student's identity, intersecting in complex ways with other aspects such as race, ethnicity, class, sexual orientation, age, and religion. Recommendations for teacher education reform in the 1990s called for more teacher reflection, not only on teaching practices but also on identities and beliefs. Critical and postmodern theorists called into question the liberal assumptions of the equity and multicultural movements. According to their analyses, White preservice teachers may express positive intentions about treating all students equally and may even acquire knowledge of cultural differences among their students, but until they critically examine the social construction of their "whiteness," they will have only surface understandings of the complexity of their work in a racialized society.

Because identity is multifaceted, examination of racial identity, which has received by far the most attention in teacher education, is intertwined with gender (class, sexual orientation, etc.) identities. However, many researchers report that convincing preservice teachers that they should critically interrogate the construction of their multiple identities and cultural assumptions can be challenging. Educators of the "missionary" teachers of earlier times did not ask their students to question their identities and intentions or to abandon their naive notions of assimilation, racism, and reproduction. Young, heterosexual, middle-class, White female students often appear in teacher education case studies as people who resist self-examination and social critique (although there are exceptions).

Critical and feminist teacher educators have made an impact in teacher education research, probably more than in practice. In this area, there is more international literature and more evidence of the influence of non-U.S. scholars (see, e.g., Britzman, 2003; Evans, 2002; Fischman, 2000). These writers ask teacher educators to help their students, both men and women, break down essentializing discourses portraying women as self-sacrificing caregivers and men as controlling disciplinarians or technicians. They would expand limited notions of gender equity to include deeper understandings of femininities/masculinities, sexuality, and sexual orientation. They envision the transformation of teacher education through frank interrogations of the self and society. Within the generally conservative cultures of colleges of education, however, this transformation of teacher education curricula seems unlikely.

Future Directions

Teacher education is currently facing political pressures on several fronts, and there may be gender implications of these pressures for the preservice teacher population and the teacher education curriculum. The first major source of pressure is the contradiction between simultaneous demands for higher standards for teacher education candidates and programs and for less time- and resource-intensive alternatives to teacher education or even open entry without formal teacher preparation. In the United States, this demand is supported by a perennial argument that colleges of education are self-aggrandizing institutions that promote ineffective quackery. More difficult entry and requirements are supposed to professionalize teaching. Easier entry, in contrast, might deprofessionalize teaching in comparison with other fields and diminish the size and mission of colleges of education. Easier entry, however, might also attract men who perceive teacher education as a college program for women. Some programs are recruiting African American men into teaching through alternative routes, even providing salary incentives that may prove controversial.

Another important policy trend is for teacher education programs to be evaluated based on the achievement scores of their graduates' students, according to production function models of education. In the context of market competition, low-quality teacher education programs would presumably be forced out of business if they could not show that their graduates are academically competitive. This policy trend is likely to have the effect of focusing teacher education curricula more narrowly on content knowledge and technical practices shown through experimental research to produce higher student test scores. Multicultural, feminist, and other critical approaches to teacher education would be even less likely if teacher education programs made such curricular changes. In addition, teacher education faculty may find it more difficult to find external, particularly federal, support for research on gender unless they can argue that such studies will contribute to higher achievement outcomes.

REFERENCES AND FURTHER READING

Britzman, D. P. (2003). *Practice makes practice: A critical study of learning to teach*. Albany: State University of New York Press.

Clifford, G. J. (1989). Man/woman/teacher: Gender, family and career in American educational history. In D. Warren (Ed.)., *American teachers: Histories of a profession at work* (pp. 293–343). New York: Macmillan.

Clifford, G. J., & Guthrie, J. W. (1988). *Ed school: A brief for professional education*. Chicago: University of Chicago Press.

Cochran-Smith, M., Feiman-Nemser, S., McIntyre, D. J., & Demers, K. E. (Eds.). (2008). *Handbook of research on teacher education* (3rd ed.). New York: Routledge.

Evans, K. (2002). *Negotiating the self: Identity, sexuality, and emotion in learning to teach*. New York: RoutledgeFalmer.

Fischman, G. E. (2000). *Imagining teachers: Rethinking gender dynamics in teacher education*. Lanham, MD: Rowman & Littlefield.

Ginsburg, M. B., & Lindsay, B. (Eds.). (1995). *The political dimension in teacher education: Comparative perspectives on policy formation, socialization, and society*. London: Falmer Press.

Hoffman, N. (1981). *Woman's "true" profession: Voices from the history of teaching*. Old Westbury, NY: Feminist Press.

Spring, J. (2005). *The American school, 1642–2004*. Boston: McGraw-Hill.

Tyack, D., & Hansot, E. (1992). *Learning together: A history of coeducation in American public schools*. New York: Russell Sage Foundation.

CHAPTER 31

Technology and Computer Science

RONALD E. ANDERSON

The nexus of gender, technology, and computer science evolves rapidly with technology advancement. Perhaps because of the newness of the field, this social change has been, and will continue to be, rather volatile. Not only is the information technology industry subject to ups and downs, but enrollments and degree counts in higher education have been seemingly capricious as well.

Computer science (CS) is not the only technology major for college students or the only technology vocation. Yet it still serves as the quintessential professional community, bridging advanced technology industries with the knowledge society. That computer science epitomizes technology fields in the early twenty-first century justifies intense scrutiny of gender roles within computer science. We need not only a map of the CS pipeline, particularly for women, but also a review of its implications and the interventions that would change it.

The complex character of the interaction between gender and technology derives largely from the sprawling, rapidly evolving nature of technology itself. In the United States, *technology* has become synonymous with *information technology* (IT) and *information and communication technology* (ICT). Computers are only a subset of ICT, albeit the most central part. Ironically, the world outside of the United States uses the word *technology* in a much more narrow way, and many Americans do not know what ICT stands for. In this essay, *technology* is used in the broad, U.S. sense.

People have been writing and talking about technology-based gender gaps for some 40 years, but almost nobody listened. Then about 15 years ago, someone coined the term "digital divide," and soon lots of attention was given to gaps based upon income, age, and race. While some tried to focus the digital divide movement on gender, journalists and others chose to concentrate on economic divisions within society.

Some believe that the gender gap has disappeared, having heard that men and women are equally likely to be using the Internet. In 2005, the official Web site of the U.S. Department of Education's Office of Technology stated, "The gender divide in computer use has been essentially eliminated, as there is no overall difference between boys and girls in overall use of computers."

Such conclusions are misguided because they fail to recognize there are numerous ways people relate to technology. Not only do access and mere use matter, but so do amount, quality, and appropriateness of use. Not only does opportunity to learn matter, but so do acquisition of technology-related skills and understandings. Not only do motivation and preference for different kinds of technology applications matter, but so do recruitment and retention into computer science curricula and technology-related jobs. Each of these dimensions is discussed here using those gender-related data that are currently available.

Gendered Access and Technology Use

For the first 35 years of computers (1940 to 1975), the principal force underlying computer use was occupation. During that period, men dominated engineering occupations, and computers were the purview of electrical engineers. However, as business and government implemented large data-processing operations, they needed data entry, and women were relegated to those routine jobs. Eventually they needed lots of computer programmers, and men primarily sought those jobs.

During this early period, computers took up huge amounts of space and cost more than most people could afford; but the microcomputers, later to be called PCs, of the late 1970s changed all that. In the early 1980s, many people took home their first computer, schools acquired them for staff and students, and companies installed them for individual workers. Using computers became not just a matter of occupation but of education, income, and personal preference.

In 1984, the U.S. census found that among 3- to 17-year-olds, 14% of American boys used a computer at home but only 9% of girls did so. This gender gap grew even larger over the next 10 years as parents sought to steer their boys into "good computer jobs." Parents were more likely to buy their sons a computer than their daughters, and that propensity remains, at least in the United States.

Not only did boys access computers more, but they also used them for much longer periods than girls. Boys took to programming and playing computer games in a big way, but girls tended to use them for practical things like learning and writing. Interestingly, this gendered pattern persisted 15 years later in the way people adapted to the Internet. Boys and men continue to be more likely to use the Internet for games and technical matters like downloading software, while girls and women are more likely to use it for practical things like searching for medical information.

Researchers Chen and Wellman (2003) analyzed Internet usage statistics for the period of the 1990s and the early 2000s for eight countries and made the following conclusions. During this period, the gender gap continued to be "declining yet persistent" in the United States, the United Kingdom, Japan, and China. It was declining in Mexico and persistent or flat in Korea. But most interesting was that the gender gap for Internet use was increasing in Germany and Italy. It is quite likely that the rising gap in these two countries relates to beliefs about gender roles, but it is also possible that it is partly explainable by the slow rise in the use of handheld Internet devices in these two countries.

Statistical trend studies in the United States show that in terms of mere access, the adult gender gap narrowed over time until it dissipated. But for measures of total time used (e.g., total online hours), the gap started very small and progressively got larger. Since 2000 the gap remains, in large part because men are considerably more likely than women to play online games.

As of early 2009, according to reports of the Pew Internet and American Life Project, 89% of Americans in the age bracket of 18 to 24 used the Internet, and 50% of those used it every day. Men are more likely to go online for no particular purpose, for using pornographic sites, or for getting online news, while women were more likely to go online to send e-mail, to search for medical or government information, and to seek help for problems with violence. This suggests that women tend to be more goal oriented and serious, or even more mature, in their utilization of the Internet.

The Pew studies have also found that women and men are equally likely to use a social networking site, such as Facebook or LinkedIn. However, females in their teens are more likely to participate in a social networking site than their male counterparts. The 2009 Pew study found that, in general, women are more likely to use social networking sites to reinforce preexisting relationships, and men use them more to meet new people.

The Computer Science Pipeline

The flow of students along the routes from high school through college degrees to job placement is often called a pipeline, although it would more aptly be labeled a funnel because fewer and fewer students successfully pass each more advanced educational milestone. When we examine this flow of students by contrasting computer science degrees for men and women, it is appropriate to call it a gendered pipeline because a wide gender gap persists throughout.

Researchers pointed out 25 years ago that not only did men get advanced degrees in computer science at much higher rates than women, but enrollments in elective computer programming and computer science courses in high school and college were far from gender parity. More general, less specialized computer courses tend to have less of a gender gap, in large part because they include instruction in applications like creating and using databases, which are topics that are of more interest to the pragmatic minds of young women.

The principal professional association of computer scientists, the Association for Computing Machinery, started college programming contests in the 1980s, and they are still popular among male students 30 years later. However, women students rarely participate in these contests. While some people infer from this that men are better at programming than women, a more plausible interpretation is that women are less attracted to cutthroat competition and to the honor that comes from winning such contests.

U.S. gender trends in computer science have been remarkable in at least seven major ways. First, enrollments and degrees in undergraduate CS have been dropping for *both* women and men, which bucks the trend for science, technology, engineering, and mathematics (STEM) fields, where enrollments have been increasing in all other fields. Some blame the decline in popularity of CS degrees on "dot.com" bubbles, others on outsourcing, but the most likely culprit is the field itself, which has rapidly become more theoretical and less associated with particular jobs or practical applications. In some colleges and universities, it has been combined with engineering, which takes away from the glamour of computer science as a profession for many prospective students.

Second, the number of computer science enrollments and bachelor's degrees earned (for both men and women) has been extremely volatile during the past three decades. Why have CS degree trends been so volatile? CS did not become popular until 1980, and the nature of CS evolved rapidly thereafter. As it became more theoretical, many students, especially women, dropped out. Also, the dot.com bubble in the early

2000s created the impression that CS jobs had been lost to industry downsizing and overseas outsourcing.

The number of CS bachelors' degrees (for both genders) peaked in 1986, dropped 30%, skyrocketed in the late 1990s in response to the dot.com boom, then crashed, peaking again in 2004, and declining slowly since. About a third of these CS degrees were awarded to women, and their percentage curve, for the most part, followed the overall peaks of the pipeline rollercoaster. However, overall in the past 25 years the gender pipeline for women's BA and BS degrees in CS narrowed from 36% to 20%, which is roughly equivalent to a shift from one-third women to one-fifth women.

Third, in two-year colleges the number of associate of arts (AA) degrees in CS awarded to women dropped wildly in the past 10–15 years. In 1996, 40% of those receiving AA degrees in CS were women. That share in 2006 had dropped to only 6%. This means that 94% of recipients of AA degrees in CS were men. Further research is needed to determine if this decline is an artifact of changes in reporting categories, institutional changes, or student preferences.

Fourth, graduate enrollment, postdoctoral fellows, and Ph.D.s in CS from 1996 to 2006 declined slightly for women, despite growth in graduate programs in all other STEM fields. One statistical trend during this period offers a basis for cheer. Specifically, in 1996, 15% of CS Ph.D. degree recipients were women, but that had risen to 22% a decade later.

A large influx of foreign Ph.D. graduate students in CS bolstered the number of women Ph.D. graduates. If the students who are not U.S. citizens are removed from the count of those receiving Ph.D.s in CS, then the Ph.D. degrees to women drops in 1996 and drops even more in 2006. Thus, for U.S. citizens, the percent of women Ph.D. degrees declined in this decade.

Fifth, about 60% of the women receiving a Ph.D. in CS remained in academe, whereas about 60% of the men took jobs in industry. If this trend continues, graduate CS program faculty will eventually reach gender parity. But the high-status CS positions in industry will become even more male dominated.

Sixth, women are more likely to pay for their own undergraduate and graduate education in CS. Not surprisingly, then, women also rely more on fellowships, research assistantships, and internships as sole sources of support. Because of this reliance on institutional supports, women are more vulnerable to shifts in educational policy regarding cuts in student funding and employment.

Seventh, gender and race do not have interaction effects, which is to say they are not mutually reinforcing nor acting in opposition. For example, racial minorities are more likely to drop out of CS, but men and women minority students are about equally likely to drop out, which implies the lack of an interaction.

Gender in Community College Technology Programs

Women constitute 60% of all students in community colleges, and they make up a majority of students in community college science and engineering technology programs as well. The latter is true only because these programs encompass technical vocations in the health industry. In these "health technology" programs 80% of the students are women, while in programs classified by National Science Foundation reports as "engineering," only 20% are women. Twice as many students overall go into health technology programs as go into engineering programs.

In community colleges, women are much more likely to get a degree in health technology, whereas men are much more likely to get a degree in engineering. This almost certainly results from women being more likely than men to value and choose behavior that is caring and kind toward others. This gender difference regarding the value of caring has been documented over many years by the very large-sample annual surveys by the Cooperative Institutional Research Program (CIRP) program at UCLA of entering undergraduate freshmen.

Monk-Turner and Baba (2007) argue that two-year college curricula are more gendered because of their function to prepare students for vocations, many of which remain highly segregated by gender. Examples of highly gendered occupations are dental technician and civil engineering technician.

Experimental Research on Gendering Processes

In an attempt to identify and map the social and psychological forces behind the gendering processes related to computers, psychologists have run experiments by getting students to play a game like the Zork adventure game on a computer. When playing the game in private, females did much better than males, but when another person was in the room, males performed far better than females. The mere presence of another person impaired female performance, even though the other person was on the other side of the room working on something completely different.

Psychologists use the concept of anxiety and self-confidence to explain this impact of the presence of another person upon computer-game performance. They argue that females in the experiments experienced "great anxiety" because they believed the stereotype that females tend to fail at computer tasks. What these psychologists fail to consider is that there are other explanations at least equally valid: Females in the experiment might have been bored with the game, and the person may have seemed more interesting than the computer; women may have been distracted by the mere presence of another person, wondering why the person was in the room; or the women may have figured out what the experimenter was hoping to find and may have been trying to please him or her by changing their behavior.

Computer games are not necessarily the best vehicle for understanding how people of different genders respond to computer work. Furthermore, other factors like social class or race may work together with gender to produce major effects. For example, Bird and Jorgenson (2003) found that among working-class families, men were more resistant than women to both recreational and work-related uses of the Internet.

Interventions That Reduce Gender Bias

Over several decades, hundreds of millions of dollars have been given by the National Science Foundation and other agencies for projects to work on the reduction of barriers to girls and women in the pipeline toward technology degrees and occupations. A body of knowledge on these interventions has been summarized by Klawe, Whitney, and Simard (2009) and by Mattis (2007). The research encompasses dozens, if not hundreds, of interventions from preschool through graduate school and the workplace. Despite all of these research projects, much more research will be needed before an effective assault on gender bias in technology education and labor can be made.

It appears that women especially have been repelled by the increasingly theoretical rather than applied nature of computer science. The two most popular applied technology programs are health information systems and information technology, often called computer information systems (CIS). CIS is often taught in schools of business or management. A number of colleges have combined CS and IT programs, trying to maintain both a theoretical and an applied track. Such institutional change would not be called a gender-related intervention because it is not oriented to improving gender equity. Nevertheless, it illustrates the potential for improving opportunities for women simply by making changes in the organization of educational institutions.

Workplace Implications of Gendered Technology

While some technology-based gender gaps have disappeared, many gender-based digital gaps remain. Some would attribute gender gaps to female timidity and anxiety, but a careful review of the data reveals that structural conditions like occupation and school curricula shape the gendering process. In addition, cultural forces, such as simplistic stereotypes, make it very difficult for girls and women to participate equally in technology opportunities.

The CIRP program at UCLA in 2003 asked all four-year college freshmen about their probable careers. It found that 5.5% of the men but only 0.5% of the women checked "computer programmer or analyst," and 3.6% of men versus 0.4% of women checked "computer science" for their "probable career." This constitutes a gender gap for computer science that is among the highest of projected career paths for freshmen. According to U.S. Department of Labor statistics, women made up 20% of the IT workforce in 2002. The CIRP findings suggest that the technology labor force gender gap may be even higher in future years.

By the time students in the United States graduate from four-year colleges, four times as many men receive computer science degrees than do women. Since the choice jobs in the computer and Internet industries require college degrees, the character of the workplace remains as gendered as it did before. Furthermore, women compared to men in the "information" industry suffer more during economic downturns, as evidenced by higher unemployment rates.

Aside from the moral and political implications of the gendered technology pipeline from kindergarten to the workplace, there are serious labor force inadequacies that derive from underutilization of women. U.S. policies have encouraged both overseas outsourcing and the immigration of computer workers from other countries to deal with national shortages of computer workers. These policies arguably have not worked well. A more well-rounded and perhaps more sensible approach would be to invest in ways to ungender the computer pipeline in higher education.

REFERENCES AND FURTHER READING

American Association of University Women. (2000). *Tech-savvy: Educating girls in the new computer age*. Retrieved May 11, 2009, from http://www.aauw.org/research/girls_education/techsavvy.cfm

Anderson, R. E., Lundmark, V., Harris, L., & Magnan, S. (1994). Inequity in computing. In C. Huff & T. Finholt (Eds.), *Social issues in computing* (pp. 352–385). New York: McGraw-Hill.

Bird, S. E., & Jorgenson, J. (2003). Extending the school day: Gender, class, and the incorporation of technology in everyday life. In M. Consolvo & S. Paasonen (Eds.), *Women and everyday uses of the Internet* (pp. 255–274). New York: Peter Lang.

Chen, W., & Wellman, B. (2003). *Digital divides and digital dividends*. Toronto, Canada: University of Toronto, Centre for Urban and Community Studies.

Cohoon, J. M., & Aspray, W. (Eds.) (2006). *Women and information technology: Research on underrepresentation*. Cambridge, MA: MIT Press.

Fox, M. F., Johnson, D. G., & Rosser, S. V. (Eds.). (2006) *Women, gender, and technology*. Urbana, IL: University of Illinois Press.

Klawe, M. Whitney, T., & Simard, C (2009). Women in computing—take 2. *Communications of the Association for Computing Machinery, 25*(2), 68–76.

Margolis, J., & Fisher, A. (2002). *Unlocking the clubhouse: Women in computing*. Cambridge, MA: MIT Press.

Mattis, M. C. (2007). Upstream and downstream in the engineering pipeline: What's blocking US women from pursuing engineering careers? In R. J. Burke and M. C. Mattis (Eds.), *Women and minorities in science, technology, engineering, and mathematics: Upping the numbers* (pp. 334–362). Cheltenham, UK: Edward Elgar.

Monk-Turner, E., & Baba, Y. (2007). Gender and college opportunities: Changes over time in the United States and Japan. *Sociological Inquiry, 27*(3), 292–303.

Morris, H. H., & Lee, P. (2004). The incredibly shrinking pipeline is not just for women anymore. *Computing Research News, 16*(3): 20–22.

Ray, S. G. (2003). *Gender inclusive game design: Expanding the market*. Herdon, VA: Charles River Media.

Tam, M. S., & Bassett, G. W., Jr. (2006) The gender gap in information technology. In J. M. Bystyzienski & S. R. Bird (Eds.), *Removing barriers: Women in academic science, technology, engineering, and mathematics* (pp. 108–122). Bloomington: Indiana University Press.

CHAPTER 32

Women's and Gender Studies

JEAN C. ROBINSON

Women's studies have now been in existence for close to 40 years and have gone through several generational changes. The most recent of these is the metamorphosis of some women's studies programs into academic units with a new name—gender studies—and with a more heightened focus both on the making and meaning of gender and on the various forms of sexuality that are part of human experiences.

The first women's studies program was established at San Diego State University (then San Diego State College) in 1970. Only one full-time women's studies instructor was hired by the campus at that time, and most of the other instructors of women's studies courses were drawn from faculty teaching in other departments. Cornell University established a women's studies program in 1972, generally considered to be the second in the United States. Women's studies spread rapidly as an academic interdisciplinary program; it now exists at more than 600 colleges and universities nationwide. Internationally, there were an additional 250 women's studies programs, centers, and departments in 2006.

That women's studies as an academic pursuit grew out of the women's movements of the 1960s has been well documented. The first campus programs were the academic response to the American feminist movement off campus. They began both when women started asking questions about women's history and no one knew the answers and when feminists inside the academy, both students and faculty, began to ask why the study of women was almost nonexistent. Because the history of women's lives had generally been ignored or subsumed within the history of men and society, there was little accumulated knowledge, fewer books, and even fewer courses that focused on a critical understanding of the ways in which women's and men's roles, histories, and opportunities were shaped by gender, class, race, and power.

The first women's studies courses at most campuses examined histories of women in the United States, studies of women's literature, and courses typically titled "Women and ——," where everything from religion to art history to political philosophy filled in the blank. These courses were embedded in programs shaped by the contemporary feminist practices. They promoted a transformation in the construction and dissemination of social knowledge by establishing nonhierarchical and thus revolutionary forms of scholarly organization on campuses. The first task, as many early texts and articles in women's studies suggested, was to discover women's experiences and to uncover the ways in which social orders shaped and oppressed women. Women's studies facilitated a more systematic accumulation of the then-marginalized information about women's lives by promoting the collection of materials on women and gender in libraries. They facilitated research on women and gender by providing spaces and funding for that research. They disseminated research by establishing academic journals, encouraging university and commercial presses to publish books and journals on women's studies topics, and, most thoroughly, by establishing a wide-ranging curriculum that focused on this research and newly gained knowledge through interdisciplinary academic programs. Since no professors or instructors had been trained specifically to do research and teaching in women's studies, the first women's studies courses were ineluctably additive. They sought to corral information and to add information and research on women's lives, creations, and roles to core disciplines.

Just as the idea of focusing solely on women was a rebellious addition to the substantive literature that constituted core knowledge, so too the administrative structures created and embraced by women's studies programs seemed to establish a new paradigm for how academic programs and departments should be run. Rather than having senior scholars make all decisions, as in most mainstream departments in the 1960s and 1970s, many women's studies programs were founded on the concept of feminist solidarity and nonhierarchical management. Instead of chairs and directors who were responsible for managing the programs, the curriculum, and the lecture circuit, there were (and often still are) coordinators and steering committees. In the early years, staff from secretaries to librarians took their place alongside research and teaching faculty to make curricular, hiring, and funding decisions. Students were invited to participate as voting members of coordinating committees and to share a leading role alongside faculty in making decisions about what an education in women's studies would and should entail.

The earnestness and passion of the early women's studies programs bore fruit in the development of large numbers of courses throughout the humanities and social sciences. Students and faculty were energized by the excitement of learning new things and of thinking about old ideas and imparted wisdom in new ways. But there were also troubles along the way.

Much of the work of running and maintaining the core curricula depended on volunteer labor. Faculty taught overloads, and lecturers were paid a pittance to teach ever-growing courses while developing the new content as they went along. Students would provide free child care so that working mothers could attend sponsored events. Few programs were given permission to hire their own faculty, so coordinators and directors had to beg departments to loan faculty for a course or two. Budgets were tiny. Faculty, staff, and students would have brown-bag lectures where the speaker was free and the announcements for the events were copied, folded, and distributed by the coordinating committee. Faculty and staff "borrowed" paper from their home departments in order to eke out the meager supplies given women's studies programs. It was a communal effort, at a time when community was highly valued in radical politics but carried low status in the academic world.

In addition to the hard work, low status, and lack of money, other challenges emerged. One was related to the very nature of feminist organization. One was related to the debates over how women's studies—and professors who taught and researched in women's studies—would gain legitimacy in the academy. The third was related to the demographics of the core of second-wave feminism.

The feminist organizing that was the forerunner to women's studies was based on the dual principles of democracy and nonhierarchy. Although the nonhierarchical organizing structure of the many women's groups could not be completely replicated in the academy, many women's studies programs sought to avoid formal structures of power. This ultimately created tensions because, as feminist theorist Joreen (Jo Freeman) suggested, the consequence of a lack of formal rules of hierarchy and democratic governance was a failure to recognize the hidden power of the supposedly equal participants. The "tyranny of structurelessness" sometimes meant that an inordinate amount of time was spent on process and not enough on securing outcomes or that someone or some group of people imposed order in the vacuum left by a lack of structure. Structurelessness and a reluctance to appoint singular leaders made it difficult to act decisively in academic environments that typically were formally structured and based on unitary authoritative leadership. Some women's studies programs foundered because they refused to adjust to the prevailing norms of chairs and deans. Other programs fought internally over how to have a functioning leadership that was still responsive to the feminist community and operated in a transparent mode.

[handwritten margin note: tried to evicate nonhierarchy]

Many if not most of the faculty involved in the early women's studies programs were young untenured women. Most had been trained in disciplinary studies and were either self-educated in women's studies or applied interdisciplinary training in other areas to women's studies research and teaching. The vast majority were employed in mainstream disciplinary departments. Yet, in order to survive, women's studies programs needed to have their own secure group of dedicated faculty who had the expertise to teach and research in women's studies. Because women's studies programs usually were not allowed to hire their own faculty, most faculty members still had to satisfy the demands of their home departments.

Women's studies teaching and research often had to be fit into the margins of one's work life. If young professors tried to make it the center, they might have to defend the legitimacy of research on women to their colleagues. Especially in the social sciences, but also in many humanities-oriented departments, the challenge was to find a way to publish work on women that was judged acceptable by non–women's studies colleagues. As often as not, these women's studies research efforts did not count for much in the home disciplinary department. Many assistant professors thus had to meet two different disciplinary and interdisciplinary sets of expectations. Too often, the women's studies line of research and teaching was dropped in order to secure tenure for the faculty member.

Simultaneously, women's studies directors and coordinators had to develop other mechanisms to ensure that professors would be released to teach courses and could obtain the credit for their work in women's studies research that it deserved. Often the resolution to the search for the legitimacy that faculty and directors faced was to move toward establishing faculty lines in women's studies. At some universities, this could be done within the framework of the existing interdisciplinary program. At other institutions, it was done through establishing women's studies lines in disciplinary departments. At still others, women's studies moved to become a freestanding department. Sometimes a combination of these three options was attempted. In almost all instances, though, the conversion meant that women's studies moved out of the volunteer-based communal structure into one that more closely resembled the tenure-line formal hierarchy of typical academic departments.

The third challenge of the women's studies programs was how to expand beyond the core demographics of the second-wave women's movement. The midwife of women's studies was the politics of American second-wave feminism. This was the feminism that understood that liberation was about sex as much as it was about equality but that found talking about sex and critiquing heterosexuality risky and intimidating. This was also the feminism that was mostly focused on issues relevant to White middle-class women. This was the feminism of Betty Friedan and the 1970s women's movement that split over lesbianism. Although women's studies programs certainly embraced the opportunity to examine sexuality in its many forms and to analyze gender as a sexualized construction, the sexual focus was often diffuse. And although women's studies programs, faculty, and students certainly embraced the opportunity to examine race, ethnicity, class, and privilege in their many manifestations, nevertheless the class, racial, and ethnic focus remained predominantly White middle-class American.

The challenge for women's studies programs was to ensure that classes, curriculum, research, and programming were inclusive, exhaustive, welcoming, and self-critical. Conversations around these issues often became fraught with anger and guilt. In the early to mid-1980s, the National Women's Studies Association almost disbanded because of the tensions within the organization surrounding these fundamental issues. Eventually, through extensive debates and by establishing venues for the regular consideration of race, sexuality, class, ethnic, religious, accessibility, and other issues, women's studies programs developed mechanisms and processes to ensure that the focus of their teaching and research was not only or primarily for and about White middle-class women.

Generally, the period of new establishment of women's studies programs started in the 1970s and extended through the mid-1980s. The transitions discussed above were neither easy to resolve nor the same at every institution. But for most women's studies programs at American colleges and universities, the mid-1980s through the mid-1990s was a period of consolidation during which answers to the dilemmas of structure, legitimacy, and constituency were found. Some of the resolutions were quite idiosyncratic, shaped both by the personalities and politics of the faculty members and students involved and by the politics and structures of the academic institutions in which they were embedded.

By the mid-1990s, though, new issues were emerging. The first formally trained generation of women's studies scholars were now being hired by women's studies programs and departments. These were women, and some men, who had learned women's studies as undergraduates and had focused on women's studies in their graduate training in interdisciplinary and disciplinary departments. Inevitably a clash emerged between the first generation of self-taught, now-tenured women's studies founding "mothers" and the new generation. There was talk about professionalizing the field, making programs into departments, hiring and legitimating only those who had the proper women's studies credentials, and perhaps most controversially, rejecting feminist politics for academic feminism. With good reasons, the young scholars sought to establish legitimacy for the rigorous and interdisciplinary approaches and paradigms they had mastered, and they saw little reason to continue the traditions and practices of that first voluntary wave of feminists in the academy.

In the late 1990s, as some women's studies programs transformed themselves into gender studies or women and gender studies departments, the midwife was again politics. The politics this time, though, was a new version of feminism—a feminism that partnered with the lesbian, gay, bisexual, and transgender movement in the United States and that, unlike the earlier women's movement, was not afraid to identify with sexual issues. Indeed, gender studies has been criticized by some women's studies proponents as forgetting about women and ignoring the continuing need for feminist activism in favor of sexuality and transgendered studies. Others, however, point out that gender is about both men and women; that it is about our constructed notions of what constitutes masculinity and femininity; and that sexual practices as well as the political construction of acceptable sexuality create many of the constraints that women and men experience.

In 2006, within the United States there were more than 600 academic interdisciplinary programs organized around the study of women and gender. Of these, slightly over 100 called themselves gender studies, or women's and gender studies, or, to a much lesser extent, feminist, gender, and sexuality studies. Are these all the same kind of studies with idiosyncratic names? At Cornell, for instance, where a shift in name and focus took place in 2002, "Feminist, Gender, and Sexuality Studies Program" describes the unit that is intended to bring attention to the intertwining of gender and sexuality with power and inequality. Cornell first added a lesbian, bisexual, and gay studies minor to the women's studies program in the early 1990s. The original women's studies program, so named to highlight the ways in which the traditional curriculum marginalized women as the "Other," no longer seemed sufficient either politically or theoretically. Similarly, at Indiana University, the shift from women's studies to gender studies, which took place in the mid-1990s, was intended to reflect the ways in which theorizing and knowledge about women and gender have evolved and become more complex.

Organizationally, women's studies and gender studies departments and programs still must resolve the generational problem. The newest trend in this decade has been to secure faculty lines within programs and departments where these core faculty have primary responsibility for the curriculum, for hiring and policy decisions, and for establishing new degree programs. These faculty are more likely to have earned doctorates in interdisciplinary programs; to have written dissertations on gender themes; and to have experience teaching about sexuality, intersectionality, and transnationalism. Adjunct or affiliate faculty, often including the first generation of self-taught women's studies professors, sometimes feel excluded from the new project of women's/gender studies, but notably few of them have tenure in the programs or departments. They have less at stake currently, since their academic home is likely elsewhere; nevertheless, they do understandably want to protect their stake in "owning" women's studies. The generational tension over ownership has lessened at some institutions when efforts to expand specifically address the inclusion of this first generation. At other colleges and universities, hostility to change (or to the old guard) and anger at being excluded has led to rehashing old debates and to creating roadblocks to moving forward.

In other parts of the world, many gender studies programs have been institutionalized without the birth pangs so commonly found in the transition from women's studies to gender studies. Because women's and gender studies tended to come later to academic institutions outside North America and Western Europe, they were more likely to be informed by scholars who had experience and knowledge gleaned from observing and interacting with specific North American or European universities. Nevertheless, institutionalizing gender studies has faced additional challenges in many places, especially in those societies where feminism is even less accepted than it is in

North America or Europe. The challenges include convincing other scholars that women and gender are even worthy of study. In Canada, Australia, and many parts of western and central Europe, however, gender and women's studies is thriving, as scholars and programs have often benefited from support from state feminist agencies in national and supranational governments.

The discourse has certainly shifted. In the heyday of women's studies, the rhetoric was often about patriarchy and oppression. Now the rhetoric is about the intersection of gender with other substantive categories of analysis and identity. Revolution takes different forms in different times, and if at first glance gender studies no longer seem to be the site for overt feminist activity, this is deceiving. From its inception, an underlying goal of women's studies and gender studies has been to spotlight women as producers and consumers of knowledge and to focus on gender constructs as a substantive and legitimate theme within the realm of the university. Gender studies, feminist studies, sexuality studies—no matter what they are called—remain revolutionary efforts that seek to reframe knowledge and power.

REFERENCES AND FURTHER READING

Chen, P. (2004). *Acting "otherwise": The institutionalization of women's/gender studies in Taiwan's universities*. New York: RoutledgeFalmer.

Griffin, G. (2005). *Doing women's studies: Employment opportunities, personal impacts and social consequences*. London: Zed.

Kennedy, E. (2005). *Women's studies for the future: Foundations, interrogations, politics*. New Brunswick, NJ: Rutgers University Press.

National Women's Studies Association. http://www.nwsa.org

Wiegman, R. (Ed.). (2002). *Women's studies on its own: A next wave reader in institutional change*. Durham, NC: Duke University Press.

IV

Gender Constructions in the Extracurriculum

The extracurriculum, sometimes called the cocurriculum, consists of organizations and activities that are recognized, regulated, or sponsored by the administration of a college or university but are not considered part of the academic curriculum. Some of these activities and organizations, such as academic clubs, service-learning programs, student government, and intercollegiate athletics, are officially sponsored by institutions of higher education. Some of these officially sponsored organizations, like women's centers, were initiated primarily by students, but others, like honors societies, were initiated by faculty or administrators. Other activities and organizations are officially recognized and regulated but not sponsored by the colleges and universities in which they exist. Included among these are fraternities and sororities as well as newer, student-initiated organizations for which gaining official recognition usually means that they can meet in campus buildings and sometimes also that they receive funding from the student activity fees paid to that educational institution. Organizations of this latter type are often political or religious in nature, and because they are controversial, educational institutions go to great effort to indicate that they are not "sponsoring" such activities, merely allowing the organizations to exist, meet, and publicize themselves on campus.

There also are activities and organizations that seek official recognition but have not yet achieved it. Groups advocating equal treatment for gays, lesbians, bisexuals, and transgendered people sometimes fall into this category, but at many colleges and universities, as chapter 33 ("Campus Resources and Support for LGBTQQIA Students, Faculty, and Staff") indicates, such groups are officially recognized and provided with resources and various kinds of support. Yet on some campuses, either such groups do not exist at all or they are treated as peer groups and denied any official support.

Many of the student clubs and activities that are now called the extracurriculum were initiated and organized by students seeking some relief from the rigid, narrow academic curricula characteristic of U.S. colleges and universities during the eighteenth and most of the nineteenth centuries in the United States. Because the extracurriculum was outside of the official academic curriculum, it was also outside of the control of faculty and college officials, who often found themselves in serious conflicts with students. It was not uncommon for students to use parts of the extracurriculum, such as debating and discussion societies, literary magazines, theatrical events, and school newspapers as instruments of criticism and attack on official school policies and practices. Even more frivolous components of the extracurriculum, such as the football games, homecoming weekends, proms, and "socials," were occasions for student hedonism and acts of rebellion against the academic seriousness and hard work advocated by faculty and campus administrators.

During the Progressive Era of 1890–1920, administrators of most colleges and universities came to an accommodation with the students' extracurricular clubs, activities, and organizations. The mechanism for achieving this accommodation was the creation of student governments. By creating governments run by students who were elected by their peers, institutions of higher education gave official recognition to the students' own status system. Those elected were not necessarily the best students nor the students whom the faculty held in highest regard but rather those who were most popular among their peers and considered by those peers to be good leaders. From the standpoint of institutions of higher education, the purpose of student government was not to give such students recognition but to establish lines of communication with them and to co-opt them. Student governments rarely had the power to make the policies that governed students' lives on campus, but they could give college administrators advice about those policies, and they could run the student courts that enforced them. Progressive Era ideology placed a heavy emphasis on citizenship and service, and colleges became increasingly successful over time in using student government to harness student energies to these progressive values.

In conjunction with the establishment of student government, many colleges and universities, especially those with more than a small number of students, created new college officials, such as deans of students, whose job it was to help plan and coordinate student activities that were compatible with the goals of the campus administration. As the number of coeducational institutions increased, most college presidents felt it necessary also to appoint a woman to guide and protect the women students and help them develop suitable activities. On many campuses, the woman who did this work was not given the title of dean and was subordinate to a man who was. For example, a campus might have a dean of students who was a man with an associate dean of women students who was a woman. No associate dean of men students would be appointed, however, as it would be assumed that the dean of students was also the dean of men. It was also not unusual on campuses that became coeducational before World War I and the passage of the Nineteenth Amendment to the U.S. Constitution granting women's suffrage for the dean of students/men to work with an all-male student government while the associate dean of women worked with an association of women students that functioned as a secondary student government concerned with the nonacademic activities of women students. Eventually, these separate women's governing bodies merged with the men's student government, although some did not do so until after the rise of second-wave feminism in the 1960s.

The outcome of historical efforts to control the extracurriculum can be seen on contemporary university campuses in the United States where there is likely to be a large office of student affairs or department of student services responsible for supervising student housing, including fraternity and sorority houses, and for working with student government to recognize and regulate a vast array of student clubs and organizations. The relationships between student governments and the college or university administrations to which they report is often fraught with tension concerning the extent to which administrators have the power to control the agenda of the student government and to veto student votes and initiatives.

Tensions also exist between student governments and the student body they supposedly represent. Some of these arise when the student government is thought to represent the interests of only a segment of the student body, while ignoring or even working against the interests of other student groups. Other tensions occur when students feel that their government is failing to represent them and is instead simply carrying out the dictates of school administrators. Also, because student governments rarely have real power on campus, they are often viewed with disdain or indifference by the student bodies they supposedly represent. Election turnouts tend to be low, and it is often difficult to get students to contribute their time and energy to the many activities for which student governments have come to be responsible.

As a result, campus personnel whose task it is to work with student governments often find themselves in the somewhat ironic position of having to figure out ways to make student governments stronger. And parts of the contemporary literature about student government, and the extracurriculum more generally, read like recruiting brochures with a heavy emphasis on the rewards and benefits that individual students can gain by getting involved. To date, no publications have appeared that analyze student government using a gender lens, although both researchers and the mass media report that, in the United States, females now outnumber males in student government positions on increasing numbers of coeducational college and university campuses.

On most contemporary campuses, substantial parts of the extracurriculum fall outside of the purview of student government and student services personnel and are instead managed by a department of athletics. Unlike departments of physical education that award credits or degrees to students whom they have successfully educated and trained as teachers, coaches, and physical trainers, departments of athletics are in charge of intercollegiate athletics. So large and dominant have these departments become both on campus and nationally that they often have budgets in excess of those of even the largest of the academic departments, and it is not unusual for the head football or basketball coach at a major university to be paid more than that university's chief academic officer, usually titled the president or chancellor.

Despite their prominence, surprisingly little research has appeared examining the ways in which college athletic programs and adjunctive programs of cheerleaders, pep squads, and spirit clubs contribute to the perpetuation of very traditional, stereotypic versions of masculinity and femininity on campus. Instead, most of the concerns about athletics and gender in higher education have focused on Title IX of the Education Amendments of 1972 and the effort to give college women equal, or at least increased, opportunities to participate in college sports. (See chapter 48 in part VI.)

Substantially more attention has been given to the ways in which Greek-letter social fraternities and sororities strive to emulate and reproduce particular types of masculinity and femininity that are considered dominant and enviable among the members and by some students outside of Greek organizations. Chapter 34 ("Fraternities") and chapter 37 ("Sororities") discuss both the advantages of these organizations, historically and at the present time, and the criticisms that have been levied against them. Some complaints, such as those focused on the tension between the academic goals of the college or university and the social, sexual, and romantic goals of the fraternities and sororities, have actually lessened somewhat as contemporary students, including those in the Greek system, have become—or are thought to be—more career oriented than their predecessors. Nevertheless, many of the targets of complaint about the Greek system today—such as the hazing, excessive partying, drinking, and sexual violence—have their roots in a traditional heterosexual system in which men compete with one another and subject women to rigorous scrutiny and objectification, while women are encouraged to be male-identified and to make themselves attractive and pleasing.

Contrasting but complementary forms of masculinity and femininity also have deep roots in the U.S. military and in the military training programs that exist on many campuses and are described in chapter 35 ("Reserve Officers' Training Corps"). Claims that these programs train strong, manly, forceful leaders help to construct women as outsiders, especially if those women want to retain forms of femininity based on being nurturant, as many of them do. Like the military colleges and academies described in part II, Reserve Officer's Training Corps (ROTC) programs are available to women but are not yet fully accessible in the sense of providing those women with feelings of acceptance and belonging.

Unlike the struggles surrounding ROTC, the challenges faced by service-learning programs have not involved availability and accessibility for women. Instead, as chapter 36 ("Service Learning and Activism") makes clear, there has been a conflict, often among women, concerning the goals that service-learning experiences should have. While all agree that service learning is mostly about students volunteering their time to help others on the campus or in the local community, sharp differences have appeared between traditional and activist versions of this volunteer work. Traditionally, women (and men) who participate in service learning help to provide ongoing services offered by voluntary associations, medical centers, schools, and other private and public agencies. Some feminists argue, however, that (women) students should not be supporting the status quo with their volunteerism, in the charity-work style of rich ladies of the mid-twentieth century. In contrast, student volunteers should be activists working for social changes that will increase gender, racial, and socioeconomic equality in U.S. society. Over time, however, what was once considered activism for equality, such as organizing and working in a battered women's shelter, is becoming accepted as routine social service activity. As this routinization occurs and as service-learning activities are increasingly centralized under the control of campus administrations, the possibility of an activist version of service learning may fade completely in favor of an increased focus on volunteerism as a way of acquiring skills, credentials, and social connections useful in future occupational careers. Such a shift, if it becomes widespread, would increase the likelihood that the inequities and accessibility problems that women face in some academic departments and affiliated careers, described in part III, might spread to service-learning activities as well.

Surprisingly, accessibility may sometimes be a problem for women who seek to participate in programs sponsored by some women's centers. Chapter 38 ("Women's Centers") gives an overview of the history, missions, and challenges that these centers have faced, stressing the efforts that they have made to promote gender equity and community among women. The fact that these goals have not yet been achieved is both a reason why women's centers are still needed even though women students outnumber men on most campuses and a reason why women's centers need to continually review their activities and programming to make certain they are as inclusive as possible. While it is certainly important for women's centers to challenge traditional, stereotypical femininity as the only or the best way to be a woman, it is also important that the centers are not seen as places *for* only certain types of nonconventional women. By emphasizing their role in building bridges, women's centers can help to make themselves and the broader campus places where multiplicities of women representing all sorts of intersectionalities can feel at home.

CHAPTER 33

Campus Resources and Support for LGBTQQIA Students, Faculty, and Staff

CHRISTIAN MATHEIS

The history of higher education, as of the United States more generally, is replete with examples of cultural and institutional discrimination toward people who are lesbian, gay, bisexual, transgender/transsexual, queer, questioning, intersex (LGBTQQI), and allies (LGBTQQIA). Nevertheless, LGBTQQIA communities and individuals are not defined solely by a common history of oppression. There are rich social forms, icons, celebrations, types of art, entertainment, language, and cultural facets that mark some of the inherent values of these communities.

In recent years, colleges and universities have been in flux about whether and how to effectively acknowledge the cultural diversity of sexualities, affectionalities, gender identities, and gender expressions present on their campuses. Some acknowledgments take the form of new or revised organizational policies that extend antidiscrimination rules and guidelines to cover "sexual orientation, identity, and preference" along with more traditional categories of race, ethnicity, religion, and gender. Following models used to recognize other underrepresented groups on campus, such as African Americans and women, a vast variety of cocurricular LGBTQQIA programs have been established on campus, including resource centers, advocacy offices, mentoring programs, health and wellness resources, and many different kinds of educational programs.

Relevant curricular offerings have also increased, and there are now many opportunities to prepare oneself for moral, political, and institutional commitments to working in support of diversity of sexuality and gender. Many graduate programs in student affairs and higher education now provide courses specifically focused on sexuality and gender and augment previously existing courses with such information. Academic and professional organizations offer conference sessions, newsletters, and professional articles, and caucuses for people who are LGBTQQI. In addition, outside of higher education, there are growing networks of nonprofit organizations—international, national, regional, and local—that can provide extraordinarily high-quality, relevant educational and professional development opportunities.

Contemporary Challenges of Culture, Community, and Language

On college and university campuses, students who are LGBTQQI certainly enjoy more support from and access to curricular and cocurricular programs than they experienced even within the past five to ten years. Within the United States many traditionally college-aged adults grew up during the modern LGBTQQIA civil rights movement. This movement, still very much under way and in search of federal and state legislative, judicial, and executive support, has played a key role in informing national elections and cultural formations in the minds of students, faculty, administrators, and alumni/ae. This national political and cultural trend has created critical opportunities for institutions of higher education to provide for sincere, valuable, and often challenging discourse surrounding a historically contentious array of issues.

Politics and cultural trends certainly matter, though the key to understanding and working with people who are LGBTQQIA is truly to focus on the real needs of real people. There are many theories of inclusion and exclusion, identity development, culture, diversity, and equality that add to our knowledge about sexual/affectional orientation and gender identity/expression. Theoretical accounts are vital, and at the same time students and educators must learn and be encouraged to engage in actual practices of responding to the needs of people and communities, locally and nationally, with timely, thoughtful, and sometimes experimental—though no less sincere—approaches. Methods of creating and sustaining good moral and political ideas must begin with, or at least always refer back to, methods of creating and sustaining good actions.

Some common strategies have emerged on college and university campuses that support holistic cultural incorporation of LGBTQQIA people: Many campuses host celebrations and cultural observances, such as Transgender Day of Remembrance, National Coming Out Day, pride festivals, and community-specific commencement programs, usually called "lavender graduation." These cultural events fulfill at least two important needs: They provide a sense of recognition, representation, and connection for LGBTQQIA communities, and they help to educate members of the larger community who have had little exposure to diversity of sexuality, affection, and gender.

These needs can also be met by the use of cultural tools, such as language. Use of inclusive language and regard for self-identification, representation, and critique through language is a hallmark of effectively recognizing and supporting people from traditionally underrepresented backgrounds of race, class, sexuality, disability, religion and spirituality, and so forth. A common objection to the use of acronyms like LGBTQQIA is that the language is too complex, that usage shifts from person to person in sometimes unpredictable ways, and that it is too challenging to recall new and dynamic terms. Contrary to this view is, first, the recognition that people can handle complexity of this kind and, second, the realization that honoring and exploring language provide for affirmation of those whose self-esteem may, in part, depend on self-determination and self-naming for a time, such as those who are exploring their own identities and self-awareness. Finally, careful attention to language broadens one's own self-understanding and attainment of knowledge. Thus, by using terminology about sexuality and gender with care, acknowledging fallibility, and practicing humility, people are likely to discover new ways of accounting for themselves and others in their communities in more rational, practical, and holistic ways. In exploring knowledge surrounding sexuality and gender, it is important to develop comprehensive attention to language and terminology—both on a national scale and on the level of the commonly used phrases in the local vernacular.

Institutional Considerations: Policies, Processes, and Systems

As students, administrators, and faculty advocate for the creation of ethically sound, socially relevant educational experiences, they must come to terms with policies and systems of practice. Nearly all institutions of postsecondary education have established public commitments through statements of mission, vision, and values. These guiding principles are some of the strongest evidence and grounding for transforming institutional operations and cultures toward equity with regard to sexuality and gender. When developing administrative strategies or grassroots plans to further improve attention to people who are LGBTQQIA, the establishment of publicly accessible, broadly accountable policies and procedures constitutes a perpetual message of commitment from generation to generation.

Recent ways in which institutional policies have been changed to express this commitment to LGBTQQIA individuals and communities include

- adding "sexual/affectional orientation" and "gender identity/expression" to nondiscrimination statements;
- moving away from exclusive, "colorblind" language like "regardless of" and "without regard to" and toward context-setting phrases such as "inclusive of" and "with regard for";
- institutionalizing academic general education requirements for study of difference, power, and discrimination in sociohistorical contexts within the United States with attention to traditionally historically underrepresented communities;
- creating specific health and wellness policies related to sexuality, affectionality, and gender identity/expression;
- establishing policies requiring the institution to contract with and retain the services of public agencies and private companies that explicitly provide for equal treatment of LGBTQQIA persons, employed or otherwise;
- welcoming transgender/transsexual students in campus housing options by developing policies for case-by-case responses to needs or for specific residence hall and cooperative spaces as "gender inclusive";
- creating hiring initiatives that specifically include sexual/affectional orientation and gender identity/expression along with race, sex, veteran status, disabilities, etc.;
- publicizing specific statements of support on local departmental levels, such as in campus safety and security, health services, housing and residential education programs, academic affairs, etc.;
- including requirements in annual professional development activities that specify focus on behaviors and approaches to successfully affirming diversity of sexuality and gender.

Resources, Services, and Cocurricular Engagement

Since the early 1990s college and universities have become home to resource centers and professional offices that focus on supporting LGBTQQIA students and community members. These centers and offices offer a wide array of programs and resources, with the specific offerings often depending on the age of the center or office, its institutional financial support, and the size of campus student populations. Often, what becomes a comprehensive resource center will begin with a few carefully designed programs. These programs include, but are not limited to, provision of a safe space, a resource library, and professional/employee associations for LGBTQQI people; educating campus groups about them; mentoring them; providing them with health and wellness resources; and increasing their access to and involvement in cocurricular and academic programs.

Safe Spaces

A safe space can be any physical site in which individuals find a welcoming environment, inclusive of their differences. Many campus facilities and work spaces have been constructed and staffed primarily to meet the needs of overrepresented, majority, or "privileged" groups. Thus the reality is that most college and university campuses are not yet safe spaces for students of color, women, people with disabilities, or people who are LGBTQQIA. Safe spaces provide LGBTQQIA students with a vital respite from general social environments in which they are unlikely to "be themselves." Lounge space, more specifically, within a resource center or program can create an environment for relaxation between classes and an inviting place to socialize or to have discussions and events. In a sense, they are a "home away from home" for those who are trying to find formal and informal community support in order to continue working toward academic and cocurricular successes. Moreover, multipurpose spaces allow resource programs to host events, such as film viewings or workshops that can increase the visibility and usability of the safe space.

Resource Libraries

Many resource programs provide basic or comprehensive media collections for students, staff, and faculty, most of which can be borrowed for personal use or classroom instruction. Resource libraries generally contain fiction and nonfiction books, magazines, journals, movies, and other media. These resources offer LGBTQQIA students an opportunity to access community-specific knowledge, fiction representations that reflect common experiences, and advanced research materials on topics ranging across relevant topics. While most resource libraries are housed in centers or with student organizations, some are housed at a main campus library or are cross-listed in electronic catalogs and can be searched via Web access from on- and off-campus locations.

Employee and Professional Organizations

Organizations for LGBTQQIA employees are also vital to campus life. Such organization can help employees who are facing challenges related to promotion or tenure, to the desire to meet people and make community connections, or to obtain information about health and wellness and other issues. With a healthy base of successful, visible, and recognizable faculty, staff, and administrators across all disciplines and functions, students are more likely to recognize their own potential for success. The role-modeling effect that comes from healthy communities of mentors, elders, and professionals cannot be overlooked, and this may be one of the most significant ways to increase recruitment and retention of students, staff, faculty, and administrators from various underrepresented populations.

Ally Programs

Often people who are heterosexual and cisgender (not transgender/transsexual) are called upon to be advocates for gay, lesbian, and bisexual people on campus. Unfortunately, many straight allies who are genuinely committed to being supportive have few skills or resources available to them. Moreover, allies sometimes have little or no readily available information to guide their own development or to use in helping others become better advocates for the gay, lesbian, bisexual, and transgender communities. Heterosexual and cisgender staff and faculty who engage in ally-development programs can have a significant, positive impact on the culture of a college or university campus. The programs that promote this impact sponsor a variety of activities:

- offering formal training and community-building programs, such as "safe zone training," at regular intervals;
- hosting regular social gatherings and meeting spaces for allies and community members;
- providing "safe zone" or "ally" stickers or posters for office and personal work areas in order to publicly display signs of commitment and hospitality as an ally;
- publishing Internet-based and hard-copy lists of members of LGBTQQIA groups in support network databases;
- creating department-specific ally-development resources, strategies, and training programs;
- extending tailored training and outreach to traditionally hard-to-reach populations such as fraternity and sorority life and collegiate athletics programs, as well as academic disciplines including but not limited to those focusing on science, technology, engineering, agriculture, and mathematics.

Peer-to-Peer Education, Speakers Bureaus, and Panel Programs

Speakers bureaus and panel programs comprise an important grassroots peer-to-peer education program on many campuses. LGBTQQIA students from diverse backgrounds are trained to educate the university and local community on sexual/affectional orientation, gender identity/expression, oppression, and diversity. Through sharing personal narrative, students are able to educate others by giving insight into their own experiences while developing vital skills in public speaking and self-representation. These programs can be tailored to fit the individual needs of various audiences, and members of speakers bureaus typically visit classrooms, residence halls, athletic programs, fraternity and sorority houses, and local schools and religious organizations and will frequently coordinate workshops for groups within the campus community. Without exception, these peer-to-peer education models provide some of the most significant outreach and lasting educational experiences in this realm of work.

Mentoring Programs

Students who are exploring their identities and seeking greater self-understanding often encounter a need for structured, confidential, and consistent advice and support. Mentoring programs connect students who are coming out or exploring their identities with other individuals who are more knowledgeable and self-accepting of their LGBTQQIA identities. Mentoring relationships help students to develop a positive base of knowledge and sense of connection by providing a supportive relationship, accurate information, and a safe person to talk with about concerns and interests. Mentors are usually graduate students, faculty, or alumni who have experienced first-hand the challenges of coming out and finding self-acceptance. They are generally chosen for their maturity, sound judgment, knowledge of community resources, and willingness to make contributions to LGBTQQIA communities by helping others. Mentor training programs are often thorough, with commitments and expectations articulated carefully in advance of establishing mentor-mentee pairings. Mentoring programs are typically conducted in partnership with campus counseling and psychological programs, through which licensed therapists and counselors can provide ongoing support and quality assessment and support mentors in effectively responding to the needs of mentees.

Health and Wellness

Whether in partnership with professional medical and health services or academic units or conducted independently, programs and resources related to the health and wellness of LGBTQQIA people are provided on many campuses. These include educational information and advice related to sexually transmitted infections, reproductive options, safe and healthy practices, and more. Campus counseling and psychological service programs also provide occasional or ongoing support for needs related to mental and emotional health. These can range from anxiety and stress-related issues to self-exploration, negotiating stressors related to family and peer interactions, relationships and intimacy, and many other factors. Like any professional service providers, those working in health fields can be a fundamental base of support so long as they are committed to ongoing learning discovery. Most care providers are reliable sources of information and referral in the event that their own expertise is limited, and students should be encouraged to seek referrals to providers who can provide adequate levels of time, support, and advice.

Student Organizations and Activities

Those who are LGBTQQIA will often seek consistent opportunities for social connections with others, most often with peers. Student organizations and clubs offer regular social and cultural events at which students can meet peers, develop friendships, and coordinate their efforts to address their shared and individual needs. Student groups organize around diverse topics, are likely to serve specialized purposes, and are unlikely to take a one-stop approach. Some common focuses of student organizations include social and cultural engagement, persons of color from traditionally underrepresented backgrounds, women's issues, planning and hosting events and celebrations, activism and politics, career and professional development, education and outreach. The proliferation of specialized groups can provide students with a wide range of opportunities for interaction and connection, allowing creativity and diversity of expression and purpose.

Academic Programs

Cocurricular resource models, as described above, are one way of promoting success for people who are LGBTQQIA, and academic programs are another crucial component. Through academic programs—majors and minors, certificate programs, course work—colleges and universities have the ability to prepare students with critical thinking skills and personal commitments to thoughtful and ethical civic engagement. These programs emerge under a variety of titles, such as women's and gender studies, sexuality studies, queer studies, and lesbian, gay, bisexual, and transgender studies. Many of these academic programs and courses are highly interdisciplinary. The concepts, data, research, and literature regarding sexuality/affectionality and gender identity/expression are not best confined to any particular discipline, nor to specific colleges, such as humanities, liberal arts, or social sciences. Rather, academic programs that spread course work and degree programs across disciplines provide an excellent basis for comprehensive study. Some course work may bridge traditionally separate academic and cocurricular approaches, such as providing first-year experience and exploratory courses that blend intellectual and experiential education.

Competency, Knowledge, and Experience

The kinds of knowledge and experience relevant to leading programs that provide services and support for LGBTQQIA people on campus may come from a wide array of disciplinary and life-experience backgrounds. Modes of learning about difference will inevitably vary, as not all people learn about difference, power, and discrimination in exactly the same ways. Some will pursue the challenges of understanding sexuality and gender through personal narratives and nonfiction examples, others may come to a better understanding through reviewing statistics and conventional research, and yet others may only learn to account for the experiences of others by carrying out activist or social change projects among peers. It is vital for the success of LGBTQQIA communities that resource programs, bases of knowledge, and strategic efforts to establish equity are designed with attention to diverse learning styles and sets of values.

With resources, opportunities for growth, institutional value commitments, and leadership, what remains is a matter of personal or group choice and integrity. Each person and community—students, faculty, administrators, alumni/ae—must evaluate their own values and behaviors, critically, in order to decide on the quality and scope of their commitment to supporting the LGBTQQIA community. Such personal and group commitments depend on deciding how much the dignity of others matters and how much to respect them. Effective institutional policies in turn emerge from and depend upon such personal and group commitments.

REFERENCES AND FURTHER READING

Blumenfeld, W. J., & Raymond, D. (1993). *Looking at gay and lesbian life* (2nd ed.). Boston: Beacon Press.

Jackson, J. F. L., & Terrell, M. C. (Eds.). (2007). *Creating and maintaining safe college campuses*. Sterling, VA: Stylus.

LGBTQArchitect. (2008). Resources. Retrieved June 8, 2009, from http://architect.lgbtcampus .org/

Meem, D. T., Gibson, M. A., & Alexander, J. F. (2010). *Finding out: An introduction to LGBT studies*. Thousand Oaks, CA: Sage.

Palmer, J. (1989, March). Diversity: Three paradigms for change leaders. *Journal of the OD Network*, 1–5.

Pharr, S., (1997). *Homophobia: a weapon of sexism*. Inverness, CA: Chardon Press.

Roper, L. (2005). The role of senior student affairs officers in supporting LGBT students: Exploring the landscape of one's life. In R. L. Sanlo (Ed.), *Gender identity and sexual orientation: Research, policy, and personal perspectives: New directions for student services, No. 111* (pp. 81–88). San Francisco: Jossey-Bass.

Xing, J. (Ed.). (2007). *Teaching for change: The difference, power, and discrimination model*. Lanham, MD: Lexington Books.

Zack, N., (2005). *Inclusive feminism: A third wave theory of women's commonality*. Lanham, MD: Rowman & Littlefield.

CHAPTER 34

Fraternities

EDWARD G. WHIPPLE AND KEITH B. O'NEILL

Fraternities, in North American colleges and universities, are organizations of men who share common ideals and values, enjoy a sense of communal brotherhood and social orientation, and have pledged allegiance to each other and to their particular organization. These groups are often named with Greek letters; frequently express ideals of scholarship, service, and leadership; and have become largely social in nature and purpose. As social organizations, fraternities can be distinguished from other groups that are known by Greek letters. Such groups—literary societies, honorary organizations, and professional organizations—may share similarities with fraternities in basic structure, origin, or purpose, but today's fraternities have become unique as outlets for male students to feel a sense of social belonging and community.

Sharing the values of brotherhood—the quality of support and friendship rooted in kindred minds and spirits—was an original aim of fraternal life and has been enhanced and passed down through generations of members. Because many fraternities were founded as academic and literary societies, striving toward scholarly achievement in academic life also has been a goal, building on the spirit of mutual challenge and support in bettering oneself academically. In addition, a vast commitment to others—a "love of humankind"—is often demonstrated through philanthropic activities of community service and the benevolent support of charity and those less fortunate.

Along with this rich and positive heritage of brotherhood, academic achievement, and philanthropy, social fraternities also have a tradition of peer rebellion against faculty and administrative authority that began with open and violent student revolts in the late eighteenth and early nineteenth centuries. Although these outbreaks were forcibly and successfully suppressed by leaders of the colleges in which they took place, acts of student rebellion against institutional control—often in the forms of pranks, rowdiness, ritualized violence, insubordination, academic cheating, and what is now called substance abuse—continued to characterize many college and university campuses. Such acts were and are not unique to fraternity members, but fraternities have provided an organizational context and brotherly support for all sorts of activities, legal or not, that have come to be regarded collectively as fun, good fellowship, and bases for social prestige.

In response to the problems created by fraternal crimes and misbehaviors and the other challenges facing fraternal life today, student affairs professionals and some faculty have begun to assess the need for greater attention to undergraduate chapters and intensified training for fraternity leaders. With particular focus on liability issues, the need for leadership, diversity, raising academic and ethical standards, and other strategies for positive membership development, there is a renewed commitment to support fraternities in returning to their roots and redefining the fraternal experience in light of each group's founding values. The ability of college men to join together with common interests and shared concerns, to pledge to uphold all that is good in an organization's heritage and subscribe to the positive beliefs handed down through the generations, to wear a member's badge and celebrate an age-old ritual, and to exemplify the best characteristics of educated gentlemen are the renewed goals of fraternal life today. Overcoming the negative stereotypes and destructive behaviors remains a challenge to truly reaching these goals.

Historical Development

America's first institutions of higher education were small colleges founded to educate preachers, teachers, and statesmen. Because of the frequent lack of intellectual excitement and social freedom in the formal curriculum, students began to create their own extracurricular activities. They formed debating societies and literary clubs; some colleges witnessed the founding of "secret" societies of students who were "pledged" and "initiated" into the traditions of the societies as defined by each group's founders. Often reflecting the aims of the philosophical-scholarly schools of ancient Greece, these groups would take on distinct characteristics—whether as literary societies, debating groups, or other academically focused bodies—that would later distinguish them entirely from each other. Sometimes the groups' mottoes or guiding values would be stated in Greek, and the organizations came to be known by the initial letters of those Greek words. These initials served through the decades as the distinct nicknames (and later, the formal names) of the organizations. These groups eventually developed a much more social focus, primarily because they began to offer housing to students. This created the modern prototype of the fraternities of today.

The Phi Beta Kappa honorary fraternity was founded in 1776 at the College of William and Mary and is the forerunner of today's Greek-letter organizations. Phi Beta Kappa established precedents that today's groups still follow, including a name composed of Greek letters; secret rituals and symbols that affirm shared values and beliefs; and a badge that, in general, only initiated members wear. Despite these similarities, it can be argued emphatically that today's Greek organizations lack the scholarly emphasis of Phi Beta Kappa, which now admits its members, including women, solely on the basis of their grades and other academic achievements.

In the past two centuries, student life at American colleges and universities expanded broadly beyond the walls of the classroom. Early leadership in this expansion was often exercised by groups of male students who shared common interests and banded together to discuss not only academic matters but also the affairs of campus and society. These groups developed into friendship networks and became brotherhoods defined by shared values, beliefs, and perspectives. These distinct brotherhoods —these *fraternities*—were a mainstay on the landscape of U.S. higher education for much of its history.

Throughout their rich histories, fraternities have often been the birthplace of leaders who have taken their place on the national and international scene in government, athletics, entertainment, and other public venues. All but 2 U.S. presidents have been fraternity members, and 16 vice presidents have been members of fraternities. Approximately two-thirds of all who have served in cabinet-level posts in any administration since 1900 have been fraternity men, and over three-fourths of U.S. Senators and Representatives have been members. Over 85% of U.S. Supreme Court Justices have been fraternity members, as have as many as 43 chief executive officers of the nation's 50 largest corporations. Fraternity membership runs wide and deep and is often the birthplace of leadership for many of those who choose it.

Fraternities have a long history of relationships with sororities, or women's fraternities. These women's organizations were founded almost a century after Phi Beta Kappa first appeared, primarily as a way for women to gain male acceptance and to ally themselves with male power on coeducational campuses. Although modeled after the men's fraternities, sororities developed their own character on the landscape of campus life. Both historically and in contemporary times, they have been less likely than fraternities to engage in rebellion against college authority, and they are generally less likely to attract attention because of antisocial or illegal behaviors. Nevertheless, they remain closely associated with fraternities as "siblings" or "partners" in campus Greek communities.

Contemporary Organization, Characteristics, and Activities

Today's college fraternities are national or international organizations comprised of undergraduate members and large networks of support provided by alumni members. Each group is governed by a national office and organizational structure, and local chapters of these groups are installed at individual campuses of colleges and universities. Fraternities that are officially recognized on this local level are supported by these national or international structures of government, resources, and leadership and are also hosted and guided by the college or university at which the chapter is located.

Many fraternities have chapters in both the United States and in Canada, making them truly international organizations; however, few if any have chapters or branches outside North America. Nationally and internationally, and usually on an annual basis, undergraduate and alumni members of fraternities gather for organizationwide events such as conferences, summer institutes, and training sessions to learn more from each other about ritual, values, scholarship, and leadership. This ongoing commitment to membership development is an investment in each organization's future; providing sound training and education for its members beyond the classroom walls helps to develop and prepare future leaders for each group and for greater society. Such activities are reminders of a shared vision of the past and the development of shared perspectives on the future.

Today's college and university campuses feature a wide range of fraternities that vary in size, purpose, mission, involvement level, age, and character. Although there are 66 nationally and internationally recognized fraternal organizations for college men, few campuses host a chapter of each organization. Instead, smaller Greek communities on the campus level are made up of chapters that have demonstrated interest and willingness to become an established part of the college or university community in that location. Campuses must recognize a chapter and often declare that a special relationship exists between the college or university and the chapter, outlining the support and contributions that each will provide, before the national organization will grant a charter at that location. Not all fraternities are affiliated with a national or international organization, however; some remain independent or "local," in order to retain more control and reduce organizational costs.

Some colleges and universities in North American do not allow fraternities (or sororities) to organize on their campuses. Among those that do, small to midsized institutions may typically host between 5 and 20 fraternities; some larger universities may feature more than 40 or 50 chapters. These organizations are governed locally by interfraternity councils, comprising chapter members from a particular campus who volunteer to help regulate and guide the fraternal community through structured governance. The North American Interfraternity Conference is the international body that provides oversight and standards for campus interfraternity councils and men's fraternities in both the United States and Canada.

Individual chapters are traditionally made up of a general membership led by officers and a committee structure. They operate on an annual calendar that features marketing, recruitment, education, social, athletic, and philanthropic events. Recruitment, formerly known as "rush," is the process by which new members are invited to learn more about the organization and affiliate with the chapter; a more intensive education period ("pledging") is the formal education or formation period for new members. Through a series of other programs, events, and activities, each chapter takes on its own personality on campus, often raising support for charities, competing against other student organizations in intramural athletics, developing a vibrant social atmosphere for members and other interested students, and otherwise making unique contributions to the campus and Greek community.

In terms of physical environments, Greek housing is often concentrated or grouped together or in close proximity on college campuses. "Greek Rows" of houses—each belonging to a particular chapter—dominate sections of campuses, and the homes of members of fraternities and sororities coexist near each other in a true and tangible, neighborly Greek community. More often than not, the shared experience of "being Greek" encourages friendships and relationships among men's and women's organizations, and chapters often cosponsor events or share responsibility for philanthropic projects. These partnerships continue to grow as today's fraternities and sororities rise to the challenge of portraying positive images for their organizations and continue to celebrate their rituals and to role-model behaviors for their peers on campus and beyond.

Among members of Greek communities on some campuses there exists a friendly, competitive tension to visibly demonstrate a positive image on college and university campuses. A vibrant spirit of community is demonstrated by interfraternity athletic contests, charity fundraisers, homecoming float decorations, house landscaping, or other types of competition. Such activities express the spirit of "doing good" (philanthropy) through community building that is a foundational value of Greek life. More often than not, campuses benefit from the good that is done by fraternities and their members, but they also suffer from the few (but significant) episodes of unhealthy choices and destructive behavior often associated with fraternity life.

Unfortunately, some unique characteristics of men's fraternal groups—common interests, shared values, distinct housing, and the occasional lack of internal leadership or supervision—often can encourage "group think" and lead to poor choices and unhealthy decision making. In recent decades, the attention of campus administrators and the media has focused on fraternity members' alcohol and drug abuse, hazing, academic cheating, sexual assault, and other acts that are either criminal in nature or that violate the values or standards of the organizations they pledged and of the institutions of higher education that host them. Currently, hazing and alcohol abuse lead the list of problems that are making colleges and universities the targets of legal action, followed closely by examples of offensive and insensitive behavior. Forty states have antihazing laws, some nearly 30 years old, but hazing continues. Research shows that members of fraternities are more likely to abuse alcohol than their non-Greek peers. Such forms of crime and misbehavior perpetuate a negative image for these groups, and exemplary chapters are often forced to battle the stereotypes created by other chapters' destructive behaviors. Because of these instances, some campuses have gone so far as to reduce or close the entire Greek community rather than to continually address the problems created by certain behavior. Yet, without proper guidance and support from alumni and institutional staff, fraternity members are left alone to (mis) manage an often dangerous environment.

Some of today's fraternities suffer the stigma of being "party houses" on campus, centers of debauchery and delinquency and devoid of any opportunities for positive role modeling. Those who support fraternities argue that these lackluster chapters have nothing in common with their founding organizations or values except the name, and other, values-driven chapters of the same fraternity on other campuses take great displeasure in sharing their name with what they regard as their less-than-worthy brethren. Thus there are tensions both within and outside of each group, making it ever more necessary to develop strong internal and external leadership for fraternities on every campus.

Diversity, Academic, and Ethical Challenges

Fraternities today are being challenged to turn themselves into ethical learning communities that can address not only ways to eliminate or reduce crime and misbehavior but also ways to improve diversity, academic commitments, and ethical standards and expectations. These challenges are broad in scope and very different from those that their founders faced more than two centuries ago, but success in dealing with them is likely to be critical to the survival of fraternities as communities of scholars, friends, learners, and leaders.

A long-standing criticism of fraternities is that they are highly exclusive and lack diversity. Although the United States and Canada have been multicultural societies since their founding, multiculturalism has received increasingly explicit attention in recent years, and colleges and universities in both countries face increasing demands to prepare graduates who can live and work effectively in a multicultural world. Greek leaders assert that the Greek experience helps students appreciate individuals from diverse backgrounds and cultures, but fraternities remain largely homogeneous in their ethnic and racial makeup. Research has shown that undergraduate students who participate in educational activities and programs focusing on diversity displayed greater openness to diversity than their peers who did not. Similarly, workshops and training programs designed to prevent sexual harassment and rape on campus have been found to reduce hostility toward and abuse of women. The challenge remains for fraternities to move toward a stronger commitment to—and appreciation of—diversity in the years to come.

Fraternity men are also being challenged to commit to high standards in academic honesty and achievement. Possibly owing to a lack of highly regulated housing environments, fraternity house residents may not be held responsible for maintaining study hours, completing homework, or attending classes; other members may suffer from poor time management and the frequent choice to socialize more than study. These choices lead to lower achievement in scholarship, greater temptation to cheat, and lower rates of degree completion for some Greek communities, thereby increasing efforts by national organizations, institutional staff, and faculty to work closely with fraternity men to better strategize and maximize their academic potential. Although there are good examples on many campuses of fraternity scholars and those who achieve highly in academics, the efforts of some fraternities to encourage their members to truly become "scholars among men" remain stigmatized.

Nevertheless, fraternities must consider cognitive outcomes (such as critical thinking, reasoning, and understanding) as a priority as they seek to redefine themselves as learning communities of scholars and leaders. Unfortunately, research has shown that early Greek involvement can negatively affect cognitive development, particularly because the first year of college tends to have lasting implications for a student's college career. Healthy involvement may lead to healthy outcomes; anything less may lead to more negative results.

Not only high academic standards but also clear, high ethical standards and expectations for student behavior are important if fraternities are to become true learning communities shaped by values, friendship, scholarship, and service. Unfortunately, studies show that fraternity membership influences ethical development in a negative way through pledge education and various social events that do not respect other people, values, or cultures. Historically, many fraternities have had codes of behavior and standards that stress moral values and personal integrity to which members commit at initiation. If these standards truly become part of the lives of chapter members, fraternities could indeed become effective and ethical learning communities. There must be a shared expectation and demand that members commit to and live out the positive values that they and their organizations espouse; to miss this goal is to disregard much that is positive in the heritage and the original purpose of their brotherhoods.

REFERENCES AND FURTHER READING

Anson, J. L., & Marchesani, R. F., Jr. (Eds.). (1991). *Baird's manual of college fraternities*. Indianapolis, IN: Baird's Manual Foundation.

Horowitz, H. L. (1987). *Campus life: Undergraduate cultures from the end of the eighteenth century to the present*. Chicago: University of Chicago Press.

North American Interfraternity Conference. (n.d.). Retrieved May 22, 2006, from http://www.nicindy.org/

Whipple, E. G. (Ed.). (1998). *New challenges for Greek letter organizations: Transforming fraternities and sororities into learning communities: New Directions for Student Services, No. 81*. San Francisco: Jossey-Bass.

CHAPTER 35

Reserve Officers' Training Corps (ROTC)

JENNIFER M. SILVA

The Reserve Officers' Training Corps (ROTC) is a program that provides military training to college students in exchange for service as a commissioned officer after graduation. More than half of these students also receive scholarship support from the Department of Defense. Currently, more than 1,000 colleges and universities across the United States offer these programs. Although the mission of the military and the mission of twenty-first-century secular higher education are often viewed in opposition to each other, ROTC provides a venue in which these two institutions interact and overlap, especially in terms of gender assumptions, ideology, and practices. Since students who participate in ROTC are, by definition, citizen-soldiers, frequently shifting between the university and the military, their experiences illustrate the ways in which meanings of masculinity and femininity are carried back and forth between two organizational cultures as well as the ways in which women negotiate the contradictory constructions of how to be a woman and a military officer. In general, this negotiation process does more to reproduce than to undermine traditional notions and ways of doing gender.

ROTC on Campus

Since its founding in 1916, just before the United States entered World War I, ROTC has been a campus-based program and has often been the target of controversies and conflicts between universities and the military, most notably during the Vietnam War era. Like the military itself, ROTC has undergone enormous changes historically (see Neiberg, 2000). By 1980, it had become a voluntary program that had jettisoned its heavy military emphasis, reduced its contact hour requirements, and included courses taught by regular civilian faculty in its curriculum. As the nation moved toward its new, all-volunteer armed forces, ROTC became the largest source of officers for all branches of the U.S. armed forces except the U.S. Coast Guard, which does not have ROTC programs. In 2004, ROTC graduates constituted 57% of army, 42% of air force, 21% of navy, and 12% of marine officers, for a combined 39% of all active duty officers under command of the U.S. Department of Defense (Office of the Under Secretary, 2004). In contrast to the 1950s when ROTC was composed primarily of White male students from private eastern schools and land-grant universities nationwide, today's ROTC programs are disproportionately located in public universities in the U.S. South and Midwest, especially those near strong military communities, and their programs enroll large numbers of women and minority students (Neiberg, 2000). Liberal arts colleges and Ivy League schools, on the other hand, have become more resistant to granting full academic status to ROTC, but students enrolled at those institutions often have the option of cross-enrollment with other schools.

ROTC programs are responsible to both the military and to the institutions of higher education in which they are embedded. In addition to meeting the graduation requirements of the college or university in which they are enrolled, ROTC students take military classes, participate in physical training sessions, and spend their summers at training camps, all in preparation for military service after graduation. When they graduate from college, they are commissioned as officers and serve a minimum of four years in the military. Those who pursue specialized skills may be required to complete more than four years. Those who want to become fighter pilots, for example, are required to complete two additional years of training and ten years of military service.

Students who participate in ROTC do so for a variety of reasons. Many are attracted by the college scholarships. Some come from military families, and some, but not most, plan to have careers in the military. Most view the military as a venue in which they can gain job skills and credentials, and recruitment materials distributed by ROTC put a heavy stress on the occupational and career advantages, such as leadership development and strategic planning skills, to be gained by officer's training and military service.

Gender in the Military and in ROTC

Both numerically and ideologically, the military is highly male-dominated: Department of Defense statistics for 2004 reveal that women comprised 18% of the air force, 17% of the army, 15% of the navy, and 6% of the marine active duty officer corps (Office of the Under Secretary, 2004). Ideologically, Jeanne Holm (1992) portrays the history of women's military service primarily in terms of a tension between the cultural desire to maintain the masculinity of warfare and the more practical need to recruit women for their labor, especially since the elimination of the draft in 1973. This tension exists in army policies that do not allow women in combat units—even as the line between combat and noncombat in modern warfare grows increasingly fuzzy— while at the same time women are actively recruited by the military and are allowed to serve unofficially in combat positions (see Francke, 1997, especially pp. 47–72, for a discussion of women who have served in combat positions but have not been formally acknowledged by the military for doing so). Although laws banning air force and navy women from flying combat missions and from serving on combat ships were repealed in the early 1990s (Holm, 1992), many of the most prestigious specialties within these branches still prohibit women from participation. In particular, women cannot be SEALs or paratroopers, and the submarine community will remain exclusively male until 2012. Thus the career consequences of exclusion play out in much the same way across the different branches of the military: Women cannot achieve the highest-status positions.

Despite these gender exclusions and their consequences, the contemporary military often presents itself as a gender-blind institution in which people can excel as individuals—as *soldiers*, neither male nor female—and be judged on the basis of ability rather than gender. This gender-blind, individual-achievement rhetoric is challenged by many experiences in ROTC, especially in the physical training sessions, where differences between males and females are highlighted by the "gender norming" of fitness standards (Fenner & deYoung, 2001). These standards consist of three components: push-ups, sit-ups, and a two-mile run. In 1999, men in the 17- to 21-year-old age category were expected to complete 42 push-ups to pass the test, while women were expected to complete 19. Both males and females were required to complete 53 sit-ups to pass. Men had to run 2 miles in 15 minutes and 54 seconds, but women were allowed an additional 3 minutes to pass this test. These are passing scores, and the standards for maxing the tests are more rigorous (Fenner & deYoung, 2001). Other branches of the military have slightly different standards, but the discrepancy between men's and women's standards remains. The military rationale for the gender differences in these standards is that women are physically weaker than men and that the standards simply equalize the *effort* required by men and women. Nevertheless, like combat exclusion policies, gender-based physical training standards continually mark women as different, leaving them without the full status of soldier.

In contrast to this emphasis on women's inferiority, there are many ways in which the military context can be viewed as potentially empowering to women, especially given that the military demands physically and mentally tough, goal-oriented, aggressive soldiers with skills of violence, weaponry, and, ultimately, death. Historically, many scholars have seen the military as a potential site for the transformation of cultural meanings of gender, arguing that its equal opportunity employment structure and "gender-blind" policies provide a vehicle for women who wish to escape constrictive civilian gender roles (e.g., Fenner & deYoung, 2001; Holm, 1992). Furthermore, these scholars view women's military participation as essential to achieving full equality with men, noting that the military is a core institution in the United States and that only by participating in it can women "realize the full rights and responsibilities of citizenship" (Holm, 1992, p. 508). Even critics of the military stress that women must have a voice within it in order to be taken seriously as citizens. Elshtain (1995), for example, views the female soldier as one possible solution to the problem of women "still [being] prepared to have men think and act politically in their behalf" (p. 243). Scholars who advocate women's military participation share the belief that the notion of a female soldier is transgressive in and of itself, challenging essentialist conceptions of women as nurturers in need of male protection.

Enloe (1983, 2004), however, raises alternative possibilities that reject this notion of transgression and focus more heavily on maintenance and reproduction. She argues that the military is primarily a patriarchal institution that depends on masculine ideology in order to carry out its goals. She accuses the military of exploiting the rhetoric of empowerment in order to use women's labor while at the same time barring women from achieving first-class status within the institution, since combat positions remain the ultimate symbol of sacrifice and service. Enloe focuses on the meanings of masculinity and femininity within the military context, arguing that the military allows women's presence only to the extent that it can ensure the reproduction of traditional cultural notions of women as nurturers and men as warriors. She asserts that combat exclusion policies differentiate between men's work and women's work, prompting military men to define combat as part of what it means to be a man in our society. In this way, women's presence in the military serves to highlight gender differences, leading to the reproduction of traditional gender stratification.

In addition, there is a vast literature documenting male institutional resistance to women's presence—and femininity itself—within the military. At the interpersonal level, multiple studies (e.g., Francke, 1997; Herbert, 1998; Miller, 1997) point to the rampant sexism, sexual harassment, and discrimination in the armed services. At the institutional level, the construction of the "soldier" categorically rejects prevailing models of femininity. Indeed, self-control, assertiveness, and determination combine to form a concept of soldierliness that is distinctly different from cultural understandings of femininity as caring, connection, and compromise. This difference raises serious questions about the likelihood that women can fully assimilate into dominant military culture, especially since—as major theorists, such as Erving Goffman (1959), Harold Garfinkel (1967), and Judith Butler (1990) have demonstrated—performing or "doing" gender in culturally recognizable ways is crucial to the development of a meaningful identity. Gender is a fundamental building block of identity, prerequisite to a sense of self and to social acceptance. Butler explains: "Discrete genders are part of what 'humanizes' individuals within contemporary culture; indeed, we regularly punish those who fail to do their gender right" (p. 178).

In an institution where the notion prevails that men are qualified to be soldiers *because they are men*, women have an ambiguous and often inferior status (Miller, 1997). In her study of how military women do gender, Herbert (1998) indicates that female soldiers face a double bind: "Held accountable as women and as soldiers," they must prove that they have culturally defined masculine qualities such as self-control and stoicism while also negotiating cultural definitions of femininity that have provided them with stable gender identities throughout their lives. Thus, to understand the gender implications of women's participation in ROTC, the question becomes, How far can women extend existing boundaries of femininity within the military context while still maintaining their identities as *women*? Given that contemporary cultures, including campus and military cultures, do not recognize the possibility of an ungendered self, this question points to the constraining nature of cultural systems of meaning, the limits of agency, and the tension between cultural reproduction and transformation.

Negotiating the Tension between ROTC Culture and Traditional Femininity

Supporting the view of the military (and ROTC) as a source of empowerment, my own study of army, air force, and navy ROTC programs (see Silva, 2008) revealed that the women who were cadets or midshipmen in those programs (hereafter called "cadets") endorsed ROTC culture as an opportunity to be strong, assertive, and skillful; they spoke enthusiastically about learning weapon systems and practicing land navigation, as well as about serving as leaders in their battalions, all of which they acknowledged as exciting, nontraditional activities for women. They also defined ROTC as an escape from some of the negative aspects of traditional femininity, understood mainly as the belief that they had to compete with each other, achieve the ideal feminine body, or act weak or incompetent in order to attract men. ROTC allowed these women to resist definitions of traditional femininity that they found restrictive, especially when compared with the climate of their universities more generally, which they saw as promoting unachievable standards of female attractiveness.

Despite these understandings of ROTC as a gender-neutral or beneficial space, both the female and male cadets in my study perceived their experiences in ROTC as gendered. The women felt that they had to constantly prove that they were capable, and many of the men said that female standards of physical training required less effort despite Department of Defense claims to the contrary. Some of the women saw their own performance as "worthy" only when they could meet the male standards, and they were willing to label themselves, or other women, as inferior when they fell short of these standards (see also Abrams, 1993).

Both men and women cadets drew upon traditional understandings of masculinity and femininity in order to delineate between men's work and women's work, linking masculinity and soldiering in a fundamental and inextricable way that is always in juxtaposition to femininity. While women felt empowered to the extent that they could defy traditionally feminine expectations, none of them questioned the social construction of masculinity and femininity, instead interpreting these concepts as natural, biological, and fixed. Braudy's (2003, p. 23) definition of military masculinity as "a ritual of differentiation and distinction: who we are versus who we are not" asserts that masculinity takes shape only when femininity is present in opposition; to be masculine is therefore to prove that one is not feminine. All but one of the cadets in my study (Silva, 2008) upheld this binary, continually setting up femininity as other, or as the lack of masculine strength and steadfastness.

Male cadets spoke most highly of ROTC women who conformed to university or civilian gender identities. Because these men took femininity as a sign of natural womanhood, and depended on femininity in order to define their own masculinity in juxtaposition, they championed ROTC women who best maintained a system of gender differentiation. This is in direct contradiction to the explicitly stated position of the U.S. military, which lays claim to gender neutrality or gender-blindness. Despite this official policy, cadets privileged both masculinity and maleness and viewed them as foundational. Thus the men's evaluation of their female colleagues contradicted and rejected both the explicit criteria promulgated by the U.S. military and the implicit criteria for defining a "good soldier." For the women, therefore, winning the respect of their male colleagues meant denying the explicit demands to be a "good soldier" in order to meet expectations of being a "good woman."

Furthermore, while the women conceived of ROTC as a space where they could expand and even redefine traditional definitions of femininity, the men were not aware of this constant gender negotiation and continued to privilege traditional femininity. Despite widespread recognition and acknowledgment that ROTC women challenged their traditional perceptions of women, none of the male cadets rethought gender more broadly. Instead, *individual* strong, capable women were redefined—sometimes in an ambivalent or even complimentary way, but always as abnormal. For women, to espouse gender neutrality explicitly at the institutional level of the military, to privilege masculinity implicitly in the ROTC setting, yet all the while to perform traditional femininity in interactions with their male colleagues, was to walk a very fine line indeed.

Yet this difficult balancing act did not cause the women in my study to reject notions of traditional femininity. Instead, they defined themselves as feminine and embraced traditional meanings of femininity—attractiveness, sensitivity, and motherhood—as fundamental sources of meaning in their lives. Because they viewed femininity as natural, they struggled to embody it, even though they knew this trait was explicitly incompatible with the military. Most found themselves unable to reconcile the contradiction between their identities as women and the qualities they deemed necessary for combat or even a military career. In other words, they saw femininity as fundamentally incompatible with the core function of the military—but never called into question the importance and centrality of femininity for themselves. On the contrary, these women viewed themselves as actively constructing meaningful identities that resisted the hegemony of masculinity in the military. Yet their focus on their individual choices obscures the cumulative effects of their actions: the reproduction of gender stratification and, ultimately, male privilege.

Although some commentators in the media and the public assume that women's participation in the military involves a fundamental transformation of gender, my own study of ROTC cadets casts doubts on this assumption. On one hand, it is true that the ROTC women I studied did, in many ways, challenge extant notions of masculinity and femininity. Through routine practices such as building muscles in physical training exercises, leading their battalions, assembling and skillfully using weapons, and presenting their bodies in a competent and nonsexual way, these women certainly defy central cultural understandings of women as weak, passive, and sexual. At the same time, however, the cadets in my study did not see or explain their actions as revolutionary, masculine, or defiant. Consequently, their incorporation into the American military system is unlikely to transform either that system or more widespread conceptions of gender. Because they understand masculinity and femininity as individual, stable, and natural attributes, they cannot see their location in a system of gender relations that is based on powerful cultural notions of what men and women are allowed to be. None of the women in my study rejected her femaleness or even her femininity as a fundamental component of her core identity. The deep, hierarchical logic of gender—mainly the notion of women as nurturing caretakers and of men as steadfast warriors—remains untouched.

REFERENCES AND FURTHER READING

Abrams, K. (1993). Gender in the military: Androcentrism and institutional reform. *Law and Contemporary Problems, 56*(4), 139–158.

Braudy, L. (2003). *From chivalry to terrorism: War and the changing nature of masculinity*. New York: Random House.

Butler, J. (1990). *Gender trouble: Feminism and the subversion of identity*. New York: Routledge.

Elshtain, J. B. (1995). *Women and war*. Chicago: University of Chicago Press.

Enloe, C. (1983). *Does khaki become you? The militarisation of women's lives*. New York: Pluto Press.

Enloe, C. (2004). *The curious feminist: Searching for women in a new age of empire*. Berkeley: University of California Press.

Fenner, L. M., & deYoung, M. E. (2001). *Women in combat: Civic duty or military liability?* Washington, DC: Georgetown University Press.

Francke, L. B. (1997). *Ground Zero: The gender wars in the military*. New York: Simon & Schuster.

Garfinkel, H. (1967). *Studies in ethnomethodology*. New York: Prentice Hall.

Goffman, E. (1959). *The presentation of self in everyday life*. Garden City, NY: Anchor Books.

Herbert, M. (1998). *Camouflage isn't only for combat: Gender, sexuality, and women in the military*. New York: New York University Press.

Holm, J. (1992). *Women in the military: An unfinished revolution*. New York: Ballantine Books.

Miller, L. (1997). Not just weapons of the weak: Gender harassment as a form of protest for army men. *Social Psychological Quarterly, 60*(1), 32–51.

Neiberg, M. (2000). *Making citizen-soldiers: ROTC and the ideology of American military service*. Cambridge, MA: Harvard University Press.

Office of the Under Secretary of Defense, Personnel and Readiness. (2004). *Population representation in the military services*. Data reported in this chapter were retrieved on May 15, 2009, from http://www.defenslink.mil/prhome/poprep2004/officers/commission.html and from http://www.defenslink.mil/prhome/poprep2004/officers/gender.html

Silva, J. M. (2008). A new generation of women? How female ROTC cadets negotiate the tension between masculine military culture and traditional femininity. *Social Forces, 87*(2), 937–959.

CHAPTER 36

Service Learning and Activism

KAREN BOJAR

The relationship between service learning and feminism is a complicated one with deep philosophical differences sometimes masked by shifting terminology. *Service learning* is often used interchangeably with *activism* and with *experiential education*, the catchall term that includes any structured learning experience outside the traditional classroom. Experiential education might include the experiences of a business major interning in an accounting firm or a women's studies major interning in a radical direct action group. The term *internship* is usually applied to experiential education involving a major time commitment and preparation for a specific career area. It is typically unpaid work. While participating in an internship may enhance a student's future career possibilities, some students may not have the time or cannot afford to give up paid work to engage in this form of experiential learning.

Service learning tends to be the term used for experiential education projects that are short term and not necessarily connected to a career area. Service learning has proved to be a politically useful term for some, since there are now national organizations, such as Campus Compact, dedicated to its promotion and funding. Some teachers who use the term focus on traditional service projects such as tutoring and working in homeless shelters, whereas others use the term to include projects that might be characterized as social change or advocacy work.

Because of these different definitions, service learning has proved to be a controversial concept, especially among those feminists who contrast it with activism aimed at challenging gender norms and changing the social structure. Nevertheless, women's studies programs have been particularly receptive to all forms of experiential learning, including service learning, but the possibilities for feminist activism and other forms of experiential learning depend upon the institutional constraints and political climate in which those programs find themselves.

Feminist Unease with Service Learning

The term *service learning*, with its connotations of traditional charitable work, has long made many feminists uneasy. Although celebrated by some strands of feminist thought as embodying an ethic of care, charitable work has been regarded with suspicion by feminists who have seen such work as implicated in female subordination or as an attempt to prop up an unjust status quo. At the 1973 convention of the National Organization for Women (NOW), the Task Force on Volunteerism passed a resolution that advocated for political activism as opposed to the "band-aid" approach of service-oriented volunteerism. The resolution stated that NOW believed that service-oriented volunteerism was a hit-or-miss, patchwork approach to solving major social problems, most of which are reflections of an economic system in need of an overhaul. Worse yet, the political energy devoted to service-oriented volunteerism actually provided administrative support for the current system, thereby preventing needed social changes from occurring.

NOW has since changed its bylaws to remove its prohibition against service-oriented volunteerism. Although the 1973 NOW statement may seem somewhat extreme, it does raise some important questions and reflects a legitimate (and prescient) concern that a parsimonious government will abdicate its responsibilities to its citizens and try to substitute "hit-or-miss" volunteer efforts for much-needed social programs.

The NOW members who argued for the removal of the prohibition against service-oriented volunteerism thought it missed something extremely important: the mutually reinforcing relationship between direct service and advocacy for social change. The political energy that NOW wanted to encourage is often developed as a consequence of the experience of direct service. Determination to attack a social problem at its roots can be an outgrowth of the experience of direct service.

The ambivalent responses of feminists to volunteerism (and by implication to service learning) is an extremely useful lens for exploring conflicts in contemporary feminist thought. The debate about volunteer work is intimately bound up with the difference/sameness debate that runs throughout the feminist thought of the past 150 years. Traditional service-oriented volunteerism is more likely to be valued by "cultural feminists" or "difference feminists" who value women's different voices and concerns and tend to emphasize women's special attributes. Volunteer work is most likely to be viewed with suspicion by the strand of feminist thought that focuses on the struggle for equality based on the assumption that men and women are fundamentally the same and should be treated the same in the public sphere. Such "equal rights feminists" are more likely to adhere to individualist values; cultural feminists are more likely to adhere to communitarian values.

Ironically, at the same time that some feminists were criticizing the volunteer ethic, a new kind of volunteer work—volunteering on the job—was emerging, a kind of volunteer work largely exempt from feminist critique and often encouraged by feminist organizations. This new kind of volunteer work has clear affinities with the kinds of charitable works women have traditionally performed throughout the history of American society. And, as in earlier periods, volunteers tend to come from the ranks of relatively affluent women. In contemporary society, volunteering on the job is mainly characteristic of professional women and tends to be most prevalent in the less-prestigious professions such as teaching and social work. For many women in education and human services, their jobs have become their volunteer work as they put in far more time than the hours for which they are paid. Volunteering on the job can become insidious when a woman's job is also her cause. Some of the most compulsive volunteers on the job are directors of women's studies programs and directors and staff of women's advocacy groups.

What Is Feminist Activism and What Makes It Possible?

The debate about activism versus volunteer work has been part of the reflective component of many service-learning / experiential-education courses. NOW's encouragement of feminist activism (loosely understood as activities that challenge prevailing gender norms) rather than traditional volunteer work has resonated with many feminist educators. However, there is no clear consensus among feminist educators as to what counts as activism or the extent to which it is to be valued over traditional volunteer work. For some, the activist project is intended to help students develop a deeper understanding of feminist issues; for others, it is intended to promote the development of skills necessary for building a powerful feminist movement. Many feminist educators would no doubt lay claim to both goals, with the emphasis shifting depending upon the level of the course. A focus on expanding awareness is more likely to be the top priority in an introductory course; an analysis of strategies for advancing the feminist agenda is more likely to be the focus of a senior seminar intended for women's studies majors.

To further complicate matters, projects that meet the usual understanding of activism might be characterized by some feminist educators as service learning. The shifting terminology and the use of the term *service learning* to characterize what might well be described as activism is apparent in recent collections exploring the relationship between service learning and activism on one hand and the academic field of women studies on the other. Naples and Bojar (2002) and Balliet and Heffernan (2000) present a wide range of possibilities that have been included under the rubric feminist activism or service learning.

Some feminist educators have found the term *service learning*, with its connotations of charity rather than social change, politically useful when they are writing grants to fund activist projects or seeking support from college administrators. Academic administrators (even liberal ones) tend to be reluctant to channel resources to anything that might be considered controversial by their boards of trustees or by local political leaders, in the case of public institutions dependent on state and local funding. The compromises feminist educators make (or choose not to make) depend on institutional constraints, local political climate, and the extent to which feminist educators are in a position to take risks.

Institutional constraints shape both the possibilities available to feminist educators and the language used to describe them. In women's studies courses that enroll large numbers of nonmajors, students are often resistant to feminism, in particular, and to activism. Furthermore, possibilities for community partners are very dependent upon location. Options abound in urban areas rich in feminist organizations. Frequently in such urban areas, institutions are managed by liberal administrators who provide support or at least are not actively opposed to efforts of women's studies programs to promote feminist activism. Once one leaves the Boston-Washington megalopolis, the Pacific Coast, and a few urban centers in the South and Midwest (Atlanta, Austin, Chicago, and Minneapolis–St. Paul), the range of potential community partners for feminist projects generally dwindles.

In addition to institutional constraints such as geographical location and political climate, another powerful constraint is time. Residential campuses provide opportunities for campus-based projects not available at commuter colleges where students rush off to jobs and family responsibilities. Finding time for activist projects is an especially urgent issue for teachers at community colleges desperately trying to pack as much as possible into their introductory women's studies courses, knowing these may be the only women's studies courses their students will ever take. The options available to them are worlds apart from those available to teachers of senior seminars for women's studies majors in four-year colleges.

Relationships among Activism, Service Learning, and Women's Studies

Women's studies as an academic discipline has been particularly receptive to experiential education in its many forms. In the minds of many women's studies practitioners, women's studies and feminist activism are inextricably intertwined. Women's studies as an academic discipline has defined itself in terms of its subject matter, methodology, and pedagogy. A commitment to experiential education has been a major theme of feminist pedagogy, and many women's studies practitioners would argue that it is central to feminist pedagogy. In the early days of women's studies programs, the link between the academic study of women's lives and the feminist movement was, for the most part, unquestioned.

However, as women's studies programs became institutionalized, a note of anxiety about compromising one's scholarship by political engagement was sometimes heard; increasingly, some feminist scholars began to see feminist activism as something of a career risk. Of course, the riskiness of a public commitment to activism varies considerably depending on one's situation. A teacher in a community college might be rewarded for what is seen as laudable civic engagement; a feminist scholar seeking tenure in a traditional academic department at an elite institution might well worry that activism might jeopardize her career. Whether feminist activism is likely to reap rewards or punishment is clearly dependent on the political climate of the institution and its surrounding community.

Some women's studies programs, heavily influenced by postmodernist theory, disengaged from activism. Feminist scholars began to write what were seen by some as unintelligible theoretical articles that sought to problematize key concepts and categories—such as the category *woman*. These scholars argued that gender boundaries are permeable, that *woman* is an unstable category, and that ultimately there is no such thing as "woman." This shift to theory coincided with a shift from women's studies to gender studies. It is not surprising that navigating these minefields has led some feminist educators to use more politically acceptable terminology such as *service learning* or *experiential education* rather than *activism* to describe activist-oriented pedagogical strategies.

Interestingly, the activist projects (often characterized as service learning) developed by feminist educators usually do not include projects related to electoral politics. The service-learning movement itself is on every level shot through with the notion that politics is dirty business. Tobi Walker (2000), who is one of the few service-learning practitioners to argue for encouraging student involvement in electoral politics, cites numerous examples of leaders of the movement—such as a director of a student-run national service organization and government officials at the Corporation for National Service—who exalt service over politics and reflect what Walker calls "a troubling tendency within the community service movement to conclude that politics is evil." Much of the literature on women's grassroots activism, such as Temma Kaplan's (1997)

Crazy for Democracy and Nancy Naples's (1997) *Grassroots Warriors*, report similar distrust of participation in electoral politics on the part of community activists and the widely held belief that "authentic" grassroots activists must stay above the fray of electoral politics.

Whether defined as service learning, experiential education, or activism, there is agreement that these activities represent a labor-intensive approach to education and that the resources available are limited. Women's studies practitioners generally agree that there is a need to build support for their efforts to include experiential/service-learning/activist components in their courses. This support could take many forms, including smaller classes, additional resources such as teaching assistants, additional compensation either in the form of increased pay or released time, and recognition for such work when decisions are made regarding promotion and tenure. This agenda might seem hopelessly utopian to those who teach at financially strapped colleges that would have great difficulty providing additional financial resources or at elite institutions that would be very resistant to considering a commitment to experiential education when awarding promotion and tenure. Yet there are other feminist goals that seemed hopelessly utopian in earlier times but have been at least partially realized. If feminist educators are committed to an experiential/activist approach, they must also build an institutional commitment to experiential education.

REFERENCES AND FURTHER READING

Balliet, B. J., & Heffernan, K. (Eds.). (2000). *The practice of change: Concepts and models for service learning in women's studies*. Washington, DC: American Association of Higher Education.

Kaplan, T. (1997). *Crazy for democracy: Women in grassroots movements*. New York: Routledge.

Naples, N. A. (1997). *Grassroots warriors: Activist mothering, community work, and the war on poverty*. New York: Routledge.

Naples, N. A., & Bojar, K. (Eds.). (2002). *Teaching feminist activism: Strategies from the field*. New York: Routledge.

Report of the National Organization for Women Task Force on Volunteerism. (1973). Reprinted in *Ms.*, February 1975, 73.

Walker, T. (2000). A feminist challenge to community service: A call to politicize service learning. In B. J. Balliet & K. Heffernan (Eds.), *The practice of change: Concepts and models for service learning in women's studies* (pp. 25–38). Washington, DC: American Association of Higher Education.

CHAPTER 37

Sororities

AMY E. WELLS AND DEBORAH WORLEY

Sororities are Greek-letter voluntary associations for college women and alumnae that aspire to foster a sense of belonging, character development, and cultural awareness through ritual, traditions, and the shared experiences of members. Inspired by secret societies, including the Masonic orders and men's Greek organizations, or fraternities, sororities have existed on American college campuses for nearly 160 years, functioning within the context of undergraduate student culture. Over four million women are affiliated with college sororities today.

Sorority membership first served college women to enrich the formal curriculum of the mid- to late nineteenth century. As coeducation progressed, sororities conferred prestigious social standing upon members in male-dominant environments and enhanced their participation in student governance. Sororities flourished over time by meeting a range of member needs including providing meals and lodging, introducing suitable associates and good marriage prospects, promoting academic success and persistence among members, providing entrée into alumni-sponsored business and employment networks, and addressing the distinct needs of different racial and ethnic groups as student populations diversified.

While some sororities reside as isolated chapters on individual campuses, sororities also exist apart from colleges and universities as large, multichapter, national or international corporations with executive offices, multimillion-dollar budgets, independent philanthropic foundations, and extensive alumnae networks. Sororities, along with fraternities, receive special endorsements such as land and administrative staff support from colleges and universities. However, the nature of the relationship between sororities and academic institutions is best described as symbiotic, meaning sororities and their host colleges and universities exist in a mutually interdependent state but are not necessarily of benefit to each other. Campus prohibitions on Greek housing or policies that delay member recruitment until sophomore year, for example, demonstrate that colleges and universities may curtail sorority growth and operation. Well-documented incidents of hazing, high-risk drinking, and eating disorders among sorority women illustrate that at times members indulge in behaviors that may undermine the academic goals of individuals and the institution.

Despite the pervasiveness of sororities, limited research exists about their short- and long-term membership and community effects as well as their larger consequences for women's and men's education. Proponents claim that sorority membership promotes academic achievement, student involvement, institutional loyalty and pride, overall satisfaction with college student life, and alumni giving. Opponents contend that sorority membership promotes frivolity; detracts from student learning; perpetuates unhealthy behaviors; and accentuates women's appearance, manners, and traditional female roles. Thus scholars, educational practitioners, students, and even sorority members themselves contest the purpose, value, and customs of sororities, and conclusions about their contribution to the collegiate extracurriculum are contradictory at best.

History and Development

Although the term *sorority* may denote various civic clubs for women, a Syracuse University Latin professor coined the term "sorority" in 1874 in reference to Gamma Phi Beta, the first women's voluntary association to actively identify itself as a sorority on a college campus. Prior to that, sororities existed as isolated secret societies without Greek nomenclature, or they were known as fraternities. The secret literary societies founded in 1851 and 1852 at Wesleyan Female College in Macon, Georgia, and known respectively as the Adelphean and Philomathean societies, are considered the first sororities. Only after the turn of the twentieth century did these two groups come to identify themselves as Alpha Delta Pi and Phi Mu fraternities and expand their membership to other campuses.

I.C. Sorosis is the first sorority founded as a national women's "fraternity" and the first sorority to start chapters in other locations, although its chapters quickly folded. Founded at Monmouth College in Monmouth, Illinois, in 1867, I.C. Sorosis became Pi Beta Phi fraternity 21 years later when members perceived an advantage in the adoption of Greek letters. Founded in 1870, Kappa Kappa Gamma followed I.C. Sorosis at Monmouth by three years, and during that same year, creators established another sorority, Kappa Alpha Theta, at DePauw University. Interestingly, these two women's groups, Kappa Kappa Gamma and Kappa Alpha Theta, intentionally adopted the principles and practices of men's organizations.

Greek-letter sororities proliferated rapidly around the turn of the twentieth century. They arose at various institutional types; operated in concert with societal norms and discriminatory constraints related to race, religion, and ethnicity; and reflected women's opportunity and participation in various fields of study. The pattern of organizational beginnings shows that sororities often began in close proximity to others where an established group sparked competition and gave models to emulate. This happened at Longwood College (then the Virginia State Normal School in Farmville, Virginia), where Kappa Delta (1897), Zeta Tau Alpha (1898), and Sigma Sigma Sigma (1898) originated, and at Stephens College in Columbia, Missouri, a junior college where three sororities—Kappa Delta Phi, Zeta Mu Epsilon, and Theta Tau Epsilon—began in 1921. Three groups primarily, but not exclusively, for African American women originated at Howard University, a historically Black university in Washington, DC, namely, Alpha Kappa Alpha (1908), Delta Sigma Theta (1913), and Zeta Phi Beta (1920). For Jewish women, three sororities began in New York City: Iota Alpha Pi (1903, Hunter College), Alpha Epsilon Phi (1909, Barnard College), and Delta Phi Epsilon (1917, Washington Square College of New York University). In addition, women created their own professional recognition societies in many academic fields, including Pi Kappa Sigma (1894, education), Nu Sigma Phi (1898, medicine), Kappa Beta Phi (1908, law),

Phi Upsilon Omicron (1909, home economics), and Gamma Epsilon Pi (1918, commerce) and others.

Particularly among the early social sororities, fierce competition or "rushing" for the "best" women brought about informal agreements among sororities. To promote the extant agreements, curb problems like concurrent membership in different groups, and stave off external regulation by college faculty and deans, representatives from nine sororities came together in 1902 to create what later became the National Panhellenic Conference (NPC). Deriving authority from the unanimous agreements that its autonomous member sororities adopt and observe, the NPC offers advocacy and support for its 26 national and international member sororities and the local Panhellenic associations that oversee Greek women's affairs on the individual campus level. Similarly, the National Panhellenic Council, Inc. (NPHC), established in 1930, acts as an umbrella organization that promotes and supports the distinct mission related to racial uplift of the nine international predominately Black Greek-letter organizations, including the three historically Black sororities already mentioned that were founded at Howard University and a fourth historically Black sorority, Sigma Gamma Rho, that was founded in Indianapolis, Indiana, in 1922 and became a collegiate sorority when chartered at Butler University in 1929.

In addition to the longstanding NPC- and NPHC-affiliated groups, a large number of local sororities emerged along with sororities designed to meet the distinct cultural needs of an increasingly diverse population of college women. Defined as a single chapter on a specific college or university campus, local sororities can be robust and lasting or fragile and fleeting. Sometimes local sororities occur when universities forbid nationally recognized Greek organizations from colonizing or when existing chapters exclude new members with diverse backgrounds or characteristics. In fact, many of the multicultural or ethnic-interest groups that thrived in the last decades of the twentieth century started and continue as local groups. These emergent sororities include groups in support of Asians (e.g., Sigma Omicron Pi, 1930; Alpha Kappa Delta Pi, 1990), Latinas (e.g., Lambda Theta Alpha, 1975; Chi Upsilon Sigma, 1980), Native Americans (e.g., Alpha Pi Omega, 1994; Sigma Omicron Epsilon, 1997), South Asians (e.g., Sigma Sigma Rho, 1998; Kappa Phi Gamma, 1998), and Muslim women (Gamma Gamma Chi, 2005) as well as lesbians, bisexuals, and transgendered women (e.g., Gamma Rho Lambda, 2003). In addition, over 20 multicultural sororities formed for the purpose of bringing about multiethnic, multiracial organizations to promote multicultural awareness (e.g., Mu Sigma Upsilon, 1981; Lambda Sigma Gamma, 1986; Theta Nu Xi, 1997). Some of these emergent groups also created their own national advocacy and support agencies, including the National Association of Latino Fraternal Organizations and the National Multicultural Greek Council, Inc., both formed in 1998.

Characteristics of and Controversies about Contemporary Sororities

To the outside world and internally, sororities evidence their priorities and shared commitments through mottoes, crests, creeds, badges, songs, colors, flowers, calls or chants, grips, hand signs, member nicknames, and rituals. These representations also reveal the public history and predominantly, though not exclusively, Christian ideals of each group, often nestled in respect and reverence for founding members or "mothers." Because Greek-letter groups often begin in proximity to other social sororities, tremendous similarity exists between organizational symbols and ideals among groups

founded in similar eras with similar purposes and with slight variation in the sororities' surface characteristics. For example, many NPC sororities use Greek and Roman
mythology, and NPHC sororities draw inspiration from African lore. Emergent groups
reflect aspects of popular culture in their public identities, including a few who employ
the terms "herstory" and "womyn" to emphasize a woman-centered purpose and
knowledge of language as gender constructed among group founders and members. In
addition, sororities also subscribe to philanthropy, and on the whole, members contribute thousands of service hours and raise millions of dollars on an annual basis for
nonprofit, service-oriented, and community-based organizations.

This focus upon philanthropic work, combined with the various rituals and representations centering on the themes of "sisterhood" and "ideal of true womanhood,"
make sororities a legacy of the clubwoman era (mid- to late 1800s through the early
1900s) when civic organizations and culture clubs, as a means to enter public affairs,
gave purpose to a burgeoning group of middle-class women liberated from the constraints of the "domestic sphere" by industrialization. Just as rising middle-class clubwomen faced constraints against participation in public affairs, college women, though
relatively privileged, faced a number of restrictions upheld by law and policy when
they sought and eventually gained access to higher education. Once women gained
admission to institutions of higher education, these restrictions included admissions
quotas, ineligibility for enrollment in classes or majors, and being banned from participation in student government and many extracurricular clubs. In addition, women
faced strict behavioral codes with rules about attire, curfews, daily activities, and use of
campus spaces. Early on, these affluent but relatively conventional college women embraced sororities as a tool for making inroads into student governance to bring about
emancipation from oppressive restrictions.

For young college women establishing independence from their families, sororities serve as an instrument of female agency within historically conservative, competitive, male-regulated or -centered educational institutions. At women's colleges, which
can be similarly male ordered, sororities provide females a vehicle for working with
faculty and administration as they navigate the passage into independent adulthood.
Sororities do this at coed institutions, too, but they also ally members with the competitive and relatively privileged fraternity men whose interests and activities (e.g.,
athletics, drinking) dominate the extracurriculum. In this way, sororities help women
date and mate the "best" men on campus.

Within this competitive, heterosexual milieu, sorority membership offers women
increased control over their identities and sexualities prior to full adulthood, with its
requisite sobriety and substantial responsibilities. Hence, sororities offer a cocoon of
sorts, permitting privileged members to indulge in lifestyle freedoms semiprivately
with reputed and like-minded associates under the public protection of their Greek
affiliation within a select or closed system. Within the campus or local context, this
competition and exclusion often evolves into a gender-differentiated prestige hierarchy, whereby whole sororities and fraternities informally pair with an opposite-gender
group having members of similar appearance, economic status, and social standing.
Because membership signifies status within the bounds of this community, simply
stating identity as a member of a particular sorority conveys meaning about a member's place within the community that other community members implicitly recognize and understand. Thus, joining a sorority in general and a "better" sorority in particular provides "better" associates, protects a woman's reputation when engaged in

permissive behaviors, and foretells future financial success, as well as membership in prestigious clubs and junior leagues.

On a typical college campus, the Greek system has spaces for all the women who would like to participate. Therefore, the membership recruitment process aligns each prospective new member with a chapter, ideally allowing for each side to have a say in the outcome of the selection, with some variation in the member recruitment or "intake" process for the historically Black, ethnic-interest, and multicultural groups. Often when women fail to attain Greek membership, it is because they limit their opportunities, seeking only to join the highest-status groups and refusing to take the places offered in groups of lesser standing within the institution-specific Greek prestige hierarchy. On the whole, sororities maintain or attain status within the undergraduate cultural context when they are reputed to be more selective than others and when the majority of members display the desired social characteristics that advance or uphold the group's status within the local system. These implicit rules about maintaining reputation also apply to participating members; for those members who overindulge in lifestyle freedoms or bring disrepute to the group face consequences such as probation, suspension, or expulsion from the group.

From the outside looking in, some observers are troubled that sorority women frequently describe their association as a "sisterhood," and members often refer to each other as "sister," or "soror" in the predominantly Black and some ethnic-interest as well as multicultural sororities. But sorting out this ideal of sisterhood and the role of sororities among relatively privileged women within the context of higher education requires wrestling with women's history in postsecondary education and the broader effects of socially constructed undergraduate campus cultures. Among participants in women's clubs, the woman's suffrage and women's rights movements, and especially among African American women, the term *sisterhood* refers to a shared struggle in the face of oppression and signals women's collective power to bring about social change. Critics of sororities, including many feminists, believe the word *sisterhood* rings hollow for sorority women, especially those in predominantly White sororities, because of their exclusivity and focus on competition for men and social status. These critics also argue that sororities promise little positive social change compared with early clubwomen who were intently concerned with social welfare activities. Given the term's sociohistorical usage, especially its ties to feminism and to struggles against racial and class oppression, these opponents challenge the appropriateness of the term *sisterhood* as a description of the bonds of association among members of social sororities. Nevertheless, the term remains popular among sorority members themselves, including White members of predominately White organizations, who often use the term as a synonym for close friendship and who often cite sisterhood within their sorority as a positive—sometimes the most positive—experience of their undergraduate years.

The desire for and high value assigned to close friendship probably also explain why sororities continue to be popular among many undergraduate women and why women from minority backgrounds, cultures, religions, and ethnic groups that were previously excluded from sororities band together to establish similar associations with similar rituals and activities, rather than other forms of student organizations. For minority women, sororities offer not only close friendships but also kinshiplike ties with other members of underrepresented groups in predominantly White college settings. The added dimension of a shared desire among members to sponsor educational, economic, political, and social advancement or "uplift" for other members of their gender, race, ethnicity, and culture fits the individual aspirations of many college-going members of these populations, too. This emphasis on uplift historically separated NPHC from NPC groups and their members. For example, the first public act of Delta Sigma Theta, now a member of NPHC, was to march in a woman's suffrage parade down Pennsylvania Avenue in Washington, DC, on March 13, 1913. The activities of Black sororities, in partnership with Black fraternities, have included providing leadership for the American Council on Human Rights, the United Negro College Fund, the National Urban League, and the National Association for the Advancement of Colored People, to name a few.

In contrast to the NPHC sororities, those in the NPC have continued to place more emphasis on sociability. Their philanthropic work has rarely had the personal relevance or exhibited the intense commitment of the uplift work of NPHC sororities that has been rooted in racial and gender identities. Thus it is surprising that even now, when women have increased their independence from men, have become more career oriented, and outnumber men in many academic fields and institutions of higher education, NPC sororities remain popular, in contrast to fraternities, whose numbers and popularity fluctuate. Given the demands of membership, including its financial costs, and the potential negative effects of being perceived as someone who focuses on superficial or status-oriented aspects of life such as appearance, popularity, wealth, and reputation, why would contemporary White women want to participate in them? Their popularity may result not only from the desire for close friendships but also from the fit between organizational ideals and the values of the women they attract. Some studies show, for example, that women in traditionally and still predominantly White sororities are politically conservative, reject feminism, and hold traditional gender attitudes regarding dating and marriage as well as conventional stereotypes about male dominion in interpersonal relationships.

Sororities' popularity also has something to do with the fact that just as sororities reflected their times, they also changed with them. Certainly, society and sororities, along with the colleges and universities that host them, indulge much more permissive behaviors and attitudes among female students than was true years ago. Not merely relics of the past, today's sororities adapt and meet new member demands for persisting in a male-ordered academy and offer keys to succeeding within the bounds of patriarchal society without undoing it or requiring that women give up becoming wives and mothers. Thus, even first-generation college students from diverse backgrounds and groups find sororities useful as a vehicle to support their career aspirations and personal success ideologies. So in addition to activities and practices that focus on appearance and perpetuate traditional notions of womanhood, sororities also strive for high scholastic achievement and leadership development among members. Sororities devote time and resources to member education on issues related to women's health, academic success, and professional networking, and their investment often pays off in members' academic persistence and success. Though much of the research examining the effects of the Greek experience does not separate effects of sorority membership from fraternity membership, researchers have found that Greek affiliation positively promotes greater feelings of belonging and involvement, increased academic effort, and higher levels of satisfaction with the college experience.

In a society where women are encouraged to want and have both successful careers and families, sororities have been found to help women achieve their romantic goals by establishing their femininity and value to men through their appearance, reputation, and attractiveness while simultaneously supporting their members' academic and career aspirations. While the advent of multicultural sororities helped to break the mold of sororities as racially and ethnically exclusive organizations, gender constructions among these groups most often fit familiar patterns, with sororities claiming association with opposite-gender "brother" groups, for example, and some groups participating in new-member hazing or high-risk drinking activities. These conflicting tendencies within and among sororities to both promote and impede women's liberation and success contradict simple claims about their benefits and liabilities and also makes clear the need for more and better research into their purposes, values, and contributions to the higher education of women in the United States.

REFERENCES AND FURTHER READING

Bank, B. J. (with Yelon, H. M.). (2003). *Contradictions in women's education: Traditionalism, careerism, and community at a single-sex college*. New York: Teachers College Press.

Blair, K. J. (1980). *The clubwoman as feminist: True womanhood redefined, 1869–1914*. New York: Holmes & Meier.

Brown, T. L., Parks, G. S., & Phillips, C. M. (Eds.). (2005). *African American fraternities and sororities: The legacy and the vision*. Lexington: University Press of Kentucky.

Holland, D., & Eisenhart, M. A. (1990). *Educated for romance: Women, achievement, and college culture*. Chicago: University of Chicago Press.

Horowitz, H. L. (1987). *Campus life: Undergraduate student cultures from the end of the eighteenth century to the present*. Chicago: University of Chicago Press.

Nuwer, H. (1999). *Wrongs of passage: Fraternities, sororities, hazing, and binge drinking*. Bloomington: Indiana University Press.

CHAPTER 38

Women's Centers

CHARLOTTE A. KUNKEL

Women's centers emerged on college and university campuses in the United States in the late 1960s mainly as a response to the large numbers of nontraditional women entering or returning to college. Women's centers initially served as information houses to help these women negotiate their reentry to and progress through higher education. The centers often counseled women about their academic studies, career aspirations, and child-care issues and helped them develop job skills such as résumé preparation and interviewing.

The pressure to establish women's centers and to expand the services they provided increased as the women's movement took hold across the country in the 1970s. Women's centers quickly became locations on the college campus in which to house education programs and support services directed toward women of all ages, including antirape, antiviolence, and sexual assault hotlines and awareness programs. Given their roots in the women's movement, many centers were and remain committed to feminist principles and ideologies, and many have close affiliations with women's studies programs or departments on their campuses.

Today, there are probably more than the 440 women's centers listed by Davie (2002) or the 460 in existence according to Kasper (2004a) that are providing services to meet a myriad of campus women's needs. New centers are being created even today (see Kunkel chapter in Davie, 2002). These centers take a variety of organizational forms, have many different missions, are relatively more or less successful than other centers, face similar but not identical challenges, and have evolved a variety of survival strategies.

Organizational Forms

Collegiate women's centers exist on all types of campuses: both public and private, community colleges, liberal arts colleges, and research universities. Students or a single determined faculty, staff, or community member started many of them, although sometimes the impetus for their founding was completely idiosyncratic, as when the administration of a college, within a large university, wanted to retain control of a newly empty building and did so by turning it into a women's center (see Willinger chapter in Davie, 2002).

Women's centers are funded by various means. Some are funded in house by administrations through student fees, others from outside grants and through private donations. Some are student based and student run, while others have full-time professional directors with administrative support. Some have operating budgets of nearly nothing, while others have six-figure budgets (Kasper, 2004b).

They are also structured in a variety of ways. Many are autonomous units, while others are affiliated with other campus offices or departments (Kasper, 2004b) such as student affairs, support services, a diversity or ethnically affiliated office, an office of women's affairs, or a women's studies department or program. Women's centers have various physical spaces as well. Some claim whole buildings, while others are lucky to have their own phone line.

Missions

Despite their variety, most women's centers see their central mission as meeting the needs of campus women. Five central needs were identified by Kunkel (1994) and are echoed in the mission statements of women's centers across the country. These needs are *safety, education, support and advocacy, equity*, and *community*.

With regard to *safety*, many women's centers are the central office for reporting sexual assaults and harassment, for counseling survivors, and thus for serving as sounding boards for sexual assault and harassment policies. Clothesline projects, "take back the night" marches, eating disorder awareness projects, and, most recently, performances of *The Vagina Monologues* are common actions or events produced or supported by women's centers. Teaching nonviolence to the whole community is a way in which women's centers can promote proactive change instead of healing survivors after the fact (Allen, 2001). Myriad local actions are simply the everyday common praxis supported by campus women's centers.

When it comes to *education*, some argue that this activity should no longer be central to the mission of women's centers, especially on campuses where women's studies programs are well established. But such arguments ignore the ways in which women's centers have been directly active in enhancing women's learning by engaging curricular issues. Many women's centers are linked to women's studies programs, and it is quite common for women's centers to sponsor speakers, workshops, conferences, and even scholarships for women that supplement the formal curriculum. Other women's centers have worked directly to change curriculum, for example, through curriculum transformation projects and summer programs training girls in science. Bryne (2000) suggests women's centers are instrumental in creating feminist pedagogy by linking theory to practice. Bryne sees the action programs sponsored by women's centers as prime opportunities for women's studies and other academic programs to develop internships, offer workshops, and organize conferences. Kasper (2004a) likewise sees the campus women's center as being fertile for the interactions of academic social workers, faculty and students alike. She urges social work faculty and students to become active in campus women's centers to gain experience in service, the community, serving clients, internships, and program evaluation.

Those who argue against women's centers also claim that the time when campus women needed special *support and advocacy* has passed. On most campuses, women constitute the majority of the students, and there are many offices on campus that serve the needs of women students as well as or better than those of men. Such arguments fail to make the important distinction between serving women and serving in women's best interests.

There are still sexist tendencies in the academy, for example, in tracking women out of science and math or into elementary education. There are still real discrepancies in both numbers of female faculty and in wages. Recently a woman student visited a professor during office hours. In the course of their conversation, the student told the professor that she was the first female professor the student had ever had. The student was in the spring of her second year, which means she probably had taken nearly 18 courses. Could a student really get through half of her college career and not have a female professor? Some informal investigation discovered there were other students who also had had only one female professor and several others who said they had had only two female professors in their entire college career. This was in 2006 at a liberal arts college.

At this particular college in that year, women comprised 37% of full-time faculty and 43% of all full- and part-time faculty. Women comprised 33% of the tenured faculty, and they numbered only 17, or 31%, of full professors. The highest administration was 33% female (2 of 6), while just 6 out of 25, or 24%, of department heads were female. In contrast, the student body was nearly 60% female. These figures are consistent with those reported nationally. The American Association of University Professors reports that in 2008 women comprised only 39% of college and university faculty nationally and earned on average only 80.7% of what male faculty earned.

In 2008, the United States had not yet achieved gender equity on college campuses in terms of numbers of faculty or wages. We have not eradicated ideologies of gender inferiority, androcentrism or male bias, or the incidence of sexual harassment and assault on campus. Some suggest college women have a greater risk for sexual assault than their non college bound peers. It is estimated that nearly 5% of college women are assaulted in a given year, although most students do not report their assault. A women's center can be a refuge for women who feel isolated, undervalued, or under siege. It can also be educational, supportive, and celebratory. Women are at the center of a women's center, which is why women's centers are still needed on college and university campuses today.

Women's centers can also give support to and advocate on behalf of women by coordinating services for women across the campus. At many colleges and universities, women's centers serve a vital role in building bridges and centralizing services for women on campus and in the community. Even if there are organizations whose services are intended to meet women's special interests such as an office of women's affairs, a committee on women, harassment officers, displaced homemaker programs, or women's colleges, these organizations do not always coordinate with each other. They may even duplicate services for women. For example, such offices as student health services, student life, a recreation or sports center, and a diversity center may each address issues of women's sexual health. Women's centers can serve as coordinators of services, building bridges among programs and service providers. In fact, women's centers probably work best when they do not try to reproduce or take over these services but are able to provide connections between these offices and to support students' efforts to gain access to existing services.

Support and advocacy for women can also take the form of action programs designed to promote gender *equity* and *community* among women. To achieve these goals, women's centers engage in a broad variety of activities, including campus and community service, research, programming, producing publications such as newsletters and working papers, and providing library collections. They have often been instrumental in college policy making about issues important to women, such as racism, homophobia, sexual assault, or academic achievement.

On many campuses, women's centers are often more focused on social action that promotes the equality of women on campus and in society than are women's studies programs or departments. Whereas activism may be welcomed by the campus women's center, a struggling women's studies department may discourage it. Historically, many women's studies programs strategically distanced themselves from activism in order to achieve legitimacy as an academic discipline. Women's centers thus became the activist arm of the women's movement on many college campuses. Nevertheless, linking feminist ideologies and knowledge to practice is vital for social change, and Parker and Freedman (1999) have written compellingly about the renewed need for collaborations between women's centers and women's studies.

Celebrations of women's achievements and women's lives are a form of activism that women's centers can engage in to meet several of the central needs of campus women. Celebrating the women before us, and the women of today, creates community at the same time as it provides education about women's achievements. Celebrating women who are all too often missing from the standard curriculum provides educational enlightenment, promotes greater gender equity, supports women by providing them with role models, and highlights the achievements they have made in society.

Exemplary Campus Women's Centers

The successes of campus women's centers depend largely on knowing their own community, on acquiring broad-based support and funding, and on integrating women and women's needs into campuswide goals. The most successful centers have a commitment to not marginalizing or ghettoizing the center by making it the only place to serve women. Women's services must be addressed throughout campus, but the successful women's center must gain recognition as an important and necessary provider of some (but not all) of these services.

There are many exceptional college and university campus women's centers. The Women's Resource and Action Center at the University of Iowa, the Women's Research and Resource center at Spelman College, the Women's Resource Center at Washington State University, the Women's Center at Miami University of Ohio, and the Newcomb College Center for Research on Women at Tulane University are five that illustrate well how varied women's centers are and the different ways in which they have become successful.

One of the oldest and largest centers in the Midwest, the Women's Resource and Action Center at the University of Iowa is unique in its outright claim to serve not only campus women but women in the community and the state. It has an advisory board of 15 to 18 members drawn from students, faculty, staff, and the local community. The center reports serving over 10,000 clients a year with a very low staff turnover rate and attributes its success to diversity, cooperation, and open and direct communication.

Spelman College is a historically Black college for women and started a women's center in 1981. The Women's Research and Resource Center has a threefold mission: curriculum development in women's studies with a focus on women of African descent, community outreach, and research on Black women (see Guy-Sheftall & Sanders chapter in Davie, 2002). The center at Spelman houses the women's studies program and has an outstanding record of achievements, including hosting a journal, holding national conferences, winning grants, and sending delegations to international world conferences. Spelman's center is exceptional for both its academic excellence and its overtly political focus on Black women's agency and activism.

The Washington State University Women's Resource Center is exceptional for its very successful transit program, which provides free door-to-door service for women walking alone at night. In 2006–7, 803 rides were provided to women on 140 nights. The transit service not only prevents sexual assault but also gives the resource center widespread campus visibility. The service also has provided training and volunteer opportunities as drivers and dispatchers for 274 students (Kasper, 2004a). The program serves as a model for educating and involving students in outreach, service learning, and activism while providing safety for women. It clearly is a campuswide effort.

The center at Miami University (Ohio) is distinctive because it focuses on student concerns rather than developing and offering its own programming. The director of the women's center reports to each of the four university divisions and procures funding from each. This funding is awarded to students and groups who come to the center with problems or requests. The center aids these students and groups in creating solutions and implementing them. In other words, the activities of the center are truly student driven.

The Newcomb Center at Tulane University is notable in that it exemplifies the successful transition from what was primarily a resource center with a mission to provide "opportunities and programs focusing on personal growth, professional awareness, and educational planning" to a research center that aims to "produce and promote research for women and foster curriculum development in women studies." This transition was indicated by the change of names from the Newcomb Women's Center, at its founding in 1975, to the Newcomb College Center for Research on Women in 1985. The center today is thriving as a research center with actively involved faculty who are interested in the study of gender (see Willinger chapter in Davie, 2002).

Challenges and Survival Strategies

Despite some notable successes, women's centers across the country are still struggling to be all that they can and to act in the best interest of campus women. Insufficient funding is most often cited as the number one obstacle inhibiting a center's mission because staffing and programming are most often contingent on funding. In times of education budget cuts, the women's center is often on the chopping block. The threat is real. Some centers have histories that include closing one year only to reopen a year or two later.

Visibility, factionalization, and prioritizing are a few more of the challenges women's centers face. Visibility is vital to women's centers' success. Publicity is one way for centers to be known—make the news. Being seen is another. Sometimes women's centers are tucked away in a location off the beaten path, but a central location is key to visibility. The perception of the center is also important. Being known around campus is one thing. Being seen as open and welcoming to all women is even more vital to a center's success. For example, if the active voices are all perceived to be White or middle class, the center may struggle with serving women of color and working-class women. If the center takes an anti-Greek stance on some issues, it may alienate sorority women.

The center works best by diversifying staff and building alliances between groups of women. These alliances can be strengthened through broad programming and outreach programs to various campus women's groups. Even the perception of a center as "feminist" is sometimes perceived as negative. Center visibility and publicity emphasizing access and relevance to all women can combat these stereotypes.

Other challenges women's centers might face are those of factionalization. When centers are student run, faculty and staff may believe they are less welcome or not intended recipients of services. When centers are closely affiliated with women's studies or have a research focus, women staff and community members may not see the center as applicable to them. Including staff women in women's center programming is often challenging. Various centers have encountered challenges concerning racism and homophobia, just as the women's movement in the United States has historically struggled with its own racism and homophobia. Women's centers must be careful not to reproduce these inequalities but to use their politics and location directly to challenge the matrix of dominations of sexism, racism, homophobia, and classism. Today there is also much more awareness of the power of involving men in eradicating inequality, and yet getting men involved is a particular challenge to women's centers.

Prioritizing goals and resources, including time, is also an issue for many women's centers. This is especially true for those with perceived competing interests, multiple interest groups, or limited resources and staff. In addition, Kasper (2004a) identifies apathy, lack of administrative support, and territorialism as reported problems of women's centers. Many campus-based women's centers report negative perceptions of feminism, antifeminist sentiment, and basic student indifference as challenges they face. Young women may not be aware of challenges that many women face, and they may think the "women's movement" of their mother's generation solved all those problems.

REFERENCES AND FURTHER READING

Allen, S. L. (2001). Activist anthropology in a women's center. *Voices: A Publication of the Association for Feminist Anthropology, 5*(1), 11–15.

Bryne, K. Z. (2000). The role of campus-based women's centers. *Feminist Teacher, 13*(1), 48–60.

Davie, S. L. (Ed.). (2002). *University and college women's centers: A journey toward equity*. Westport, CT: Greenwood Press.

Kasper, B. (2004a). Campus-based women's centers: A review of problems and practices. *Affilia, 19*(2), 185–198.

Kasper, B. (2004b). Campus-based women's centers: Administration, structure, and resources. *NASPA Journal, 41*(3), 487–499.

Kunkel, C. A. (1994). Women's needs on campus: How universities meet them. *Initiatives, 56*(2), 15–28.

Parker, J., & Freedman, J. (1999). Women's centers/women's studies programs: Collaborating for feminist activism. *Women's Studies Quarterly, 27*(3–4), 11.

V
Gendered Faculty and Administration

Both in the United States and in many other countries, educational institutions are characterized by a labor force that contains unequal numbers of men and women. The size and nature of this gender inequality varies considerably as one moves across occupational positions and educational levels. Essays in part V focus primarily on faculty and administrative jobs in higher education, but even in only these two occupational categories at the same educational level, the distribution of men and women varies considerably across job types and educational contexts. Across the whole educational system, it seems fair to say that men tend to outnumber women in the faculty and administrative jobs that command the highest salaries and give their incumbents the most autonomy, power, and prestige. In contrast, women tend to move closer to gender equality, and sometimes to outnumber men, in academic jobs that pay less.

The American Association of University Professors (AAUP) issues annual reports on the economic status of faculty in higher education throughout the United States. These reports consistently observe that the economic status of faculty members varies tremendously by gender, with men consistently earning much more than women. So commonplace has this finding become that the most recent report of this kind (available at www.aaup.org/AAUP/comm/rep/Z/ecstatreport08-09/default.htm) skips immediately from salaries per se to the major factor that determines salary and then focuses on gender differences in that determining factor.

Interestingly, despite loud claims on many campuses that faculty salaries are based on the merit system, the AAUP makes no attempt to assess gender differences in merit, but focuses instead on differences in academic ranks. Some might argue, of course, that movement up the academic ranks is based on merit, but that argument has been challenged by analysts of evaluation policies for academics (see chapter 45 in part VI). In any case, the AAUP ignores merit arguments in favor of noting simply that academic rank is the most important variable for predicting faculty compensation.

The AAUP report goes on to state that although a woman's likelihood of advancing to the rank of tenured full professor improved over the last decade—with significant variations among institutional types—women were still less likely than men to be at the top rank in 2008–9. The gender differences are most marked at doctoral-granting universities, where there were seven men for every woman at the rank of full professor in 1995–96 and approximately four male full professors for each woman at that rank in 2008–9. At four-year institutions and those granting master's but not doctoral degrees, the gender ratios among full professors were four men for every one woman in 1995–96 and two men for every one woman at full professor rank in 2008–9. At community colleges, there were two men full professors for each women full professor in 1995–96, and by 2008–9 women had achieved virtual parity with men. The AAUP report concludes that women are achieving greater rates of success in moving up the faculty career ladder, but substantial impediments to their advancement still exist.

Ironically, the community and four-year colleges at which women are more likely to advance up the professorial ranks are also the institutions that pay the lowest faculty salaries. So even though a woman taking a full-time, tenure-track assistant professorship at a community college can anticipate a fairer chance of advancement to full professor than a woman taking the same kind of position at a major state university, the salary of the first woman will always lag behind the salary of the second. This salary gap, though large over the span of a career, is likely to be small in comparison to the gap between salaries and benefits currently paid to tenure-track faculty versus adjunct faculty, even when these two kinds of faculty work in the same institution in the same department. And part-time faculty almost never receive salaries or benefits that are proportionately commensurate with those of full-time faculty. The fact that women are more likely than men to hold part-time and adjunct positions means that not only their salaries but also their chances of academic advancement are much lower.

Another impediment to both career advancements and higher salaries, discussed in chapter 39 ("Academic Career Patterns"), may be the academic field in which a faculty member was educated and is employed. As noted in part III, some of these fields, such as computer science, engineering, and mathematics, continue to be male-dominated numerically and culturally. They also command higher salaries, on average, when compared with fields of study such as the humanities, family and consumer sciences, or education that enroll and employ larger proportions of women. Chapter 39 also notes that academic salaries and advancement are heavily affected by the increasingly entrepreneurial nature of universities, an argument similar to the depiction of academic capitalism in the first chapter of part I. Successes in attracting grants from government agencies, public and private foundations, and corporations and in obtaining patents for one's inventions and innovations that can stimulate new business enterprises are becoming more important bases for faculty evaluations than the ability to teach well or to produce high-quality scholarly publications. Few are the faculty in the humanities and other academic departments with high proportions of women faculty who can compete with the scientists and engineers on campus when it comes to attracting external funding.

Even the women who are members of male-oriented departments in which resources and opportunities for outside funding abound (relative to other departments on the same campus) may have more difficulties climbing the career ladder than their male counterparts. The chapters in this section offer three major reasons for this gender contrast within departments: mentoring, family-work conflicts, and the masculinized culture of higher education, especially universities that grant doctoral degrees.

With regard to mentoring, chapter 39 indicates that women often have less access to the networks, sponsors, and mentors that help men in their departments succeed.

Recognition of the potential benefits of mentoring for academic women, particularly in male-dominated fields, has become widespread, and organizations such as the National Science Foundation that seek to increase the recruitment and retention of women in science, engineering, and technological fields have become willing to give financial support to mentoring programs designed to achieve these goals. An overview of such programs and an examination of their effectiveness can be found in chapter 43 ("Mentoring Women Faculty").

Much has also been written about family-work conflicts, and a consensus has emerged among researchers that the movement of women into the labor force, including academic jobs, has not been accompanied by an equally strong and large movement of their male partners into child-care and homemaking responsibilities. To those who argue that academic couples, with their more flexible work schedules and more gender-egalitarian ideologies, might be more able and willing than other couples to redress this imbalance, chapter 42 ("Faculty Workloads") offers a more pessimistic prognosis. The authors provide substantial evidence to support the argument that men and women in academic positions are working harder than ever. The heavy demands that must be met to gain tenure and promotions make it increasingly unlikely that men who hold academic jobs will be willing to spend more time helping out at home. Thus the burdens of home and family life will continue to fall more heavily on women, and these burdens will be particularly severe for academic women because the heaviest demands of childbearing and early child-rearing are likely to occur at the very time that occupational demands are at their peak. In recognition of the severity and ubiquity of this problem, efforts are being made at many institutions of higher education to formulate and implement policies that would give support to academic women (and men) who are trying to succeed professionally while also being good parents and family members. See, especially, the last chapter in part VI.

In addition to family demands, academic women are often subject to additional job-related demands that their male colleagues can avoid. These demands and the stresses that accompany them are described in chapter 41 ("Advising and Mentoring Graduate Students"), as well as chapters 39 and 42. Chapter 41 also echoes the themes of the overworked academic and work-family conflicts central to chapter 42 and alerts readers to the masculinized disciplinary cultures and other contextual influences that structure the experiences of graduate students and their supervisors.

The masculinized culture of higher education is also central to the analysis of academic leadership contained in chapter 40 ("Administrative Leadership Styles"). Not only are higher-level administrators far more likely to be men than women, but those men are much more likely to be comfortable with and to perpetuate the competition, hierarchical structure of authority, and coercive power that are the hallmarks of masculinized institutions. Even though some women administrators may be more comfortable with a communal leadership style that is more relationship oriented than the agentic style of their male counterparts, chapter 40 presents several reasons it may not be possible for women administrators to behave in a supportive and collaborative manner. Women's underrepresentation in top administration makes it difficult if not impossible for even the most successful woman to challenge the masculinized practices and assumptions that characterize her employer institution and have come to be expected and accepted by its governing board, its other administrators, and most of its faculty.

CHAPTER 39

Academic Career Patterns

MARY ANN DANOWITZ AND LYNDSAY J. AGANS

During the past three and a half decades, women have increased their presence among faculty members in the United States. According to the National Center for Education Statistics (NCES), women now are 42% of the 917,000 faculty members in four-year colleges and universities (U.S. Department of Education, 2006). However, their careers and the positions they ultimately hold differ from those of men. Within the faculty group, women are less likely to hold full-time positions than men (55% compared with 62%), and they are more likely to be employed in off-track positions (not leading to tenure), where they hold 47% of the part-time positions but only 23% of the full-time faculty positions (U.S. Department of Education, 2006). The significance of full-time tenure-line employment is considerable. Incumbents receive higher wages and employment benefits; they influence the research agenda and the allocation of university resources, shape the direction of a field, decide what is to be taught, and select and mentor graduate students.

Preparation for a faculty career takes place through graduate education in departments of research-oriented universities. Doctoral students' experiences induct them into the discipline or field by developing skills, influencing their research productivity, and shaping their first networks—which become the foundation for a career of research and teaching. Progress in an academic career principally occurs by successfully negotiating three gatekeeping processes—hiring, tenure review, and promotion—in order to arrive at the visible and valued achievement of a tenured, senior position, the institutionalized optimum faculty employment standard (see chapter by Glazer-Raymo in Sagaria, 2007).

Faculty careers progress through a well-defined sequence of positions, while administrative careers are less well defined. Since the 1970s, middle management positions have increased exponentially, but the relationships among those positions, faculty positions, and senior-level administrative positions are poorly defined. While the proportion of women in the higher levels of university administration has also increased, they remain a small minority of college and university presidents nationwide and worldwide. In contrast, there has been a striking feminization of lower levels of campus administration, especially in those positions that provide external services to client groups.

Sex Differences in Faculty Careers

Despite the increasing proportions of degrees awarded to women, their employment differs across fields, which profoundly influences women's careers. Women are most underrepresented among academics in engineering (10%), natural sciences (23%), and business (27%). They are better represented in agriculture / home economics (36%), social sciences (36%), fine arts (37%), and humanities (41%). In the health sciences, they are close to parity with men (48%), and in education the majority of faculty are women (58%) (U.S. Department of Education, 2006).

Entry into a full-time tenured faculty career begins with passing through the formal gate of hiring into a tenure-track position, usually directly after a doctoral program or, as in the life and physical sciences, after a postdoctoral appointment. The appointment is likely to begin at the assistant professor level for a maximum probation period of seven years. In many fields, qualified female candidates are not being hired into tenure-track positions proportionately to their presence in the Ph.D. pool. Nelson's (2005) study of faculty representation in the top 50 ranked departments in 14 disciplines showed that women were underrepresented even in fields such as biology, where women earn more Ph.D.s than men. The percentage of women in those departments ranged from a high of 45% (in sociology) to a low of 17% (in chemistry). Nelson's study further corroborated research showing that lack of representation is particularly acute for women of color who may be subject to tokenism, a process whereby they are treated as representatives or symbols of their group and not as individuals (Beutel & Nelson, 2006).

The second gatekeeping process is tenure review. Tenure and promotion reviews are conducted in accord with institutional mission. There is usually a peer review process in which research, teaching, and service are evaluated and weighted to correspond with institutional priorities. Thus, in a research-extensive university, a faculty member is evaluated principally for the quality and quantity of her or his publications and grants. An individual is either granted tenured and promoted to associate professor or her or his contract is not continued.

Women in the social sciences, sciences, and engineering are less likely to receive tenure than male colleagues. Among women tenure-track faculty who were employed in Research I universities (those awarding 50 or more doctoral degrees per year in at least 15 disciplines) in both 1995 and 2001, 54.5% of the women received tenure, compared with 59.2% of the men. Of individuals not tenured in a Research I university, women (8.5%) are half as likely as men (15.3%) to move to jobs outside the academy, but women are more likely to be unemployed (2.5%) than men (0.6%) (National Academy of Sciences, 2006). Moreover, women are more likely to leave a tenure-track position for an adjunct appointment than men.

Across Research I universities, tenure rates are roughly 50% or higher. Although rates vary by institution, they also vary by field. Field-specific analyses show that women are 1%–3% less likely than men to receive tenure in physical sciences, 2%–4% more likely than men to receive tenure in the natural sciences and engineering, and 8% less likely than men to earn tenure in the social sciences (Ginther & Kahn, 2006).

Career progression and the tenure review process are likely to differ for men and women in some fields. In the aggregate, women are promoted more slowly than men. The difference begins early, with men being promoted and tenured earlier in their career than women. After tenure, men are also promoted more quickly to full professor than women. These patterns were discerned principally from institutional studies, such as those at the University of California, Berkeley; MIT; and Duke University. These differences become even greater by race. According to the National Academy of Sciences (2006), within 15 years of earning the Ph.D., African American women were almost 10% less likely than men to be promoted to full professor. Possible explanations are that women are expected to meet higher standards for promotion, they may feel less ready to apply for promotion to full professor, and they have children.

The gatekeeping process to the rank of full professor is more unyielding for women, as they are less likely than their male counterparts to be promoted to the senior rank. Although sex discrimination has been illegal in academe since 1972, there continue to be fewer women at each career step. According to the NCES, women account for approximately 36% of assistant professors, 31% of associate professors, and 16% of full professors in research universities (U.S. Department of Education, 2006). This pattern represents different career progressions and experiences for men and women resulting in terrible losses, both in opportunities for individual women and in institutional potential for solving problems and increasing economic performance (see Sagaria & Agans chapter in Yokoyama, 2006).

When tenure-track faculty members change jobs, they are likely to do so for multiple reasons—most important, salary and promotion, regardless of field. Female faculty members at four-year colleges and universities are less satisfied than their male counterparts with advising, course workload, the quality of their benefits, job security, and salary levels, and this affects their intent to leave—a good indicator of actually leaving (Rosser, 2004). A national study of actual job changers among tenure-track faculty members in engineering and the life, physical, and social sciences corroborated the Rosser study regarding the importance of pay and promotion for women and men. Across fields, however, female academics consistently rated working conditions, family, and job location higher than males among reasons for changing jobs (National Academy of Sciences, 2006). Important research and programs have developed to increase awareness and to push for policy changes to reduce the potential conflicts between faculty work and family life. Women faculty members often face a challenge of achieving a desirable balance between their work and family life. While the tenure track is stressful and academic work never ends, the pretenure period often corresponds with childbearing years and may create additional dilemmas for women who want to have or adopt children. Although many women find complementary relationships between their work and family life, for others it is more complicated. Data from 160,000 faculty in California indicate that women faculty are less likely than their male peers to be married or living in a committed relationship; they report they receive less supervisory and institutional support than men; and they are 38% less likely than men to achieve tenure (Mason & Goulden, 2004). While institutions are recognizing the added challenges women face, higher education is still in the early stages of providing the support that is necessary to recruit and retain more women faculty.

The Context of Faculty Careers

Economic, social, and political forces are driving universities to become more entrepreneurial and market driven by preparing individuals for the labor market and producing profitable research. In this context, institutional prestige, reputation, and ranking correspond to competitive advantage and economic strength. Consequently, some universities are strategically reallocating funds to priority areas and reducing costs by restructuring; reducing tenure-track, full-time faculty lines; and increasing adjunct, part-time faculty. Recipient departments of reallocated funds are often those expected to contribute to the institution's external research funding and prestige. So retrenchment and selective investment strategies mostly have redirected funds from the humanities, social sciences, and education, where the majority of women faculty members are found, toward life and physical sciences, medicine, and engineering, which have a small percentage of women faculty. Thus strategic redirection of funds has disproportionately adversely affected women (see chapter by Sagaria & Van Horn in Sagaria, 2007). A department's institutional centrality (and its resources) influences a faculty member's working conditions, which may have career consequences that can differ for men and women. Volk, Slaughter, and Thomas (2001) found that departments powerfully influence faculty members' access to institutional resources. Graduate-degree-granting departments with a high proportion of full-time male faculty tend to receive more grants and contracts and to be more highly resourced than departments characterized by female faculty, high use of female adjuncts, and undergraduate teaching and degree-granting programs.

An academic career in a research university also very much depends on productivity and recognition, usually in the form of peer-reviewed publications and significant books. Moreover, advancement involves judgment and recommendations of academic referees. Yet a substantial body of research shows that these judgments can be arbitrary and linked to sponsorship and networks that may disadvantage women in fields where they are in the minority. Although women's productivity in many fields is now equal to men's (National Academy of Sciences, 2006), women continue to experience subtle, often unexamined gender bias by both men and women, which is even more oppressive with the interlacing of racism that women of color in predominately White institutions confront.

In many fields and disciplines, women are the leaders and most distinguished scholars regardless of whether they are a part of a numerical majority or minority. Even more women will be able to thrive as colleagues and institutions continue to chip away at the factors that contribute to cumulative gender disadvantages (Clark & Corcoran, 1986). The small preferences and subtle forms of discrimination that can accumulate can create large differences in prestige, power, and position.

Administrative Careers

The changing nature of colleges and universities, especially the shift to being highly managed entrepreneurial organizations, has resulted in a significant increase in the need for and actual numbers of administrators and staff. The NCES reports that in 2005 women held approximately 51% of the 164,656 executive, administrative, and managerial positions in four-year colleges and universities in the United States (U.S. Department of Education, 2006). Describing administrative careers is complicated because of the lack of current research and agreement in terminology for job groups, categories, and levels of jobs. The senior-level, or top-level, refers to positions of institutionwide leadership such as presidents or chancellors (chief executive officers) along with those who are likely to report to those positions while having administrative and financial authority and responsibility for major functional areas of an institution, such as provost (chief academic officer) and vice presidents such as chief financial officer and chief student affairs officer. In many colleges and universities, this level may also include deans of academic units. Midlevel positions include directors of units across various functional areas including development (institutional advancement or fund raising), campus life, athletics, campus planning, technology, and assessment. The next job group comprises staff and professional positions located at various institutional levels. Some, such as legal counsel, require highly specialized skills and knowledge, while others, such as academic advising, require more general qualities and skills. Thus, the prerequisite education for administrative positions is directly related to functional areas.

Careers advance through job changes and with the help of opportunity structures, networks, sponsoring, and mentoring. Recruitment for midlevel and professional positions is usually from an internal labor market (inside the organization), a local labor market, and, at times, the national and international labor market. The search is likely to be national for executive positions and those requiring highly specific advanced skills or extensive experience.

More women of color, White women, and men of color than White men depend upon opportunity structures and internal institutional job changes to build their career (Johnsrud & Rosser, 2000). Although there is little systematic information about opportunity structures because they differ from one institution to another, university reports by women's commissions and diversity committees are likely to be reliable sources about campus climates and opportunity structures.

Sagaria and Johnsrud (1992) found that in a public research university policies intended to benefit women and men of color and White women had unintended adverse consequences for them because White senior male administrators were likely to hire individuals like themselves, a finding studies from various sectors have corroborated. Describing the experiences of a small group of female provosts, Lively (2000) observed that women can benefit from internal hiring for senior-level positions when a university has racial, ethnic, and gender diversity among administrators and staff and when senior administrators are willing to take risks with hiring decisions.

Networks, sponsors, and mentors are particularly important when there is not a definable career path to a position and competencies must be extrapolated from one job to another, such as in new positions like director of diversity. Sponsors and mentors have also been important in creating new positions for protégés. In particular, this strategy has advanced the careers of women who have taken on additional or new responsibilities in order to meet changing institutional priorities and needs (Miner & Esler, 1985).

Search committee chairs and hiring officials are the gatekeepers of administrative advancement. Individuals in those roles are more likely to exclude someone unknown to them than someone whom they know and do not perceive as likely to be a risk, threat, or embarrassment to them. Because search committees rely heavily on known sources to make personal judgments based upon personal preferences and biases, Black and White women and Black men without an advocate who is known by a White male search committee member are more likely to be screened out of competition for positions than White men (Sagaria, 2002). Furthermore, fit—a philosophy and style compatible with those of search chairs and being able to work well with others—is an important criterion for being offered a job. However, White men are less likely to perceive women and men of color and White women as a "good fit." Therefore, a sponsor or mentor may be able to reduce or eliminate concerns that White men may have that a female's assertiveness is perceived as too aggressive or argumentative, which can prevent women candidates from being hired (Sagaria, 2002).

Search firms are increasingly becoming gatekeepers for advancement to senior administrative positions. In half of the presidential searches reported to the American Council on Education, search firms were involved in the process. These firms rely on referrals and informal networks throughout the country to identify and recommend candidates. Until more women gain senior administrative positions, this may be more of a disadvantage for women than for White men because White women and women and men of color tend to have different networks than White men, who occupy the majority of senior-level positions (see chapter by Tuitt, Danowitz Sagaria, & Viernes Sotello Turner in Smart, 2007).

The growth of new managerialism (Pritchard & Deem, 1999) has resulted in an increase in the number of women in higher education administration in the United States and United Kingdom. For example, institutional support systems positions in the University of California system increased by 104% between 1966 and 1991, nearly two and a half times faster than instructional positions (Gumport & Pusser, 1995). Administrative and nonteaching professional positions have been the fastest-growing group of positions. This trend has continued to the present with the creation of a new administrative sector. As universities have become more entrepreneurial, to drive down costs and increase the rate of return from faculty members, there has been a feminization of the lower tiers of administration. In these positions, with their focus on accountability, external relations, and client services, women are expected to challenge opposition to management practices and to monitor faculty activities (Pritchard & Deem, 1999).

Most notable is the advancement of women into senior-level positions. Women now account for 23% of university presidents or chief executive officers (American Council on Education, 2007). This is an impressive increase from approximately 10% in 1986, although it has slowed in recent years and it has yet to achieve representation proportional to the number of women in the administrative cohort. Nevertheless, it is especially significant that women now lead more major research universities, including Brown, Harvard, Michigan, Michigan State, Pennsylvania, Princeton, and the University of Miami. While there are multiple career paths to the presidency, the majority of the women leading research universities, unlike their male counterparts, have stayed close to the traditional presidential career path of faculty member, department chair, dean, provost, and president. Many women on this path have been able to use their provost position to convince boards of trustees of their potential as a president. As more women assume senior leadership positions, leadership stereotypes are being challenged to open up new ways to consider how to lead higher education. These female leaders also are opening more gates through creating networks (Lively, 2000) and providing sponsorship and mentoring that have great potential to create more career opportunities for current and future female faculty, administrators, and staff.

REFERENCES AND FURTHER READING

American Council on Education. (2007). *The American college president* (2007 ed.). Washington, DC: Author.

Beutel, A. M., & Nelson, D. J. (2006). The gender and race-ethnicity of faculty in top social science research departments. *Social Science Journal, 43*(1), 111–125.

Clark, S., & Corcoran, M. (1986). Perspectives on the professional socialization of women faculty: A case of accumulative disadvantage. *Journal of Higher Education, 57*(1), 20–43.

Ginther, D., & Kahn, S. (2006). *Does science promote women? Evidence from academia, 1973–*

2001 (NBER SEWP Working Paper). Cambridge, MA: National Bureau of Economics Research.

Gumport, P., & Pusser, B. (1995). A case of bureaucratic accretion: Contests and consequences. *Journal of Higher Education, 66*(5), 493–520.

Johnsrud, L. K., & Rosser, V. J. (2000). *Understanding the work and career paths of mid-level administrators.* San Francisco: Jossey-Bass.

Lively, K. (2000). Women in charge. *Chronicle of Higher Education, 46*(41), A33–35.

Mason, M. A., & Goulden, M. (Nov. 2004). Do babies matter? (Part II) Closing the baby gap. *Academe.* Retrieved December 29, 2008, from http://www.aaup.org/pubsres/academe/woor/NO/Feat/04ndmaso.htm?PF

Miner, A. S., & Esler, S. E. (1985). Accrual mobility: Job mobility in higher education through responsibility accrual. *Journal of Higher Education, 56*(2), 121–143.

National Academy of Sciences. (2006). *Beyond bias and barriers: Fulfilling the potential of women in academic science and engineering* (Report of the Committee on Maximizing the Potential of Women in Academic Science and Engineering, National Academy of Sciences, National Academy of Engineering, and Institute of Medicine). Washington, DC: National Academies Press.

Nelson, D. K. (2005). *A national analysis of diversity in science and engineering faculties at research universities.* Retrieved October 25, 2006, from http://cheminfo.chem.ou.edu/~djn/diversity/briefings/Diversity%20Report%20Final.pdf

Pritchard, C., & Deem, R. (1999). Wo-managing further education: Gender and construction of the manager in the corporate colleges of England. *Gender and Education, 11*(3), 323–342.

Rosser, V. J. (2004). Faculty members' intentions to leave: A national study on their work life and satisfaction. *Research in Higher Education, 45*(3), 285–309.

Sagaria, M. D. (2002). An exploratory model of filtering in administrative searches. *Journal of Higher Education, 73*(6), 677–710.

Sagaria, M. D. (Ed.). (2007). *Women, universities, and change: Gender equality in the European Union and the United States.* New York: Palgrave Macmillan.

Sagaria, M. D., & Johnsrud, L. K. (1992). Administrative promotion: The structuring of opportunity within a university. *Review of Higher Education, 15*(2), 191–212.

Smart, J. (Ed.). (2007). *Higher education: Handbook of theory and research* (Vol. 22). Dordrecht, The Netherlands: Springer.

U.S. Department of Education. (2006). *Integrated postsecondary education data system (IPEDS), Winter 2005–06.* Washington, DC: National Center for Education Statistics.

Volk, C. S., Slaughter, S., & Thomas, S. L. (2001). Models of institutional resource allocation: Mission, market, gender. *Journal of Higher Education, 72*(4), 387–413.

Yokoyama, K. (Ed.). (2006). *Gender and higher education: Australia, Japan, the U.K. and USA.* Hiroshima, Japan: Higher Education Institute Press.

CHAPTER 40

Administrative Leadership Styles

MARGARET E. MADDEN

In education, as in other types of organizations, gender and situational characteristics interact to construct patterns of gender differences that vary with circumstances. When gender differences are evident, they tend to be characterized by agentic and communal behavior. Agentic leadership is task oriented, assertive, and directive; communal leadership focuses on interpersonal relationships, supporting others, and not seeking attention. The extent of gender differences in leadership style depends on characteristics of schools, such as the prevalence of gender stereotypes and discrimination; proportions of women and men in leadership and subordinate roles; hierarchical organization; emphasis on stereotypically masculine tasks; and historical reliance on masculine leadership models that stress coercive power and competition. In educational settings, women prefer leadership styles that focus on organizational and social transformation, collaboration, and empowerment of others. Even in educational settings that have the characteristics that promote masculinized leadership patterns, women have developed coping strategies that allow them to be successful leaders, contributing to a larger proportion of women leaders at all levels of education and to transforming both institutions and the definition of leadership.

Gender Differences in Leadership

Are there gender differences in leadership styles in educational contexts? While there is considerable scholarly research on gender in educational literature, little of it addresses this question, and that which does is generally anecdotal or qualitative and relies on very small samples. Research on gender and leadership in broader managerial contexts is helpful, in that it demonstrates quite clearly that leadership behavior is strongly influenced by social context; that is, gender differences exist in some social situations but not in others. Social scientists can make equally plausible cases to support both the absence and existence of gender differences in leadership styles. The key to understanding this apparent contradiction is the context in which leadership occurs. Hence, rather than dwelling on the extent of differences, it is more productive to discuss situational characteristics that are correlated with gendered stylistic patterns.

What are those stylistic patterns? Alice H. Eagly and her colleagues use the distinction between agentic and communal attributes to describe these differences. Agentic leadership behavior includes focus on tasks and problems, assertive speech, influence attempts, and calling attention to oneself; communal behaviors include focus on relationship and interpersonal problems, tentative speech, supporting others, taking direction from others, and not seeking attention (Eagly & Johannesen-Schmidt, 2001). Popular and academic literature that purports to describe gendered leadership styles generally proposes a distinction along the lines of agentic and communal behavior, using terms such as *task-oriented* and *interpersonally oriented style*, *participative* and *directive*, or *democratic* and *autocratic*. A review of multiple studies on leadership behavior by Carli and Eagly (1999) found that women display more positive social behavior and agreement than men, whereas men are more task oriented and disagree more than women.

However, this distinction is not a dichotomous dimension; rather, agentic behavior is defined more by the status of participants in an interaction regardless of their gender. In contrast, communal behavior is related to gender, with women engaging in it more, especially when interacting with other women. Research looking at the interaction of gender roles and organizational roles implies that women and men in the same leadership role behave more similarly than not, so some gender variations may be the result of gender differences in the roles occupied by women and men. Informal actions that are not functional aspects of a given leadership role, such as the topics of casual office conversation, may be the most discretionary and most likely to vary with gender.

An important element of gendered leadership patterns is the influence of stereotypic expectations of women's and men's behavior. Female and male leaders are evaluated differently in experimental studies where behaviors are equated; women using direct language, disagreement, and autocratic behavior are regarded more negatively than men exhibiting the same behavior. Women leaders appear to be more constrained by gender stereotypes than men. Thus women may learn that they are more effective when they employ communal leadership strategies, possibly to the extent that they internalize gender-stereotypic expectations and leadership styles. These kinds of factors lead to the argument that congruity of leader roles and gender roles is a critical factor in people's choice of leadership behavior, evaluations of that behavior by others, and effectiveness as leaders (Eagly & Carli, 2007). Therefore, the question of whether women and men lead differently is meaningless without concurrent analysis of relevant contextual variables.

Furthermore, emphasis on the question of whether women and men have different leadership styles encourages analyses that overgeneralize, or essentialize, female and male differences. As with most gender differences, women's and men's behavior overlaps greatly, and there is much more variability within each gender than between them. Focusing solely on gender differences legitimizes a dualistic view of gender that can be seen in much of the literature on leadership in education, greatly oversimplifying the role of gender and exaggerating differences out of context.

The Context of Education

What are characteristics of the educational context that influence the extent to which gender interacts with leadership style preferences? While there is little controlled experimental evidence about these interactions, much of the literature on leadership in education implicitly discusses context variables that promote or mitigate gender differences. Although many of the resources for this chapter concern higher education in the United States, authors writing about elementary and secondary school principals and superintendents and about educational systems in other English-speaking countries describe similar characteristics.

As in most areas of human endeavor, historically men have been leaders in education at all levels. Women leaders in higher education emerged at women's colleges or as deans of women in early coeducational schools at the beginning of the twentieth century. Interviews with women leaders from different generations demonstrate that leadership styles vary with changing sociohistorical contexts. For example, in one study, those who came of age during the Great Depression and World War II emphasized the value of education for achieving equality for women and often adopted male models of leadership (Astin & Leland, 1993). Those who came of age during the 1960s, with the civil rights, anti–Vietnam War, and feminist movements, focused on concerns about equal opportunity in education and other work settings and the inclusion of women in scholarly and curricular concerns. Those who were ascending to leadership position in the 1990s extended those values to creating alternative modes of leadership.

Also, like other areas of human behavior, education is heavily influenced by gender discrimination and stereotyping. Work on the nature of gender stereotypes is instructive for understanding dynamics in regard to leadership. Stereotypes of out-groups often invoke the characteristics of sociability and competence, which for women take the form of the false dichotomy between sociable housewife and competent career woman, as if sociability and competence were mutually exclusive (Goodwin & Fiske, 2001). Such stereotypes interact with other situational factors, as when women in male-dominated businesses experience contradictory expectations more than those in gender-balanced offices. The gender imbalance in higher education, which is more pronounced in higher leadership positions and more prestigious institutions, indicates that women are under more pressure to perform competently than male peers. Countering stereotypes may be necessary to establish credibility as leaders, hence the advice frequently offered to women pursuing academic administrative careers to develop extensive expertise in finance, strategic planning, and research to overcome stereotypes of women's weaknesses. Furthermore, gender stereotypes and other stereotypes certainly interact. For example, gendered ethnic stereotypes that African American women are aggressive and hostile and Asian, Native American, and Hispanic women are deferent and passive impact perceived leadership ability (Task Force on Women in Academe, 2000). In general, women are stereotyped as less likely to demonstrate important leadership behaviors than men. The incongruity between leadership roles and female gender roles leads to prejudicial actions, such that men are more likely to have opportunities and to emerge as leaders than women.

The hierarchical organization of education is another contextual factor. Either overtly or implicitly, hierarchies assume gendered constructs. Hierarchies are endemic to education. Schools are ranked in prestige and reputation, disciplines vary in status, size of tuition is equated with value, and faculty salaries are related to institutional prestige. While it would be simplistic to argue that hierarchy and masculine values are perfectly correlated, traditional hierarchical management does mimic masculine qualities, in the extreme taking the form of a "military model" designed to control the role of emotion and caring in organizations (Hatcher, 2003). Feminist writers often note that organizations change to value human needs more when a critical mass of women employees is reached, particularly women leaders (Regan & Brooks, 1995). While the numbers of women in education at all levels have increased, women administrators remain in the minority and are in the smallest proportion in the most prestigious colleges or positions. As schools adopt business models, hierarchical line management has replaced collegial governance in many places, perhaps undermining changes normally facilitated by increased proportions of women.

Male dominance in education has been ignored, perhaps because it seems obvious. However, ignoring male dominance has led to failure to thoroughly analyze how deeply embedded gender constructs are in organizations. Meta-analyses of studies of leadership effectiveness corroborate the relationship between perceived effectiveness and situational expectations, as women leaders are seen as less effective when the proportion of male subordinates is greater, in highly masculinized environments like military organizations, and when a larger percentage of male raters are evaluating them (Eagly & Carli, 2007). In highly masculinized organizations, men are the numerical majority, tasks are stereotypically masculine, the main goal is task completion, and hierarchy and coercive power are stressed (Yoder, 2001). Leadership in masculinized contexts depends on status, self-promotion, competition, and autocratic behavior, all of which are viewed negatively when engaged in by women. Despite some evidence that education provides more opportunity than other work settings, in that women are perceived as somewhat more effective in education, government, and social services than in other kinds of organizations, education remains masculinized to some extent. For example, historical accounts of leaders in the community college arena focus on a few "great men" who have shaped the role of these colleges in higher education using frontier, pioneer, athletic, and military images (Amey & Twombly, 1993). To the extent that leadership characteristics are inferred from these metaphors, the leadership styles of women and ethnic minorities are seen as deficient, limiting their access to leadership positions.

Gender is a status characteristic in our culture, giving men an edge in any situation where status matters. Women attempting to improve their own stature face a double bind because self-promotion by women can backfire. Women who are modest about their successes are recognized more than women who are moderately self-promoting. Furthermore, women must demonstrate greater competence than similar men to gain recognition, even when they have achieved high-status positions. As educational management adopts corporate models, women may be further disadvantaged. Solving financial and political problems has become more prominent in the role of president. Women college presidents comment often that they feel they must work harder than male presidents to gain the confidence of their boards of trustees and are given a second chance less often after failure (Brown, Van Ummersen, & Sturnick, 2001). Women of color believe they are especially vulnerable in this regard.

Too little is known about the interaction of gender with other cultural identities, such as ethnicity, sexual orientation, or disability, but gender and these other identity characteristics undoubtedly interact with status in complicated ways. Some educators feel that race stereotypes overpower gender expectations in treatment from others; others feel that gender is more salient; others say that gender and ethnicity are so intertwined that the debate is pointless. The role of these highly salient characteristics requires considerable further research.

Gendered Leadership Styles

Although readers must be mindful of these complex multivariate interactions and gaps in knowledge about leadership, analyses of leadership style do suggest patterns associated with gender that may be the result of either gender-related values or choices based on an understanding of what is effective in gendered contexts.

Women leaders often value institutional transformation explicitly, considering the ultimate reward for their persistence in academic administration to be creating a more congenial environment for future generations of both female and male administrators. Women leaders also report commitment to broader social transformation. For example, African American administrators frequently mention an obligation to give back to the community and mentor others (e.g., Miller & Vaughn, 1997). Other administrators focus on transforming the very nature of leadership by transforming the culture of one's own organization or broader societal notions of leadership. Social values go beyond focusing only on women to explicitly include work against racism, violence, and heterosexism as well (Strachan, 1999).

Another theme in writings by women administrators is the importance of understanding power relations (Strachan, 1999). To succeed and transform leadership, people must understand their position and relative power in an organization. While acknowledging that women must be politically attuned to these power dynamics in their institutions, women academic leaders often say they are ambivalent about the perceived need to play power games to advance before being able to change the rules of the game. They also feel ambivalent about being pleased by their ability to use power to accomplish goals, simultaneously recognizing that it plays into the masculine definitions of leadership (e.g., Brown et al., 2001). In addition to finding it difficult to become assimilated while articulating a critique of male management models, feminist administrators are seldom concerned with obtaining power or establishing strong personal claims to authorship. But leaders must understand the leadership culture of their organizations, since the masculinized context so frequently found in higher education includes the assumption that effective leadership depends on status and power manifested through autocratic behavior (Yoder, 2001). Understanding politics essentially means understanding the nature of formal and informal power in academe in general and in a particular institution. One way of reconciling ambivalence about playing power games is to define power as the ability to influence outcomes rather than the ability to influence people, as one writer notes, using a metaphor of "expanding the pie" of influence, rather than a "fixed boundary" view of power (Valverde, 2003).

This ambivalence is one of many strains women leaders discuss. Organizational transformation often evokes resistance, which creates stresses for women administrators, such as isolation, difficulty balancing work and personal life, self-doubt, and institutional intransigence. Fortunately, women educators also give advice about survival strategies to aspiring administrators. For instance, African American women administrators consistently describe specific tactics they use to cope with ethnic and gender discrimination, such as emphasizing the importance of self-knowledge and self-care. They counsel African American educators to develop a strong sense of their own values, beliefs, and abilities and to adopt reflective leadership attuned to long-term goals when short-term tactics require compromise (e.g., Valverde, 2003).

Another prominent theme is defining situations rather than being defined by them, emphasizing that survival depends on interpretation and the meanings applied to situations, as well as on actions. If, rather than using military metaphors to describe leaders, one uses metaphors of weaving, cultivating, and networking, leadership becomes a process of creating, empowering, facilitating, collaborating, and educating instead of a personality characteristic (Amey & Twombly, 1993). Women often try to articulate how they lead with the express purpose of educating others about alternative modes of leadership.

Avoiding simplistic dichotomies and listening to many opinions are also values reported by women leaders. But senior administrators or boards of trustees, who define leadership as making fast and firm decisions, may misunderstand inclusive discussion; those who expect administrators to "fix things" easily will not recognize the leadership needed to arrive at complex solutions. Once again, this evokes the double bind: Women who are directive and autocratic are less effective than those who are not.

Collaboration is another important element of women's leadership styles and is consistently considered a fundamental tenet of feminist leadership. Collaboration is effective because participatory decision making is satisfying for participants and produces results and plans that people feel they own. Not only do women use collaborative leadership more often than men, they are expected to and are less effective if they choose more authoritarian leadership tactics. While much of this research focuses on women leaders in general, descriptions of women's leadership styles in higher education are consistent with researchers' conclusion that women are expected to be warmer and more collaborative in their leadership styles than men, who are expected to be more task oriented (Eagly & Carli, 2007). For example, in interviews, women administrators emphasize interdependence with followers, community service orientation, and ability to create conditions of trust, caring, fairness, objectivity, focus, and vision. Skills they depend upon included empowerment, team building, and facilitation, along with problem solving and risk taking. In the framework of relational psychology, authors discuss academic presidential leadership based on connectedness rather than control and domination. Women define their identity in terms of interdependent relations, viewing the world as made up of interconnected physical and social entities governed by needs other than control.

Despite its value, collaboration is not an easy solution to leadership problems. As noted previously, it may limit women's ability to be seen as leaders. Women presidents may be misunderstood, marginalized, or trivialized when they choose strategies different from conventional views of leadership, inadvertently reinforcing the stereotype of women as nurturers. In masculinized institutional cultures, hostile members or those fearful of the consequences of outspokenness may undermine collaboration so thoroughly that a leader has no opportunity to demonstrate the benefits of collaboration.

The expectations that women will always be collaborative can also create dilemmas for women leaders. Female and male faculty of colleges with women presidents perceive their presidents to be less collaborative than the presidents believe themselves to be. Women faculty who are passionate about wanting collaborative presidents may have naive expectations about situational constraints under which presidents operate. The strengths that women leaders may bring can be overshadowed by expectations that they have complete freedom or control over decision making. Women presidents are keenly aware of this paradox, reporting that they try hard to identify when collaboration is inappropriate, as one respondent said, to distinguish when the outcome of a decision is more important than the process (Brown et al., 2001). For example, college leaders themselves often report anecdotally that highly masculine leadership behavior is expected by boards of trustees or central system administrators, creating a situation in which some important constituency will be dissatisfied with any leadership style.

Women from ethnic backgrounds that conflict with their preferred feminist modes of leadership encounter other dilemmas. For example, Native American (Warner, 1994) and Samoan (Strachan, 2003) educational leaders report that being respectful of elders —men in their cultures—sometimes clashes with empowering women or makes it difficult for them to supervise men. Women also sometimes report the confusion between new leadership styles and selfless giving and motherhood. Because motherly nurturance is not expected to be reciprocated, women feel their efforts are taken for granted and not seen as evidence of leadership ability. Nurturing behavior, therefore, may discourage others' kindness and reduce recognition of leadership skills.

The desire to collaborate and help others may pose career problems for women, who see service to the community and to others similar to them as important, while service in academic departments does not necessarily enhance prospects for administrative leadership positions. In higher education, for instance, scholarly work is sometimes more important than administrative experience in selection of administrators (Task Force on Women in Academe, 2000).

Negotiating paradoxical values and expectations is necessary to survive long enough to be a change agent. Women who are uncomfortable with a double standard about appropriate leadership behavior often choose to work to change either gender-based expectations about leadership or conceptions of leadership to include more facilitative and socially positive behavior.

Thus, women lean toward leadership styles that emphasize organizational and social transformation, sensitivity to power dynamics, and collaboration. Educational contexts produce paradoxes that require women to negotiate through sociohistorical and stereotypic expectations, hierarchical organizations and masculinized cultures, and interactions of status with gender and other identity characteristics. Despite these constraints, women leaders have developed strategies to cope with these expectations and are making gradual but steady advancement in leadership positions in education at all levels.

REFERENCES AND FURTHER READING

Amey, M. J., & Twombly, S. B. (1993). Re-visioning leadership in community colleges. In J. S. Glazer, E. M. Bensimon, & B. K. Townsend (Eds.), *Women in higher education: A feminist perspective* (pp. 475–492). Needham Heights, MA: Ginn Press.

Astin, H. S., & Leland, C. (1993). In the spirit of the times: Three generations of women leaders. In J. S. Glazer, E. M. Bensimon, & B. K. Townsend (Eds.), *Women in higher education: A feminist perspective* (pp. 493–506). Needham Heights, MA: Ginn Press.

Brown, G., Van Ummersen, C., & Sturnick, J. (2001). *From where we sit: Women's perspective on the presidency*. Washington, DC: American Council on Education.

Carli, L. L., & Eagly, A. H. (1999). Gender effects on social influence and emergent leadership. In G. N. Powell (Ed.), *Handbook of women and work* (pp. 203–222). Thousand Oaks, CA: Sage.

Eagly, A. H., & Carli, L. L. (2007). *Through the labyrinth: The truth about how women become leaders*. Boston, MA: Harvard Business School Press.

Eagly, A. H., & Johannesen-Schmidt, M. C. (2001). The leadership styles of women and men. *Journal of Social Issues, 57*(4), 781–797.

Goodwin, S. A., & Fiske, S. T. (2001). Power and gender: The double-edged sword of ambivalence. In R. K. Unger (Ed.), *Handbook of the psychology of women and gender* (pp. 358–366). New York: Wiley.

Hatcher, C. (2003). Refashioning a passionate manager: Gender at work. *Gender, Work, and Organization, 10*(4), 391–412.

Madden, M. E. (2005). Gender and leadership in higher education. *Psychology of Women Quarterly, 29*(1), 3–14.

Miller, J. R., & Vaughn, G. G. (1997). African American Women executives. In L. Benjamin (Ed.), *Black women in the academy: Promises and perils* (pp. 179–188). Gainesville, FL: University Press of Florida.

Regan, H. B., & Brooks, G. H. (1995). *Out of women's experience: Creating relational leadership.* Thousand Oaks, CA: Corwin Press.

Strachan, J. (1999). Feminist educational leadership: Locating the concepts of practice. *Gender and Education, 11*(3), 309–322.

Strachan, J. (2003). Feminist educational leadership: Not for the fainthearted. In C. Reynolds, (Ed.), *Women and school leadership: International perspectives* (pp. 111–126). Albany: State University of New York Press.

Task Force on Women in Academe. (2000). *Women in academe: Two steps forward, one step back.* Washington, DC: American Psychological Association.

Valverde, L. A. (2003). *Leaders of color in higher education.* New York: Alta Mira.

Warner, L. S. (1994). A study of American Indian females in higher education administration. *Initiatives, 56*(4), 11–17.

Yoder, J. D. (2001). Making leadership work more effectively for women. *Journal of Social Issues, 57*(4), 815–828.

CHAPTER 41

Advising and Mentoring Graduate Students

SANDRA ACKER

The terms *advising* and *mentoring* are used in different ways within and across countries by those involved in graduate education. In this chapter, *advising* and *supervising* are used as synonyms that refer to the assignment of a relatively experienced academic with responsibility for the research work (thesis or dissertation) of an associated student. Although *mentoring* is sometimes used as another synonym, it usually refers to a more intense, extended, and idealized relationship than advising. Both advisory and mentoring relationships take place in institutions that are infused with gendered divisions of labor, hierarchies, and expectations. They are shaped by elements of power and control, positionality, diversity, and contextualization—issues to be explored in this chapter.

Advising is only one aspect—albeit an important one—of the graduate experience. Depending on the national, institutional, departmental, and disciplinary context, students may enjoy more or less funding, fulfill various course and examination requirements, and work alone or with a research team. Sometimes the metaphor of the "journey" is used, especially for doctoral studies, to signify the attainment of a distant goal reached by traveling across difficult and unknown terrain. Although there is a widespread belief that advising makes a critical difference in reaching the goal, there is not much consensus on exactly what impact it has or how it should be done.

What Is the Advisory Role?

The advisory role is surprisingly difficult to define. Although the advisor is similar to a teacher, instructors do not usually have a long-term relationship with a student based on a piece of work that extends over a number of years and is examined by other academics. Graduate students (also called postgraduates or research students in some countries) have as their main goal the production of a booklike piece of work called a thesis or dissertation based on original research. The advisor/supervisor, who normally has some expertise and authority in the area of the student's research, is charged with the responsibility of assisting the student to conceptualize, plan, carry out, and write up the results of the research. Beyond the student-teacher depiction, the relationship has been expressed in more colorful terms such as *master-servant, guru-disciple, parent-child*, and so forth. Supervisors have been characterized by analogies as diverse as midwife and business manager. All such depictions imply that an advisor will facilitate the production of the thesis and initiate the student into the secrets of academe. The midwife advisor might help the student give birth to the knowledge already inside; the business manager advisor might make sure the student has schedules, goals, objectives, and the means of accomplishing them.

Some writers believe that the process of thesis production and the associated supervisor-student relationship can be made subject to control and prediction. The model could be called the "technical-rational" approach to supervision and finds its place in many policy documents and self-help textbooks for students and supervisors (for critiques see Acker, Hill, & Black, 1994; Kamler & Thomson, 2008). The ultimate goal is to improve the chances that a student will finish the "journey." Others prefer a "negotiated order" model, which stresses the mutual negotiation and interaction between the participants. Any advice that can be given about best practice, this model says, will have to be modified by what happens in real life as well as by the expectations and understandings each person brings to the table. For example, not all students intend a career in academe, while supervisors generally think that is the desirable goal, at least for superior scholars. Or, if a student desires nurturing and warmth from the supervisor but the supervisor prefers a strictly professional approach prizing student independence, either the parameters will need to be negotiated in some way or the relationship may deteriorate.

Some literature about women's preferred styles of learning suggests many women students would prefer a nurturing supervisory style. A Canadian study found women academics in faculties of education struggling to meet the expectations of the many women students who wanted to work with women supervisors and expected a high level of interest and mentoring from them (Acker & Feuerverger, 1996). Whatever these patterns, studies also show that the majority of students are satisfied with the advising they receive (although a small minority are very dissatisfied) if only because they do not have many other experiences with which to compare their situation.

Knowledge and Control

One way to think about the supervisory process is as a site for expression of power or control. As a "deeply uncertain practice" (Grant, 2005), supervision involves elements of knowledge and power that are shifting rather than constant. Students may not even know what they need to learn, as many aspects of academic life are tacit or unspoken, part of a "hidden curriculum" (Acker, 2001) learned "on the grapevine" (Gardner, 2007). They are subject to what the French theorist Michel Foucault would see as "disciplinary technologies"—deadlines, rules, forms, timetables, reports, examinations—the cumulative effect of which is to produce docility or conformity. In addition, they need to learn the subject-area conventions that make up a disciplinary culture (for example, whether writing a book or a refereed journal article is preferable). Departments may provide various ways for graduate students to become informed, such as orientations, workshops, and seminars, but advisors are in a key position to communicate the rules of the game to their students, both directly and by example. Nevertheless, it may not occur to advisors that their students do not already know these things.

Other features of the supervisory dyad relate to power relationships. Generally, there is a generation gap, with the supervisor being older, although in some professional fields, students may not be chronologically "young," having already accumulated work experience outside the ivory tower. Gender also invokes power. Given the numerical dominance of men in the academy, especially in higher ranks and in scientific specialties, one is more likely to find men supervising women than the reverse. The supervisor may control financial resources that have an impact upon the student.

Nevertheless, some writers believe that students have more power than they normally realize. If the pairing does not match the expected power dynamics—for example, if the supervisor is female and the student is male, or the student is older than the supervisor, or the supervisor but not the student is from a minority ethnocultural group—some readjustment and possibly even some conflict is likely to take place (Acker, 2001). Some students with clear goals find themselves taking the lead in advisory sessions. As the research progresses, the student will come to know more than the supervisor about the specific topic area. In some cases, the advisor relies on the student to do an important part of the work of a research team. More generally, students' success brings credit to their supervisor; conversely, poor completion rates or rumors of inadequate supervision will do some harm to the supervisor's reputation and equanimity.

The power of the supervisor may also be mitigated where it is conventional to have supervisory committees or cosupervision. It may also be reduced intentionally, as in efforts to develop feminist mentoring (Humble, Solomon, Allen, Blaisure, & Johnson, 2006), analogous to feminist pedagogy, one of the critical or liberatory pedagogies that attempts to work against the grain of teacher authority normally found in classrooms and in hierarchical relationships between faculty and students. Humble and her colleagues (2006) point out that conventional mentoring is not very compatible with radical pedagogies because it aims to socialize individuals into an existing environment rather than to create conditions for change. The concept of feminist supervising or mentoring is almost unknown and could bear further development.

Is It Mentoring?

The title of this chapter suggests that advising and mentoring go together. In common usage, mentoring would be the stronger concept, evoking a long-term investment in the welfare and future of a protégé(e), going well beyond the specific goal of producing a thesis or completing a doctorate. Mentoring has also been a popular innovation in efforts to assist women and minority members of organizations or to support persons from disadvantaged communities in order to improve their life chances. Graduate students—again, especially women and minority students—are sometimes encouraged to find mentors who will help them achieve career success.

However, as Helen Colley (2003) shows, the idea of mentoring is suffused with romantic myths and gendered paradigms. Although the original template for mentoring may have been males helping males, the dominant model is now one in which the female-associated virtues of endless caring and self-sacrifice are incorporated into the mentor persona. In her study of mentoring in a program for disadvantaged youth, Colley describes a dysfunctional pairing of two young women who become trapped within a perpetual cycle of accepting and caring from the mentor and indifference from the mentee.

Studies of women and minority academics suggest a parallel downside to mentoring: namely, the extra layer of work expected by students, other faculty, the academic herself, and even the wider community, quite possibly occurring at the same time that junior faculty members need to put extensive efforts into research production to secure their own positions (Tierney & Bensimon, 1996). Problems are exacerbated in situations where the representation of women or minorities among the faculty is less than among the student body. In Canadian faculties of education, for example, women are about 42% of full and associate professors (most of whom hold permanent positions and are likely to be allowed to supervise theses) but 70% of doctoral students (Canadian Association of University Teachers, 2008, pp. 12, 27). If students try to affiliate with supervisors in the same gender or ethnic group, then a numerical pressure point and a predictable overload for women and minority faculty is likely, such as the one reported by Romero (1997), whose interviews with Chicana faculty (women in the United States of Mexican descent) revealed that they were highly isolated, inundated with students and other workload responsibilities, and conscious of a class, race, and gender disparity between themselves and majority faculty.

An extended one-to-one relationship may easily become intense and emotional and present uncomfortable aspects of dependence or desire. At the very least, there are boundary issues that must be negotiated. Not all boundary problems lie in the sexual realm. For example, questions sometimes arise about who should lay claim to the intellectual property generated by the student.

In considering mentoring, one should also beware of too-easy generalizations, such as assuming that same-sex mentor-student pairings are always better. In contrast, there are some hints in the literature that women supervisors (in part, because they may be more junior in the academy) have fewer resources to put at the disposal of their students. A study by Kurtz-Costes, Helmke, and Ülkü-Steiner (2006) found that women students in predominantly male departments like chemistry did not want to work with the women faculty in their field because they found them too "driven" and unlikely to be role models for combining family and work.

In practice, mentoring in its sense of an intense and extended relationship is probably hit or miss. Few academics can take on a protégé(e) for life. There are too many students, and some will inevitably be disappointed.

Positionality, Diversity, and Contextualization

Positionality is important: The group someone belongs to and where they are located in the institution (and society) influences both opportunities and perceptions. Sometimes graduate students are written about as if they are all interchangeable: "the" graduate student. Yet the graduate student population is increasingly diverse. Forty or more years ago, the situation was different: Most students were male, White, middle-class, young, living on campus, and studying full time. Many social trends have changed this picture. In some places, numbers have risen steeply, while the composition of the student cohorts has changed. For example, in Great Britain, the number of full-time postgraduates more than quadrupled in the 30 years from 1970 to 2000, while the international student proportion rose from 13.7% to 41.1% (Chiang, 2003, pp. 9–10). Students now have a variety of backgrounds and characteristics, although some marginalized and minoritized categories of the population (e.g., aboriginal students, those from working-class backgrounds, disabled students) are still greatly underrepresented.

Women remain concentrated in certain fields such as education, health, and social work and scarce in others such as engineering and computer sciences, but overall they are found in much greater numbers than in the past. In many countries (including the United States and Canada), they are now a small majority among master's degree recipients and approaching parity at the doctoral level.

Different disciplines require and permit different modes of study (Gardner, 2008).

Students who work in laboratory environments are likely to see their supervisors regularly and may well be working on a joint project, while the library-based (or, increasingly, home-based) student or part-time student may have relatively little such contact. Chiang (2003) refers to the main models as "teamwork" and "individualist" research training structures and uses chemistry and education, respectively, as illustrations. Regardless of the structure, some students may be better positioned than others for excelling and networking. It is likely that academics are most comfortable with others like themselves, a predilection that has in the past ensured the continuity of male domination in universities through same-gender patronage. An extension of the same point may account for cases in which academics show discomfort with international students and adhere to some cultural stereotypes. However, there is little likelihood that instructors and students can be matched with any precision: Gender alone does not address the myriad of other characteristics (age, class background, religion, race, sexual orientation, etc.) that make up someone's identity (Valentine, 2007). There are also preferences regarding style and closeness or distance of supervision and reasons for undertaking further study and research, all of which vary idiosyncratically.

Students who work on professors' research projects or who can afford to spend large amounts of time in a department may be first in line for important socialization and mentoring experiences. Conversely, those who are working outside the academy to make ends meet, looking after children as a single parent, responsible for caring for an elderly dependent, or commuting several hours to the university may not have the same advantages. Studies of women academics suggest that they are often working against the biological clock to establish their careers; those with children get little sleep as they struggle to keep up with expectations still based on a family-free male model (Acker & Armenti, 2004; Wolf-Wendel & Ward, 2006). Although there are not many similar studies of graduate student women, it is likely that many of the same problems exist. Gender, class, race, ethnicity, dis/ability, and other attributes all singly and together influence the experiences of graduate students.

It is important to remember that the supervisor-student dyad is not located in a vacuum. The impact of particular disciplinary cultures and structures has already been mentioned. Many institutional features are relevant. Institutional and departmental status, resources, size, location, cultures, and policies influence the opportunities graduate students have. For example, some universities provide training or workload credit for supervisors, while others do not. It is likely that students, especially early in their programs, do not have a full appreciation of most of these contextual factors that impinge on their experience.

Funding policies, both internal and external to the university, are especially important in shaping the graduate environment (Acker & Haque, in press). In Great Britain, changes in the social science funding council's practices in the 1980s led to universities providing more research training, keeping better track of students, and putting pressure on students to complete their research more quickly (Leonard, 2001). Funding policies may have gender-differentiating effects. In the United States in the 1960s, there were prestigious foundations—and indeed universities—that routinely excluded women from their lists of scholarship recipients.

A myriad of other policies and practices also have an impact on graduate students and sometimes women in particular. Again, in the United States in the 1960s, childcare facilities were practically unknown, and hiring policies openly discriminated against academic couples. Although there is now child-care provision in many universities, it may be difficult to access, and student parents may lose their university funding while on a maternity or parenting leave. Overt discrimination against couples (which mainly affected women) has declined, yet accommodating partners is still a problem for universities. On the surface, universities have come a long way, but the barriers are now more subtle, located in disciplinary cultural traditions, women's competing external responsibilities, and a residue of bias.

Contextual influences go beyond individual institutions to labor market conditions, state policies, and even international events. At the same time as apparently more enlightened policies like maternity leave and child-care provision spread, academic work—and by extension graduate study—has been altered by global trends. Academics do more work in the same or less time, often with fewer resources. Their output is also repeatedly audited, not only by the traditional peer-review procedures assessing the suitability of research for publication but by new modes of what some call performativity: reaching a level of accomplishment *and* showing publicly that the level has been reached, for example, by reports to external assessors or annual reviews. Universities are thought to have become more like businesses and are managed by "executives" who put the emphasis on the bottom line and market-driven priorities.

Although this level of analysis may at first seem remote from the experiences of graduate students and their supervisors, it has important shaping effects. International students may be recruited for the money and contacts they bring with them; in some countries faculty are expected to teach abroad or to find other ways of initiating entrepreneurial activity. Successful graduate student degree completions may be one of the ways in which departments can demonstrate value for money and thus receive further funding. More insidiously, academics are so stretched that they have less and less time to look after their students. Kamler and Thomson (2008, p. 509) question whether the proliferation of self-help books for doctoral students is related to the fact that advisors have less time to spend with them. Increased reliance on temporary and part-time faculty also means fewer individuals available for supervision. And finally, students see these harried and distracted academics and wonder what attractions are left in academe. An ironic outcome may lie ahead: students—including women—look at their mentors and decide *not* to be like them.

REFERENCES AND FURTHER READING

Acker, S. (2001). The hidden curriculum of dissertation advising. In E. Margolis (Ed.), *The hidden curriculum in higher education* (pp. 61–77). New York: Routledge.

Acker, S., & Armenti, C. (2004). Sleepless in academia. *Gender and Education, 16*(1), 3–24.

Acker, S., & Feuerverger, G. (1996). Doing good and feeling bad: The work of women university teachers. *Cambridge Journal of Education, 26*(3), 401–422.

Acker, S., & Haque, E. (in press). Doctoral students and a future in academe? From the iceberg to the shore. In L. McAlpine & G. Kerlind (Eds.), *New visions of academic practice: Becoming an academic in the social sciences*. Basingstoke, UK: Palgrave Macmillan.

Acker, S., Hill, T., & Black, E. (1994). Thesis supervision in the social sciences: Managed or negotiated? *Higher Education, 28*, 483–498.

Canadian Association of University Teachers (2008). *CAUT almanac of post-secondary education in Canada 2008–2009*. Ottawa: Author.

Chiang, K.-H. (2003). Learning experiences of doctoral students in U.K. universities. *International Journal of Sociology and Social Policy, 23*(1/2), 4–32.

Colley, H. (2003) *Mentoring for social inclusion: A critical approach to nurturing successful mentoring relations*. London: RoutledgeFalmer.

Gardner, S. (2007). "I heard it through the grapevine": Doctoral student socialization in chemistry and history. *Higher Education, 54*, 723–740.

Gardner, S. (2008). "What's too much and what's too little?" The process of becoming an independent researcher in doctoral education. *Journal of Higher Education, 79*(3), 326–350.

Grant, B. (2005). Fighting for space in supervision: Fantasies, fairytales, fictions and fallacies. *International Journal of Qualitative Studies in Education, 18*(3), 337–354.

Humble, A., Solomon, C., Allen, K., Blaisure, K., & Johnson, M. P. (2006). Feminism and mentoring of graduate students. *Family Relations, 55*(1), 2–15.

Kamler, B., & Thomson, P. (2008). The failure of dissertation advice books: Toward alternative pedagogies for doctoral writing. *Educational Researcher, 37*(8), 507–514.

Kurtz-Costes, B., Helmke, L., & Ülkü-Steiner, B. (2006). Gender and doctoral studies: The perceptions of PhD students in an American university. *Gender and Education, 18*(2), 137–155.

Leonard, D. (2001). *A woman's guide to doctoral studies*. Buckingham, UK: Open University Press.

Romero, M. (1997). Class-based, gendered and racialized institutions of higher education: Everyday life of academia from the view of Chicana faculty. *Race, Gender & Class, 4*(2), 151–173.

Tierney, W., & Bensimon, E. (1996). *Promotion and tenure: Community and socialization in academe*. Albany: State University of New York Press.

Valentine, G. (2007). Theorizing and researching intersectionality: A challenge for feminist geography. *Professional Geographer, 59*(1), 10–21.

Wolf-Wendel, L., & Ward, K. (2006). Academic life and motherhood: Variations by institutional type. *Higher Education, 52*, 487–521.

CHAPTER 42

Faculty Workloads

SARAH E. WINSLOW-BOWE AND JERRY A. JACOBS

The story of gender equity and education is, at all levels, one of progress and bottlenecks. In higher education, for example, women are now the majority of college and graduate school enrollees and degree recipients, but they have made fewer inroads as faculty, especially in the natural sciences and engineering (Jacobs, 1996). One important element of this story is the high level of career commitment expected from faculty. Although the public often does not fully understand the nature and rhythm of faculty life, faculty positions are, in fact, highly demanding. The demands of these jobs are pervasive. Moreover, the requirements of faculty positions are often more intensive during the childbearing and child-rearing periods of young faculty's lives.

The data discussed in this essay were drawn from the 1998 National Study of Postsecondary Faculty (NSOPF) administered by the National Center for Education Statistics of the U.S. Department of Education (2001). The survey, designed to collect information on faculty and other instructional staff in institutions of higher education, is currently the most comprehensive study of postsecondary faculty. This cross-sectional survey has been administered three times, during the 1987–88, 1992–93, and 1998–99 academic years. For the present analysis, the sample was restricted to those faculty members at four-year institutions who considered their academic appointment to be their primary job and who did not spend the majority of their time in administrative activities. This resulted in a final sample size of 11,162 faculty members, of whom 10,092 were full time. Selective reports from the 1992 administration of the same survey are also presented. Because the NSOPF did not solicit information on spouses of faculty members, information about those married couples in the 1990 census in which either spouse reported her or his occupation as "postsecondary teacher" were rearranged to fill this gap.

The Faculty Workweek

Time is a valuable yet finite resource about which individuals have to make allocation decisions. Juliet Schor brought this issue into the spotlight in her 1991 book, *The Overworked American*, arguing that, after a century-long decline, working time began to increase in the 1980s. The lengthening of the average workweek, Schor contended, is the principal source of time pressure faced by individuals. Jacobs and Gerson (2004) found that a diversifying workforce has been accompanied by a bifurcation in working time, with more jobs requiring either very long or short workweeks. This time divide among jobs tends to mirror the class divide as well, with long working hours concentrated among managerial and professional workers and shorter working hours for workers with more modest educational and occupational credentials.

Working time among academic faculty reflects this larger pattern. Professors put in very long hours. Full-time male faculty report working 54.8 hours per week on average; their female counterparts report working almost as many hours (52.8 hours per week). Although a sizable minority of male (34.4%) and female (27.0%) full-time faculty do some paid consulting work, the amount of time they spend doing such work is minimal (approximately 5 hours per week). Thus the majority of faculty working time is devoted to their main position, with outside consulting representing a minor fraction of total work effort.

Faculty work more hours per week than do those in most other occupations, even those in comparable professional positions. In 2000, the average employed man worked 43.1 hours per week, while the average male professional or manager worked 46.0 hours per week, a full 9-hour day less than professors (Jacobs & Gerson, 2004). Female professors exceed their same-sex counterparts in paid working time by an even larger margin. The average employed woman worked 37.1 hours in 2000, and female professionals and managers worked 39.5 hours on average.

Moreover, extremely long workweeks are pervasive in academia. The averages detailed above clearly indicate that a 50-hour workweek is normative, with roughly two-thirds of faculty reporting working such long hours. But a 60-hour workweek is also common; among full-time faculty, 38.1% of men and 32.5% of women report working at least 60 hours per week.

Long hours are pervasive across institutional types and academic rank. While faculty in research institutions report working the longest hours (an average of 55.8 for men and 54.0 for women), the average workweeks of full-time faculty in other institution types are quite similar. For example, male full-time faculty in liberal arts colleges work 54.0 hours per week, and their female counterparts put in 53.4 hours per week. Both male and female full-time faculty at all institutional groups average above 50 hours per week. Similarly, faculty at all ranks put in over 50 hours per week. Assistant professors work long hours, but so too do tenured associate and full professors. Male assistant professors put in slightly longer hours than do their female counterparts (55.8 hours per week for the men versus 53.5 hours for the women). For men, there is a slight posttenure slump, with the length of the workweek declining by 2 hours, only to rise again for full professors. For women, the workweek grows steadily as they advance from the ranks of assistant to associate to full professor. The gender gap in working time for assistant professors is a bit larger among those working 60 or more hours per week—43.2% of men and 33.5% of women put in these long workweeks. But long hours are not restricted to those on the tenure track. Even lecturers and instructors put in over 50 hours per week.

Working Time from the Perspective of Families

Individual workweeks are only one part of the time crunch facing faculty members. American family structure has changed dramatically in recent decades, and this has profound implications for analyses of work-family conflict. Whereas just over half of married couples fit the breadwinner-homemaker model in 1970, by 2000 three in five were dual-earner couples. Census data indicate that dual-earner couples are common in academia, particularly among female faculty. Just over half (56.2%) of married male faculty and nearly all (88.5%) of married female faculty have spouses working full time. Moreover, a sizable minority is married to other faculty members, and most have spouses in a managerial or professional occupation. Women faculty are more likely to be married to male faculty (18.2% versus 12.5%), but the partners of both groups are typically professionals or managers (69.5% for female faculty, 70.7% for male faculty).

What does this mean for the work-family conflicts facing academic faculty? In earlier work, Jacobs and Gerson (2004) argued that, in order to fully understand the time crunch facing American men and women, researchers must examine working time from the perspective of families. The family workweeks of married faculty are long: 84.1 hours per week on average for male faculty and 89.3 hours per week for female faculty. A sizable minority are in couples devoting 100 or more hours per week to paid employment (17.3% for men versus 25.4% for women). Thus the pressure generated by the long faculty workweeks discussed above are compounded by the fact that most faculty, especially most women faculty, have spouses who themselves are putting in long hours. Are academic careers family friendly? One might argue that the answer is yes. Faculty members do not have to punch a time clock and are not closely monitored on an hourly basis as is the case in many occupations. The measure of control and flexibility inherent in academic work allows faculty, especially those who are parents, to be available when children are sick or when breakdowns in child-care arrangements inevitably occur. However, much of this compatibility rests on the implicit assumption that faculty members are able to wait until after receiving tenure to have children.

The strategy of delaying childbearing until after receiving tenure is quite appealing in that the most demanding phase of child care would occur after the pressure and risk associated with being an untenured assistant professor is completed. But clearly this strategy depends on getting tenure relatively early in life. In other words, the "tenure first, kids later" approach relies on a certain ordered, uninterrupted life-course sequencing in which one receives his or her Ph.D. at age 27 or 28 (which itself relies on the assumption of beginning graduate school immediately or soon after receiving one's undergraduate degree and completing the degree in five or six years) and receives tenure at roughly the age of 34. This poses an important empirical question: How old are assistant professors? If this ordered life-course sequencing is occurring, one would expect assistant professors to be in their early 30s. Is that the case?

The average age of male assistant professors is 42.4; for women, it is slightly older at 43.7. The average age of assistant professors is higher in some fields, such as education and nursing, than others, such as the physical sciences. But the average exceeds 37 years of age in all of the academic specialties. Thus the dilemma of whether to wait until tenure to have children is a daunting one in all areas of academia, with the data suggesting that most assistant professors are too old to wait until receiving tenure to start their families.

Why is it that assistant professors are older than the ordered life-course sequencing perspective would lead one to expect? One reason is that faculty members are not receiving their degrees until after their 30th birthdays. The average age at degree is 33.4 for men and 35.5 for women. Again, there is variation across academic fields with faculty in some fields, such as education, obtaining their degrees much later in life than in other fields, such as architecture and engineering. Nonetheless, in all fields the average age for doctoral degree recipients is at least 30. As a result, questions about getting married and having children before achieving tenure, whether that is when one is in graduate school, holding postdoctoral fellowships or other temporary positions, or as an assistant professor, arise in all fields of academic specialization.

Another possible explanation for an age profile that does not support the "tenure first, kids later" pattern might be that faculty members are starting families before receiving their Ph.D.s. While the cross-sectional data available do not allow exact pinpointing of these events, one may make some life-course inferences about these data. For example, women obtaining Ph.D.s in the physical sciences are slightly younger than their male counterparts (average age of 30.2 for women versus 31.4 for men). Thus it is likely that few women in this area are having children in advance of receiving their Ph.D.s, since there is no evidence of a slowdown relative to their male counterparts. In other fields, such as the arts and humanities, education, and biological sciences, women are obtaining their doctoral degrees two or more years after their male counterparts. Childbearing in advance of the degree may well be the explanation for these differences.

Finally, it may be the case that academics do not progress directly from degree receipt to a tenure-track faculty position. The data indicate that assistant professors have been at their current institution for an average of just over three years. This figure is exactly what one would expect given a six- or seven-year tenure clock, but it leaves several years unaccounted for. In other words, age at degree plus years at current institution does not add up to the respondent's current age. What explains this gap? In some fields, like biology, respondents typically worked five or more years at another institution, presumably as a postdoctoral fellow, before starting as an assistant professor. The number of years elapsed before starting as an assistant professor is much lower in other fields, including business and the social sciences. Thus the fact that assistant professors are often in their late 30s or early 40s is due to a combination of obtaining the doctoral degree in their early 30s and spending several years in postdoctoral fellowships or temporary positions after the receipt of the degree. Taken together, these results indicate that the "tenure first, kids later" strategy is not a viable option for many in academia. For many faculty members, the most demanding years of child rearing are likely to coincide with the demands and uncertainty of the pretenure years.

Workload, Productivity, and Satisfaction

How can we make sense of the long workweeks put in by faculty members, particularly in light of the fact that, for many, they are combined with a spouse's lengthy employment hours and the demands of raising children? Are these hours self-imposed, or are they rooted in institutional and professional expectations?

An optimistic view might hold that academia is a context in which devotion to work is self-imposed. Professors do not punch a time clock, and even at the most teaching-intensive institutions, classroom time rarely exceeds 15 hours. The time demands experienced by faculty are thus in some sense discretionary. Moreover, this argument holds that faculty members love their work and deeply identify with their professional role. In this sense, academia represents a secular "calling" with faculty embracing the "work devotion" schema outlined by Blair-Loy (2003). That faculty do not relinquish their professional titles or affiliations upon retirement (i.e., "professor" simply becomes "professor emeritus") suggests that many professors keep working diligently into retirement as long as their strength and stamina allow. All of this might logically lead to the conclusion that, if the faculty workweek seems excessive to some, it certainly does not to faculty because it is what they choose to do.

In contrast to the view that faculty work time is self-imposed, an alternative view is that professors often find themselves caught in a set of institutional and professional expectations. In other words, normative expectations about what it means to be a good or successful academic drive many faculty members to put in excessive hours. While the institutional-demands perspective would acknowledge the many attractions of academia, such a view stresses the practical challenges that large numbers of faculty confront at both elite and less selective colleges and universities.

If professors' long workweeks are due to "structural constraints," what are these structures and what are the sources of these constraints? There are four main sources of growing time pressures on faculty. First, the rising cost of higher education has brought renewed public scrutiny and, with it, calls for more emphasis on teaching. While the source of the scrutiny may differ across institution type (with public institutions often responding to budget cuts and private institutions justifying rising tuition by focusing on how much faculty attention students receive), the pressure to increase the quantity and quality of time devoted to teaching has been evident in public and private institutions of higher education. Second, the increased emphasis on teaching has been accompanied by rising expectations for research productivity. Both the form and the content of the tenure review system, formerly most developed in the elite schools, have been adopted by colleges and universities at all levels of higher education. Third, technological changes associated with the information economy have paradoxically increased the time demands and intensity of faculty jobs. Although this claim cannot be assessed with NSOPF data, anecdotal evidence strongly suggests that faculty spend countless hours reading and responding to e-mail and are often assumed by students to be available 24 hours per day. Moreover, the adoption of computers was also accompanied by a decline in secretarial support for faculty.

Finally, the rise of part-time employment in academia increases the pressures on full-time faculty members. Part-time employment in academia has risen sharply over the past 30 years as extremely low-paid part-time faculty are available to teach for a small fraction of the cost of full-time members of the standing faculty. In 1999, more than two in five (42.5%) postsecondary faculty were employed part time, a substantial increase from 21.9% found in 1970 (National Center for Education Statistics, 2001). The growth in the number of part-timers increases pressures on full-timers in two ways. First, the reduction in the number of full-time positions makes entry into the ranks of full-time faculty that much more competitive. Furthermore, since part-timers are rarely asked to serve on committees or to take on other administrative roles, the growth of part-time employment means that a smaller fraction of faculty are saddled with a growing amount of administrative responsibility. In sum, a perspective emphasizing structural constraints and normative expectations suggests that multiple course preparations, endless committee meetings, seemingly limitless productivity standards, and a relentless stream of e-mails make today's faculty work experience less than the idealized world of academia suggested by the self-imposed viewpoint outlined above.

Which of these views fits the data more closely? While it is clear that faculty overwhelmingly report being satisfied with their jobs (84.8% of men and 81.8% of full-time women report being somewhat or very satisfied with their jobs), they do voice complaints about salary, benefits, and their workload. By focusing on whether faculty report dissatisfaction with their workload, we can assess the extent to which the length of the faculty workweek is self-imposed and willingly chosen. If the self-imposed perspective is correct, then we would expect that those who put in the longest hours express few if any complaints about their workload, since these faculty love teaching and research and cannot get enough of it. On the other hand, if one's workload is largely driven by institutional and professional demands such as increasing course loads and expectations for publishing, then we may find a significant number of professors who are not satisfied with their jobs. A key question, then, is whether satisfaction with workload increases with time on the job. If so, then those working the longest may not be doing so completely voluntarily. Instead, work patterns may be the result of many pressures, some stemming from the institution, others from normative expectations set by other faculty. A related question concerns the connection between working time and research productivity: Do long workweeks play a key role in contributing to success in publishing? If so, this relationship may provide insight into the reasons for the amount of time faculty spend on the job.

Faculty dissatisfaction with workload increases with hours on the job. For example, one in three (30.3%) female faculty working less than 50 hours per week report being dissatisfied with their workload, compared with more than two in five (44.1%) of those working more than 60 hours per week. The idea that greater hours are associated with more complaints about an excessive workload may seem simple, but it runs counter to the notion that people working the longest hours are all doing so simply out of a love of their jobs. So what explains the excessive workweeks that are so pervasive in academia? The data clearly indicate that those who put in the longest workweeks are likely to publish more books and articles. The differences between those putting in over 50 hours per week and those putting in less than 50 hours per week are substantial. However, the impact of working over 60 hours per week is even more dramatic and seems especially critical for women. If research productivity is indispensable for success in academia and if a 60-hour workweek is key for success in publishing, then working 60 or more hours per week essentially becomes a requirement of academic jobs.

Academic positions are highly sought after and very satisfying, but they are also very demanding and pose significant challenges to those striving to maintain a fulfilling family life. This remains particularly true for married women faculty whose husbands are typically very busy professionals themselves. The risk of maintaining the current systems is the loss of talent, both in terms of faculty lost through the "leaky pipeline" as well as those deterred from pursing careers in this profession. The first step in addressing these concerns is to understand that there is a problem that needs to be addressed. Policies designed to manage the demands of faculty jobs can be devised (see Jacobs, 2004) but only after recognizing that some limits need to be set on the demands posed by academic positions.

REFERENCES AND FURTHER READING

Blair-Loy, M. (2003). *Competing devotions: Career and family among women executives*. Cambridge, MA: Harvard University Press.

Jacobs, J. A. (1996). Gender inequality and higher education. *Annual Review of Sociology, 22*, 153–185.

Jacobs, J. A. (2004). The faculty time divide. *Sociological Forum, 19*(1), 3–27.

Jacobs, J. A., & Gerson, K. (2004). *The time divide: Work, family, and gender inequality*. Cambridge, MA: Harvard University Press.

Jacobs, J. A., & Winslow, S. (2004a). Overworked faculty: Job stresses and family demands. *Annals of the American Academy of Political and Social Science, 596*(1), 104–129.

Jacobs, J. A., & Winslow, S. (2004b). Understanding the academic life course, time pressures and gender inequality. *Community, Work, and Family, 7*(2), 143–161.

National Center for Education Statistics. (2001). *Background characteristics, work activities and compensation of faculty and instructional staff in postsecondary institutions* (NCES 2001- 152). Washington, DC: U.S. Government Printing Office.

National Center for Education Statistics. (2002). *Digest of education statistics.* Washington, DC: U.S. Government Printing Office. Retrieved April 5, 2004, from http://nces.ed.gov/programs/digest/

Schor, J. (1991). *The overworked American: The unexpected decline of leisure.* New York: Basic Books.

Winslow, S. (2005). Work-family conflict, gender, and parenthood, 1977–1997. *Journal of Family Issues, 26*(6), 727–755.

Winslow-Bowe, S. E. (2006). *Husbands' and wives' relative income: Persistence, variation, and outcomes* (Unpublished doctoral dissertation). University of Pennsylvania, Philadelphia.

CHAPTER 43

Mentoring Women Faculty

JILL M. HERMSEN, JACQUELYN S. LITT, JENI HART, AND SHERYL ANN TUCKER

"Numerous studies of college and university faculty have shown that women have fewer mentors and face greater professional isolation, slower rates of promotion, and increased likelihood of leaving an institution before gaining tenure than do their male counterparts" (Wasburn, 2007, p. 52). Research demonstrates that barriers to women's professional advancement are caused, at least in part, by bias. Valian (1998) identifies unconscious biases as mental processes that evaluate men as more effective, productive, and competent professionals and leaders. Coupled with bias, institutional structures are gendered in terms of leadership, organizational structure, policies, and norms. Collective practices at work, such as masculine cultures and the mobilization of masculinity marginalize women in both formal and informal interactions (Martin, 2001).

Studies of women faculty reveal that they feel lower levels of satisfaction than men, feel marginalized in departments, desire more women faculty in leadership and senior positions, and experience isolation. Faculty isolation translates into fewer opportunities for advancement, fewer rewards, and less visibility for women. In addition, women faculty also report greater concerns than men about work-life balance, increased service responsibilities, ongoing requests from students for mentoring and informal advising, assignment of larger and introductory classes, and lack of leadership opportunities.

Institutions reproduce systems of advantage in ways that negatively affect women. Even the perception of a "typical" faculty career is based on a gendered model of faculty advancement (Hart & Litt, 2010). These processes, which permeate academic culture, mean men accumulate professional advantage as they progress through their careers. The concern among academic leaders, women faculty, and the National Science Foundation's ADVANCE program have inspired calls to action to address the individual and institutional factors that create disparate levels of advantage. A primary intervention has been the development of formal mentoring programs for women in academia.

Mentoring women faculty is understood to address unconscious bias, isolation, and gendered organizations. Mentoring is offered through professional associations, specific professional development programs (e.g., Higher Education Resource Services [HERS]) and is a mainstay of the National Science Foundation ADVANCE programs. Yet some scholars emphasize that mentoring is only part of a broader package of institutional change. In their study of a faculty mentoring program, Laursen and Rocque (2009) distinguish individual goals (i.e., career skills and access to resources) from organizational needs and systemic change. Organizational needs include mentees' desires for community and collegiality, while systemic change includes institutional flexibility (e.g., work-life programs). Combining the three (i.e., mentoring, organizational needs, and systemic change) may produce the most comprehensive approach to eliminating barriers to women's success.

Short of the kind of institutional changes Laursen and Rocque (2009) recommend, mentoring has emerged as a primary way colleges and universities are addressing the status of women. This chapter describes the rationales behind these programs, provides examples of different models, and analyzes the implications for women's professional achievement. This discussion is not intended to be a formal review of the literature but rather a synopsis of key issues to consider in mentoring women faculty. Given that much of the literature is focused on tenured/tenure-track faculty at four-year colleges and universities, this chapter focuses on mentoring programs for those faculty. This is not to negate the importance of focusing on other institutional types (e.g., community colleges) or groups of faculty (e.g., adjunct and other non–tenure track). Rather, it is a reflection of the lack of attention given to some types of institutions and faculty in the literature.

Definitions of Mentoring

The term *mentoring* is used to describe a variety of activities and programs. It is traditionally used to describe a "top-down, one-to-one relationship in which an experienced faculty member guides and the supports the career development of a new or early-career faculty member" (Sorcinelli & Yun, 2007, p. 58). More recently, *mentoring* describes a "broader, more flexible network of support, in which no single person is expected to posses the expertise required to help someone navigate the shoals of a faculty career" (Sorcinelli & Yun, 2007, p. 58).

Some feminists have critiqued traditional mentoring as a process that reproduces "sameness" based upon a male-centered faculty model, which alienates anyone whose personal and professional goals deviate from the normative model of success. A feminist approach to mentoring is based upon mutuality between those involved. Moreover, such an approach is focused on empowerment and challenging the academic status quo. Thus a successful mentoring relationship should enhance self-esteem, address gender inequities, and promote retention of women faculty (Benishek, Bieschlke, Park, & Slattery, 2004).

While there is some agreement in the literature on the traits of mentors and the range of mentoring activities, there is not a consistent definition of mentoring (Zellers, Howard, & Barcic, 2008). For the purposes of this chapter, *mentoring* is defined as an interactive process that relies on collaboration to provide information, guidance, and support to improve performance, overcome problems, enhance networks and relationships, and increase professional success.

Goals of Mentoring Programs

Just as there are varying definitions of mentoring, there are myriad goals associated with mentoring relationships. Some programs and participants focus on specific career goals (e.g., "achieving tenure and promotion"), whereas others focus on personal goals (e.g., "finding work-life balance"). We strongly support an approach that allows participants to enhance their careers on their own terms, recognizing that mentoring benefits both individuals and their institutions.

Individuals access and leverage resources in an institution through social capital. Social capital is contingent on positions in the social hierarchies as well as connections to others. The more extensive people's social ties, the more access they have to resources. Mentoring develops social ties. Yet mentoring functions differently for men and women. For example, women faculty report more barriers to gaining mentors, although mentoring is desired (Gibson, 2006). Departmental cultures also can influence whether women receive mentoring, how they experience the mentoring relationship, and whether they conceive of the possibility of academic success.

Despite the barriers, women describe support as essential for their individual success and often urge their junior colleagues to find good mentoring relationships (Gibson, 2006). This may be because mentored faculty have smoother integration into the organization, enhanced career satisfaction, higher rates of promotion, and more substantial contributions to their institution and profession (Zellers et al., 2008). In addition, mentees report greater clarity in their professional goals. According to some accounts, mentoring may be particularly important for women whose professional and personal styles might be more "relational" than those of men in their pursuit of advancement (Laursen & Rocque, 2009).

Mentors also benefit from mentoring programs. For example, mentors not only feel a sense of satisfaction that comes with helping other faculty members succeed but also are exposed to new networks, ideas, and perspectives, which can rejuvenate their own work (Zellers et al., 2008). Mentors also may gain knowledge of unconscious bias and gender organizations, which, in turn, benefits women faculty and the institution.

Mentoring programs are typically assumed to provide skill development and networks to individuals. Yet mentoring also confers institutional benefits. Most obviously, these programs have the potential to improve faculty productivity and satisfaction, which are essential to developing excellent academic institutions. Institutions benefit from a more positive work culture, more collegial relationships, increased faculty investment in institutional activities, and broader perspectives of the institution (Zellers et al., 2008). Moreover, the sharing of institutional knowledge leads to improved understandings of the working of higher education and promotes a culture more open to change and new and improved policies and practices.

Types of Mentoring Programs

There are many different types of mentoring programs, ranging from one-on-one relationships to peer mentoring to professional development workshops. Given this range, it is clear that one size does not fit all in terms of programs and that mentors and mentees should be consulted when creating a program. Programs based on faculty feedback are likely to be more successful than those created in a vacuum and announced to the faculty (Litt, Tucker, & Hermsen, 2009).

Formal mentoring programs appear to serve women better than informal programs. "The traditional school of thought views mentoring as a spontaneous human phenomenon in which any effort to formally manage the process negates the chemistry or magic believed to be inherent to these relationships" (Zellers et al., 2008, p. 562). Assuming mentoring will emerge from informal relationships presents problems for women because women feel excluded from the informal networks in their departments. Informal mentoring also makes it challenging for women to find mentors with experiences similar to their own, a trait women look for in mentors. Also, the low number of women faculty, particularly those in senior or leadership roles, results in those faculty assuming more mentoring responsibilities. Therefore, formal programs are seen as a way to offset the lack of informal mentoring for women on campus.

One-on-One Mentoring

One-on-one mentoring programs match one mentee with one mentor. The mentor typically has advanced skills or experience with the topics the mentee wants to address through the relationship. For these programs, it is essential to focus on creating good matches between mentees and mentors. Some programs use a formal matching process, soliciting input from mentees and mentors when making the match. A good match is one in which the mentee and mentor are in sync in terms of goals (see discussion above regarding mentee goals), interests, and personalities.

In terms of gender, there are aspects of one-on-one relationships that must be considered when forming mentoring partnerships. There are issues associated with cross-gender mentoring pairs (e.g., paternalistic views, differences in work-life balance concerns). Yet, given the shortage of senior women faculty and administrators, matching women and men in mentoring relationships is often a necessity.

Group Mentoring

Group mentoring provides several benefits to women. It has "the potential to provide women, non-White men, and other minorities with access to same-culture mentoring in environments in which White men represent the majority" (Zellers et al., 2007, p. 565). Also, group mentoring reflects a more feminist approach to mentoring. Finally, group mentoring can alleviate the pressure on women to provide a larger share of individual mentoring responsibilities.

Group mentoring takes many forms. For peer mentoring, similar faculty (e.g., by rank, with similar concerns) meet to discuss issues with one another. These peer mentoring sessions allow mentees to serve as resources for one another, while also providing opportunities for free-flowing discussion and networking. This sort of mentoring is particularly powerful for women who feel a strong sense of isolation, as it allows them to establish relationships with similarly isolated faculty and with faculty who have better connections. Another option is to have a group of similar faculty meet with another faculty member for guidance. This format is a hybrid of the one-on-one mentoring and peer mentoring structures. Finally, a different arrangement is for one faculty member to meet with a group of faculty for mentoring. This format is more similar to a "board of directors" style of mentoring wherein one person receives guidance from a range of individuals representing different areas of expertise (de Janusz & Sullivan, 2004). These formats are just a few examples of the types of group coaching options available in mentoring programs.

Professional Development Workshops

Mentoring can also be provided in professional development workshops, especially those formats that allow for substantial discussion among participants and with the facilitator. Workshops are particularly useful when they are on topics of broad concern to faculty, such as work-life balance, leadership, negotiation, communication, and recognition.

Other Mentoring Programs

The three types of mentoring programs profiled above (i.e., one-on-one, group, and professional development workshops) are just some of the options provided in formal mentoring programs within institutions. There also are programs offered, with various formats among institutions, by professional associations and through Web sites dedicated to mentoring.

Mentoring Differences by Faculty Rank

While much of the discussion above could apply to faculty in general, mentoring can and should specifically address the experiences of women at different faculty ranks.

For female junior faculty, mentoring often starts as an orienting and socializing experience. While mentoring is a process that should continue throughout the career cycle, mentoring untenured women as soon as they arrive on campus is essential (Gibson, 2006). Finding both formal and informal mentors can be challenging. While male faculty can and do serve as valuable mentors for junior faculty women, some women have raised concerns about the ability to discuss certain issues with male mentors (Gibson, 2006). Also, the lower numbers of women in senior faculty positions in certain disciplines and certain institution types leads to a gender gap among potential mentors (i.e., there are too few senior women to serve as mentors). This is of particular concern to women seeking advice and support from mentors concerning work-family issues. Work-family includes a variety of aspects, but for many junior women childbirth is a primary concern, as the biological and tenure clocks often coincide. Since the numbers of senior women faculty are small, group mentoring, or multiple-mentor models, can help alleviate some of the demands on mentors. Also, Peluchette and Jeanquart (2000) found that faculty with multiple mentors were the most research productive *and* emotionally supported. They also found that generally faculty who started their careers feeling productive and supported continued their careers in the same way.

Moreover, higher education as a gendered organization (Acker, 1990) may encourage a "grooming" model of mentoring. Grooming suggests that mentors should help mentees follow one particular model of a faculty member. This model is predicated on a male model of what a faculty member should be. However, women may not be interested in assimilating to such an andocentric organization, which has implications for the nature of mentoring for these faculty. Mentoring could encourage faculty to develop their own sense of a successful academic life. In addition, the singular (gendered) model of success presupposes that asking for advice or assistance is a signal scholars are too dependent on others. This idea may make it difficult for junior women to seek out mentors, since they may already face biases because they are women, further amplifying the challenges faced by women faculty. As a result, creating a culture of mentoring for all junior faculty is vital.

For female associate and full professors perhaps the largest challenge in mentoring is the lack of resources provided for their posttenure career combined with increased service responsibilities. Institutions focus on helping junior faculty achieve tenure and promotion to associate professor through protection from service, course releases, bridge funding, providing research assistants, and so on. Once tenured, most of that protection and support disappears. Although formal support wanes for both women and men, the time to promotion to full professor is often longer for women (e.g., in the humanities; see Modern Language Association, 2009), and women full professors are less likely to be in positions of academic leadership (Stout, Staiger, & Jennings, 2007).

In addition to the lack of support, other issues remain significant for senior faculty. Whether with new babies, older children, or elder care, juggling different kin expectations can create new responsibilities that can be as time consuming as those experienced in the junior years, if not more so. Since there is no promotion and advancement "clock," there are often fewer departmental or institutional mechanisms to support family-related leave. Mentors can support women through this career transition, helping them to manage the changing responsibilities while at the same time expanding their networks and helping them gain recognition for their contributions.

Efficacy of Mentoring Programs

Although mentoring programs are often designed to address specific individual and institutional needs, it is not clear that they are successful in meeting those needs. As Zellers and her colleagues (2008) note, "Recent literature is relatively consistent in identifying mentoring program success factors but is less clear in determining how one measures the 'success' of a formal mentoring program" (p. 578). Thus there is substantial attention given to best practices of mentoring programs but less focus on overall program efficacy. Measures of program success included in the literature range from objective career outcomes of program participants (e.g., promotion rate) to subjective experiences of the participants (e.g., feelings of belonging) (Zellers et al., 2008).

In addition to the limited discussion of overall program effectiveness, the literature is also limited in terms of discussing the negative components of mentoring and formal mentoring programs. Some of the challenges of mentoring programs and critiques of mentoring that are offered, however, are specific to gender. For example, there is discussion about issues related to (1) cross-gender mentoring relationships that influence the quality of the relationship; (2) the use of mentoring to socialize individuals into the dominant, gendered power structure of the organization; and (3) the view that mentoring is remedial and thus designed to correct problems or address weaknesses, which is particularly problematic for women, since unconscious gender bias already causes others to see women as less effective, less dedicated to their jobs, less productive, and less competent than men.

There is a need for more empirical research about the gender aspects of faculty mentoring and on the efficacy of mentoring programs in addressing not only feelings of isolation but also unconscious gender bias. Notwithstanding these gaps, the literature does provide some perspectives on mentoring women faculty. Despite the varying definitions of mentoring and its traditional depiction of one-on-one relationships, new models of mentoring programs are emerging to address the needs and concerns specific to women. Although programs can vary greatly in their goals and the types of mentoring offered, it is clear that mentoring programs can provide women faculty with the information, guidance, and support they need to meet their personal and professional goals while also helping institutions improve the context for all academics.

ACKNOWLEDGMENT
This chapter is based on work supported by the National Science Foundation under Grant No. 0618977. Any opinions, findings and conclusions, or recommendations expressed are those of the authors and do not necessarily reflect the views of the National Science Foundation.

REFERENCES AND FURTHER READING

Acker, J. (1990). Hierarchies, jobs, bodies: A theory of gendered organizations. *Gender and Society, 4*, 139–158.

Benishek, L., Bieschlke, K., Park, J., & Slattery, S. (2004). A multicultural feminist model of mentoring. *Journal of Multicultural Counseling and Development, 32*, 428–442.

de Janusz, S. C., & Sullivan, S. E. (2004). Multiple mentoring in academe: Developing the professional network. *Journal of Vocational Behavior, 64*(2), 263–288.

Gibson, S. K. (2006). Mentoring of women faculty: The role of organizational politics and culture. *Innovative Higher Education, 31*(1), 63–79.

Hart, J., & Litt, J. S. (2009). Mechanisms of integration and exclusion: Dissecting the gendered production of gender inequity in STEM faculty. Unpublished manuscript, University of Missouri, Columbia MO.

Kemelgor, C., & Etzkowitz, H. (2001). Overcoming isolation: Women's dilemmas in American academic science. *Minerva, 39*(2), 153–174.

Laursen, S., & Rocque, B. (2009). Faculty development for institutional change: Lessons from an ADVANCE project. *Change.* Retrieved May 28, 2009, from http://www.changemag.org/Archives/Back%20Issues/March-April%202009/full-advance-project.html

Lin, N. (1999). Social networks and status attainment. *Annual Review of Sociology, 25*, 467–487.

Litt, J. S., Tucker, S. A., & Hermsen, J. M. (2009). Mentoring tenured faculty: Rationales and programs. *Department Chair, 20*(1), 5–7.

Martin, P. Y. (2001). "Mobilizing masculinities": Women's experiences of men at work. *Organization, 8*(4), 587–618.

Modern Language Association of America. (2009). *Standing still: The associate professor survey: Report of the Committee on the Status of Women in the Profession.* New York: Author. Retrieved May 21, 2009, from the Modern Language Association Web site, http://www.mla.org/pdf/cswp_fina1042909.pdf

Peluchette, J. V. E., & Jeanquart, S. (2000). Professionals' use of different mentor sources at various career states: Implications for career success. *Journal of Social Psychology, 140*(5), 549–564.

Sorcinelli, M., & Yun, J. (2007). From mentor to mentoring networks: Mentoring in the new academy. *Change, 39*(6), 58–61.

Stout, P. A., Staiger, J., & Jennings, N. A. (2007). Affective stories: Understanding the lack of progress of women faculty. *NWSA Journal, 19*(3), 124–144.

Valian, V. (1998). *Why so slow? The advancement of women.* Cambridge, MA: MIT Press.

Wasburn, M. H. (2007). Mentoring women faculty: An instrumental case study of strategic collaboration. *Mentoring & Tutoring, 15*(1), 57–72.

Zellers, D. F., Howard, V. M., & Barcic, M. A. (2008). Faculty mentoring programs: Reenvisioning rather than reinventing the wheel. *Review of Education Research, 78*(3), 552–588.

VI
Gender and Higher Education Policies

OVERVIEW

Policy is an elusive concept. It basically refers to official statements of intentions to act on certain problems. Or, for purposes of this book, *policy* can be defined as official statements of intentions to act on problems surrounding gender and higher education. But even this definition remains obscure until the terms *official statements, intentions to act,* and *problems of gender and higher education* are clarified. This can best be accomplished by reading all of the chapters in part VI plus related chapters in other parts of this book that are mentioned in this overview. Taken together, they provide a wide-ranging, richly detailed, and sophisticated understanding of the nature of policies concerned with gender and higher education. Each chapter is designed to stand alone, however, and each provides valuable, expert information about the specific gender policies, educational policies, or policy-making groups referenced in its title.

As the chapters show, *official statements* are institutionally and organizationally formulated and enacted. Although individuals, groups, voluntary associations, and campus committees, such as those described in chapter 49 ("University Women's Commissions and Policy Discourses"), can and do influence policies, they cannot issue official statements of policy unless they hold legitimate positions of authority over educational matters. Those who do have such authority in the United States include the three branches of the federal government; state and local governments; and educational officials at all levels. The official policy statements of these authorities can take various forms, including reports, laws, executive orders, court decisions, governmental or agency regulations, faculty and student handbooks, and course syllabi.

Some of these statements—such as Title IX of the Education Amendments of 1972 which prohibits sex discrimination in all federally aided educational programs—deal explicitly with both education and gender. Title IX and its impact on college athletics are discussed in detail in chapter 48 ("Title IX and College Athletics"), which also describes the many controversies surrounding this legislation.

Two other kinds of statements should also be considered to be education and gender policies. One of these consists of general but official statements against gender discrimination that cover all institutions, not just education. Executive Order 10925, creating the Equal Employment Opportunity Commission; the Equal Pay Act of 1963, the Civil Rights Acts of 1964 and 1991; and Executive Order 11375, adding "sex" to the mandate for affirmative action in the workplace, are primary examples. These orders and laws, plus laws like Title IX that deal specifically with both education and gender, are often referred to as affirmative action policies. An overview of all of these policies, their history, and current status is presented in chapter 44 ("Affirmative Action"), which also shows the important role that U.S. courts have played in shaping presidential and congressional actions into public policy.

The second kind of statement that should be included among education and gender policies consists of official policy statements specific to education that do not deal explicitly with gender, even though they may have important gender effects. Examples of this kind of policy include the 1961 court decision known as *Dixon v. Alabama State Board of Education*, which gave students in public institutions of higher education the right to due process and had the effect of ending the power of public colleges and universities to act in loco parentis. Chapter 47 ("Students' Rights") shows how this case and subsequent court cases, in combination with affirmative action and privacy legislation, have increased students' rights—especially the rights of women students—at public and, to a lesser extent, private colleges and universities.

Defining official policy statements as *intentions to act*, rather than as actions, emphasizes the fact that policies may or may not lead to effective action. One reason they don't is the enormous complexity of policy interpretation and implementation. A law, executive order, or court decision is not an unambiguous rule that everyone understands in the same way; that can, must, and will be supported and followed by everyone; and that has clear and anticipated consequences. The ambiguity of laws is nicely illustrated by the fact that although Title IX was enacted into law in 1972, it was not until 1975 that the U.S. Congress specified how Title IX should apply to school and college athletics, and it was not until 1976 that the Department of Health, Education, and Welfare (DHEW) disseminated the guidelines and regulations for implementing the law. Nor did these guidelines clarify Title IX for all times and all people. Additional clarifications were issued by DHEW in 1979; by Congress in the form of the Civil Rights Restoration Act in 1988; and by the Office for Civil Rights of the Department of Education (DOE) in 1996.

Many of these clarifications were stimulated by court challenges that were raised to determine whether DHEW and, after 1980, DOE had correctly interpreted the law; whether all programs in an educational institution were covered by Title IX or only those that received federal funds; whether athletic programs for men and women could be "separate but equal"; whether schools should be required to pay compensation to students whose rights under Title IX had been violated; etc. Even if the judicial opinions that resulted from these challenges had been totally unambiguous, which they weren't, there still would be problems in using court decisions to define the law without congressional or executive action. One problem results from the fact that decisions made by most federal courts are limited to the jurisdiction of that court, and even Supreme Court decisions, which affect the whole country, are limited to situations that are similar to the one on which the Court based its judgments. The famous *Brown v. Board of Education of Topeka, Kansas*, decision in 1954, for example, outlawed educational segregation by race but not by gender.

The policy process does not involve only those in government whose job it is to enact, interpret, and enforce laws about gender and education. The process also involves college and university administrators, faculty, parents, and students, all of whom have their own interpretations of what gender is or should be, what gender equity means, what the intention of the law "really" is, how seriously they must take it, and what effects it will or should have on campus programs and practices. Consensus about these issues among the many actors involved is unlikely to be high, particularly when the policy in question is controversial, as gender policies inevitably are.

Although the enormous complexity of policy interpretation and implementation often prevents effective action, complexities and misunderstandings can sometimes be used as excuses for inaction that is designed to cover up deliberate resistance to policies. This resistance is particularly likely when policies are designed to shift power arrangements by increasing resources of previously underprivileged groups, thereby reducing the relative advantage of previously dominant groups. Policies of this type include those intended to promote gender and other forms of educational equality. As demonstrated in the chapters of part VI, such policies have challenged and continue to threaten the relative power and advantages of White males. These policies have already produced more opportunities for girls and women and, if fully implemented, would bring about even more extensive changes in educational structures and processes. Opposition to them has come from all levels of the political and social hierarchy, and it is not surprising that the most effective resistance has come from the very highest levels. President Reagan and his cabinet, for example, were known for their decisions to simply stop funding the enforcement of laws passed by earlier sessions of Congress with which Reagan disagreed. These included civil rights laws, such as Title IX, and it was not surprising that, by the end of Reagan's years in office, Congress felt it necessary to pass the Civil Rights Restoration Act, mentioned above, over Reagan's veto.

Official resistance to gender equity policies such as Title IX indicates a reversal of the way in which the government had previously defined the major problems of gender and education. In response to the efforts of the women's liberation movement, now called second-wave feminism, the federal government in the 1960s and 1970s had accepted and acted on the assumption that the major problem of gender and education was the same as that of race and education: namely, the problem of inequities in schooling, particularly the disadvantages girls and race-ethnic minorities were then experiencing in comparison to White boys. Under the broad umbrella of gender inequities were specific problems that no longer exist, such as the underrepresentation of women in higher education generally, and many problems that are still of concern, such as the underrepresentation of girls and women, compared to boys and men, in the STEM fields, discussed in Part III, and the sexual harassment and violence directed at girls and women throughout their years of schooling. Information about the incidence of the latter problem in higher education is presented in chapter 46 ("Sexual Harassment Policies and Practices"), which also discusses the impact of sexual harassment on college students and faculty, as well as the various policies and practices that have been developed to combat harassment and to make higher education a supportive place rather than a hostile environment for women.

For reasons of fairness and to provide equivalent role models for boys and girls, second-wave feminists also fought for policies that would foster gender parity among teachers and school officials at the elementary and secondary levels and among all academics and administrators in higher education. In particular, it was argued that more women should be recruited into academic and administrative positions and into teaching subjects such as science and mathematics in which male teachers predominated.

Like faculty members, educational administrators should be made aware of their different behaviors toward males and females and should be required to treat and evaluate students and faculty members of both sexes in an equitable manner, free of stereotypic assumptions about gender differences. Unfortunately, as chapter 45 ("Evaluation Policies for Academics") makes clear, efforts to apply the so-called merit system equally to faculty women and men are doomed to failure because of the shortcomings of the theory of neoclassical economics on which the merit system is based. Nevertheless, gender equity has been the goal of the liberal feminists who continue to call for more equitable application of merit principles. In contrast, chapter 45 offers some alternative principles to guide evaluations.

The official policies designed to eliminate gender and racial biases on campuses and in other organizational venues had barely begun to be implemented in the United States when they encountered major opposition of three types. First were the failures to enforce the official policies. As suggested in the discussion of Title IX above, this form of resistance was most successful when applied by the executive branch of the federal government. Not only was this branch of government charged with the duty of enforcing official equity policies nationwide, but it also was given the funding to do so. Once the president and cabinet members denied those funds to the Equal Employment Opportunity Commission and other enforcement agencies, many campus officials felt free to stop expending their own resources on equity and affirmative action programs, and most athletic directors continued or went back to pouring most of their resources into men's rather than women's athletics.

The second kind of opposition to gender equity policies goes beyond passive nonenforcement and nonfunding to overt and hostile attempts to eliminate these policies altogether. Several of the following chapters, especially chapters 44 and 48, identify many of the persons and groups responsible for these attempts. Court challenges have been a common tactic of those who oppose affirmative action, but efforts to change state and federal laws through either lobbying efforts or voter initiatives have gained momentum.

The third and most recent type of opposition to equity policies takes the form of a claim that such policies are no longer needed. While difficult to sustain when it comes to race-ethnicity, this argument has gained increasing purchase in debates about gender and higher education. In support of the argument, proponents point to the higher enrollment and graduation rates of women versus men, to the movement of women students and faculty into formerly male-dominated fields, to the movement of women up the faculty ranks, to the feminization of lower-level administration, and to the narrowing of the gaps between women and men in higher-level faculty and administrative positions. Although the successes wrought by affirmative action on behalf of women are impressive and widespread, all of the chapters in this section and most throughout this book make clear that some barriers to women's progress remain and these barriers are unlikely to be overcome by individual effort alone. Policies that affirm women's rights continue to be needed, and attempts to render such policies obsolete are premature.

Responsibility to continue the policy battle for equity and women's rights falls not only to officials assigned this task under laws and organizational rules but to everyone who believes in these goals and who understands that they have not yet been met. It is widely known that the major impetus for higher education policies focused on gender came from participants in the women's liberation movement that we now call second-

wave feminism. What is less widely recognized is that in institutions of higher education themselves it was often women's commissions or the status of women's committees
such as those described in chapter 49 that goaded and cajoled college and university
administrators not only into establishing the commissions themselves but also into
implementing their recommendations on behalf of women. These recommendations
ranged from increasing faculty women's salaries and hiring more women faculty to
obtaining family sick days and family leave for staff and establishing women's centers
and women's studies programs. On many campuses, women students and alumnae
also brought pressure to bear on administrators in favor of a more woman-friendly curriculum and extracurriculum, recognition of faculty contributions to women's education, and greater safety on campus. These efforts and the many successes to which they
led call attention to the fact that gender and education policies are not just a matter
of official enactment and top-down enforcement by administrators but also a matter of
policy initiatives and struggles to get them adopted that have often come from people
on the lower rungs of academe.

On many campuses today, a major policy struggle under way is the effort to gain
needed supports for faculty, especially women faculty, in their efforts to deal with childbearing and adoption, child-rearing, and work-family conflicts more generally. The
debilitating nature of these conflicts is discussed in part V, especially chapter 42. Chapter 50 ("Work-Family Conflicts and Policies") looks at these conflict from a more policy-
oriented perspective. After describing the nature and sources of work-family conflicts,
chapter 50 describes the policies that have been proposed (and on some campuses,
enacted) to reduce them.

The fact that family-friendly policies are now at the top of the policy agenda on
so many campuses is not without its ironies. Despite attempts to make these policies
gender neutral by advocating family leaves rather than maternal leaves, tenure-clock
stoppages for all primary care givers regardless of gender or marital status, and even
sometimes by treating pregnancy like any other medical condition, there are few people on campus or elsewhere who do not recognize these policies as primarily designed
to benefit women. It is women who must deal with their own pregnancies and who
have borne primary responsibility for the care of infants, children, sick partners, and
aging parents. As a result, it is women who most need, are most likely to use, and will
gain most from family-friendly policies. Thus the struggle to adopt, implement, and
fund these policies is a struggle that calls attention to women's roles as mothers and
homemakers and to women's differences from men. This is a different way of constructing women than the emphasis on gender sameness and male-female equality
central to liberal feminism, the theoretical perspective that has been the source of
most of the official gender and education policies discussed in this book.

Yet we are beginning to see an increasing number of policy analyses and initiatives
that, like family-friendly policies, are based more on differences and diversity than
on sameness, more on radical, poststructural, and Marxist or feminist reproduction
theories than on classical or feminist liberalism. Chapter 45, for example, criticizes
merit systems of evaluation because they ignore structural disadvantages and assume
that *all* faculty perform on a level playing field.

Chapter 49 shows that university women's commissions, even with the most
prowoman intentions in the world, often use discourses that construct *all* university-
affiliated women as people who are vulnerable outsiders in a male domain. Both chapters 45 and 49 call for an improved policy process, but it's not easy for Americans to

think about fairness and equity outside of the box of sameness and "objective" outcomes. As the chapters in parts II and IV on military colleges and ROTC reveal, it is even hard for people to recognize as fair those norms for physical training that are based on equivalent *effort* by men and women rather than on equivalent *performance* by all.

It is doubtful, however, that goals of gender fairness and equity in higher education (or elsewhere) can be reached unless policies aimed at achieving them recognize certain basic differences between women and men, in particular the differences surrounding reproduction. Radical feminists have long argued that pregnancy should not be treated as if it is an illness or a condition similar to something experienced by men. Nor should motherhood be treated as if it is the same as fatherhood. Some reproduction-related differences, like pregnancy, are biological, but others, like the assignment of primary child care responsibilities to women rather than men, are deeply embedded cultural and historical traditions. In either case, it is unlikely that gender equity policies that ignore these differences will be successful. Only when entrenched differences are recognized and policies are formulated accordingly can pregnant and mothering students have equal opportunities with men and other women to continue and complete their educations. And as chapter 50 makes clear, only if their employers adopt, fund, and implement policies of this kind will pregnant and mothering faculty and administrators be evaluated fairly in comparison to men and to women without children.

Those who want to give women full access to all the best that higher education has to offer must work for policies that take account not only of mothering but also of the full range of gender multiplicities and intersectionalities. Chapter 49 points out that university women's commissions often base their reports and policy recommendations on ideals of professionalism and leadership that are suitable for some professors and administrators but may disempower other university women by making them feel that their accomplishments are of little importance. This is the kind of criticism of liberal feminism's elitist tendencies that has been around since the 1960s, and it calls attention to the need for policies that are crafted to take into account the differences among university women, and the differences among university men as well. The policies and programs for LGBTQQI students, faculty, and staff discussed in part IV are important steps in this direction, as are all the chapters throughout the book that called attention to race-ethnicity and social class.

Policy initiators and policy makers concerned with gender in higher education also need to take into account the many different cultural and structural locations of women and of men in higher education that have been identified in this book. These structural locations, such as different college types, academic departments, extracurricular organizations, faculty ranks, and administrative levels, carry with them different rights, responsibilities, and powers. For many years now, most policies concerned with higher education and gender have focused primarily on moving women into more powerful positions, a strategy that takes structure for granted. Not surprisingly, the women who have most benefitted from these policies have often been the best educated, most credentialed White women. Perhaps it is time to enact more policies directed at changing the existing structure in ways that decrease power differentials or create new positions of power for those types of women and men who are currently most disadvantaged.

CHAPTER 44

Affirmative Action

JUDITH GLAZER-RAYMO

Affirmative action as public policy originated as a federal antidiscrimination measure to eliminate racial bias in the hiring and employment of minorities; sex discrimination was not considered in the original concept. At the height of the civil rights movement in the 1960s, political leaders responded to the demands of social policy activists with statutes, executive orders, and other laws that would bring about significant changes for racial and ethnic minorities. Women's rights activists viewed these changes as opportunities to issue demands for legislation that would end discriminatory policies and promote women's advancement in the workplace. In this chapter, a brief historical summary of federal statutes and presidential executive orders provides some context for understanding the origins and development of affirmative action as public policy. I then focus on two Supreme Court decisions that have defined the meaning of affirmative action in higher education admissions—*Bakke* and *Grutter*—and four statewide voter initiatives that are now redefining this policy with important ramifications for women and minorities. I conclude by assessing the outcomes of affirmative action and the new and continuing challenges that confront proponents of this policy in the second decade of the twenty-first century.

Historical Summary

Executive Order 10925, issued by President John F. Kennedy on March 6, 1961, created the Committee on Equal Employment Opportunity; this order mandated that contractors of federally funded projects "take affirmative action to ensure that hiring and employment practices are free from racial bias" (Brunner, 2008). Kennedy also signed the Equal Pay Act in 1963, enacting the nation's first federal law prohibiting "sex-based wage discrimination between men and women in the same establishment who perform jobs that require substantially equal skill, effort, and responsibility under similar working conditions." His successor, President Lyndon Johnson, oversaw the enactment of the historic Civil Rights Act of 1964, codifying the principles of the 1954 Supreme Court ruling that had ended racial segregation, *Brown v. Board of Education of Topeka* (347 U.S. 483, 1954). Two sections of that act had particular significance for women: Title VI reaffirmed equal employment opportunity guarantees and barred racial or ethnic discrimination in any programs or activities receiving federal assistance; Title VII prohibited discrimination in employment based on race, sex, religion, color, or national origin. It also created the Equal Employment Opportunity Commission (EEOC), charged with interpreting and enforcing Title VII. (The EEOC now also enforces the Equal Pay Act, the Age Discrimination in Employment Act, and the Americans with Disabilities Act.)

The following year, Johnson issued another historic document: Executive Order 11246, requiring government contractors "to take affirmative action" in hiring and employing minorities. It also established the Office of Federal Contract Compliance Programs to ensure that employers with federal contracts comply with nondiscrimination and affirmative action laws and regulation. Two years later, under pressure from women's organizations, Johnson signed Executive Order 11375, adding "sex" to the mandate for affirmative action on the utilization of women and minorities in the workplace. Seeking support from women and African American voters, in 1971 President Richard Nixon directed the Department of Labor to issue Revised Order No. 4, requiring federal contractors to develop affirmative action programs based on institutional analyses of the underutilization of minorities and women and the adoption of good-faith goals (not quotas) and timetables for correcting any deficiencies.

The 1970s were a turning point for women in higher education. In 1972, omnibus higher education legislation extended Title VII's affirmative action coverage to all full-time faculty and professional staff, "assigning investigative authority and oversight of affirmative action plans to the EEOC, including good faith efforts to employ women and minorities," and extended the Equal Pay Act to executive, professional, and administrative employees. All colleges and universities would now be required to perform workforce analyses of the utilization of women and minorities on their campuses and to adopt goals and timetables for their equitable recruitment, promotion, and compensation. In October 1972, a directive to 2,500 colleges and universities with federal contracts stated emphatically the need for good-faith efforts in fulfilling the mandates.

Perhaps the most consequential legal provision for women occurred in companion legislation with the passage of the Education Amendments of 1972, specifically its Title IX, granting legal protection to girls and women in K–12 and postsecondary education. It stated succinctly: "No person in the United States, on the basis of sex, can be excluded from participation in, be denied the benefits of, or be subjected to discrimination under any education program or activity receiving Federal financial assistance." Title IX regulations added an affirmative action provision: "In the absence of a finding of discrimination on the basis of sex in an education program or activity, a recipient may take *affirmative action* to overcome the effects of conditions which resulted in limited participation therein by persons of a particular sex."

Also of interest to women's rights activists, the Civil Rights Act of 1991, signed by President George H. W. Bush, upheld affirmative action as a remedy for "intentional employment discrimination" and "unlawful harassment in the workplace," extending compensatory damages to include sex and disabilities, in addition to race or national origin, and permitting punitive damages against offending organizations. Title II of this act created a Glass Ceiling Commission to investigate the existence and make recommendations on the elimination of artificial barriers to the advancement of women and minorities in the workplace. This commission issued position papers and a report directed mainly at employment practices in the nation's largest corporations, but there is little evidence that substantive changes resulted from its ruminations.

Implementation of affirmative action laws and regulations has been an incremental process. Affirmative action officers were appointed, commissions on the status of women established (for details, see Glazer-Raymor, 1999, pp. 168–188; 2008, pp, 26–29), and class action suits filed. A major turning point for feminists occurred with the defeat of the Equal Rights Amendment (ERA) to the U.S. Constitution in 1982. Approved by Congress and sent to the states for ratification in 1972, its proponents failed by three states to gain the necessary two-thirds majority of the states. Grassroots activism faded following the ERA's defeat, and academic women turned their attention instead to the creation of feminist scholarship in their disciplines and to the development of women's and gender studies programs.

Throughout the 1980s and 1990s, the political climate shifted to other social policy issues. The administrations of Ronald Reagan (1981–1988) and George H. W. Bush (1989–1992) led to appointments of conservative justices to the federal courts and increases in political activism among opponents of affirmative action. Alliances were formed and white papers issued by Washington, DC–based think tanks such as the Heritage Foundation and the Center for Individual Rights (CIR). Two sets of strategies evolved: (1) legal challenges to admissions policies at prestigious flagship state universities; and (2) statewide voter initiatives seeking constitutional bans on affirmative action in states' public agencies and educational institutions.

The Courts and Affirmative Action

Since the inception of affirmative action as a guiding principle in access and equity in employment, judicial decisions have had a central role in redefining and extending its meaning as public policy. Although the courts have tended to defer to educational institutions in the decision-making process, a series of Supreme Court rulings serve as important markers in establishing the parameters (and perhaps the timetable) of affirmative action policy. In this section, I review selected Supreme Court decisions that have influenced higher education policy makers, sustaining affirmative action as constitutionally viable but narrowing the standards for its viability.

The *Bakke* Decision

In 1978, the Supreme Court agreed to hear a reverse-discrimination case, *Regents of the University of California v. Bakke* (438 U.S. 265, 1978). This case was brought by a White male engineer, Allan Bakke, who had been denied admission twice to the University of California, Davis, medical school although minority candidates with lower scores had been admitted. Bakke claimed he had been discriminated against on the basis of race under the equal protection clause of the Fourteenth Amendment and Title VI of the Civil Rights Act of 1964, which states that programs receiving federal assistance cannot discriminate on the basis of race. Six separate opinions were rendered by the Supreme Court, which split 5–4 on the constitutionality of racial classification schemes indicating the divisive character of this issue. Justice Lewis Powell cast the deciding vote, and his opinion became the litmus test for devising higher education admissions policies for the next 25 years. Powell ruled out the use of fixed quotas in admissions, stating in part, "In such an admissions program, race or ethnic background may be deemed a 'plus' in an individual applicant's file," in addition to such qualities as "exceptional personal talents, unique work or service experience, leadership potential, maturity, demonstrated compassion, a history of overcoming disadvantage, ability to communicate with the poor, or other qualifications deemed important." For the next 25 years, the diversity rationale provided a template for tailoring college and university admission policies to increase minority access, establishing to some extent its use in states without a history of racial segregation.

The *Croson* and *Adarand* Decisions

Two affirmative action cases decided by the Supreme Court that underscored this uneven development were *Richmond v. J. A. Croson Co.* (488 U.S. 469, 1989) and *Adarand Constructors v. Pena* (515 U.S. 200, 1995). They held that all racial classifications imposed by state or local governmental agencies (*Croson*) and federal agencies (*Adarand*) must adhere to a standard of "strict scrutiny," the highest level of Supreme Court equal-protection review. Strict scrutiny meant that affirmative action programs would now have to be "narrowly tailored to fulfill compelling governmental interests" and that the principle of strict scrutiny would be applicable to all levels of government, "whether to state and local government through the Fourteenth Amendment or to the federal government via the due process clause of the Fifth Amendment" (Ancheta, 2008b, p. 31). Indicative of the disjointed incrementalism of public policy, gender classifications (in contrast to racial and ethnic classifications) were not part of this decision and, under the law, would continue to be subject to intermediate scrutiny.

The VMI Decision

Evidence of this can be seen in the Supreme Court ruling that overturned the single-sex status of the publicly supported Virginia Military Institute (VMI) in *United States v. Virginia* (518 U.S. 515, 1996). In her majority opinion, Justice Ruth Bader Ginsburg drew an analogy to cases of racial discrimination now held to the "strict scrutiny" standard, stating that the VMI ruling "raised the bar in cases of gender discrimination, elevating the gender standard from 'intermediate' to 'heightened intermediate scrutiny.'" The VMI ruling was handed down during the administration of President Bill Clinton, who took a centrist position on affirmative action policy. Illustrative of that position, in July 1995, following the 5–4 decision in *Adarand*, Clinton issued a memorandum calling for the elimination of any affirmative action program that "(a) creates a quota; (b) creates preferences for unqualified individuals; (c) creates reverse discrimination; or (d) continues even after its equal opportunity purposes have been achieved" (Brunner, 2008, p. 3).

The *Hopwood* Decision

Also in 1995, Cheryl Hopwood and three other White applicants to the University of Texas Law School who had been rejected for admission challenged its affirmative action program, asserting that less qualified minority students had been accepted. On March 18, 1996, in *Hopwood v. Texas* (78 F.3d 932, 5th Cir., 1996), the Court of Appeals for the Fifth Circuit (Texas, Louisiana, and Mississippi) suspended the law school's admissions policy and in its ruling sidestepped *Bakke*, stating that "educational diversity is not recognized as a compelling state interest." The Supreme Court declined to hear this case on writ of certiorari, and in 1997, race-neutral criteria went into effect in the state universities in Texas. The State of Texas created "the Top 10 Percent Plan, which gave the right to any Texas high school graduate in the top ten percent of his or her high school class to enroll in any state university" (LaNoue & Marcus, 2008, p. 19). In 2000, the State of Florida also introduced a percentage plan for college admissions as part of the governor's "One Florida" initiative, with the objective of ending affirmative action in that state (Brunner, 2008).

The *Grutter* Decision

In 2000–2001, the CIR challenged the use of race in violation of the Fourteenth Amendment and Title VI of the Civil Rights Act of 1964. Two actions contested the legality of the University of Michigan's undergraduate admissions policy (*Gratz v. Bollinger* [539 U.S. 244, 2003]) and of its law school's admission policy (*Grutter v. Bollinger* [539 U.S. 306, 2003]). As in *Hopwood*, two White women, Jennifer Gratz and Barbara Grutter, were selected as the lead plaintiffs. In agreeing to hear these cases, the Supreme Court revisited *Bakke* after a quarter century of implementation. In 2003, the Supreme Court heard both cases, rendering two split decisions in what collectively became known as the *Grutter* decision. A 5–4 vote narrowly upheld the University of Michigan Law School's affirmative action program, stating that "the Law School has a compelling interest in attaining a diverse student body" that "is at the heart of [its] proper institutional mission." In her opinion for the majority, Justice Sandra Day O'Connor reiterated the findings in *Croson* and *Adarand* that all racial classifications imposed by government must be narrowly tailored to further compelling governmental interests. In *Gratz*, the Court rejected 6–3 Michigan's undergraduate admission policy for assigning a point system in the review of minority applications and, in the view of the majority, violating the equal protection clause.

Justice O'Connor acknowledged the importance of the many amicus briefs filed in support of the University of Michigan by corporations, labor unions, professional associations, and military and academic leaders, asserting that "context matters when reviewing race-based governmental action under the Equal Protection Clause." In the context of higher education, using the language of "sunset provisions" and "termination points" for "all race-conscious admissions programs," O'Connor stated her expectation that "25 years from now, the use of racial preferences will no longer be necessary" to achieve diversity in the student body. This comment caused a great deal of speculation within the educational establishment, considering that 25 years had passed since *Bakke*, in which similar issues had been debated.

Grutter did overturn *Hopwood*, resulting in the reinstatement of affirmative action at the University of Texas. Since the 1970s, White women had made significant progress in higher education, attributable in part to the enactment of affirmative action laws and regulations. Nevertheless, gender was rarely mentioned in the arguments presented by litigants who preferred the rhetoric of color-blindness, gender neutrality, and individual rights. Legal challenges raised the stakes for compliance with affirmative action mandates and for adherence to the diversity rationale; in this contentious environment, women's voices were eclipsed by the priorities of competing identity and interest groups.

The State Voter Initiative Strategy

As *Hopwood* was being argued by the CIR in the federal courts, California's leadership initiated another line of attack against affirmative action policy. In July 1995, after a year of "political and economic conflict," the University of California (UC) Board of Regents approved two resolutions: SP-1 to end race and gender preferences in university admissions (approved 14–10) and SP-2 to do the same in employment and contracting (approved 15–10) (Pusser, 2004, p. 1). These votes signified a with-drawal of support for affirmative action in admissions, employment, and contracting for the prestigious UC system of research universities, which was "all the more remark-able since the UC Regents were the defendants in the *Bakke* decision that had codified affirmative action policies in higher education" (Pusser, p. 1).

California's Proposition 209

Two regents, Governor Pete Wilson and African American business executive Ward Connerly, led a powerful coalition in both the UC Regents' vote and in the subsequent campaign for passage of Proposition 209, a voter initiative banning affirmative action in all public agencies in California. This proposition declared: "The state shall not dis-criminate against, or grant preferential treatment to any individual or group on the basis of race, sex, color, ethnicity, or national origin in the operation of public employ-ment, public education, or public contracting." Unsuccessful attempts to block its adoption as a constitutional amendment resulted in a one-year delay, but Proposition 209 became effective in November 1997.

Washington's State Initiative I-200

In 1998, the State of Washington also conducted a successful ballot initiative, I-200, banning affirmative action as a statute rather than a constitutional amendment. With support from conservative allies in the Republican Party, Ward Connerly, a leader of the Proposition 209 campaign in California, formed the American Civil Rights Co-alition, an adversarial interest group dedicated to the termination of affirmative ac-tion state by state. Of concern to college and university presidents and chancellors who had made public commitments to access and diversity in their institutions, these voter initiatives were troubling and unsought interventions. For women and minori-ties, they threatened to become effective wedge issues, a strategy heightened by the deliberate selection of White working-class women as the lead plaintiffs in court cases in Texas and (subsequently) in Michigan, pointedly contrasting their academic quali-fications with those of minority men and women (Glazer-Raymo, 2008).

Michigan's Proposal 2

Brisk responses from the litigants immediately followed the *Grutter* decision. Hav-ing failed to accomplish their objective of a judicial ruling ending affirmative action at the federal level, Ward Connerly and his American Civil Rights Coalition vowed to re-sume the state voter initiative strategy, enlisting Jennifer Gratz, the plaintiff in *Gratz v. Bollinger* as cochair of the campaign. Intentionally selecting Michigan for this purpose, the Michigan Civil Rights Initiative (MCRI) sought passage of Proposal 2, a constitu-tional amendment banning affirmative action in the state's public agencies. This pro-posal asked voters to ban public agencies and institutions (including Michigan's public colleges and universities, community colleges, and school districts) from using affir-mative action programs that "discriminate against or grant preferential treatment to any individual or group on the basis of race, sex, color, ethnicity, or national origin in the operation of public employment, public education, or public contracting" (West-Faulcon, 2009, p. 1132, n45). The voters approved this initiative by a wide margin—58% to 42%—revitalizing the anti–affirmative action movement and presumably attract-ing resources to support ballot initiatives in other states. A coalition to defend affirma-tive action, integration, and immigration rights challenged the constitutionality of the MCRI as violating the equal protection clause and conflicting with federal statutes, specifically Title VI of the Civil Rights Act of 1964 and Title IX of the Education Amendments of 1972. Since the MCRI stipulated a disclaimer that it "does not prohibit action that must be taken to establish or maintain eligibility for any federal program, if ineligibility would result in a loss of federal funds to the state," the district court determined that it "deftly avoids conflicts and at once resolves conflicts in favor of federal law" (*Coalition to Defend Affirmative Action v. Regents of the University of Michigan*, 539 F.Supp. 2d 924 [E.D. Mich. 2008]). In fact, each of the state anti–affirmative action laws contains a provision that "the section shall be implemented 'to the maximum extent' permissible by federal law and the United States Constitution" (West-Faulcon, 2009, p. 1132, n48).

The Super Tuesday Strategy

Having gained momentum in the MCRI vote, Connerly and his adherents initiated petition campaigns for ballot initiatives in five additional states: Arizona, Colorado, Missouri, Nebraska, and Oklahoma. The strategy was to elevate this issue into the national spotlight as a means of getting out the conservative vote for what its proponents referred to as "Super Tuesday," the November 2008 presidential election. Civil rights and politically affiliated organizations vowed to oppose this strategy, revealing even further the partisan nature of this debate.

Colorado voters narrowly rejected Amendment 46 by 51%–49%. In Nebraska, where 91% of the electorate is White, Initiative 424 was approved 58%–42%, amending that state's constitution to "end race and gender preferences," banning quotas and set-aside programs based on race or sex in "public employment, public education, and public contracting." Challenges claiming irregularities in qualifying petitions in Arizona, Missouri, and Oklahoma prevented supporters of these initiatives from obtaining places on their state ballots. Nebraska officials predicted that scholarship and other financial aid programs or structured outreach programs would probably be affected, as they initiated an evaluation of existing programs and practices.

For women, the impact of ballot initiatives has been more subtle. Public institutions in states with statutory or constitutional bans on affirmative action will no longer find it necessary to submit affirmative action plans; monitor equity guidelines; provide incentives to departments, schools, and institutes for the employment of women faculty and professional staff; or consider gender, race, or ethnicity in awarding contracts. In California, statutes have been amended or repealed to remove references to race or gender, including "precollege outreach and preparation programs, scholarships and fellowships, and professional training programs" (Kaufmann, 2007, p. 5). In addition, California followed the lead of Texas and Florida in mandating "percentage plans" requiring that "students who rank in a specified top percentage of their high school graduating class be admitted to a campus in the state university system" (p. 7).

Assessing Affirmative Action's Status

Affirmative action has been in effect since the 1960s. Throughout its development, it has been subjected to continued scrutiny by its proponents and by those who oppose its continuation. Claims advocating its constitutionality have been advanced on behalf of a number of interest groups. Undoubtedly, it has played a significant role in advancing the status of women and minorities on a number of levels and across a wide array of institutions. Whether or not it has outlived its original purposes continues to be debated in the courts, and a body of case law has evolved on which future decisions will be based. *Grutter* anticipated that only 25 more years would be necessary to accomplish affirmative action in higher education institutions, meaning that by 2028, adherence to such policies could become moot.

A more conservative Supreme Court has shown little inclination to support consideration of race (and by implication, gender and ethnicity) in recent rulings. Following O'Connor's retirement, the court's conservative arguments were evident in joint rulings handed down in June 2007, opposing the consideration of race as a factor in voluntary school district integration policies in *Parents Involved in Community Schools v. Seattle School District No. 1* (551 U.S. 701, 2007) and *Meredith v. Jefferson County Board of Education*. The majority opinion for the 5–4 decision, written by Chief Justice John Roberts, stated that these two plans failed to meet "strict scrutiny, the most exacting standard of review used by the courts to evaluate policies under the Equal Protection Clause" requiring that racial classification policies be narrowly tailored to achieve a compelling government interest (Ancheta, 2008a, p. 301).

Political Dimensions

The state initiative strategy lost some momentum in November 2008 with its narrow defeat in Colorado and the inability of its proponents to mount referenda in three other states. Since California is considered a bellwether state, Proposition 209's impact is being documented in statistical data reports on enrollments in flagship institutions as well as in faculty employment and contracting awards. In her review of how state anti–affirmative action laws are arguably in violation of "disparate impact" provisions of Title VI of the Civil Rights Act of 1964, Kimberly West-Faulcon (2009) provides extensive statistical documentation of the consequences of Proposition 209 in the decade since its approval, particularly the declines in admission rates of underrepresented minorities in California's universities. Susan Kaufmann (2007) also reports declines in targeted scholarships, fellowships, and grants, in outreach programs to underrepresented minorities, in opportunities for bidding on contracts by women and minorities, and in "decreases in the hiring of women faculty and faculty of color at the University of California." (p. 7). Other states with affirmative action bans are likely to experience similar reversals.

Kimberle Crenshaw (2007) argues persuasively that Michigan, California, and Washington (and now presumably Nebraska) "constitute the new post–affirmative action frontier," effectively stating that "all identity-conscious policies constitute forms of preferential treatment and discrimination" (p. 1). She underscores the fact that the MCRI "campaign to eliminate race and gender conscious remedies has been largely underappreciated for the radical intervention that it actually represents" and rather than acquiescing to Justice O'Connor's 25-year dictum, has succeeded in terminating affirmative action policy "as a decision by the electorate" (p. 3). The retreat from affirmative action in gender policy has been ongoing since the 1980s, when the backlash against women's rights led to the defeat of the ERA. Periodic attempts to revive the campaign for its ratification in three additional states have earned only symbolic support in the U.S. Congress. By 2050, the U.S. Census Bureau predicts that people of color will be more than 50% of the population. These data suggest that more needs to be done to inhibit further erosion of support for affirmative action as "a facilitator of change, a corrector, a remover of obstacles" (Crenshaw, 2007, p. 8).

Economic Dimensions

Evidence is mounting that the economic recession in 2009 is having an impact on public and private higher education. Budget freezes, endowment losses, and reductions in revenues are affecting commitments to demographic and income diversity in admissions, employment, and capital construction. Tuition costs are spiraling higher, and in some private universities the costs of tuition, room, and board now exceed $50,000 per year. State budget reductions also affect the available resources for hiring in public colleges and universities, with implications for the availability of full-time tenure-track and professional staff positions. The uncertainty of student loan programs and the fear of job losses and of cutbacks in health and pension benefit plans have shifted priorities from access and equity to economic survival of the fittest. Whether or not the diversity rationale prevails remains to be determined, particularly now that women are being singled out as responsible for the "new gender gap," in which their participation as undergraduate and graduate students exceeds that of their male cohorts. In 2007, of 17.5 million students enrolled in higher education, women comprised 57.2% of undergraduates and 59.8% of graduate students (Glazer-Raymo, 2008, p. 3). Nevertheless, an equally troubling gender gap persists in the lower tenure rate for women full-time faculty (47% compared with 70% for their male counterparts) and in the disproportionate number of women in the growing ranks of contingent faculty. As can be seen by assessing the outcomes of the 1963 Equal Pay Act, women also continue to earn less than their male counterparts (77 cents on the dollar according to the Institute of Women's Policy Research), and in higher education male faculty enjoy a long-standing salary advantage over women faculty of from 5% to 9% across all ranks and institutional types (pp. 8–9).

The Social Policy Dimension

Cogent arguments can be made regarding the intersection of race, gender, ethnicity, and social class in organizational hierarchies. The data regarding affirmative action's history as public policy show that women have been major beneficiaries of some of its provisions. Nevertheless, the record is mixed; the academic power structure is still predominantly White and male, and although more women are being appointed to senior-level positions, gender and race disparities in faculty, administrative, and trustee leadership persist. As the nation's first African American president, Barack Obama has indicated his support for affirmative action; nonetheless he has also commented that he does not expect his two young daughters will need its protection. The diversity rationale has been the linchpin of affirmative action policy since *Bakke* in 1978, and while *Grutter* reaffirmed the importance of diversity in higher education, affirmative action bans have had the reverse effect. The reality may be that without affirmative action women would not have been able to achieve access to the status professions, but there is still plenty of evidence that the protections granted to women under Title VII, Title IX, and the rules and regulations enforcing these laws will be necessary to ensure that remaining barriers to women's progress into the highest levels of their professions, including higher education, are eradicated.

REFERENCES AND FURTHER READING

Ancheta, A. N. (2008a). A constitutional analysis of *Parents Involved in Community Schools v. Seattle School District No 1* and voluntary school integration policies. *Rutgers Race and the Law Review, 10*, pp. 297–339.

Ancheta, A. N. (2008b). *Bakke,* antidiscrimination jurisprudence, and the trajectory of affirmative action law. In P. Marin & C. L. Horn (Eds.), *Realizing Bakke's legacy: Affirmative action, equal opportunity, and access to higher education* (pp. 15–40). Sterling, VA: Stylus.

Brunner, B. (2008). Timeline of affirmative action milestones. Retrieved March 17, 2009, from http://www.infoplease.com/spot/affirmativetimeline1.html

Crenshaw, K. W. (2007). Framing affirmative action. *Michigan Law Review, 105*, 123–132. Retrieved March 17, 2009, from http://www.michiganlawreview.org/firstimpressions/vol105/crenshaw.pdf

Glazer-Raymo, J. (1999). *Shattering the myths: Women in academe.* Baltimore: Johns Hopkins University Press.

Glazer-Raymo, J. (2008). The feminist agenda: A work in progress. In J. Glazer-Raymo (Ed.), *Unfinished agendas: New and continuing gender challenges in higher education* (pp. 1–34). Baltimore: Johns Hopkins University Press.

Kaufmann, S. W. (2007). The history and impact of state initiatives to eliminate affirmative action. In M. Kaplan & A. T. Miller (Eds.), *Scholarship of multicultural teaching and learning: New directions for teaching and learning, No. 111* (pp. 3–9). San Francisco, CA: Jossey-Bass.

LaNoue, G., and Marcus, K. L. (2008). "Serious consideration" of race-neutral alternatives in higher education. *Catholic University Law Review, 57*(Summer), 991–1054.

Pusser, B. (2004). *Burning down the house: Politics, governance, and affirmative action at the University of California.* Albany: State University of New York Press.

West-Faulcon, K. (2009). The river runs dry: When Title VI trumps state anti–affirmative action laws. *University of Pennsylvania Law Review, 157*(April), 1075–1160.

CHAPTER 45

Evaluation Policies for Academics

SANDRA HARDING

Merit is often invoked as the objective basis upon which recruitment, tenure, and promotion decisions are made within the academy and outside of it. In many institutions of higher education in the United States, merit is also the major criterion that is said to be used to determine appropriate annual increases in the salaries of individual faculty members. Merit, it is argued, is the fairest way to evaluate faculty because it assures that the best and brightest will rise to the top and that evaluations will be unaffected by personal biases of evaluators in favor of or against specific individuals or certain groups of faculty. Thus it has been claimed that basing important personnel decisions on a merit system of evaluation will diminish gender inequalities in the academy, such as the poor placement of women and racial or ethnic minorities.

The concept of merit is troublesome, however, because it is grounded in a neoclassical economic theoretical perspective that limits one's understanding of, and responses to, organizational inequality. In principle, merit-based appointments ought to provide an equitable basis for recruitment, salary, and promotion decisions yielding more equitable outcomes for women because women, and other minorities, have a chance to be judged as equally meritorious. Where structural disadvantage exists for whole groups, however, the application of the merit principle is difficult if not impossible. Reliance on more socially embedded theoretical perspectives on inequality provides a way of explaining such structural disadvantage and calls into question the existence of an even playing field where all players can be judged on the same merit criterion.

These challenges to the theoretical framework of neoclassical economics suggest two alternatives to the merit systems currently used in higher education. At the very least, merit ought to be defined and measured in more inclusive ways so that women have a chance to be judged as equally meritorious with their male counterparts. A more radical response would be to eliminate merit from our lexicon and look to new ways of addressing gender inequality in universities. What may be happening instead is that market principles of neoclassical economic theory are being adopted by universities, in combination with merit, to determine who obtains favorable evaluations.

Neoclassical Economics and the Merit System

Neoclassical economics is rooted in the work of Adam Smith (1776/1937). According to this perspective, the market is competitive and business organizations operate best when allowed to interact in free and unfettered competition. Society is not as important as individuals, "atomized" individuals, who each make quite independent choices for or against some particular product or service. The idea is that such choices are made using particular criteria, like price, quality, and availability, and the organization that delivers the best mix of these "wins" the support of consumers. To achieve this, business must maximize efficiency (inputs to outputs); the most efficient organization wins under free market conditions. In this way, according to this theoretical perspective, some producers are appropriately rewarded over others.

This perspective is based on a series of simplifying assumptions like perfect information, rational action, and free entrance into and exit from the market. It also relies on an "invisible hand" to set things right. A key tenet of this perspective is that, left alone, the market itself is efficient and will deliver the best result for society.

Moreover, this theoretical perspective marries individualism and the idea of a meritocracy to explain how society works. According to this perspective, individuals act in the market as rational, independent players, and, as far as their placement in society is concerned, individuals succeed only through their own talents and hard work. Race, ethnicity, gender, and social class are irrelevant in this view of the world. Instead, an open social system is assumed, meaning that an individual's placement in society is not constrained by anything other than his or her own merits. The key idea is that anyone can move up the social hierarchy if he or she is able and willing to work hard enough.

As a theoretical perspective, neoclassical economics is optimistic, perhaps overly so. Certainly classical theorist Adam Smith expected wealth to be generated without end under free market conditions. Society as a whole would benefit from the upward spiral of economic growth delivered by the free flow of market forces as needs were met in the marketplace and efficient owners became richer and rewarded workers by sharing this wealth with them, to the greater good of all. There is an explicit judgment here that owners and workers who succeed do so through their own merits and will be rewarded in proportion to their merit.

Neoclassical economics has become the dominant paradigm promulgated by most business schools, and most of the disciplines that drive their approaches are embedded within it. It is also the dominant paradigm in the West, in general. But this is not to suggest that this is the only, or even the best, explanation of economy and society. Alternative explanations also inform our understanding.

Alternatives to Neoclassical Economics

In general, these alternative perspectives developed in reaction to neoclassical ideas. Karl Marx offered one of the earliest reactions to Smith's theory. Marx lived in England during the Industrial Revolution, and he did not see the upward spiral of wealth for all that Smith had so optimistically predicted. Instead, he witnessed the horrors and atrocities of life in the sweatshops and "satanic mills" of the time. Marx, philosopher, revolutionary, and then social scientist, set himself the task of trying to figure out what went wrong: why Smith's perfectly reasonable theory did not result in wealth for all and a universal increase in the quality of life.

In the end, Marx (1857–1858/1965, 1867/1918) argued that the system of production itself, the free market or capitalism, is the problem. It sets people against one another, as only some people have ownership and control of the means of production, while others have only their labor to sell. Under free market conditions, as producers try to become the most efficient and responsive in their industry, it is rational for owners and managers to try to extract as much from workers as possible and give them as little as possible in return. This would not work in the long term, according to Marx, as not only would workers become wretched in such a system, but they could no longer afford to buy the very products they produce. Without a mass consumer market, business itself would collapse. This is the key contradiction in capitalism that Marx thought would lead, ultimately, to the destruction of that system of production. Moreover, Marx argued that capitalist society is inherently unequal, by virtue of the existence of the power differential between these two groups: owners of capital and labor. A meritocracy cannot exist where whole groups in society, particularly labor in his view, begin at a disadvantage. To suggest that everyone has an equal chance to move up the social system and to accumulate wealth is simply a deception, according to Marx.

Later theoretical development in explanations of business, economy, and society were reactions to the ideas of both Smith and Marx. These works include those of Max Weber and the critical theorists. Although Weber (1958a, 1958b, 1988) is most famous for his analyses of formal organizations, particularly bureaucracies, and for his analysis of why market capitalism developed when and where it did, he also wrote extensively about social stratification, and much of that writing is relevant to the notion of meritocracy. Weber argued that society is layered and people reside at different locations in the social stratification system depending on their economic class (similar to Marx), social honor or status, and political power. Movement up the hierarchy is possible, but it is not simply a matter of individual effort and hard work, and most people remain roughly where they started. Placement in the hierarchy depends less on individual effort than on group memberships. In other words, people are located at positions in the social stratification system as much by their race-ethnicity and social class as by their individual merits. Occupational groups were of particular interest to Weber, who saw them as not only establishing relationships to capital and wealth (as did Marx) but also determining status (prestige) and power.

Another theme of Weber's work relevant to the concept of meritocracy was his concern that economic efficiency was becoming the major criterion against which all human behaviors were being judged. Because bureaucracy, with its routinized systems, files, and hierarchy of control, was technically the most efficient form of social organization, Weber was convinced that it would come to displace all other forms. He anticipated that increasingly business—and education—would be run by large bureaucracies because of the technical and economic efficiencies they permit. He was concerned that single-minded pursuit of this economic principle was propelling this criterion for action into center stage. He was most concerned that, ultimately, society would lose the ability to judge social action and organization on anything but purely economically rational grounds. In fact, he saw that society was coming to value the economic criterion of efficiency so highly that efficiency was becoming the only legitimate basis for action. Under these conditions, making decisions based on grounds like equity or justice cannot be understood to be rational. Weber's analysis led him to the pessimistic conclusion that humanity is trapped in an iron cage of a narrow and distorted economic rationality and there is no way out.

Like Marx and Weber, theorists of the so-called Critical School provide critical insights into the nature of social organization. Forerunners of this school, writing in the 1920s, tried to explain why, despite the atrocious conditions under which much of the Western world lived, workers did not revolt and usher in a new society as Marx had optimistically hoped. Lukacs (1923/1971) came to the view that most people were kept happy enough through access to sufficient food and entertainment not to seek to change the basis of society. Gramsci (1971) argued, similarly, that it had become conventional wisdom that economy and society are naturally unequal and competitive, that it is good and proper that some people are wealthier than others, and that this is merely their just dessert for their talent and hard work. According to these theorists, things do not change even under difficult conditions where whole groups are systematically disadvantaged, as these same people fail to see how things could be otherwise. Gramsci called this taken-for-granted, conventional wisdom that dominates our thought and action a "cultural hegemony."

Critical School theorists, like Horkheimer and Adorno (1947/1972) and, more recently, Habermas (1984), picked up on this idea of a cultural hegemony, and Habermas, in particular, set himself the task of trying to work out how this overly economic-rational view of the world might be challenged. His solution is startling. Habermas argues that what we need is more rationality, not less. To rely only on an economically rational view of the world—precisely what neoclassical economics does—is to consider valid only one of a number of equally valid bases for social action. At the moment, we judge social action and explain the nature of organization and gender inequality using only economic principles. More particularly, we judge most social action on the basis of its economic efficiency. The more economically efficient the answer to a particular problem, the better. This is what counts. But, as Weber (1968) argued, there are other bases that we can use both to judge social action and to guide notions of the appropriateness of social organization. These other bases include truth, truthfulness, and rightness (social justice). Although Habermas (1984) argues that societies need more rationality, they do not need more of the narrow and, consequently, distorted rationality that only judges action using the economic criteria that are dominant in Western thinking at the present time.

Although not explicitly concerned with merit systems, the theories of Marx, Weber, and the Critical School make it easy to understand that an objective meritocracy, where individuals are located along a social hierarchy solely on the basis of individual aptitude and action—on their own merit—is not possible. There is no level playing field. There is no objective place to stand. People are located at positions in the socio-economic hierarchy as much by their race-ethnicity, social class, and other group membership as by their individual merits. Under such conditions, to judge on "merit" is nonsense, as not all groups have a chance to be equally meritorious. To be non-White and poor is to be at a disadvantage when decisions are made based on some supposedly objective, merit-based criterion.

Feminist Theories

Although Marx, Weber, and the theorists of the Critical School moved social thought away from the emphasis on competition and individual merit of neoclassical economics, their emphasis on social stratification and group disadvantage rarely extended to women. It fell to the feminists to examine the merit system through a gender lens, but when they did so, some were more likely to reject merit systems of evaluation than others.

Most likely to embrace the merit system and the neoclassical economic theory on which it is based have been advocates of *liberal feminism*. From this perspective, women have lagged behind men economically because they have been prevented from achieving the same education, training, and job experiences that men have historically enjoyed. Once the barriers holding them back are removed and an equal opportunity structure is created, women and men will be able to compete on a level playing field, and there is every reason to assume that, over time, women will become just as meritorious as men and do just as well as men economically. In support of their theory, liberal feminists point to the advances over the past 40 years that women have made, relative to men, in educational attainments, employment status, and salaries. If women have not yet achieved the same economic level as men, argue the liberals, the remedy lies in individual efforts to increase their merit by, for example, taking more math and science courses in school, choosing college majors such as engineering that lead to more lucrative jobs, demonstrating higher levels of job commitment, and being more assertive and competitive.

Other forms of feminist theory are more likely to reject the merit system and other individualistic solutions to gender inequality. These feminists see gender as more than an individual characteristic. Instead, it is a major organizing principle in our society. To some, called *Marxist feminists* or *socialist feminists*, gender is as important or almost as important as social class in determining where people stand (rich men highest, poor women lowest) in the organizations and institutions of societies. To others, called *Black feminists* or *multicultural feminists*, gender is as important as race or ethnicity in making this same determination (White men highest, Black or minority women lowest). To still others, *radical feminists*, gender is the most enduring and most important basis for organizing societies, and the gender hierarchy as patriarchy is based on a system of male superiority and power over females.

In contrast to liberal feminism, all of these latter forms of feminism share in common the notion that the differences between men and women are not differences of individual characteristics, such as merit, but are categorical differences based on the hegemonic power of men to determine how people (including less powerful men, but especially all women) will be evaluated and treated. The playing field for men and women is far from level. Hegemonic men control the field and the ways in which the game can be played and scored. They define what is and is not meritorious; these definitions will be used to maintain their own power, and they will not give up this power willingly. An individual academic woman might find herself accorded high status if she were able to acquire all of the credentials and accomplishments regarded (by hegemonic men) as meritorious. But she would probably also be regarded as atypical, or even mannish. And if increasing numbers of women began to acquire those meritorious credentials and accomplishments, they would probably find that the criteria for merit had shifted in ways that downplayed their achievements and put increasing emphasis on the achievements of their male colleagues.

Despite their greater support for the merit system, liberal feminists would join with other feminists to argue that the poor representation of women at the seniormost levels of universities and other organizations is not simply a matter of choice. There is an argument that women choose family or family/career or career, thereby making an active decision about their career trajectory. While many women choose to commit to family, the argument runs, many successful men have made a career choice, often with the help of supporting partners who take primary responsibility for the domestic domain, subjugating their own extradomestic goals in support of this choice. However, feminist and other alternative theoretical perspectives indicate that, in many cases, such "choices" are an illusion. Social structures and expectations reinforce the position of whole groups in society. In this case, women remain primarily responsible for social reproduction roles, and this severely constrains the choices women may make. While individual women may have some choice—particularly those who, through the seniority of their position, can afford to pay for child care and domestic assistance or who do not have a family or who receive the support of a partner who elects to subjugate his/her extradomestic goals to that woman's career—general social expectations mean that most women's choices are tightly constrained. They must negotiate both social reproduction and production or work roles, taking the lead in domestic and family matters, even as they seek to measure up against supposedly objective merit-based criteria.

Alternatives to the Merit System

The difficulty of shifting away from current merit-based approaches is underscored when alternatives to the status quo are considered. One approach may be to fundamentally redefine "merit," perhaps even eliminating it from our lexicon, so that recruitment and promotion decisions can be made on other bases. This approach would require universities to reevaluate current recruitment and promotion criteria on the basis of a review of existing positions and ranks with a view to establishing what is actually required to perform these roles competently. The idea is to establish criteria for competence. This would mean challenging assumptions that, for example, the candidate with the most publications "wins" when all that is really required is evidence of some appropriate level of productivity. Moreover, continuous service may not be as important as the caliber or quality of that service. Once a pool of competent candidates has been established, recruitment, tenure, salary, and promotion decisions can be made on other, appropriate and work-related criteria. Remedying the underrepresentation of particular groups may be one such criterion. The core idea here does not involve appointing individuals who are not competent to undertake a particular role. Rather, it involves accurately specifying the role and then selecting among competent candidates on other, relevant criteria.

Another alternative is to turn this process on its head. For example, if women are underrepresented in a particular area, the approach may be to invite applications in the first round only from women (Bacchi, 1993). This latter approach constitutes the sort of direct and unapologetic affirmative action that is, in all likelihood, necessary to ensure appropriate levels of participation by women and minorities in senior positions. Whether approaches like these are best described as redefining merit or eliminating merit is open for debate. Regardless of this labeling, such approaches are sensible only if the notion of a meritocracy aligned with the dominant hegemony of economic rationalism is dismissed. The idea that fair and objective judgments can be made and rewards allocated solely in proportion to worth, or individual merit, is at best naive and at worst a deception.

Alternative perspectives encourage a broader view of social organization and inequality that permit strategies aimed at delivering equitable outcomes. By contrast, neoclassical economic assumptions and the troublesome concept of merit, as currently conceptualized and applied, work against improvement in the status of women and other minorities. Rather than an adoption of evaluation policies based on alternative perspectives, however, recent years have seen an increased reliance on neoclassical economic assumptions about not only individual merit but also the importance of market competition. In the United States in particular, but to some extent internationally, market considerations now affect academic salaries to a far greater degree than they once did. Academics in fields perceived to be in high demand are likely to be recruited at higher salary levels than those in fields that are overcrowded, and the most certain way to gain a large salary increase at one's home university is to obtain an attractive salary offer from a comparable university elsewhere. Grantsmanship also enters the picture with large salaries being demanded by and awarded to those who are able to bring large research grants to their campuses. Such market considerations have an impact on merit systems in that they promote definitions of merit that are increasingly based on financial considerations. The worth of faculty members comes increasingly to be defined by the grants and the salary offers that they can obtain. And although advocates of the merit system would argue that there is nothing stopping women academics from getting grants, it is easy to document the fact that the larger grants and salaries are likely to be found in those academic fields that are dominated by men. Once again, the evidence suggests a clash between the merit and market values of neoclassical economic theory and the goal of improving the status of women and other minorities.

REFERENCES AND FURTHER READING

Bacchi, C. (1993). The brick wall: Why so few women become senior academics. *Australian Universities Review, 36*(1), 36–41.

Gramsci, A. (1971). *Selections from prison notebooks.* London: New Left Books.

Habermas, J. (1984). *The theory of communicative action: Vol. 1: Reason and the rationalisation of society* (T. McCarthy, Trans.). Boston: Beacon Press.

Harding, S. L. (2002). The troublesome concept of merit. In G. Howie & A. Tauchert (Eds.), *Gender, teaching, and research in higher education: Challenges for the 21st century* (pp. 248–260). Burlington, VT: Ashgate.

Horkheimer, M., & Adorno, T. (1972). *Dialectic of enlightenment.* New York: Herder. (Original work published 1947)

Lukacs, G. (1971). *History and class consciousness.* London: Merlin Books. (Original work published 1923)

Marx, K. (1965). *Pre-capitalist economic formations.* New York: International Publishers. (Original work published 1857–1858)

Marx, K. (1918). *Capital.* London: William Glaisher. (Original work published 1867)

Smith, A. (1937). *The wealth of nations.* New York: Random House. (Original work published 1776)

Weber, M. (1958a). *From Max Weber* (H. H. Gerth & C. Wright Mills, Eds.). New York: Oxford University Press.

Weber, M. (1958b). *The Protestant ethic and the spirit of capitalism* (T. Parsons, Trans.). New York: Scribner.

Weber, M. (1968). *Economy and society* (Vols. 1–2) (G. Roth & C. Wittich, Eds.). Berkeley: University of California Press.

CHAPTER 46

Sexual Harassment Policies and Practices

MICHELE PALUDI

Margaret Mead once argued that a new taboo is needed in educational institutions, one that requires faculty and administrators to make new norms based on caring as a central and active value. The need to make sexual harassment a taboo continues in colleges, as evidenced by the high incidence of harassment reported by students and faculty. An adequate policy for getting to the heart of harassment problems in the educational system requires not only a clear definition of harassment, policy statements against the behavior, and the enactment of laws to enforce such policies; it also requires the efforts and support of the campus administration at all levels and continual training of all individuals, as well as procedures that *encourage*, not just allow, complaints. Success requires action to prevent and remedy sexual harassment as well as to train the entire campus on legal and psychological aspects of sexual harassment. With both a policy and the procedure for carrying it out in place, not only will the campus be on stronger footing in any legal action, it will find that, human relations–wise, the entire campus benefits from an environment of cooperation and respect.

Definitions and Legislation

Sexual harassment is defined legally as unwelcome sexual advances, requests for sexual favors, and other verbal or physical conduct of a sexual nature when any one of three criteria is met: (1) submission to such conduct is made either explicitly or implicitly a term or condition of the individual's employment or academic standing; (2) submission to or rejection of such conduct by an individual is used as the basis for employment or academic decisions affecting the individual; or (3) such conduct has the purpose or effect of unreasonably interfering with an individual's work or learning performance or creating an intimidating, hostile, or offensive work or learning environment.

As these criteria indicate, there are two types of sexual harassment situations that are described by this legal definition: quid pro quo sexual harassment and hostile-environment sexual harassment. *Quid pro quo sexual harassment* involves an individual with organizational power who either expressly or implicitly ties an academic or employment decision or action to the response of an individual to unwelcome sexual advances. Examples include a professor promising to reward a student for complying with sexual requests (e.g., promising a better grade or a letter of recommendation for graduate school or employment) or threatening a student for failing to comply with sexual requests (e.g., threatening to not give the student the grade earned). *Hostile-environment sexual harassment* occurs when an atmosphere or climate is created by staff or peers in the classroom or other area on campus (e.g., biology lab) that makes it difficult if not impossible for a student to study and learn or for a professor to work because the atmosphere is perceived by the individual to be intimidating, offensive, or hostile.

This legal definition identifies the conditions under which a behavior may constitute sexual harassment but generally does not give specific examples. Empirical definitions of sexual harassment are derived from men's and women's descriptions of their experiences of sexual harassment. Examples include *unwanted sexual attention*, which includes verbal and nonverbal unsolicited comments, gestures, or attempts at physical contact (e.g., a professor attempts to touch or kiss a student or repeatedly asks the student for dates), and *sexual coercion*, which includes job-related or education-related threats or benefits that are contingent upon compliance with sexual demands (e.g., a department chairperson promising to vote to promote a faculty member only if she is sexually cooperative or threatening not to support her promotion if she refuses the sexual demands) (Fitzgerald, Gelfand, & Drasgow, 1995). *Contrapower sexual harassment* involves a subordinate sexually harassing a superior, such as a male student in a women's studies course sexually harassing the female professor (DeSouza & Fansler, 2003).

Because U.S. courts have recognized that sexual harassment is a form of sex discrimination, it is covered by antidiscrimination legislation such as Title IX of the 1972 Education Amendments, which states: "No person in the United States shall, on the basis of sex, be excluded from participation in, or denied the benefits of, or be subjected to discrimination under any educational program or activity receiving federal assistance." For employees, sexual harassment is covered under Title VII of the 1964 Civil Rights Act. Title VII specifically states that it is an unlawful employment practice for an employer to "fail or refuse to hire or to discharge any individual" or to discriminate in the "compensation, terms, conditions or privileges of employment" on the basis of an employee's or prospective employee's race, color, religion, sex, or national origin.

In order to promote effective and equitable resolution of sexual harassment complaints, it is necessary for educational institutions to have an explicit antiharassment policy that complies with the provisions of Title IX and Title VII. The Office for Civil Rights (OCR) and the Equal Employment Opportunity Commission (EEOC) have emphasized that educational institutions have an affirmative duty to issue a strong policy prohibiting sexual harassment on which students and employees are trained, conduct a full investigation of all complaints of sexual harassment, and administer appropriate disciplinary action toward individuals who have violated the campus's policy statement. Title IX covers employees and students in organizations with educational programs and activities who are recipients of federal financial assistance. Title VII protects employees from sexual harassment in organizations even if they are not recipients of federal financial assistance.

Campuses, similar to workplaces, should exercise "reasonable care" to ensure a sexual harassment–free and retaliatory-free environment for students, faculty, and staff. This "reasonable care," derived from the Supreme Court ruling in *Faragher v. Boca Raton* (524 U.S. 775, 1988), includes the following at a minimum: establishment and dissemination of an effective anti–sexual harassment policy, an effective investigatory procedure, and the provision of training in sexual harassment in general and in the campus's policy and procedures specifically.

Incidence of Sexual Harassment of College Students and Professors

In the first large-scale study with college students, Fitzgerald and her colleagues (1988) investigated approximately 2,000 women at two major state universities. Half of the women respondents reported experiencing some form of sexually harassing behavior. The majority of these women reported experiencing sexist comments by faculty. The next-largest category of sexually harassing behavior was seductive behavior, including being invited for drinks and a back rub by faculty, being brushed up against by their professors, and having their professors show up uninvited at their hotel rooms during out-of-town academic conferences.

More recently, Hill and Silva (2005) reported findings from their nationally representative survey of 2,036 undergraduate students (1,096 women and 940 men) commissioned by the American Association of University Women Educational Foundation. Their research found that approximately one-third of the students reported physical harassment, including being touched, grabbed, or forced to do something sexual. Hill and Silva (2005) also reported that men and women are equally likely to experience sexual harassment, although in different ways. For example, women were more likely to report experiencing sexual comments and gestures, while men reported experiencing homophobic comments. Furthermore, Hill and Silva found that men are more likely than women to harass.

The incidence of sexual harassment appears to be higher for certain student groups than for others. Graduate students, for example, report more harassment than undergraduates. Other groups reporting higher-than-average experiences of sexual harassment include women of color, especially those with "token" status; students in small colleges or small academic departments, where the number of faculty available to students is quite small; women students in male-populated fields, such as engineering; students who are economically disadvantaged and work part time or full time while attending classes; lesbian women, who may be harassed as an expression of homophobia; physically or emotionally disabled students; women students who work in dormitories as resident assistants; women who have been sexually abused; inexperienced, unassertive, or socially isolated women, who may appear more vulnerable and appealing to those who would intimidate or coerce them into an exploitive relationship (Woods & Buchanan, 2008).

Peer sexual harassment is also common among college students. The main form of peer sexual harassment experienced by female students involves lewd or sexual comments from classmates. Peer sexual harassment of Chinese women by male college students occurs twice as frequently as faculty-student sexual harassment (Tang, Yik, Cheung, Choi, & Au, 1996).

In addition, the incidence of contrapower sexual harassment in colleges and universities is widespread, especially for women professors who are sexually harassed by male students. Grauerholz (1989) noted that approximately 48% of women professors in her research reported contrapower sexual harassment from male students that ranged from sexist comments to sexual assault. Similar findings have been reported by women professors regarding sexual harassment from colleagues and superiors in the academy at several universities.

Fitzgerald and Omerod (1993) and Ilies, Hauserman, Schwochau, and Stibal (2003) concluded that it is reasonable to estimate that one out of every two women will be harassed at some point during her academic or working life, a proportion indicating that sexual harassment is the most widespread of all forms of sexual victimization. This estimate has been supported by countless numbers of empirical research studies, using various methodologies to collect incidence data in various parts of the world, including Australia, Brazil, China, Italy, Israel, Pakistan, Puerto Rico, Sweden, and Turkey (see chapter by DeSouza & Solberg in Paludi & Paludi, 2003).

Incidence versus Reporting

Research with college students and faculty indicates that despite the fact they reported experiencing behaviors that fit the legal definition of sexual harassment, they did not label their experiences as such. Individuals' responses to sexual harassment can be classified into two categories: internally and externally focused strategies (Fitzgerald, Gold, & Brock, 1990). Internal strategies represent attempts to manage the personal emotions and cognitions associated with the behaviors individuals experienced. The following classification system for internally focused strategies has been posited:

- Detachment: Individual minimizes the situation.
- Denial: Individual denies behaviors and attempts to forget them.
- Relabeling: Individual reappraises the situation as less threatening and offers excuses for the other's behavior.
- Illusory control: Individual attempts to take responsibility for the harassment.
- Endurance: Individual endures the behavior because she either does not believe help is available or fears retaliation.

Externally focused strategies focus on the harassing situation itself, including reporting the behavior to the individual or organization charged with investigating complaints of sexual harassment. These strategies include

- Avoidance: Individual attempts to avoid the situation by staying away from the harasser.
- Assertion/confrontation: Individual refuses sexual or social offers or verbally confronts the harasser.
- Seeking institutional relief: Individual reports the incident and files a complaint.
- Social support: Individual seeks support of others to validate their perceptions of the behaviors.
- Appeasement: Individual attempts to evade the harasser without confrontation and attempts to placate the harasser.

Internal strategies represent the most common response overall. Most victims do not tell the harasser to stop. Typically, harassers are more powerful—physically and organizationally—than victims, and sometimes the harasser's intentions are unclear. The first or first few harassing events are often ignored by victims, especially when they are experiencing hostile-environment sexual harassment. Research has also indicated that victims of sexual harassment fear retaliation should they confront the perceived harasser (Fitzgerald, Gold, & Brock, 1990; Hill & Silva, 2005). Students and faculty who are high in performance self-esteem and who hold egalitarian gender-role attitudes are more likely to report incidents of sexual harassment than those who are low in self-esteem and hold traditional gender-role attitudes.

Research suggests that men who are likely to engage in sexual harassment with women or men are those who emphasize male social and sexual dominance and who demonstrate insensitivity to others' perspectives. It is possible for women to sexually harass men. However, the behavior is unlikely because of women's relative lack of formal power and the socialization that stigmatizes sexually assertive women. Most of men's experiences of sexual harassment are instigated by other men. Men may be reluctant to disclose this information because of homophobic concerns still prevalent in U.S. society. Furthermore, the sexual harassment of lesbian, gay, and bisexual students and faculty is widespread.

Impact of Sexual Harassment on College Students and Faculty

Research with college students and faculty has documented the high cost of sexual harassment to individuals. Research indicates that there are career-related, psychological, and physiological outcomes of sexual harassment. For example, women students and faculty have reported decreased morale and decreased satisfaction with their career goals. Furthermore, women students and faculty have reported feelings of helplessness and powerlessness over their academic and work career, strong fear reactions, and decreased motivation. Individuals have also reported headaches, sleep disturbances, eating disorders, and gastrointestinal disorders as common physical responses to sexual harassment (see chapter by Lundberg-Love & Marmion in Paludi & Paludi, 2003; Willness, Steel, & Lee, 2007).

Policies and Procedures Opposing Sexual Harassment

Although the existence of laws and policies opposing sexual harassment are no guarantee that it will be reported, there is considerable evidence indicating that students are less likely to experience professor/student sexual harassment and peer sexual harassment if they attend colleges that have a policy prohibiting sexual harassment that is widely disseminated and enforced. A policy alone will not prevent sexual harassment, but it is the foundation on which to build a strategy of prevention.

According to the OCR and the EEOC, a comprehensive approach for eliminating harassment includes developing and disseminating strong written policies specifically prohibiting harassment. These policies should take into account the significant legal factors relevant to determining whether unlawful harassment has occurred and should be tailored to the needs of the particular campus. Components of an effective policy statement that have been identified in the sexual harassment literature as accomplishing the OCR's and the EEOC's recommendations include a statement of the purpose of the policy, legal definition of harassment, behavioral examples of harassment, a statement concerning the impact of sexual harassment, a statement of the campus's responsibility in responding to complaints, a statement concerning confidentiality of complaint procedures, a statement concerning sanctions available, a statement prohibiting retaliation and establishing sanctions for retaliation, a statement concerning false complaints, and identification of individual(s) responsible for hearing complaints, including their backgrounds, telephone numbers, and office locations.

A campus that carries out each of these measures will be doing what is necessary to establish a program that will meet the needs of students and faculty and stand the ultimate test in courts, if that should ever become necessary. A court test of a policy probably will never occur if the policy is designed to meet the standard it would be tested for: its ability to prevent and handle problems before they get out of control and before the level of legal liability is reached.

Once the policy is in place, it must be clearly and regularly communicated. The OCR and EEOC recommend that the policy statement be reissued each year by the senior administrator and displayed prominently throughout the campus. In addition, the policy statement should be published in student, faculty, and employee handbooks. The responsibility for communicating the policy statement must be made a part of the job description of anyone on the campus with authority to enforce the policy. It is also recommended that students and employees sign a statement that they have been given a copy of the policy and that they understand their rights and responsibilities (Paludi & Paludi, 2003).

Research also suggests that procedures for investigating complaints of sexual harassment must take into account the psychological issues involved in the victimization process. These issues include individuals' feelings of powerlessness and isolation, changes in their social network patterns, and wishes to gain control over their personal and career development. Research has indicated that the experience of participating in an investigative process can be as emotionally and physically stressful as the sexual harassment itself. Therefore, it is important not only to build in several support systems but also to help complainants and alleged perpetrators cope with the process of the complaint procedure. Counselors may work with the investigator for this purpose.

Although each college typically establishes its own complaint procedure that fits its unique needs, the OCR and the EEOC have identified three guidelines that apply to investigations of sexual harassment. One of these is that the campus has an obligation to make the environment free of sexual harassment and free of the fear of being retaliated against for filing a complaint of sexual harassment. A second guideline is that individuals should be informed that the campus will not ignore any complaint of sexual harassment. And the third guideline is that investigations of sexual harassment complaints will be completed promptly.

In addition to these guidelines, the OCR and EEOC offer several "practical considerations" for establishing effective grievance procedures. These considerations take the form of questions that should be answered in the document describing the procedures for grievances: How many levels will the procedure have, and what will be the time frame for each level? Who may file complaints on behalf of the injured party? Should an evidentiary hearing be part of the process? Should administrators review the investigator's decision in all instances or only when the decision is appealed?

Training and Other Educational Programs

Campuses are required to take reasonable steps to prevent and end sexual harassment of their students as well as their faculty, administrators, and employees, including facilitating training programs on sexual harassment awareness. Training programs involve more than a recitation of individuals' rights and responsibilities and what the law and campus policy requires. Training also requires dealing with individuals' assumptions and misconceptions about power as well as the anxieties about the training itself. Stereotypes about women, men, sex, and power often remain unchallenged unless individuals participate in effective trainer-guided intervention programs (Paludi & Paludi, 2003).

In addition, training programs on sexual harassment must provide all individuals with a clear understanding of their rights and responsibilities with respect to sexual harassment. Training must also enable individuals to distinguish between behavior that is sexual harassment and behavior that is not sexual harassment. Training programs also provide individuals with information concerning the policy statement against sexual harassment and investigatory procedures set up by the campus. Finally, training programs have as their goal to help empower individuals to use their campus's procedures for resolving complaints.

Research indicates that training increases the tendency to perceive and report sexual harassment and makes individuals more sensitive to incidents of sexual harassment especially when case analyses are used. Training also assists sexual harassment contact persons with listening and helping skills and confidence, and it increases knowledge and changes attitudes (see Paludi & Paludi, 2003).

To supplement the training programs in sexual harassment awareness, additional educational programs have been recommended in the literature. Among these are including information on sexual harassment in new student and employee orientation materials; facilitating a "sexual harassment awareness week" and scheduling programs that include lectures, guided video discussions, and plays; reporting annually on sexual harassment; encouraging faculty to incorporate discussions of sexual harassment in their classes; and encouraging students to start an organization with the purpose of preventing sexual harassment.

Interventions created to combat sexual harassment should involve students in making policies intended to alter the campus climate with regard to these forms of victimization in order to promote positive interaction between students; this will serve to promote inclusion and empowerment for students. Interventions should also send a clear message to teachers, administrators, parents, and all campus staff as well as students that sexual harassment will not be tolerated. It is only when the entire campus is informed that successful change can occur.

Remedies through the Office for Civil Rights

The OCR enforces Title IX of the Education Amendments of 1972. When its investigations indicate a violation of Title IX has occurred, the OCR provides an opportunity to the campus to voluntarily correct the problem. If the campus refuses to correct the situation, the OCR initiates enforcement action.

Remedies sought by the OCR for harassment include corrective and preventive actions to stop the harassment and minimize the chance of its recurrence. This can take the form of counseling or discipline of the harasser and training for students and staff on how to recognize harassment and what to do if they are harassed or observe harassment. Other corrective and preventive actions include psychological or other counseling; compensatory education to make up for any time lost from the educational program as a result of the harassment; adjustment of any grades affected by the harassment or the opportunity to repeat a course without additional cost. If the complainant was forced to leave the academic program because of the harassment, reimbursement for any costs that occurred as a result or an opportunity to reenroll should be provided.

Remedies through the Equal Employment Opportunity Commission

The EEOC enforces Title VII, which prohibits sexual harassment in employment as well as other forms of employment discrimination based on sex, race, religion, age, national origin, pregnancy, and disability. Title VII also prohibits retaliation against individuals who complain of sexual harassment or other forms of prohibited job discrimination. Employees who have exhausted their organization's sexual harassment procedures may file a charge with the EEOC before they are allowed to go to court for themselves. For a private lawsuit to be filed under Title VII, the EEOC must issue a "right to sue" letter to the employee who made the complaint. The employee has 90 days in which to file a private lawsuit in federal or state court. Remedies available for sexual harassment in employment include corrective actions to end the sexual harassment and minimize its reoccurrence, reinstatement into a job lost or denied as a consequence of sexual harassment, and compensatory and punitive damages.

Exercising "reasonable care" on college campuses for students and faculty will ensure all individuals can reach their full potential. No longer should sexual harassment be a hidden gender-equity problem on campuses.

REFERENCES AND FURTHER READING

DeSouza, E., & Fansler, A. G. (2003). Contrapower sexual harassment: A survey of students and faculty members. *Sex Roles, 48*, 529–542.

Fitzgerald, L., Gelfand, M., & Drasgow, F. (1995). Measuring sexual harassment: Theoretical and psychometric advances. *Basic and Applied Social Psychology, 17*, 425–427.

Fitzgerald, L., Gold, Y., & Brock, K. (1990). Responses to victimization: Validation of an objective policy. *Journal of College Student Personnel, 27*, 34–39.

Fitzgerald, L., & Omerod, A. (1993). Sexual harassment in academia and the workplace. In F. Denmark & M. Paludi (Eds.), *Psychology of women: A handbook of issues and theories* (pp. 553–582). Westport, CT: Greenwood.

Fitzgerald, L., Shullman, S., Bailey, N., Richards, M., Swecker, J., & Gold, Y. (1988). The incidence and dimensions of sexual harassment in academia and the workplace. *Journal of Vocational Behavior, 32*, 152–175.

Grauerholz, E. (1989). Sexual harassment of women professors by students: Exploring the dynamics of power, authority and gender in a university setting. *Sex Roles, 21*, 789–801.

Hill, C., & Silva, E. (2005). *Drawing the line: Sexual harassment on campus.* Washington, DC: American Association of University Women Educational Foundation.

Ilies, R., Hauserman, N., Schwochau, S., & Stibal, J. (2003). Reported incidence rates of work-related sexual harassment in the United States: Using meta-analysis to explain reported rate disparities. *Personnel Psychology, 56*, 607–63.

Paludi, M., & Paludi, C. (Eds.). (2003). *Academic and workplace sexual harassment: A handbook of cultural, social science, management, and legal perspectives.* Westport, CT: Praeger.

Tang, C., Yik, M., Cheung, F., Choi, P., & Au, K. (1996). Sexual harassment of Chinese college students. *Archives of Sexual Behavior, 25*, 201–215.

Willness, C., Steel, P., & Lee, K. (2007). A meta-analysis of the antecedents and consequences of workplace sexual harassment. *Personnel Psychology, 60*, 127–162.

Woods, K., & Buchanan, N. (2008). Sexual harassment in the workplace. In M. Paludi (Ed.), *The psychology of women at work: Challenges and solutions for our female workforce* (pp. 119–132). Westport, CT: Praeger.

CHAPTER 47

Students' Rights

JOHN WESLEY LOWERY

When one considers the topic of students' rights in U.S. higher education, it is important to recognize that the rights of college students at public institutions of higher education are fundamentally different from those of students attending private institutions of higher education. As the Supreme Court noted in *Tinker v. Des Moines Independent Community School District* (393 U.S. 503, 1969), "It can hardly be argued that either students or teachers [at public institutions] shed their constitutional rights . . . at the schoolhouse gate." However, private institutions of higher education have no legal obligation to afford students the rights guaranteed by the Constitution. The courts will instead demand that private institutions afford students the rights promised in various institutional documents including the student handbook. Beyond constitutional rights, public institutions will also be expected to afford students those additional rights set forth in institutional documents. The courts have treated those documents as the foundation of a contractual relationship between institutions and students. Another source of students' rights in higher education is federal legislation, which typically places obligations on all institutions that are recipients of federal financial assistance.

From Unfettered Authority of Colleges to Due Process for Students

For the first 300 years of the history of American higher education, colleges and universities were assumed to have basically unfettered authority over their students. In 1913, the Kentucky Supreme Court formally articulated the legal theory that would continue to hold sway for another 50 years. In *Gott v. Berea* (156 Ky. 376), the court ruled that college and university authorities stand in loco parentis, or literally in place of the parents, "concerning the physical and moral welfare, and mental training of the pupils." Therefore, the court observed, "we are unable to see why to that end they may not make any rule or regulation for the government, or betterment of their pupils that a parent could for the same purpose." The court placed few limits on the rules that colleges and universities could establish beyond those rules that were "unlawful or against public policy."

For almost five decades following this decision, the courts rejected virtually every attempt to challenge an institution's authority to discipline students in the manner the institutions considered appropriate. During this period, most institutions enforced rules that severely limited student behavior and often placed greater restrictions on women students than men. Common parietal rules during this period included curfews for women students—although less commonly for men—prohibitions against smoking in public, dress codes, and restrictions on riding in cars.

The turning point in the history of students' rights occurred in 1961 with the decision from the U.S. Court of Appeals for the Fifth Circuit in *Dixon v. Alabama State Board of Education* (294 F. 29 2d 150). This case arose as a result of disciplinary action taken by the State of Alabama against a group of students at Alabama State College for Negroes in Montgomery (now Alabama State University). Six students filed suit against the Alabama State Board of Education after they were removed from the institution for their involvement in civil rights protests. The students participated in demonstrations at a segregated lunch counter in the basement of the Montgomery County courthouse as well as in a demonstration on the steps of the state capitol. The day following the demonstration at the state capitol, which involved more than 600 students, Governor John Patterson convened a meeting of the State Board of Education to consider disciplinary action against 29 students whom the governor considered the "ring leaders" of these civil rights protests. The students did not attend the hearing. In fact, the students were not even informed that the board was meeting. The State Board of Education voted, based largely upon information from the governor, to expel nine students and to place the other students facing charges on probation. The students were notified of this action in writing by Dr. Trenholm, president of Alabama State, in letters dated March 4 or March 5.

Represented by Montgomery attorney Fred Gray, who had also defended Rosa Parks, six of the expelled students brought suit in federal court against the Alabama State Board of Education claiming that their constitutional rights had been violated. After the district court ruled for the state, the students appealed the decision to the U.S. Court of Appeals for the Fifth Circuit with the support of the Legal Defense and Education Fund of the National Association for the Advancement of Colored People, including Thurgood Marshall and Jack Greenberg. The appeals court ruled that when the state takes action against an individual, the Constitution demands that due process be afforded, and due process requires notice and some opportunity for a hearing before students at a tax-supported college are expelled for misconduct. "In the disciplining of college students," the court noted, "there are no considerations of immediate danger to the public, or of peril to the national security, which should prevent the Board from exercising at least the fundamental principles of fairness by giving the accused students notice of the charges and an opportunity to be heard in their own defense."

It is difficult to overestimate the significance of the court's ruling in *Dixon*. Although the U.S. Supreme Court did not hear the *Dixon* case, it later described the ruling as a landmark decision in the area of student discipline in public higher education. While the *Dixon* case is now more than 40 years old, the court's decision remains the foundational statement of due process for students in public higher education. The rights to notice of the charges and an opportunity for a hearing at which to present a defense against the charges remain at the heart of students' due process rights in public higher education. More broadly, *Dixon* represents the federal courts' first application of the U.S. Constitution to the legal relationship between public institutions of higher education and students. This decision is grounded in the Fourteenth Amendment's due process clause.

In the years that followed, numerous courts have reinforced and expanded the rights articulated in *Dixon*, and despite some difference in legal interpretations, courts usually have accorded students the right to hear the evidence against them and to present oral testimony or, at minimum, written statements from witnesses. There are, however, issues upon which various courts have reached different conclusions. Most notable is the right to counsel in student disciplinary proceedings. In *Gabrilowitz v. Newman* (582 F.2d 100 [1st Cir., 1978]), the Court of Appeals for the First Circuit concluded that, because the student was facing criminal charges resulting from the same set of facts, he was entitled to receive advice of his attorney during the disciplinary hearing. However, the U.S. Court of Appeals for the Seventh Circuit in *Osteen v. Henley*, (13 F.3d 221, 223 [7th Cir., 1993]) concluded that the right to counsel was potentially even more limited.

In addition to the specific requirements of due process, the Supreme Court also requires that institutions avoid rules that are unconstitutionally vague. In *Connally v. General Construction Company*, (269 U.S. 385, 1926) the Court noted that rules must be clear and specific enough that people are not forced to guess at their meaning and are not likely to differ as to its application. Because the Supreme Court has not directly addressed the rights enjoyed by college and university students at public institutions, the specific requirements of due process are not as clearly established as other areas of constitutional law, and requirements may vary somewhat from one jurisdiction to another.

It is important to recognize, however, that not all disputes between a student and the institution demand the same level of due process. The Supreme Court has clearly distinguished between the process required when students are dismissed for academic reasons and the process required when they are dismissed for reasons related to their conduct. In *Board of Curators of the University of Missouri v. Horowitz* (435 U.S. 78, 1978), the Supreme Court ruled that students facing suspension or dismissal for academic performance are only entitled to be informed of the faculty's dissatisfaction with their academic performance and that the faculty's decision was careful and deliberate.

Other Constitutional Rights

In addition to their rights under the due process clause of the Fourteenth Amendment, students at public colleges and universities in the United States are also granted rights under the First and Fourth Amendments and the Fourteenth Amendment's equal protection clause. While private institutions are not required to afford students constitutional rights, private institutions are also expected to ensure the rights described within the institution's contracts with students. Under the First Amendment, students at public colleges and universities are entitled to freedom of speech, freedom of the press, freedom of assembly, and freedom of association.

Many of the cases through which these rights were established took place during the student protest era of the 1960s and early 1970s. In *Healy v. James* (408 U.S. 169, 1972), for example, the Court noted that state colleges and universities are not immune from the sweep of the First Amendment and that First Amendment protections should apply with no less force on college campuses than in the community at large. The courts have granted the greatest protections under the First Amendment to expression that takes place in a public forum. While institutions cannot base restrictions on the content of student expression, institutions can place reasonable time, manner, and place restrictions on student protests. More recently, the courts have invalidated institutional policies that prohibit or punish racist or intolerant speech. In the late 1980s and early 1990s, the courts overturned hate speech codes at a number of institutions including the University of Michigan, the University of Wisconsin, and George Mason University. Hate speech codes are institutional policies that were developed to prohibit racist or intolerant speech, particularly when directed at women or students of color. In more recent cases, the courts have invalidated such policies even if they have never been enforced because, by their very existence, they have a "chilling effect" on freedom of speech. These cases, along with Supreme Court precedents, make it clear that public institutions are extremely limited in their ability to lawfully restrict student speech. However, institutions can constitutionally punish conduct or behavior, as distinct from speech, that is motivated by bias or intolerance.

While the First Amendment does not include a clear right of association, the Supreme Court has noted that it is implicit in rights articulated in the First Amendment. In the previously cited *Healy v. James* decision, the Supreme Court ruled that Central Connecticut State College had violated the First Amendment in refusing to recognize a student chapter of Students for Democratic Society because the college's president disagreed with the group's beliefs. However, the court did identify three forms of behavior for which an institution could justifiably refuse to recognize a student organization: refusing to follow reasonable campus rules, interrupting classes, and engaging in illegal activity or inciting imminent lawless action. In subsequent cases, the court's decision was extended to require that institutions that grant student groups access to institutional funding and the right to reserve rooms on campus must also do so without regard to the content of the group's beliefs. In *Rosenberger v. Rector and Board of Visitors of the University of Virginia* (515 U.S. 819, 1995), the Supreme Court ruled the institutions making funding decisions for student organizations must be viewpoint neutral in the decision-making process. The Supreme Court returned to the issue of funding student organizations when students at the University of Wisconsin challenged, as violating the First Amendment, the use of their mandatory student activity fees to support student organizations with which they disagreed. In *Board of Regents v. Southworth* (529 U.S. 217, 2000), the Court ruled that mandatory student activity fees did not violate the First Amendment as long as the fees were distributed in a manner that was viewpoint neutral.

Students at public institutions also enjoy protections under the Fourth Amendment against unreasonable searches and seizures. However, these rights are generally less extensive than the rights enjoyed by citizens in their homes. The primary exceptions that limit students' Fourth Amendment rights are institutions' ability to conduct certain administrative searches. For example, institutions can legally engage in searches for the purpose of protecting health and safety. Violations of institutional policy discovered in the course of these searches can be used as the basis for disciplinary action or even criminal prosecution. The courts have also often allowed warrantless searches when the purpose of the search is the enforcement of institutional policies rather than criminal prosecution. Other exceptions include searches conducted with consent, items in plain view, and searches conducted in emergency circumstances. Like other areas of constitutional law, these restrictions do not apply to administrations at private institutions unless they are acting at the direction of the police.

Rights against Discrimination

College and university students also enjoy two types of protection against illegal discrimination. First, students at public colleges and universities are protected in part by the Fourteenth Amendment's equal protection clause. The Fourteenth Amendment served as the foundation for the Supreme Court's decisions in both *Brown v. Board of Education* (347 U.S. 483, 1954) which made racial segregation in public schools illegal, and *United States v. Virginia* (518 U.S. 515, 1996), which ordered that women be admitted to Virginia Military Institute and The Citadel in South Carolina.

Second, students at colleges and universities that receive federal financial assistance are also protected under a number of pieces of federal civil rights legislation. All public universities and almost all private universities are recipients of federal financial assistance that includes not only direct federal aid to the institution but also any federal financial aid received by students. There are only a small number of private institutions of higher education that do not allow their students to participate in any federal financial aid programs. These institutions include Christendom College (Virginia), Bob Jones University (South Carolina), Grove City College (Pennsylvania), Hillsdale College (Michigan), Patrick Henry College (Virginia), and Principia College (Illinois). At institutions that receive any federal funds, the relevant aspects of federal civil rights legislation to students include

*   Title VI of the Civil Rights Act of 1964 (42 U.S.C. §2000d): "No person in the United States shall, on the ground of race, color, or national origin, be excluded from participation in, be denied the benefits of, or be subjected to discrimination under any program or activity receiving Federal financial assistance."
*   Title IX of the Education Amendments of 1972 (20 U.S.C. §1681 et seq.): "No person in the United States shall, on the basis of sex, be excluded from participation in, be denied the benefits of, or be subjected to discrimination under any program or activity receiving Federal financial assistance."
*   Section 504 of the Rehabilitation Act of 1973 (29 U.S.C. §794): "No otherwise qualified individual with a disability in the United States . . . shall, solely by reason of her or his disability, be excluded from the participation in, be denied the benefits of, or be subjected to discrimination under any program or activity receiving Federal financial assistance."

Two issues related to federal civil rights legislation require additional consideration: affirmative action and sexual harassment. The Supreme Court addressed the legality of affirmative action programs in higher education in its 2003 decisions in *Gratz v. Bollinger* (539 U.S. 244) and *Grutter v. Bollinger* (539 U.S. 306). Justice O'Connor, writing the majority opinion in *Grutter*, reinforced Justice Powell's decision 25 years earlier in *Regents of University of California v. Bakke* (438 U.S. 265, 1978). Justice O'Connor ruled that the equal protection clause of the Fourteenth Amendment does not prohibit the narrowly tailored use of race in admissions decisions to further a compelling interest in obtaining the educational benefits that flow from a diverse student body. However, the legal issues related to affirmative action were not resolved fully by the *Gratz* and *Grutter* decisions, as the court has yet to articulate the parameters of a narrowly tailored admissions process.

The issues addressed by Title IX of the Education Amendments of 1972 reach far beyond admissions. The courts have extended protections against sexual harassment in the business context to the educational field. The Supreme Court has addressed sexual harassment in education twice in recent years, in *Gebser v. Lago Independent School District* (524 U.S. 274, 1998) and *Davis v. Monroe County School District* (526 U.S. 629, 1999). Although both of these cases involve K–12 settings, the rulings also apply to colleges and universities. Under the *Gebser* ruling, colleges and universities can be held liable for monetary damages for sexual harassment as a violation of Title IX. In order to succeed in a sexual harassment claim against an institution for sexual harassment by an employee, a student must demonstrate that actual notice was made to officials who have authority to act and who responded with deliberate indifference. The *Davis* ruling extended *Gebser* to address student-on-student sexual harassment that creates a hostile environment in violation of Title IX. The student must demonstrate that the sexual harassment was so severe, pervasive, and objectively offensive that it can be said to deprive the victims of access to the educational opportunities or benefits provided by the school. In addition to lawsuits, students can also file complaints with the U.S. Department of Education for violations of Title IX. While the student cannot receive monetary damages, the Department of Education has the authority to order institutions to make policy changes.

Student Privacy Rights

The Family Educational Rights and Privacy Act (FERPA) was passed by Congress as part of the Education Amendments of 1974. FERPA was an amendment to this larger piece of legislation sponsored by Senator James Buckley. FERPA conferred upon parents, or eligible students, three primary rights related to their education records: (1) the right to inspect, review, and access education records; (2) the right to challenge the content of education records; and (3) the right to consent to the disclosure of education records. In the context of higher education, it is important to understand that, by definition, the rights under FERPA rest with the students regardless of their age. This differs significantly from the K–12 context, where the rights rest with parents until the student turns 18.

The records covered under FERPA comprise what the regulations refer to as "education records," which are defined very broadly to include all records that are directly related to a student and maintained by an educational agency or institution or by a party acting for the agency or institution. There are various documents or records that are excluded from the definition of education records, including sole-possession records, records of law enforcement units, employment records (except when a student is employed as a result of his or her student status), certain medical records, and alumni records. Students may request access to their education records, and institutions are required to provide a student access to, but not generally copies of, the education records in question.

FERPA also generally limits the release of students' education records without written consent. However, Congress has enacted numerous exceptions to the written consent requirement since FERPA's passage. These exceptions include

* release to school officials with legitimate educational interest,
* release to the parents of dependent student as defined by the Internal Revenue Service,

- release in a health or safety emergency,
- release of directory information,
- release of the final results of a disciplinary proceeding to the victim of alleged crime of violence,
- release of information regarding violations of institutional alcohol policies or laws to the parents of student under the age of 21, and
- release of information regarding the final results of a disciplinary proceeding to the public when a student is found responsible for a violation that corresponds to the definitions of a crime of violence.

Congress has continued to expand the exceptions to the written consent requirement in recent years. The Supreme Court also ruled that students could not use 42 U.S.C. §1983 as the grounds for a civil lawsuit against an institution for violations of FERPA. The court placed the responsibility for enforcement of FERPA's mandates on the U.S. Department of Education (*Gonzaga University v. Doe*, 536 U.S. 273, 2002).

Gender and Students' Rights

There are inherent gender issues in any discussion of students' rights in U.S. higher education. In the era of in loco parentis, male and female students were subjected to disciplinary systems that severely constrained behavior and addressed violations of those rules in a manner that did not place a high value on students' rights. However, it should be acknowledged that female students faced even greater restrictions on their behavior. The decisions in *Dixon* and other student discipline cases of the 1960s and 1970s, coupled with broader societal changes, helped to remake student life on campus. While all students enjoyed new freedoms on campus, the past restrictions may have made this change more profound for female students.

In more recent years, rules governing students' rights have dealt with gender in two distinct ways. Some have explicitly focused on gender, especially on abolishing gender and other forms of discrimination. Others purport to be gender-neutral rules concerning the rights of all students, regardless of gender. Not surprisingly, the former are often more controversial than the latter. Title IX, for example, has evoked controversies on campuses, in courts, and in Congress ever since its original passage. Even today, it is viewed by some as having failed to achieve equity for women in school sports, while others see it as a law that has imposed reverse discrimination on men by eliminating some of their athletic scholarships and teams in favor of giving undeserved support to women.

Even when rules are gender neutral in formulation, they may not be so in perception or in practice. Rules of conduct, for example, may make no mention of gender but may raise important gender issues in those student discipline cases that arise from the roles of male students as perpetrators and female students as victims of violations of the code of student conduct. While not the most commonly adjudicated cases on campus by far, cases that involve students as both victims and perpetrators create a tension between the rights of the accused student and the rights of the accusing student. Under the laws and court cases summarized here, public institutions of higher education have a legal obligation to address the rights of both groups, whatever their gender composition, when dealing with student disciplinary cases, including student-on-student sexual harassment and physical assaults.

REFERENCES AND FURTHER READING

Dannells, M. (1997). *From discipline to development: Rethinking student conduct in higher education* (ASHE-ERIC Higher Education Report, 25(2) San Francisco: Jossey-Bass.

Downs, D. A. (2005). *Restoring free speech and liberty on campus.* Oakland, CA: Independent Institute.

Kaplin, W. A., & Lee, B. A. (2006). *The law of higher education* (4th ed., Vols. 1–2). San Francisco: Jossey-Bass.

Lancaster, J. (Ed.). (2006). *Exercising power with wisdom: The bridge from legal to developmental practice.* Asheville, NC: College Administration Publications.

Paterson, B. G., & Kibler, W. L. (Eds.). (1998). *The administration of campus discipline: Student, organizational, and community issues.* Asheville, NC: College Administration Publications.

Silverglate, H. A., & Gewolb, J. (2003). *FIRE's guide to due process and fair procedure on campus.* Philadelphia: Foundation for Individual Rights in Education.

Stoner, E. N., II, & Lowery, J. W. (2004). Navigating past the "spirit of insubordination": A twenty-first century model student conduct code with a model hearing script. *Journal of College and University Law, 31*(1), 1–77.

CHAPTER 48

Title IX and College Athletics

CYNTHIA FABRIZIO PELAK

The number of girls and women participating in school-based sports in the United States has skyrocketed over the past three decades (National Women's Law Center, 2002). In 1971, girls made up 7.4% of all high school athletes and 15% of all college athletes. By 2000, females made up 42% of the athletes at both the high school and college levels. In 2000 there were three million girls participating in high school sports and 150,000 participating in college sports. The single factor that best explains the 800% increase in girls' participation in high school sports and the 400% increase in women's participation in intercollegiate sports is Title IX of the Education Amendments of 1972, the equal opportunity law that prohibits sex discrimination in education. Despite the progress toward gender equity in school-based sports, women still do not enjoy equal or equitable opportunities in athletics relative to men. Although there is widespread public support for Title IX and gender equity in sports, separate is still not equal in the context of gender-based school sports (McDonagh & Pappano, 2007). This chapter focuses on Title IX and college athletics and discusses the emergence and development of the legislation, enforcement of the law, legal and political challenges to the law, and the current status of gender equity in collegiate athletics.

Emergence and Development of Title IX Legislation

Building on the successes of the civil rights movement, in the late 1960s and early 1970s women's rights activists worked on drafting legislation to address discrimination against women by the state. Using the language of the Civil Rights Act of 1964 as a model, advocates for gender equity in education developed the Title IX legislation that prohibits sex discrimination within U.S. educational institutions that receive federal monies. In 1972, Congresswoman Edith Green and Senator Birch Bayh introduced the Title IX legislation to Congress, and without much fanfare or controversy Congress passed the bill into law that same year (Suggs, 2005). On June 23, 1972, President Nixon signed Title IX of the Education Amendments into law. In part, the statute reads: "No person in the United States shall, on the basis of sex, be excluded from participation in, be denied the benefits of, or be subjected to discrimination under any educational program or activity receiving Federal financial assistance" (20 U.S.C. §1681 et seq.).

Although Title IX applies to all types of educational programs and addresses issues such as sexual harassment, the law quickly became associated with gender equity in athletics. There was little discussion during the congressional debates of how the anti-discrimination bill was to affect athletics. However, in 1974 when the Department of Health, Education, and Welfare (DHEW) was drafting the Title IX regulations on college sports, debate over how Title IX was going to affect men's college sports emerged. Senator John Tower of Texas proposed an amendment to Title IX that would exempt revenue-producing sports (e.g., men's football) from being tabulated when determining Title IX compliance. Congress rejected the Tower amendment. Senator Jacob Javits of New York then put forth an alternative amendment that cleared the way for the passage of Title IX regulations for interscholastic and intercollegiate athletics. In 1975, Congress passed and President Ford signed into law the Title IX regulations.

The Title IX regulations established the following: (1) sex discrimination is prohibited in any interscholastic, intercollegiate, club, or intramural athletics; (2) separate sports teams for women and men are allowed; however, if a sport is not offered to one group, the excluded sex must be allowed to try out for the team, provided that the sport is not a contact sport; and (3) equal opportunity in treatment and participation must be provided, but equal expenditures for female and male teams are not mandatory. Elementary schools were given one year to comply with the regulations, and secondary and postsecondary educational institutions were given three years to comply. Currently, the Office for Civil Rights (OCR) of the U.S. Department of Education oversees Title IX compliance, complaints, and violations. The OCR assesses Title IX compliance on a programwide basis. The ultimate penalty for noncompliance is the withdrawal of federal financial assistance to the school. To date, no institution has lost federal funding because of noncompliance.

In 1979, Title IX regulations were further developed and adopted by DHEW through the document "Policy Interpretation: Title IX and Intercollegiate Athletics." This document set out the basis of the three-prong test of Title IX compliance. In 1996, these compliance requirements were clarified by the OCR through the document "Clarification of Intercollegiate Athletic Policy Guidance: The Three-Part Test." According to these policy statements, gender equity in athletics at federally funded institutions is based on three dimensions: *participation, scholarships*, and *other benefits of sports programming*. Postsecondary institutions have the flexibility of complying with Title IX in the area of *participation* through any one of three prongs, which has become known as the "three-prong test." The first way for a school to comply with the participation requirements is to demonstrate that female and male students participate in intercollegiate athletic programs in numbers substantially proportionate to their undergraduate enrollment at the school. This prong is known as "substantial proportionality" and requires a comparison of the ratio of female and male athletic opportunities to female and male full-time undergraduates. The second way a school can meet the participation requirement of Title IX is to show a history and continuing practice of program expansion for the underrepresented sex. The third way an institution can comply is to demonstrate that the athletic department is fully and effectively accommodating the interests and abilities of the underrepresented sex.

The OCR has no preferred way for an institution to comply with the Title IX participation regulation; however, the first prong of substantial proportionality has been deemed a "safe harbor" for Title IX compliance (U.S. Department of Education, 2003). During the 1990s, courts repeatedly ruled that if an institution complies with the substantial proportionality prong, the institution is essentially immune from lawsuits and complaints filed with the civil rights office (Suggs, 2003). Courts have cited figures of plus or minus 3 to 5 percentage points as the criterion to determine if a school is offering proportional opportunities in athletics to women and men students. According to a report by the U.S. General Accounting Office (2000), from 1994 through 1998 the OCR reviewed 74 cases involving Title IX participation complaints. Of these, 28.4% (21 schools) were held in compliance under prong one, and the rest of the schools complied under prongs two or three.

In the area of *scholarships*, Title IX requires that an educational institution ensure that the athletic scholarships given to female and male student athletes are awarded in about the same ratio as the percentages of females and males participating in the athletic program. If women make up 42% of the athletes at the institution, then women must receive about 42% of the scholarship money awarded by the athletic department. In the area of *other benefits of sports programming*, an institution must ensure that female and male athletes are treated equitably in the provision of (1) equipment and supplies, (2) scheduling of games and practice times, (3) travel and daily allowance, (4) access to tutoring, (5) coaching, (6) locker rooms, (7) practice and competitive facilities, (8) medical and training facilities and services, (9) publicity and promotions, (10) recruitment of student athletes, and (11) support services.

Enforcement, Controversies, and Legal Challenges

Since the law was enacted, there have been many rounds of heated debates and controversies about how Title IX should be enforced (Staurowsky 1995, 1996; Suggs 2005). As DHEW was drafting the Title IX regulations for athletics in the late 1970s, the National Collegiate Athletic Association (NCAA), which offered few programs for women, rallied against the regulations. Conservative members of Congress, such as Senator Jesse Helms, also attempted to curtail Title IX enforcement. Nonetheless, the positive effect of the legislation on girls' and women's participation in athletics was immediate. Even before the three-year grace period had ended in 1978, women's sports grew by leaps and bounds. Schools hired women coaches, added girls and women's teams, and converted existing girls and women's intramural programs into varsity programs. These changes reflected and contributed to the growing women's movement in the United States during the period.

However, by the early 1980s, progress toward equal opportunities for girls and women in sports slowed. The election of President Reagan in 1980 ushered in a backlash against civil rights laws and gains. In 1980, the U.S. Department of Education was established, and the OCR began to oversee Title IX enforcement. In the mid-1980s, control of women's intercollegiate sports shifted from the women-dominated Association for Intercollegiate Athletics for Women to the male-dominated NCAA, even though the takeover was contested in a legal battle that reached the U.S. Supreme Court. Another major setback to gender equity for women in sports came with the 1984 court case of *Grove City College v. Bell* (465 U.S. 555). In this pivotal case, the Reagan administration argued that only entities within universities and colleges that were direct recipients of federal funding should have to comply with Title IX regulations. The U.S. Supreme Court agreed, and the ruling effectively exempted athletic departments from Title IX regulations. The power of Title IX in the area of athletics was immediately lost.

As the political and economic climate started to change in the late 1980s, Congress passed, over a veto by President Reagan, the Civil Rights Restoration Act of 1987, which restored the original power of Title IX in the area of athletics. The Civil Rights Restoration Act, which passed in 1988, explicitly states that all programs supported and offered by a school that receives federal monies must comply with Title IX regulations. Athletic departments were no longer exempt from Title IX. As an indication of the political and legal shift regarding Title IX, in 1990 the OCR issued a Title IX Investigation Manual for schools to evaluate Title IX compliance. With Title IX restored, female athletes seized the moment to use the courts to force schools to comply with Title IX. In 1992, one of the most critical Title IX legal cases—*Franklin v. Gwinnett County Public Schools* (503 U.S. 60)—came before the U.S. Supreme Court. The case involved a sexual harassment allegation from a high school student against a coach at her school. The student claimed that school officials knew about the harassment but did nothing to stop it. In its decision, the Supreme Court ruled for the first time that plaintiffs suing institutions for Title IX violations could seek monetary damages for alleged intentional sex discrimination. The decision immediately gave Title IX greater enforcement leverage. Schools that had ignored the law were put on notice that financial penalties could be awarded by the courts in Title IX cases. Schools took note, and athletes began demanding their rights.

In situations where schools dropped women's sport teams to deal with financial shortfalls, women athletes were particularly successful in their strategy of turning to the courts. Simply threatening a lawsuit was also an effective strategy to gain more opportunities and resources for women in athletics (Pelak, 2002). One of the most important victories for Title IX during the 1990s was the class action suit against Brown University, which was filed in 1992 and made its way to the Supreme Court in 1997. The case was initiated when Brown University dropped its varsity programs for women's gymnastics and women's volleyball. The Brown case revolved around the appropriateness of the three-prong test and particularly the issue of proportional representation of women students in athletics. Lawyers for the administration of Brown University claimed that men are more interested in sports, and thus it is appropriate to offer male students more opportunities to participate in sports. The Supreme Court disagreed and refused to hear the Brown case. Thus the ruling by the Court of Appeals for the First Circuit that Brown University was in violation of all prongs of the three-part test for equitable participation held, and Brown University was forced to reinstate women's gymnastics and women's volleyball (Haworth 1997).

This was a symbolically important Title IX case because Brown University spent millions of dollars fighting the case and had a large number of groups and institutions sign onto the case on their behalf, including 60 colleges and universities, numerous collegiate coaching associations, various athletic and higher-education associations, USA Wrestling, USA Swimming, United States Water Polo, 48 U.S. representatives, and 1 U.S. senator. In the end, the administration of Brown University and the many other opponents of Title IX lost the case. The court decision made it clear that a stereotype purporting that women do not want to participate in competitive athletics was not a valid argument at the turn of the twenty-first century.

The 1990s also brought new legislation that encouraged heightened enforcement of Title IX. In 1994, Congress passed the Equity in Athletics Disclosure Act (EADA), which requires coeducational institutions that participate in any federal student financial aid program and have an intercollegiate athletics program to disclose, with annual reports, certain information regarding their athletics program. The EADA requires athletic departments to report roster sizes of women's and men's teams, as well as budgets for recruiting, scholarships, coaches' salaries, and other expenses. These data are proving to be useful in highlighting the persistent gender inequalities in collegiate athletics and are helping in local efforts to make educational institutions more accountable. The National Women's Law Center, which has litigated many of the Title IX lawsuits and lobbied heavily in favor of strong enforcement of Title IX, has used the EADA data to file complaints against institutions with gender imbalances in their athletic departments. During the 1990s, the Clinton administration also demonstrated strong support for enforcement of Title IX. Norma Cantj, assistant secretary of education for civil rights in 1993, fought hard to improve enforcement of Title IX. And as mentioned above, in 1996 the OCR issued a policy guidance document that clarified in a strict fashion the regulations around equity in participation opportunities known as the three-prong test.

With the successes of Title IX court cases and enforcement during the 1990s, a backlash emerged. Opponents of Title IX claimed that gender equity regulations were hurting men's sports and that the way the courts were applying the three-prong test was an illegal quota. Male wrestlers and their supporters, who believed that Title IX was the reason men's wrestling programs and other nonrevenue men's sports were being cut, led the organized opposition. In 2002, the National Wrestling Coaches Association and other Title IX opponents filed a federal lawsuit against the U.S. Department of Education challenging Title IX regulations and policies. After the Supreme Court refused to hear the case, the wrestlers and others opposing Title IX regulations found a sympathetic ear in the Bush administration. In 2002, Roderick Paige, the new secretary of the Department of Education under President George W. Bush, convened a Commission on Opportunity in Athletics supposedly to see that athletic opportunities were expanding and to ensure fairness to all athletes. The women's rights community was outraged by the commission, which they saw as an effort to undermine Title IX enforcement and reinforce male dominance in athletics. The commission proceedings were fraught with tensions, and observers claimed that concern for the inequities that women still face in athletics was rarely expressed during commission debates (Suggs, 2005). At the end of the six months of proceedings, the commission submitted a report with recommendations to the U.S. secretary of education. Commission members and women's sports advocates Donna de Varona and Julie Foudy strongly disagreed with the report and submitted a minority report urging the Department of Education to step up enforcement of Title IX. One year later, the OCR issued a clarification of Title IX policy that did nothing to change existing Title IX regulations but emphasized the flexibility of the three-prong test and discouraged schools from dropping sport teams to comply with Title IX regulations.

According to the empirical evidence, blaming the decline in men's wrestling teams on Title IX regulations is simply unfounded (National Women's Law Center, 2002). Between 1984 and 1988, a time when Title IX did not apply to athletic departments because of the *Grove City* court case, the number of NCAA men's wrestling programs dropped by 55, from 289 to 234. Since Title IX was not in effect during these years, it is hard to blame the loss of the wrestling programs on the gender equity legislation. In contrast, between 1988 and 2000, a 12-year period in which Title IX applied to athletic departments, about the same number of men's wrestling programs were dropped. If Title IX were responsible for the loss of wrestling programs, one would expect that far more programs would have been dropped during the 12-year period than the earlier 4-year period. Moreover, during this same period, women's gymnastics also suffered a substantial decline. Between 1982 and 2000, 90 of the 179 women's gymnastics programs belonging to the NCAA were dropped, representing almost of half of the existing programs.

Schools decide to drop teams for a number of reasons, including decreasing interest in specific sports, liability considerations, and to preserve the budgetary dominance of masculine flagship sports such as football. Despite the claims by the wrestling coaches and other opponents of Title IX, the evidence shows that between 1981 and 1998 the overall number of men's sport teams increased and men's intercollegiate athletic participation rose (National Women's Law Center, 2002). While certain men's sports like wrestling have declined, other men's sports, such as baseball, crew, football, lacrosse, and soccer, have increased. Likewise, some women's sports, such as field hockey and gymnastics, have also declined, while other women's sports, such as ice hockey and soccer, have increased. Blaming the loss of wrestling or other non-revenue-producing men's sports on Title IX is misplaced and contributes to an unhelpful antagonism between women's and men's sports programs (Staurowsky, 1996). Rather than focusing on bloated expenditures or inflated participation rates in high-profile men's football and basketball programs, opponents of Title IX scapegoat women athletes, who still are not enjoying equitable opportunities in school-based sports.

The most recent U.S. Supreme Court decision on Title IX with implications for collegiate athletics is *Jackson v. Birmingham Board of Education* (544 U.S. 167, 2005). The case involved an Alabama high school teacher/coach who complained to his supervisor about the inferior facilities and resources for girl's sports at the school and was fired shortly thereafter. In its 2005 decision the Supreme Court established that individuals including coaches and teachers have a right to action under Title IX if they are retaliated against for protesting discrimination. Moreover, the court ruled that men who are retaliated against for speaking up against sex discrimination in education are protected by Title IX just as women would be protected. This decision demonstrates the increasing institutionalization of the prohibition of sex discrimination in education.

The most recent change to Title IX compliance regulations was issued by the Department of Education in 2005, without any notice or opportunity for public comment. In the document *Additional Clarification of Intercollegiate Athletics Policy Guidance: Three-Part Test—Part Three* the Department of Education created a new method for colleges to demonstrate compliance with the third prong of the three-part test (U.S. Department of Education, 2005). The "clarification" allows schools to use a single e-mail survey of students to measure the level of interests in athletics among students and potentially show that they are fully meeting the interests and abilities of the underrepresented sex in athletics. This regulation keeps alive that false assumption that females are not as interested in participating in sports as males are. Advocates of gender equity in education denounced the new regulations as creating a loophole in the Title IX law (National Coalition for Women and Girls in Education, 2008). In reality, the new regulation may backfire on those seeking to prevent equitable opportunities for women in college athletics. First, the relatively small number of opportunities in collegiate athletics in comparison with high school athletics suggests that there will always be more women college students interested in and skilled to participate in college athletics than are actually accommodated. Second, the high level of public support and consciousness about gender equity in sports, at least in principle, suggests that women's sports advocates on campus could effectively organize a campaign to encourage women students to "vote" their collective interests regardless of whether they are personally interested in participating in sports. Therefore, an institution's desire to comply with Title IX with an e-mail survey of students may actually create a political opportunity for women's rights advocates to educate the campus community about the existing gender inequalities at the school. Nonetheless, the new regulation is a reminder that gender equity in collegiate sports is still highly contested.

States have also acted, or failed to act, to encourage gender equity in school-based sports. At least 20 states have either passed legislation or have legislation pending that aims to improve gender equity in athletics. Some states have also provided monetary assistance in the form of tuition waivers for women athletes and monies for building facilities for women's athletics. In 1998, the National Organization for Women negotiated an out-of-court settlement with the California State University system to comply with a state law that mandates immediate progress toward gender equity in athletics. There are, however, important differences in Title IX compliance across states. Research has found that schools in southern states offer far fewer opportunities to girls and women in athletics than schools in other states. Educational institutions in the Northeast and Far West offer the most equitable athletic opportunities for girls and women in the country. A recent study showed that 70% of colleges and universities in the southern United States use some form of sexist naming for their women's sports teams and that the use of a sexist name is associated with a lower level of opportunities for women in athletics at southern institutions (Pelak, 2008). Unlike state athletic associations at the high school level, the powerful NCAA has not been held subject to Title IX or constitutional protections. In *National Collegiate Athletic Association v. Smith* (525 U.S. 459, 1999), the Supreme Court held that the NCAA was not subject to Title IX simply because it receives funding from federally funded schools. The decision, however, left open other legal arguments for coverage of national athletic associations in Title IX compliance. Although the NCAA is not currently subject to Title IX legislation, the association has an interest in encouraging member institutions to comply. In 1991, NCAA published a landmark gender equity study of its member institutions. The study found that women were only 30% of athletes on varsity teams, and women's teams of NCAA member schools received only 23% of operating budgets of athletic departments.

Although the NCAA has not been a perennial supporter of Title IX, during the 1990s its actions and statements regarding Title IX became more positive. In response to the findings of its 1991 gender equity study, the NCAA established a Gender Equity Task Force in 1993. The task force has continued to track gender inequalities at NCAA member schools and has served as an important body to encourage institutional progress on gender equity. One process that the NCAA put into place during the 1990s is the requirement that Division I schools conduct a self-study of gender equity as part of their cyclical certification process. In addition, when the OCR issued a clarification that allowed Internet surveys of undergraduate students to be used as a way to measure women's interest in athletics, the NCAA came out opposing the new policy interpretations because it believed, along with women's rights advocates, that the Internet surveys could be used to dismantle progress on Title IX compliance. These and other efforts have encouraged NCAA member schools to take positive steps toward increasing women's opportunities in athletics, and they demonstrate the NCAA's growing commitment to Title IX.

The Current Status of Title IX in Collegiate Athletics

Despite the progress made toward achieving gender equity in education-based sports, girls and women are still not receiving their fair share of opportunities, resources, and attention. As the percentage of women students increases at college campuses across the country, athletic departments are finding it increasingly difficult to reach gender proportionality in athletics. In 2003–4, just over 57% of college students were women, but only 42% of college athletes were women. The percentage of female college student-athletes appears to be stalled around 42%. Monetary expenditures, such as scholarships and team budgets, remain woefully unequal, even after the turn of the twenty-first century. Although gender relations in athletics have changed dramatically over the past 35 years, much work remains to be done. The resistance to fully dismantling male dominance in athletics and the persistence of stereotypes that purport that boys and men deserve more opportunities in athletics than girls and women suggest that equitable opportunities in education are secured only through continued struggle.

REFERENCES AND FURTHER READING

Haworth, K. (1997). Colleges, sporting groups, and lawmakers back Brown University's appeal in Title IX case. *Chronicle of Higher Education, 43*(30), A36.

McDonagh, E. and L. Pappano. (2007). *Playing with the boys: Why separate is not equal in sports.* New York: Oxford University Press.

National Coalition for Women and Girls in Education. (2008). *Title IX at 35: Beyond the headlines.* Washington, DC: Author. Retrieved from http://www.ncwge.org/pubs-reports.html

National Women's Law Center. (2002). *The battle for gender equity in athletics: Title IX at thirty.* Washington, DC: Author. Retrieved from http://www.nwlc.org

Pelak, C. F. (2002). Women's collective identity formation in sports: A case study from women's ice hockey. *Gender and Society, 16*(1), 93–114.

Pelak, C. F. (2008). The relationship between sexist naming practices and athletic opportunities at colleges and universities in the southern United States. *Sociology of Education, 81*, 189–210.

Staurowsky, E. (1995). Examining the roots of a gendered division of labor in intercollegiate athletics: Insights into the gender equity debate. *Journal of Sport and Social Issues, 19*(1), 28–44.

Staurowsky, E. (1996). Blaming the victim: Resistance in the battle over gender equity in intercollegiate athletics. *Journal of Sport and Social Issues, 20*(2), 194–210.

Suggs, W. (2003). A federal commission wrestles with gender equity in sports. *Chronicle of Higher Education, 49*(17), A41.

Suggs, W. (2005). *A place on the team: The triumph and tragedy of Title IX.* Princeton, NJ: Princeton University Press.

U.S. Department of Education. (2003). *Further clarification of intercollegiate athletics policy guidance regarding Title IX compliance.* Washington, DC: Office for Civil Rights, U.S. Department of Education. Retrieved from http://www.ed.gov/print/offices/list/ocr/title9guidance additionalFinal.html

U.S. Department of Education. (2005). *Additional clarification of intercollegiate athletics policy guidance: Three-part test—Part three.* Washington, D.C.: Office for Civil Rights, U.S. Department of Education. Retrieved from http://www.ed.gov/about/offices/list/ocr/docs/ title9guidanceadditional.html

U.S. General Accounting Office. (2000). *Gender equity: Men's and women's participation in higher education* (Report to the Ranking Minority Member, Subcommittee on Criminal Justice, Drug Policy and Human Resources, Committee on Government Reform, House of Representatives, Report No. GAO- 01- 128). Washington, DC: Author.

CHAPTER 49

University Women's Commissions and Policy Discourses

ELIZABETH J. ALLAN AND LISA PLUME HALLEN

University women's commissions have been in existence for more than 40 years and have played an important role in revealing gender inequities in higher education and in shaping policies to remediate those inequities. As a result these commissions are generally viewed as feminist agents of social change. When policy discourse analysis is used to analyze women's commission reports (see Allan, 1999, 2003, 2008), however, evidence emerges showing ways in which these reports can undermine the expressed goals of women's commissions by producing or reproducing images of women as vulnerable outsiders and supplicants to the institution, for example. In light of this evidence, readers should consider their own discursive tendencies in their roles as educators, students, and leaders, and members of women's commissions should to be alert to the shaping of subject positions that may ultimately prevent or impede achieving their stated goals.

University Women's Commissions and Women's Status

Since their inception in 1968, numerous university women's commissions have produced reports used as benchmarks for documenting status, conditions, and positions of women and for making policy recommendations at particular institutions. Women's commissions are "conceptualized within a liberal feminist framework" and have generally served the following three purposes: (1) to demonstrate administrative support for the improvement of women's status; (2) to give women a collective voice on campus; and (3) to serve as a sounding board for women's concerns (Glazer, 1997, p. 66). Issues frequently addressed by commissions include the representation of women in various institutional arenas; sexual harassment; women's inclusion in the curriculum; campus safety; personnel policies related to maternity leave and family caregiving; pay equity; sex discrimination in promotion and tenure; and the lack of women in upper-level administrative and leadership positions.

Commission reports represent a culmination of months, often years, of collaborative work on the part of the committed staff, students, and faculty who are typically appointed to serve by university presidents (Blum, 1991; TenElshof, 1973). Often, the genesis of a women's commission on a particular campus can be traced back to both the pressures of grassroots organizing by women and the threat of Executive Order 11246 and Title IX sanctions (TenElshof, 1973). Thus it is not uncommon to find that university women's commissions have had direct reporting lines to the university's affirmative action or equal opportunity office. Most often, however, they are formally recognized university investigative committees that report directly to the institution's president, provost, or governing board. The work of these commissions generally concludes with the distribution of a report highlighting the status of women and policy recommendations to enhance equity at their institution.

At times, commission reports have catalyzed follow-up studies. For example, in the early 1970s, Robinson (1973) reviewed findings of 125 reports generated by university women's commissions across the United States and concluded that a pattern of discrimination against women existed in higher education. By the early 1990s, more commission reports had been generated, and it was not uncommon for comparisons to be made between newer reports and those issued 20 years earlier. For instance, in October 1991, the *Chronicle of Higher Education* cited new evidence indicating that a hostile environment still existed for women in academe (Blum, 1991) and pointed out that many commission report findings of the 1990s yielded nearly identical conclusions to those issued in the 1970s.

Nearly 10 years after the *Chronicle* report, a study on the status of women faculty at the Massachusetts Institute of Technology (MIT) prompted the chair of MIT faculty to write, "The key conclusion one gets from the report is that gender discrimination in the 1990s is subtle but pervasive" (Massachusetts Institute of Technology, 1999, p. 3). This finding is underscored by Valian (1999), who reports, "The data demonstrate that women in academia are substantially underrewarded. . . . [E]ven when productivity is controlled for, women earn less and achieve tenure more slowly than men do" (pp. 248–249). As a follow-up to the MIT faculty report on the status of women, a 2004 article in the *Chronicle of Higher Education* contends that women who do get hired at major research universities often face a "toxic atmosphere" (Wilson, 2004, p. A8), and in November 2006, *Inside Higher Education* reported that Johns Hopkins University had endorsed findings from the 2006 Report of the University Committee on the Status of Women, including the prioritization of gender parity, women's concerns, and work-life balance for faculty (Thacker, 2006, p. 1). More recently, a 2007 article in the *Chronicle of Higher Education* echoed similar concerns at North Dakota State University, where a "revolving door" had left the campus "thin on women, particularly at the top" (Wilson, 2007, p. A6), and in 2008, the *Chronicle* reported that female faculty and graduate students at Rutgers accused the political science department of "bias and hostility" (Moser, 2008, p. A14).

Commission work and related scholarship has helped portray gains made as well as persistent problems in the attainment of gender equity. For instance, overall, women are earning research doctorates at roughly the same pace or slightly better than men, yet more men than women are tenure-track professors, and salaries of male professors are consistently higher than those of female professors across ranks (Bradburn & Sikora, 2003; National Center for Educational Statistics, 2004, 2005; Knapp et al., 2004). In response to this and other climate-related matters for women, Wilson (2004) notes that many academic women are surprised because they "believed that gender inequities would be behind them now." (p. A8) Theda Skocpol, holder of an endowed chair in government and sociology at Harvard University, is noted as saying, "I feel like I'm in a time warp. This has a very 70s feel, like stuff we thought we had overcome" (quoted in Wilson, 2004, p. A8).

Though some gains have been made for women in the academy in terms of hiring, representation, and pay, discrepancies continue to plague higher education. In a recent report, the American Association of University Professors noted that substantial impediments to women's advancement to the senior faculty ranks continue to exist and only in community colleges have women achieved parity with men at the highest academic ranks (2009, p. 27). Thus even today, inequities persist, and university women's commission reports continue to serve as vehicles for communicating messages to academics, and sometimes the general public, about persistent sex/gender equity problems in higher education.

The Emergence of University Women's Commissions

Working both within and against the formal structure and policies of the institution, university women's commissions occupy an inherently contradictory space. Women's commissions are part of the formal institutional governance structure because administrative officials within the university typically establish them; hence the commissions maintain formal reporting lines within the administrative hierarchy. Yet the primary focus of their role is to address concerns about the position of women in academe, including the institution's treatment of, devaluation of, and discrimination against women. Thus women's commissions are also positioned to work against the institutional status quo. The manner in which university women's commissions are established and the contradictory location they occupy within the institution set them apart from other types of women-focused groups in higher education.

Generally speaking, the primary task of a university women's commission is to assess women's status and make recommendations for improvement. This is typically accomplished through the development of policy reports, which have traditionally included a compilation of statistics about women's access to the university and various arenas within the institution, the representation of women in the leadership of the university, promotion and tenure rates, and salary equity. Climate-related matters are also addressed, including child-care and family-leave concerns, sexual harassment, safety, and the representation of women in the curriculum (Glazer, 1997; Glazer-Raymo, 1999; Moore & Sagaria, 1993; Robinson, 1973; TenElshof, 1973).

Research about University Women's Commissions

Although women's commissions in universities have been generating reports for over three decades and have served as a primary vehicle by which women in universities have contributed to policy-making efforts, historical accounts and governance studies of higher education have largely ignored these groups. Ginsberg and Plank (1995) note that "the multiple uses to which commissions can be put have made them an integral part of the policy-generating and policy-making process" (p. 4). When studies have focused on university women's commissions, they have most often been examined through a feminist lens and case study methodology in which they are treated as exemplars of a change strategy, a movement, or a political strategy by women (Rossi & Calderwood, 1973; Rosenberg, 1982; Stewart, 1980). Recently, commissions have been the focus of research related to empowerment of women in U.S. universities (Moore & Sagaria, 1993), affirmative action policy in U.S. higher education (Glazer, 1997), gender equity policies at a South African university (Walker, 1997), and gender equity policies in Canadian educational institutions (deCastell & Bryson, 1997).

While scholarly studies about women's commissions vary in approach, most employ a case study method and draw upon observation and interview data to arrive at their findings. These studies are primarily descriptive and have provided insights on the organization and function of commissions as policy-focused groups of women advocating for institutional change in higher education. Allan's (1999, 2003, 2008) study differs in that she analyzed the reports produced by women's commissions in order to examine how the discourses taken up by them contribute to producing or reproducing particular images and constructing women's status in the context of higher education policy making. Allan's approach aligns with the work of deCastell and Bryson (1997), who apply poststructural perspectives to describe the "paradoxical consequences of institutionalized equity policies" (p. 85) that may actually be undermined by the uncritical acceptance of concepts such as equity that can carry exclusionary assumptions. Thus they suggest that substantial conceptual clarification and strategy are needed for those involved with equity policy efforts. Allan's findings underscore deCastell and Bryson's assertion that feminists need to find ways to intervene strategically with the means of discursive production in order to avoid subordinating "nominally feminist agendas to the greater ends of orderly and hegemonically controlled institutional reform" (p. 100).

Policy Discourse Analysis and Women's Status

Women's commission reports serve as a focus for policy discourse analysis because they represent a primary means by which women in universities have articulated concerns and made recommendations designed to improve their status in these institutions over the past five decades. Since women's commission reports are used to communicate ideas to mass audiences, the images they convey may have far-reaching effects by shaping perceptions of self and others in relation to the social world.

Over several decades, research has served as a powerful vehicle for documenting gender inequity and uncovering attitudes, beliefs, behaviors, and social systems contributing to the problem. Discursive analysis of women's commission reports emerged from Allan's feminist interest in examining and working to strengthen women's policy-making efforts in the context of higher education. While findings from this research may appear critical of commission efforts, it would be a misunderstanding to consider the research a censure of commission work. To the contrary, many women have benefitted from policy changes and enhanced campus awareness of gender equity inspired by the work of women's commissions. Nevertheless, Allan's research reveals ways in which women's commissions have worked against women's interests in social change and equity by reinforcing traditional views of gender.

The findings, briefly presented here, are drawn from women's commission reports and supporting data gathered from four U.S. public land-grant research universities over a 25-year period (Allan, 1999, 2003, 2008). The sample consisted of 21 "official reports" in addition to 150 secondary sources, including survey data, newspaper articles, meeting agendas and minutes, letters and memos to and from commission members, journal articles, and preliminary research reports used by women's commissions in preparing official reports.

The Vulnerable Woman

Throughout the reports examined, women working and studying in universities are often depicted as "scared," "intimidated," "at risk," "falling behind," and "in jeopardy." Allan contends that these characterizations are made possible through discourses of distress and dependency and are supported by a dominant discourse of femininity that constructs dominant cultural norms of female behavior as an outcome of "natural" womanhood (Coates, 1996; Mills, 1992).

This discourse of femininity reinforces White, middle-class, and heterosexual norms about how women "should" behave. It therefore supports sexism, heterosexism, and racism (Smith, 1990) and reinforces male dominance and heterosexism by shaping femininity in ways that promote women's acceptance of their dependence on men (Coates, 1996; Mills, 1992). Unfortunately, dominant discourses are quite powerful. They tend to eclipse or silence other ways of making sense, and they resist alternate discourses, making other possibilities of describing and addressing a problem more difficult to identify. However, multiple and competing discourses exist within a single strategy (Foucault, 1976/1978; Weedon, 1997). For example, women's commission reports are generally considered a women's empowerment strategy operating through a feminist discourse, which positions them against patriarchy. However, the findings of Allan's study (1999, 2003, 2008) show that these reports can also reinforce discourses that disempower women.

Discourses of distress and dependency, supported by a dominant discourse of femininity, (re)produce subject positions that situate women as vulnerable and dependent on the (typically male-dominated) university administration to provide for them and keep them safe. The "problem" of safety for women is a theme reiterated in women's commission reports. Certainly, safety is an equity issue. However, the articulation of the problem typically relies upon a dominant discourse of femininity. In order to establish that safety and security are legitimate concerns, women are typically portrayed by the reports in ways that emphasize their vulnerability. This discourse constructs the vulnerable woman as the fearful object or potential object of male anger, aggression, and violence. This approach tends to identify the problem as women's concerns about safety (i.e., women's distress) rather than the violence itself. Thus the discourse of distress supports dominant constructions of femininity in that it focuses attention on women's (in)ability to remain safe.

Women on the Outside

Women's commission reports often described the attainment of equity in terms of access, and they rely on discourses that are typically offered in quantifiable terms. The reports examine numbers of women compared with men in various university arenas and make the case that women remain underrepresented in important areas of the university. They urge the improvement of women's status by including more women in positions and activities from which they have been marginalized or excluded. Such statements are illustrative of a dominant discourse of access that serves to (re)produce the woman outsider subject position. Quite simply, the reports construct women as outsiders in the very process of their appeal for women to become insiders. The focus on promoting women's access—their moving into, inside, and being included within different and more desirable locations of the institution and its culture—positions them as outsiders.

The outsider subject position is accomplished through discourses of access that produce a dominant image of women as supplicants who are urgently seeking permission to enter a previously male domain and to participate in activities that have expressly or tacitly excluded them. This positioning may ironically undermine the intended goals of women's full participation, as it reinforces structural and cultural dominance of male power within the institution by persistently petitioning that power rather than creating or drawing upon alternative configurations.

Outstanding Women

While the discourse of access serves to position women as outsiders, a discourse of professionalism shapes characterizations of women inside the institution with a focus on individual improvement through professional development, leadership, and career training. This discourse works to construct a belief that all women will benefit from the professional/career advancement of individual women.

The embodiment of the professional woman subject position serves to (re)produce inequity among women. In commission reports and other gender equity initiatives, women are often viewed as a collective, all of whom are working toward, or should work toward, progress and advancement. Some women will find their sense of self aligns with the discourse—they may see themselves as accomplished scholars or administrators, for example, and feel validated by the policy problems and solutions delineated in the commission reports. However, since most women working in universities are not faculty members or administrators, they are likely to relate to the discourse in a markedly different way. Women whose experiences do not align with the professional woman as constructed through this dominant discourse are positioned as deficient and receive the message that it is desirable to rectify their "deficiency" through increased education, training, and professional development.

Women who aspire to have careers, to become leaders, and to engage in professional development are positioned as improving not only their own lives but the lives of all women. Ironically, the discourse produces difference among women as it works to promote sameness by professionalizing all women. For example, the professionalism discourse (re)produces a particular view of leadership. This view accords "leaders" an elite status and provides that leaders, like professionals, require specialized training. In this sense, leadership is not portrayed as a set of traits or qualities that are "natural" to women or that women might learn in the course of their daily lives. Thus the discourse in commission reports implies that some women are lacking in female leadership role models at least in part because of the lack of women who are adequately prepared to be "leaders" as that term is dominantly defined.

The shaping of the faculty/professional ideal may seem self-evident in the context of a university—after all, it is an academic institution, an enterprise designed to promote learning and provide training for professionals. Indeed, it is precisely this predictability that demonstrates the normalizing power of the discourse of professionalism. The discourse supports particular versions of achievement and success that become taken for granted and accepted as "normal" or given. As such, these versions of achievement are no longer seen as choices among the many possible perspectives. The dominance of the discourse—and its taken-for-granted "goodness"—make it difficult to see how accorded meanings of achievement or leadership might serve to disempower many women whose sense of self does not align with these particular meanings. This is especially invidious when commission policy reports are intended to empower and improve the status of women working and learning in higher education.

Thinking Differently: Discursive Effects and University Women's Commissions

How might the research highlighted here inform more effective practice? As Ball (1994) cautions, "there are real struggles over the interpretation and enactment of policies. But these are set within a moving discursive frame which articulates and constrains the possibilities and probabilities for interpretation and enactment" (p. 23). Keeping this caveat in mind, we offer the following suggestions for improving practice of university women's commissions and similar policy-related groups: (1) Promote keener awareness and understanding of policy as discourse among commission participants; (2) analyze the discursive framing of policy reports including policy silences and assumptions inherent in policy problems and solutions; (3) in the process of policy development, examine the possible implications of discourses drawn upon to articulate policy problems and recommendations; and (4) consider how the articulation of problems and solutions in the policy reports might contribute to constructing particular images of women. As strategies for recognizing and analyzing discursive effects, these recommendations are offered to further the development of alternative and perhaps more empowering ways to address the issues and concerns of women on campus.

REFERENCES AND FURTHER READING

Allan, E. J. (1999). *Constructing women's status: Policy discourses of university women's commission reports* (Unpublished doctoral dissertation). The Ohio State University, Columbus.

Allan, E. J. (2003). Constructing women's status: Policy discourses of university women's commission reports. *Harvard Educational Review, 73*(1), 44–72.

Allan, E. J. (2008). *Policy discourses, gender, and education: Constructing women's status*. New York: Routledge.

American Association of University Professors. (2009). *On the brink: The annual report on the economic status of the profession, 2008–09*. Washington, D.C.: Author.

Ball, S. J. (1994). *Education reform: A critical and post-structural approach*. Buckingham, UK: Open University Press.

Blum, D. E. (1991). Environment still hostile to women in academe, new evidence indicates. *Chronicle of Higher Education, 38*(7), A1.

Bradburn, E. M., & Sikora, A. (2003). *Gender and racial/ethnic differences in salary and other characteristics of postsecondary faculty: Fall 1998* (NCES No. 2002-170).

Clune, M. S., Nunez, A., & Choy, S. P. (2001). *Competing choices: Men's and women's paths after earning a bachelor's degree* (NCES 2001-154). Washington, DC: National Center for Education Statistics, U.S. Department of Education Office of Educational Research and Improvement.

Coates, J. (1996). *Women talk: Conversation between friends*. Cambridge, MA: Blackwell.

deCastell, S., & Bryson, M. (1997). En/Gendering equity: Paradoxical consequences of institutionalized equity policies. In S. deCastell & M. Bryson (Eds.), *Radical in(ter)ventions: Identity politics, and difference/s in educational praxis* (pp. 85–103). Albany: State University of New York Press.

Foucault, M. (1978). *The history of sexuality: Volume 1: An introduction* (R. Hurley, Trans.). New York: Vintage Books. (Original work published 1976)

Ginsberg, R., & Plank, D. N. (1995). Commissions and change. In R. Ginsberg & D. N. Plank (Eds.), *Commissions, reports, reforms, and educational policy* (pp. 3–16). Westport, CT: Praeger.

Glazer, J. (1997). Affirmative action and the status of women in the academy. In C. Marshall

(Ed.), *Feminist critical policy analysis: Vol. 2: A perspective from post-secondary education* (pp. 60–73). Washington, DC: Falmer Press.

Glazer-Raymo, J. (1999). *Shattering the myths: Women in academe.* Baltimore: Johns Hopkins University Press.

Knapp, L. G., Kelly-Reid, J., Whitmore, R. W., Huh, S., Zhao, L., Levine, B., et al. (2004). Staff in postsecondary institutions, Fall, 2003, and salaries of full-time instructional faculty, 2002–2004. *Education Statistics Quarterly, 7*(1 & 2). Retrieved January 10, 2007, from http://nces.edu.gov/programs/quarterly/vol_7/1_2/5_10.asp

Massachusetts Institute of Technology. (1999). *A study on the status of women faculty in science at MIT.* Retrieved June 12, 2009, from http://web.mit.edu/fnl/women/women.html

Mills, S. (1992). Negotiating discourses of femininity. *Journal of Gender Studies, 1*(3), 271–85.

Moore, K., & Sagaria, M. (1993, February). *Women, a strategy framework and empowerment in U.S. universities.* Paper presented at V Congreso Internacional E. Interdiciplinario. San Jose, Costa Rica.

Moser, K. (2008). Women accuse Rutgers political-science department of bias and hostility. *Chronicle of Higher Education, 55*(8), A14.

National Center for Educational Statistics. (2004). *Digest of Education Statistics.* Chapter 3: Postsecondary Education. Retrieved January 10, 2007, from http://nces.edu.gov/programs/digest/d04/tables/dt04_237.asp

National Center for Education Statistics. (2005). *Postsecondary institutions in the United States: Fall 2003 and degrees and other awards conferred: 2002–03* (NCES 2005- 154). Retrieved January 10, 2007, from http://nces.edu.gov/programs/digest/d04/tables/dt04_237.asp

Robinson, L. H. (1973). Institutional variation in the status of academic women. In A. S. Rossi & A. Calderwood (Eds.), *Academic women on the move* (pp. 199–238). New York: Russell Sage Foundation.

Rosenberg, R. (1982). Representing women at the state and local levels: Commissions on the status of women. In E. Boneparth (Ed.), *Women, Power, and Policy* (pp. 38–46). New York: Pergamon.

Rossi, A. S., & Calderwood, A. (Eds.). (1973). *Academic women on the move.* New York: Russell Sage Foundation.

Smith, D. E. (1990). *The conceptual practices of power: A feminist sociology of knowledge.* Boston: Northeastern University Press.

Stewart, D. W. (1980). *The women's movement in community politics in the U.S.: The role of local commissions on the status of women.* New York: Pergamon.

TenElshof, A. (1973, Winter). Purpose and focus of a campus commission on the status of women. *Journal of NAWDC,* 84–89.

Thacker, P. (2006, November 21). Hopkins endorses gender parity. *Inside Higher Ed.* Retrieved from http://www.insidehighered.com/news/2006/11/21/hopkins

Valian, V. (1999). *Why so slow? The advancement of women.* Cambridge, MA: MIT Press.

Walker, M. (1997). Simply not good chaps: Unraveling gender equity in a South African University. In C. Marshall (Ed.), *Feminist critical policy analysis: Vol. 2: A perspective from post-secondary education* (pp. 41–59). Washington, DC: Falmer Press.

Weedon, C. (1997). *Feminist practice and poststructuralist theory* (3rd ed.). Cambridge, MA: Blackwell.

Wilson, R. (2004). Where the elite teach, it's still a man's world: The women who do get hired at major research universities often find a "toxic atmosphere." *Chronicle of Higher Education, 51*(15), A8.

Wilson, R. (2007). At North Dakota State, women are few and far between: Why does one university seem so far behind the times? *Chronicle of Higher Education, 54*(10), A6.

CHAPTER 50

Work-Family Conflicts and Policies

RACHEL E. HILE

Work-family conflicts result from difficulties in responding satisfactorily to the competing demands of both the work role and the family role in an individual's life. Outsiders often assume that the unique working conditions of professors buffer them from significant work-family conflicts: professors perform some of their work from home, have summers off from active teaching duties, and have more flexible schedules than most workers. However, some of these very qualities lead to significant work-family conflicts among faculty members. Required on-site hours are shorter than in other jobs, but research demands, in addition to off-site grading and class preparation as well as on-site evening and weekend events, can encroach upon a professor's personal and family commitments.

In higher education, the increasing reliance on part-time and non-tenure-track faculty creates a more complicated gendering of teaching work, with tenure-track faculty positions gendered "male" and marginalized teaching positions gendered "female." That is, a tenured or tenure-track faculty member is expected to have a "male" orientation that privileges work over family responsibilities; academics whose family responsibilities prevent them from committing to tenure-line positions will be seen as having a "female" emphasis on family over work. In part, the cultural gendering of these teaching positions leads to different sources of work-family conflicts for the individuals who hold them.

Faculty members often create solutions to work-family conflict at the individual or family level, but this "privatization" of the problems of achieving work-family balance ignores the possibility of creating broader cultural change within academia through institutional responses to work-family conflict. Ideas about gender and gendered interpretations of specific educational work roles have important influences on the work-family conflicts experienced by faculty members. Although individual- and family-level accommodations can do much to alleviate work-family conflict, a larger reconceptualization of ideas of work and gender is necessary for fundamental and lasting change.

Sources of Work-Family Conflict

At its most fundamental level, work-family conflict arises from conflicts between life roles as workers and as family members. Whereas specific instances of conflict occur when work requirements affect family life (W→F conflict) or when family needs interfere with one's work performance (F→W conflict), work-family conflict exists as well at a psychological level, resulting from both individual and cultural ideas about gender and role balance.

Americans tend to believe that individuals understand and perform their roles hierarchically and that it is impossible for women in particular to be equally committed to both family and work roles. Because a man's culturally endorsed family role of "breadwinner" coincides neatly with his work role, a man can avoid some of the psychological distress that a woman faces when her expected family role of "nurturer" comes into conflict with her worker role. Women are more likely to believe that, in their actions and thought, they must prioritize either work or family. For this reason, women often understand the choices they make in specific situations as reflecting a broader orientation, either "choosing family over work" or "choosing work over family," either of which can lead to distress.

The cultural idea that individuals will order and perform their roles hierarchically leads to the expectation that individuals who consciously and emphatically prioritize one role over the other will experience less work-family conflict. What this idea ignores, however, is the extent to which cultural prescriptions regarding role hierarchies and gender constrain such choices in advance. Those who consciously "choose" to opt out of either family or work commitments make these choices in the context of a culture that believes that work-family conflict will always result when a woman attempts to succeed at both work and family roles. Although women who explicitly reject either the family or the work role may experience fewer episodes of situational work-family conflict, they are not immune to such conflict at the psychological level.

Work-Family Conflicts of College and University Faculty

The rigidity of the career hierarchy in higher education creates significant tensions between work and family. The normative career path, gendered male, involves moving smoothly through graduate school and then to a tenure-track job, where one advances at regular intervals from assistant professor to associate professor to full professor. The assistant professor years put the most pressure on young professors, as they struggle to prove themselves worthy of tenure. For female professors, the coincidence of the pretenure years with prime childbearing years leads to problems in adapting the female lifespan to this male-oriented model.

Over the past several decades, increasing numbers of women have earned doctoral degrees and begun academic careers, such that percentages of male and female assistant professors are roughly equal. However, disparities in percentages of women and men holding positions at the associate and full professor levels indicate that more women than men fail to receive tenure (West & Curtis, 2006). Both gender bias and parental status affect women's ability to succeed in academia. Wolfinger, Mason, and Goulden (2008) found that a woman who is married *or* who has children under the age of six is significantly less likely to obtain a tenure-track job. This disparity between married women with children and their single, childless counterparts gives way later in the career path to a gender differential unrelated to family status: Wolfinger and her colleagues found that men's and women's different rates of achievement of tenure and promotion to full professor cannot be explained with reference to marital and parental status.

The rigidly hierarchical career model of professorial work leads to a work culture that is remarkably intolerant of employment interruptions. Because of this, the practice —common outside academia—of temporarily drawing back from full engagement in the workforce during especially demanding caregiving periods remains essentially unavailable for academics. The tight academic job market renders temporarily cutting back on one's academic work even more problematic: Graduate students feel the need to get a tenure-track job as soon as possible, knowing that a few years after graduation their ability to land a tenure-track job will start to decline. Pretenure faculty know that if they leave a tenure-track job to care for children, they might never get another one.

The career expectations of the tenure-line professor decrease flexibility in terms of being able to limit work obligations, and the academic career creates additional challenges to successfully balancing work and family. Because of the scarcity of tenure-line academic positions, many academics live and work too far from their families of origin to receive substantial or ongoing support in caring for children. Distance from the family of origin creates its own constellation of problems as well for professors responsible for caring for their own parents at the end of life. Other work-family balance challenges that affect significant numbers of academics arise from the difficulties of balancing two academic careers in the same family, which may lead to spouses living separately for several months of the year, the strains of underemployment for one spouse, or the stress of two demanding careers.

Part-time and non-tenure-track faculty members face different challenges. Called lecturers, instructors, or adjuncts, they are disproportionately female (West & Curtis, 2006), and they have less job security and are paid less—usually significantly less— than professors. Many women in marginalized academic positions hold the jobs they do because of family-related aspirations or commitments that conflict with the expectations of the academic career model. Such women include those without doctoral degrees for reasons related to family or those with doctoral degrees whose family work renders the demands of a professorial academic career unappealing or impossible. The decision to work for lower pay and status than are accorded to tenured and tenure-track faculty, though sometimes narrated as a free choice, is made in response to the cultural ideology that views women, but not men, as "choosing" either work or family over the other.

Individual-Level Solutions to Work-Family Conflicts

Many people develop individual- and family-level responses to work-family conflict rather than envisioning a culturewide reconceptualization of the connections between gender and work and family roles. Whether at the individual or family level, these private strategies aim either to reduce work encroachments on family life or to minimize family intrusions into the workplace. Research on the former has focused on general populations of dual-earner couples, whereas much of the research focused on academic populations has examined the latter.

Becker and Moen (1999) report that the majority of dual-earner couples avoid at the family level the stresses of two high-pressure careers by means of strategies to scale back in order to protect the family from work encroachments. They identify three specific strategies: placing limits on work engagements, having a "one-job, one-career" marriage (most often, the man has the career and the woman the "job"), and trading off, allowing priority to both partners' work lives but at different times in the life course.

Because of the unusually high pressure of the pretenure years for professors and the difficulty of returning to the tenure track after exiting academia for whatever reason, these strategies are less available for those in academia, and so efforts to reduce F→W conflict become salient, particularly for female assistant professors with children. Research by Finkel and Olswang (1996) quantifies female junior faculty members' sense of the necessity of limiting F→W conflict in order to achieve tenure. Of their sample of 124 female assistant professors, 30% had decided not to have children, and an additional 49% had chosen to postpone childbearing. Forty percent of their study participants cited "time required by children" as a serious barrier to achieving tenure, including 82% of the subsample of women with at least one child under the age of six.

A female assistant professor's decision to avoid or delay childbearing, a "free choice" made in the context of a culture that requires women to choose work or family, is a clear example of "bias avoidance"—that is, a behavior intended to minimize any seeming or actual intrusions of family life on work commitments in order to be taken seriously as a professional (Drago, Crouter, Wardell, & Willits, 2001). Female academics who do have children in the pretenure years often attempt to limit F→W conflict by making their maternal status as invisible as possible. Such efforts can begin with timing conception attempts to ensure summer childbirth, thus avoiding interruptions of the academic semester. More problematic is the underutilization of family-friendly policies increasingly in place at colleges and universities, including paid parental leaves, flexible scheduling, and the option of stopping the tenure clock for a year. Although studies have repeatedly demonstrated wide support for such policies among both male and female professors, actual utilization rates suggest that the majority of eligible faculty members do not request to use them.

Researchers assume that academic parents do not fully utilize family-friendly policies because of concerns that, even when institutionwide policies support them, they may still be penalized at the department level when decisions about tenure are made. An assistant professor's colleagues, like the larger culture, may perceive work-family balance as a zero-sum game, such that an "orientation" to work or family necessarily implies a corresponding deficit of attention to the other sphere. In a workplace governed by this model, any utilization of family-friendly policies will be perceived as signaling a lack of scholarly seriousness.

These private strategies to balance the demands of work and family often provide individuals with a satisfactory experience of succeeding at multiple life roles. However, the difficulty with private solutions to problems rooted in culture and ideology is that approaching problems with work-family balance as a series of free choices made by individuals ignores the ways in which the possible choices—and the necessity of "choosing" work or family at all—are constrained by cultural forces that remain invisible as long as they are ignored. Fundamental change—as opposed to individual- and family-level accommodations to the way things are—requires broader public solutions to the problem.

Policies to Reduce Work-Family Conflicts among Academics

Whereas many discussions of work-family reconciliation policies argue for governmental leadership in instituting such policies, the unique qualities of faculty jobs and career trajectories compared with nonacademic careers require that colleges and universities implement policies to address specific challenges faculty members face in combining family work and academic careers. Starting in the early 1990s and continuing to the present, college and university administrators have implemented increasing numbers of family-friendly policies, including parental leave policies, stopping the tenure clock, job sharing, employment assistance for spouses, and other policies. As policies relating to parental leave and tenure-clock stoppage become widely accepted, researchers and faculty activists interested in work-family conflict are envisioning policy changes that go even farther to make academia welcoming to those who seek to balance their commitments to work and to family.

In their analysis of work-family reconciliation policies, Janet C. Gornick and Marcia K. Meyers (2003) discuss policies for family leave, limiting the workweek, and child care. Their ideas, modeled on European responses to work-family conflict, rely heavily on governmental leadership. Governmental policies in these areas would meet the needs of administrative staff and others holding nonteaching positions within higher education, but adjustments to those categories of policy needs are required in order to address the needs of faculty members. In addition, policies to effect cultural change are necessary to increase utilization of family friendly policies already on the books.

Family Leave Policies

In the United States, since the passage of the Family and Medical Leave Act of 1993 (FMLA), eligible employees have been entitled to receive up to 12 weeks of unpaid, job-protected leave in a 12-month period, which can be used to care for a newborn, a newly adopted child, or a sick family member. The legislation, written with the typical year-round, 40-hour-a-week job in mind, requires adaptations to meet the needs of faculty members, whose teaching responsibilities fall into 10-week quarters or 16-week semesters with inflexible start and end dates. While staying in compliance with the requirements of FMLA, colleges and universities need to create policy adaptations that more realistically address the actual work schedules of faculty members.

Research on work-life reconciliation policies outside of academia has demonstrated that workers are more likely to take the leave allowed by FMLA if the leave is paid rather than unpaid. Within academia, workers will be more likely to utilize leave policies that acknowledge the 10- or 16-week trajectory of the quarter or the semester rather than clinging to the FMLA's arbitrary designation of 12 weeks of leave, which might lead to situations in which a professor teaches for the first 2 weeks of a semester, takes 12 weeks off to care for a newborn, and then returns to full classroom duties in time for the final 2 weeks of the semester. Particularly for faculty members teaching specialized upper-level courses, such a scenario is not only ridiculous but unfeasible as well, given the difficulty of finding a qualified teacher to cover the course for 12 weeks. At present, institutions in the vanguard of work-family reconciliation policies for academics are implementing parental leave policies that allow an entire quarter or semester's release from teaching duties.

Faculty Workweek Policies

European countries have shortened their workweeks by reducing the hours in a standard workweek and instituting limits on hours worked or overtime hours. If such policies were to be enacted in the United States, they would legally affect only the workweeks of wageworkers but would presumably lead to culturewide changes in the idea of the workweek that would in turn lead to decreases in the workweeks of salaried employees. In the absence of such culturewide adjustments to the idea of the workweek, and given academics' extremely long workweeks (54.8 hours per week for the average male and 52.8 hours per week for the average female faculty member; see Winslow-Bowe and Jacobs in part V of this book), policy interventions within academia are required to shorten the academic workweek.

The idea of stopping the tenure clock for faculty members who become parents seems largely uncontroversial, but the contentious history of the idea and its continuing low utilization rates suggest continuing concerns on the part of faculty members that utilizing family-friendly policies will have negative professional effects on them. In 1974, the American Association of University Professors (AAUP) Committee on the Status of Women in the Academic Profession recommended that faculty members be able to request that the tenure clock be stopped for a year because of the birth or adoption of a child but only if the faculty member took an extended, unpaid leave of absence from the university. The AAUP changed this position only in 2001, when the *Statement of Principles on Family Responsibilities and Academic Work* recommended that faculty members be granted a one-year stoppage of the tenure clock upon becoming new parents, regardless of whether the parent takes a leave of absence. The effect of the 2001 recommendation is thus to reduce the workweeks of new parents who continue their full-time academic employment. Low utilization rates of tenure-clock stoppage policies have led many colleges and universities recently to make the stoppage automatic, rather than requiring that faculty members request it.

Whereas some form of a tenure-clock stoppage policy is becoming more common in academic workplaces, the next frontier of policies to limit the academic workweek involves legitimizing part-time tenure-line work and limiting the workweeks of all faculty, not just parents. For example, recognizing that child rearing involves a time commitment considerably longer than the one year of a stopped tenure clock, Robert Drago and Joan Williams (2000) propose the creation of half-time tenure-track faculty positions, which would allow parents to work half time for up to 12 years before coming up for tenure. Jerry A. Jacobs (2004), however, believes that such policy changes, by focusing attention exclusively on the work-family conflicts of faculty members with children, ignore the root problem: the ever-increasing demands on professors' time. In his view, the creation of part-time tenure tracks, which he suspects would be populated almost entirely by women, would thus serve to reinstitutionalize gender inequity, and tenure-clock stoppage, by giving parents extra time to "catch up," diverts attention from the fact that some departments' tenure requirements cannot be met by anyone with any reasonable definition of work-life balance. In Jacobs's opinion, addressing the root cause of work-family conflict requires policy changes to limit the workweeks of *all* professors, not just those with children.

Child-Care Policies and Programs

Parents in academia would benefit from institutional leadership in providing or subsidizing child care that responds to the unusual scheduling needs of faculty members. Most child-care providers tailor their hours and policies to the needs of the typical 40-hour-a-week worker, leading to potential problems for academic parents. Work schedules for academics change frequently (1) from semester to semester, sometimes including evening and weekend classes; (2) within the semester, for the week of final exams; and (3) from the school year to the summer, when some parents might wish to decrease children's hours in nonparental care. Child-care providers who require parents to commit to an unchanging, full-time, year-round schedule may not provide the flexibility that faculty members need.

Colleges and universities can respond to these potential problems by providing on-campus day-care facilities that address the similar scheduling needs of both student and faculty-member parents. Along with other family-friendly policies, available and affordable child-care options can help with recruitment and retention of faculty members.

Policies to Promote Cultural Change

Effecting culturewide changes in levels of work-family conflict requires cultural interventions to change decision makers' attitudes toward work-family balance. Policies to promote cultural changes have arisen in response to low utilization rates for family-friendly policies in both academia and the nonacademic world. Sweden provides a useful example of disparities between the ideal, expressed in policy, and reality: Despite egalitarian policies designed to maximize women's workforce participation and men's parental involvement, Swedish women take the majority of leaves and perform the majority of child care; men are reluctant to take family leaves for fear of being perceived as less serious workers. In a study focusing on the effect of Nordic countries' family-friendly policies on gender inequity specifically in the academic workplace, Audrey Mayer and Paivi Tikka (2008) compared the status of women in academic positions in the United States with those in Finland and Sweden and found similar conditions for female academics in the United States and in the Nordic countries, suggesting the difficulty in equalizing gender imbalance through policies alone.

Until our understanding of work shifts to allow recognition of women and men with significant caregiving responsibilities as valuable and effective workers, fundamental change will be impossible. To speed such changes along, some are attempting to facilitate work-family balance by means of cultural interventions. The cultural intervention efforts of Cinamon and Rich (2005) in the K–12 workplace could serve as models for similar interventions at the college and university level. Cinamon and Rich used a two-pronged approach in their program for alleviating work-family conflict, one focusing on school managers (e.g., school principals and administrators) and one on teachers at high risk for work-family conflict (e.g., novice teachers who are also parents of young children). For both targeted groups, intervention focused on changing both attitudes and actions; for managers, this involved sensitivity training to enhance managers' understanding of work-family conflicts of educators as well as skill-oriented work to increase managers' effectiveness in dealing with work-family conflicts from the perspective of family-friendly managerial practice.

In higher education workplaces, making such cultural interventions at the department level is essential for changing the climate for parents in academia, since department-level colleagues, rather than administrators, sometimes play the most important role in tenure decisions for junior faculty members. The limited use of sensitivity training initiatives such as those just described, even at universities that are leaders in family-friendly policy implementation, suggests that administrators should follow up such initiatives with concrete measures to shift attitudes of the senior faculty who actually decide the fates of junior faculty members' careers.

REFERENCES AND FURTHER READING

American Association of University Professors. (2001). *Statement of principles on family responsibilities and academic work*. Washington, DC: Author. Retrieved November 24, 2008, from http://www.aaup.org/AAUP/pubsres/policydocs/contents/workfam-stmt.htm

Becker, P. E., & Moen, P. (1999). Scaling back: Dual-earner couples' work-family strategies. *Journal of Marriage and the Family, 61*(4), 995–1007.

Cinamon, R. G., & Rich, Y. (2005). Reducing teachers' work-family conflict: From theory to practice. *Journal of Career Development, 32*(1), 91–103.

Drago, R., Crouter, A. C., Wardell, M., & Willits, B. S. (2001). *Final report of the Faculty and Families Project.* University Park: Pennsylvania State University. Retrieved November 20, 2008, from http://lser.la.psu.edu/workfam/facultyfamilies.htm

Drago, R., & Williams, J. (2000). A half-time tenure-track proposal. *Change, 32*(6), 46–51.

Finkel, S. K., & Olswang, S. G. (1996). Child rearing as a career impediment to women assistant professors. *Review of Higher Education, 19*(2), 123–139.

Gornick, J. C., & Meyers, M. K. (2003). *Families that work: Policies for reconciling parenthood and employment.* New York: Russell Sage Foundation.

Jacobs, J. A. (2004). The faculty time divide. *Sociological Forum, 19*(1), 3–27.

Mayer, A. L., & Tikka, P. M. (2008). Family-friendly policies and gender bias in academia. *Journal of Higher Education Policy and Management, 30*, 363–374.

West, M. S., & Curtis, J. W. (2006). *AAUP gender equity indicators 2006: Organizing around gender equity.* Washington, DC: American Association of University Professors. Retrieved November 20, 2008, from http://www.aaup.org/AAUP/pubsres/research/geneq2006toc.htm

Wolfinger, N. H., Mason, M. A., & Goulden, M. (2008). Problems in the pipeline: Gender, marriage, and fertility in the ivory tower. *Journal of Higher Education, 79*, 388–405.

CONTRIBUTORS

Sandra Acker is Professor in the Department of Sociology and Equity Studies in Education at the University of Toronto in Canada. She has worked in the United States, Britain, and Canada as a sociologist of education, with interests in gender and education, teachers' work, and higher education. Her current research is focused on university tenure practices, women academics in leadership positions, and doctoral student experiences. She is the author of *Gendered Education* (1994) and *The Realities of Teachers' Work: Never a Dull Moment* (1999) and coeditor of *Whose University Is It Anyway? Power and Privilege on Gendered Terrain* (2008).

Lyndsay J. Agans is Clinical Assistant Professor in Higher Education and P-20 Educational Programs in the Morgridge College of Education at the University of Denver. Her scholarship focuses on the intersections of education, technology, and sustainability in a globablized world and the implications for student and faculty development.

Elizabeth J. Allan is Associate Professor of Higher Education at the University of Maine, where she is also an affiliate faculty member with the Women's Studies Program. She is the author of *Policy, Gender, and Education: Constructing Women's Status* (2008); *Reconstructing Policy in Higher Education: Feminist Poststructural Perspectives* (2009); and articles and book chapters concerned with gender, diversity, and campus climates in higher education. She is the recipient of the American Educational Research Association Division J Outstanding Publication Award (2005).

Ronald E. Anderson is Professor Emeritus at the University of Minnesota, where he taught sociology for 35 years. His legacy includes 7 books, over 100 articles, 150 presentations at professional meetings, 15 large research grants, and over 50 smaller research projects. He began studying gender and technology in 1979.

Lucy E. Bailey is Assistant Professor of Social Foundations and Qualitative Research and a core Women's Studies faculty member at Oklahoma State University. Her research interests focus primarily on feminist and qualitative methodologies, nineteenth-century American women's history, and critical gender and race issues in education. She is coeditor of *Wanted—Correspondence: Women's Letters to a Union Soldier* (2009). Her current research focuses on methodological issues in researching ancestors and an interpretive biography of a nineteenth-century didactic author and ancestor.

Barbara J. Bank is Professor Emerita of Sociology and of Women Studies at the University of Missouri in Columbia. During her years at UMC, she helped to initiate and develop the Women Studies Program, served as Director of Graduate Studies and Department Chair of Sociology, and was honored with a Fulbright Senior Scholar Award, visiting fellowships at the Australian National University, and awards for excellence in teaching and for outstanding contributions to the education of women. Her many scholarly presentations and publications, including *Contradictions* *in Women's Education: Traditionalism, Careerism, and Community at a Single-Sex College* (2003), reflect her long-standing interests in social psychology, gender studies, and the sociology of youth and education. She is also the organizer and editor of *Gender and Education: An Encyclopedia* (2007).

Brent L. Bilodeau is Director of the Lesbian, Bisexual, Gay, and Transgender Resource Center at Michigan State University. His research focuses on leadership in lesbian, bisexual, gay, and transgender student organizations and on the experiences and identities of transgender college students. His book *Genderism: Transgender Students, Binary Systems and Higher Education* (2009) is based on his dissertation, which won the 2007 Dissertation of the Year Award from the Queer Studies Special Interest Group of the American Educational Research Association.

Karen Bojar is Professor of English and Coordinator of Women's Studies at Community College of Philadelphia, where she has taught for the past 30 years. She has published extensively on feminist pedagogy and the relationship between women's studies, service learning, and feminist activism. She has a long history in grassroots feminist politics. Currently, she serves as President of Philadelphia NOW, chairs its political action committee, and is on the board of the Pennsylvania NOW-PAC. She is also a board member of NARAL-PA Foundation.

Stephanie Woodham Burge is Assistant Professor of Sociology at the University of Oklahoma in Norman. Her research interests include gender and education, work and family, and aging and the life course.

Mary Ann Danowitz is a Visiting Professor in the Institute of Gender and Diversity in Organizations at the Vienna University of Economics and Business Administration in Austria. She has held faculty appointments at the University of Denver, Ohio State University, and the College of William and Mary. She has been a Fulbright professor in Austria and Indonesia and a visiting scholar in Australia, Germany, and Malaysia. Her research focuses on leadership, academic careers, governance and administration in higher education, gender and racial/ethnic equality, and comparative perspectives on diversity management and gender. Her most recent book is *Women, Universities, and Change: Gender Equality in the European Union and the United States* (2007).

Diane Diamond received a doctorate in Sociology in 2005 from Stony Brook University in New York and is currently teaching at the College of the Holy Cross in Worcester, Massachusetts. She has written on gender integration and assimilation at the United States Military Academy at West Point and Virginia Military Institute. Her research interests include women in male-dominated institutions, tokenism, and the debate over gender equity and gender equality.

Jo-Anne Dillabough is Reader in Sociology of Education at the University of Cambridge in the U.K. and retains her post as Associate Professor in the Department of Educational Studies at University of British Columbia in Vancouver, Canada. She is coauthor of *Lost Youth in the Global City: Class, Culture and the Urban Imaginary* (2010) and coeditor of *Troubling Gender in Education* (2009); *Education, Globalization, and Social Change* (2006); and *Challenging Democracy: International Perspectives on Gender, Education and Citizenship* (2000). Her scholarly work has been concentrated in three interrelated areas: the "sociology of education" and social theory, particularly in relation to critiques of democracy and the study of marginalized communities; the sociocultural analysis of youth, economic disadvantage, and social exclusion; and most recently, the relationship between youth exclusion, international human rights issues, and critical analyses of the law.

Becky Eason is Associate Director of the Institute for Educational Research and Public Service at the University of Kansas, where she received her doctorate in Higher Education in 2002.

Berenice Malka Fisher is Professor Emerita of Educational Philosophy at New York University. Her articles and chapters address topics as diverse as women role models, the impact of disability on women's friendships, and feminism and political theater. Her book, *No Angel in the Classroom: Teaching through Feminist Discourse*, received the 2002 Distinguished Publication Award of the Association for Women in Psychology. Her current interests include feminist education, political discourse, and the peaceful resolution of political conflict.

Becky Francis is Professor of Education at Roehampton University in the United Kingdom. Her expertise and extensive publications center on the production of subjectivities in educational contexts, social identity and educational achievement, and feminist theory. Her recently coauthored books include *Feminism and "The Schooling Scandal"* (2009); *Understanding Minority Ethnic Achievement: Race, Gender, Class and "Success"* (2007); and *Reassessing Gender and Achievement* (2005). She has also coedited several readers on theory and practice in gender and education, including the *Sage Handbook of Gender and Education* (2006).

Mary E. Frederickson is Associate Professor in the Department of History at Miami University in Oxford, Ohio. Named the Miami University Distinguished Educator for 2006, she is the author of numerous articles in labor and women's history and coeditor of *Sisterhood and Solidarity: Worker's Education for Women* (1984). She is currently editing an anthology titled *Gendered Resistance: Women Opposing Sexual and Economic Subjugation in Global, Historical and Contemporary Contexts*. Her book entitled *Looking South: Essays on Race, Gender, Class, and Labor* is in press.

Marybeth Gasman is Associate Professor of Higher Education at the University of Pennsylvania in Philadelphia. She has written extensively on historically Black colleges and is the author of *Envisioning Black Colleges: A History of the United Negro College Fund* (2007), which won the American Education Research Association's Outstanding Book Award, and the lead editor of *Understanding Minority Serving Institutions* (2008) and *Historically Black Colleges and Universities: Triumphs, Troubles, and Taboos* (2008). In 2006, she was given the Early Career Award by the Association for the Study of Higher Education.

Judith Glazer-Raymo is Lecturer in the Higher and Postsecondary Education Program at Teachers College, Columbia University, and Professor Emerita of Education at Long Island University. Her research and scholarship focus on gender equity, graduate education restructuring, and higher education policy and leadership. Her recent publications include her edited book, *Unfinished Agendas: New and Continuing Gender Challenges in Higher Education* (2008), published as a sequel to her book *Shattering the Myths: Women in Academe* (1999), for which she received the Outstanding Publication Award from the Postsecondary Division of the American Educational Research Association (AERA). She is also senior editor of *Professionalizing Graduate Education: The Master's Degree in the Marketplace* (2005) and of monographs, book chapters, and articles. She is the recipient of the Leadership Award (2008) and the Research Achievement Award (2004) from the Association for the Study of Higher Education, the Trustees

Award for Scholarly Achievement from Long Island University (2001), and the Willystine Goodsell Award for scholarship, activism, and community building from the AERA (2001).

Lisa Plume Hallen is a doctoral candidate at the University of Maine. Her research interests include access and curriculum, secondary to postsecondary policies, and discourse analysis.

Sandra Harding is Vice-Chancellor and President of James Cook University in Queensland, Australia. She is a sociologist whose key scholarly interests revolve around the sociology of work, organization, and inequality. Her current research is focused on the conditions for enterprise development and organization survey methodology. She has a keen professional interest in education policy and management.

Jeni Hart is Associate Professor of Higher Education in the Department of Educational Leadership and Policy Analysis at the University of Missouri in Columbia. Her work centers on women faculty and on climate issues in the academy.

Robert Heasley is Associate Professor of Sociology at Indiana University of Pennsylvania. From 1986 to 1991, he was a member of the board of directors of the National Organization for Changing Men (now the National Organization for Men against Sexism) and currently serves as President of the American Men's Studies Association. His current work focuses on "queer masculinities of straight men"—expanding the discourse on the intersection between masculinities and sexualities in men's studies. He has worked with schools and community programs toward ending men's violence, school-based bullying, and homophobia.

Jill M. Hermsen received her Ph.D. in educational leadership and policy analysis in 2008 from the University of Missouri in Columbia, where she is currently the Program Director for Mizzou ADVANCE and Focus on Faculty, two senior-faculty mentoring programs. Her research interests center on the job satisfaction and work engagement of higher education faculty and staff members.

Abbe Herzig is Research Assistant Professor in the Department of Educational Theory and Practice in the School of Education, University at Albany, State University of New York. She is also a statistician in the Health Ratings Center of Consumers Union and has consulted on diversity-related projects for the Pew Charitable Trusts, the United Nations, the Legal Defense Fund of the NAACP, and the School of Engineering at Rutgers University. Her research and teaching concern equity, diversity, and social justice in mathematics education. She recently completed a six-year study of factors supporting the success of women and people of color in postgraduate mathematics, supported by an Early Career grant from the National Science Foundation. From 2004 to 2007, she was also a coprincipal investigator on a Mathematics-Science Partnership grant from the New York State Department of Education to provide sustained professional development to teachers of elementary and middle-school mathematics in Albany and Schenectady.

Rachel E. Hile is Assistant Professor of English at Indiana University–Purdue University at Fort Wayne. Her research focuses on early modern English literature, and she is the editor of *Parenting and Professing: Balancing Family Work with an Academic Career* (2005).

Jerry A. Jacobs is Merriam Term Professor of Sociology at the University of Pennsylvania. He has served as editor of the *American Sociological Review* and President of the Eastern Sociological Society. His research has addressed a number of aspects of women's employment including authority, earnings, working conditions, part-time work, and entry into male-dominated occupations. He is coauthor of *The Time Divide: Work, Family, and Gender Inequality* (2004). His research has been funded by the National Science Foundation, the Spencer Foundation, the Sloan Foundation, Atlantic Philanthropies, and the Macy Foundation. His current research projects include a study of women's entry into the medical profession, funded by the Macy Foundation, and a study of working time and work-family conflict among university faculty.

Maulana Karenga is Professor of Africana Studies at California State University, Long Beach. He is a senior/founding scholar of Black Studies and author of the standard introductory text *Introduction to Black Studies* (4th ed., 2009). He is the creator of Kwanzaa and author of *The African American Holiday of Kwanzaa: A Celebration of Family, Community and Culture* (1998). An authority in classical African ethics, he is also author of *Odu Ifa: The Ethical Teachings* (1999); *Maat, The Moral Ideal in Ancient Egypt: A Study in Classical African Ethics* (2004, 2006); and *Kawaida and Questions of Life and Struggle: African American, Pan-African and Global Issues* (2008).

Annette Kolodny is Professor Emerita of American Literature and Culture at the University of Arizona, where she served as Dean of the College of Humanities and subsequently as College of Humanities Professor of American Literature and Culture. Her successes and challenges in implementing feminist and family-friendly policies during her years as dean are detailed in her 1998 book, *Failing the Future: A Dean Looks at Higher Education in the Twenty-First Century*. Her many works of feminist scholarship, including "Dancing through the Minefield: Some Notes on Defining a Feminist Literary Criticism"; *The Lay of the Land: Metaphor as Experience and History in American Life and Letters* (1975); and *The Land before Her: Fantasy and Experience of the American Frontiers, 1630–1860* (1984) have won numerous awards and been translated and reprinted worldwide. Her most recent scholarship concentrates on Native American studies and issues of race. She is currently completing a book titled *In Search of First Contact: The Vikings of Vinland, the Peoples of the Dawnland, and the American Struggle for Identity*.

Charlotte A. Kunkel is Associate Professor of Sociology at Luther College in Decorah, Iowa. She specializes in gender studies and has taught widely in sociology and women's studies. She actively pursues research and scholarship that promotes equality for all. Her current interests include academic freedom, diversity education, and women's transnational identities and immigration.

Jacquelyn S. Litt is Dean of Douglass Residential College and Campus at Rutgers, the State University of New Jersey. She was formerly Chair of the Women's and Gender Studies Department at the University of Missouri in Columbia where she was also the principal investigator for Mizzou ADVANCE, a project supported by a grant from the National Science Foundation to increase the representation and advancement of women in science, technology, engineering, and math. She authored *Medicalized Motherhood: Perspectives from the Lives of African-American and Jewish Women* (2000), which was awarded an Outstanding Achievement in Scholarship Honorable Mention from the Race, Gender, and Class Section of the American Sociological Association in 2002; received the Distinguished Faculty Award (2004) from the Iowa chapter of the American Association of University Women; co-edited *Global Dimensions of Gender and Carework* (2006), and is working on a new monograph, *Women of Katrina: Crossing Borders, Weaving Networks, and Taking Care*.

John Wesley Lowery is Associate Professor of Student Affairs in Higher Education in the College of Education and Educational Technology at Indiana University of

Pennsylvania. He has written extensively on topics related to student affairs and higher education, particularly legal and legislative issues.

Margaret E. Madden is Provost and Vice President of Academic Affairs at the State University of New York at Potsdam. A social psychologist, she specializes in the psychology of gender and was President of the Society for the Psychology of Women (Division 35 of the American Psychological Association) in 2004. Recent publications focus on enhancing the representation of gender and ethnicity in the psychology curriculum and analyses of women's and gender issues in higher education administration.

Renée J. Martin is Professor in the Judith Herb College of Education at the University of Toledo in Toledo, Ohio. She is the recipient of two National Women Educator awards for the development of social justice curriculum, a recipient of the university's Outstanding Teacher Award, and has received two Outstanding Woman awards. She is the editor of *Practicing What We Teach: Confronting Diversity in Teacher Education* (1995) and of a two-volume series titled *Transforming the Academy: Struggles and Strategies for the Advancement of Women in Higher Education* (Vol. 1, 1996; Vol. 2, 2007).

Christian Matheis is Student Advocate at Oregon State University in Corvallis, Oregon. He has researched and written on sexuality, affectionality, and gender in higher education, with emphasis on policy reform, social change, and community development through teaching and applying ethics and political philosophy.

Amy Scott Metcalfe is Assistant Professor of Higher Education in the Department of Educational Studies at the University of British Columbia. Her research examines the organizational space between higher education institutions, the state, and markets, and she has developed a theory of "intermediating organizations" to describe these relationships.

Susan Staffin Metz is an educational researcher at Stevens Institute of Technology and is a founder and past president of WEPAN, Women in Engineering Proactive Network. She has implemented multi-institutional initiatives to increase access and retention of women in engineering. Her work was recognized by the White House as a recipient of the President's Award for Excellence in Science, Mathematics, and Engineering Mentoring, and she received the Maria Mitchell Women in Science Award.

Leslie Miller-Bernal is Vice President for Academic Affairs and Dean of Wells College in Aurora, New York. She has written about the comparative experiences of women in single-sex and coeducational colleges and is the author of *Separate by Degree: Women Students' Experiences in Single-Sex and Coeducational Colleges* (2000) and co-editor of *Going Coed: Women's Experiences in Formerly Men's Colleges and Universities, 1950–2000* (2004) and *Challenged by Coeducation: Women's Colleges since the 1960s* (2007).

Keith B. O'Neill is a doctoral student in the Higher Education Administration program at Bowling Green State University in Ohio. He has been active in the National Association of Student Personnel Administrators, the Ohio Association of Student Personnel Administrators, and Sigma Pi fraternity.

Michele Paludi is President of Human Resources Management Solutions and Participating Full Professor of Management at Union Graduate College. She has published several texts on sexual harassment, including *Ivory Power: Sexual Harassment on Campus* (1990), which received the Myers Center Award for an Outstanding Book on Human Rights in the United States.

Cynthia Fabrizio Pelak is Assistant Professor of Sociology at the University of Memphis in Tennessee. She has published articles concerned with gender, race, class, and sports in the United States and South Africa, including the persistence of sexist naming practices of women's athletic teams at universities and colleges in the southern United States. She is currently researching collective memory of the Black freedom struggle at the National Civil Rights Museum in Memphis.

Peggy Placier is Associate Professor of Education Policy Studies at the University of Missouri in Columbia, where she has been practicing and conducting research in teacher education for 16 years. She is particularly interested in critical discourse analysis of school policies both past and present.

Kristen A. Renn is Associate Professor of Higher, Adult, and Lifelong Education at Michigan State University. Her research interests focus on issues of identity in higher education, including mixed-race college students, women's colleges in the United States and abroad, and lesbian, gay, bisexual, and transgender issues.

Tiffani A. Riggers is a doctoral student in the Higher Education and Organizational Change program at UCLA. Her research interests include college student moral, ethical, and spiritual development; first-year experiences; leadership programming; and the impact of mentoring relationships for college students.

Jean C. Robinson is Associate Dean for Undergraduate Education in the College of Arts and Sciences, Professor of Political Science, and Affiliate Professor of Gender Studies at Indiana University in Bloomington, where she served as Coordinator/Director of the Women's Studies Program during 1977–1982 and 1991–1992. She has written extensively on gender and social policies in China, Eastern Europe, and France, including *Living Gender after Communism* (2007). She also contributed a chapter on cultural change in women's studies to *Women's Studies on Its Own* (2002).

Sue V. Rosser is Dean of Ivan Allen College, the liberal arts college at Georgia Institute of Technology, where she is also Professor of History, Technology, and Society. From 1995 to 1999, she was Director of the Center for Women's Studies and Gender Research and Professor of Anthropology at the University of Florida, Gainesville. In 1995, she was Senior Program Officer for Women's Programs at the National Science Foundation. From 1986 to 1995, she served as Director of Women's Studies at the University of South Carolina, where she also was Professor of Family and Preventive Medicine in the Medical School. She has edited collections and authored 11 books and more than 120 journal articles on the theoretical and applied problems of women and science and of women's health. Her most recent single-authored book is *The Science Glass Ceiling: Academic Women Scientists and Their Struggle to Succeed* (2004); she coedited *Women, Gender, and Technology* (2006) and edited *Women, Science, and Myth* (2008). She has held several grants from the National Science Foundation to improve teaching and curricula in science and mathematics.

Linda J. Sax is Associate Professor of Higher Education in the Graduate School of Education and Information Studies at UCLA. Her work focuses on gender differences in the impact of college, as discussed in her recent book *The Gender Gap in College: Maximizing the Development Potential of Women and Men* (2008). She is the recipient of the 2005 Scholar-in-Residence Award from the American Association of University Women and the 1999 Early Career Award from the Association for the Study of Higher Education.

Jennifer M. Silva is a doctoral candidate in Sociology at the University of Virginia. She specializes in cultural sociology with a focus on social class, race, and gender inequality. Her current research examines how changing economic fortunes shape young adults' experiences of coming of age, with particular attention to the ways in which social class, gender, and race structure their transition to adulthood. She was recently awarded a Woodrow Wilson Women's Studies Dissertation Fellowship.

Sheila Slaughter is the first occupant of the Louise McBee Professorship of Higher Education at the Institute of Higher Education at the University of Georgia. A distinguished scholar of higher education, her most recent book is *Academic Capitalism and the New Economy: Markets, State, and Higher Education* (2004). Her scholarship concentrates on the relationship between knowledge and power as it plays out in higher education policy at the state, federal, and global levels.

Wayne J. Stein is Professor of Native American Studies and Higher Education Studies at Montana State University in Bozeman. He works closely with the seven tribal colleges of Montana and several others around the country. He has also consulted with several tribes interested in starting their own tribal colleges. His scholarship has focused primarily on tribally controlled colleges and universities, but he has done some research and writing in the areas of Indian gaming and faculty of color in higher education. He is author or coauthor of three books, including *The Renaissance of American Indian Higher Education: Capturing the Dream* (2002). He formerly served as President of Sitting Bull College and Vice President of Academic Affairs at Fort Berthold Community College. His tribal affiliation is Turtle Mountain Chippewa.

Susan Talburt is Director of the Women's Studies Institute at Georgia State University in Atlanta. She is the author of *Subject to Identity: Knowledge, Sexuality, and Academic Practices in Higher Education* (2000) and coeditor of *Youth and Sexualities: Pleasure, Subversion, and Insubordination in and out of Schools* (2004).

Rosemarie Tong is Distinguished Professor of Health Care Ethics in the Department of Philosophy and Director of the Center for Professional and Applied Ethics at the University of North Carolina at Charlotte. She has published over 125 articles on topics related to reproductive and genetic technology, biomedical research, feminist bioethics, global bioethics, and feminist theory. She has also authored or edited 15 books. Her most recent books are *New Perspectives in Health Care Ethics: An Interdisciplinary and Cross-Cultural Approach* (2007) and the third, much-expanded edition of *Feminist Thought: A More Comprehensive Introduction* (2008). She is an executive board member of the Association of Practical and Professional Ethics and serves on the advisory board of the International Network of Feminist Approaches to Bioethics. Currently, she speaks nationally and internationally on feminist topics at academic conferences, universities, and medical schools.

Barbara K. Townsend died on June 11, 2009. At that time, she was Professor of Higher and Continuing Education and Director of the Center for Community College Research at the University of Missouri in Columbia. A former community college faculty member and administrator, her research interests included community college faculty, community college missions, and transfer and articulation policies. Her most recent book is the coauthored *Community College Faculty: Undervalued and Overlooked* (2007). She was the recipient of numerous professional awards including the Council for the Study of Community Colleges' Senior Scholar Award (2000), the University of Missouri Status of Women Committee's Distinguished Service Award (2009), and the American Educational Research Association Division J's Award for Exemplary Research (2009).

Sheryl Ann Tucker is Associate Dean of the Graduate School and Professor of Chemistry at the University of Missouri in Columbia. Beyond her chemistry research, she is actively engaged in increasing the participation and success of under-represented groups in science. She was honored for this work by the White House, receiving a Presidential Award for Excellence in Science, Mathematics, and Engineering Mentoring (2005).

Virginia B. Vincenti is Professor of Family and Consumer Sciences in the University of Wyoming's Department of Family and Consumer Sciences in Laramie. She has published extensively on the history, philosophy, and contemporary issues of home economics / family and consumer sciences. She has coedited *Rethinking Home Economics: Women and the History of a Profession* (1997), presented her research at international conferences in Thailand, New Zealand, South Korea, and Finland and keynoted international conferences in Japan and Switzerland.

Christine von Prümmer is Senior Researcher and Head of the Evaluation Unit at the German FernUniversität, a single-mode distance teaching university. Since the early 1980s, her research and writing have focused on gender in distance education and gender issues in virtual, open, and distance learning environments. She is co-author of the seminal paper "Support and Connectedness. The Needs of Women Distance Education Students" (1990) and the author of *Women and Distance Education: Challenges and Opportunities* (2000). See also her homepage at http://www.vonpruemmer .de/christine/.

Chris Weedon is Professor of Critical and Cultural Theory at Cardiff University, Wales. Her books include *Feminist Practice and Poststructuralist Theory* (1987); *Cultural Politics: Class, Gender Race, and the Postmodern World* (1994); *Feminism, Theory, and the Politics of Difference* (1999); *Identity and Culture* (2004); and *Gender, Feminism, and Fiction in Germany, 1840–1914* (2007).

Amy E. Wells is Associate Professor of Higher Education in the Department of Leadership and Counselor Education at the University of Mississippi. She has written on the history and development of education in the South, Rockefeller philanthropy, and multicultural Greek organizations.

Evangeline A. Wheeler is Associate Professor of Psychology at Towson University in Maryland. She writes on issues of concern to African Americans and is currently at work on an edited volume of essays in emancipatory psychology.

Edward G. Whipple is Vice President for Student Affairs and Adjunct Associate Professor of Higher Education and Student Affairs at Bowling Green State University in Ohio. He has served in a variety of administrative roles in Greek life and student affairs and has published a number of articles on topics related to these areas. He has served in leadership positions at the national level with the National Association of Student Personnel Administrators, the National Association of State Universities and Land-Grant Colleges, the Association of Fraternity Advisors, and with Phi Delta Theta International Fraternity.

Sarah E. Winslow-Bowe is Assistant Professor of Sociology at Clemson University in South Carolina. Her research interests focus on gender inequality, the intersections of work and family, and the life course. In addition to her publications on gender inequality and work-family issues in academia, she has written about trends in work-family conflict from the 1970s through the 1990s and the relationship between welfare reform and women's enrollment in postsecondary education. Her current research examines persistence and variation in wives' income advantage and its relationship to reported levels of marital conflict. This research has been supported by the Woodrow Wilson Foundation and recognized by Sociologists for Women in Society and the Family Sections of the American Sociological Association and the Society for the Study of Social Problems.

Lisa Wolf-Wendel is Professor of Higher Education in the Department of Educational Policy at the University of Kansas, where she coordinates the master's program in higher education administration. Her expertise centers on college students and equity issues in higher education, and her research typically explores the characteristics of programs, policies, or institutions deemed exemplary in responding to diversity issues. She is coauthor of *Taking Women Seriously: Lessons and Legacies for Educating the Majority* (1999).

Deborah Worley is Assistant Professor of Higher Education in the Department of Educational Leadership at the University of North Dakota. She has extensive experience in student affairs units, including career services and experiential education, and has also volunteered in the Greek community as a sorority advisor. Her research emphases include student assessment, cocurricular involvement, and students' success beyond the college years.

INDEX

The letter *t* following a page number denotes a table.